PERSONALITY AND THE BEHAVIOR DISORDERS

IN TWO VOLUMES

PERSONALITY

and the

BEHAVIOR DISORDERS

A HANDBOOK BASED ON EXPERIMENTAL
AND CLINICAL RESEARCH

Edited by

J. McV. HUNT

DIRECTOR, INSTITUTE OF WELFARE RESEARCH, COMMUNITY SERVICE
SOCIETY OF NEW YORK. FORMERLY, ASSOCIATE PROFESSOR OF
PSYCHOLOGY, BROWN UNIVERSITY

VOLUME I

THE RONALD PRESS COMPANY ⸱ NEW YORK

Copyright, 1944, by

THE RONALD PRESS COMPANY

All Rights Reserved

8

PRINTED IN THE UNITED STATES OF AMERICA

EDITOR'S PREFACE

The study of personality and its development draws heavily upon nearly all of the life sciences. In the recent past, anyone endeavoring to become familiar with the scientific knowledge about the behavior of whole individuals inevitably found himself wandering back and forth across the traditional boundaries between the sciences. This work brings together forty contributors representing the life sciences and seeks to present the major portion of theory, investigative fact, and clinical practice from all those scientific fields that have contributed to this knowledge.

This is not a work feasible for the pen of any one man, for the topics covered range through the structure and assessment, the dynamic development and determinants, and the disorders and therapy of personality. Furthermore, many of the thirty-five chapters survey developments of the last decade in subfields where the details of theory and research are known only to small coteries of workers. Each chapter has been written by one or more authorities in the subject concerned. Each author has endeavored to survey his field with technical jargon minimized or defined immediately, and with ample documentation to serve as a bridge to the original literature, so that his expositions may serve both as a text for students beyond the elementary level and as a reference work for mature clinicians, investigators, and teachers.

Understanding the individual person, until almost the last half-century, was left largely to the artist, or the moral philosopher. Whole organisms, and especially human beings as molar objects, were unadapted to traditional laboratory approaches. The various scientific subjects bit off their diverse parts to chew them in isolation. Only as the inductive implications of clinical observation were gradually clarified did it become possible to design experimental studies of the whole organism and its development. Due partly to the growing impact of the work of Galton and of Freud, and partly to the cumulative effects of the application of the scientific method, the volume of scientific output on personality has snowballed. It has recently become clear, moreover, that the traditional boundaries between the sciences have obstructed progress in this field, and that a cross-disciplinary approach is required. To assemble this literature and gather the results of this investigation into more compact exposition and to foster this cross-disciplinary approach to the study of personality have been the two principal aims in the design of this work.

It is unreasonable to expect uniformity of terminology and point of view at this time in this dynamic field. In fact, the editor has deliberately invited contributors who represented not only various life sciences but even divergent points of view within these sciences. Yet this work is not a symposium of systematic views, for each author gives a survey of the fact and research strategy of his subfield. For instance, no account of psychoanalytic doctrine as such appears, but several authors are analysts, and psychoanalysis is described as a clinical method of research. Moreover, its influence upon many of the subfields may easily be discerned. Again, no exposition of the tenets of the psychobiological schools appears, but several authors were trained in this school and its influence may be noticed in many of the subfields. The same goes for behaviorism, etc.

Because the emphasis of this book is upon the whole organism or person, the first term in the title is *Personality*. The term, however, is not limited to its common cross-sectional connotations; instead, a person is understood to be a socio-biological process beginning with conception and ending with death. Accordingly, both the cross-sectional problems concerned with description, assessment, and classification of present characteristics and their interrelationships must be considered, as well as the longitudinal problems concerned with the dynamic relationships between behavioral events and characteristics at one time, and those at a later time in the life of the individual. Within each of these two classes of problems, many perfectly valid systems of relationships may be abstracted for study which may account for some of the differing meanings given to the term personality. It is admitted that *personality* is not altogether a fortunate term with which to designate the scientific sudy of persons—in fact, the editor would prefer the term *personology* were it in current use.

It is fitting that *Behavior Disorders* should form a coordinate term in the title of this book. In the past, and even today, a large portion of our knowledge of persons has derived from the clinical observation and treatment of the abnormal. We use *behavior* instead of *mental*, also, to avoid implying dualism. Like this postulate of a monistic person, other postulates growing out of clinical study foreshadow a systematic science of molar behavior in which the individual organism will be the focus of concern. For instance, the convictions that normal and abnormal personalities differ only in degree, that the distinction between them is relative, and that the fundamental dynamic laws of behavior and personality development are the same for the normal and the abnormal have been gaining adherents rapidly. Furthermore, it is becoming more and more apparent that the dynamic laws of the life process are broader than the human species. Thus, in the strategy of research, it becomes entirely feasible to utilize infrahuman forms. Several chapters are here devoted to the uncovering of these dynamic laws by way of experiments with animal subjects. Clinical observation, however, will probably continue indefinitely to be the final testing ground for these laws at the human level.

This work is truly a collaborative product. As the editor, I am deeply grateful for the suggestions and counsel I have received from the authors and from many others, and for the fine cooperative spirit I have met consistently. Nevertheless, I must stand responsible for the general pattern of organization in this Handbook. Thanks are due the many publishers, foundations and associations who granted permission to quote from material previously published under their several auspices. I am greatly indebted to Professor Walter S. Hunter for encouragement and counsel from the time this work was first considered. I am also very greatly indebted to my wife, Esther Dahms Hunt, who has compiled the index of authors, and who has edited all of the bibliographies and made them conform to the system of citation given in the *World List of Scientific Periodicals* (2nd ed.) and used, for example, by the *Psychological Abstracts.*

If this work serves to disseminate existing knowledge of persons, to foster the cross-disciplinary approach in the several related fields, to save bibliographical effort for busy clinicians, scholars, and teachers, and to broaden the coverage of the textbooks of the future, the authors and the editor will have been amply rewarded.

J. McV. HUNT

Brown University

CONTENTS

VOLUME I

PART I

PART II

CONTENTS

PART III

BEHAVIOR DYNAMICS, EXPERIMENTAL BEHAVIOR DISORDERS, AND HYPNOTISM

PART IV

DETERMINANTS OF PERSONALITY—BIOLOGICAL
AND ORGANIC

VOLUME II

PART V

DETERMINANTS OF PERSONALITY—EXPERIENTIAL AND SOCIOLOGICAL

PART VI

SOME OUTSTANDING PATTERNS OF BEHAVIOR DISORDER

PART VIII

THERAPY AND THE PREVENTION OF BEHAVIOR DISORDERS

PART I

THEORETICAL APPROACHES TO PERSONALITY

Chapter 1

THE STRUCTURE OF PERSONALITY

By Donald W. MacKinnon, Ph.D.

The truth of William James's dictum that "the history of philosophy is to a great extent that of a certain clash of human temperaments" (1907, p. 6) is nowhere more apparent than in man's attempt through the ages to describe his own personality, character, and temperament. The present chapter which seeks to summarize what man has thought about these problems is, then, of necessity in large measure a record of clash of opinion and conflict of theory rather than a survey of a large body of established fact concerning the structure of personality.

History of the Concept of Personality

The meanings of the term personality are almost legion. The early history of the classical Latin word *persona* from which the word personality is derived has been discussed by a number of writers. Allport (1937) has summarized this literature and collated it with the subsequent meanings which the term personality has acquired in theology, philosophy, law, sociology, and psychology. In all, 50 meanings are distinguished by this author. Yet in spite of the diversity of connotative significance to be found among these definitions, two basic and fundamentally opposed meanings occur again and again. They are, on the one hand, the definition of personality in terms of outward superficial appearance, and on the other, in terms of the inner, essential nature of man. Two meanings could hardly be more antithetical yet both have found acceptance, not only in the past, but in the present writings of psychologists. The former, often referred to as the mask definition of personality, has been derived from the original meaning of *persona* as the mask worn by the ancient actor to signify his role in the drama, while the latter, known as the substance definition of personality, derives from the emphasis which has been placed upon the inner nature or substance of man in the various juristic and philosophical but especially theological discussions of person and personality. Although it is perhaps fair to say that in philosophical discussions of personality the emphasis has been upon the inner aspects of the self and that in psychology it has been upon the outer aspects—a difference revealed in the more frequent use of the term *Personalität* in German philosophy and of *Persönlichkeit* in

3

German psychology (Ehrlich, 1930) and in Stern's (1930) distinction between *Personalismus*, the abstract philosophical inquiry, and *Personalistik*, the concrete psychological inquiry—nevertheless, reviews of the psychological definitions of personality reveal clearly the influence of both meanings upon psychological thought (Allport and Vernon, 1930; Allport, 1937).

Mask definitions of personality which emphasize the most superficial aspects of behavior have been offered most often by behaviorists. Personality is "the sum of activities that can be discovered by actual observation over a long enough time to give reliable information. In other words, personality is but the end product of our habit systems" (Watson, 1924, p. 220). "Personality is the characteristic behavior of an individual" (Sherman, 1928, p. 174).

Substance definitions of personality, on the other hand, have been written by psychologists who have been willing to conceptualize inner psychological states, processes, and structures and relationships among them in order to make the observed behavior of the individual more meaningful. Typical definitions of this sort are: "Personality is the entire mental organization of a human being at any stage of his development. It embraces every phase of human character: intellect, temperament, skill, morality, and every attitude that has been built up in the course of one's life" (Warren and Carmichael, 1930, p. 333), and "Personality is the sum-total of all the biological innate dispositions, impulses, tendencies, appetites, and instincts of the individual, and the acquired dispositions and tendencies—acquired by experience" (Prince, 1924, p. 532). In many ways the psychoanalysts, and more recently Murray (1938), have contributed most to the substantive conceptualization of personality but they have not sought to condense their extensive writings on personality into brief definitions of the term.

Types of Definition of Personality.—In their survey of the literature in this field Allport and Vernon (1930) have distinguished five types of definition of personality.

1. *Omnibus or rag-bag definitions* consider personality a mere summation of parts or units of some sort. From this viewpoint personality is an "und Summe," not a configuration, a resultant, not an emergent. Valentine's definition of personality as "the sum-total of one's habit dispositions" (1927, p. 21) and Prince's definition cited above are good examples of this type of definition, expressive, as are all such definitions, of an atomistic and elementaristic psychology.

2. *Integrative definitions* of personality stress the organization of the factors which make up personality and consequently are usually also substance definitions. Warren and Carmichael's definition quoted above falls in this class.

3. *Hierarchical definitions* of personality, like integrative definitions, emphasize the organization of personality but place particular stress upon

the vertical rather than the simple horizontal organization of personality. The classical example is James's discussion of the four levels of the Self: the material Self, the social Self, the spiritual Self, and finally the Self of Selves or Pure Ego (James, 1890). Shand (1914) and McDougall (1923, 1926, 1933), however, have developed this type of definition most fully. A hierarchy of sentiments dominated by the enduring sentiment of self-regard constituted for McDougall the very core of personality which he designated character. "The native propensities are the chief part of the raw material which becomes organized to form character. The process of organization is of two stages. The first stage is the formation of sentiments. The second stage is the building of the sentiments into an harmoniously cooperating system. Such a system of sentiments is character. The strength of character is a matter of the degree of harmony and integration attained by the system, and perhaps also by the degree to which the whole organization is solidified by exercise" (1933, p. 188).

4. *Definitions of personality which emphasize adjustment* have usually been behavioristic. Some of them, such as "Personality means the definitely fixed and controlling tendencies of adjustment of the individual to his environment" (Bowden, 1926, p. 152), are free from evaluative connotations. But it is a curious fact that the behaviorists who were so intent on being rigorously scientific have often introduced into their definitions of personality considerations of social approval and evaluative criteria in general. Thus, for example, J. B. Watson suggested that personality be considered "an individual's total assets (actual and potential) and liabilities (actual and potential) on the reaction side" (1924, p. 417) and Rexroad defined personality as "the balance between socially approved and disapproved traits" (1929, p. 355).

5. *Definitions of personality in terms of distinctiveness and uniqueness* have been offered in part as a corrective for the confusion which has resulted when personality and culture have been treated as essentially synonymous. In the writings of some anthropologists the cultural patterning of personality has been stressed to the point of ignoring almost completely the problem of individual differences. The paradox of this position is clearly expressed in Marcuse's statement that "Personality is the convergence of all essential cultural tendencies in one mind. The more culture one has, the harder it is to be a single personality" (1926, quoted from Allport and Vernon, 1930, pp. 684–688). As Schoen has written, "If all the members of any one social group acted alike, thought alike, and felt alike, personality would not exist" (1930, p. 397). With these considerations in mind personality has been variously defined as "the organized system, the functioning whole or unity, of habits, dispositions and sentiments that mark off any one member of a group as being different from any other member of the same group" (Schoen, 1930, p. 397) and as "that combination of behavior forms in the individual . . . which distinguish that individual from others of a group" (Yoakum, 1924, p. 442).

Closely related to this type of definition is Woodworth's well-known adverbial definition which emphasizes the quality or style of the unique personality. "Personality refers not to any particular sort of activity, such as talking, remembering, thinking or loving, but an individual can reveal his personality in the way he does any of these things" (Woodworth, 1929, p. 553).

Allport's own definition of personality, developed in the light of his extensive review of the literature, is that "Personality is the dynamic organization within the individual of those psychophysical systems that determine his unique adjustments to his environment" (1937, p. 48).[1]

American *vs*. German Conceptions of Personality.—A comparison of the traditional approaches to the problem of the structure of personality in American and European, especially German, psychology reveals an interesting opposed emphasis in the two streams of thought.

American psychologists have tended to emphasize the parts or units which, summed or integrated, could be thought to constitute personality, especially those elements which they had reason to believe were common to all individuals. By assuming the existence of common elements they made their problem of measurement easier. It is probably fair to say that the insistence in American psychological thought upon the primary place of measurement in science has favored the widespread acceptance of atomistic definitions of personality. The emphasis upon the measurement of traits of personality common to all individuals and normally distributed in the population has led to a critical attitude toward the scientific validity of the study of the single case. To most American psychologists it has seemed clear that the study of configurations, each of which is unique, cannot constitute science. Even the assumption of discrete classes or types of personality has been looked upon with suspicion. As Allport (1937) has pointed out, American psychologists have been concerned with a nomothetic approach to problems of personality almost to the exclusion of idiographic considerations. Finally, American psychologists as natural scientists have assumed that the problems of structure and function of personality are ultimately to be explained in terms of mechanisms, whether these be conceived of as physiological, neurological, or psychological.

German psychologists, on the other hand, have been more inclined to think of personality as a unique whole which cannot fruitfully or legitimately be analyzed into smaller component parts. Not only have they not been interested in measuring aspects or traits of personality; they have believed it impossible to do so, for while qualitative differences may be described the uniqueness of each personality precludes any commonality to which units of measurement may be applied. With what to most

---

[1] The definitions which have been included in this section are only illustrative. For a thorough review of this field, see Allport and Vernon, 1930, and Proceedings of the second colloquium on personality investigation, 1930.

American psychologists has seemed a cavalier disregard of statistical considerations many German psychologists have described disparate categories or types of personality. And finally with much more sympathy for a Geisteswissenschaftliche psychology than their American colleagues, a fair number of German psychologists have argued that personality cannot be explained but has rather to be understood and that in the attempt to understand personality, mechanisms, whether they be physiological, neurological, or psychological, are of no avail. Rather, there is required a knowledge of the historical past and cultural present in the setting of which the meaning of personality is to be understood.[2]

Character.—In early writings the terms personality and character were used quite interchangeably but in the modern period two different meanings have been commonly attributed to the term character, both of which differentiate it from personality (Allport and Vernon, 1930).

In the first of these meanings character is considered to be the ethical or moral aspect of personality or personality considered from the standpoint of some social or ethical norm. Such a conception of character agrees well with the layman's use of the term, for in common parlance only two kinds of character are recognized—good and bad. The terms used to designate the opposed types of character are numerous: strongweak, noble-base, high-low, etc., but always the ethical connotation is obvious. Even to say that a person is lacking in character is recognized as meaning that the person in question lacks a good character or, in other words, has a bad character.

In its second and less frequently employed modern meaning, character is identified with a part of the personality, namely, conation. Some writers have argued that it is possible to treat the conative aspects of personality without moral or ethical evaluation. Thus, Filter defines character as those conative traits which are of a nonmoral nature and adds that in character "the emphasis is upon the force of activity rather than upon its direction, upon the quality of behavior in terms of strength, persistence, readiness, rapidity, etc., rather than upon its value as right or wrong, good or bad, wise or foolish, etc." (1922, pp. 323–324). However, most writers who consider character to be the conative aspect of personality either wittingly or unwittingly introduce evaluative considerations into their discussions with the result that in actual practice their use of the term character cannot be distinguished from the traditional one. McDougall, defining character as a system of sentiments under the control of the self-regarding sentiment, says that character is "that in a man which gives, or, rather, is the ground of, consistency, firmness, self-control, power of self-direction or autonomy" (1933, p. 185). Similarly, W. S. Taylor defines character in terms of "degrees of ethically effective organization of all the forces of an individual" (1926, p. 86). Since there

---

[2] See, for instance, Angyal's (1941) conception of the life history as a Gestalt. (Editor)

can hardly be an effective organization and integration of personality without some degree of inhibition, the capacity to inhibit impulses has assumed a central position in discussions of character. Following upon his comprehensive survey of the literature in this field, Roback suggests that character is "an enduring psychophysical disposition to inhibit instinctive impulses in accordance with a regulative principle" (1931, p. 450).

The psychoanalysts have perhaps been most explicit in identifying character with a part of the personality—the ego and super-ego as against the id. The dynamics of character-formation and the psychology of the ego have been extensively investigated by them. Allport (1937), however, has criticized this common practice of separating the will from the rest of the personality and designating it character. He insists that it is the personality as a whole that wills and not one part of it; willed activities emanate from the most complex systems of the personality. Character enters the picture, according to Allport, only when personal effort is evaluated from the standpoint of some code. This would appear to be an attempt to keep the psychology of personality pure and uncontaminated by social and ethical considerations, but since the personality is so definitely shaped by the norms of the culture in which it is conditioned, the advisability or even the possibility of discussing personality apart from any consideration of social values may well be questioned. One might agree with Allport that "character is personality evaluated, and personality is character devaluated" (1937, p. 52) but hesitate to accept his proposition that the psychologist does not need the term character at all.

Temperament.—Although temperament has sometimes been used synonymously with personality there has been in the past as well as today considerable agreement among writers that temperament is but one aspect of personality, namely, "the general affective nature of an individual as determined by his inheritance and life history" (Warren, 1934, p. 273). In general, however, more emphasis has been placed upon innate factors than upon individual experiences as the determinants of temperament. In the literature at least three different aspects of temperament have received varying stress: the emotional, the physiological, and the kinetic (Allport and Vernon, 1930).

Temperament has often been considered to be primarily a matter of the characteristic emotional experiences of an individual. With such a concept in mind psychologists have described various facets of temperament—most frequently variations on Hippocrates's phlegmatic, choleric, sanguine, and melancholic types—and have suggested various dimensions of temperament, e.g., speed and intensity of emotional response (Wundt, 1903); emotional frequency and change (frequency of emotional upsets and rapidity of succession or alternation of moods), emotional breadth (the range and variety of objects which arouse emotion), and emotional strength (the superficial-deep dimension of emotional experience) (F. H. Allport, 1924), etc.

The criticism most frequently made of such discussions of the emotional function in temperament is that however adequate they may be at the descriptive and phenomenological level they have nothing to say about the factors which are responsible for temperament. They do not explain temperamental differences.

The emphasis upon physiological function has usually constituted an attempt to correct for this deficiency and to explain the various types of emotional temperament by relating them to assumed underlying physiological and biochemical states. This explanatory approach to the problems of temperament dates from the writings of Hippocrates and finds its present-day expression in the more speculative theorizing of Berman (1921) and Cobb (1927), and in the combination of solid work and conservative theory of Hoskins (1933), Lipschütz (1925), Rowe (1932), and others.

Finally, the kinetic emphasis is found in the writings of the relatively few psychologists who have thought of temperament as a matter of the type of motor response characteristic of an individual. Bloor writes that "if there is in human behavior an irreducible factor which may be known as temperament . . . its manifestations must be looked for along the lines of rapidity of natural responses and in duration of the disturbances produced" (1928, p. 156). This emphasis upon the kinetic was the theoretical basis upon which Downey constructed her Will-Temperament Tests. She wrote, "Temperament, it appears, reveals itself in various patterned forms of activity. These patterns are determined by: (1) The amount of nervous energy at the disposal of the individual; and (2) The tendency of such nervous energy to discharge immediately into the motor areas that innervate the muscles and glands; or, on the contrary, to find a way out by a roundabout pathway of discharge" (1923, p. 59). In the light of such a theory temperaments are conceived to range between two extremes; hyperkinetic temperaments characterized by an explosive discharge of energy and quick action resulting from "a high level of activity or from great simplification of pathways in the nervous system (absence of inhibition)," and hypokinetic temperaments characterized by a low level discharge of energy and slow action resulting from "a low level of activity or from undue elaboration of impulses in the brain centers" (1923, p. 59).

The emphasis upon kinetic functions in temperament, like the emphasis upon physiological and emotional functions, does not constitute a new definition of temperament but merely singles out for special attention one aspect of temperament as it is usually defined. A definition giving due weight to all three functions of temperament and broad enough to include most shadings of meaning which have been attributed to the term is the following: "Temperament refers to the characteristic phenomena of an individual's emotional nature, including his susceptibility to emotional stimulation, his customary strength and speed of response, the quality of his prevailing mood, and all peculiarities of fluctuation and intensity in mood; these phenomena being regarded as dependent upon constitutional make-up, and therefore largely hereditary in origin" (Allport, 1937, p. 54).

Personality and Tripartite Psychology.—It is interesting to consider the terms personality, character, and temperament in relation to the tripartite psychology which distinguishes cognition, affection, and conation as the basic functions of mind. Character is the more or less enduring and consistent pattern of a person's conation; temperament, his more or less enduring and consistent pattern of affection; intelligence, his more or less enduring and consistent pattern of cognition. Curiously, character and temperament have loomed large in all discussions of personality, but not intelligence. Character and temperament have frequently been used synonymously with personality and not infrequently confused with it, but not so intelligence. It is interesting to speculate about the reasons for this neglect of intelligence in discussions of personality, but it is a neglect which cannot be justified, for certainly intelligence is as integral a part of the personality as are character and temperament. Intelligence, character, and temperament may be singled out for separate investigation and description; no one of them alone, however, constitutes personality. Instead the more or less enduring qualities of these functions and their functional interdependence constitute personality.

Theories of the Structure of Personality

While the definitions reviewed in the preceding section serve as an introduction to the various theories of the structure of personality, they fail to indicate their nature in any detailed way. But before going on to a systematic review of these theories consideration should be given to the claim which has sometimes been made that it is meaningless to conceive of the personality as possessing enduring structure in its own right.

Psychologists who deny that the personality has intrinsic structure have done so on a number of grounds. One of the most interesting arguments in defense of this rather extreme position has been based on an analogy between the field of sensory and perceptual psychology and that of personality.

The work on color conversion has in one instance been made the basis for the development of such an argument (H. Helson, personal communication). Strictly speaking, the color of any object or material cannot be specified apart from the conditions under which it is viewed, for the same object will appear now to have one color and now another depending upon its surroundings, the illuminant in which it is placed, and the nature of the viewing situation. It is, then, obviously impossible, if one is speaking precisely, to say, e.g., that a given object is red just because under conditions of daylight illumination it has the phenomenal appearance of redness. Similarly, it has been argued that such general characteristics as honesty or ascendance cannot be attributed to a personality on the basis of observations of either honest or ascendant behavior on the part of the person in question in either one or a number of situations, for the same person may in other situations act dishonestly and in still others assume a submissive role. It has no more meaning to speak of an honest man than to refer to a red object.

Against such arguments as these there is no answer so long as one remains on the level of phenomenal appearance. But if either the personologist or the colorimetrist wishes to predict how the object of his scientific investigation, a person in the one case, a sample in the other, will behave—i.e., will be observed to have varying phenomenal appearances—he must go below the surface of phenomenal appearance and force the object of his interest to reveal something of its structure. The colorimetrist does this by spectrophotometry, and once he has determined the spectrophotometric specifications of his sample he can predict what its phenomenal color will be under known conditions of background, illumination, and viewing. Unfortunately the personologist has no instrument comparable in precision to that of the spectrophotometer with which to determine the hidden structure of his human subject's personality, but in principle his procedure must be the same as the colorimetrist's. The instruments and techniques which have been developed thus far for the purpose of revealing the structure of personality are at best crude and will yield little more than first approximations, but one must not make the error of assuming that where it is difficult to see a structure none exists. A perfect crystal reveals no structure to the naked eye.

It may be objected that the colorimetrist has tools which enable him to determine the characteristics of the environment of his sample with a precision which will always be lacking to the personologist who seeks to determine the life-space of an individual. Granted. But the difference again is not one of principle but of technical difficulty.

Just because it has been so difficult to determine the structure of personality many psychologists have chosen to remain on what has seemed to them the firmer and safer ground of describing the more external and objective aspects of behavior. Out of this sort of cautious preoccupation with the externals of personality has come the widespread acceptance of mask definitions of personality, the attractiveness of phenotypical classifications of types of personality, and the appeal of what has seemed to many to be the superior scientific status of an objective and behavioristic conception of personality.

Theory of Types of Personality

In studying personality psychologists have tended to be primarily motivated by one of two interests: either a nomothetic interest in that which is common to all personalities, or an idiographic interest in that which is unique in any one person. Thus two types of psychology of the personality have developed, one primarily interested in the establishment of general laws, the other predominantly concerned with understanding the individual case.

Conscious and sophisticated attempts at reconciliation of these opposed approaches to problems of personality have been made recently by a number of investigators, most notably by Lewin (1935, 1936, 1938), Allport (1937, 1942), and Murray (1938), but unconscious and sometimes methodologically naïve attempts at reconciliation of these opposites have been made since the day when man first began to make general statements about individual differences. Just as in all sciences a good deal of qualitative spade work has preceded the development of quantitative refinements, so in the history of psychology attempts to describe personality and to draw pictures of what might be considered universal types were made long before the work of Francis Galton (1883) laid the foundation for a quantitative approach to the problem of individual differences.

Literary Characterology.—The attempt to draw word portraits of universal types of human beings is known as literary characterology. This form of writing originated among the ancient Greeks. Although Plato in his dialogues and Aristotle in his Nichomachean Ethics described certain types of human beings, the minor literary form of character writing seems to have been developed by Aristotle's pupil, Theophrastus. According to one legend, Theophrastus wrote his Characters at the age of 99 after long wondering, "why it is that while all Greece lies under the same sky and all Greeks are educated alike, it has befallen us to have characters variously constituted" (Roback, 1931, p. 9).

Thirty of Theophrastus's Characters have been preserved (Aldington, 1924). Each of them follows the same pattern: a definition of a trait and a description of a personality in which this trait is dominant and manifested in a variety of ways.

Not all human types were described by Theophrastus. Those which he did depict show considerable overlap, and nowhere did he offer any explanation of the development of his various characters. Yet in spite of these shortcomings Theophrastus's characters were so skilfully drawn that it is not difficult for the modern reader to recognize the same types among his contemporaries. Take, for example, the flatterer.

THE FLATTERER

Flattery may be considered as a mode of companionship degrading but profitable to him who flatters.

The Flatterer is a person who will say as he walks with another, "Do you observe how people are looking at you? This happens to no man in Athens but you. A compliment was paid to you yesterday in the Porch. More than thirty persons were sitting there; the question was started, Who is our foremost man? Everyone mentioned you first, and ended by coming back to your name." With these and the like words, he will remove a morsel of wool from his patron's coat; or, if a speck of chaff has been laid on the other's hair by the wind, he will pick it off; adding with a laugh, "Do you see? Because I have not met you for two days, you have had your beard full of white hairs; although no one has darker hair for his years than you." Then he will request the company to be silent while the great man is speaking, and will praise him, too, in his hearing, and mark his approbation at a pause with "True"; or he will laugh at a frigid joke, and stuff his cloak into his mouth as if he could not repress his amusement. He will request those whom he meets to stand still until "his Honour" has passed. He will buy apples and pears, and bring them in and give to the children in the father's presence; adding, with kisses, "Chicks of a good father." Also, when he assists at the purchase of slippers, he will declare that the foot is more shapely than the shoe. If his patron is approaching a friend, he will run forward and say, "He is coming to you"; and then, turning back, "I have announced you." He is just the person, too, who can run errands to the woman's market without drawing breath. He is the first of the guests to praise the wine; and to say, as he reclines next to the host, "How delicate is your fare!" and (taking up something from the table) "Now this— how excellent it is!" He will ask his friend if he is cold, and if he would like to put on something more; and before the words are spoken, will wrap him up. Moreover he will lean towards his ear and whisper with him; or will glance at him as he talks to the rest of the company. He will take the cushions from the slave in the theatre, and spread them on the seat with his own hands. He will say that his patron's house is well built, that his land is well planted, and that his portrait is like.

In short the Flatterer may be observed saying and doing all things by which he conceives that he will gain favour. (Jebb, 1909, pp. 39–43)

In such sketches as that of the flatterer Theophrastus set up a style of writing which has been followed from his day to the present in which an attempt is made to describe a common human type briefly yet so succinctly that it will be recognized everywhere and at all times as valid.

It is impossible to review here the work of all or even the most outstanding of the literary characterologists—Chaucer, Ben Jonson, Joseph Addison, Richard Steele, Samuel Johnson, George Eliot, Samuel Butler— nor is it necessary to do so since this has been done so admirably in great detail by Roback (1931) and in briefer, more popular form by Jastrow (1915). The former has also compiled a most valuable bibliography of characterology (1927).

It should be noted, however, that while many character writers have deviated from the particular form set by Theophrastus, certainly the most successful of them have revealed in their writing a belief that men act consistently and each with his own characteristic style. This is particularly well illustrated in the writing of Jean de la Bruyère (1645–

1696), one of the most psychological of all literary characterologists. His sketches are actually portraits of individuals rather than descriptions of types, yet their universality is so great as to place them among the more general character sketches. Instead of taking a dominant trait and showing how it reveals itself in many forms of behavior, as did Theophrastus, La Bruyère pictured the psychological congruence of many traits in a single person. The consistency of personality traits and the expression of them in a unique style of life are, however, depicted as so extreme in La Bruyère's writing that his pictures sometimes cease to be portraits and become instead caricatures. Yet La Bruyère's Portraits (Aldington, 1924) create in the reader the same feeling of psychological verisimilitude as does the best of all character writing.

One finds in the writings of the literary characterologists two implicit theories concerning the structure of personality. One theory—perhaps best revealed in the Characters of Theophrastus—has emphasized the importance of some dominant trait as a dynamic and directive force in giving stability and consistency to the personality. The other theory—clearly manifest in the writings of La Bruyère—has stressed the existence of a unique style of life coloring the various traits of a person and revealing itself in all that he does.

It may be charged that characterologists have done violence to the richness of personality in abstracting a single trait or a limited number of traits and confining their description of character to these, but it must be remembered that they have seen these traits as pervasive ones which color the whole personality. If characterologists have not described the whole person in their sketches, at least they have concentrated their attention upon those traits which reveal themselves in all that the person does. They have pictured characteristic traits of the person. The present-day successors of characterologists working within the framework of psychology are the typological psychologists who, like the characterologists, place their emphasis upon the whole personality although they describe only an abstracted part of the whole. It is this, of course, which has justified critics in claiming that both typologists and characterologists engage in too easy and too uncritical generalization in their descriptions of personality.

From the standpoint of science which seeks not only to describe but also to explain the phenomena which it studies, the greatest shortcoming of literary characterology is the fact that it rests content with a mere description of types of human beings.

Types of Temperament.—The attempt to explain the development of types of temperament is not a product of present-day science but rather of science in the Golden Age of Greek medicine. It even antedated literary characterology. It is in Hippocrates's theory of humoral pathology that one finds the first clear attempt to relate differences in the emotional basis of personality or temperament to differences in what would today be recognized as the biochemistry of the body. This theory which was based upon Empedocles's doctrine of the four elements—earth, air, fire, and water—assumed that the corresponding humors of the body —black bile, blood, yellow bile, and phlegm—would when mixed in proper proportions constitute health but when mixed in improper proportions result in disease. It assumed further that the more enduring imbalances of the humors would result in four corresponding types of temperament—melancholic, sanguine, choleric, and phlegmatic. The assumed relationships in the Hippocratic theory are represented in Table I.

TABLE I

CLASSICAL THEORY OF TEMPERAMENTS

Cosmic Elements	Their Properties	Corresponding Humors	Corresponding Temperaments
EMPEDOCLES cir. 450 B.C.		HIPPOCRATES cir. 400 B.C.	
Air	warm and moist	Blood	Sanguine
Earth	cold and dry	Black Bile	Melancholic
Fire	warm and dry	Yellow Bile	Choleric
Water	cold and moist	Phlegm	Phlegmatic

(From Allport, 1937, p. 63)

As one moves in the placement of emphasis from description to explanation, one moves from a concentration of interest upon problems of characterology to those of temperament. And if one sees as the basic notion in the classical humoral theory of temperament the idea of a correspondence between the general affective and emotional nature of the individual and his biochemical make-up, then that theory has had a continuous though continually changing history from the time of Hippocrates to the present. There is today, of course, no evidence of humors. Hormones play the role in modern endocrinology which was assigned by the ancients to humors, for there is increasing evidence in endocrinological researches that the hormones determine not only many aspects of the physical constitution but also the temperamental characteristics of the individual.

The earlier history of humoral psychology has been reviewed by many writers (Klages, 1932; Laehr, 1900; Pillsbury, 1929; Roback, 1927, 1931; and Stern, 1911). The later history, during which time increasing emphasis has been placed upon the correlations between endocrine function, temperamental characteristics, and physique, is reviewed by Sheldon in Chapter 18 of this volume.

Dichotomous Typologies.—In the latter part of the nineteenth century a sudden increase of interest in the description of types of personality and in the development of systematic typologies was stimulated by the preoccupation with problems of classification of mental disorders to which Kraepelin in the field of the psychoses and Janet in the field of the psychoneuroses made such brilliant contributions. The work of these two men in establishing in their respective fields of interest a simple, basic dichotomy of types set a pattern for typological psychology which has been followed from their day to the present by many psychologists but especially by psychiatrists and psychopathologists.

When Emil Kraepelin (1899) embraced both mania and melancholia under the single heading of manic-depressive psychosis upon the demonstration that both conditions are symptomatic of a single morbid process and distinguished this psychosis from dementia praecox, he established a fundamental dichotomy in the field of the functional psychoses. Kraepelin's diagnosis of dementia praecox did not go unchallenged for long and the concept of dementia praecox as a definite disease entity was later supplanted by Bleuler's (1924) notion of schizophrenia as a group of psychotic reactions, but the idea of a fundamental difference between the two most important functional psychoses continues to exert a strong influence on psychiatric thought.

Pierre Janet (1894, 1903) did the same thing for the psychoneuroses when he established a dichotomy between hysteria and psychasthenia. This dichotomy has stood the test of time little better than Kraepelin's. Psychasthenia was from the beginning a scrap-basket category out of which other psychoneurotic conditions were almost immediately differentiated, but this simple two-fold classification once made has continued to influence psychiatric thought to a marked degree.

These early dichotomous classifications of the functional psychoses and psychoneuroses, together with the general acceptance within psychiatry of the distinction between predisposing and exciting factors in the development of mental disease, resulted in a seeking for those characteristics of personality which might be thought to predispose the individual to develop one or the other of the major psychoses or psychoneuroses. Thus the search began for traits which would distinguish two presumably opposed types of prepsychotic and prepsychoneurotic personality. Over the course of years, as a result of this interest, a long line of dichotomous types of personality, temperament, physique, and personality traits has been drawn; on the one hand, those assumed to be associated with either manic-depression or hysteria, and on the other, those presumably associated either with dementia praecox (schizophrenia) or with psychasthenia.

Each investigator, in presenting his particular typology, has usually explicitly pointed out the relation of his schema to the opposed types of psychosis and psychoneurosis and either explicitly or implicitly indicated its relation to other dichotomies already described. Thus there has developed gradually a rather elaborate scheme of typological formulations which has influenced, often directly but more often in indirect and subtle ways, the development of psychiatric and psychological thought about problems of personality.

In presenting this schema in Table II there is no implication that the factors listed on one side of the table are all positively correlated with each other and negatively correlated with the factors on the other side of the table although this is the assumption which has frequently been made. It is presented rather, as it was presented earlier in a simpler form (Barry, MacKinnon, and Murray, 1931), to make explicit what has too often been implicit. At least it would seem worth while to present as clearly as possible the relationships which have been assumed to exist between types, for theories are usually not experimentally checked until they have been explicitly formulated.

It is not easy to trace all of the specific notions which have contributed to the development of this schema, though some stand out in clear relief. Both the Paris and Nancy schools of psychiatry stressed the association of suggestibility and hypnotizability with hysteria.

Jung and Kretschmer have perhaps most directly and most explicitly contributed to the development of this typological schema. Having proposed (1909) the concept of introversion to account for the personality of the schizophrenic, Jung subsequently (1916) pointed out "the essential relationship" between psychasthenia and schizophrenia. When later (1923) he developed the dichotomy between introversion and extraversion he wrote of hysteria as the extravert's neurosis and of psychasthenia as the neurosis of the introvert. In addition he suggested the close relationship if not essential identity between his typology and those which had been previously proposed by other investigators. The most important of these suggested correlations for the development of the above schema was that between introversion-extraversion and the deep-narrow —shallow-broad types of mental process which had been described by the psychiatrist Otto Gross (1902). In order to explain differences in perseveration of mental processes Gross had assumed a correlation between the intensity of any experience and the tendency for that experience to persist secondarily and to determine the subsequent course of mental associations. He described two opposed types of mental process: a deep-narrow type in which characteristically the primary function, highly toned and loaded with affect, involves the expenditure of a great deal of energy and is of necessity followed by a lengthened period of restitution or long secondary function, and a shallow-broad type in which a less intense primary function is followed by a short secondary function.

It seemed to Spearman (1927) that Gross's long secondary one was essentially what G. E. Müller (1900) had called perseveration. On theoretical grounds as well as on the basis of experimental studies Spearman concluded that perseveration or the lag or inertia of mental processes was the central factor in the deep-narrow type of mental process (Gross),

TABLE II

TABLE OF TWO-FOLD TYPOLOGIES

PSYCHOTIC TYPES	
Manic-depression	Dementia Praecox (Kraepelin)
Manic-depression	Schizophrenia (Bleuler)
PSYCHONEUROTIC TYPES	
Hysteria	Psychasthenia (Janet)
PSYCHOTIC PERSONALITY TYPES	
Cycloid	Schizoid (Kretschmer)
PSYCHONEUROTIC PERSONALITY TYPES	
Hysteroid	Obsessoid (Janet)
NORMAL PERSONALITY TYPES	
Shallow-Broad	Deep-Narrow (Gross)
Extraverted	Introverted (Jung)
Nonperseverative	Perseverative (Spearman)
Objective	Subjective (Stern)
Cyclothymic	Schizothymic (Kretschmer)
Syntropic	Idiotropic (Wertheimer & Hesketh)
Color-type	Form-type (Scholl)
Extratensive	Introversive (Rorschach)
B-type	T-type (Jaensch)
Integrate	Disintegrate (Jaensch)
PERSONALITY TRAITS	
Suggestibility	Nonsuggestibility (Janet)
Hypnotizability	Nonhypnotizability (Janet)
Short secondary function	Long secondary function (Gross)
Extraversion	Introversion (Jung)
Nonperseveration	Perseveration (Spearman)
Color-abstraction	Form-abstraction (Külpe)
B-type eidetic imagery	T-type eidetic imagery (Jaensch)
Integration of psychic processes	Disintegration of psychic processes (Jaensch)
MORPHOLOGICAL TYPES	
Pyknic	Leptosomic (Kretschmer)
$\dfrac{\text{Height}}{\text{Chest volume}}$ low	$\dfrac{\text{Height}}{\text{Chest volume}}$ high (Wertheimer & Hesketh)

in introversion (Jung), and in the subjective type (Stern). Thus Spearman contributed to the development of the typological schema.

Stern (1938) also has pointed out the essential identity of all typologies which divide people on the basis of an inward or outward directedness of interest and experience: his own objective and subjective types, Jung's extraverted and introverted types and Kretschmer's opposites, cyclothyme and schizothyme.

When Rorschach (1942), on the basis of a study of subjects' interpretations of the symmetrical ink-blots of his *Psychodiagnostics* (for this method, see Chapter 6 by White), distinguished two types of persons— the introversive type, primarily responsive to stimulation from within, and the extratensive type, primarily responsive to external stimulation— it seemed clear to most investigators that there was at least a great similarity between the typologies of Rorschach and of Jung.

One cannot read the traits attributed by Rorschach to the extratensive and introversive types without thinking of the extravert and introvert types of Jung yet at the same time recognizing certain vital differences in the two typologies. The extratensive type which is indicated by a predominance of color over motor responses in the interpretation of ink-blots is described by Rorschach in the following terms: "stereotyped intelligence, more reproductive ability, more 'outward' life, labile affective reactions, more adaptable to reality, more extensive than intensive rapport, restless labile motility, skill and adroitness" (Rorschach, 1942, p. 78). On the other hand, the traits of the introversive type in which kinaesthetic interpretations predominate over color responses are said to be "more individualized intelligence, greater creative ability, more 'inner' life, stable affective reactions, less adaptable to reality, more intensive than extensive rapport, measured stable motility, awkwardness, clumsiness" (Rorschach, 1942, p. 78). Yet Rorschach (1942, p. 82) insisted that his use of the concept introversion had almost nothing in common with Jung's use of the term except the name.

The predominance of color responses in the interpretations of the extratensive type has suggested a relationship between this type and the color type. Külpe (1904) in his tachistoscopic experiments on abstraction was the first to observe and to report individual differences in the perception of colored forms: one of his Ss tended to report form, another color, the third sometimes color and sometimes form. The abstracter of form Külpe called a "formal" type, the abstracter of color a "material" type. But neither Külpe nor a number of investigators who confirmed his findings considered the problem of form abstraction *vs.* color abstraction from the point of view of psychological types until Scholl (1927a, 1927b) reported the correlation of definite psychological and somatic characteristics with color and form dominance in perception. Following Scholl a number of investigators have sought to determine the relation of color and form dominance in perception to other traits of personality. The relations of color and form types to the types of

Rorschach, of Jaensch, and of Kretschmer have all been investigated. Although the results of these investigations have been by no means uniform or clear they have nevertheless contributed to the development of the notion of typological relationships pictured in Table II (shown on page 18).

On the basis of their investigation of eidetic imagery E. R. and W. Jaensch (1926, 1930) have developed over the course of some years an extremely complex typology. Distinguishing two types of eidetic imagery each of which seemed to be intimately associated with different psychological and somatic traits the Jaensches proposed the existence of two broad biotypes of personality—B and T types. In the former eidetic images very much like memory images but more vivid and subject to voluntary control were observed in individuals with Basedow's syndrome (exophthalmic goiter resulting from hyperfunctioning of the thyroid gland). In the T-type eidetic imagery more nearly resembling after-imagery and not subject to voluntary control was observed to be associated with a tetanoid state resulting from hypofunctioning of the para-thyroid glands.

The criticism that these early eidetic types were too narrow to account for the great range of personalities was made at once and accepted by the Jaensches. But if their first typology was too simple, their correction of it has certainly been extremely complex. In their revised typology the B-type and T-type have become merely the exaggerated expressions with physical symptoms of two broad and basic biotypes designated the integrate and disintegrate types.

The integrate type of person is said to be characterized by an interpenetration of all mental processes, in the extreme case revealing no distinction between after images, eidetic images, and memory images. In effect, all imagery is of an eidetic character. In integrates, a change of experience in one sense modality tends to induce corresponding changes in other modalities. The integrate type is said to be plastic, intuitive, empathic, and often artistic. His experience is characterized by "coherence with the outer world," which is to say that his perceptual constancies are particularly marked. He is concerned with the outer world.

The disintegrate type of person, on the other hand, has very little clear-cut imagery. After images and memory images are differentiated; eidetic imagery is lacking. In general his mental processes are more clearly differentiated and more independent than the mental processes of the integrate. Whereas the integrate is plastic, the disintegrate is said to have a tendency to invariance, to be inflexible and rigid.

The following table summarizes the chief characteristics of the integrate and disintegrate types as given by Jaensch and suggests the reasons why in the schema of typological relationships the integrate type and its extreme expression in the B-type have come to be associated with the types and traits listed in the left-hand column and the disintegrate type and its extreme form, the *T*-type, have come to be associated with the types and traits of the right-hand column of Table II.

TABLE III

CONTRASTING CHARACTERISTICS OF THE INTEGRATE AND
DISINTEGRATE TYPES (Jaensch)

INTEGRATE	DISINTEGRATE
1. All psychophysical functions react as a closed whole.	1. All psychophysical functions react more or less separately from each other.
2. Feeling emphasized.	2. Will emphasized.
3. Open to the environment. Outwardly and inwardly vigorous, moving with others, adaptable, with hearty mood changes. More childishly gay and pulsating.	3. Closed against the world. Outwardly a mask, inwardly often fully controlled affect, or at one and the same time excitable and apathetic. More earnest, austere, given to reflection.
4. Plastic nature.	4. Rigid nature.
5. Artistically or aesthetically inclined.	5. Conscientious, men of conflict.
6. Visionary.	6. Theorist.
7. Lively, often rapidly changing association of ideas.	7. Slow, dragging association of ideas.
8. Changeable.	8. Persevering.
9. An artist in life and a skilful practical person.	9. A hard and harsh person.

Exaggerated Forms with Outer Marks	
B-Type	*T*-Type

The Jaensches have described yet other types, for example, another integrate type characterized by synaesthesia. Limitation of space does not permit an exposition of all these variations. Indeed, the more recent developments of the Jaensches' typology deserve no space, for whatever scientific validity their typology may have once possessed has been lost in its prostitution in the service of National Socialist theories of race.

Kretschmer's contribution to the scheme of typological relationships indicated in Table II is to be found in his study of the physique and temperament of manic-depressive and schizophrenic patients which led him to distinguish two psychotic personality types, the schizoid temperament of schizophrenics and the cycloid temperament of manic-depressive patients.

The schizoid and cycloid are described by Kretschmer as "those abnormal personalities which fluctuate between sickness and health, which reflect the fundamental psychological symptoms of the schizophrene and the circular psychoses in the lighter form of a personal oddity" (1926, p. 122).

The person of cycloid temperament is described as fundamentally sociable, good-natured, friendly, and genial; when elated and manic he is cheerful, humorous, jolly and hasty; when depressed he is quiet, calm, easily depressed, and soft-hearted. In his social reactions he is characterized by a readiness of response, a tendency to give himself up to the immediate present situation, seeking in a relatively uninhibited manner to give immediate expression to his emotions and his moods. He lives with others emotionally and takes an active part in his social environment. His attitude tends to be the realistic one of "live and let live." The psychic tempo or psychomotility of the cycloid temperament is described as even, natural, well-rounded and fluid, varying between an acceleration in mania and a slowing down in depression.

The person of schizoid temperament, on the other hand, is said to be characteristically unsociable, quiet, reserved, serious, humorless, and eccentric. According to Kretschmer, he is not, as many have thought him, either unduly sensitive or lacking in sensitivity but is both over-sensitive and cold at the same time. The psychic oversensitivity of the schizoid temperament is revealed in such traits as timidity, shyness, fineness of feelings, nervousness, excitability, and fondness of nature and books. Coldness and insensitivity, on the other hand, are said to be observed in such traits as pliableness, indifference, dull-wittedness, and silence. The social reactions of the schizoid are at best inferior and often essentially lacking. Autism is a fundamental trait which in some cases is a symptom of hypersensitivity, in others an expression of a lack of affective resonance for the world about. The mode of expression and psychomotility of the schizoid is not natural and adequate to the situation as in the case of cycloids but is characterized by a lack of immediacy. This is frequently seen in stiff, cramped, restrained, and stylized gestures and movements. In describing the schizoid psychic tempo Kretschmer says that "many schizoid temperaments may be ranged between two poles, i.e., between abnormal tenacity and abnormal jerkiness. On the one hand, we find people who are toughly energetic, stubborn, mulish, and pedantic, and, on the other, those whose natures are particularly unstable, whimsical, jerky, rash, and incalculable. And we find all possible mixtures and transitions between the two groups. If the cycloid temperaments may be said to vary between fast and slow, then the schizoids vary between tenacious and jerky. The cycloid temperamental curve is a wavy one, the schizoid curve is often jagged" (Kretschmer, 1926, p. 177).

When the traits of the cycloid and schizoid are toned down and expressed in the behavior of average or normal men, they constitute cyclothymia and schizothymia. Whereas the terms cycloid and schizoid are used when certain types of personality are looked upon as abortive forms of manic-depression and schizophrenia, as transitional stages between health and illness, the terms cyclothyme and schizothyme imply nothing as to health or illness but "are inclusive terms for large general biotypes, which include the great mass of healthy individuals with the few corresponding psychotics which are scattered among them" (Kretschmer, 1926, p. 208).

In addition to relating his general biotypes and prepsychotic personality types to manic-depressive psychosis and schizophrenia, Kretschmer related all of these in turn to the types of physique which he differentiated and designated as pyknic and leptosomic (asthenic and athletic). According to Kretschmer, cyclothymia in its normal as well as in its prepsychotic and psychotic manifestations tends to be associated with the pyknic build while schizothymia in its various expressions is more often observed in persons of leptosomic physique.[3]

In an attempt to get away from having to assign individuals to the bodily types on the basis of subjective judgments of qualitative aspects of their anatomical and physiological markings, Wertheimer and Hesketh (1926) devised an anthropometric index:

$$\frac{\text{Leg length} \times 10^3}{\text{Transverse chest diameter} \times \text{Sagittal chest diameter} \times \text{Trunk height}} \times 100$$

Presumably a low index would be indicative of a pyknic build, a high index indicative of an asthenic physique. Wertheimer and Hesketh report a low average index in manic-depression, a high average index in schizophrenia. In their study of the traits of prepsychotic personalities they substituted for Kretschmer's terms the terms syntropic and idiotropic to refer respectively to those who look for satisfaction in contact with others and those who find satisfaction in difference, in detachment, and in isolation from the personal and social environment.

Types are crude pictures of personality. That is why they are so easily drawn, why they invariably overlap, and why such a scheme of interrelationships as pictured in Table II is so easily developed and yet so difficult to prove or disprove, for only that which is precisely stated can be definitely tested. To be sure, many of the relationships assumed to exist among the dichotomous typologies have been investigated both clinically and experimentally but with little success so far. For the most part these studies have been made by partisan investigators; the details of experimental procedure have not been clear; the bases of selection of subjects, extremely important in studies of this sort, have not been specified; and the statistical treatment of results demanded by the very

---

[3] A fuller exposition as well as a critical evaluation of this aspect of Kretschmer's work will be found in Chapter 18 of this book.

nature of these investigations has been lacking. The problem of the relationships among the various dichotomous typologies remains a problem.

The charge may be brought, as indeed it often has been, that all such two-fold classifications fail to do justice to the richness and variety of the human personality. Allport charges that "any doctrine of types is a halfway approach to the problem of individuality, and nothing more" (1937, p. 13). The obvious inadequacies of oversimplified dichotomies have frequently led those who have developed them or other investigators seeking to improve them to describe subclasses (e.g., simple, hebephrenic, catatonic, and paranoid types of schizophrenia; introverted and extraverted thinking, feeling, sensation, and intuition). However, the attempt to correct for the inadequacy of a typology through a further elaboration and differentiation of additional types may defeat the very purpose for which the typology was originally developed. The resultant elaborated typology may become too unwieldy to handle. The prime example of a typology gone to seed is Fourier's (1851) classification of human passions into 3 classes, 12 orders, 32 genera, 134 species, and 404 varieties which in turn yield 810 types of character!

The validity of dichotomous typologies has also been questioned on statistical grounds, for when the traits of personality on the basis of which types of personality have been distinguished have been measured by tests, questionnaires, and rating scales a plot of the measurements has invariably yielded a unimodal rather than bimodal curve of distribution, provided the population tested has been an unselected one.

Actually types are never based on single traits. They are always configurations of many traits in which the emphasis is upon the whole. It is only in the form pattern of personality as a whole that the type can be found. This has been pretty well recognized by the typologists who have given us the first descriptions of types, but it has all too often been ignored by those who have sought to replace the crude qualitative descriptions of types by a measurement of their component parts. For this reason most statistical studies of types have been beside the point. Here we have come upon the question as to whether the total personality can be studied objectively. Since this question in turn raises many problems concerning the nature of traits of personality, an attempt will not be made to answer this question until the theory of traits has been discussed.

Before leaving the discussion of types, however, the question may well be asked: What theory of the structure of personality is implicit in the doctrine of types? All typologies are based upon the assumption that the personality is characterized by a more or less enduring structure. Typologists may disagree as to the nature of this underlying structure, some conceive of it in psychological terms, others conceptualize it physiologically, and yet others think of it in terms of neural structures. It is not by chance that most typologists have been biologically oriented. Typologists may emphasize different traits or characteristics as most fundamentally differentiating the basic types of personality, but on one point they agree, namely, that there are intrinsic traits of personality.

Theory of Specific Stimulus-Response Elements of Personality

The theory of personality structure which has been developed in the behavioristic approach to personality is, among the various theories, closest to the position that the personality possesses no enduring structure, for it attributes a minimum of structure to it, namely, nothing more than a mere aggregation of stimulus-response elements (see Chapter 2 by Guthrie).

According to this theory there are no broad, general traits of personality, no general and consistent forms of conduct which, if they existed, would make for consistency of behavior and stability of personality, but only independent and specific stimulus-response bonds or habits. Proponents of this view argue that it is meaningless to speak of individuals as aggressive, extraverted, persistent, ascendant, etc., for such terms cannot properly be applied to persons but only to the quality of the behavior which they will reveal in specific situations. Believing that behavior is in a narrow sense specific to the situation in which it occurs, they caution us against an uncritical generalization of behavior. According to these theorists the range of prediction of behavior is greatly circumscribed, for they hold that having observed a certain quality of behavior, let us say aggression, in a single action in a specific situation, one can predict no more than that the same individual will act aggressively in the same situation again or in a situation very similar to it and that the greater the number of identical elements in any two situations, the greater the probability that the behavior in the two situations will be the same.

This theory of personality has been variously called the theory of specific habits, the theory of specificity, and the anti-trait theory. Historically it has developed in the wake of the violent reaction against the excesses of a faculty psychology which certainly overemphasized the value of formal discipline and the extent to which the effects of training may be transferred from one situation to another. The revolt against faculty psychology was first led by William James and later ably furthered by E. L. Thorndike, both of whom instigated what has turned out to be a long line of experimental investigations of transfer of training which has revealed much less in the way of effective transfer than the earlier champions of formal training had assumed. The investigations, however, which in the opinion of many have given the *coup de grace* to any theory of broad traits of personality are the very extensive studies of the Character Education Inquiry directed by Hartshorne and May (1928, 1929, 1930). In these investigations hundreds of children were presented with a variety of concrete performance tests and their responses to different test situations examined for evidence for or against the existence of such alleged general traits as deception, helpfulness, cooperativeness, persistence, and self-control.

The findings with reference to deception are typical of the findings with reference to all the alleged general traits. Having created situations in which subjects might deceive the experimenter by cheating, by stealing, or by lying, the investigators found that a subject who deceived in one situation did not necessarily deceive in all situations. From an analysis of their data Hartshorne and May concluded that a single test of deceit reveals little about deception in general, and that in so far as individual subjects behave similarly in different situations, they do so in proportion as the situations are alike. They interpret their findings as evidence against the existence of a general trait of deception in these words, "an individual's honesty or dishonesty consists of a series of acts and attitudes to which these descriptive terms (honesty and dishonesty) apply" (1928, p. 380). Their final conclusion about all the alleged general traits which they investigated is that they are "groups of specific habits rather than general traits" (1930, p. 1).

Allport (1937) has criticized the findings and conclusions of Hartshorne and May on the grounds that these investigators, in studying *good* and *bad* qualities rather than natural qualities, complicated the already difficult problem of studying personality by introducing social and ethical concepts of honesty and service which "seldom correspond precisely to the form of mental organization found in adults, and still less to the unsocialized dispositions of children" (1937, p. 252). Moreover, since such socialized traits as honesty and self-control have to be learned, one would not expect to find them as broad generalized traits in very young children. Accordingly, the limitation of the study to children in the fifth to eighth grades would seem to have been an unhappy selection of subjects. It is noteworthy, however, that even within this narrow age range there is ample evidence from the study that children grow more consistent with age and especially with reference to positive social ideals. But possibly Allport's most telling point is that although the low correlations between tests in the Character Education Inquiry show that children do not possess the particular traits of deception, helpfulness, etc., which were investigated, they do not prove that there are no other broad traits of personality. Lying may not be related to stealing and in this sense there may be no evidence of a general trait of dishonesty, but both of these habits which by themselves were shown to be *fairly* consistent may be integral parts of other broad traits which were not investigated.

Figure 1 represents Hartshorne and May's conception of a trait of dishonesty as well as other traits which were not investigated in the Character Education Inquiry but whose possible existence Allport describes as follows:

It may be that child *A* steals pennies because he has a consistent personal trait of *bravado* based upon his admiration for the gangsters he reads about in the tabloids and sees on the screen; child *B* steals because he has a persistent *interest in tools and mechanics* that drives him to buy more equipment than he can honestly afford; child *C*, suffering from a gnawing *feeling of social inferiority*, steals pennies to purchase candy to buy his way into favor with his playmates. Child *D* does not steal pennies, but he lies about his cheating, not because he has a general trait of dishonesty, but because he has a general trait of *timidity* (fear of consequences); child *E* lies because he is afraid of hurting the feelings of the teacher whom he adores; child *F* lies because he is *greedy for praise.* Each of these children behaved as he did toward these tests, not because he had specific habits but because he had some deep-lying and characteristic trait. All that the C.E.I. discovered was that the particular trait of honesty as defined in the usual ethical terms and tested in various conventional situations, was not one of which the children possessed constant individual degrees, especially in the face of perhaps a stronger tendency of each child to express some trait other than honesty through the behavior of lying and stealing. The children did not all have the *same* trait, but they had nevertheless their own traits. (1937, pp. 251–252.)

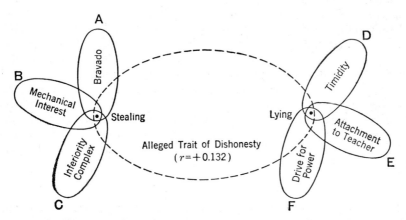

Figure 1.   Critique of One Statistical Conception of Trait

Dotted ellipse represents the trait as conceived by investigators in the Character Education Inquiry, solid ellipses, possible personal traits overlooked by them. (From Allport, 1937, p. 251)

Allport further points out that the interpretation of complex statistical results is always to some extent arbitrary. Thus while Hartshorne and May interpret their results as evidence of specificity, Maller (1934) who also worked in the Inquiry, sees in the same data evidence of a general trait of character, "*c*," defined as "the readiness to forgo an immediate gain for the sake of remote but greater gain" (p. 101). Thus two antithetical hypotheses, one of specificity, the other of generality, find support in a single body of data depending upon the interpretation and evaluation of a matrix of correlations.

Additional criticisms of all investigations which have yielded evidence of specificity are made by Allport (1932) in another place. He points out that the research methods which have yielded evidence of specificity have been completely inadequate for the demonstration of the most fundamental consistencies of personality, for if such consistencies exist they exist only in the pattern or style of the total personality and not in the arbitrarily isolated variables measured by tests and questionnaires. But even such tests and questionnaires, inadequate as they are, reveal some measure of consistency, for what else is the meaning of the split-half reliability of scales which may range between +.75 and +.85? Finally, the theory of specificity is supported largely by the results of mass or group investigations in which there is a neglect of the individual, whereas congruence and integration of behavior can probably be fully observed and demonstrated only in the intensive study of individuals. In this connection MacKinnon's (1938) investigation of honesty and deceit with fewer and more mature subjects (college and university students) is indicative of the different sort of results which will be obtained when a different method of investigation is employed. In a situation in which subjects were left free to obey or violate prohibitions placed upon the seeing of solutions to problems which they were trying to solve, two different yet within themselves consistent and congruent patterns of personality traits were observed to differentiate the violators and nonviolators of the prohibitions.

Certainly a great deal of behavior is specific to the situation in which it occurs. Even such an uncompromising champion of traits as Allport does not deny that certain traits are more specific than others, but he would deny that the existence of some specific traits constitutes ground for a sweeping denial of consistency of personality. In spite of occasional specificity Allport insists that generality prevails in the organization of the personality.

A final consideration of the rival claims of trait and anti-trait theorists and a final evaluation of the evidence for and against the opposed theories of specificity and generality in personality will be postponed until the trait theory of personality has been presented. Logically between the theory of specific stimulus-response elements and the theory of traits comes the theory of factors of personality.

Theory of Factors of Personality

As has been pointed out above, the theory of specificity grew in large measure out of the revolt against a faculty psychology which assumed that the common and universal elements of mind and personality were certain generic powers or agencies such as memory, attention, ambition, imagination, intellect, feeling, will. These were called faculties and it was by reference to them that the phenomena of consciousness and behavior were to be explained. Faculty psychologists were, to be sure, more interested in the problems of mind-in-general than personality. Possibly for this reason they assumed that the elements of personality were the same as the elements of mind-in-general (Allport, 1937, p. 238).

This was to some extent even true of Franz Joseph Gall (1758–1828), the founder of phrenology, who unlike most faculty psychologists was very much concerned with the problem of individual differences and sought to explain them by reference to faculties. Gall, however, was not satisfied with the faculties postulated by the psychologists of his day, for, as he wrote, "We nowhere find that a man or a woman has become celebrated by the Understanding and the Will, by Attention, Comparison, Desire. . . . Every man, except an idiot, enjoys all these faculties. Yet all men have not the same intellectual or moral character. . . . We need faculties, the different distribution of which shall determine the different species of animals, and the different proportions of which explain the difference in individuals" (1835, Vol. I, pp. 87–88).

For this purpose Gall described 27 determinate faculties or radical powers relative intensities of which might account for differences in individuals. These faculties were not arrived at in any *a priori* manner but were, he insisted, empirically determined. Furthermore, they were independent of one another, or at least he hoped they were. In giving less emphasis to the nomothetic or universal attributes of mind which had been stressed by other faculty psychologists and in seeking to establish empirically differentiating faculties which could be assumed to be independent of one another, Gall was years ahead of his contemporaries in his treatment of the problem of individual differences and was in more than one sense of the word the forerunner of the modern factor analysts. Of course, factors are no more identical with faculties than are hormones with humors, yet in both cases there is a historical continuity of thought which should not be overlooked. The change from the earlier to the later concepts has in both cases been dependent upon the factual and conceptual development of sciences other than psychology. Just as endocrinology has made possible the transition from humors to hormones, so recent advances in mathematical and statistical theory have made it possible to replace faculties with factors.

The search for factors as the most important and basic elements of personality has been stimulated by the striking success of the psychometricians in seeking and finding the units of intelligence by means of a factor analysis of the intercorrelations of intelligence test scores. The pioneer in the development of factorial methods for the discovery of the components of intelligence was Spearman (1904). His methods have been vastly modified and improved by a large number of workers.[4] As these methods have been developed they have been used not only to discover the component elements of intelligence but also of personality. This transfer of the method and its basic assumptions from problems of intelligence to those of personality has been made rather uncritically. Allport, however, has questioned "whether intelligence, an obviously artificial construct of the nomothetic order, might [not] in principle, offer a different type of scientific problem from the vital and integrated personality" (1937, p. 242).

There is neither space nor need in the present chapter to discuss the mathematics of factor analysis, but something must be said about the logic of the method as background for understanding the theory which assumes that the basic units of personality are the factors discovered in the analysis of a matrix of correlations of ratings and of test and questionnaire scores. For such purposes Burt's treatment of factor analysis (1941) is particularly valuable because he suggests that factor analysis be considered a logical method rather than a mathematical one, since mathematics is best to be thought of not so much as the science of quantity as the science of logical relations.

The various methods of factor analysis have as their aim the discovery of the smallest number of independent factors or variables which will be adequate for the description and classification of traits of mind and personality. Not content with the dichotomous classifications of the typologist, the factor analyst subdivides his first crude qualitative classes until he has replaced them with quantitative grades. The quantitative variables which thus replace qualitative attributes can be represented as vectors which vary in length (the quantitative element) and in direction (the qualitative classification).

On so much the factor analysts are in agreement. But if one asks, "How many kinds of factors are there?" one does not get a clear or single answer. Spearman (1904) has postulated two kinds of factors: one general factor and a number of specific factors. Some have reduced Spearman's two factors to a single general factor. Others have argued for three kinds of factors: a general factor, group factors, and specific factors. Still others have insisted that there must be an indefinite number of common factors. Approaching this problem through an examination of the logical basis of factor analysis, Burt writes that, "If our factors are logical principles rather than psychological principles, we should be able to state, a priori and in advance, how many kinds we may in theory expect, though whether all the kinds will be found in this particular table or in that must depend upon the traits or tests actually selected for study, i.e., upon the experimental design" (1941, p. 101).

---

[4] It lies outside the scope of the present chapter to review and criticize this development of factor analysis. One of the most readable, relatively nontechnical, summaries of this development is to be found in Dael Wolfle, Factor Analysis to 1940, *Psychometric Monographs*, No. 3, Chicago: University of Chicago Press, 1940.

According to Burt, four possible statements may be made about the traits of individuals measured in any investigation:

(1) *All* the traits possess a particular characteristic, *g,* and thus form a general, all-inclusive class;

(2) *Some* of the traits possess a particular characteristic, p_1 (which the rest do not possess), and thus form a narrower sub-class; and again others possess the characteristic p_2 (which the rest do not possess) and thus form a second sub-class, and so on;

(3) *This* particular trait possesses one particular set of characteristics, u_1, which none of the others possess and which thus, as it were, forms a sub-class of one, and similarly for each of the other traits.

Further, if we repeat our tests, we may be able to add that this particular trait possesses (*a*) one particular set of characteristics, s_1, *always,* i.e., every time we measure it (the series of repeated measurements thus forming, as it were, a sub-subclass), and (*b*) other sets of characteristics, $e_1, e_2, \ldots$ *occasionally,* i.e., one set on this occasion, another on that. (1941, p. 102)

These four statements give a logical classification of four factors: two main groups, each with two subclasses.

A. *Common* factors, i.e., those influencing several tests or traits. These are of two kinds, viz.:

(1) *Universal* or General factors, common to all the traits.

. . . . .

(2) *Particular* factors, each common to a certain group of traits only, and hence usually termed "*Group*-factors": they have sometimes been called "special factors," "overlapping specific factors" ("overlapping," because any single trait may contain more than one of them), or "general factors of limited range"—phrases which all rather blur the real nature of the distinction.

B. *Individual* or Unique factors, i.e., those influencing one test or trait alone, viz.:

(3) *Singular* factors, each peculiar to a single trait, and usually called "*Specific* factors" (sometimes also "individual" or "unique" factors); when the characteristics they cover are regarded as irrelevant to the main inquiry, these factors, like the following, are frequently described as "errors," and then, in contrast to the following, are designated "constant" or "systematic errors."

(4) *Accidental* factors, each peculiar to the particular occasion on which the particular trait was measured, and therefore sometimes called "factors of error" or of "unreliability" (the latter term in factor-analysis merely means inconsistency). Here the errors are the results, not of some gross and traceable bias, but of a very large number of very small causes. Hence the minor fluctuations for which they are responsible show the random distribution characteristic of

"chance," and the factors themselves are consequently often called "random errors" or "chance factors." (Burt, 1941, pp. 102–103)

These four factors are summarized by Burt in his four-factor theorem which states that:

> The measurement of any individual for any one of a given set of traits may be regarded as a function of four kinds of components: namely, those characteristic of (*i*) all the traits, (*ii*) some of the traits, (*iii*) the particular trait in question whenever it is measured, (*iv*) the particular trait in question as measured on this particular occasion. (1941, p. 103)

Four factors are thus distinguished: general, group, specific, and error factors which, as Burt points out, correspond quite closely to the categories of the scholastic logicians: *genus, species, proprium,* and *accidens.*

Burt (1941) has argued that the four-factor theorem is fundamental and that other factor theories are derived from it by omitting factors of one kind or another and emphasizing certain of the factors that remain. Which theory will be most applicable will depend upon the traits selected for investigation in any particular study, but in general he believes that some form of multiple factor theory or a "theory of common factors" will best serve to discover factors which are psychologically significant. Others express preference for other theories. There is no common agreement. A good deal of the controversy among factor theorists results from a failure to recognize the relative nature of the distinctions made between different kinds of factors. Guilford (1940), who himself favors the use of Thurstone's method, states with commendable frankness that "At this stage of things factorial, any choice of method or theory is largely a matter of prejudice, in view of the absence of any final proof which compels assent" (p. 368).

Here again, his logical approach prevents Burt from making this common error. With admirable clearness he has insisted that:

> the differences throughout are principally differences of degree; the "general factor" is simply the "group-factor" that has the most widespread occurrence; and the "specific factors" are simply the "group-factors" that are most narrowly limited in their operation. Give me a list of tested traits which are said to be governed by a general or universal factor only such as Spearman's *g*: I can always add one or more tests or traits which do not contain the factor, and so reduce the general factor to a group-factor. Name any specific factor, said to be peculiar to one tested trait alone: I can always add one or more slightly different tests or traits, guaranteed to contain the factor (or the constant elements of it), and so convert that specific factor into a group-factor. . . . Thus *the distinctions between general, group-, and specific factors are formal rather than material, relative rather than fixed.* (1941, p. 167)

A good deal of the controversy among factor theorists would not have occurred had they remembered that:

> genus and species are "not absolute terms, but purely correlative." "The same term may be at the same time a genus to the lesser classes it contains, and a species of the next more general class: by itself no term can be styled a genus or a species." [1] In the same fashion we may say: by itself no factor can be styled general, group-, or specific; such designations have reference solely to the particular set of tests and traits that have been correlated. (Burt, 1941, pp. 167–168)
>
> [1] J. Welton, *Manual of Logic*, I, p. 81.

Thus Spearman's "g" may appear as a general factor if only cognitive abilities are measured but let measurements of emotional and moral reactions also be included and "g" will be a group-factor.

Burt concludes:

> Accordingly, so far as the psychological interpretation of the factors is concerned, the most convenient theory to adopt will be the most comprehensive: namely, that which simply states that the mental reactions of our examinees can always be described in terms of *a number of factors of a greater or a lesser degree of generality*. How many *kinds* of factors we are to recognize becomes a minor issue. In principle, as will now be clear, we must regard all factors as group-factors, and treat the general factor and the specific factors as merely extreme and limiting cases; and in that sense we have to deal with one kind of factor only. (1941, p. 168)

This seems an admirably simple and eminently sound solution of the whole controversy over the number and kind of factors.

But what are factors? Are they reals to which causal efficacy is to be attributed or are they merely statistical fictions? Of course, one might avoid this troublesome question if one were to define factors as "what factor-analysts seek and find" (Burt, 1941, p. 210). However, most factor theorists have been more explicit than this about the nature of factors.

At one extreme are those who think of factors as faculties or abilities. Thurstone (1935) refers to simple, primary, or fundamental abilities. Holzinger (1937) writes of underlying abilities. Though Spearman does not think that factors should be identified with faculties or abilities, it is clear that he thinks of them as causal reals. He earlier interpreted factors as organs or fundamental functions of the mind. He has described "g" as energy and "s" as neural mechanisms or engines. Strictly speaking, if factors are defined as abilities, factor analysis would not be applicable to the study of personality in the broad sense but only to the investigation of intelligence. Possibly for this reason, some investigators have defined factors more broadly, though those who have equated factors to abilities have not refrained on that account from applying factor analysis in the study of personality. In any case, many have agreed with Kelley (1935) that factors should be considered as elementary or unitary traits of personality. Guilford (1940) would prefer to think of factors as the fundamental dimensions of the mind.

At the other extreme of conceptualization are those factor theorists who deny real existence to factors. Anastasi (1936, 1938) believes that factors are statistical fictions—"shifting mathematical components" is the term she uses—since she has found both factors and factor loadings to change as the result of experiential influences on her subjects. To think of factors as abilities is, she believes, to revert to faculty psychology. Her position seems to Guilford (1940) to represent a search for absolutes. Allport (1934, 1937), outside the fold of factor analysts, is in fundamental agreement with Anastasi as to what factors are. To him they are primarily mathematical artifacts; they have no psychological meaning.

Thomson thinks that much controversy would be avoided "if factors were admitted to be only statistical coefficients, possibly without any more 'reality' than an average, or an index of the cost of living, or a standard deviation, or a correlation coefficient" (1939, p. 42). For Burt, factors are principles of classification.

He writes:

> Rigorously speaking, factors cannot be regarded as substances or as parts of a substance, or even as causal attributes inhering in a substance. They are not separate "organs" or isolated "properties" of the mind; they are not "primary abilities," "unitary traits," "mental powers or energies." They are principles of classification described by selective operators. *The operand on which these operators operate is not "the mind," but the sum total of the relations between minds and their environment.* The relational structure of this operand the factorist must presume to be knowable, but its causal or substantial nature he must treat as unknown or at any rate irrelevant. (1941, p. 227)

Of course, to ask what is the nature of a factor is to ask a metaphysical question and perhaps the failure of factor theorists to agree upon an answer should not be held too much against them.

A more scientific and possibly more relevant question to ask would be, "What is the origin of any factor?" or "What makes for factors?" Anything that makes for correlations also makes for factors. When a factor is found, regardless of the particular method of analysis employed, there is evidence that there are common causes in the variables which have been analyzed. The causes of factors are as numerous as the causes of correlation (Wolfle, 1940).

A criticism frequently made of the attempt to isolate the fundamental factors of personality by factorial analysis is that the factors which are extracted depend upon the particular items which are included in the original tests, rating scales, and questionnaires. If no logical basis under-lies the original selection of items, it is difficult to see how such logic can be introduced by the mere application of factorial methods. In a very real sense the factors with which one comes out are the resultants of the items with which one starts. Just as no amount of statistical manipula-tion can improve incomplete or inaccurate data, so the factors extracted from the analysis of the intercorrelations of test scores and ratings possess the same errors which the tests and ratings possess.

As Vernon (1938) has pointed out, "the factors can only cover those facets of personality which are represented in the test battery, hence their universality is limited by the comprehensiveness of the sampling of human traits" (pp. 109–110). He believes further that since sub-jective attitudes distort ratings and since objective measures of conduct have as yet been little developed, none of the factorizations yet made have disclosed the real elements of personality. Finally, and this he considers the most fundamental objection, any set of extracted factors are not the only possible ones. An infinite number of factorizations of any given set of variables is possible, the relative merits of which have to be decided on logical and mathematical grounds. Unfortunately the mathematical ground seems all too often to be shifting sand if one may judge from the conflict and controversy in the field of factor theory.

Whether factor analysis can reveal the underlying structure of per-sonality or merely the logical structure of the personality tests employed in such investigations is a fundamental problem. It is fair to say that most analysts believe the former, their critics the latter. On this point Kelley (1935) is very explicit. He believes that the unitary or basic traits of personality can be isolated by factorial methods and that eventually the relatively small number of elements necessary for the complete description of personality will be established. Tryon (1935), Burks (1936), Allport (1937), and Vernon (1938), although taking different positions as to the structure of personality, are nevertheless in agreement in believing that the factorist's conception of personality is false, that it is contradicted by the majority of facts established in biology and psychology.

The more scientifically sophisticated factorists think of factors as *systems* of coordinates, as simple and parsimonious frames of reference for the classification and interpretation of the underlying variables of personality. For them, factors are not faculties or traits existent in concrete personalities, but rather convenient descriptive categories which enable the factorist to generalize and simplify test results and "make predictions about people with a maximum degree of efficiency" (Vernon, 1938, p. 110). This is the clearly stated position of Burt (1941).

When factors are conceived of as a system of coordinates it is quite clear that there is no claim that factors are traits existent in the per-sonality, and arguments from biology, psychology, or from any science other than mathematics and logic are largely irrelevant. The factorists who take this position, however, must be reminded that their factors cannot be considered the building stones out of which the structured personality is built.

The factorist has criticized the clinician for depending exclusively upon subjective judgment in the isolation and description of the fundamental traits of personality. He charges that in the analysis of personality and in the classification of its fundamental traits the clinician lacks objective criteria which are supplied by factorial methods. To this the clinician has replied that the factors discovered by analysis are dependent upon the original test items and the decision as to which items shall be included is the result of a subjective judgment, and that after factors have been extracted their identification or interpretation is made again in terms of subjective considerations. The clinician is disturbed that so often the factors isolated by factor analysis lack psychological significance and are so heterogeneous as to defy meaningful designation. Most factorists, on the other hand, are not troubled by their failure to identify the factors they have isolated. To them it seems fully as scientific to designate them x, y, or z as to relate them to the variables of personality which the clinician has described; their psychological meaning is not important. To be sure, Thurstone (1935) has insisted that factors be psychologically meaningful, but this position has by no means been taken by all factorists.

But then the question can be raised as to whether one has through the application of factorial methods discovered anything about the elements of personality or their interrelationships. Of course, it is hardly to be expected that the factors isolated by analysis will correspond exactly to either the layman's or the clinical psychologist's conceptions of traits of personality. If they did not cut across such conceptions and unite traits previously considered separate and elemental and break up other supposed basic traits into simpler components, the application of factorial methods would be mere mathematical mumbo-jumbo. Unless factor analysis yields something other than that with which it starts, the labor and time spent in its application might better be used for some other purpose. It must be remembered that a factor is an abstraction from a number of tests of different traits, therefore some heterogeneity of traits entering into a single factor is to be expected. But this is at times so great as to raise doubts as to whether the isolated factors can possibly be either fundamental traits of personality or significant reference points in any significant system of classification. There is no reason why a common factor might not be a blend of two traits ordinarily considered as separate, but unfortunately many examples are to be found in the literature which make neither logical nor psychological sense.

It must be clear that not every factor discovered can be thought of as a fundamental trait of personality or a significant rubric for the classification of personality. Most factor methods fail to provide criteria for significance. Thurstone (1935, 1938), however, believes that the rotation of axis insures psychological significance of the factors discovered by the application of his method. But in this as in all methods the final interpretation of a factor depends upon the psychological insight of the investigator. The name given to any factor should at this stage of factor analysis be thought of as no more than an hypothesis about its nature. In this connection more serious consideration might be given to Copeland's (1935) proposal that the imbalance between the mathematical meticulousness and the psychological laxness of factor analysis be corrected by obtaining group judgments of the psychological meaning of extracted factors instead of relying as at present upon the subjective interpretation of the single investigator.

A fundamental premise of factor analysis is that factors are uncorrelated with each other. This assumption has been made on formal grounds by all factor analysts with the exception of Thurstone and Tryon because to assume independent factors simplifies considerably the mathematics of factor analysis. Actually there are many reasons for believing that the fundamental traits of personality are not completely independent. The assumption of the factorists that they are mathematically independent has been severely criticized (Allport, 1937; Vernon, 1938) as being a return to faculty psychology with its concept of independent abilities or faculties. They point out, quite rightly, that such unrelatedness of traits in the person seems unlikely in view of all that is known about the development and structure of the nervous system and the personality.

This criticism is relevant if directed at the conception of factors which identifies them with traits or abilities. It must be remembered, however, that there is no common agreement as to the nature of factors and such a criticism is irrelevant when factors are conceived to be nothing more than categories of classification. Even if factors are conceived of as traits or abilities it may be expedient for certain purposes to conceive of them as independent even though it is clear that their independence is not complete. Wolfle has suggested that "Intelligence test scores and academic grades depend, in part, upon the same causes and so are correlated. But they are easily separated in thought. Height and weight have some common determiners and are correlated measures. But it seems more convenient and natural to use these correlated measures than to search for two strictly independent functions of body size" (1940, p. 29).

Those who criticize factor analysis for assuming the existence of independent factors should criticize the use of a psychograph on the same ground although I am not aware that they have done so. One of the severest critics of the structure of personality implied in the logic of factor methods has discussed with approval the representation of personality by means of the psychograph (Allport, 1937). But as Burt (1941) has pointed out, the only difference between the drawing of a psychograph and the factorization of a personality is that the latter introduces greater mathematical precision. The factorist's representation of a factor by a vector and the use of coordinates rather than ordinates does not involve a great jump in principle, for

> In using coordinates instead of ordinates, he [the factorist] implies that the lines whose lengths represent the numbers or weights are to be drawn in different directions and to start from a common origin instead of standing parallel on a common base line. It is as though we saw three pins of different length, lying side by side on the pin-paper, and then took them out and stuck them round a pin-cushion instead; the two little patterns formed by the pin-heads—the old "curve" on the flat paper and the new three-dimensional pattern round the cushion—would be two alternative ways of representing the same complex fact, namely, the differences in length of the pins. With *n* traits instead of three, the vectorial pattern will be specified by coordinates in *n* dimensions; but, if the student has trouble over picturing patterns in *n*-dimensional space, I suggest he translates the *n*-dimensional configurations into flat zizag "profiles" by treating the coordinates as ordinates. (Burt, 1942, pp. 78–79)

Whether one uses ordinates or coordinates, one is using mathematics for the representation of certain facts. In neither case is an actual picture of a concrete person being drawn; confusion arises only if one expects fictional concepts which have been developed for the rational correlation of certain phenomena to mirror those phenomena in all their concrete actuality.

Let Burt speak for the factor theorists in reply to the charge that through the application of factor analysis to the study of personality the person as experienced is lost. He says:

> I am therefore far from supposing that factor measurements by themselves can yield an adequate picture of the "living personality" that stands behind the measurable performances. For such a reconstruction a factor measurement is about as helpful as the barring and metronome-figures are in indicating the changing rhythm of a symphony. A complete set of factor measurements for a sample population, with no comments and no case histories, would be as informative as the bare notes on an orchestral score with no marks of expression and no concert-goer's notes. To translate a musical experience into black dots on a number of parallel staves is indeed to "disrupt a living whole into little bits in the interest of a quantitative technique": yet that is no reason for consigning all scores to the fire. Provided factor analysis tells the truth and nothing but the truth, we need not condemn it for failing to tell the whole truth. (1941, pp. 137–138)

Certainly, factor analysis does not tell the whole truth. It tells very little about the single case; for such a study it is not the method of choice. But certainly an interest in that which is general is as important as an interest in that which is unique. It is no criticism of any method that it is limited in its applicability to but one kind of problem.[5]

So much for the theory of factors. We may now ask what have been the results of the application of factor analysis to the study of personality. It is generally recognized that the application of factorial methods to the study of personality has been conspicuously less fruitful than the application of the same methods to the study of intelligence. This has been due, at least in part, to the fact that the ratings, tests, and questionnaires which have been devised for the measurement of traits of personality have had lower validity and reliability than those used in the measurement of intellectual ability (Wolfle, 1942). And yet amid the confusion of reported findings some order is beginning to emerge.

What are the settled and established findings? I prefer to let a factorist answer the question. Wolfle (1942) finds that over fifty factors of personality have been reported in the literature. However, many of these have been reported but once, many have been poorly defined, and many are questionable on yet other grounds. Eliminating these, Wolfle finds seven factors which fulfill the criterion of having been reported in three or more studies. These seven factors are:

1. "w" or will (Webb, 1915; Studman, 1935; Cattell, 1933; Reyburn and Taylor, 1939; Brogden, 1940)

2. "c" or cleverness (Garnett, 1919; Cattell, 1933; Reyburn and Taylor, 1939)

3. "s" or shyness (Guilford and Guilford, 1934, 1936, 1939; Williams, 1935; Maurer, 1941; Flanagan, 1935; Mosier, 1937; Darrow, 1932)

4. A factor of self-confidence (Flanagan, 1935; Guilford and Guilford, 1936; Maurer, 1941; McCloy, 1936; Mosier, 1937; Williams, 1935)

5. "f" or fluency of mental activity [Studman, 1935; Mosier ("the cycloid temperament"), 1937; Guilford and Guilford ("emotional immaturity"), 1936; Darrow, 1932; Moore, 1933; Thurstone, 1934]

6. "d" or mental depression (Guilford and Guilford, 1939; Mosier, 1937; Thurstone, 1934)

7. A factor of hypersensitivity (Mosier, 1937; Guilford and Guilford, 1934; Reyburn and Taylor, 1939; Woodrow, 1939)[6]

(For some applications of these factors in the description of the behavior disorders, see Chapter 33 by Hunt and Cofer.)

---

[5] In this connection, see also Angyal's (1941) discussion of the basic aspects of personality. (Editor)

[6] The writer is not convinced that the factors reported in these investigations are identical with Mosier's factor of hypersensitivity.

It may be that "factor analysis provides a powerful analytic tool for isolating the important variables of human personality" (Wolfle, 1942, p. 397), but only if it is used with the best of psychological insight and combined with the keenest of clinical observation. Too many factor studies have overlooked the fact that the significance and the stability of the factors which will be discovered will depend upon the psychological meaningfulness of the traits which are measured. The most elaborate statistical procedures cannot introduce psychological meaning into a collection of meaningless or psychologically irrelevant measurements (Kelley, 1935). Even Copeland's (1935) proposal that the judgment of a single investigator be replaced by the judgment of a group of psychologists will do little to relieve the psychological poverty of factor analysis if the original tests and ratings and questionnaires are inadequate in their conceptualization of personality traits.

There is one investigation of the variables of personality which in seriousness of intent, in breadth of vision, and in significance of findings stands in a class by itself among the clinical attempts to describe personality. That study is the *Explorations in Personality* directed by Murray (1938) at the Harvard Psychological Clinic. To factorize the matrix of intercorrelations of ratings in such a study would be a Herculean labor, but until factor studies are conducted on that scale of magnitude and with data of that degree of psychological relevance for the description of personality, the results of the application of factor analysis in the study of personality will continue to be meager and trivial.

Theory of Traits of Personality

Radically different from the conceptual representation of personality as either an aggregation of specific stimulus-response bonds or a constellation of mathematically independent factors is the layman's notion that people possess more or less stable and enduring traits of personality in terms of which they may be described and on the basis of which they can be distinguished from one another. Unlike the specificist, the layman does not hesitate to use adjectives to describe persons, for he believes that most people act consistently even in widely different situations. In the light of what he knows about a person today he feels safe in predicting not only the kind of person he will be tomorrow but also what he will do in certain concrete situations.

These common-sense notions about personality are in essential agreement with that theory of the structure of personality which is known as the theory of traits or the theory of generality. This theory, in direct opposition to the anti-trait theory, sees generality rather than specificity as predominating in the organization of personality, and to account for the consistency of personality which it stresses the theory postulates broad, generalized, complex, overlapping, but relatively stable and enduring dispositions to action as the important and genuine components of personality.

Whereas the anti-trait theory is a mask theory of personality, the trait theory is one of substance. Trait theories have been developed in as many forms as there have been different conceptions of traits. There is neither space nor need to review them here; some have been discussed briefly in the historical section of this chapter. Allport, who has given one of the fullest, most recent, and most adequate theories of traits, defines a trait as "a generalized and focalized neuropsychic system (peculiar to the individual), with the capacity to render many stimuli functionally equivalent, and to initiate and guide consistent (equivalent) forms of adaptive and expressive behavior" (1937, p. 295).

This particular concept, like all concepts of trait, is a fictional concept devised for the purpose of correlating rationally the observed phenomena of generality of behavior and consistency of personality. The specificist who so redefines traits as to deny their existence as genuine components of personality feels no need for a concept of trait, for he is not convinced of the facts of generalized behavior or of personal consistency. If he denies that there is any generality or consistency, it is clear that he is shutting his eyes to a large body of fact. On the other hand, the generalist who denies any specificity or inconsistency of behavior is equally blind. It may be argued whether generality is the rule or the exception in the organization of personality but not whether there is both generality and specificity of behavior. Clearly a broader formulation that will recognize and account for both specificity and generality is needed. Before discussing such a reformulation of theory, however, let us survey some of the facts.

Genetically generality is prior to specificity. Total mass action precedes specific response and, as though to compensate for the differentiation of behavior which if unchecked would result in complete disunity and chaos, an integration of differentiated responses occurs simultaneously with the process of individuation (Coghill, 1929, 1930; see also Chapter 21 by Ribble). Thus the neurological basis of behavior and personality provides the mechanisms for both specificity and generality.

Experimental investigations of specificity and generality of behavior have been numerous. In their findings evidence for both specificity and generality can be found (for method of estimating traits see Chapter 4 by Maller and Chapter 5 by Jones).

The specificity of speed of decision and of confidence has been reported by Trow (1923, 1935). Other traits reported to be specific are: speed of work (Dowd, 1926), accuracy (Hartmann, 1928), leadership (Cowley, 1928), and introversion (Guthrie, 1927; Hovey, 1929; Weber and Maijgren, 1929; Newcomb, 1929). On the other hand, generality has also been reported for such traits as speed in both simple and complex mental reactions (Kennedy, 1930; Vernon, 1930; MacFarland, 1930), personality tempo (Braun, 1927), leadership in young children (Goodenough, 1928; Thomas, 1928), nervous habits (Olson, 1929), attitudes (Cantril, 1932; Lentz, 1938; Wickert, 1940), and introversion (Marston, 1925). In some instances, as can be seen in these lists, a trait reported as specific by one investigator has been reported as general by another. In other instances, a single investigator has demonstrated both specificity and generality as in Cantril's (1932) study of general and specific attitudes and in Trawick's (1940) investigation of trait-consistent individuals.

In the field of expressive movements something more than thoroughgoing specificity but something less than complete generality and consistency of response has been demonstrated by Allport and Vernon (1933), Eisenberg (1937), and Carlson (1938).

In investigations of the ability of subjects to estimate unknown aspects of personality from a limited knowledge of a few traits, the number of correct judgments has been shown frequently to be considerably better than chance. Such successful judging of traits of personality can be understood only if a large measure of personal consistency is assumed. Typical of such investigations have been those by Pear (1931), Herzog (1933), and Estes (1938).

The most striking and significant demonstrations of personal consistency, however, have been made through the application of the matching method in the study of personality. Here is a method which, it is claimed, makes possible the objective study of the total personality (Allport, 1933; Vernon, 1935, 1936). Whether the total personality can be investigated by this method is questionable, but certainly it does less violence to the personality as a whole than most methods of research in this field. It has been defined as a "method for establishing quantitative relationships between qualitative aspects of personality" (Vernon, 1936). It permits one to demonstrate the relation between psychological characteristics of personality which cannot be treated by the usual correlational procedures. It had its roots in the observation that subjects who knew the works of Michelangelo, Leonardo da Vinci, and Raphael could identify the handwriting of these artists when seen for the first time. The method consists of presenting judges with various modes of expression or aspects of personality gathered from different subjects unknown by the judges—for example, pictures of profile, phonographic records of voice, specimens of handwriting, stenographic reports of subjects' ways of telling a folk tale, artistic and literary creations, thumbnail sketches of the personality of the subjects, etc.—and asking the judges to put together those items which have been derived from a single person. If the matching of items in such an experiment is better than chance, it must be due to the perception on the part of the judges of some quality or style pervading the various expressions of a single personality or, in other words, to the perception of some form of personal consistency. A number of investigators have demonstrated matching considerably above chance (Arnheim, 1928; Wolff, 1929, 1930; Allport and Cantril, 1934; Allport, Walker, and Lathers, 1934; Cantril and Rand, 1934; Bender, 1935; Cantril and Allport, 1935; Eisenberg, 1938; Eisenberg and Zalowitz, 1938; Eisenberg and Reichline, 1939; Fay and Middleton, 1939, 1939a, 1940). There can be no doubt after Vernon's (1936) excellent review and critique of the method of matching and the results of its application to the study of personality that here is a method of great usefulness for the demonstration of generality and consistency in the modes of expression of personality.

Resolution of the Conflict of Theories

No longer can there be any doubt that there is both specificity and generality of behavior. Both personal consistency and inconsistency must be recognized.

Proponents of a radical anti-trait theory who deny any generality of behavior or any consistency of personality commit the "situation error," the error of assuming that all behavior is determined solely by the specific *situation*, physical and social, in which the individual finds himself. On the other hand, supporters of an extreme trait theory who deny any specificity of behavior or any inconsistency of personality commit the "organism error," the error of thinking of behavioral traits as fixed attributes of an *organism* as stable and as unchanging as a finger print or as a birth mark (Murphy and Murphy, 1931). A field theory of personality which sees behavior and personality as functions of a total field of which they are subparts is the form of theory which today seems best suited for the conceptual representation of personality. Such a theory is slowly emerging from the work of many investigators (see especially Murray, 1938; Lewin, 1935, 1936, 1938; Allport, 1937; Burt, 1941; Angyal, 1942; and Chapter 3 by Mowrer and Kluckhohn). On the psychological side this theory will take account of both mask and substance aspects of personality, fully recognizing that much that looks like specificity of behavior, and is specificity if viewed from the standpoint of action *qua* action, is actually an expression of generality and consistency if the setting of the behavior and its meaning for the total personality is considered. On the logical and mathematical side this theory will recognize that the traits or factors of personality range from the most specific to the most general and that the difference between specificity and generality is formal rather than material, relative rather than fixed.

BIBLIOGRAPHY

ALDINGTON, R. 1924. A book of "characters." New York: Dutton.
ALLPORT, F. H. 1924. Social psychology. Boston: Houghton Mifflin.
ALLPORT, F. H., WALKER, L., & LATHERS, E. 1934. Written composition and characteristics of personality. *Arch. Psychol., N. Y., 26*, No. 173.

ALLPORT, G. W. 1932. Review of P. M. Symonds's Diagnosing personality and conduct. *J. soc. Psychol., 3,* 391–397.

—— 1933. The study of personality by the experimental method. *Character & Pers., 1,* 259–264.

—— 1934. Review of R. C. Perry's A group factor analysis of the adjustment questionnaire. *Character & Pers., 3,* 169–170.

—— 1937. Personality: a psychological interpretation. New York: Holt.

—— 1942. The use of personal documents in psychological science. *Soc. Sci. Res. Coun. Bull.,* No. 49.

ALLPORT, G. W., & CANTRIL, H. 1934. Judging personality from voice. *J. soc. Psychol., 5,* 37–55.

ALLPORT, G. W., & ODBERT, H. S. 1936. Trait-names: a psycho-lexical study. *Psychol. Monogr., 47,* No. 1.

ALLPORT, G. W., & VERNON, P. E. 1930. The field of personality. *Psychol. Bull., 27,* 677–730.

—— 1933. Studies in expressive movement. New York: Macmillan.

ANASTASI, A. 1936. The influence of specific experiences upon mental organization. *Genet. Psychol. Monogr., 18,* 245–355.

—— 1938. Faculties *versus* factors: a reply to Professor Thurstone. *Psychol. Bull., 35,* 391–395.

ANGYAL, A. 1941. Foundations for a science of personality. New York: Commonwealth Fund.

ARNHEIM, R. 1928. Experimentell-psychologische Untersuchungen zum Ausdrucks problem. *Psychol. Forsch., 11,* 1–132.

BARRY, H., JR., MACKINNON, D. W., & MURRAY, H. A., JR. 1931. Studies in personality. A. Hypnotizability as a personality trait and its typological relations. *Hum. Biol., 3,* 1–36.

BENDER, I. E. 1935. A study in integrations of personalities by prediction and matching. Syracuse, N. Y.: Syracuse University Library.

BERMAN, L. 1921. The glands regulating personality. New York: Macmillan.

BLEULER, E. 1924. Textbook of psychiatry. New York: Macmillan.

BLOOR, C. 1928. Temperament. London: Methuen.

BOWDEN, A. O. 1926. A study of the personality of student leaders in colleges in the United States. *J. abnorm. soc. Psychol., 21,* 149–160.

BRAUN, F. 1927. Untersuchungen über das persönliche Tempo. *Arch. ges. Psychol., 60,* 317–360.

BROGDEN, H. F. 1940. A factor analysis of forty character tests. *Psychol. Monogr., 52,* No. 3, pp. 39–55.

BURKS, B. 1936. Personality theories in relation to measurement. *J. soc. Psychol., 7,* 140–150.

BURT, C. 1941. The factors of the mind. New York: Macmillan.

CANTRIL, H. 1932. General and specific attitudes. *Psychol. Monogr., 42,* No. 5.

CANTRIL, H., & ALLPORT, G. W. 1935. The psychology of radio. New York: Harper.

CANTRIL, H., & RAND, H. A. 1934. An additional study of the determination of personal interests by psychological and graphological methods. *Character & Pers., 3,* 72–78.

CARLSON, W. S. 1938. Further studies in expressive movement. *Psychol. Rec., 2,* 310–316.

CATTELL, R. B. 1933. Temperament tests: I. Temperament. *Brit. J. Psychol., 23,* 308–329.

COBB, I. B. 1927. The glands of destiny. London: Heinemann.

COGHILL, G. E. 1929. Anatomy and the problem of behavior. New York: Macmillan.

—— 1930. Individuation versus integration in the development of behavior. *J. gen. Psychol., 3,* 431–435.

COPELAND, H. A. 1935. A note on "The vectors of mind." *Psychol. Rev., 42,* 216–218.

COWLEY, W. H. 1928. Three distinctions in the study of leaders. *J. abnorm. soc. Psychol., 23,* 144–157.

DARROW, C. W., & HEATH, L. L. 1932. Reaction tendencies relating to personality. In Lashley, K. S., *Studies in the dynamics of behavior.* Chicago: University Chicago Press. Pp. 59–261.

DOWD, C. E. 1926. A study of the consistency of rate of work. *Arch. Psychol., N. Y., 13,* No. 84.

DOWNEY, J. E. 1923. The will-temperament and its testing. Yonkers, N. Y.: World Book.

EHRLICH, W. 1930. Stufen der Personalität: Grundlegung einer Metaphysik des Menschen. Halle: Niemeyer.

EISENBERG, P. 1937. A further study in expressive movement. *Character & Pers., 5,* 296–301.

—— 1938. Judging expressive movement: I. Judgments of sex and dominance-feeling from handwriting samples of dominant and non-dominant men and women. *J. appl. Psychol., 22,* 480–486.

EISENBERG, P., & REICHLINE, P. B. 1939. Judging expressive movement: II. Judgments of dominance-feeling from motion pictures of gait. *J. soc. Psychol., 10,* 345–357.

EISENBERG, P., & ZALOWITZ, E. 1938. Judging expressive movement: III. Judgments of dominance-feeling from phonograph records of voice. *J. appl. Psychol., 22,* 620–631.

ESTES, S. G. 1938. Judging personality from expressive behavior. *J. abnorm. soc. Psychol., 33,* 217–236.

FAY, P. J., & MIDDLETON, W. C. 1939. Judgment of occupation from the voice as transmitted over a public address system and over a radio. *J. appl. Psychol., 23,* 586–601.

—— 1939a. Judgment of Spranger personality types from the voice as transmitted over a public address system. *Character & Pers., 8,* 144–155.

—— 1940. Judgment of Kretschmerian body types from the voice as transmitted over a public address system. *J. soc. Psychol., 12,* 151–162.

FILTER, R. O. 1922. A practical definition of character. *Psychol. Rev., 29,* 319–324.

FLANAGAN, J. C. 1935. Factor analysis in the study of personality. Stanford University: Stanford University Press.

FOURIER, C. 1851. The passions of the human soul. (2 Vols.) London: Bailliere.

GALL, F. J. 1835. On the functions of the brain and each of its parts, etc. Vol. 1. Boston: Marsh, Capen & Lyon.

GALTON, F. 1883. Inquiries into human faculty and its development. London: Macmillan.

GARNETT, J. C. M. 1919. General ability, cleverness and purpose. *Brit. J. Psychol., 9,* 345–366.

GOODENOUGH, F. L. 1928. Measuring behavior traits by means of repeated short samples. *J. juven. Res., 12,* 230–235.

GROSS, O. 1902. Die zerebrale Sekundärfunktion. Leipzig: Vogel.

GUILFORD, J. P. 1940. Human abilities. *Psychol. Rev., 47,* 367–394.

GUILFORD, J. P., & GUILFORD, R. B. 1934. An analysis of the factors in a typical test of introversion-extroversion. *J. abnorm. soc. Psychol., 28,* 377–399.

—— 1936. Personality factors S, E, and M, and their measurement. *J. Psychol., 2,* 109–127.

—— 1939. Personality factors D, R, T, and A. *J. abnorm. soc. Psychol., 34,* 21–36.

GUTHRIE, E. R. 1927. Measuring introversion and extroversion. *J. abnorm. soc. Psychol., 22,* 82–88.

HARTMANN, G. W. 1928. Precision and accuracy. *Arch. Psychol., N. Y., 16,* No. 100.

HARTSHORNE, H., & MAY, M. A. 1928. Studies in deceit. New York: Macmillan.

—— 1929. Studies in service and self-control. New York: Macmillan.

HARTSHORNE, H., MAY, M. A., & SHUTTLEWORTH, F. K. 1930. Studies in the organization of character. New York: Macmillan.

HERZOG, H. 1933. Stimme und Persönlichkeit. *Z. Psychol., 130,* 300–369.

HOLZINGER, K. J. 1937. Student manual of factor analysis. Chicago: Department of Education, University Chicago.

HOSKINS, R. G. 1933. The tides of life. New York: Norton.

HOVEY, H. B. 1929. Measures of extroversion-introversion tendencies and their relation to performance under distraction. *J. genet. Psychol., 36,* 319–329.

JAENSCH, E. R. 1930. Eidetic imagery. New York: Harcourt, Brace.

JAENSCH, E. R., & *Mitarbeiter.* 1930. Studien zur Psychologie menschlicher Typen. Leipzig: Barth.

JAENSCH, W. 1926. Grundzüge einer Physiologie und Klinik der Psychophysischen Persönlichkeit. Berlin: Springer.

JAMES, W. 1890. Principles of psychology. Vol. 1. New York: Holt.

—— 1907. Pragmatism. New York: Longmans Green.

JANET, P. 1894. L'état mental des hystériques. Paris: Rueff.

—— 1903. Les obsessions et la psychasténie. Paris: Alcan.

JASTROW, J. 1915. The antecedents of the study of character and temperament. *Pop. Sci. Mon., 86,* 590–613.

JEBB, R. C. 1909. The characters of Theophrastus. London: Macmillan.

JUNG, C. G. 1909. The psychology of dementia praecox. *Nerv. ment. Dis. Monogr.,* 1936, Ser. 3.

—— 1916. Psychology of the unconscious. New York: Moffat Yard.

—— 1923. Psychological types. New York: Harcourt, Brace.

KELLY, T. L. 1935. Essential traits of mental life. Cambridge: Harvard University Press.

KENNEDY, M. 1930. Speed as a personality trait. *J. soc. Psychol., 1,* 286–299.

KLAGES, L. 1932. The science of character. Cambridge: Sci-Art.

KRAEPELIN, E. 1899. Psychiatrie. (6th ed.) Leipzig: Barth.

KRETSCHMER, E. 1926. Physique and character. New York: Harcourt, Brace.

KÜLPE, O. 1904. Versuche über Abstraktion. *Ber. I Kongr. exp. Psychol.,* 56–68.

LAEHR, H. 1900. Die Literatur der Psychiatrie, Neurologie und Psychologie von 1459–1799. (3 Vols.) Berlin: Reimer.

LENTZ, T. F. 1938. Generality and specificity of conservatism-radicalism. *J. educ. Psychol., 29,* 540–546.

LEWIN, K. 1935. A dynamic theory of personality. New York: McGraw-Hill.

—— 1936. Principles of topological psychology. New York: McGraw-Hill.

—— 1938. The conceptual representation and the measurement of psychological forces. *Contr. psychol. Theory, 1,* No. 4.

LIPSCHÜTZ, A. 1925. Innere Sekretion und Persönlichkeit. *Jb. Charakterol., 2 & 3,* 229–259.

MACFARLAND, R. A. 1930. An experimental study of the relationship between speed and mental ability. *J. gen. Psychol., 3,* 67–97.

MACKINNON, D. W. 1938. The violation of prohibitions in the solving of problems. In Murray, H. A., *et al., Explorations in personality.* New York: Oxford University Press. Pp. 491–501.

MALLER, J. B. 1934. General and specific factors in character. *J. soc. Psychol., 5,* 97–101.

MARCUSE, L. 1926. Die Struktur der Kultur. *Jb. Characterol., 2,* 131–140.

MARSTON, L. R. 1925. The emotions of young children. *Univ. Ia. Stud. Child Welf.,* No. 3.

MAURER, K. M. 1941. Patterns of behavior of young children as revealed by a factor analysis of trait "clusters." *J. genet. Psychol., 59,* 177–188.

MCCLOY, C. H. 1936. A factor analysis of personality traits to underlie character education. *J. educ. Psychol., 27,* 375–387.

MCDOUGALL, W. 1923. Outline of psychology. New York: Scribner's.

—— 1926. Outline of abnormal psychology. New York: Scribner's.

—— 1933. The energies of men. New York: Scribner's.

MOORE, T. V. 1933. The essential psychoses and their fundamental syndromes. *Stud. Psychol. Psychiat. Catholic Univ. Amer., 3,* No. 3.

MOSIER, C. I. 1937. A factor analysis of certain neurotic tendencies. *Psychometrika, 2,* 263–286.

MÜLLER, G. E., & PILZECKER, A. 1900. Experimentelle Beiträge zur Lehre vom Gedächtnis. *Z. Psychol.,* Ergbd. *1,* 1–300.

MURPHY, G., & MURPHY, L. B. 1931. Experimental social psychology. New York: Harper.

MURRAY, H. A., *et al.* 1938. Explorations in personality. New York: Oxford University Press.

NEWCOMB, T. M. 1929. The consistency of certain extrovert-introvert behavior patterns in 51 problem boys. *Teach. Coll. Contr. Educ.*

OLSON, W. C. 1929. The measurement of nervous habits in normal children. *Univ. Minn. Child Welf. Monogr. Ser.*, No. 3.

PEAR, T. H. 1931. Voice and personality. London: Chapman & Hall.

PILLSBURY, W. B. 1929. The history of psychology. New York: Norton.

PRINCE, M. 1924. The unconscious. New York: Macmillan.

Proceedings of the second colloquium on personality investigation. 1930. Baltimore: Johns Hopkins University Press.

REXROAD, C. N. 1929. General psychology for college students. New York: Macmillan.

REYBURN, H. A., & TAYLOR, J. G. 1939. Some factors of personality. A further analysis of some of Webb's data. *Brit. J. Psychol.*, *30*, 151–165.

ROBACK, A. A. 1927. A bibliography of character and personality. Cambridge: Sci-Art.

—— 1931. The psychology of character. New York: Harcourt, Brace.

RORSCHACH, H. 1942. Psychodiagnostics. Berne: Hans Huber.

ROWE, A. W. 1932. The differential diagnosis of endocrine disorders. Baltimore: Williams & Wilkins.

SCHOEN, M. 1930. Human nature. New York: Harper.

SCHOLL, R. 1927a. Untersuchungen über die teilinhaltliche Beachtung von Farbe und Form bei Erewachsenen und Kindern. *Z. Psychol.*, 1926, *101*, 225–280.

—— 1927b. Zur Theorie und Typologie der teilinhaltlichen Beachtung von Form und Farbe. *Z. Psychol.*, 1926, *101*, 281–320.

SHAND, A. F. 1914. Foundations of character. London: Macmillan.

SHERMAN, M. & I. C. 1928. The process of behavior. New York: Norton.

SPEARMAN, C. 1904. "General intelligence," objectively determined and measured. *Amer. J. Psychol.*, *15*, 201–293.

—— 1927. The abilities of man. London: Macmillan.

STERN, W. 1911. Differentielle Psychologie. Leipzig: Barth.

—— 1930. Studien zur Personwissenschaft. I. Personalistik als Wissenschaft. Leipzig: Barth.

—— 1938. General psychology. New York: Macmillan.

STUDMAN, L. G. 1935. The factor theory in the field of personality. *Character & Pers.*, *4*, 34–43.

TAYLOR, W. S. 1926. Character and abnormal psychology. *J. abnorm. soc. Psychol.*, *21*, 85–86.

THOMAS, W. I. & D. S. 1928. The child in America. New York: Knopf.

THOMSON, G. H. 1939. The factorial analysis of human ability. Boston: Houghton Mifflin.

THURSTONE, L. L. 1934. The vectors of mind. *Psychol. Rev.*, 1934, *41*, 1–32.

—— 1935. The vectors of mind. Chicago: University Chicago Press.

—— 1938. Primary mental abilities. Chicago: University Chicago Press.

TRAWICK, M. 1940. Trait-consistency in personality: a differential investigation. *Arch. Psychol., N. Y.*, No. 248.

TROW, W. C. 1923. The psychology of confidence. *Arch. Psychol., N. Y.*, *10*, No. 67.

—— 1925. Trait consistency and speed of decision. *Sch. & Soc.*, *21*, 538–542.

TRYON, R. C. 1935. A theory of *psychological* components—an alternative to mathematical factors. *Psychol. Rev.*, *42*, 425–454.

VALENTINE, P. F. 1927. The psychology of personality. New York: Appleton-Century.

VERNON, P. E. 1935. Can the "total personality" be studied objectively? *Character & Pers.*, *4*, 1–10.

—— 1936. The matching method applied to investigations of personality. *Psychol. Bull.*, *33*, 149–177.

—— 1938. The assessment of psychological qualities by verbal methods, a survey of attitude tests, rating scales and personality questionnaires. Report No. 83, Medical Research Council, Industrial Health Research Board. London: His Majesty's Stationery Office.

WARREN, H. C. (Ed.) 1934. Dictionary of psychology. Boston: Houghton Mifflin.

WARREN, H. C., & CARMICHAEL, L. 1930. Elements of human psychology. Boston: Houghton Mifflin.

WATSON, J. B. 1924. Behaviorism. New York: People's Institute Pub.

WEBB, E. 1915. Character and intelligence. *Brit. J. Psychol., Monogr. Suppl., 1,* No. 3.

WEBER, C. B., & MAIJGREN, R. 1929. The experimental differentia of introversion and extraversion. *J. genet. Psychol., 36,* 571–580.

WERTHEIMER, F. L., & HESKETH, F. E. 1926. The significance of the physical constitution in mental disease. Baltimore: Williams & Wilkins.

WICKERT, F. 1940. The interrelationships of some general and specific preferences. *J. soc. Psychol., 11,* 275–302.

WILLIAMS, H. M. 1935. A factor analysis of Berne's "Social behavior pattern in young children." *J. exp. Educ., 4,* 142–146.

WOLFF, W. 1929. Gestaltidentität in der Charakterologie. *Psychol. Med., 4,* 32–44.

—— 1930. Über Faktoren Charakterologischen Urteilsbildung. *Z. angew. Psychol., 35,* 385–446.

WOLFLE, D. 1940. Factor analysis to 1940. *Psychomet. Monogr.,* No. 3.

—— 1942. Factor analysis in the study of personality. *J. abnorm. soc. Psychol., 37,* 393–397.

WOODROW, H. 1939. The common factors in fifty-two mental tests. *Psychometrika, 4,* 99–108.

WOODWORTH, R. S. 1929. Psychology. New York: Holt.

WUNDT, W. 1903. Grundzüge der physiologischen Psychologie. Vol. 3. (5th ed.). Leipzig: Engelmann.

YOAKUM, C. S. 1924. The definition of personality. *Rep. Brit. Assn. Advanc. Sci.,* 92nd mtg., p. 442.

Chapter 2

PERSONALITY IN TERMS OF ASSOCIATIVE LEARNING

By Edwin R. Guthrie, Ph.D.

PSYCHOLOGICAL STUDIES OF PERSONALITY have, on the whole, been developed from a viewpoint very different from that to be stressed in this chapter. The typical studies have been concerned with a cross-sectional analysis of the characteristics and traits of individuals and groups or have been devoted to the search for an entity which, it is assumed, is *"the"* personality; the influence of old theological notions concerning the soul may well be present in the latter kind of attack on the problem. Allport (1937), Murphy, Murphy, and Newcomb (1937), and Stagner (1937) have reviewed many of the numerous studies of these types. In contrast to the above orientations, we shall be concerned in this chapter with an obvious, practical approach to understanding men. This approach is through the understanding of how men adjust themselves to their circumstances through learning, and the use of the past experience of the individual for the prediction of his behavior in future situations.

To present this point of view, it is first required that some statement be made concerning the nature of behavior and of associative learning and that a description of adjustment in terms of associative learning be presented.[1] The sources of variability in behavior and the nature of habit must also be reviewed. Personality is defined in terms of habit-adjustment, and this is applied to the problem of describing personality traits.

The thesis as stated above sounds highly abstract, but it can be put in far simpler terms. It is our contention that practical and sound description of personality traits must be made in terms of learned skills and adjustments rather than in terms of general traits like "introvert," "ascendant," or the like.

Behavior and Associative Learning

In the human organism the structural basis of behavior lies in receptors, a connecting nervous system, and muscles and glands. Muscles and glands have their specialized functions. Muscles contract and glands

---

[1] This thesis is developed in further detail elsewhere (Guthrie, 1938).

secrete. In the strict sense all human behavior consists in muscular contraction and glandular secretion. Human personality must in one sense be reducible to such activities of effectors.

But almost no one is interested in his neighbor's muscles and glands. What really interest him are the probable changes in his own situation that may result from his neighbor's activity. Most words for his neighbor's activity name not patterns of muscular contraction but common and typical effects of such patterns.

We may distinguish acts from movements. Acts name the consequences of movements. Going to lunch, driving home, putting a coin in a slot, telling a story—these are achievements that might in each case be brought about by a wide variety of movements. You can go to lunch in a wheel chair, or by inducing someone to carry you. The coin could be put in the slot with the teeth or the toes, or the right or the left hand. The name of the act does not name the muscles involved or attempt any description of the order and extent of their contraction.

Personality traits are even less determinate in terms of actual organic response (see Allport and Odbert, 1936). "He is likable." There is an infinity of ways in which a man may cause liking in others. "Honesty" does not name a pattern of muscular response but a large indefinite class of responses whose common property is that their verbal description will not excite widespread condemnation. There are a million ways to be honest in any situation—not a million names of ways but a million or an infinity of patterns of actual movement. No two persons are honest by identical movements when put in a test situation.

The detailed muscular contractions by which a man acts honestly or dishonestly have no interest for most persons, and this has led writers on personality to an almost total disregard of the nature of learning and the role of learning in the development of personality traits. Thus, in their great concern for cataloging acts, Allport (1937) and Lewin (1935) have neglected the most important aspect of personality—how acts are learned. These and other writers in the field have attempted to disregard the physical basis of behavior and the fact that learning and habit must be primarily functions of sense organs, nervous system, and muscles. The basic laws of learning must apply to movements, not to acts, since it is muscles that are innervated and not the external world on which muscles operate. There is no direct connection between sense organs and the coin or the slot in which we place the coin. The direct connection is between sense organs and the muscles that move the coin to the slot.

All acts are made up of movements. An act is a class of movements defined by the end result.

The phenomena of association and habit are primarily phenomena of movement. In association what is associated is a movement pattern with a stimulus pattern. A habit is a movement pattern that is self-facilitating. The initial parts of the movement have become cues for the rest (Guthrie, 1940).

Acts and personality traits are not defined in terms of movement but in terms of the effect of movement. Both act and trait can be realized by a wide variety of movements. It does not follow, as most writers have assumed, that association and habit can be disregarded or given a subordinate place in understanding personality. The reason that this does not follow is that in any particular man the achievement of an act is completely dependent on his acquisition, through learning, of a *specific* and *stereotyped* movement or set of movements for the accomplishment of the effect that defines the act.

Let us illustrate this. When a child learns for the first time to button one of his garments this accomplishment will be found to be highly specialized. Only when the garment is in a specific position and he is standing in a particular way is the particular stereotyped movement series called out that will bring results. One small change in situation and his movements, even if they occur, do not result in fastening the button.

In time he acquires a repertoire of movements, and buttoning can result in a wide variety of stances, garment styles, initial behavior, etc. But even when this skill has been developed, the *specificity* and *stereotyping* are as much present as ever. It is the repertoire that has increased, not the stereotyping that has broken down.

In other words, every man has his peculiar, individual, stereotyped style of walking, riding, playing tennis, being entertaining, being irascible, being honest, truthful, gregarious, or what you will. Allport has an occasional "hunch" that this is true. "The *reason* for a present act of conduct," he says (Allport, 1937, p. 466), is to be sought in the present desires and intentions of the individual (though these in turn may arise from deep-lying personal traits and interests) ; but the style of execution is always guided directly and without interference by "deep and lasting personal dispositions." Allport, like most writers on personality, has a strange and profound lack of interest in the nature of these "deep and lasting personal dispositions," and their manner of acquisition and change.

The thesis of this chapter is that such "deep and lasting dispositions" must be treated in terms of *stimulus, movement,* and *association.* It is here contended that even the choice of movement, which Allport appears to believe *may* be independent of these deep-lying determiners, has its possible alternatives defined in past learning. The *reason* for a present act must include the associative history of that act in the individual.

This curious statement of Allport's is in line with his apparent notion that association is a mode of change in behavior that is sometimes used by men, sometimes not. Certain low forms of learning are associative, but the better bits are insightful and nonassociative. This is a view shared by Wheeler (1929) and the Gestalt psychologists (see Koehler, 1925) and well described by Katona (1940) in his book *Organizing and*

Memorizing. It is not shared by such theorists as Guthrie (1930, 1935, 1940), Hunter (1934), Hull (1935), Miller and Dollard (1941), Skinner (1938), Spence (1936, 1937), and others.

The view taken in this chapter is that association is a general characteristic of behavioral change and that its rules are not violated in insight, choice, etc., but that these forms of behavior like all others conform to associative principles. The principle of association is here comparable to the principle of gravitation. Not many phenomena can be explained by gravitation but no phenomena violate its formula. It will not predict which horse will win but no one of the entries will be found a nonconformist.

Adjustment in Terms of Association

The mark of a living creature is that to such changes in the world about it as threaten its continued existence it reacts by itself changing in such a manner as to remove the threat. To acid in its surrounding water medium or to a heightened temperature the paramecium responds by an active but undirected darting about. This may carry it to an innocuous region and so let it survive.

So far as we know definitely the paramecium will continue to behave thus in the presence of heat or acid. The evidence that paramecium can change its style of response is highly questionable.

There are other creatures that obviously do more than react to threatening changes with protective change in themselves. These are creatures that react to *recurring* threats by changing their style of reaction. The ways of paramecium are the same from one day to another except for maturation and senescence which are much the same in all individuals. In creatures that we grant to have "minds" this is not the case. One day a bird is without fear at the sight of the hunter. The next day it is very shy. The bird has changed its style of reacting and the change is lasting. It has, due to a threatening change in its environment, become a different creature and so preserved its essential identity. The life of man consists of a continuous adjustment of this kind (see Shaffer, 1936). To some change in his environment he makes an immediate response. When the response is adequate and removes the threat, it may remain his response in that situation. But when the response is not adequate and the threat remains, he may continue active and new responses appear. When one of these responses does away with the threat, it remains his response to that threat. Hull (1929), Mowrer (1939), Miller and Dollard (1941), and Estes and Skinner (1941) have presented somewhat similar discussions but employing different concepts.

To be more concrete, when a child is agitated by some stimulus to activity—say cold, hunger, pin-prick, or the like—the maintained stimulation builds up excitement and a reinforcement of action. In small children there is probably an instinctive attachment of crying and excitement. The child cries. Its mother is likewise disturbed, comes and removes the discomfort.

When this particular annoyance happens again, the last response associated with it was crying. We now expect the child to cry again.

But suppose that the mother did not come and that the child continues active and crying. Eventually some other behavior may supplant crying. This other behavior (such as getting under the covers in case of cold) removes the disturbing cold. The next day, being again cold, the last associated response was covering up. This is what we shall expect to happen now.[2]

A small boy following about a group of older boys is disregarded by them and has no place in their activity. But he is by the sight of their play continuously stimulated to take part. He eventually accumulates a high degree of excitement. One line of action, as it fatigues, is displaced by another. Eventually, in his rage he is (and some past associations would be involved) led to start throwing rocks at the older boys. They are frightened into giving him their attention and admitting him to their play. The new device becomes his associative reaction to "being left out" and so long as it remains effective is a part of his personality. Each repetition widens the range of circumstances in which his violent solution is associatively available.

A boy enters a school in which there is on the playground little supervision and much bullying and fighting. Another boy attacks him or snatches his cap. He cries and his crying attracts the attention of the teacher who comes out, and commands the return of the cap, and takes him out of the situation. When, a week later, he is again a victim of similar aggression, his last response, crying, remains his associated reaction. But if crying had not been effective and he had run through his

---

[2] The effectiveness of reinforcement in governing learning is not regarded by the present writer in the same light as it would be regarded from the point of view of the "law of effect." Reinforcement is here seen as terminating a sequence of behavior and, perhaps, the initial and maintained stimulation which originally leads to the behavior sequence. The function of reinforcement ("reward") is to "protect" the associations made. This is done through the removal of the organism from the environment in which the responses were made (and so new associations to those environmental stimuli cannot be made) and/or by changing the condition of the organism so that its internal stimulation will now be different than before. In the latter case conflicting associations will not be formed, even though the organism remain in an objectively constant external environment; the responses of the organism will now be different as the maintained stimulation has been modified by virtue of the reinforcement. Learning from this point of view is thought to occur in one trial. New trials bring new learning and the first habits are supplanted. Other writers have differed in their attitude toward reinforcement—for example, Hilgard (1937), Culler (1938), Skinner (1938), and Razran (1939). For a more complete statement of the present formulation as well as for an analysis of the views of the above four writers, see Guthrie (1940). Hull (1931, 1932, 1937), Mowrer (1939), and Miller and Dollard (1941) present still different analyses of the function of reinforcement. Hilgard and Marquis (1940) discuss the whole question of reinforcement in some detail (see also section on learning in Chapter 3).

repertoire of behaviors as each was exhausted, ending up with a violent attack on the aggressor that frightened him away, the aggression being removed, the last association with it is the reprisal and this is what we expect the next week when another aggressor turns up.

To threatening or disturbing events in the world the individual continues to react so long as the disturbing situation continues or until exhausted. If exhaustion occurs and the disturbing situation is still present, we become habituated and learn to tolerate evils that were at first intolerable.

Variability in Response

The outstanding feature of human behavior is its repetitiousness, and repetitiousness is our chief predictive basis when we attempt to describe the nature of a man. Two separate features of behavior affect the degree of stereotyped repetition to be found in individuals. One of these is the fact that the events in our environment exhibit both repetition and change. We are never exposed to an exact reproduction of any situation. Hence, we must be content to estimate or evaluate the extent to which one situation repeats the significant stimulus pattern of another. Even in the reaction-time experiment in which one signal is mechanically like the last, we are never caught in exactly the same posture or readiness. Our attention in one instance differs from our attention in the other and posture and attention must be included as determiners of our response. On the playfield one aggression is never the exact repetition of the last and never catches the boy in exactly the same phase of activity. Hence we must qualify our predictions and speak of "tendencies" rather than of responses. This boy has been observed to cry when pushed about by the playground bully. If we have no other information about him this is what we expect him to do when a third boy jostles him. We may, however, have noted previous friendly responses to the third boy which would change or make doubtful our prediction.

The failure of situations of the same name or description to be the same in fact is then a bar to any exact anticipation of what is coming.

Actually our information as to what people will do in certain classes of circumstances goes much farther than the above statements would lead us to expect. *People can sometimes be trusted to do the expected thing in a large variety of situations.*

This is the phenomenon of *habit*. Its basis is undoubtedly the fact that an essential part of any situation is the current response. What a man is doing at any time is a most important determiner of what he will do next. A crying child resists the most bizarre blandishments of the grownups around him. What the traffic officer will say to you when he reaches the side of your car depends very little on your own statement. Traffic officers are poor listeners. In order to overcome their previous habits of politeness and good nature and to finish conversations, they have long ago hit upon a truculent manner and a "line" of talk that minimizes debate. By watching the officer's approach some estimate of what his line will be can be obtained.

This important component of all situations that consists in prevailing action also serves for association. A series of movements may have been guided by an adventitious sequence of events but the next time the series is started it is not so dependent. Its own cues may be enough to see it through. A tight collar may have led a man in a maiden speech to pull at it while talking. This mannerism may remain for years though all subsequent collars have been larger. The movement was originally started and guided by the pressure of collar on the neck. It now guides itself and can be started by odd components of the situation "beginning a speech."

When any movement series has once been performed it becomes to some extent independent of the external situation and needs only an initial push. Our style and manner of greeting acquaintances, telling an anecdote, making love, eating a meal, driving a car, selling an insurance policy, of doing anything that we do often, become more characteristic of us than of the situations we confront. Most of our execution may be useless or embarrassing in particular situations. It can be better predicted by observing us in a previous situation than by observing many others in situations like the present one. We become all too predictable to our friends and our family. They know what song we will sing in the shower, the point at which we go off-key and the point at which we falter and stop. They know how we will react to their arguments, what we will say as we drive past a certain point in the road, how we will respond to a request for a contribution or to serve on a committee, or to criticism or flattery.

We are predictable in terms of our habits to an extent that belies the variety of the situations we encounter. And each habit has its own history. It was at first the result of a combination of stimuli and a sequence that was unique—adventitious. If it does not cause trouble and so new learning, it has been fixed and stereotyped.

Habit-Acts

Thus far we have been discussing *habit-movements* describable if we had time in terms of muscular action patterns. Habits are also to be found in acts as well as movement, defined by their results rather than by the specific muscular contractions that make them up. We habitually lunch at a certain restaurant though this means indefinitely varied means of getting there. We are in the habit of taking or refusing a dessert for lunch, though our expression of our wishes varies with the situation.

Act-habits are built up of movement-habits through association. How this is done can be very simply described. Acts are defined in terms of their results or goals. A goal may be defined as an inciting situation that can be eliminated by the proper movement or set of movements. The inciting capacity of the goal may depend on past associations (as in the case of "acquired drives," Miller, 1941)(or on the original nature of man.)

If the sight of a bright-colored rattle at a distance stirs an infant to restless activity, the infant may learn to get it by crying or reaching. In either case the rattle in the hand so completely changes the situation by the new noise and movement of the rattle that the means of acquisition remain attached to the sight of the rattle at a distance.[3]

But the rattle is seldom twice at the same distance from the baby or in the same direction. The repetition of the exact movements used in first obtaining the rattle is not successful and these movements are supplanted by others (fatigue alters the situation, or there is a change of situation as a result of moving, etc.). Eventually other movements obtain the rattle and in time the child acquires a repertoire of movement-sets fitted to various distances and positions. The child now has an act-habit (or as Hull, 1934, has called it, a habit-family hierarchy), namely, picking up the rattle. This act-habit, composed of a large set of movement-habits, can be affected as a whole by associative inhibition. In fact it behaves very much like a movement-habit in the child's experience.

A person who has been regularly and often made uncomfortable when his teeth are unbrushed, when a rug is turned, when a picture is hanging askew, when a water-faucet is dripping, when his arithmetic problem is undone, when he misspells a word, when he is dressed differently from his companions, when he mispronounces a word, may eventually establish the set of adjusted movements that corrects the trouble as a set of responses to the sight or signs of the trouble itself. The original incitement may have come from the scolding of others, but the unfinished job, the unachieved result is a substitute inciter.

The compulsive act in abnormal psychology is only a misplaced or embarrassing example of the same mechanism. When the sight of the hands instead of the sight of dirt on the hands becomes a stimulus for anxiety which is relieved only by washing them, we have a compulsion. In the same manner we find established act-habits that conform to custom. When a man's dress or behavior causes others to make him uncomfortable or keeps others from cooperating with him, he may be rendered uneasy and in the course of that uneasiness hit upon the correction and establish this as an act-habit defined by the custom. Mowrer (1939) has presented a somewhat similar account of the development of neurotic acts and has reformulated, in these terms, Willoughby's (1935) account of the function of magical rites in primitive societies. Mowrer's discussion is couched in terms of the "law of effect," however, which, as has been mentioned above, does not accord with the writer's point of view.

---

[3] See footnote 2.

Habit Systems

Movement-habits and act-habits may enter into identifiable systems. The basis of such systems lies in the systematization of institutions and culture to which the individual is exposed, as is well illustrated by the discussions of Plant (1937) and Sherif (1936). An army officer, a college professor, a bootblack, a policeman, are subjected to more or less common treatment by the public. What is expected of them is standardized and stereotyped. By such means their behavior is forced into certain norms from which a departure brings "punishment" and new training for conformity. There are occupational habit-systems based on the use of certain tools, the manner of life of a trade group, as well as on public reaction. The work of Foley (1937, 1940) illustrates this point very well. He showed that the motor speed and tempo preferences of his subjects were related to the speeds to which they had become "conditioned" as a consequence of their occupational experience. Further, Efron and Foley (1937) and Efron (1941) have shown that characteristic reaction patterns may change as a result of changed social environment. They found that the gestural patterns characteristic of certain immigrant groups were modified after a period of residence of these groups in the United States.

Public attitudes are organized about the names of occupations and such names of social status become important habit-cues for regulating behavior. When the army officer is confronted with a package, the recall of his class name may carry with it associated prohibitory phrases. Occasionally an order forbids officers to carry packages. His role is an important determiner of much of a man's behavior. Verbally familiar with many roles, the adoption of a new one may cause profound shifts in a person's behavior. Election to office, public disgrace, public recognition of ability, new titles, all operate through the cue of the role and previously learned behavior associated with such cues. Roethlisberger and Dickson (1939) in *Management and the Worker* describe the heightened output of girls who had been selected for an experiment on the effects of rest periods on output. The effect of the changed role so overshadowed the effects of the rest periods that no statement could be made about the actual effects of rest periods.

The behavior of a person—his attitudes, opinions, prejudices, etc.—is also influenced in a somewhat similar way by the components of the social situation in which he finds himself. Thus Katz (1941) has found that the results of a public opinion poll, conducted in a low-rent district of a large city, were significantly influenced by the status of the interviewers. "White-collar" interviewers apparently elicited different responses than did "working-class" interviewers, and the former group probably selected its respondents on a slightly different basis than did the working-class interviewers.

Definition of Personality

For the purpose of this chapter personality is defined as those habits and habit systems of social importance that are stable and resistant to change.[4]

Many habits are recognized as transient in the sense that they may be expected to change readily with common changes in environment. We change our residence and find no difficulty in breaking the habit of going to the previous apartment. The season changes and we alter our clothing to suit.

There are other habits and habit systems we regard as more profound. A housewife has fought disorder for so long that we judge that the sight of it will continue indefinitely to make her uncomfortable until it is corrected. A certain man has been so habituated to lavish spending that we judge the reduction of his income will not effect a tendency to economize. After the depression many firms found that men habituated to executive positions at large salaries were now not employable in subordinate places at less salary. Their role and habits of command were so well entrenched that these were characteristic and would outlive a change of circumstances.

Systems of deep-laid habits that make up the personality may be formed about a wide variety of circumstances. Since habits are always adjustments to change, so is personality to be regarded as founded on learned adjustment.

Personality as Habit-Adjustment

Mental life consists in adjusting to recurring change by changes in the behavior of the organism itself. And since by personality we mean the stable behavior of the organism, this consists largely of adjustive changes and *can be well described in terms of the world that is adjusted to.* We can in many instances describe a man without examining him at all when we know the character of the world in which he lived. If, for instance, he is born into a Negro family, or into the family of fisherfolk, or if his family contains a blustering and tyrannical father and a timid mother, if he is born into the family of a preacher to a wealthy congregation, we know in advance many of the traits he will develop (see Guthrie, 1938).

Of what advantage would it be for the managers of opinion polls to know some ready means for classifying people as extrovert or introvert, as ascendant or submissive, as temperamentally radical or conservative? Would they then take prompt measures to control their samples for the

---

[4] For the history of the concept of personality, see Chapter 1 by MacKinnon.

proper proportion of these traits as they now control them for economic status, occupation, age, etc.? This is highly doubtful. Their experience has shown that status, age, and occupation are important determiners of opinion on specific issues (Gallup and Rae, 1940). When we know that a man is the head of a family, has been on relief for one year, has a high school education, for 15 years worked as a carpenter, has been living in southern Illinois, we have a much shrewder notion of his opinion on politics, art, religion, and morals, and a much shrewder notion of his future and of his reactions to social situations than we have by learning his extroversion index, his aggressiveness centile, or his honesty score.

Some of the adjustments dictated by the environment are as obvious and certain as the use of language and conventional dress. Others depend on accident and circumstance.

Crude efforts to describe adjustment in terms of a limited number of "drives" would not represent man as effecting an adjustment to his environment, but would represent his sex drive or his nutritional drive as that which gets adjusted. This is incorrect. It is the whole man that is adjusted. Drives cannot be listed in a simple list because they must include all the ways in which he may be stimulated through sense organs, endocrine secretions, drugs. There is no point in describing a distended bladder as a drive. It is quite effective as a stimulus and its distension results in learning methods of relief that avoid other sources of annoyance like parental criticism or parental punishment. All habits may do what drives are supposed to do; their self-reinforcing structure makes interference with their execution the source of restlessness and varied behavior that leads either to their execution in a form that avoids the obstacle, or to substitute habits.

When threatened, the organism changes in such a way as to remain the same. It preserves its constant states by altering its nature. It is now a new organism and in their turn the changes that are part of the new organism are protected from change by other changes.

A system of servile habits may be developed as a protective adjustment to a master; liberation may find these servile habits persistent and defended against change. They are part of the man—the essence of his personality.

Neurotic behavior has this characteristic. It is first developed as an adjustment to trouble. The nervous breakdown is one way of meeting trouble. The symptoms excuse or explain a defeat; they save face. The habit-role, say of a concert pianist, is protected by a "piano-player's paralysis" that keeps the inadequacy hidden and enables the man to go on acting the part of a good pianist. An adjustment has been hit upon. But in its turn this paralysis will offer stubborn resistance to cure. It will survive medical examination, argument, evidence of all sorts. The role "concert pianist" when threatened with exposure and disgrace changes to "concert pianist with a special paralysis that prevents playing." When interrogation hints that this is a mere pose and in no sense genuine, there is new distress and some modification (such as denouncing the doctor) will preserve it in its essentials.

A cultivated German is placed in extreme distress by continuous criticism of everything German. Rebuttal of this criticism brings more and worse attack. He develops attitudes of counter-attack and criticizes things American. If the two nations should declare war, German criticism of America is now met with ostracism or internment or violence. The role of German is given up for another that preserves what has now become essential—bitterness toward the United States, and he becomes a labor radical. The cultural habits he acquired in his German education are changed but a basic loyalty to things German is preserved in his response to Germany's critics.

In recent years American Communism has given many examples of this identity in change. A boy lives with a domineering father. If the father's dominance were thorough and consistent, the boy would probably adjust by developing a complaisant and obedient attitude. But if dominance is irregular or inconsistent, the boy's adjustment may involve the survival of independent behavior with strong emotional reinforcement. There is common sense evidence that suppressed act-habits may effectively disappear, but act-habits that encounter obstacles become emotionally reinforced. The father becomes a cue for opposition and resistance.

If, now, the father dies or leaves the picture, this attitude is not affected. It may be called out by command, prohibitions, the symbols of authority, the state, the boss. But since domineering fathers are not pure types and their difference from other fathers is only one of degree, we can find in the rebel the converse of his father-hate, and Marx, Lenin, or Stalin plays the role of God, the Father, objectifying a childhood adjustment to a physical father infinitely wiser and stronger than the child.

In his attitudes of both resistance and obedience there is evidence of early intrenched habits that have become parts of the rebel's personality. They were originally adjustments to an actual father, changes effected through years of childhood. They are now defended by the associative learning that brought them about in the first place. Evidence concerning relationships between the psychological characteristics of the individual and the family constellation of his youth is presented by Stagner and Krout (1940).

We are all aware that descriptions like the above are lacking in more than one essential as scientific generalizations. We have not adequately defined dominance, offered means of measuring it, or made any general survey on which statements could be based. They are rather obscurely inferred from the nature of learning and some vague statements about the emotional effects of interference and opposition. Yet we can all think immediately of cases which fit the description, once granted that we can objectively rate dominance and rebellion. As they stand, the generalizations are of little value because it is not even established that membership in the Communist Party is an instance of revolt. It could well be a docile acquiescence to the politics of father or friends; that this might be true is suggested by Allport's (1929) finding that 79% of 400 college students supported the same political party as their fathers. Before we can speak with confidence in this field it would be necessary to establish the validity of general trait categories as well as the validity of their measurements.

Personality Traits

Is there a measurable general personality trait, like rebellion against authority, or neatness, or promptitude?

It is here argued that such traits may in one sense be asserted and at the same time pronounced of little significance or value. Our reaction to any situation whatever depends on our experience and the associations of that situation. The reaction, given the particulars of the situation, is specific. Every neat person has his own mode of being neat—the comparatively stereotyped movements by which neat results are accomplished in that situation.

Habitual movements resulting in neat effects may have been organized through long-time exposure to a family tradition or they may have been organized by the necessities of a way of life. The sailor on a sailing ship, living in cramped quarters and dependent in emergencies on having available and ready the gear of his ship, and living with other sailors, is gradually forced to acquire a large repertoire of acts that keep things ship-shape. He has been punished or admonished in the presence of disorder, unready gear, uncoiled ropes, unsecured hatches, until the sight of disorder motivates him strongly to react, and the reactions that remove the disorder remain as his characteristic behavior in its presence. They so remain because they are protected from unlearning. In order to learn to behave differently (or indifferently) in the presence of disorder, disorder must be present and thus be differently reacted to.

The systems of habit that make up identifiable personality traits are imposed on the individual through his learned adaptation to his family, his calling, his culture in general, the exigencies of his environment (see Davis and Dollard, 1940; Kardiner, 1939; Klineberg, 1940). Our ability to describe persons depends on our ability to name classes of situations to which he has learned such adaptations. More information is conveyed about a man when we name his calling than when we attempt to name the vague qualities that constitute extraversion or dominance or indecision. When we know that a man is a professional soldier, we know much about his skills and abilities, his style of thinking, his carriage, his opinions, his ambitions. We know this because we know the conditions of life to which he has had to adapt himself—what he must have learned.

We may raise the question why it is that writers on personality have disregarded so completely this obvious source of dependable information about the nature of man. In practical life we learn about his potential behavior from his record of training, his occupation, and his experience. But writers on personality are searching for something beyond this. They are possibly in search of a theological entity, the soul, and willing to disregard the conspicuous but banal information concerning him that lies at hand.

What they seek are descriptive traits that apply to all his behavior, and so may be taken to express the real man in a way in which he is not expressed by his knowledge and his skills, his prejudices, his opinions. These are obviously based on his training and describable in terms of learning.

In fact, we do find some evidence of such traits. There are people who have acquired with their occupation the manner fitted to the occupation, the deference of the waiter, the aggressive good-fellowship of the Y.M.C.A. secretary, the air of "being in the know" of the practiced lobbyist, the bedside deportment of the physician, the ready classroom omniscience of the high school teacher, the air of decision and authority practiced on the bench, the habits of qualification of the college professor.

All of these are learned by experience and they remain associated with the recurring occupational situations which they "solve" because lapses into other manners provoke distress and awkwardness and are unlearned. These specific manners are the ones that have worked.

But few of the owners of these manners can be trusted to exhibit them in situations remote from the occupation. The querulous behavior of the famous judge when he inquires of his wife the location of his black tie for evening wear, or his garrulous accounts of his golf game in the locker room have little resemblance to his aloof command exhibited on the bench. The question what he is *really* like *in himself* has no answer.[5] He is never "in himself." He is either in court or at home or at the country club and in all three places he behaves as he has there learned to behave. His three personalities derive in part from the nature of his court, his home, his club. They also bear evidence of accident in the sense of mannerisms that have merely failed to be eliminated because they did not interfere with success.

What has been said about personality traits may be summarized. Human behavior is made up of specific movement-responses to situations and these are determined in terms of association. A man tends, when faced with any feature of a situation, to repeat the behavior he exhibited when such a feature was last present. Such associative tendency may be, of course, completely blocked by current distracting or inhibiting situ-

---

[5] To a certain extent, and in a connotation perhaps different from that usually given by this phrase, we may mean by "what he is really like in himself" the common sources of his behavior in a variety of situations—generalized fears, anxieties, desires for prestige, etc.

ations, but remains the chief basis for predicting what the man will do when the feature in question is present.

These specific movement-responses become organized into skills which consist in the development of large groups of specific movement-responses all of a sort to achieve success or relief. Such a repertoire of specific movements adjusted to variations in the disturbing situation tends to remain because success or relief usually protects the constituent parts of the repertoire from being unlearned.

Certain general features of behavior, personality traits, appear as a result of exposure to recurring general features of situations. Most conspicuous are occupational skills. Perhaps most interesting to the psychologist of personality are skills or mannerisms in dealing with personal relations that go beyond occupation. These, like all skills, are the result of adapting through associative learning to recurring difficulties with persons.

The search for universal traits, or traits that attach to all of an individual's behavior, is mistaken in its conception and bound to fail. It has led to a neglect of profitable material at hand for the prediction of behavior (such as occupational traits) and to waste and clumsiness in dealing with the adjustment of behavior in the clinic.

Interference in Personality Adjustment

In the clinic practical results are of first importance and the perfection of theory may be postponed. For this reason we find clinical practice in different places exhibiting certain basic uniformities, while there are prodigious differences in theory (Murphy and Jensen, 1932).

But in the end all theories are tools and their value is determined by the ease with which they can impart to other persons the ability to deal successfully with persons.

The clinical psychologist is, first of all, practicing an art which he learns by experience and example. Some of the most successful have made no serious effort to put into words the methods by which they work. Many of those who have ventured into print with accounts of how their results are achieved have been quite mistaken in what they thought was effective. A manner, of which the clinician is not in so many words aware, may have been the largest contributing factor in his success. Even his diagnoses may have had nothing to do with his actual therapeutic measures and may have been invented after the fact, the results of a certain pressure to name and to classify, to tell "what ails the patient."

Freud and his followers made the first extensive efforts to state their therapy in terms of a general theory. That general theory was handicapped by several things. One of these was that the psychoanalysts were almost universally ignorant of the more modern concepts of psychology and talked in terms of common sense. They used instead of scientific concepts the popular mythology of the mind in which explanations are in terms of agents.

But they tackled a problem that had been neglected, the problem of how the patient "got that way." And their explanation may have been put in mythological terms, but they did take into account the nature of the events leading up to the patient's condition, and they did this in terms of a crude, popular associationism. Perversions, fixations, transfer, repression, the censor, the development of the *ego* and *super-ego* out of the *id* were all stated in terms of the situations and experience to which the patient had been exposed. Free association was the method of recovering the history of a symptom and depended on the notion that the original experience had been describable in associative terms.

The contribution of psychoanalysis was not its mythology but that it sought explanations of personality traits in the circumstances that attended the appearance of such traits. Underlying all psychoanalytic theory is an implicit associationism. The psychoanalysts remain almost completely vague as to what it is that is associated, and no distinction is made between ideas and movement, though these are assumed to be representative of the scholastic categories of mind and matter. But the psychoanalysts are fairly definite in assuming that new cues are established by the fact of their attendance on response. Dislike, suspicion, love, resentment, etc., are already attached to one situation. The purely adventitious presence of another neutral cue when one of these responses is in evidence gives the neutral cue the power to elicit the response.[6]

Of the real nature of learning there is no psychoanalytic theory (see also Chapter 9 by Sears). The bringing into full consciousness of the original circumstances of an association is supposed to separate cue from its undesired response. That this can obviously be done when the original circumstances are not recalled as well as when they are has not been noticed by the psychoanalysts. Nor has the fact that the revived memory may be quite fictitious and still serve its purpose been noticed by them. In terms of a systematic associationism the requisite for detaching a stimulus from an undesirable response is only that the stimulus be presented and, by one means or another, the response be prevented (Guthrie, 1935).   •

---

[6] Some psychoanalysts have considerably modified Freud's theoretical views, for example, Horney (1937, 1939) and Fromm-Reichmann (1941), and others have attempted to utilize conditioning principles in relation to psychoanalytic practice (French, 1933; Kubie, 1934; Schilder, 1937). The reformulation of psychoanalytic concepts in terms of learning theory has been begun by Hull (1939), Miller (1935), Mowrer (1939), Sears (1936, 1937), and others. In Ch. 12 of their book, Hilgard and Marquis (1940) summarize much of this work. Brown (1937) and Lewin (1937) have approached the problem from the standpoint of topological psychology. The experimental analysis of psychoanalytic mechanisms has received much attention from psychologists of whom the following list is representative: Dollard, Doob, *et al.* (1939); Doob and Sears (1939); Hovland and Miller (1940); Hovland and Sears (1938, 1940); Hunt (1941); Miller (1939); Mowrer (1940); Sanders (1937); Sears and Sears (1940); Sears and Hovland (1941). Rosenzweig (1937) has reviewed the earlier experimental work.

Psychoanalysts have noted that repression is one of the conditions favoring the preservation of a phobia. They have not noted that the reason for this is that the repression has prevented the occurrence of the stimuli to which associative inhibition must be attached. When an event has attached to the sight or mention of blood a tendency to syncope, and also there have been learned many habits that serve to avoid this subject (repression), the subject is protected from cure as well as from syncope.

Practical clinical work takes naturally to statement in terms of conditioning and association. The patient himself may be entertained with dramatic tales of the battling agents within him and accept such an account because he thinks in dramatic terms. But such an account lacks among other things honesty. The actual measures taken to get rid of undesirable habits or undesirable attitudes or undesirable traits must be stated in terms of association. The phobia which is now dependent on a perception elicitable by a variety of cues and words can be eliminated if these cues and words are presented at a time when a control of the total situation makes the terror impossible. The fearsome reminder becomes no longer fearsome when it has been associated with amusement or contempt or even with the indifferent performance of a routine task.

Practical Descriptions of Personality

The practical meaning of a personality trait is potential behavior. By asserting that a man has the trait, we mean that in certain types of future situations he will behave in a particular way of interest to us. Since we are not interested in his manner of performance so much as in the effects of that performance on us, it is not movements but types of results that we must use for the description. If, for instance, we say that a man is grateful, we mean he will, when reminded of the personal object of his gratitude, behave in ways to be classed as beneficial rather than harmful to that object. We may attempt a general trait description: He is grateful in general. By this we can only mean that specific attitudes resulting in beneficial behavior toward others are readily established in him.

But by far the greatest importance is to be attached to many categories very different from general gratitude, or general bravery, or general honesty. These are not profitable dimensions of personality. They are too difficult to measure and almost impossible to use after they have been measured. In one serious attempt to measure such a trait, that of honesty (Hartshorne and May, 1928), it was found to be a very *specific* pattern of behavior. The useful categories in describing what may be expected of a man include his skills which can be often readily measured. They include his types of adjustment described in terms of the situation to which he has been exposed. He is a hardened campaigner, an experienced broker, an experienced carpenter; he has been for ten years a head-waiter. If we know these types of experience, we

Avoiding the issue

may safely assume that he has learned skills that meet the problems of these trades and occupations.

Or we may mention that he is far below the average height. This is a problem situation in most societies and to it he has presumably made some type of adjustment, and there is a limited number of ways in which one can adjust to this handicap in our society. We mention that he is outrageously ugly or outrageously handsome, and we may safely assume certain typical adjustments to these departures from normal experience. We may mention that he is lame, or physically weak, that he has been brought up almost exclusively by a doting mother, that he has lived a life of great poverty, that he has always lived among men who were his inferiors in strength, that he has served a term in prison, that he was for three years a member of the Communist Party, that he grew up on a farm or in the city. Each of these sets of circumstances gives a basis for predicting his behavior in a wide variety of situations. Each of them conveys practical and useful information.

In the application blank we may require the statements of sponsors as to his introversion or extraversion, his general honesty, his loyalty, his industry. But the useful information on this blank is more likely to be his past record of occupation, his specific skills, his financial status, his marital and police record. His past affiliations, political and religious, offer better and more specific predictions of his future than any of the traits that we usually think of as personality traits. But it is just this predictive value that is required of a personality trait *and nothing more*.

When we know how men adjust themselves through learning to their situation, and know also the situations to which they have been exposed, have the record of their adjustment, we know the men themselves and there is no need to speculate concerning the deeper reaches of the soul until we can explore these with similar knowledge.

BIBLIOGRAPHY

ALLPORT, G. W. 1929. The composition of political attitudes. *Amer. J. Sociol.*, 35, 220–238.
—— 1937. Personality; a psychological interpretation. New York: Holt.
ALLPORT, G. W., & ODBERT, H. S. 1936. Trait-names; a psycho-lexical study. *Psychol. Monogr.*, 47, No. 211.
BROWN, J. F. 1937. Psychoanalysis, topological psychology, and experimental psychopathology. *Psychoanal. Quart.*, 6, 227–237.
CULLER, E. 1938. Recent advances in some concepts of conditioning. *Psychol. Rev.*, 45, 134–153.
DAVIS, A., & DOLLARD, J. 1940. Children of bondage. Washington: American Council on Education.
DOLLARD, J., DOOB, L. W., MILLER, N. E., MOWRER, O. H., & SEARS, R. R. 1939. Frustration and aggression. New Haven: Yale University Press.
DOOB, L. W., & SEARS, R. R. 1939. Factors determining substitute behavior and the overt expression of aggression. *J. abnorm. soc. Psychol.*, 34, 293–313.
EFRON, D. 1941. Gesture and environment. New York: King's Crown Press.
EFRON, D., & FOLEY, J. P., JR. 1937. Gestural behavior and social setting. *Z. SozForsch.*, 6, 152–161.

ESTES, W. K., & SKINNER, B. F. 1941. Some quantitative properties of anxiety. *J. exp. Psychol., 29,* 390–400.

FOLEY, J. P., JR. 1937. An experimental study of the effect of occupational experience upon motor speed and preferential tempo. *Arch. Psychol., N. Y.,* No. 219.

—— 1940. The occupational conditioning of preferential auditory tempo: a contribution toward an empirical theory of esthetics. *J. soc. Psychol., 12,* 121–129.

FRENCH, T. M. 1933. Interrelations between psychoanalysis and the experimental work of Pavlov. *Amer. J. Psychiat., 89,* 1165–1203.

FROMM-REICHMANN, F. 1941. Recent advances in psychoanalytic therapy. *Psychiatry, 4,* 161–164.

GALLUP, G., & RAE, S. F. 1940. The pulse of democracy. New York: Simon & Schuster.

GUTHRIE, E. R. 1930. Conditioning as a principle of learning. *Psychol. Rev., 37,* 412–428.

—— 1935. The psychology of learning. New York: Harper.

—— 1938. The psychology of human conflict. New York: Harper.

—— 1940. Association and the law of effect. *Psychol. Rev., 47,* 127–148.

HARTSHORNE, H., & MAY, M. A. 1928. Studies in deceit. New York: Macmillan.

HILGARD, E. R. 1937. The relationship between the conditioned response and conventional learning experiments. *Psychol. Bull., 34,* 61–102.

HILGARD, E. R., & MARQUIS, D. G. 1940. Conditioning and learning. New York: Appleton-Century.

HORNEY, K. 1937. The neurotic personality of our time. New York: Norton.

—— 1939. New ways in psychoanalysis. New York: Norton.

HOVLAND, C. I., & SEARS, R. R. 1938. Experiments on motor conflict: I. Types of conflict and their modes of resolution. *J. exp. Psychol., 23,* 477–493.

—— 1940. Minor studies of aggression: VI. Correlation of lynchings with economic indices. *J. Psychol., 9,* 301–310.

HULL, C. L. 1929. A functional interpretation of the conditioned reflex. *Psychol. Rev., 36,* 498–511.

—— 1931. Goal attraction and directing ideas conceived as habit phenomena. *Psychol. Rev., 38,* 487–506.

—— 1932. The goal gradient hypothesis and maze learning. *Psychol. Rev., 39,* 25–43.

—— 1934. The concept of the habit-family hierarchy and maze learning. *Psychol. Rev., 41,* 33–54; 134–152.

—— 1935. The mechanism of the assembly of behavior segments in novel combinations suitable for problem solution. *Psychol. Rev., 42,* 219–245.

—— 1937. Mind, mechanism, and adaptive behavior. *Psychol. Rev., 44,* 1–32.

—— 1939. Modern behaviorism and psychoanalysis. *Trans. N. Y. Acad. Sci.,* Ser. II, *1,* 78–82.

HUNT, J. McV. 1941. The effects of infant feeding frustration upon adult hoarding in the albino rat. *J. abnorm. soc. Psychol., 36,* 338–360.

HUNTER, W. S. 1934. Learning: IV. Experimental studies of learning. In Murchison, C., *A handbook of general experimental psychology.* Worcester, Mass.: Clark University Press. Pp. 497–570.

KARDINER, A. 1939. The individual and his society; the psychodynamics of primitive social organization. New York: Columbia University Press.

KATONA, G. 1940. Organizing and memorizing. New York: Columbia University Press.

KATZ, D. 1941. The effect of the social status, or membership character, of the interviewer upon his findings. *Psychol. Bull., 38,* 540.

KLINEBERG, O. 1940. Social psychology. New York: Holt.

KOEHLER, W. 1925. The mentality of apes. New York: Harcourt, Brace.

KUBIE, L. S. 1934. Relation of the conditioned reflex to psychoanalytic technic. *Arch. Neurol. Psychiat., Chicago, 32,* 1137–1142.

LEWIN, K. 1935. A dynamic theory of personality. New York: McGraw-Hill.

—— 1937. Psychoanalysis and topological psychology. *Bull. Menninger Clin., 1,* 202–211.

MILLER, N. E. 1935. The influence of past experience upon the transfer of subsequent training. New Haven: Dissertation, Yale University.

——— 1939. Experiments relating to Freudian displacement to generalization of conditioning. *Psychol. Bull., 36,* 516–517.

——— 1941. An experimental investigation of acquired drives. *Psychol. Bull., 38,* 534–535.

MILLER, N. E., & DOLLARD, J. 1941. Social learning and imitation. New Haven: Yale University Press.

MOWRER, O. H. 1939. A stimulus-response analysis of anxiety and its role as a reinforcing agent. *Psychol. Rev., 46,* 553–565.

——— 1940. An experimental analogue of "regression" with incidental observations on "reaction formation." *J. abnorm. soc. Psychol., 35,* 56–87.

MURPHY, G., & JENSEN, F. 1932. Approaches to personality. New York: Coward-McCann.

MURPHY, G., MURPHY, L. B., & NEWCOMB, T. M. 1937. Experimental social psychology. New York: Harper.

MURRAY, H. A. 1938. Explorations in personality. New York: Oxford University Press.

PLANT, J. S. 1937. Personality and the cultural pattern. New York: Commonwealth Fund.

RAZRAN, G. H. S. 1939. The law of effect or the law of qualitative conditioning. *Psychol. Rev., 46,* 445–463.

ROETHLISBERGER, F. J., & DICKSON, W. J. 1939. Management and the worker. Cambridge: Harvard University Press.

ROSENZWEIG, S. 1937. The experimental study of psychoanalytic concepts. *Character & Pers., 6,* 61–71.

SANDERS, M. J. 1937. An experimental demonstration of regression in the rat. *J. exp. Psychol., 21,* 493–510.

SCHILDER, P. 1937. Psychoanalysis and conditioned reflexes. *Psychoanal. Rev., 24,* 1–17.

SEARS, R. R. Functional abnormalities of memory with special reference to amnesia. *Psychol. Bull., 33,* 229–274.

——— 1937. Initiation of the repression sequence by experienced failure. *J. exp. Psychol., 20,* 570–580.

SEARS, R. R., & HOVLAND, C. I. 1941. Experiments on motor conflict: II. Determination of mode of resolution by comparative strengths of conflicting responses. *J. exp. Psychol., 28,* 280–286.

SEARS, R. R., HOVLAND, C. I., & MILLER, N. E. 1940. Minor studies of aggression: I. Measurement of aggressive behavior. *J. Psychol., 9,* 275–294.

SEARS, R. R., & SEARS, P. S. 1940. Minor studies of aggression: V. Strength of frustration-reaction as a function of strength of drive. *J. Psychol., 9,* 297–300.

SHAFFER, L. F. 1936. The psychology of adjustment. New York: Houghton Mifflin.

SHERIF, M. 1936. The psychology of social norms. New York: Harper.

SKINNER, B. F. 1938. The behavior of organisms; an experimental analysis. New York: Appleton-Century.

SPENCE, K. W. 1936. The nature of discrimination learning in animals. *Psychol. Rev., 43,* 427–449.

——— 1937. The differential response in animals to stimuli varying within a single dimension. *Psychol. Rev., 44,* 430–444.

STAGNER, R. 1937. Psychology of personality. New York: McGraw-Hill.

STAGNER, R., & KROUT, M. H. 1940. A correlational study of personality development and structure. *J. abnorm. soc. Psychol., 35,* 339–355.

WHEELER, R. H. 1929. The science of psychology. New York: Crowell.

WILLOUGHBY, R. R. 1935. Magic and cognate phenomena; an hypothesis. In Murchison, C., *A handbook of social psychology.* Worcester, Mass.: Clark University Press. Pp. 461–519.

Chapter 3

DYNAMIC THEORY OF PERSONALITY

By O. H. Mowrer, Ph.D., and Clyde Kluckhohn, Ph.D.

FOR THE PURPOSES of this chapter, the phrase "dynamic theory of personality" will be taken to mean a composite of concepts and postulates which stem mainly from three relatively independent lines of scientific development: psychoanalysis, social anthropology, and the psychology of learning. Each of these disciplines has evolved its own specialized terminology and methods of research, and each has achieved distinctive results. Perhaps the greatest single contribution of psychoanalysis has been to show the continuity of principles governing "normal" and "abnormal" behavior alike; social anthropology has had a similar influence in breaking down the categorical distinctions formerly made between "civilized" and "savage" societies; and learning experiments have done much to integrate our understanding of those attributes and capacities which have been regarded as uniquely "human" and the behavioral characteristics manifested by the rest of the "animal" world. But psychoanalysis, anthropology, and learning theory do not merely complement each other in respect to their contributions to present scientific knowledge and outlook; they also possess certain inherent affinities and a potential unity. The possibility of converging these three disciplines into a single comprehensive system of personality theory—which currently holds the attention of a number of workers in each of these fields—arises chiefly from the circumstance that they all embrace the following basic assumptions: [1]

(a) The behavior of all living organisms is *functional.*

(b) Behavior always involves *conflict,* or *ambivalence.*

(c) Behavior can be understood only in relation to the *field,* or *context,* in which it occurs.

(d) All living organisms tend to preserve a state of maximal *integration,* or *internal consistency.*

---

[1] The reader should be warned that we are using the word "theory" in its loose, popular sense. The *rigorous* systematization (see Hull, *et al.,* 1940) of psychoanalysis, anthropology, and learning theory is a task for the future.

Psychologists, and social and biological scientists in general, have long been divided into two major factions: the "mechanists," on the one hand, and the "purposivists," on the other. For the former, interest has centered primarily upon .he formula, *stimulation* ⟶ *movement*; whereas the latter have been intent upon the relationship between *movement* and the *effects thereof*. Believing that in such controversies the whole truth is rarely all on one side, or even on both sides considered separately, a number of modern writers—whom we may call "dynamicists"—have come to the conclusion that if we wish to have a really adequate theory of behavior, we must take as our starting point the more complex formula:

$$\text{Stimulation} \longrightarrow \text{Movement} \longrightarrow \text{Effects}$$

In order to represent the psychological presuppositions of some writers, the concept of *consciousness* would have to be introduced in this formula between *stimulation* and *movement*. Others would insist that *consciousness* be identified as an attribute of all three factors in the above formula.[2] While recognizing the possible validity of both views, we do not believe that we need to employ the term consciousness at all in order to define dynamicism, which is our sole immediate objective. We cannot, however, fail to note that symbolic processes (SP)—"reasoning," "planning," "intending," "imagining," "considering," "thinking," etc.—do unquestionably sometimes intervene between stimulation and movement, thus:

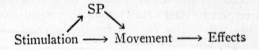

$$\text{Stimulation} \longrightarrow \text{Movement} \longrightarrow \text{Effects}$$

Although we shall refer from time to time to these symbolic processes, their genesis and function are still far from completely analyzed scientifically. We mention them at this point, not because they are essential to the present argument, but as a means of indicating that we do not in any sense systematically exclude them.

What we wish to emphasize at this juncture is that dynamicism represents an attempt to conceive the behavior of living organisms, including man, sufficiently broadly to end the dilemma of mechanism *vs.* purposivism. The various psychologists[3] who have been interested in this

---

[2] We are indebted to Professors H. W. Holmes and E. G. Boring for useful comment in this connection.

[3] See Allport (1937), Köhler (1940), Lewin (1935), McDougall (1932), Murray (1938), and Woodworth (1918). Thorndike (1900), though not a self-styled dynamicist, is especially noteworthy in this connection because of his early formulation and vigorous advocacy of the Law of Effect. See also Walker (1942) and Angyal (1941).

task differ somewhat in their particular approaches, but all would probably accept the logic of our analysis up to this point. We must now turn to the examination of the four fundamental propositions already listed.

(a) The concept of *function*, or *functionalism*, has been used with so many different connotations that it must be restricted if it is to have any concise meaning here. For us the view that living organisms make movements when stimulated and that this is the end of the matter is definitely *not* a functional theory of behavior. Physical machines and other inanimate objects may be said to "respond" to forces which impinge upon them, but it is only living organisms which possess in any high degree what may be called the capacity for *self-regulation*. There are, however, two important schools of thought as to how this is achieved. Under the sway of Darwinian biology, many writers of the last century conceived of the behavior of all living organisms as being determined primarily by *instincts*. These were defined as genetically inherited patterns of behavior which were relatively fixed as far as the lifetime of a given individual was concerned but which were capable of changing from generation to generation through the mechanism of natural selection ("survival of the fittest"), or *adaptation*. More recently, writers have stressed the importance of *habits*, which are defined as ways of behaving which have been acquired by the individual during the course of his life history. It is true, of course, that heredity, in both the genetic and the cultural sense, is a potent force in determining what a given individual's life experiences will be and thereby greatly influences the kinds of habits that are developed; but the habits that come as a result of both the genetic and the cultural determinants must be equally understood in terms of learning.

Learning theory represents an attempt to explain the genesis and nature of habits, and in order to make this theory adequate to its task the concept of *adjustment* (reward, satisfaction, gratification) has come into prominence. According to the instinct theory, behavior functions, or is functional, if it keeps the individual alive, healthy, and reproducing; according to learning theory, behavior functions, or is functional, if it leads to the elimination of the stimulation, or tension, which caused it. Failure to distinguish between adaptation (which develops and changes inherited ways of behaving) and adjustment (which develops and changes habits) has been the cause of endless confusion. Living organisms are so constructed that adjustive acts are, in the overwhelming majority of cases, also adaptive. Thus, eating food when hungry ordinarily functions both to satisfy the hunger and to keep the organism alive. However, an animal *may* eat palatable but poisonous food, in which event its behavior is adjustive but not adaptive. Although the concept of adaptation is useful in explaining instincts and also culture in the most general sense, it is only by adopting the adjustive conception of individual behavior that psychoanalysis, anthropology, and learning theory have made their

greatest advances as separate sciences and present the favorable possibility which they do for systematic unification.[4]

In its simplest, most basic form, adjustment implies that living organisms tend to go into action and to remain in action until the source of
their activity is removed. The proposition that "the behavior of all living
organisms is functional" thus comes to mean merely that their behavior
tends to result in the elimination of the stimulation, or irritation, which
produces it. In the next section we shall expand this conception of function as it relates to the learning process. But to suggest its relevance to
psychoanalysis and anthropology, we need only cite Witmer, who says:
"The light which psychoanalysis shed on individual behavior by its insistence that there was meaning and purpose in the most incoherent talk
of a psychotic is the same that functional anthropology brought to the
study of group behavior" (1939, p. 98).[5]

(b) The proposition that behavior always involves *conflict*, or *ambivalence*, is so indigenous to psychoanalysis that no comment is needed
on this score (see Chapter 14 by Miller and Chapter 9 by Sears). The
next section of the present chapter will likewise indicate its basic position in learning theory. Many anthropologists and other social scientists
have similarly emphasized the role of conflict in determining the patterns
of a culture, but the following quotation from Malinowski puts the matter
especially vividly and succinctly:

> Primitive law is not a homogeneous, perfectly unified body of
> rules, based upon one principle developed into a consistent system.
> So much we know already from our previous survey of legal facts in
> the Trobriand Islands. The law of these natives consists on the con-
> trary of a number of more or less independent systems, only partially
> adjusted to one another. Each of these—matriarchy, father-right, the
> law of marriage, the prerogatives and duties of a chief and so on—has
> a certain field completely its own, but it can also trespass beyond its

[4] For a more complete and adequate statement than is here possible of the relationship between instinct, culture, and habit, see Linton (1936). The relationship
between these three phenomena may, however, be at least briefly suggested by
noting that instinct theory rests on the concept of needs in the abstract, ultimate
sense, i.e., what an organism must do *in order to* achieve specified ends; whereas
learning theory involves the notion of needs as concretely and immediately felt,
with habits developing *because* of these needs. The understanding of culture, as a
system of "socially inherited habits," requires both of these conceptions.

[5] See: Bateson, Chapter 23 of this book; also Chapter 7 by French, Chapter 20
by Ribble, and Chapter 34 by Appel, dealing with psychoanalytic theory and therapy.
The relatively frequent occurrence in English psychoanalytic literature of the word
"instinct" is very misleading in this connection. This word has been unfortunately
used in translating the German word *Trieb,* used by Freud and others, which would
have been more felicitously interpreted as *drive* or *impulse.* It should also be noted
that in espousing functionalism (as here defined), both psychoanalysis and anthropology find it necessary to distinguish between "manifest" and "latent" functions,
i.e., between the various levels of drives which are reduced by a given action or
form of behavior.

legitimate boundaries. This results in a state of tense equilibrium with an occasional outbreak. The study of the mechanism of such conflicts between legal principles, whether overt or masked, is extremely instructive and it reveals to us the very nature of the social fabric in a primitive tribe. (1926, p. 100) [6]

(c) Gestalt psychologists have particularly stressed the importance of *field*, or *context*, in the determination of behavior; but their predilection for using visual and spatial imagery in their thinking and writing and then reifying their figurative constructs has done much to counteract their otherwise helpful influence in this connection. In simpler, more literal terms, psychoanalysis, anthropology, and learning theory all take for granted that the particular behavior produced by a given source of stimulation will be influenced by many different factors. The discussion of discrimination in the next section will suggest the extent to which the "total stimulus situation" is taken into systematic account by modern learning theory. The psychoanalytic emphasis upon the individual's "life history" as a determinant of what he does in a given situation is an acknowledgment of a slightly different, but no less important, form of "context." [7] And the following quotation, again from Malinowski, will illustrate the explicit recognition accorded to this principle in the field of social anthropology:

> The study by direct observation of the rules of custom as they function in actual life . . . reveals that the commandments of law and custom are always organically connected and not isolated; that their very nature consists in the many tentacles which they throw out into the context of social life; that they only exist in the chain of social transactions in which they are but a link. I maintain that the staccato manner in which most accounts of tribal life are given is the result of imperfect information, and that it is in fact incompatible with the general character of human life and the exigencies of social organization. (1926, p. 125)

(d) The proposition that "all living organisms tend to preserve a state of maximal *integration*, or *internal consistency*," is to some extent implied by the three preceding propositions, but its importance is such as to warrant independent formulation. According to proposition (b), conflict is an ever-present feature of behavior, i.e., every act, however gainful, also entails some sacrifice or loss; no form of adjustment (stimulation reduction) can occur without some dis-adjustment (stimulation increase). But this fact is in no way inconsistent with the proposition that living organisms show a tendency to select those modes of adjust-

---

[6] See Lynd (1939) and Mead (1942) for analyses of conflict in American culture.
[7] See Kluckhohn and Mowrer (1944) for a contextual scheme for analyzing the determinants and components of personality; also Horn (1944), and the conclusion of Chapter 1 by MacKinnon.

ment which involve the least possible conflict, i.e., which will afford maximal integration.[8]

By calling attention to repression and other dissociative processes, psy‑choanalysis may at first seem to be stressing an inherent trend away from rather than toward integration. But further examination will reveal the somewhat paradoxical view that all disintegrative processes derive their energy from the basic propensity of living things to function in such a way as to preserve and increase integration. Just as an organism may encapsulate or even extrude tissues or foreign substances which are no longer behaving harmoniously with respect to the rest of the body, so may the dominant psychic processes attempt to protect themselves by severing relations with other, disturbing processes. Perhaps the clearest and most complete statement of the concept of integration at the societal level is given by Sumner and Keller (1927) under their concept of the "strain toward consistency."

Because of the limits of space, the foregoing discussion, sketchy as it is, must suffice for showing the common acceptance by psychoanalysis, anthropology, and learning theory of the four basic propositions which were stated at the beginning of this section. For us, these propositions are the "minimum essentials" of a *dynamic* theory of personality.[9] Al‑though we draw many more principles from the three disciplines men‑tioned as we develop this theory more completely, these other principles need not be explicitly considered at this point.

It now remains to review some of the connotations which the term personality has previously had (for detailed discussion of these, see Chapter 1 by MacKinnon) and to arrive at that definition which coin‑cides best with the foregoing discussion and with the remainder of this chapter. A few years ago, when Watsonian Behaviorism was at the height of its popularity, personality was commonly defined as "the sum‑total of habit systems" which an individual possesses (Watson, 1930, p. 304), "the sum-total of an individual's habit dispositions" (Valentine, 1927, p. 393), "the sum-total of an individual's tendencies to reaction, both native and acquired" (Baar, 1928, p. 166). As we shall see shortly, this type of definition is objective and accurate from a formal standpoint; but since Behaviorism relied almost wholly upon associationism as a theory of learning (see Chapter 2 by Guthrie), and since associationism

---

[8] The time dimension is obviously involved here: gains and losses are computed not only in terms of the present but also the future. For an analysis of the process whereby future prospects become translated into immediate psychological realities, see the following section on the principles of learning; also Mowrer (1939).

[9] Since the text of this chapter was completed, an article by Masserman (1942) has come to our attention which represents an effort to show the "essential unity" of biology, psychology, psychiatry, and psychoanalysis, in which this author also lists "four general psychobiologic principles of behavior." It is perhaps indicative of the agreement and objectivity that is developing in this field that the four prin‑ciples listed by Masserman parallel to a remarkable degree the four propositions which have been independently formulated by the present writers.

is distinctly nondynamic in its general outlook,[10] such definitions lack much of the cogency and utility which they logically imply.

In keeping with the general reaction against naïve Behaviorism, attempts to define personality have also shifted in their emphasis, and we find May saying:

> The notion seems to be that an individual's personality may be completely described in terms of *his reactions*. This view of personality is a direct outgrowth of behavioristic psychology in its endeavor to get away from psychological entities and subjective categories. . . . The view presented here is a reemphasis of the root meaning of the word and holds that personality cannot be completely described in terms of reactions but that the individual as a stimulus must also be taken into account. An individual's personality is not defined wholly by his responses to others but also by the responses that others make to him as a stimulus. . . . When asked to describe an individual's personality one does not begin by giving an inventory of his reactions, but rather by describing the impression he makes on others, or by describing the way he influences others. (1932, pp. 82–83)

Allport has taken exception to May's emphasis on the "social stimulus value" of the individual as an index of personality and has advanced various considerations which do indeed expose certain limitations. He says:

> Definitions of personality in terms of the outer appearance of a man, that is, in terms of his "stimulus value" for others, are as common as they are troublesome [p. 39]. . . . Completely unsuitable are biosocial formulations in terms of social reputation or superficial charm. The distinction between reputation (social effectiveness) and the true personality is one that will be observed rigidly [p. 47]. . . . Might we not merely say that, psychologically considered, personality is what a man really is? [p. 48]. . . . The biosocial view stands in sharp contrast to the *biophysical* conception . . . which holds that personality, psychologically considered, is what an individual *is* regardless of the manner in which other people perceive his qualities or evaluate them. (1937, p. 40)

It is perhaps well to remind ourselves at this point that "personality" is simply a word and that we can profitably avoid all questions as to what it *really* means or *ought* to mean. Anyone can use and understand this term as he pleases, limited only by considerations of consistent,

---

[10] The associationists are unable to escape from the mechanism-purposivism quagmire. Admitting that "unconditioned reflexes" have biological utility (see Cannon's concept of homesotatis, 1932), Pavlov (1927, p. 13) speaks of the "great advantage to the organism" in being able to form "conditioned reflexes." But the "advantage" which Pavlov posits is not one of adjustment, but adaptation—a concept which leads straight to the purposivism which Pavlov and his followers have otherwise so energetically sought to avoid. See Mowrer and Lamoreaux (1942).

efficient communication. The disagreement between the two writers just cited arises, we believe, from the fact that this word has been and is still commonly used ambiguously, to refer to two distinguishable phenomena. In holding that the term personality should be reserved for one rather than the other of these phenomena, neither of these writers denies that the other phenomenon exists. Once we see clearly what these two phenomena are, the question of terminology becomes relatively unimportant.

Having already pointed out that a dynamic conception of behavior demands that *effects*, as well as stimulation and movement, be taken into account, we may now note that these effects fall into three categories: effects upon the actor himself, effects upon others, and effects upon the impersonal environment.[11] The behavior formula previously suggested may therefore be expanded as follows:

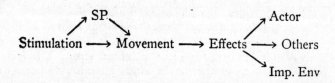

From principles described in the next section it follows that most, if not all, of the movements, or responses, which an individual makes have the immediate net effect of either rewarding or punishing him. These responses may also affect other individuals or the impersonal environment in such a way as to produce more or less delayed, indirect effects back upon the actor, which are again either of a rewarding or a punishing character. In both cases, the actor's movements tend to become either fixated (by reward) or inhibited (by punishment). Relatively stable, predictable habits thus develop and merge into an organized, integrated pattern. This, we believe, is essentially what Allport means by the expression "true personality," what the individual "really is."

Before a "personality," thus defined, can become an object of scientific study, it must, of course, have "social stimulus value," i.e., it must be perceived by other human beings, either directly or through recording or

---

[11] Two points should be noted here. First, it is no accident that the catch phrase, "interstimulation and response," which was borrowed by certain sociological writers directly from Behaviorism, has dismally failed to provide an adequate psychological underpinning for sociology. We now see that so-called stimulation and response are relatively meaningless unless their *effects* are also carefully analyzed in terms of reward and punishment. Secondly, some writers have objected to the concept of adjustment as used in this chapter on the grounds that it implies too great passivity on the part of living organisms and does not sufficiently stress the experience of *mastery*. In pointing out that behavior can be adjustive only when it has effects and that these effects may involve either the actor, others, or the impersonal environment, we feel that this objection is fully met. See Cattell (1943).

measuring instruments of some kind; but, as Allport remarks, this is equally true of rocks and stars.[12] Because the individual may be a part of the universe of observers of his own "personality," the situation is to this extent different from what it is in other sciences, and elaborate controversies have flourished as to whether each man "knows" himself best or can perhaps be more adequately described and understood by others (see Chapter 4 by Jones, on subjective evaluations of personality). Recent emphasis on "unconscious motivation" suggests that there are at least some situations in which the *effects* of an individual's behavior may give a clearer indication of his "wishes" than does his own conscious awareness. But this is a different matter from saying that personality *is* the effect of an individual's habitual actions. That there is a genuine distinction between an individual as "an integrate in action" [13] and his "reputation" is indicated perhaps most decisively by the fact that when an individual dies, "personality" in the first sense comes to an end, but in the second sense it may continue or even grow for centuries.

In emphasizing this distinction we realize that as long as an individual is alive his "personality" in the first sense is in more or less constant interaction with his "personality" in the second sense. The fact that a man is rewarded and punished by the kind of reputation he has makes him solicitous of that reputation, not only during his lifetime but also (by generalization) afterwards. But since a man's effect on others obviously does survive after his physical demise, because being "famous" and "immortal" are much the same thing in common speech, confusion between an individual's "biophysical" personality and his "biosocial" personality, to employ Allport's terms, very naturally arises. However, the fact that different *operations* must be engaged in if one wishes to study an individual's actual habit structure and his social reputation, makes this distinction valid and necessary.

Although we thus recognize the two-fold meaning of the term, we shall employ "personality" in this chapter to refer to the individual as an organized, adjusting, behaving entity, not to the way in which this individual may influence other individuals (or things). We acknowledge

---

[12] The development of so-called personality tests and measuring scales (see Chapter 5 by Maller) obviously represents an attempt to objectify our perception of personality in much the same way that we have learned to put visual scales on balances as a means of objectifying our perception of physical mass. That personality scales have been notoriously less satisfactory than balances may be due in part to the circumstance that we have not always properly defined what we have been trying to measure. It might be illuminating in this connection to see to what extent the indices, or criteria, which are used in learning experiments might also be utilized as measures of "personality."

[13] This expression is here used to include (1) the meaning, or *function*, which an individual's actions have for him, (2) the *conflicts* which exist between his various habit systems, (3) the environment, or *field*, to which he is accustomed, and (4) the more or less unique way in which he is held together, or *integrated*. These four criteria, derived from the four basic assumptions of dynamic theory, thus provide a comprehensive scheme for defining "personality" in general and for identifying any "personality" in particular.

that before any "personality" can become an object of scientific study, that individual must indeed *have* "social stimulus value," i.e., other human beings must be able to observe and make coherent statements about him; but this is not to say that this "social stimulus value" *is* the individual's personality. The order of effects which an object of scientific study has upon the observing scientist is very different from the type of effects, namely, the rewards and punishments, which are instrumental in determining both an individual's "reputation" with others and his own habit structure. It is, we believe, in the latter sense that clinicians most often use the term personality; and this definition is also most consistent with our emphasis on learning; for what an individual is or becomes is determined, not primarily by the way in which his actions reward or punish others, but by the way in which these actions directly or indirectly affect the individual himself.[14]

Principles of Learning

A dynamic theory of personality, as delineated in the preceding section, must necessarily place a central emphasis upon the psychology of learning. While consonant with learning theory, psychoanalysis and anthropology have, on the whole, been concerned with phenomena which represent such a high order of complexity that they have not been able to isolate and systematize the basic facts of learning as has laboratory experimentation. Without these two sciences, contemporary learning theory falls considerably short of presenting a sufficiently comprehensive view of human conduct and its vagaries, but without learning theory psychoanalysis and anthropology lack a solid, well-anchored foundation. What we can say here about learning will unavoidably be the barest kind of sketch, but without such a statement some of the main objectives of this chapter could not be even approximated. Naturally we cannot present more than illustrative evidence for any of the various principles which are here listed, nor can we even develop the purely theoretical structure to its fullest possible extent. Only within the last decade has learning theory approached being a coherent, self-consistent system. Consequently there is still a sparsity of published writings to which the reader can be referred for more complete statements and more extended documentation. However, the following should prove of greatest relevance and use in this connection: Thorndike (1931), Shaffer (1936), Davis and Dollard (1940, Ch. 1), Miller and Dollard (1941, Chs. 1–5), McConnell, *et al.* (1942), McGeoch (1942), and Hull (1943).

---

[14] Elsewhere an attempt has been made to explore and elaborate the concept of personality as "social stimulus value" (Kluckhohn and Mowrer, 1944). In adopting a different conception for the purposes of this chapter, we make no judgment as to which is ultimately "right," i.e., most generally useful. Such a judgment would demand an analysis of the nature of *observation of* vs. *participation in* social events and of the factor of reciprocity in relation to all social roles (Linton, 1936) which would take us far beyond the scope of this chapter.

The great unifying principle in the version of learning theory that is here espoused is the proposition that all behavior is *motivated* and that all learning involves *reward*.[15] The formula for the most elementary type of learning is: motivation $\longrightarrow$ variable behavior $\longrightarrow$ motivation reduction. Motivation is here defined as any state of affairs which puts an organism into action. Motives may be *primary*—such as hunger, thirst, heat, cold—or they may be *secondary* (emotional)—such as fear, anger, love.[16] Variable behavior may take the form of gross overt activity, or sensory exploration (looking about, listening, smelling, etc.), or symbolic exploration (thinking, phantasying, dreaming, talking, calculating, etc.). Every motive thus constitutes a problem situation, and the resulting behavior represents an attempt to solve it. If and when a "right," or "successful," response occurs, the motive is reduced, or adjustment is said to occur.[17] By virtue of the occurrence of this sequence something happens within the organism's nervous system

---

[15] See the discussion of *function* in the preceding section. The psychoanalytic equivalent of this conception of reward is, of course, the *pleasure principle*. Anthropologists are likely to mean roughly the same thing when they speak of behavior as being *functional*. Bateson (1942, p. 96) has argued that the Balinese do not see life as composed of conative sequences ending in satisfaction, but rather see it as composed of rote sequences inherently satisfying in themselves (see also Bateson, 1941). Such an interpretation is not, however, representative of current trends in anthropology.

[16] Here we are making three assumptions which some readers may not find immediately acceptable: (1) that emotions are learned, (2) that they function as motives, and (3) that there is no essential distinction between what we have called secondary drives, or emotions, and what others have termed *derived* drives (see Murray's [1938] concept of cathexes). However, we believe that these assumptions not only make a more coherent and simpler theory of behavior than is otherwise possible; we also believe that they are empirically justified (Mowrer, 1939, 1940; Miller and Dollard, 1941).

[17] At first blush this statement may seem to be contradicted by common experience. No one denies that much stimulation is of such a character as to cause the affected organism to try to reduce or eliminate it, but it may be contended that there are other forms of stimulation that are inherently pleasurable, which the affected organism will attempt to preserve or even increase. We recognize, of course, that human beings sometimes go to concerts, attend theatres, and seek "thrills"; we know that they go to dances, play games, and enjoy other, often strenuous, activities; and we also are aware that they sometimes derive deep satisfaction from making sacrifices and enduring suffering. In the face of these facts, there are two alternatives. On the one hand, one can conclude that stimulation (tension) increase and decrease have no relation to the fixation or inhibition of behavior. In this case one either has to find some other objective variable which *does* correlate with these two phenomena, or one has to abandon the whole problem as metaphysical and beyond the scope of science. (Miller and Dollard, 1941, following Freud, 1922, have considered the possibility that tension reduction is rewarding only to a certain point, below which it is punishing. Such a possibility cannot be categorically dismissed, but the fact remains that no one has yet empirically established such a hypothetical point. See later discussion of the antagonism of the sympathetic and parasympathetic divisions of the autonomic nervous system.) The theoretical position which we take, on the other hand, provides a simple, parsimonious hypothesis, namely, that stimulation is increased by living organisms only as a means of achieving, now or later, *still greater stimulation reduction*. In a later section we shall extend this analysis to certain problems connected with sexuality and moral masochism (see the psychoanalytic "reality principle").

which we call learning and which is operationally manifested by the fact that on subsequent recurrences of the same problem situation the "right" response occurs with increasing promptness and proficiency. The process whereby the "connection" between a given motive and a given response is strengthened is called *reinforcement*.

It is now well established that of those variable responses (sometimes called "random," or trial-and-error, behavior) which precede a rewarding state of affairs, that response which occurs closest in time to the reward is most strongly reinforced. But it has also been shown that other responses which lead up to the reward are somewhat strengthened, increasingly in the order of their temporal proximity to the reward. These facts have led to the formulation of the concept of the *gradient of reinforcement*.[18] Many important deductions have been made from this concept, including so fundamental a thing as the shape of the curve of learning; but the most relevant point to be noted in the present connection is that for learning to occur most rapidly and efficiently, there should be a minimum of delay between the occurrence of the "right" response and the reward.[19]

A theory of learning must, of course, be able to account no less adequately for the empirical fact that the likelihood that a given motive will elicit a given response can be *decreased* than for the fact that the likelihood that a given motive will elicit a given response can be *increased*. If we call the latter type of change in behavior *learning,* then we may call the former *inhibition*. But if disastrous confusion is to be avoided here, certain fundamental considerations must be clearly noted. It was formerly supposed that just as reward is the *sine qua non* for learning, so was "punishment" thought to be essential for inhibition. Punishment was assumed to be the opposite of reward, and just as reward directly strengthens stimulus-response connections, punishment was supposed to weaken them. While it is descriptively true to say that punishment "weakens" a given habit, what happens in such a case can and should be explained on the basis of the principle of reward, without invoking an independent principle. In any situation in which punishment is said to be involved, what actually happens is that a second, more powerful motive is introduced which demands an adjustment which is incompatible with the adjustment, or habit, upon which attention was originally focused. A *conflict* is thus produced, wherein the reward provided by escape from a new motive is pitted against the reward provided by escape from (reduction of) an original motive. As a result, a new habit is set up which is antagonistic to the old one. In this way, if the

---

[18] For a good historical account of this concept and a review of the empirical facts from which it was derived, see Hilgard and Marquis (1940).

[19] Roberts (1930) was the first to show the role of *secondary* reward in bridging the gap between instrumental acts and delayed primary rewards. See Wolfe (1936) and Miller and Dollard (1941); also the concluding paragraphs of the present section.

new habit is stronger, the earlier habit becomes inhibited, or superseded, but this is not to say that the original habit has been "taken out by the roots," so to speak, or that any process or principle other than that of reward is involved.[20] The basic learning formula is thus made to account both for those situations in which the likelihood that a given motive will elicit a particular response is increased and for those situations in which this likelihood is decreased.

Not only is reward necessary to the acquisition of a given habit, it is also essential to the continued performance of that habit. Repetition of a response, as such, is now known to have no tendency whatever to make this response more likely to occur on future occasions. In fact, if conditions are such that the response is completely unrewarding, repetition tends to eliminate, or *extinguish*, the response. Some writers have taken the position that this method of inhibiting a response involves principles different from those involved in the inhibition of a response by the method of "punishment" (Hilgard and Marquis, 1940). But such a dichotomy is unwarranted and misleading. Experimental results which are now available show that the extinction of a nonrewarded response proceeds at a rate proportional to the *effortfulness* of that response (James, 1941; Mowrer and Jones, 1943). From this and other findings which have been subsumed under the Law of Least Effort (Wheeler, 1940), it is now clear that the inhibition of behavior which occurs through extinction is no less a *motivated* phenomenon than is the type of inhibition that is produced by so-called punishment. With continued, nonrewarded repetition of a habit, a new motive is created, namely, *fatigue*, and since the consummatory, or "right," response to this motive, namely, *rest*, is incompatible with the original habit, a conflict situation is created in which the outcome is determined by the same factors that control conflicts in general. The phenomena of "spontaneous recovery" of extinguished responses, the differential effects of massed *vs.* distributed practice, and the differential effects of depressant and excitant drugs upon acquisition and extinction can all be explained in a manner consistent with the conflict- or fatigue-theory of extinction (Mowrer, 1941; Miller and Dollard, 1941; Hull, 1943; Mowrer and Jones, 1943).

The next principles to be considered are those governing *generalization* and *discrimination*. If a child finds that a given kind of behavior produces desired results in his parents, he is likely to try this behavior with other persons, i.e., he generalizes, or transfers, habits which have been learned in one situation to other more or less similar situations. If the generalized responses work with persons other than the parents, then no problem is involved; but frequently this is not the case. The child finds that behavior which brought reward from the parents elicits either

---

[20] See the phenomena of repression and regression as described by psychoanalysis (Chapter 9 by Sears); also experimental studies of "retroactive inhibition" (McGeoch, 1942).

indifference or active punishment from others. This means that the child must learn to make a discrimination, i.e., he must learn that one kind of behavior will work with some persons but will not work with others. Obviously, such a differential patterning of responses presupposes that parents and nonparents should be different in clearly discernible ways, other than in the way in which they react to the behavior in question. By this route we come to the importance of *cues*, i.e., incidental stimuli which enable the child to learn to respond in one way with one person and in another way with another person. But how, precisely, does this kind of learning occur? Discriminative learning is such a commonplace, both in social and nonsocial settings, that its explanation may seem self-evident; but from a systematic standpoint it is a relatively complex affair.

In any situation in which a motive is eliciting goal-directed behavior, other forms of less intense stimulation are always present to some extent —visual, auditory, olfactory, tactile, kinaesthetic, etc. The nervous system of all higher organisms is so constructed that when the goal is reached, i.e., when the motive is reduced, not only is there a reinforcement of the connection between the motive and the "right" response; a connection is also established, by *associative* reinforcement, between this response and the various incidental stimuli which were present at the time of the occurrence of the rewarding state of affairs. By a process which is now fairly well understood but is too intricate to discuss here, the occurrence of the associative reinforcement allows the organism to learn to make one response to a given-motive-plus-a-particular-cue-or-cue-constellation and to make a different response to the *same*-motive-plus-a-*different*-cue-or-cue-constellation (see Mowrer and Lamoreaux, 1942). In short, through the mechanism of associative reinforcement, cue-, or sign-learning occurs which enables the organism to *time* and *place* his responses so as to make them match the external realities optimally. This temporal and spatial ordering of behavior is, of course, never perfect, but it provides an important and highly useful step in enabling the individual to achieve a higher level of integration than would otherwise be possible. As we shall see later, individuals who fail to make accurate discriminations often find themselves in more or less serious difficulty.

By a slight extension of the principle of associative reinforcement, we come to the phenomenon of *conditioning*. Many writers have made the error of equating conditioning and all learning, but clarity seems best served if this term be reserved for that special sphere of learning in which an incidental stimulus becomes so strongly connected, by associative reinforcement, with a "right," or "goal," response that this stimulus can alone elicit the response, *in the absence of the original motive*. Such stimuli may be referred to as *signals*, in contradistinction to *cues*. Both, however, are properly called *signs*, to indicate that they both gain their significance, or meaning, from the same process, namely, associative reinforcement.

Everyday as well as laboratory examples of conditioning are so familiar that it is probably not necessary to explicitly mention any here. It is also obvious that conditioned responses gain their utility in the behavioral scheme of things by virtue of the fact that they enable living organisms to make adaptive responses *anticipatorily*, before the motive of which the signal is premonitory has actually impinged upon the organism. Although found in varying degrees in most lower organisms, this capacity to "live in the future" is, of course, most highly developed in human beings and is related to the extraordinary degree to which human beings have elaborated the sign-behavior and sign-produced behavior which we call communication, or language. Without the capacity to use and understand words, or their equivalents, the transmission of culture, i.e., the systematic instruction of each succeeding generation by preceding ones, would be impossible—as would probably also be the common neuroses and "functional" psychoses as we know them.

According to the theory elaborated above, the simplest and most basic form of learning is manifested in the progressive modification of that type of behavior which is commonly referred to as trial-and-error. This, however, has two major limitations, the first of which is that in its prototypical form it does not provide for differential reactions to the same motive when the "field," or "total stimulus situation," is different. The evolution of associative reinforcement and the resulting capacity for discrimination provided the means of surmounting this deficiency. The other problem is that in trial-and-error learning, there is no provision for the establishment of *new* stimulus-response connections. In other words, in order for a given connection to be "learned" (i.e., strengthened), it must first occur, and in order to occur it must, of necessity, already exist, at least weakly. However, with the advent of conditioning, absolutely novel connections became possible, thereby creating the possibility of dramatically higher orders of behavior adjustability.

We thus see the illogic of the tendency of some writers to regard the "conditioned reflex" as the "fundamental unit of habit"; it is actually a comparatively complex and probably relatively recently-evolved type of learning ability.[21] But it is equally shortsighted to regard conditioning as in any sense an end point in the emergence of "intelligence." We have already noted that conditioning lays the foundation for the development of language, but no less important is the fact that it also provides for a new order of motives, i.e., the *emotions*. Not many years ago it was fashionable to regard these secondary, or derived, motives as instinctively given and as representing, therefore, the "lower" side of man's nature. It now appears that the emotions are one of the main factors that have lifted man to his present station of preeminence in the animal world. As drives which are themselves the result of prior learning, they provide

---

[21] The reader should be warned that this view, while perhaps gaining in popularity, is still far from generally accepted by learning theorists. For a review of the literature on conditioning in the various biological phyla and at various "levels" of the vertebrate nervous system, see Hilgard and Marquis (1940).

the basis for an entirely new level of psychological activity and development. We now know (Mowrer, 1939; Miller and Dollard, 1941; Mowrer and Lamoreaux, 1942) that once an emotion has developed on the basis of prior conditioning, it may in turn serve as a motive and source of reinforcement for new trial-and-error learning, generalization, discrimination, and even further ("higher-order") conditioning (see, for example, Finch and Culler, 1934). The way is thus opened for the analysis and understanding of the most intricate and highly evolved types of behavior.

The connection between emotion and learning has been scandalously neglected by laboratory researches to date, but it now appears likely that within a decade or two this oversight will be corrected. As this occurs the popularity of *ad hoc* mentalistic hypotheses concerning behavior will surely lessen, and the last links in the chain of concepts connecting learning theory and psychoanalysis—which has been concerned with emotional phenomena from the outset—will be forged. Anthropology, having long been interested in the "whole man," has already done much and will do more to amplify and broaden both learning theory and psychoanalysis so as to make them meet and merge into a unified scientific structure.

Space permitting, the foregoing discussion of learning principles should have been elaborated to include more explicit reference to the relation between these principles and the emergence and functions of language. As the major vehicle of culture-transmission, language, written and spoken, has long been a focal point of anthropological interest; and the whole area of symbolism, interpretation, and meaning has come under close psychoanalytic scrutiny. Although much remains to be done, considerable progress has also been made by students of learning (Miller and Dollard, 1941, Ch. 5) toward giving language research a firmer underpinning than philology or philosophy has ever provided (Ogden and Richards, 1938). It is sufficiently evident that when speech became a human attribute, a host of dramatic new possibilities emerged; but these new capacities grew out of pre-verbal mentality and were not created *de novo*. The pre-verbal, nonrational principles of learning thus provide, we believe, a far sounder basis for understanding "reason," "thought," "attention," "memory," "volition," "insight," "judgment," etc., than the latter do for understanding the former; and lacking the space required to trace the continuity of the nonrational and rational processes, we have chosen to slight the latter.[22] Actually, this neglect

_____

[22] Lewin's (1942, pp. 222–223) recently proposed distinction between "learning as related to motivation" ("need habits") and "learning as related to cognition" ("executive habits") seems unfortunate to us, not because we do not also recognize the importance of "cognitive structure" (if by this Lewin means the symbolic processes, cf. Linton, 1936, p. 82), but because this distinction perpetuates what is to us a fallacious dichotomy. Our position is that *all* habits (including habits of speech, thought, and even feeling) require motivation both for their acquisition and for their perpetuation.

is less serious than it might at first seem, for the reason that, like learning theory, psychoanalysis and social anthropology are both basically nonrationalistic in their approaches. In fact, the inability of rationalistic psychologies and philosophies to account for the so-called irrationality of madmen and "heathens" was perhaps the principal factor which forced scientific students of human behavior to look for a wider and more fundamental frame of reference.

In the following sections of this chapter the reader will find somewhat fewer specific references to the principles of learning than the preceding discussion may lead him to anticipate. Given unlimited space, we should have attempted to make explicit the connections between each cultural and clinical concept and the underlying learning principles; but rather than exclude other material, we shall rely upon the reader to fill in many of the interstitial logical steps (see other chapters dealing with cultural and clinical phenomena in terms of learning theory). Since we do not trace these connections in all their possible detail, the question may arise as to why we make such a relatively extended statement of basic learning theory. Our answer is that we regard .learning theory, not as in any sense in competition with psychoanalytic theory or anthropological theory, but rather as providing a "lower common denominator" for both. And since our entire subsequent argument hinges on this assumption, and since "learning theory" still means different things to different people, we have gone to some length to state the particular version which we accept and which is latent, if not explicit, in the following sections.

Infancy and Early Socialization [23]

In addition to the reasons already adduced for building a theory of personality upon psychoanalysis, anthropology, and the psychology of learning, there remains another consideration which should now be made explicit. Anthropology, more than any other science, has been concerned with the evolution, diffusion, and perpetuation of human culture. The utility which the accumulated inventions, knowledge, and values of past generations have for modern man is clearly attested by the prodigious amounts of time and money that go into the task of *education*. However, the human animal accepts the burden of this heritage only under protest and may, in some instances, find it altogether intolerable. When this happens, one commonly discovers that the educative process—broadly conceived as the total preparation of the individual for responsible adult membership in his social group—has been pushed too fast or too far, with the result that such individuals require special *reeducation* if they are to be put back on the path of normal development and function.

---

[23] In the interest of conserving space, this section, as originally submitted, has been considerably abridged. The editor takes responsibility for any change in emphasis or meaning intended by the authors. (Editor)

Unwise *teaching* thus creates or at least importantly contributes to the need for *therapy*, and it is here that we turn to psychoanalysis for the best in both theory and practice.

Human life is of necessity lived in terms of individual motivations and of cultural patterns. However, the relationship between what a given individual wants and what other individuals (either as individuals or as surrogates of culture) expect or demand of him is never entirely harmonious and may, in extreme cases, become stridently antagonistic. It is not remarkable, therefore, that there should be some lack of understanding and sympathy between those persons whose professional activities center around the preservation and perpetuation of cultural patterns and those persons whose main business it is to strive to protect and rehabilitate disorganized individuals. This opposition creates a kind of equilibrium which helps to keep societies from tipping too much toward "individualism" or too much toward social conservatism. However, the more knowledge that the teacher and the therapist have in common, the less strain and working at cross purposes there will be. Here the psychology of learning promises to perform a uniquely useful function: being on good terms with both the educational and reeducational professions, it should be able to function as a means of mediating important reconciliations and rapprochements.

In this and the remaining sections of this chapter, the dilemmas of growing up and living in a modern civilized society will be traced, with one eye on the individual as *pupil* and the other on him as potential *patient*. In following the course of socialization, main emphasis will fall upon socialization *in America*, but reference will frequently be made to other societies, both civilized and "primitive." In a sense, the remainder of this chapter may be said to constitute merely an extended commentary on "the individual *in* society": i.e., the conception of "personality" as a resultant of the fact that every individual has motives (both biologically given and determined by learning) but must so pattern his adjustments as to make them conform to the expectations and limitations of other individuals. These paragraphs, then, constitute a skeleton. The remainder of the chapter is an attempt, as it were, to supply the moving flesh and blood. But this enterprise will also afford an opportunity to bring out at least a few additional points of purely theoretical interest which could not be included in the more formal statements of the two preceding sections.

The Early Months of Infancy.[24]—It is a commonplace that the period of infancy and early childhood is of peculiar importance in personality formation. Just as the first few weeks of foetal life are crucial in determining whether an individual will be physically normal or a monstrosity, so also are the first few years after birth uniquely fateful

---

[24] For a more extended discussion of infantile experiences and for an account of the more strictly Freudian theory of development during this period, see Chapter 20 by Ribble.

in establishing personality trends (Erikson, 1940). Although infants are now known to be capable of simple learning immediately after birth and perhaps even for some time before (Marquis, 1931, 1941; Wickens and Wickens, 1940), such intra-uterine learning as occurs under ordinary circumstances is neither prescribed nor controlled culturally. Since there is so little relation between what an unborn child does and what happens to him, there is scant opportunity for habit formation. Movements which result in changes in bodily position probably relieve postural tensions and are therefore reinforced (Holt, 1931), but since this and other foetal behavior is ordinarily neither rewarded nor punished by *other persons,* there is nothing during this period that can properly be called education, or socialization. Since foetal conduct does not affect other individuals, except the mother, it is not ethically evaluated. And even the mother does not consciously hold the foetus accountable for her discomfort. Prenatal development consists, therefore, almost exclusively of physical growth, including the neural, sensory, and motor maturation which brings learning capacity into being; but since the unborn child is so completely protected by nature, alike against the possible demands of other persons and the vicissitudes of the external physical environment, this capacity lies largely unexploited until the advent of birth.

According to Rank (1929), an infant is always more or less emotionally traumatized by passage down the birth canal. However, the fact that individuals who have been delivered by Caesarian section do not, as adults, differ temperamentally in any easily discernible way from persons who have been normally born (but see Fries, 1941b) deprives the "birth trauma" theory of the sweeping significance which Rank has claimed for it. In the absence of physical injury—neural lesions, hemorrhage, suffocation (see section on anoxia in Chapter 19 by Shock and Chapter 20 by Ribble), strangulation, fractures, dislocations, etc., birth seems to have little enduring psychological importance. It does, however, have one momentous consequence: it severs forever the physical connection between child and mother, which for the first nine months of life provides nearly perfect insulation against want and obviates the necessity for independent adjustment. As Ròheim (1942, p. 162) has remarked, the newborn infant "has to bear the loss of intra-uterine happiness; he learns what it means to desire something without receiving it."

In most mammals the behavior of the mother toward newly born offspring is instinctively tender, protective, and indulgent, which does much to cushion the shock of beginning a biologically independent existence. But since the instinctive control of maternal behavior has largely disappeared in human beings, the treatment of the neonate falls almost wholly under cultural domination. While this fact makes for tremendously greater flexibility in determining the kinds of persons into which human infants may be made, it carries an attendant danger. If instincts have the disadvantage of being inflexible, they also have, given a stable and appropriate environment, a wisdom born of countless generations of evolutionary selection. It is consequently understandable how difficult it is to insure that all human parents shall have acquired, on the basis of *individual* experience, comparable competence in playing the parental role. In those few remaining "primitive" societies in which the cultural patterns have been slowly perfected over hundreds of years and have not been disrupted by contact with Western civilization, the problem of how parents should behave in their relationship with children hardly exists. Individual fathers and mothers may vary slightly from community standards, but there is little question about what is "right." In contrast, our own society presents a welter of inconsistencies.

For optimum development, it would appear from our theoretical considerations that a newborn child should be as continuously satisfied as possible during the first few months of extra-uterine life. This means answering every cry or indication of want with such rewarding care as feeding, warming, rocking, stroking, drying, etc. Keeping the infant's anxieties and tensions at a minimum improves gastro-intestinal function which is so important for the processes of maturation (see Chapter 20 by Ribble; Aldrich and Aldrich, 1939; Bakwin and Bakwin, 1942; Lucas, 1934). As important as this is, responsively answering the child's expressions of need should have equally desirable behavioral consequences. Such treatment should promote confidence and trust in a predictable world, for each primitive striving is rewarded. It would encourage an alert outgoing attitude, for the sounds and cutaneous impressions from the world become associated with satisfying events. It should foster social responsiveness which, in turn, is rewarding to parents. And it should facilitate the early establishment of positive emotional attachments to parents. This parental love is an acquired drive, which is one of the best allies which parents have in later inducing their children to make renunciations and to acquire skills; it provides the basis for what psychoanalytic writers have termed the fear of the "loss of love."

It is a common observation that a child will not make the same sacrifices for a stranger that he will for a well-loved person. A child can afford to accept discipline and training from a loved and trusted person who stands for compensating rewards and security. These theoretical considerations can hardly be said to have been validated by direct experimental evidence. But clinical evidence is clearly confirmatory (see Chapter 20 by Ribble). Clinical experience suggests that if we are to understand the determinants of personality development during infancy we must look beyond such conditions as cleanliness, nutrition, and rest. Health and physical growth are significant, of course, but so also is the psychological growth, i.e., learning, which inevitably begins with birth.

In this connection it is instructive to notice a characteristic contrast between the practices of nonliterate and folk societies and those which have recently tended to prevail in Euro-American middle classes. The tacit assumption in nonliterate societies has been that the interests of the

infant himself and of the community of which he is a part are best served
if those who are responsible for him are, in the beginning, constantly
attentive and responsive to the infant's slightest expressions of want and
discomfort. Gradually, this indulgence, which serves to provide some
degree of continuity with the complete absence of want during prenatal
existence, changes into a gentle tutelage which fosters the development
of the elementary skills and restraints demanded by the social group but
which also lays the basis for later attitudes of friendliness, affection, and
trust. By withholding the adult cooperation which is so essential to the
infant, the parent has constantly at his command a device for increasing
the infant's variable, exploratory behavior and for then selectively rewarding (by responding to) those new, more adult-like responses which
make their appearance. Although physical birth is an unavoidably
abrupt event, the change from complete foetal narcissism to the self-
sufficiency and social responsibility of later life can thus begin cautiously
and proceed little by little. Present clinical evidence suggests that if the
transition from the moral and physical sanctuary of intra-uterine existence to the rigors and responsibilities of independent, adult life is
gradual and guarded the infant is more likely, other things being equal,
to escape maiming and traumatic experiences from the imposition of
human culture.

The contrasting position may be well illustrated by the following
passage from a widely read U. S. Government bulletin on infant care:

> Through training in regularity of feeding, sleeping, and elimina-
> tion, the tiny baby will receive his first lessons in character building.
> He should learn that hunger will be satisfied only so often, that when
> he is put into his bed he must go to sleep, that crying will not result
> in his being picked up or played with whenever he likes. He will
> begin to learn that he is part of a world bigger than that of his own
> desires. (Children's Bureau Publication No. 8, 1940, p. 3)[25]

Although commonly interpreted as being in the child's own best
interests, the scheduling of infant care has many undesirable consequences
which are gradually gaining recognition. Schedules are not infrequently
observed so meticulously that an infant, although he may have cried continuously for an hour or more, is not allowed to have food until precisely
the appointed time. The notion that crying is physically good for an
infant in that it "makes his lungs strong" is clearly a rationalization.
The fear that responding to the crying of a small infant will "fixate"
this response is based on dangerous half knowledge. Rewarded responses
indeed tend to become habitual, but there is also the principle of Least
Effort, which states that instrumental acts will be performed as eco-

---

[25] In the revision of this pamphlet put out in 1942, the point of view illustrated
in this quotation has been changed considerably in the direction indicated by the
argument in this chapter (see Children's Bureau Publication No. 8, 1942, pp. 30–31,
45, 49, 50, and 65). (Editor)

nomically of effort as possible. Crying is hard work, and the repetitive expenditure of this effort without reward is conducive either to the development of apathy and resignation or insecurity and anxiety. Crying as a mode of communication obviously is not permanently acceptable because speech is a more efficient and refined means. But crying is an infant's only resource in the beginning, and its success or failure almost certainly leaves an imprint on the individual's later self-confidence and general social responsiveness. Not only are privations which are enforced before the child learns to speak usually adjusted to more slowly than if the child can be given a verbal explanation, but they are likely to foster an inability to "voice" problems later in life so that the individual will less often "know" the real source of his emotional and social discomforts.

Another misunderstanding must be anticipated. Responsively gratifying his needs during these early months does not mean that a child is "spoiled." The "spoiled" child shows just the traits we have predicted from scheduling care, and he is either one who has never met any conditions for being rewarded or who has been inconsistently rewarded. The parent who responds to a clock rather than to the behavior of the child is, from the child's point of view, not responsive at all (Richards, 1932). If the rewards which a child receives bear no consistent relation to his behavior, education will not proceed efficiently in its substantive aspects, and an apathetic or an anxious or a hostile individual is likely to result [Kilpatrick's (1926) "concomitant learnings"]. If a reward occurs either before or significantly after a response has been made which the cultural agent (mother or teacher) wishes to make habitual, that end will not be achieved (see the following section). The response that immediately precedes a reward will be the one that seems to the organism to "get results" and will tend to be learned. Thus, the hypothesis that scheduling infant care contributes most effectively to his education and "character building" is patently inconsistent with modern learning theory.

Another reason commonly given for scheduling the care of infants and more or less ignoring the psychological considerations which have just been advanced is that this gives parents, particularly mothers, more freedom and leisure. We must face the fact that certain goals prescribed for young married women in American society are incompatible, for example, with feeding an infant whenever he wishes to be fed. But these incompatible cultural goals are relatively ephemeral; they have not long been a part of the structure even of American culture. Our cultural goals are constantly being altered, and insistence upon their fixity may mask a neurotic unwillingness to make sacrifices. Actually, since another new cultural goal is fewer and better children through the utilization of birth control, the sacrifices required by child care would involve only a small fraction of the adult's life span. Furthermore, it can be argued that the sacrifices would be more apparent than real, that the long-time gain in the mother's satisfactions from responsive and teachable children would far outweigh the temporary giving up of the competing advantages.

Later Infancy.—Later infancy presents a somewhat different problem. In all societies this is a period in which physiological autonomy is at least to some extent surrendered to cultural control (Frank, 1938). The child must gradually learn bowel and bladder control. As his fundamental capacities mature, he must learn to walk and talk. And he must be taught to avoid dangerous situations. In general our theory demands at this stage that no behavior be arbitrarily demanded of a given child that does not exist in his repertoire, for a response must occur if it is to be rewarded. Our theory also demands that the rewards be administered when the desired behavior occurs and that the emotional climate be reassuring.

A number of common problems of this period should be mentioned. Many parents seem unduly concerned, not only about the regularity of the child's eating, but also about the quantity of food he consumes. He *must* have food whether he wants it or not. Forced feeding of finicky or resentful or apathetic children has been recommended and practiced to a surprising extent. The results have been unfavorable in most instances. Instead of eating being a pleasure, which can be used as reward and an educative device, it thus becomes actually a form of punishment. Modern discoveries concerning vitamins and calories have been of great value, but as McCollum has observed: "The question of *how* to feed children is certainly just as important as the question of *what* to feed them. But this is a problem on which the child psychologists will be more helpful than the biochemists" (1934, p. 49). Experiments by Katz (1932) on children and Richter (1941) on rats show that young organisms are surprisingly wise in maintaining a balanced and sufficient diet if allowed to determine their own choices (see also Chapter 19 by Shock). Sheldon (1940) has similarly done a service in pointing out the ambiguity of weight-height indices of nutritional status. Children, like adults, vary in body type, and what is "normal" weight for one child may be over- or underweight for another child of exactly the same age.[26]

In our culture the tendency has recently been not only to deny children the emotional warmth formerly granted them, but also to enforce certain renunciations upon them at the earliest possible moment. Parents have been made to feel that they must "uncompromisingly deal with 'bad

---

[26] For an interesting investigation of common parental misconceptions regarding the causes of disease and ill health in children, see Jacques (1942). Why American parents should show such exaggerated concern over the physical welfare of their children and so little sensitivity to their emotional needs is an interesting and probably very complicated question. But it is not unlikely that a factor is the unconscious guilt they feel as a consequence of the scheduling and similar impersonal practices in which they indulge.

habits' the moment they appear . . . destroying them in their early stages before they become fixed" (Levy, 1928). Such procedures seem to make for more or less enduring scars: insecurities, compulsions, revolts. When a child is punished for urinary or bowel incontinence before he is clearly capable of recognizing or announcing his need, or before he can walk to a toilet and manipulate his clothes, he can only respond with resignation or hostility toward the punishing person. When substitute gratifications, like thumb-sucking, which are developed in response to earlier privation (Levy, 1928, 1934), are inordinately punished, the child is faced with similar alternatives. Dentists have probably placed a one-sided emphasis upon the orthodontic results of thumb-sucking. As Fries (1941a) expresses it, ". . . arousing parents' emotion against thumb-sucking as though it was a criminal activity fosters an emotional problem between parent and child which may be far more difficult to straighten than any malocclusion."

Such punishment from parents is likely to result in a heightening of the ambivalence, or conflict, which necessarily exists to some degree in the attitude of the child toward the parents. And this heightened ambivalence commonly generalizes to persons outside the family, including, in later life, teachers, employers, marriage partners, and others (see Chapter 28 by Malamud). Moreover, so long as parents merely punish behavior which they dislike, and do not reward the behavior they like, the child's path of development is left largely undefined for him, except in the negative sense (Whiting, 1941). Thus, parents who squander the opportunities which infancy affords for using the dependency of this period to build up attitudes of trust and affection are later likely to find, as specific skills and restraints have to be established, more in their children that they dislike than they like and to feel obliged to resort to "force."

Such cultural dicta as "spare the rod and spoil the child" give neurotic parents a socially justified way of easing their own tensions. As Fries (1941a) suggests: "A good idea can be misused by a neurotic mother to meet her own needs, so that when a command is read such as, 'The child must be taught to use his toothbrush the right way,' a nagging mother may read a command to nag into it; a sadistic mother finds in it an excuse for sadistic force."

While accepting the logic of so ordering the care of the infant for maximally favorable educational consequences, some persons feel that punishment still "has its place." If, for example, babies are not spanked for toddling out into a busy street, how are they to learn, without serious or fatal injury, that the street is a dangerous place? Or, if the small child's hands are not slapped when he reaches for a sharp knife or scissors, how is he safely to learn that these instruments might be harmful? Instead of expecting the child to make nice discriminations between dangerous and safe situations, the simpler procedure is to protect him during at least the period in which language is undeveloped by keeping him away from temptation and harm. At the same time it is possible to let him "practice" doing unwise things in controlled and graded situations. If the parent warns and then permits the child to experience in mild form the natural consequences of not heeding a warning, later injunctions concerning more serious dangers will have, by the principle of generalization, an imaginative reality for the child which could hardly be achieved by warnings backed up only by token injuries arbitrarily administered by the parents. The dangers of contamination and infection can be dealt with along similar lines by a resourceful parent. Such procedures allow the parent to be the solicitous interpreter of a potentially punishing world and further foster the affective ties which are so important when still later renunciations must be demanded. In turn, these affective ties tend to be generalized to others outside the family, and thereby foster a responsive and flexible individual.

Cultural Implications.—This view of the needs of the infantile period has implications which far transcend mere individual adjustment and personal happiness; it bears also upon the question of the stability of the whole culture. As Frank has pointed out, "If the tuition in these required patterns of conduct is administered with gentleness and reassurance, the child learns the required conduct without a feeling of resistance, resentment, hostility, or aggression; authority for that child becomes an unquestioned aspect of all ordered forms of behavior" (1939, p. 24). But because of the harshness with which their own infantile tendencies were subdued, many adults in our culture feel impelled to be equally harsh with their children. Their own "morality" is often so compulsive that they find it hard to accept any behavior in children which is not tolerated in adults. Acts which are only a phase of the infant's development and merely part of their exploration of reality are damned as "naughty" and treated as if they were manifestations of innate depravity which must be eliminated at once.

A vicious circle is thus set up. Harshness in the training of infants lays the basis for obsessive ambition later, and this in turn makes for severely competitive behavior in later life.[27] Such competitiveness not only pervades the economic and vocational spheres but also instigates parents to vie with "the neighbors" in seeing whose baby can be most precipitously trained in respect to weaning, cleanliness, sex-tabuing, and aggression control. The sources of "the neurotic personality of our time" (Horney, 1937) lie in these features of infant training as well as in the admittedly perplexing and thwarting experiences which adults face in our society. The two aspects constitute, indeed, a mutually reinforcing system.

---

[27] See the contrast between the Arapesh and the Mundugumor of New Guinea (Mead, 1935; also Money-Kyrle, 1939, Ch. 6).

The conditions under which tuition occurs are partly, but only partly, prescribed by the culture. Mothers vary greatly in the flexibility or rigidity with which they follow the cultural pattern. Even if prescriptions are rigorously adhered to, one mother will handle the child impersonally, another with active distaste, another with emotional warmth. Thus the idiosyncratic components (Kluckhohn and Mowrer, 1944) of the mother's personality and of the personalities of other adults who interact with the child constitute from birth onward idiosyncratic determinants in the formation of the new personality. One child has a mother who wanted him and is loving even within the restrictions of the culture. Another child has a mother whose unstable security will not permit her the least flexibility in following cultural dicta, or one who resents the child for tying her to an unhappy marriage, or one who treats the child primarily as an object upon which she can work out her own emotional problems. A first child will be treated differently from the last child in a series. Even if two children are identical twins, it must not be taken for granted that idiosyncratic factors can be neglected. One of the writers knows a family where the mother gives a disproportionate amount of her affection to one twin boy and the father devotes his to the other boy even though the twins resemble each other so closely that intimate friends cannot distinguish them. The father says, "Oh, I love both the twins, but Johnny is my boy, and Bill is hers. It has been that way right from the start." Such circumstances must have important implications for the personalities of these two boys.

No culture fails to make demands for behavioral restrictions, nor can any culture succeed in keeping the infant entirely happy and undisturbed. This fact must never be lost sight of. But the striking variations among the personality components characteristic of different cultures suggest that how soon these renunciations are demanded, by whom they are demanded, and in what emotional context, are important factors shaping these social personality components. Mead (1940a, p. 93) maintains there is a systematic relationship between the cultural forms, the methods by which the newborn is inducted into them, and the personality structure of individuals so educated. Elsewhere she says:

> The mother teases and flirts with the child until she produces either a state of hysterical delight or of violent weeping, and then, refusing to become involved herself, she turns casually to something else. By the time the Balinese child is three or four years old, it learns not to respond to this one-sided situation; it withdraws more and more into itself; and the basis is formed for the insulated type of personality which is typically Balinese and which fails to enter into close emotional relationship with anyone, relying instead upon ritual and art as means of emotional expression. (1939b, p. 3)

Mead may well be right in these claims, but DuBois probably states the general principle more correctly when she remarks:

> It is important to stress that a single discipline of childhood or a single traumatic experience is rarely sufficient in itself to set cultural personality types. Repeated experiences in different behavioral, value, and institutional contexts alone will create personality constellations . . . of force and consistency. . . . (1941, p. 272)

It should be emphasized that, like biological heredity, infant experiences, while placing certain constraints upon personality, give mainly potentialities (Money-Kyrle, 1939, Ch. 6). Whether these potentialities become actualized or not, or the extent to which they become actualized, depends upon later social and other conditions which structure the individual's experiences.

A concrete illustration from Navaho culture will perhaps clarify these two points.

A feature of Navaho personality, manifested especially in relations with whites, is a certain sort of passivity. This is not the "sexual passivity" described by psychoanalysts nor a general "passivity" as technically defined by some clinicians. What we have in mind may best be indicated by a contrast. When a white American feels "on the spot," the usual precept is, *"Do something."* The Navaho precept in this case would be, "Do nothing: that is the way to be safe." A Navaho woman, known to one of the writers, was in a government hospital. She was highly acculturated and had gone to the hospital on her own initiative, convinced that white doctors could cure her whereas the native practitioners could not. She was happy, save for missing a few foods to which she was accustomed. Although she was told repeatedly by the nurse that she could have almost any special foods that she wanted, she left the hospital rather than even mention the matter. Surely, in this situation, almost any white American would have at least voiced his wish and probably complained or aggressively protested.

This kind of passivity among Navahos is documented by abundant case material. Its source appears in not one but several patterns of life experience. Being carried about by the mother and others during childhood, and the necessity for adjusting to often violent movements when the carrier is on horseback probably give a long training in physical passivity. However, this early predisposition is reinforced by the experience of the dangers of retaliation when grievances are openly expressed. Navahos live considerable distances apart, and the society is inadequately policed. In most cases the safe thing to do is to avoid giving offense. Finally, Navahos have found that the most effective adjustment to the threat of exploitation at the hands of whites is not by active but by passive resistance (Kluckhohn, 1943, footnote 93). *All* of these influences would appear to enter into the frequently observed manifestations of this passivity. Moreover, when contact with white culture was superficial, this feature of Navaho personality was unobtrusive. This fact indicates that only an external condition of adult life brings out fully a predisposition, the basis for which has been laid in the experiences of infancy and early childhood.[28]

This discussion of Navaho passivity leads to another caution, namely, that substantially the same personality trait may be caused by different patterns of childhood experience. Gorer (1938) describes for the Lepchas a sort of passivity similar to that found among Navahos, but the passivity of the Lepchas has its origin in the use of specific rewards, consisting of food, affection, and other indications of approval, for the passive behavior. Furthermore, one must be prepared to find that the same basic discipline or event in early life may result in quite different personality trends, depending upon the juxtaposition of various other disciplines, the problems which individuals in each particular society have to meet, and, always, the differing biological equipment of different individuals.

Later Socialization

In the preceding section attention has been directed to the necessity of being indulgent and protective towards the human infant. This does not mean, to be sure, that infantile indulgence *alone* will make a secure adult personality. Navaho Indian infants receive a maximum of protection and gratification, but the anxiety level among adults is very high—presumably because of post-infancy traumas of socialization and because of the interaction between the conceptual picture of the world furnished by the culture and the external pressures to which Navaho society is at present subject (Kluckhohn, 1943). But it does appear that infantile indulgence constitutes the firmest foundation upon which, if later circumstances are reasonably favorable, a secure and confident adult personality can be developed. A delayed, gradual, and gentle imposition of renunciations is also the surest basis for flexibility of personality (see below). If renunciations are hurriedly and harshly imposed, the infant's "ego" (totality of skill habits) is likely to be so weak that repression will be his only means of resolving the conflicts thus produced. The more this occurs, the more later behavior is likely to be compulsively automatic and rigid in the face of changing reality demands. Habits built upon harsh, uncushioned renunciations are poorly calculated to meet the needs of ongoing social and economic life. On the other hand, the parent dare not indefinitely and always take the part of the child. To do so would create this constellation, "The world is always wrong, and I am right," so that the child would continue to expect the external world to adjust rather than himself making many necessary accommodations. If the child is allowed to develop a strong, stable ego

---

[28] This emphasis on the multiplicity of determinants of personality is paralleled in psychoanalysis by the concept of "overdetermination" (Freud, 1905, pp. 40, 73) and in learning theory by the proposition that a single act or habit may simultaneously serve several functions and thereby derive multiple reinforcement.

before too strong a "super-ego," or conscience (totality of restraint habits) is acquired, the two can later develop side by side, more or less harmoniously. It is the child whose ego is kept impoverished and weak by an unsympathetic, unresponsive personal environment who is likely to have difficulty later on. Contrary to popular impression, a child with a strong "ego" is not "egotistical"; an egotistical child is one whose ego is weak and who has to compensate and defend himself constantly by overweening behavior.

Although children should be allowed to be *dependent* and demanding during the early part of life, this is in no way inconsistent with the view that such a state of affairs must sooner or later come to an end. Human beings must not only eventually become *independent* of their parents, but they must reach a stage of such self-sufficiency, or *dependability*, that they can and will assume the support of other dependent persons: children, the aged, unfortunates, etc. Concretely, the process of transforming the dependent child into a dependable adult consists of his learning the "thou shalts" and the "thou shalt nots" of social living. The patterning of these demands varies from culture to culture, as do the methods used to enforce the socialization process, but the process is universally much the same in principle and the problems which are encountered are likewise very similar. In its most general terms the dilemma of socialization can be expressed in the words of Murphy, Murphy, and Newcomb:

> To the child the adult represents society in its protective and prohibitive aspects, and the main problem of the child is to accept its protection without becoming too dependent upon it, and to accept the prohibitions without being too cramped or limited by them. The direction of contemporary research indicates that adults themselves are most concerned by undue "dependence" on the one hand and undue "resistance" on the other; relations with adults are considered adequate when the child is independent in relation to the activities in which the adult approves his independence, and cooperative or obedient in those activities which the adult still chooses to dominate. (1937, p. 588)

Thus the child who becomes prematurely independent—i.e., gives up "protection" too soon—is likely to remain unsocialized, which is equivalent to saying that he will become anti-social or at least asocial. On the other hand, the child who is too dependent and remains so is certain to manifest neurotic tendencies of one kind or another. Normal development thus steers a precarious course between too little and too great dependence, and this ratio is constantly changing with the increasing age of the child. The fact that many lower animals achieve a high degree of self-sufficiency in a few months or even in a few weeks or days means that they do not develop the dependency attitudes that are prerequisite to socialization; it is accordingly understandable why such animals have no "culture." But they are spared the danger of too great dependency with its attendant predisposition to conflict and neurosis. It is interesting to note that neuroses can be produced only in domestic or laboratory animals which have a forced dependency on human beings (see Anderson and Liddell, 1935, and the introduction to Chapter 13 by Finger). Were it not for this dependency, they would simply run away when trouble arises. But when there is dependency, *physical* flight is not a possible solution.[29]

We have spoken of independence and self-sufficiency as the ideals of adult adjustment. Actually, of course, no human being who continues to participate in the life of his society is wholly independent. He constantly relies upon his family and friends for emotional support and upon his neighbors for services of all kinds. Wheeler (1928) has pointed out that one of the great attractions of social life is that an individual can be weaker and less effective and still survive in a social setting than in a nonsocial setting. It is this dependence on others that makes adult human beings amenable to social restraints and injunctions. The need for social approval in adults is but a generalized extension of the need for parental approval and has the same basis, namely, genuine dependence. The society is thus to the adult what the smaller social unit of the family is to the child. The phenomenon of adult dependency is further illustrated by religions, for in almost all of them the deities may be seen as magnified parents or other familial persons represented in ways which bear systematic relationships to the particular social organization.

A comprehensive analysis of the process whereby children are trained for adult participation in their society and its implications for personality would involve a complete analysis of their society and culture. Since this is impossible here,[30] we shall try to clarify our conception of the main principles involved by describing an experimental paradigm of the socialization process. Aside from its expository advantage, there is another gain in examining this paradigm. Scientific experimentation is impossible in certain of the fields in which we need new light and insights most urgently. We cannot study human psychopathology experimentally, nor has it seemed feasible to date to attempt experimental studies of socialization. Variations are constantly being tried, both in families and in societies. But these lack proper controls and take at least one generation to carry out.

---

[29] It is noteworthy that contemporary psychoanalytic theory stresses the *defensive*, i.e., anxiety-reducing, nature of neurotic symptoms. The adjustive character of so-called unrealistic habits thus comes into line with the more obvious utility of so-called realistic habits. Learning is presumably involved in both cases, the main difference being that in "normal" learning there is an obvious connection between the individual's motives and his actions, whereas, in "abnormal" learning, the individual's motives are not sufficiently understood to make the connection between them and what he does seem "reasonable."

[30] For a relatively detailed statement of the various stages and dilemmas through which children pass in growing up in American society, see Murray (1938) and Wolf (1941).

Fenichel has summarized this difficulty as follows:

The difficulties involved in constructing a psychoanalytic characterology must not be underrated. The various schools of psychology that have attacked the problem of character are in no position to render aid, for none of them is scientifically objective and free from extrascientific evaluations. In this matter, none of these schools can be scientifically objective, since except for the psychology of the elementary psychic processes, which is of no use in theoretical psychoanalysis [nor in personality theory generally], there is no scientific psychology; and writers on character seem especially prone to introduce evaluations into their discussions. (1934, p. 400)

Experimentation with animals offers some hope of progress in this connection (see Chapter 12 by Liddell, Chapter 13 by Finger, and Chapter 14 by Miller). The value of animal experiments in demonstrating and clarifying the basic principles of motivation and learning needs no documentation. However, this work has been of limited use since it has been mainly restricted to the study of learning in situations in which there was comparatively little interplay of opposing forces, competing drives, conflict, or habit dynamics. The paradigm that will here be described has the double advantage of illustrating basic learning principles and at the same time of stressing some of the variables that are believed to be of basic importance in personality development. This paradigm is proposed as merely suggestive of what occurs in the socialization of a human being. In fact, the next section will be devoted to pointing out the ways in which the paradigm fails to parallel human conditions. It is, however, a simple way of isolating certain problems and principles which cannot be so clearly seen in the complexities of human behavior.

Aichorn (1935) and various other writers on the topic of character and personality development have spoken of aberrations in this realm as due to the individual's having "taken the wrong path" in the pursuit of his life goals and ambitions. Prompted by this and similar figures of speech, Whiting and Mowrer (1944) designed a *D*-shaped elevated maze which permitted rats to go from the starting box (upper left-hand corner of the *D*) to the food box (lower left-hand corner) by either of two routes, the one relatively short and direct, the other longer and more roundabout. After a few exploratory trials, all animals "fixated" on the shorter of these two routes to the goal, as would have been predicted. This adjustment may be thought of as comparable to the relatively easy, simple ways which infants are allowed to engage in as means of reaching their goals. Thus, in the beginning, for example, an infant is allowed to reach the goal of reducing bladder tension by urinating whenever and wherever he needs to.

But just as a time is sooner or later reached when parents and other adults begin to put pressure on the small child to "control himself," so was a change likewise introduced in the adjustment which the rats had to make on the *D*-maze. After a uniform amount of practice, or "indulgence," in reaching the food box by the shorter route, a "rule" was made that the rats must now "grow up" and take the longer, alternative route to their goal. Here, as in the socialization of children, several methods were available for enforcing this rule. As between two alternative modes of behavior, choice or preference is determined by four major factors: amount of reward, amount of delay, amount of effort, and amount of danger of discomfort that is involved. In the beginning the two paths to the goal in the *D*-maze did not differ in respect to amount of reward or amount of danger involved. Preference for the shorter route was established on the basis of less effort and less delay. Obviously a change in preference could have been produced by appropriately manipulating any of these four variables. However, it seemed desirable to select methods which are nearest to cultural practices. Accordingly, the animals, after receiving a standard amount of practice in reaching the goal by the short route, were divided into three groups. In one of these groups the new rule against going to the goal by the short route was enforced by an electric shock, administered from a grill located in the middle of the short path. In a second group, the rule was enforced by a physical barrier (a piece of plate glass) which obstructed the short route. And in the third group, the rule was enforced by withholding reward (food) if the animal reached the food box by the short, "disapproved" route.

Although all three groups of animals acquired the habit of taking the longer rather than the shorter route, they differed strikingly in the promptness with which they accomplished this. The nonreward animals made this shift most slowly, the shock animal made it most rapidly, with the barrier animal intermediate. These results parallel human experience in socializing children. Children who are punished for infantile behavior tend, in general, to abandon such behavior more quickly than do children with whom physical barriers and differential reward are employed. It is consequently understandable why there is a widespread temptation to use punishment in this connection: it produces the quickest results.

Granting that in the experiment just described something was accomplished with rats which is roughly comparable to what occurs in the socialization, or education, of children, one feature of the experiment is especially significant, namely, that the rats were *dependent* upon the experimenter for food. Had this not been the case, all efforts at "educating" them would have been in vain. In the first place, satiated animals would not have been motivated to learn the new route to the food. Moreover, if shock had been used with satiated animals they would have simply "left the field," i.e., they would have become inactive or would have "run away" by climbing or jumping off the maze. In other words, punishments and other "disciplinary" measures are effective only if there is a need on the part of the learner which can be satisfied only if he meets the conditions set by the teacher, i.e., stays in the "field."

Whiting (1941) has given a clear illustration of the way in which dependence upon others is a necessary condition for the learning of the socially essential skills and conformities in a primitive society, and Ernest Haggard has kindly supplied the writers with the following story, written by a 10-year-old American boy, which illustrates the way in which this principle operates from the perspective of childhood.

> Their [the Katzenjammer Kids'] mother becomes sick, they didn't know it, but they're going to have a baby brother. He is born alright. They don't like babies, and they plan to blame something on it, like stealing the jam, and make the mother give up the baby, and they don't know it, but the baby is too little to walk, so he couldn't get into the jam. So they smear jam all over the baby's face. Then the mother came in, and realizes that Hans and Fritz were trying to blame it on the baby. She gets the Captain, and they were going to the boys' room to spank 'em, and the Katzenjammer Kids had moved out, because they heard them discussing how they were going to get even. *Then, after a while, it becomes dark out, and cold, and they want to get back in,* but can't because they're afraid they'll get spanked. Finally they decide to go in the house, and tell the truth—that they tried to blame it on the baby, and they don't get spanked. (Italics ours, boy's own spelling.)

The heroes of this story are heavily dependent upon their parents and, as a result, eventually submit to the conditions of truthfulness, non-aggression, etc., which the parents set for them. One of the authors of this chapter has intensively studied a confirmedly delinquent boy of eight in whom this type of dependency was, on the other hand, almost completely absent. He consistently ran away from school and successfully resisted all efforts to make a "proper" boy of him. This youngster could take surprisingly good care of himself when on the "loose," and had, therefore, no urgent reason to learn the tiresome things that adults constantly wished him to learn. The opportunity to establish love and dependence in infancy and early childhood having been squandered (he was a rejected child), there seemed to be no way of bringing this boy under the sway of normal social controls and pressures.[31]

The parent or teacher who does not make himself in some way useful to the child entrusted to him for training, who does not respond to the child's needs, create affection, and encourage at least some dependence, will find that his only recourse is to use force and that this will be a short-term expedient at best. The following quotation, from *Mothers' Magazine* (1832) expresses the philosophy that such a teacher must evolve to rationalize such practices.

> Cost what it may, break the child down to obedience to the first command. And when this is once done, if you are careful *never* to let disobedience escape punishment of some kind or other, and punish-

---

[31] For a particularly skilful treatment of the same theme, see Colodi's *Pinocchio.*

ment that shall be effectual and triumphant, you will find it not difficult to maintain your absolute authority. (Quoted from "Our Children," 1934, p. 115)

As the simple animal experiment just described illustrates, it is entirely possible to achieve progression from an originally preferred ("bad") habit to another ("good") habit without recourse to punishment. Although these other methods have the disadvantage of not being so prompt in their effects as is punishment, they have other advantages which will be discussed shortly which seem to more than offset their relative slowness.

In the D-maze experiment not only was the relation between the method of interfering with the originally preferred habit and the ease of producing progression studied, but the influence of the absolute length of the alternative, longer path was also investigated. As might have been expected, it was found that if the alternative route to the goal was only a little longer than the originally preferred route, progression to it could be accomplished very much more readily than if the discrepancy in length was greater. This effect held regardless of the method that was used to produce the progression. The implications of this observation for human socialization are clear. Other things equal, the more complex and arduous the socialization demands made of children, the more resistance they will show to fulfilling these demands.[32]

Whatever the shortcomings of the socialization analogue just described, it has the virtue of portraying socialization as an active, dynamic process which does not occur spontaneously but has to be arduously accomplished by the endeavor of parents, teachers, and other surrogates of the culture. "Social maturity" and "social maturation" are entirely legitimate concepts, providing they do not carry the implication that social maturation occurs on the same basis that physical growth occurs.

Dennis, after a careful study of two infants reared under conditions of restricted practice and of minimum social stimulation, concluded that "while maturation is a major factor in infant development, its importance lies chiefly in making learning possible" (1941b, p. 187). We should likewise keep in mind that children stop crying (and give up many other infantile habits) when frustrated, not because of progressive atrophy of the lachrymal glands or change in the vocal cords, but because they *learn* not to engage in this behavior. If the difficulties and vagaries of adult

---

[32] Among the many interesting problems which might have been investigated in this connection is the question as to whether habit progression from an easy to a difficult adjustment can be made more or less easily if there are intermediate stages than if the transition is made in a single step. Clinical experience seems to indicate that numerous small readjustments provide the most favorable conditions for progression, but the evidence is not as complete as might be desired. The D-maze paradigm also offers an opportunity for investigating a number of other factors which almost certainly influence the socialization process but which could not be studied within the limits of a single experiment.

personality are to be understood, childhood must be viewed realistically as a period of recurrent crises and problem-solving dilemmas. Euphemistic references to the perpetual happiness of childhood only cloud our comprehension of the vital events that happen during this period and obscure any systematic theory of adult personality.

It is true, of course, that some types of habit progression do indeed occur more or less automatically. Thus, children normally pass from crawling to walking as a mode of locomotion without very much, if any, external pressure. This is presumably due to the fact that walking is an intrinsically better (preferable) way of achieving the same end than is crawling. As soon as walking becomes physically possible for the child, the constant exploration which keeps occurring when an adjustment, such as crawling, is only partially satisfactory, would naturally be expected to lead to the discovery of the superior adjustment of walking (as soon as myelination, ossification, and like development processes permit). But examples of this kind are relatively rare. Far more common are those instances in which the infantile adjustment is the preferable one and the socially imposed adjustment is a distinctly inferior alternative from the child's point of view.

It is this circumstance, that human beings know many of the "best things in life" first and then have to give them up, that makes growing up so difficult and which tends to make adult life dull and colorless for many individuals. As Erikson has succinctly put the matter, "The incompatibility of fixation and progression is the most common kernel of infantile neuroses" (1940, p. 119).

Special Aspects of Human Socialization

Despite the parallels between human socialization and the learning dilemma presented by the D-maze experiment, there are a number of noteworthy differences. In the first place, the task which the rat faces in the D-maze is incomparably simpler than the one which a child encounters in the socialization maze. The behavior in the maze which will lead to reward is relatively easily distinguished from behavior which will lead to no reward (or punishment). If certain parts of the maze are consistently avoided and other parts are consistently transversed, success will consistently follow. On the other hand, the "social maze" which children have to learn is only partly spatial. Sources of reward and of disappointment or punishment, namely, parents and other adults, are not neatly anchored at fixed points. They can and do move about. Furthermore, one and the same person is sometimes rewarding, sometimes punishing. One and the same type of behavior may on one occasion lead to reward, on another occasion to nonreward or worse. The child must obviously learn to take his cues from the *behavior* (linguistic, gestural, postural, etc.) of others (see Miller and Dollard, 1941, Ch. 6 ff.). His maze is therefore highly *personal*, whereas that of the rat was largely impersonal, since the behavior of the experimenter in no case gave a lead as to what was expected of the animal.

From one point of view the child has, however, a decided advantage over the rat. Originally, before the child acquires language, his learning must proceed much as does that of the rat, namely, by trial and error. But with the development of the elaborate system of habits for responding to signs, which we call *language*, the child becomes capable of *following instructions*, i.e., profiting from the experiences of others in problem-solving situations. He acquires knowledge. This frees the learner from the obvious limitations of trial-and-error learning and simple conditioning, in which each individual organism has to discover the solution to every problem for himself, and enables him to profit from the tremendous cultural accumulations of countless preceding generations.

If, in the case of the *D*-maze experiment, we had been able to "tell" the rats that they should now take the longer path to food and had given them some verbal coaching in how to follow this new route, they might well have shifted suddenly, without a single error, from the short to the longer route. By the mere symbolic presentation of the consequences (barrier, no reward, shock) of taking the familiar, easier route, the rats could have been spared the frustration and pain which they actually received.

There is, however, an important danger in learning through instruction, namely, the possibility that the teacher, through ignorance or design, will misuse symbols and thereby produce changes in the learner's behavior which are not realistically justified. Because of the extensive use of instruction, as opposed to first-hand experience, in the education of children, a certain amount of deception, willful or unwitting, is foisted upon most children. Learning of this kind is *unrealistic* and must either be unlearned subsequently or remain as a more or less important source of irrationality. The importance of using words with the greatest care and scrupulousness has only recently begun to be adequately stressed scientifically (Korzybski, 1941; Woodger, 1937).

In the *D*-maze experiment, the tabu placed upon the short path to the goal was, in one way, wholly arbitrary. Aside from the interest of the experimenters, there was no reason why the rats should not have continued indefinitely to take the short path to the goal. In human society the situation is, of course, different. As May says, ". . . culture is a statement of the design of the human maze, of the type of reward involved, and of what responses are to be rewarded" (1941, p. 5). The human maze is not the arbitrary design of any single individual nor of any single generation of men. A culture tends to represent the distilled quintessence of many generations of trial-and-error adjustments to peculiar environmental problems. From the standpoint of most acculturated individuals the maze design is, to be sure, not understood. As Mayo observes, "Piaget's researches seem to indicate that even in a civilized community with an elaborate educational system the individual must pass through a stage in which he develops appropriate and ordered responses to social signals without any real capacity to understand or judge social situations" (1933, p. 164). This is indeed precisely why love for and trust in a cultural agent is the only immediate and effective reason for submitting to socialization. Nevertheless, even though "the wisdom of the culture" is directly apparent to but few individuals, every social tabu finds or has found its ultimate *raison d'être* in some kind of social utility. The great moral injunctions are, in general, socially functional. If people seldom understand this intellectually, they nevertheless *feel* it.

Another difference between the human maze and the *D*-maze lies in the competitive nature of much of our social life. Let us imagine that in the *D*-maze experiment rats had been run not singly but in pairs. This would have meant that sometimes a given animal would have been rewarded for doing the "right" thing, sometimes not, for the simple reason that the other rat had done the right thing *first*. That children often encounter complications of this kind is indicated by the extensive literature on the topic of sibling rivalry (Levy, 1937, 1939). The ease with which a child can be socialized is definitely related to the exclusiveness and consistency with which parents can respond to him. If other children make competing demands, the effectiveness of the parent as a teacher will necessarily be somewhat decreased, although such a situation offers advantages for teaching some things that are hard to teach to the "only child."

To the consequences for personality which inhere in the competitive element in human learning generally, there may be added cultural and idiosyncratic factors which are mutually implicative. Different cultures stress and minimize the competitive angle. Mead has noted that

> . . . competitive and cooperative behavior on the part of the individual members of a society is fundamentally conditioned by the total social emphasis of that society; that the goals for which individuals will work are culturally determined and are not the response of an organism to an external, culturally undefined situation, like a simple scarcity of food. (1937, p. 16)

In our society there is no way of measuring success except by comparison with another's, and there are no fixed positions to which an individual can attain without fear of subsequent loss. The difficulty does not lie wholly in competition as such. In some cultures there seems to be competition in sport or in science with little fear of ego deflation. But in our culture, from childhood on, the dominant motif is that "a gain to your ego means a loss to mine." This is doubtless one of the reasons that sibling rivalry is so peculiarly intense among us. However, there is wide idosyncratic variation. Parents who are secure play down competitive responses among their children. Children who are relatively free from tension are the most out-going in their relations with other children (Hartshorne and May, 1928).

By the nature of the situation, it is clear that the learning of the rat in the *D*-maze was *impersonal*, i.e., not dependent upon the behavior of the experimenter. This means that the experimenter had no cue-value and that the rat developed no very definite "attitudes" (expectations, anticipations) with respect to him. Depending upon which method was used to interfere with the originally fixated adjustment, the rats certainly developed different attitudes toward the maze (since it shocked them in some cases, merely withheld reward in other cases). But their behavior toward the experimenter was certainly modified comparatively little in relation to what it would have been if he had struck the rat as a means of punishment and fed the rat from his hand as a means of reward.

In human socialization, the latter conditions are the usual ones. Rewards and punishments are personally administered, which means that children necessarily develop, in the one case, positive, approach, appetitive, affectionate attitudes toward the parent or parent surrogate; while in the other case, they develop negative, avoidant, affective attitudes.[33] In other words, the parent takes on sign-value for the child, and since signs, be they positive or negative, have motivational value, the parent is soon in a position both to reward and punish the child on the basis of the so-called secondary, or derived, motives. Parental disapproval makes the child uncomfortable and motivates him either to "leave the field" or to engage in behavior which will elicit parental approval.

Since parents ordinarily administer rewards and punishments of both a primary and secondary nature, children necessarily have mixed feelings toward them. The parents are ordinarily ambiguous individuals, being sometimes "good" and sometimes "bad" from the child's point of view. This admixture of behavior creates a kind of conflict in the child's relationship to the parent which is known as ambivalence. From many points of view, it is obviously desirable that the negative elements of fear and hate in this attitude should be as small as possible and the positive element of love and affection be as high as possible. Child training involving punishment increases the former, whereas reward-training strengthens the latter.

To speak as if only the relation between parents and child were important is, of course, an oversimplification. The relation of one parent to the other, culturally and idiosyncratically, reacts upon the child. It is

---

[33] In many societies an attempt is made to enable parents to act as socializing agents without, however, having to bear the onus which attaches to parents who personally punish their children. The use of ghosts (Dennis, 1941a), Kachinas (Benedict, 1934), relatives outside the immediate family (Malinowski, 1926), and other surrogates of parental and social authority (Whiting, 1941) has certain advantages, but the increase in other unrealistic and supernaturalistic beliefs which is thus created seems to outweigh this advantage, if a long view is taken.

said that in Chinese culture the father makes fewer demands upon the mother's love and attention than is the pattern in our society—the Chinese mother belongs much more exclusively to the child. This pattern is doubtless implemented by concubinage, but it may also be that since the father when himself a child was given great security he does not need to be mothered so much.

Likewise, the basic family constellation may take a bewildering variety of forms, each probably favoring some and not other personality trends. Mead has succinctly described some observed variations:

> The father may be the principal focus of emotion, with children of both sexes primarily oriented towards him (Manus). The mother may be the center of attention and the process of growing up for males may mean transfer of emotional attention from mother to the male group, with no great importance ever attached to the father-child (Iatmul). The ties may run across the sex lines, so that the daughters are attached to the father, the sons to the mother, with father and son definitely aligned against each other (Mundugumor), etc. Similarly, in sibling relationships there may be primogeniture with a fixed status for the eldest son and congruent attitudes of acceptance or resentment on the part of the younger sons (Tanala), in an absence of primogeniture there may be covert (Samoa) or open rivalry for the father's property or power (Chuckchee), sibling attitudes may be centered in the filial generation with the brothers competing with the father for the sister (to be used as a pawn in a marriage game) (Mundugumor), the relationship between elder and younger brother may be dynamic in the society (Iatmul), or the relationship between elder and younger brother may become a focussing point (Tchambuli). The rivalry which developed between siblings may be channelled as rivalry for the mother's breast, and later for her love, so that attention is concentrated on what is desired from the mother, not on the other individual who desires it (Balinese). Or the mother may treat the child as if he were as strong and definite a person as she, in which case when a new baby is born, the dispossessed child, the *knee baby,* may become a rival of the mother for the baby (Iatmul). (1940b, p. 7)

Even if, in the *D*-maze, the rat did develop definite attitudes toward the experimenter, this would be of little importance or significance. On the other hand, as Dollard (1938, p. 15) says: "Social patterns are transmitted by persons who become the targets of positive and negative feeling from the child as the result of facilitating and frustrating behavior on their part." It is of the utmost importance what attitudes children develop toward their socializers, for it is these attitudes which they largely generalize, or "transfer," to other persons. It is, in other words, on the basis of their experiences with their parents and other early teachers that children's expectations develop of what to expect from people in general. The child who carries into his contacts with other persons outside the family an attitude of cooperation and expectation of fair-play is likely to be a good citizen. The child, on the other hand, who has known nothing but mistreatment and exploitation will expect this from society in general and will behave accordingly.

Since it is from the parents and other members of the immediate family that the child acquires his first and most enduring conceptions of human beings in general, the phenomenon of transference as here delineated obviously has an importance greater than can be properly documented at this time. However, one striking difference between societies should be noted in this connection. In our culture the family is small, more or less exclusive, and closely-knit. In many other societies, on the other hand, the family is extended and diffuse. Instead of having only one person whom he addresses as "mother," a child may have five or ten such persons, and the same will be true as regards father-persons. Nor is this merely a matter of address; all persons designated as "father" or as "mother" have definite responsibilities toward the child in question. Likewise, certain children other than blood siblings will be designated as "brother" or "sister." This extension of the kinship system, or proliferation of the immediate, biological family out into the community at large has obvious implications. As Devereux says: ". . . from an early age the Mohave child's libido is distributed more or less uniformly over a large area of the body social and the intense individualized object cathexis characteristic of our society does not obtain among them" (1939b, p. 529). This arrangement means that the transference problem will be less acute; if a parent dies, there will be less emotional shock (because of more diverse affection) and less likelihood of physical privation, since other "parents" will assume the increased responsibility.

Another conspicuous and important difference between socialization and D-maze learning lies in the fact that in the former situation the parent ordinarily exemplifies the type of behavior which he wants the child to learn, whereas the experimenter certainly does not set any such model for the subject in the D-maze situation. Imitation is thus ruled out at the outset, as is the possibility of everything resembling identification. The rat makes no attempt to "be like" the experimenter, whereas this is a very real and normal aspiration in the child-parent relationship. The importance of this process is indicated by the fact that parents who are themselves mismatched from the point of view of character and social values frequently have children with more or less severe personality disturbances. In the most favorable family situation, in which husband and wife are mutually affectionate and approving, the little boy can take his father as a model and thereby achieve the support not only of his father but of the mother as well. From the father's point of view, the child is highly acceptable, "a chip off the old block"; and for the mother he is likewise acceptable as a recreation of the man she loves and admires. Similarly, the little girl, by patterning herself after the mother, wins the solid approval of both parents. But if there is serious conflict between parents, the child, boy or girl, is sure to find himself facing a critical dilemma: regardless of which parent is chosen as a model, it means that the love and approval of the other will be lost. Clinicians find that children who have faced this problem are almost invariably damaged by the experience.

It is not possible here to discuss in detail the mechanism of identification (see Chapter 9 by Sears), but certain fundamental features are evident. In the case of children, being *like* a parent ordinarily results in their being *liked by* the parent. In other words, imitative or identificatory behavior is likely to be rewarded, and is therefore likely to be extended and perpetuated. G. H. Mead (1934) suggests that identification consists both in taking the attitude of others toward one's own act and in associating others' attitudes toward an act or object with one's own response to the situation (see Young, 1938).

But idiosyncratic and cultural conditions can complicate the achieving of a satisfactory identification. If father and mother are in conflict, a child cannot identify with either without coming into conflict with one or the other of them. When, under these disharmonious circumstances, a so-called cross-sex identification occurs, personality difficulties are almost inevitable, as Krout and Stagner (1939) have shown. Even though identification is psychologically normal, difficulty may also arise if the person identified with does not happen to provide a socially appropriate model, as Fenichel (1934, p. 450) has pointed out. Criminal and other socially undesirable types of personalities may be perpetuated in this fashion. Likewise, the personality of a child may be very different according to whether he is born early or late in the life of a parent (see Mead, 1930, p. 140).

Our own society provides excellent examples of how cultural conditions may complicate the identification problem. Mead points out that "The degeneration of the father's role into that of a tired, often dreaded, nightly visitor has done much to make his son's happy identification with him impossible" (1930, p. 234). Further, "The failure of children to identify with their fathers is intensified in this country by the rapidly shifting standards and the differences in outlook between parents and children" (p. 236). This dilemma is peculiarly crucial for the children of immigrants in that both of their parents fail to present suitable models for identification in the "new world." But identification of the son with the father is frequently the more difficult, for

> the male child must, if he is to make any sort of happy adult adjustment, identify himself somewhat with his father or with some other grown man. No matter how close, how affectionate, how deserving of admiration and allegiance his mother may be, she does not offer the male child a way of life. If his allegiance to her is too close, it will stunt his emotional development; if he identifies himself with her it is at the risk of becoming an invert, or at best of making some fantastic and uncomfortable emotional adjustment. The heaviest

prices which family life demands from children are those which result from an antagonism to the father and an overdependence upon the mother, for a boy child, and the opposite set for a girl. (Mead, 1930, pp. 236–237)

One of the most puzzling, but at the same time most important, problems in the whole field of personality theory concerns the phenomenon of "conscience." Conscience may be defined, by a slight modification of Mead, as "a capacity to anticipate in imagination the unpleasant emotional tone which is associated with disobedience to the admonitions of parents or other cultural surrogates, and the pleasant emotional tone which is associated with their fulfillment" (1940b, p. 3). Many glib statements are made about the genesis and function of conscience, but a theory which is satisfactorily reducible to its concrete behavioral referents remains to be devised. That conscience is related to "identification" is well established, but the problem cannot be disposed of by the statement that the conscience, or super-ego, is formed by "incorporation of the ego-ideal." One concept ("conscience") cannot be explained simply by relating it to another concept, and "ego," "id," and "super-ego" are not behavioral facts—they are language. "Conscience" requires an inductive basis from empirical data. Dollard, et al., have made a theoretical advance when they say, "Super-ego or conscience is now believed to be established primarily through the existence of affectional bonds (i.e., expectations of reward and security) between a child and his parents" (1939, p. 132). Introjection is a phenomenon which is well-documented clinically, and there is no doubt that in many cultures most of the content of conscience in the effectively socialized person is formed by the internalization of parental demands (which turn out, of course, to be mainly the demands of the culture). But the formulation of Dollard, et al., is too narrow; it does not have either sufficient cross-cultural or idiosyncratic perspective. In some cultures the value-standards of grandparents or of age mates seem to be absorbed at least equally with those of parents. And, especially when identification has not proceeded normally, the conscience seems to be centrally dominated by a rejection or even a reversal of the standards of one or both parents.

Perhaps an analysis of the D-maze analogue of socialization will enable us to bring some of the questions in this field into sharper focus. First we should ask whether it is possible for infrahuman organisms to have conscience. It is clear that animals can have anxiety, i.e., can anticipate painfully intense stimulation. However, the type of anxiety that pertains to "conscience" is of a special kind. If a person is considering whether he should or should not perform a dubious act, i.e., if he is "struggling with temptation," we can hardly speak of his conscience "hurting" him. Perhaps we could say his conscience is "warning" him that he will feel uncomfortable if he commits the act. Only after the action has been performed could we say that his conscience is indeed "hurting" him. These reflections suggest the hypothesis that conscience is a form of anxiety, but that the danger signals which set it off are cue-stimuli resulting from the individual's own behavior, behavior which if "found out" is likely to be followed by chastisement. It is thus essential that punishment may be indefinitely postponed, but that if the guilty act is discovered, either by humans or by supernaturals, it may then be punished, however much later this may be. In short, conscience seems to stem from the indeterminacy but inevitability of punishment for forbidden acts.

Taking this definition, conscience can scarcely be said to have existed in our D-maze subjects. In the animals in which nonreward or barrier was used as a means of producing habit progression, there was no punishment to anticipate. And in the case of the animals that were shocked for taking the wrong path, the punishment always occurred while the act was in progress. Once the short path had been traversed, either with or without shock, the animal was then "safe." He was never punished subsequently for this misdemeanor. Merely as a hypothesis, we may conjecture that these animals never experienced "guilt." This supposition would seem to be supported by an observation that will be reported in detail later, namely, that once the shocked rats discovered that the shock was no longer present on the short route, they immediately reverted to this route. If our hypothesis is correct, this would not have been the case had the rats sometimes been punished, let us say, a few minutes after they had safely traversed the short path, rather than while on this path.

Let us contrast the human situation. In human beings punishments are only rarely administered for a forbidden act while the act is in progress. Forbidden actions may be performed secretly, and only later will their detection lead to punishment. The ultimate in this practice is the concept of punishment after death, when concealment of sins is supposed (in Christian and some other cultures) to become wholly impossible. The test of the effectiveness of conscience in the "guilt" form is: Does inhibition through anxiety occur even when parents or other cultural agents are not present and are not likely later to gain knowledge of the act?

Dependence, or "fear of the loss of love," has sometimes been proposed as the essential condition for the formation of conscience. As we have seen, this is an essential condition for all forms of education, save the simplest forms of escape and avoidance behavior. In our experimental analogue, there was definite dependence—but *not* "fear of the loss of love." The animals were dependent upon the experimenter for food. They could not solve the learning dilemma to which they were exposed either by running away or refusing to work. But, as our results suggest, this factor of dependence was not alone sufficient to establish conscience-like behavior.

Another distinction is to be noted. In our experiment, punishment followed choice of the "wrong" path, but never did it follow actual eating. Only on rare occasions did the shocked animals show any hesitancy to eat once they reached the food box. But had they been punished for taking the wrong path *after they had eaten,* then eating as well as taking the wrong path would become anxiety-laden and "dangerous." Eventually, the subjects would have made a discrimination between eating-after-taking-wrong-path and eating-after-taking-right-path, but in the beginning at any rate, the effects of punishment in the one case would generalize to both cases. Educators are not always careful to apply punishments in such a way as to inhibit only means, instead of both means and ends. Once anxiety has become attached to an end, as well as to means of reaching this end, learning of the right means may be greatly retarded, since the goal has been rendered dangerous and therefore less worth trying for.

Aggression and Sexuality

We have already examined a number of respects in which the *D*-maze paradigm differs from the actual socialization of human beings. A further difference remains which is of such importance as to deserve special consideration. It will be recalled that although the *D*-maze learning situation involved a conflict, this conflict was nevertheless resolvable. Human beings, on the other hand, are confronted in the course of their education with certain dilemmas to which there is no solution which is altogether satisfactory. In most of the problem-solving situations in which children are placed, the solution consists, as it did in the *D*-maze, merely in abandoning an earlier, easier route to a given goal and learning another, alternative one. But the goal, as such, remains accessible; only the means, or the habitual way of reaching the goal, has to be revised.

There are, however, two types of goal behavior, namely, aggression and sexuality, which, in most societies, are dealt with somewhat differently. Here it is not so much a matter of successive revisions of particular habits as it is of inhibiting, at least for certain periods or under certain conditions, all manifestations of the underlying impulses. Obviously a complete tabu on goal-directed behavior in these realms gives rise to special problems for the growing, adjusting child, and it is not surprising that the consequences are often far-reaching and fateful.

Since the problem of aggression is somewhat less complex than that of sexuality, let us consider it first. There are, it should be noted, two well-developed but contradictory contemporary theories of aggression. The one, stemming mainly from the later writings of Freud (1922), holds that aggression is a component manifestation of the *death instinct.* As such it is assumed to represent the fulfilment of a basic biological need, more or less comparable to hunger, thirst, etc., which is relatively independent of the vicissitudes of daily living. According to this view, each individual requires a certain quantum of gratification of this aggressive, destructive impulse which, if not attained in one way, will be achieved in some other (Menninger, 1938).

The rival theory of aggression holds that so-called aggressive behavior is instigated by an emotion which is aroused by thwarting, or frustration (Freud, 1917; Dollard, *et al.*, 1939). Thus the instigation, or "need," to behave aggressively is assumed to be highly variable, differing from individual to individual as well as in the same individual from time to time. If an individual's habitual modes of action lead smoothly to accustomed gratifications and the fulfilment of expectations, little or no impulse to aggression will be generated; but if obstacles arise in the habitual paths to established goals, there will be correspondingly strong instigation to forms of behavior commonly termed aggressive. The assumed sequence, then, is frustration-anger-aggression, the latter serving the commonly advantageous function of removing (overriding, pushing aside, attacking, killing) the source of the frustration and thereby clearing the path to the desired goal. The biological utility of this frustration-anger-aggression sequence is obvious, it accords well with common sense and with laboratory studies, and it seems to be more generally accepted even in psychoanalytic circles (see Horney, 1939, pp. 125–126; Alexander, 1940) than the highly speculative *death-instinct* theory.[34]

To avoid possible misunderstanding, it must be pointed out that we realize that aggression is only one of a number of possible responses to situations which are commonly defined as frustrating (see Whiting, 1942). Our position in this regard is that of Miller, who says, "Frustration produces instigations to a number of different types of response, one of which is an instigation to some form of aggression" (1941, p. 338). It should also be pointed out that this "reactive" theory of aggression, in the form in which it has just been presented, does not involve any commitment as to whether the frustration-anger-aggression

---

[34] A special connection between the problem of aggression and the function of eating must, however, be noted. Whatever is eaten is necessarily "destroyed"; and since other living organisms, sometimes even of the same species (as in cannibalism), are a part of the human diet, satisfaction of hunger commonly involves behavior (killing, butchering, cooking, biting) with distinctly aggressive, or "sadistic," connotations. Hence, any failure on the part of an individual to discriminate clearly between "damaging," or "destructive," behavior toward other living organisms which is motivated merely by hunger, and behavior which is motivated by anger is likely to lead to severe conflict. Behavior of the latter kind, at least when directed toward other members of the human in-group or even toward pets and beasts of burden, is either prohibited altogether or strictly sanctioned and culturally patterned. Consequently, any unconscious equating of, or failure to discriminate between, behavior of this type and the activities involved in the satisfaction of hunger is certain to produce intra-psychic tension and "guilt." Some persons resolve this conflict by becoming vegetarians. In extreme instances, as in severe depressions, human beings may refuse to eat any food whatsoever. The fact that infrahuman organisms seem never to suffer from this type of conflict in a state of nature (although they may under domestication) supports the hypothesis, here adopted, that the guilt and conflict connected with "oral aggression" in human beings is an indirect, generalized product of the tabu placed upon the frustration-anger-aggression sequence as a requisite condition of harmonious social living.

sequence is native or acquired. How the connection between frustration and the visceral mobilization and the characteristic subjective states constituting anger are established, whether by maturation or by learning, is at present an open question. However, it is clear that the particular *instrumental* behavior manifested by an angry individual is largely, if not entirely, a matter of habit. When provoked to anger, an organism will, we may assume, tend to learn those responses which will remove the cause of the frustration and thereby reduce anger. Since frustrating situations often differ very considerably, the nature of the reaction made to them should obviously be subject to the kind of flexibility and variability that learning alone makes possible. Although the authors know of no experiment in which the learning of particular aggressive acts has been systematically studied, the indications are that in human beings and, even to some extent in lower animals, individual experiences of success and failure play their usual important role.

If each human being were a law unto himself, as an animal in a state of nature tends to be, then capacity to behave in an effectively aggressive manner would be precious indeed. But the fact is that human beings live socially and are, therefore, often dependent upon the very persons who frustrate them. Without careful control of in-group aggression, even the simplest forms of social organization, to say nothing of civilization, would not be possible. This was one of the first lessons which the sons of Adam and Eve had to learn, and men have been chafing ever since under the restraints imposed by that lesson (Freud, 1930). As Murphy notes:

> Human society is based largely upon the capacity of individual human beings to interpret and respond to the behavior of other human beings, the more cooperative and closely knit the structure of a given society becomes, the more demands are put upon individuals to respond to the needs of others. (1937, p. 3)

As we have seen, the teaching of those restraints and skills which are deemed essential for adult social participation commonly requires that simple, naturally preferred ways of acting be interfered with and replaced by more complicated and arduous modes of behavior. Socialization is thus inevitably frustrating and necessarily generates resistance and tendencies to behave aggressively toward the socializing agents, notably parents and teachers.[35] In our culture the traditionally approved action in such cases consists of trying to bring the rebellious child to terms by means of physical punishment, or counter-aggression. The consequences which these coercive measures have for personality formation will depend, in part, upon the sources of the child's hostility and upon

---

[35] The rats used in the *D*-maze experiment showed a marked tendency to gnaw at the maze (which was made of wood) when the originally preferred route to the goal was interfered with. Although not "punished" in any way, this behavior largely disappeared as the new, alternative path to the goal became accepted as a substitute.

the general nature of his adjustment up to that point in his life
history.

If a child does something for which the parent has been punished, the
parent who has been at all identified with the child can only make peace
with his own anxiety by inhibiting the child's behavior. Furthermore,
the method which he uses to achieve this end is likely to resemble the
method used in setting up his own inhibiting anxieties. Thus, a young
Mohave Indian woman who had been exposed to the school aspect of
our socialization process has testified to the truth of this principle: "We
have been spanked so much in school that now we spank our own
children too" (Devereux, 1939a, p. 98).

Granted that necessarily "it is the business of culture to frustrate
and to check the aggressions mobilized by those frustrations," deformed
and distorted personalities can be avoided to the extent that adequate
substitute responses are institutionalized. It would also appear that
frustration and ensuing tendencies toward aggression can be reduced if
the principle of cooperation rather than coercion and competition be used
in teaching and in structuring social relationships generally. The encouragement of cooperation can succeed only to a limited extent so long as it
is against the major trends of our society. For, as Mead (1937) has
fully documented, the phrasing of cooperation and competition is intimately dependent upon the other major interests and emphases of that
society. But if change is to come, if we are prepared to recognize the
unhealthy and unhappy personalities of our time as the products of the
morbid value we give to competitive coercion, the change had best begin
with our socialization processes. Du Bois observes that:

> To eliminate . . . institutions without altering standardized meth-
> ods of education, may well produce serious social and personal dis-
> locations. . . . It is possible that when we understand better our own
> culture we shall have learned that basic social changes of a non-
> disruptive nature must be anticipated in the early and intimate
> conditioning of children. (1941, p. 281)

Even in societies where socialization is less coercively and competitively
organized, some frustration and aggression still occur. But some societies tend to let the aggression exhaust itself through its futility rather
than to try to curb it with counter-aggression. This procedure seems
much less undermining as far as the individual's security is concerned,
much less damaging to personality generally. The fear of counter-
aggression which is commonly used to inhibit original aggressive trends
may manifest itself as neurotic guilt, depression, displaced hostility, and
other clinically recognized forms of irrationality.

Up to this point we have spoken of the frustration and the resulting
tendencies toward aggression which are generated by those socialization
measures which prohibit easy, infantile ways of behaving and prescribe
more complex, adult-like ways; and we have also considered the frustra-

tion, encountered by children and adults alike, which results from failure in competitive struggles. It should be noted, however, that in both cases the goal is at least hypothetically accessible. In the first instance all the child has to do to reach his goal is to learn and adhere to the socially approved rather than the socially disapproved route. And in the second instance, all that is required, theoretically, is that the individual bestir himself and contend more vigorously. That the aggression which tends to be manifested in both of these situations falls under a more or less strict tabu may be understood as representing an attempt (a) to reduce opposition to socialization and (b) to prevent the disruption of group harmony and solidarity.

But in the realm of infantile sexuality a special complication arises. Here it is neither a question of teaching new habits to replace earlier ones nor of controlling and regulating competition, but rather of inhibiting, during part or all of childhood, all goal-directed behavior and gratification. Regardless of whether sexuality is manifested in a solitary or social setting, regardless of whether it involves the oral, anal, or genital erogenous zones, many human societies impose a comprehensive ban which is enforced, albeit laboriously, with great strictness and severity. An attempt will shortly be made to analyze the reasons for this stern tabu, but first let us note some of its immediate conditions and consequences.

Traditionally, sexual impulses have been supposed to assert themselves for the first time in the life of the growing child at puberty. It is true that prior to this point human beings are not capable of procreation. But it now seems as artificial to maintain that sexuality does not exist before puberty as it would be to hold that all sexuality thereafter is directly procreative. It is likewise true that prior to puberty the intensity of the sexual impulses is relatively weak, as compared with after puberty, and because of this it can be relatively easily inhibited during the early years of life. This is not to say, however, that the impulse is psychically obliterated nor that its inhibition leaves no mark upon the personality.

Traditionally, sexuality has likewise been limited to activities involving the genital organs. This again appears to be an unjustifiably limited view of the matter. It now appears that thumb-sucking and other forms of "mouth play," anal exploration and manipulation, as well as direct genital and urino-genital activity are all related manifestations of the same basic need or impulse (A. Freud, 1935). This is not the place to review in detail all the arguments in support of this hypothesis (see Chapter 20 by Ribble), but it should at least be noted that these areas have a kind of equivalence, in that inhibition of gratification in one sphere is likely to be followed by increased activity in another. This is especially noticeable when attempts are being made to inhibit the various forms of infantile "naughtiness" and in dealing with the so-called perversions at the adult level.

Why oral, anal, and genital erotic activities should possess this equivalence is not at present fully understood. According to Freud's view there is a unitary sexual force, the libido, which can be manifested in any of several ways. But this does not tell us specifically what the libido is, where it is located, or the precise manner in which it is gratified. A more definite, but still very tentative possibility is that the equivalence of oral, anal, and genital stimulation arises from the fact that all of these regions are connected with the parasympathetic division of the autonomic nervous system, which mediates the appetitive, vegetative functions of the body as a whole, and which is functionally antagonistic to the sympathetic division of the automatic,[36] which mediates the affects, anger and anxiety. The latter are, of course, unpleasant states and anything which will reduce them tends to be pleasurable and rewarding.

It is well known that fear and anger, if intense, have a paralyzing effect on sexuality along with the other appetites. But in milder form, the affects may themselves be inhibited or at least reduced by stimulation of the appetites. Melanie Klein (1932) has taken the position that one of the great forces behind sexuality in children and adults alike is the escape from anxiety which it affords. It is true that in adult life, orgasm also provides for the reduction of localized glandular pressures and tensions, but that the preceding period of so-called excitement is also rewarding, possibly for the reasons just given, is equally evident. In children it is apparently the fore-period type of excitement that constitutes the main element of sexuality and, by hypothesis, owes much, if not all, of its pleasurable consequences to the counteracting of unpleasant effect.

It is a common observation that children resort to thumb- or finger-sucking most frequently when they are lonely, disappointed, or apprehensive. That genital manipulation is likewise resorted to, before the tabu is successfully established, in times of emotional crisis is less well-authenticated but seems probable.

> It must be obvious that these fears, if fed by unwise and inconsistent restrictions, lead to an increase in habits as *pacifying activities in moments of extreme subjective danger.* Developmental habits, such as sucking and biting mannerisms, fingerplay involving hair, nose, etc., body-rocking, head-banging, wetting and soiling, spitting, smearing, motor restlessness, tic-like mannerisms, genital and anal masturbation, speech mannerisms, lying, etc., become fixed under the

---

[36] The rather rigid dichotomy of the Eppinger and Hess formulation now seems to be not entirely valid, since the two branches of the autonomic are very closely integrated. We understand that Dr. Bender of Mount Sinai Hospital, New York, has recently shown that in certain species one may have a parasympathetic response instead of a sympathetic response to fright-producing situations such as Cannon (1929) dealt with in his classic work on the cat. The conception seems to be growing that an acute response in the sympathetic will evoke a counter coup of the parasympathetic and vice versa. The initial reaction may also be different in different groups of animals. But, *in general,* the contrast probably holds for human beings (see Lund, 1939, and Gellhorn, 1943).

influence of unresolved anxiety, i.e., become compulsive habits. If they then are "broken," only neurosis or character deformation through excessive inhibition can result. (Erikson, 1940, p. 722)

On the basis of this analysis it may now be asked why the oral, anal, and urino-genital regions are so much more highly erogenous than other areas of the body which might be designated. Why should they be so uniquely capable, when stimulated, of producing feelings of well-being and pleasure? The most obvious answer is that this arrangement puts a premium on eating, drinking, urinating, defecating, and procreating—biological activities which are essential to the survival of the individual and preservation of the species. The fact that the nipple of the mature female breast is similarly sensitized makes the nursing of young immediately rewarding, over and beyond the relief obtained by emptying the turgid breast, and accords well with the general thesis just suggested. The fact that lactation is mediated by the parasympathetic nervous system and can be inhibited by chronic emotional tension is also in keeping with the same point of view.

When sexuality, broadly defined, is viewed in this light, the fact that it is so widely tabued and punished in children constitutes a paradox which is not easily accounted for. The conclusion can hardly be avoided that the systematic inhibition of infantile sexuality has the most profound consequences, among them being the loss of important sources of pleasure and comfort and more or less chronic resentment at the deprivation thus sustained (Dollard, et al., 1939). Why, we must ask, is such a maiming prohibition imposed upon children? Surely there must be some good and sufficient reason for any educative practice which is so exacting and momentous in its consequences.

One possibility is that any form of infantile sexual gratification is instinctively repulsive to adults and is therefore inhibited by them. More probably, however, the causal sequence is the reverse, namely, because their own efforts at libidinal gratification in childhood were accompanied by pain and humiliation, most individuals, as adults, are disturbed when they see such behavior in other children, especially their own. Although the evidence is not definitive on this point, it appears that human beings differ markedly in the extent to which they tolerate sexual activities in children, according to the society or subsociety in which they were themselves socialized, and that a given individual may have divergent attitudes in this connection at different periods of his life, depending upon the rigidity and permanence of his childhood training.

According to a common bit of folklore, autoerotic practices lead inevitably to insanity. It is probably true that most individuals who become either psychotic or neurotic have masturbated, but the incidence of such behavior is probably equally high in the population at large (Willoughby, 1937). Some psychotics and neurotics do masturbate compulsively and exhibitionistically, but the myth has other reinforcements.

First of all, there is the tendency on the part of many parents to use this dire prognostication as a means of frightening their children in the hope of more effectively enforcing the tabu. But there is apparently at least an element of oblique truth in it. Because of feelings of guilt, inferiority, unworthiness, and enduring wickedness which the masturbation temptation creates in many individuals, social timidity, reclusion, isolation, and depression may develop to such an extent that the individual is indeed more or less incapacitated for normal life. But, as various writers have suggested, it is not the autoerotic practices which are in and of themselves so damaging, emotionally and socially, but the attendant conflict and inner stresses.

More to the point, perhaps, is the argument that sexuality must be discouraged in childhood lest the harmonious functioning of the family group be disturbed. The extended literature on possible reasons for the incest tabu need not be reviewed here, but it should be noted that if libidinal interests were unrestrained within the family, sexual and personal competitions might develop which would be highly disruptive in their effects. Every known stable society more or less rigidly enforces some form of incest barrier. We must conclude, therefore, that this type of restraint is in some way essential and functional. Logically, the opposition to incest need not include a tabu upon all sexuality, including infantile autoerotic practices and sex play directed toward non-kinsmen. In fact, certain societies are fairly explicit in making such a discrimination (Mead, 1935). Why, then, should the tabu on infantile sexuality be so all-inclusive in other societies?

Commonly implied but rarely enunciated is the assumption that the ban on both childhood and adolescent sexuality is useful in inducing the individual to take up the responsibilities of married life. If sexual satisfactions can be achieved autoerotically or through illicit intercourse, it is widely believed that many men and women would never willingly assume the socially essential role of parents and providers for their offspring. The Kwoma, who have been studied by Whiting (1941), are one of the few peoples who are explicit on this score, telling the young boy that he must not manipulate his penis for the reason that "It does not belong to you; it belongs to your future wife." Marriage, with its attendant duties and obligations, is thus maintained as the only socially approved means of escaping sexual tensions and finding legitimate gratifications. This tabu thus fosters what may be called a "flight into marriage."

In the past, social groups have been much interested in encouraging marriage as a setting for procreation and expansion of population. There are now signs that in the relatively near future the advantage will come to lie with those societies which budget their populations in keeping with their natural resources, instead of trying to expand them as rapidly as possible. But even if the procreative function of the family should be less emphasized. the tabu on masturbation and other solitary sex practices will almost certainly remain. Heterosexuality is a *social* adjustment and as such presupposes that the participating individuals shall acquire certain attitudes and interpersonal skills without which no individual probably ever attains full integration into his group and a feeling of personal happiness. Only in this way can certain infantile patterns and attitudes be resolved and maximal social participation and maturity attained.

Freud (1930) and others have pointed out the interdependence between the whole culture-complex known as civilization and the phenomenon of sexual repression. These writers have mainly stressed in this connection what may be called the "divine-discontent" theory. According to this view, literature, art, science, and the other creative pursuits are the sublimated, or "sublimed," expressions of the baser forces of sexuality which are inhibited, in whole or in part, from their biologically simpler and more direct manifestations. But there is another aspect of this process which is less generally appreciated. In the process of being forced to inhibit behavior which leads to direct sexual gratification, the individual is often made to feel that erotic impulses are degrading and "wrong"; and since these impulses are part of the individual, the individual is to this extent made to feel degraded, wicked, and divided against himself. This means that he carries a more or less chronic feeling of culpability and a load of social anxiety. As a consequence, the individual has a compelling "need for social approval," and this in turn has the effect of making him engage in activities which will be judged socially useful. Each accomplishment brings with it, therefore, a feeling of relief and reward, but this agreeable state of affairs is almost certain to be transitory. The old feeling of vulnerability and inferiority and uselessness returns and drives the individual into another compulsive cycle of creative, socially desirable activity. This view makes the phenomenon of neurotic "ambition" understandable, and shows why for some persons the failure to attain "success" is likely to be so devastating.

This connection between what is essentially a neurotic character trait and the craving for social recognition and approval has been discussed at length by Horney (1937, 1939); and the fact that it involves a certain "secondary gain" in our society is indicated by the popularity of books and articles with the be-glad-you're-neurotic theme. Fenichel's remark that the "effort to free himself of a sense of guilt through the applause of the environment is a basic element in the psychology of the artist" (1934, p. 462) seems to be scarcely less applicable to certain types of individuals found in other professions and vocations. Fenichel further develops this thesis as follows:

> Reaction formations always have a certain compulsive quality that betrays their counter-cathectic nature. There are for example the "hard workers" who are under the constant necessity of working to keep from becoming unbearably tense, like the compulsion neurotic that represses his compulsion. One of Reich's patients aptly enough

called himself a "robot." It is not necessary to point out why work of this sort would be less valuable—in objective respects also—than that accomplished by a sublimation. We may refer here to the "Sunday neuroses" described by Ferenczi, determined, among other reasons, by the absence on Sunday of the opportunity to work, that is, to use work as a reactive defense. (pp. 447–448)

It should not be supposed, of course, that the erotic impulses are the only sources of guilt and social anxiety in children; humiliations and ridicule experienced in connection with elimination, cleanliness training, weaning, jealousy, aggressiveness, and the like are undoubtedly contributing factors in this connection. However, since a socially acceptable means of achieving sexual satisfaction is more difficult of attainment than are approved adjustments in these other spheres, inferiority feelings engendered by sex tabuing are probably the most pervasive and persistent. This means that, in favorable cases at any rate, the sex tabu provides a device for rendering the individual more or less permanently obedient to social regulations and to the will of the group. Since he is secretly guilty of a very great "crime," he dares not risk any defiance or noncooperation. He is like the criminal who dares not offer even legitimate resistance to the police for the reason that he is afraid of being caught and punished for some crime which he has actually committed.[37]

Closely related to the foregoing discussion is the possibility that children are denied freedom in the matter of sexual gratification on the grounds that this would allow them to react to life's hardships "unrealistically." The child who can console himself for a disappointment by putting his thumb in his mouth may be less likely to attack the frustrating situation. Alcohol, tobacco, escape literature, poetry, movies, and the other "opiates" which our culture provides for adults are restricted if not completely prohibited for "minors." We seem to assume that these devices, along with libidinal gratification, will permit the child to escape from the dilemmas in which he is placed by the socialization demands without adequately learning the skills and restraints which are expected of him.

The restraints placed upon childhood sexuality presumably have somewhat different meanings and consequences for personality in the case of boys and girls. The problems of "penis envy," "castration threat," and the origins of "female masochism" (see Horney, 1935) are still much

----

[37] The guilt which most individuals are made to feel in connection with their basic socialization has other important ramifications. Whatever their other functions may be (see Reik, 1932), primitive pubertal and initiation rites may serve to provide a final expiation and atonement for childish sinfulness and thus purify and prepare the individual for full adult participation in the life of his community. In addition to fulfilling this "need for punishment," such practices also symbolize the individual's submission to the authority of his community and signify his willingness to take up adult responsibilities. Infantile circumcision and religious baptism are, according to certain psychoanalytic writers, both attenuations of ancient ordeals of a much more drastic nature.

disputed, but, while being cautious in giving full allegiance to any particular cult of interpretation, we must grant to the contrasts in the external genitalia some implications for personality development. Conn (1940) has, however, shown a wide range of variation in children's reactions to the discovery of genital differences. Mead (1935) is undoubtedly right in insisting that much of the contrasting behavior which a society expects from the two sexes at various age levels is arbitrary from the point of view of actual biological differences, but this must not lead us to overlook the existent differences in biological equipment, potentialities, and experiences. Men, for example, simply do not menstruate or have babies, and like the experiences themselves, the looking forward to them on the part both of the individual and of society tends to create different habits in men and women. Biological differences and differing cultural expectancies join in giving a distinctive phrasing to various events in the socialization process. In cultures where the mother is the principal early socializer, the fact that her sex is that of her daughter but not that of her son creates an importantly different constellation. Perhaps herein lies the clue to the explanation of the observation that boys sometimes seem to find weaning a more traumatic experience than do girls. At least temper tantrums are notably more frequent among newly weaned Navaho and Hopi (Dennis, 1941a, p. 268) boys than among girls. From our culture, too, comes evidence that a specific socialization pattern has varying significance for girls and boys (Stagner and Krout, 1940, p. 352). Thus are laid the foundations for the typical differences in adult personalities between the two sexes.

Another complication which we have touched upon incidentally but which deserves most explicit mention and a more extended treatment than our space will permit is the fact that class, caste, minority ethnic groups, and other units of social differentiation have deep effects upon personality formation and deformation (Davis and Dollard, 1940; Davis, 1941). However, as the authors just cited show, the determinants of personality which arise from these sources readily lend themselves to analysis in terms of the general approach followed in this chapter.

Critical Stages in the Life History

In the *D*-maze paradigm only two stages, the original shorter route to the goal of food and the alternative longer route, are involved. On the other hand, personality development, as we have seen, must involve a succession of interrelated stages or habit progressions, each with its own dynamic pattern of needs and more or less adequate adjustments thereto. The sequence of development, or personality growth, is not wholly spontaneous or self-determined. Most stages or aspects of stages will persist just so long as they work for the organism. But when his environment, and primarily the interpersonal relations of this environment, demand changes of these adjustments or even of these needs before the individual can be satisfied, he will change. Thus personality growth is rather a product of the continuous and often tempestuous interaction of the physically maturing human animal and his older, more powerful mentors upon whom falls the responsibility of "transmitting the culture" and who in so doing convert this animal into an acceptable human being.

If this foregoing conception of psychosocial development be valid, certain characteristics of the adult personality and its vagaries are predicted. First, adult personality may thus be crudely visualized as a tower of innumerable layers of habits, each layer having many characteristics in common with both the preceding and the following ones but also possessing its own unique features. A personality must thus be studied hierarchically, for habitual responses at one level of complexity can obliterate any direct manifestation of habitual responses at another level. We need to know which responses will be dominant under specific conditions. This is the core of Moreno's (1934) theory. Secondly, one must expect this adult personality to consist in an unstable equilibrium which cannot be maintained under even the most favorable conditions without some emotional strain and threat of retrogressive change. Although he conceived this dilemma somewhat more narrowly than does an eclectic student of personality, Freud nevertheless induced what is probably the clearest conception of its implications as follows:

> The second danger in a development by stages such as this we call *regression*; it also happens that those portions which have proceeded further may easily revert in a backward direction to these earlier stages. The impulse will find occasion to *regress* in this way when the exercise of its function in a later and more developed form meets with powerful external obstacles, which thus prevent it from attaining the goal of satisfaction. It is a short step to assume that fixation and regression are not independent of each other; the stronger the fixations in the path of development the more easily will the function yield before the external obstacles, by regressing on to those fixations; that is, the less capable of resistance against the external difficulties in its path will the developed function be. If you think of a migrating people who have left large numbers at the stopping-places on their way, you will see that the foremost will naturally fall back upon these positions when they are defeated or when they meet with an enemy too strong for them. And again, the more of their number they leave behind in their progress, the sooner will they be in danger of defeat. (1920, pp. 295–296)

Distinct from but dynamically related to this phenomenon of regression is what Freud (1915) has called *repression*. Each pattern of adjustment is abandoned and replaced by its successor only after a certain amount of struggle and conflict. But it is often of momentous significance whether this inhibition is achieved through what we perceive as voluntary "choice" and conscious *suppression* of the earlier way of behaving or is achieved by the automatic process of *repression,* whereby the earlier behavior is not only blocked from direct motor expression but is also excluded from memory. Thus in the latter instance, *progression* is linked with *repression,* and *regression* by an abrogation of the repressed or, as Freud has said, by a "return of the repressed." Regression and the return of the repressed are, however, rarely complete and uncomplicated. The same anxieties and conflicts which produced the original habit progression and repression are almost certain to be reactivated by and to modify the would-be regressive behavior so that it may resemble little the original behavior toward which the regression occurs. The elaborate disguises which make this behavior more or less incomprehensible both to afflicted individuals and to others and the strange fears and violent hostilities which have no obvious connection with immediate realities are among the most blatant features of neurotic behavior. Before the advent of psychoanalysis these apparently unreasonable and bizarre phenomena remained without rational explanation.

Freud and his followers have been accused of stressing too much their dictum that every adult neurosis is but the reactivation of an earlier, infantile neurosis, or conflict (Adler, 1930; Horney, 1937, 1942). What is done for purposes of therapy is more or less irrelevant for the present discussion. Strictly speaking, the *present life* of the neurotic individual is all that either he or the therapist can deal with, so that Lewin (1935) has a certain justification for maintaining that all psychological causation is a-historical. But granting this, the fact remains that the individual at any given point in his adult life is a product not only of his present circumstances but also of the prior situations to which he has successively adjusted. Seen in this light, the question as to whether it is present or past frustrations that *cause* neurosis implies a non-dynamic conception of personality which Freud and most of his followers have never supported. Implied in all of Freud's writings is the assumption that every neurosis presupposes at least *two* frustrations: (a) that which has been responsible for the relinquishment of an earlier fixation, or adjustment, and (b) that which interferes with the subsequently acquired habit and precipitates the regressive trend toward the earlier one.

This dynamic interrelation of past and present frustrations in the production of neurosis may well be illustrated, in greatly simplified fashion, by returning to the *D*-maze experiment. It will be recalled that progression to the longer alternate route to the goal was effected in all cases by frustrating (electric shock, physical barrier, or non-reward) the originally preferred habit of reaching the goal. The resulting conflict and eventual abandonment of the original route, while roughly analogous to "education" or "socialization," would hardly qualify as a "neurosis." But if, for example, those animals which had been shocked as a means of frustrating the short-path habit were later prevented by a physical barrier from reaching the goal via the longer route, behavior might very well have been manifested which would have been considered "disproportionate" to the situation. An observer without knowledge of the earlier training might even think it "neurotic." But when the animal's *life history* in this situation is taken into account, the disturbed behavior is far less puzzling than it would be if only the cross-sectional view were taken.

Although the resulting conflicts and tendencies toward regression would undoubtedly show interesting differences in this *D*-maze situation, according to which particular combination of original and subsequent frustrations was employed (shock, block, or nonreward), the differences have not been studied. The relation between the amount of effort, or "work," involved in executing the later habit and the strength of the tendency to revert to the original habit "spontaneously," however, has been investigated (Whiting and Mowrer, 1944). It was found that regardless of the method used to produce habit progression, there was a persistent tendency for all animals to revert to the original and shorter path. That this tendency was indeed due to the greater effortfulness of the alternate path was shown by the fact that progressively longer alternates progressively increased the tendency to revert to the original path.

That this factor of effort is not unrelated to the problem of regression in human beings is clear from the following consideration. It is known that the discomfort occasioned by exertion, or work, varies according to whether an organism is rested or fatigued, in good health or ill, is strong or weak, is stimulated or depressed by drugs, etc. The effects of these factors in producing regressive behavior on the *D*-maze have not as yet been investigated, but they are capable of producing at least temporary regressive tendencies in human beings (Barker, Dembo, and Lewin, 1941). The common experience of "irritability" when one is fatigued, the general belief that "overwork" can cause "breakdowns," and treatment by "rest cures" (see Chapter 34, by Appel), show at least a partial appreciation of the role that effort plays in the dynamic equilibrium of personal stability, even when no external obstacle or frustration is operative.

In the preceding section, attention has been called to the fact that children face two particularly difficult problems—the tabu on all direct sexual gratification, and also the tabu on aggression. These problems are made especially acute, but we must remember the fact that one of the most valuable aids to the child in attempting to find socially acceptable ways of behaving is the behavior models which parents present. By emulating, or *identifying* with the parents, the child achieves a kind of short-cut solution to many dilemmas which might otherwise be extremely difficult of solution. But even when father and mother are ideally matched, the child's role is not an easy one. Both parents are almost certain to display aggression from time to time, often against the child himself, and soon or late the fact will emerge that they lead a sex life. To the extent that the child is prohibited from behaving similarly, his identification will necessarily remain incomplete, with more or less serious conflict and inner tension. Clinicians find that this conflict ordinarily reaches its height somewhere between the third and sixth year, at which time something very momentous happens. Since the attempt to be *like the parents* as regards their sexual and aggressive behavior almost inevitably results in conflict and disapproval, the child commonly resolves the problem by *repression*. In this way and only in this way can he achieve peace within himself and come to terms with the outer social world. But this success is achieved at considerable cost. As Anna Freud has said:

> Whoever has had the opportunity of being much with three- to four-year-old children, or of playing with them, is amazed at the wealth of their fantasy, the extent of their vision, the lucidity of their mind and the inflexible logic of their questions and conclusions. Yet the very same children, when of school age, appear to the adult in close contact with them rather silly, superficial and somewhat uninteresting. (1935, pp. 74–75)

It is well known that adults ordinarily do not remember much of their lives prior to their fifth or sixth year. Why this should be the case is not entirely clear, but the Freudian theory holds that this "infantile amnesia" is the result of the overgeneralized nature of the repression of infantile sexual and aggressive impulses. By the act of repression the child becomes "divided against himself" (Anna Freud, 1935, p. 88), but he also "arrives at a kind of peace" (p. 78). With this repression comes the so-called *latency period* which normally lasts until puberty. In some societies where the tabu on sexuality and aggression is comparatively gentle, the latency period is less intense, shorter, or altogether absent (see, e.g., Mead, 1928; Róheim, 1932, 1934; and Beaglehole and Beaglehole, 1941). Whether these children remember their early lives any better than do other children—a crucial test of the hypothesis just presented—is apparently not known.

It should be noted that by subduing the child's erotic and hostile, rebellious impulses one also renders him more cooperative in a certain sense and more amenable to education than he would otherwise be. Because the child ordinarily remains more or less dependent upon the parents at least until puberty, it is as if he made a contract with them at the onset of latency to be "good" in return for their continued support and protection. Moreover, since the child's wicked, anti-social impulses have only been repressed and not altogether destroyed, the child carries with him through this period a certain amount of "unconscious guilt," which, as previously noted, tends to make him avid for "social approval" and consequently willing to acquire the skills and knowledge that society expects of him. Far from being "the blissful period of childhood," life is often grim and earnest to children in the latency period. Only when their super-ego becomes less harsh can children develop other than a sadistic sense of humor (Klein, 1932, p. 37).

Klein has provided a sensitive description of personality features of children at this stage in our culture:

> Children in the latency period present special difficulties of their own in analysis. Unlike the small child, whose lively imagination and acute anxiety enable us to gain an easier insight into its unconscious and make contact there, they have a very limited imaginative life, in accordance with the strong tendency to repression which is characteristic of their age; while, in comparison with the grown-up person, their ego is still undeveloped, and they neither understand that they are ill nor want to be cured, so that they have no incentive to start analysis and no encouragement to go on with it. Added to this is the general attitude of distrust and reserve so typical of this period of life—an attitude which is in part an outcome of their intense preoccupation with the struggle against masturbation, and this makes them deeply averse to anything that savours of sexual enquiry or touches on the impulses they are keeping under with so much difficulty. (1932, p. 94)

However, with the advent of puberty the picture alters dramatically. The sexual impulse now increases to previously unknown intensities and places great strain upon the infantile repressions. At the same time, frustration augments, with correspondingly heightened instigation to aggression, which likewise presses against the forces of repression with renewed energy. Physically larger and more capable, the adolescent now faces an old conflict in a new setting. Normally, this "second edition" (A. Freud, 1935, p. 79) of the so-called Oedipus complex of infancy is dissolved by the "return of the repressed" and a repudiation of dependency upon the parents. In childhood the repressions called for by the parents were tolerable and the relative helplessness of the child made them necessary and useful. But now that the repressions are infinitely harder to maintain and the need for parental support and protection is diminished, the conflict of early childhood, now reactivated, tends to be settled in a quite different way. With this escape from the repressions of the latency period, identification with the parents now becomes more or less complete and a new level of adjustment is achieved. The period of apprenticeship has ended and real life has begun.

Parents often assist this familiar struggle for emancipation in their children. Consciously or unconsciously their attitudes toward sexual interests and activities change and the youth is given greater range in self-assertion and independence. Requiring a number of years to reach completion, this process is, however, sometimes made extremely difficult, if not permanently blocked, by the death of a parent, especially the parent of the same sex, during the adolescent period. Many primitive societies are protected against this tragedy by the device of the extended kinship system previously mentioned. Why this device has been largely discarded in most highly civilized societies—save in the lower social classes—is an intriguing problem. Civilization has reduced the hazards of life. This may make such an arrangement less necessary. But perhaps equally important is the difficulty of producing in an extended family the intense and relatively rigid indentifications which civilization demands.

Summarizing, it may be said that the typical developmental course for human beings in our society is as follows: The fact that aggressive and sexual prerogatives are denied to the small child throws him into conflict and prevents complete identification with the otherwise loving and protective parents. This dilemma is resolved by means of repression, which introduces the latency period. At puberty, this solution is undone and accomplished anew by repudiation of the parents' earlier tabus and attainment at last of more or less complete identification with them.

But not all adolescents experience this fortunate dissolution of the repressions of the latency period. For some individuals this transition is accomplished relatively easily, for others with greater difficulty, and for still others practically not at all. The latter type of individual, displaying what is often termed "morbid dependency," "delayed adolescence," and the like, is almost certain to manifest personality disturbances of one kind or another. Strictly speaking, the adolescent abrogation of childhood repressions is a kind of regression in that the individual goes back to interests and activities which were largely given up with the onset of latency. It is true that this change is regressive in a rather special and limited sense, but the fact remains that if the forces of repression, which institute the latency period, are too strong, they may not only prevent the return of the repressed impulses before puberty but also afterward. The individual whose psychic structure is so rigid that this normal change cannot occur is destined to experience inner stresses and character deformations of a more or less serious nature (see Popenoe, 1934, p. 45).

However, nature has placed a limit upon the period of dependency. The child does eventually, after 12 or 15 years, reach something approximating adult physical status. But most literate societies are not content to let the "training" of the oncoming generation stop at this point. Instead, they insist that it continue for at least a decade longer. This fact necessarily creates important complications. Not only are the physical and economic opportunities to escape from the limitations of the latency period not available at puberty to most children; parents are also constantly tempted to make the repressions of infancy so severe that they will withstand the onslaught of puberty and keep the individual "good" for an indefinitely longer period. That the early teen-years show the first sharp upswing in the incidence of psychoses and serious neuroses thus becomes understandable. As Klein (1932, p. 125) remarks, "In some instances repression has led to such an extreme limita-

tion of personality that the adolescent has only one single definite interest left—say, a particular sport."

In most civilized societies, the adolescent has not only his earlier
training to overcome but also encounters numerous external barriers
to the attainment of full adult status. As various writers have pointed
out (Sollenberger, 1939), most adolescents, although physically mature,
continue to be treated both by their parents and by society at large as if
they were still prepubescent children. This state of affairs reflects the
fact that although physically and even emotionally ready for active adult
life, most adolescents are far from having completed the education that
parents and society require of them. Our culture, at the manifest level,
places a very great and (cross-culturally) a very unusual premium on
rationality. Parents are forever demanding that the youngster behave
rationally. But actually any culture is a considerable bar to the free
exercise of rationality. Parents make conflicting demands—that the
child be rational but also that he not question the wisdom of the culture.
The adolescent who is painfully orienting himself to some form of compromise between his own needs and cultural demands discovers that
his parents are by no means as rational as the ideals which they have
preached to him would presuppose. This is a potent source of antagonism between parents and children and leads to mutual displays of
aggression. Adults have compromised rationality with their culture and
they very much resent any reexamination of these questions by their
children.

Even in those instances in which the adolescent escapes these gross
pathological disturbances, lesser difficulties are likely to beset his way.
If sexuality and aggressiveness have been too thoroughly inhibited, if,
to borrow a phrase from Anna Freud, "sparrows have been shot with
cannon balls" (1935, p. 97), not only will the intended effect of making
the child compliant and virtuous during latency and adolescence be
achieved, but he may be more or less permanently incapacitated for
assuming the roles which adults must play, as parents and economic
producers. That impotency and frigidity, not only in the sex realm but
toward life as a whole, commonly stem from all *too* efficient childhood
training is the consensus of clinical experience. Or, the repressed,
thwarted individual may overcompensate and develop a "power drive"
which makes him a menace to society and himself alike.

In adolescence one sees many complicated interactions of biological
drives, with their limitations, and social demands. As Frank (1941, p.
298) points out:

> . . . adolescence may be a period of organic incongruity when the
> individual child must attempt to live with organ systems and func-
> tional capacities of widely varying levels of maturity and functional
> efficiency. These organic incongruities or discrepancies may be a
> serious hazard to the individual if, as so frequently happens, he or
> she attempts to live up to this most advanced maturity, such as

stature; or if the individual is called upon by parents, teachers, and others to live according to his or her most advanced development.

A youngster whose previous socialization has been inadequate may focus upon biological events of this period unrealistically. Frank (*ibid.*, p. 7) gives a good illustration: ". . . often the adolescent girl may utilize headaches, malaise, or her menstrual function as an outlet for gaining attention or evading some requirements or the demands of life."

For those individuals who survive adolescence and achieve an acceptable marital and vocational adjustment, the next hazard is parenthood. At this juncture the individual must pass from mere self-sufficiency to the status of providing for others as well as himself. The learner must also become a teacher; the socialized child must become an adult socializer. This new task will be met with great or little competence, with patience or harshness, depending upon the individual's own earlier familial experiences and to a somewhat less extent upon the nature of his adjustments in the various other spheres of his adult life. In general, parents and other teachers who as children have themselves been strongly repressed will deal similarly with their own offspring and pupils. Having been taught to despise and abhor certain impulses in themselves, they will be angered or made anxious by manifestations of these impulses in the children for whom they are responsible. Sometimes this abhorrence of the spontaneous, unrepressed behavior of infancy and early childhood is so strong in both men and women that they cannot tolerate babies, with the result that they deliberately refrain from parenthood or, if this is an inadvertence, reject their offspring and their responsibilities for them from the outset. Fairly often one hears someone say, "I like children but I am not interested in babies." What this usually means is that the speaker does not like infantile behavior. His own repression of infantile ways has been too severe.

With the birth of children, still another difficulty is likely to arise for both husbands and wives. As the wife changes from sweetheart to mother and as the husband changes from lover to father, an old conflict is rearoused. Unconsciously, each partner at this point may begin to identify the other with his or her own parent of the opposite sex. When this happens, the incest tabu of childhood is reactivated, with an ensuing inhibition of sexuality of more or less serious proportions. Although other factors often contribute, this problem is the core of much marital discord (Flügel, 1921; Levy and Monroe, 1938).

Prophylaxis, or marital hygiene, is still a relatively unexplored area, but one factor must be noted. If the sexual interests of infancy must be punished, it should theoretically make considerable difference which parent undertakes this task. If fathers enforced the incest tabu in sons and if mothers did the same with daughters, there would presumably be less basis for the marital dilemma just described than would exist with mothers punishing sons and daughters alike, and with fathers behaving likewise. With mothers exclusively punishing their sons for sexual behavior and with fathers exclusively punishing daughters, the basis would seemingly be laid for the maximum incidence of not only disturbed marriages but also overt homosexuality. The clinical evidence for this deduction has been discussed under the heading of "inverse Oedipus complex" (Fenichel, 1934).

Illness, enforced idleness, accidents, failure in professional and economic struggles, the death of loved persons, and social and natural catastrophies all provide potential sources of frustration to which different individuals may react variously (see Reinhardt, 1937; Brown, 1936, p. 255). Whether a person will regress or progress in the face of such adversities is complexly dependent upon the many factors which have been previously reviewed. Marxist writers have tended to attribute crime, neuroses, demoralization, and all other character aberrations to unfavorable economic conditions. Bourgeois clinicians, on the other hand, are likely to stress only the unconscious (infantile) determinants of behavior. The total causation of these phenomena can apparently be adequately understood and controlled only if *both* sets of factors are taken into dynamic account.

The effects of old age upon personality have as yet been but little explored in any systematic fashion (but see Lewton, *et al.*, 1940). Waelder (1941, p. 6) is probably right in grouping old age with latency and maturity as the periods when there is likely to be the greatest psychological stability, but while stability and a greater mildness do seem to be old age features of many personalities, others seem characterized by strong reaction-formations.

BIBLIOGRAPHY

ADLER, A. 1930. Problems of neurosis. New York: Cosmopolitan Book.

AICHORN, A. 1935. Wayward youth. New York: Viking.

ALDRICH, C. A., & ALDRICH, M. M. 1939. Babies are human beings. New York: Macmillan.

ALEXANDER, F. 1940. Psychoanalysis revised. *Psychoanal. Quart., 9,* 1–37.

ALLPORT, G. W. 1937. Personality—a psychological interpretation. New York: Holt.

ANDERSON, O. D., & LIDDELL, H. S. 1935. Observations on experimental neurosis in sheep. *Arch. Neurol. Psychiat., Chicago, 34,* 330–354.

ANGYAL, A. 1941. Foundations for a science of personality. New York: Commonwealth Fund.

BAAR, J. 1928. Psychology (for reviews). New York: Globe.

BAKWIN, R. M., & BAKWIN, H. 1942. Psychologic care during infancy and childhood. New York: Appleton-Century.

BARKER, R., DEMBO, T., & LEWIN, K. 1941. Frustration and regression: an experiment with young children. *Univ. Ia Stud. Child Welf., 18,* No. 1.

BATESON, G. 1941. The frustration-aggression hypothesis and culture. *Psychol. Rev., 48,* 350–355.

—— 1942. Comment. In *Science, philosophy and religion.* New York: Country Life Press. Pp. 81–98.

BEAGLEHOLE, E., & BEAGLEHOLE, P. 1941. Personality development in Pukapukan children. In Spier, L., *Language, culture, and personality.* Menasha, Wis.: Sapir Memorial Publication Fund. Pp. 282–299.

BENEDICT, R. 1934. Patterns of culture. Boston: Houghton Mifflin.

BROWN, J. F. 1936. Psychology and the social order. New York: McGraw-Hill.

CANNON, W. B. 1929. Bodily changes in pain, hunger, fear and rage. (2nd ed.) New York: Appleton-Century.

——— 1932. The wisdom of the body. New York: Norton.

CATTELL, R. B. 1943. The description of personality: I. Foundations of trait measurement. *Psychol. Rev.*

CONN, J. H. 1940. Children's reactions to the discovery of genital differences. *Amer. J. Orthopsychiat., 10,* 747–754.

DAVIS, A. 1941. American status systems and the socialization of the child. *Amer. sociol. Rev., 6,* 345–354.

DAVIS, A., & DOLLARD, J. 1940. Children of bondage. Washington, D. C.: American Council on Education.

DAVIS, C. M. 1928. Self-selection of diet by newly weaned infants. *Amer. J. Dis. Child., 36,* 651–679.

DENNIS, W. 1941a. The socialization of the Hopi child. In Spier, L., *Language, culture, and personality.* Menasha, Wis.: Sapir Memorial Publication Fund. Pp. 259–271.

———1941b. Infant development under conditions of restricted practice and of minimum social stimulation. *Genet. Psychol. Monogr., 23,* 143–189.

DEVEREUX, G. 1939a. Mohave culture and personality. *Character & Pers., 8,* 91–110.

——— 1939b. The social and cultural implications of incest among Mohave Indians. *Psychoanal. Quart., 8,* 510–533.

DOLLARD, J. 1938. Hostility and fear in social life. *Social Forces, 17,* 15–27.

DOLLARD, J., MILLER, N. E., DOOB, L. W., MOWRER, O. H., & SEARS, R. R. 1939. Frustration and aggression. New Haven: Yale University Press.

DU BOIS, C. 1941. Attitudes toward food and hunger in Alor. In Spier, L., *Language, culture, and personality.* Menasha, Wis.: Sapir Memorial Publication Fund.

ERIKSON, E. H. 1940. Problems of infancy and early childhood. In *Cyclopedia of medicine, surgery, and specialties.* Philadelphia: F. A. Davis. Pp. 714–730.

FENICHEL, O. 1934. Outline of clinical psychoanalysis. New York: Norton.

FINCH, G., & CULLER, E. 1934. Higher order conditioning with constant motivation. *Amer. J. Psychol., 46,* 596–602.

FLÜGEL, J. C. 1921. The psychonanalytic study of the family. London: International Psycho-analytic Press.

FRANK, L. K. 1938. Cultural control and physiological autonomy. *Amer. J. Orthopsychiat., 8,* 622–626.

——— 1939. Cultural coercion and individual distortion. *Psychiatry, 2,* 11–28.

——— 1941. General considerations: certain problems of puberty and adolescence. *J. Pediat., 19,* 294–301.

FREUD, A. 1935. Psychoanalysis for teachers and parents. New York: Emerson Books.

FREUD, S. 1904. The psychopathology of everyday life. In *The basic writings of Sigmund Freud.* (Trans. & ed. by A. A. Brill.) New York: Modern Library, 1938.

——— 1905. Fragment of an analysis of a case of hysteria. In *Collected Papers.* Vol. 3. London: Hogarth, 1925. Pp. 13–146.

——— 1915. Repression. In *Collected papers.* Vol. 4. London: Hogarth, 1925.

——— 1917. Mourning and melancholia. In *Collected papers.* Vol. 4. London: Hogarth, 1925.

——— 1920. A general introduction to psychoanalysis. New York: Liveright.

——— 1922. Beyond the pleasure principle. New York: Liveright.

——— 1923. The ego and the id. (Trans. by J. Riviere.) London: Hogarth, 1927.

——— 1926. The problem of anxiety. New York: Norton, 1936.

——— 1930. Civilization and its discontents. London: Hogarth.

FRIES, M. 1941a. Psychiatry in dentistry for children. *J. N. J. St. dent. Soc.,* April. P. 3 in reprint.

—— 1941b. Mental hygiene in pregnancy, delivery, and the puerperium. *Ment. Hyg., N. Y., 25,* 221–236.

GELLHORN, E. 1943. Autonomic regulations—their significance for physiology, psychology, and neuropsychiatry. New York: Interscience Publishers, Inc.

GORER, G. 1938. Himalayan village. London: Michael Joseph.

HARTSHORNE, H., & MAY, M. A. 1928. Studies in deceit. New York: Macmillan.

HAYAKAWA, S. I. 1941. Language in action. New York: Harcourt, Brace.

HILGARD, E. R., & MARQUIS, D. G. 1940. Conditioning and learning. New York: Appleton-Century.

HOLT, E. B. 1931. Animal drive and the learning process. New York: Holt.

HORN, D. 1944. Some syndromes of personality. (To be published)

HORNEY, K. 1935. The problem of feminine masochism. *Psychoanal. Rev., 22,* 241–258.

—— 1937. The neurotic personality of our time. New York: Norton.

—— 1939. New ways in psychoanalysis. New York: Norton.

—— 1942. Self-analysis. New York: Norton.

HULL, C. L. 1943. Principles of behavior. New York: Appleton-Century.

HULL, C. L., *et al.* 1940. Mathematico-deductive theory of rote learning. New Haven: Yale University Press.

JAMES, W. T. 1941. Experimental observations indicating the significance of work on conditioned motor reactions. *J. comp. Psychol., 32,* 353–366.

JAQUES, E. 1942. Misconceptions of parents concerning child health and behavior. *Amer. J. Orthopsychiat., 12,* 202–214.

KATZ, D. 1932. Hunger und Appetit, Untersuchungen zur medizinischen Psychologie. Leipzig: Barth.

KILPATRICK, W. H. 1926. Foundations of method. Informal talks on teaching. New York: Macmillan.

KLEIN, M. 1932. The psycho-analysis of children. London: Hogarth.

KLUCKHOHN, C. 1943. Navaho witchcraft. *Pap. Peabody Museum of Harvard Univ.,* Vol. 22.

KLUCKHOHN, C., & MOWRER, O. H. 1944. "Personality and culture": a conceptual scheme. *Amer. Anthrop., 46,* No. 1.

KÖHLER, W. 1940. Dynamics in psychology. New York: Liveright.

KORZYBSKI, A. 1941. Science and sanity. (2nd ed.) New York: International Non-Aristotelian Library & Publishing Press.

KROUT, M. H., & STAGNER, R. 1939. Personality development in radicals: a comparative study. *Sociometry, 2,* 31–46.

LEVY, D. M. 1928. Finger sucking and accessory movements in early infancy. *Amer. J. Psychiat., 7,* 881–918.

—— 1937. Studies in sibling rivalry. *Res. Monogr. Amer. Orthopsychiat. Assn.,* No. 2.

—— 1939. Sibling rivalry studies in children of primitive groups. *Amer. J. Orthopsychiat., 9,* 205–215.

LEVY, J., & MONROE, R. 1938. The happy family. New York: Knopf.

LEWIN, K. 1935. A dynamic theory of personality. New York: McGraw-Hill.

—— 1937. Psychoanalytic and topological psychology. *Bull. Menninger Clin., 1,* 202–211.

—— 1942. Field theory of learning. *Yearb. nat. Soc. Stud. Educ., 41,* 215–242.

LEWTON, G., *et al.* 1940. Old age and aging. *Amer. J. Orthopsychiat., 10,* 27–88.

LINTON, R. 1936. Study of man. New York: Appleton-Century.

LUCAS, W. P. 1932. Healthy attitudes toward health. In *Our children.* New York: Viking. Ch. 7.

LUND, F. H. 1939. Emotions—their psychological, physiological and educative implications. New York: Ronald Press.

LYND, R. S. 1940. Knowledge for what? Princeton: Princeton University Press.

MALINOWSKI, B. 1926. Crime and custom in savage society. London: Harcourt, Brace.

—— 1929. The sexual life of savages. London: Routledge.

MARQUIS, D. P. 1931. Can conditioned responses be established in the newborn infant? *J. genet. Psychol., 39,* 479–492.

—— 1941. Learning in the neonate: the modification of behavior under three feeding schedules. *J. exp. Psychol., 29,* 263–282.

MASSERMAN, J. H. 1942. Psychobiologic dynamisms in behavior. *Psychiatry, 5,* 341–347.

MAY, M. 1932. The foundations of personality. In Schilles, P. S., *Psychology at work.* New York: Whittlesley. Pp. 81–101.

—— 1941. Foreword. In Miller, N. E., & Dollard, J., *Social learning and imitation.* New Haven: Yale University Press.

MAYO, E. 1933. The human problems of an industrial civilization. New York: Macmillan.

McCOLLUM, E. V. 1932. The chemistry of growth. In *Our children.* New York: Viking. Ch. 5.

McCONNELL, T. R. (Ed.) 1942. The psychology of learning. 41st Yearbook of The National Society for the Study of Education. Bloomington, Ill.: Public School Pub.

McDOUGALL, W. 1932. The energies of men—a study of the fundamentals of dynamic psychology. London: Methuen.

McGEOCH, J. A. 1942. The psychology of human learning. New York: Longmans, Green.

MEAD, G. H. 1934. Mind, self, and society from the standpoint of a social behaviorist. Chicago: University Chicago Press.

MEAD, M. 1928. Coming of age in Samoa. New York: Morrow.

—— 1930. Growing up in New Guinea. New York: Morrow.

—— 1935. Sex and temperament in three primitive societies. New York: Morrow.

—— 1937. Cooperation and competition among primitive peoples. New York: McGraw-Hill.

—— 1939a. From the South Seas. New York: Morrow.

—— 1939b. Researches in Bali, 1936–39; on the concept of plot in culture. *Trans. N. Y. Acad. Sci. Ser.* II, 2, 1–4.

—— 1940a. Social change and cultural surrogates. *J. educ. Sociol., 14,* 92–110.

—— 1940b. Conflict of cultures in America. *Proc. Middle Sts Assn. Coll. second. Schs.*

—— 1942. And keep your powder dry. New York: Morrow.

MENNINGER, K. A. 1938. Man against himself. New York: Harcourt, Brace.

MILLER, N. E. 1941. The frustration-aggression hypothesis. *Psychol. Rev., 48,* 337–342.

MILLER, N. E., & DOLLARD, J. 1941. Social learning and imitation. New Haven: Yale University Press.

MONEY-KYRLE, R. E. 1939. Superstition and society. London: Hogarth.

MORENO, S. L. 1934. Who shall survive? *Nerv. ment. Dis. Monogr.,* No. 58.

MOWRER, O. H. 1939. A stimulus-response analysis of anxiety and its role as a reinforcing agent. *Psychol. Rev., 46,* 553–565.

—— 1940. Anxiety-reduction and learning. *J. exp. Psychol., 27,* 497–516.

—— 1941. Motivation and learning in relation to the national emergency. *Psychol. Bull., 38,* 421–431.

MOWRER, O. H., & JONES, H. 1943. Extinction and behavior variability as functions of effortfulness of task. *J. exp. Psychol.* (In press.)

MOWRER, O. H., & LAMOREAUX, R. R. 1942. Avoidance conditioning and signal duration—a study of secondary motivation and reward. *Psychol. Monogr., 54,* No. 5.

MURPHY, G., MURPHY, L. B., & NEWCOMB, T. M. 1937. Experimental social psychology. New York: Harper.

MURPHY, L. B. 1937. Social behavior and child personality. New York: Columbia University Press.

MURRAY, H. A. 1938. Explorations in personality. New York: Oxford University Press.

OGDEN, C. K., & RICHARDS, I. A. 1938. The meaning of meaning. (5th ed.) New York: Harcourt, Brace.

PAVLOV, I. P. 1927. Conditioned reflexes. New York: Oxford University Press.

POPENOE, P. 1932. What a child is born with. In *Our children.* New York: Viking. Ch. 4.

RANK, O. 1929. The trauma of birth. London: Harcourt, Brace.

REIK, T. 1932. Ritual—psychoanalytic studies. New York: Norton.

REINHARDT, J. M. 1937. Personality traits and the situation. *Amer. social Rev., 2,* 492–500.

RICHARDS, A. I. 1932. Hunger and work in a savage tribe. London: Routledge.
RICHTER, C. P. 1941. Biology of drives. *Psychosom. Med., 3*, 105–110.
ROBERTS, W. H. 1930. The effect of delayed feeding on white rats in a problem cage. *J. genet. Psychol., 37*, 35–58.
RÓHEIM, G. 1932. Psycho-analysis of primitive cultural types. *Int. J. Psycho-Anal., 13*, 1–225.
—— 1934. The riddle of the Sphinx. London: Hogarth.
—— 1942. The origin and function of culture. *Psychoanal. Rev., 29*, 131–165.
SHAFFER, L. F. 1936. The psychology of adjustment. Boston: Houghton Mifflin.
SHELDON, W. H. 1940. The varieties of human physique. New York: Harper.
SOLLENBERGER, R. T. 1939. Adolescence. In Dollard, J., *et al., Frustration and aggression.* New Haven: Yale University Press.
STAGNER, R., & KROUT, M. H. 1940. A correlational study of personality development and structure. *J. abnorm. soc. Psychol., 35*, 339–355.
SUMNER, W. G., & KELLER, A. G. 1927. The science of society. New Haven: Yale University Press.
THORNDIKE, E. L. 1900. The associative process in animals. Boston: Ginn.
—— 1931. Human learning. New York: Appleton-Century.
VALENTINE, P. F. 1927. The psychology of personality. New York: Appleton-Century.
WAELDER, R. 1941. The scientific approach to case work with special emphasis on psychoanalysis. *Family, 22*, 179–185.
WALKER, K. F. 1942. The nature and explanation of behavior. *Psychol. Rev., 49*, 569–585.
WATSON, J. B. 1930. The new behaviorism. New York: Norton.
WHEELER, R. H. 1940. The science of psychology. (Rev. ed.) New York: Crowell.
WHEELER, W. M. 1928. The social insects—their origin and evolution. New York: Harcourt, Brace.
WHITING, J. 1941. Becoming a Kwoma—teaching and learning in a primitive society. New Haven: Yale University Press.
WHITING, J. W. M., & MOWRER, O. H. 1944. Habit progression and regression—laboratory study of some factors relevant to human socialization. *J. comp. Psychol.* (In press.)
WICKENS, D. D., & WICKENS, C. 1940. A study of conditioning in the neonate. *J. exp. Psychol., 26*, 94–102.
WILLOUGHBY, R. R. 1937. Sexuality in the second decade. *Monogr. Soc. Res. Child Developm., 2*, No. 3.
WITMER, H. L. 1939. Some parallels between dynamic psychiatry and cultural anthropology. *Amer. J. Orthopsychiat., 9*, 95–101.
WOLF, A. W. M. 1941. The parents' manual—a guide to the emotional development of young children. New York: Simon & Schuster.
WOLFE, J. B. 1934. Effectiveness of token-rewards for chimpanzees. *Comp. Psychol. Monogr., 12*, No. 60.
WOODGER, J. H. 1937. The axiomatic method in biology. Cambridge: Cambridge University Press.
WOODWORTH, R. S. 1918. Dynamic psychology. New York: Columbia University Press.
YOUNG, K. 1938. The impact of society upon the child. *Univ. Ia Child Welf. Pamph.*, No. 61.

PART II

CROSS–SECTIONAL METHODS OF ASSESSING PERSONALITY

Chapter 4

SUBJECTIVE EVALUATIONS OF PERSONALITY

By Edward S. Jones, Ph.D.

Appraisal of people is one of our commonest social activities. The executive, the salesman, the lawyer, and the teacher are continually judging the capacities or the social attitudes of others. To bring logical rigor, order, and control to such personal evaluations presents many possibilities and many difficulties.

By our usual standards to be scientific requires objectivity, but one's personal estimation of his fellows in social situations is in essence subjective. A judgment may be changed radically by anything affecting the judge. Carelessness, the mood of the moment, the various types of bias regarding both conduct and people are continually intruding upon apparently sober judgment. Even where a series of objective life records are available, the evaluator tends to select those items which fit his previous impression of an individual. Thus, in many circles, subjective evaluation of personality is relegated automatically to the unscientific junk-heap.

In practice, however, the appraisal of certain aspects of personality is, and probably always will remain, a personal, subjective estimate based on vague cues. Artistry will always play its part, even though the process of judging persons is brought into the atmosphere of science. In one college, for instance, after the executive board had gone to the trouble of collecting from the alumni a large number of personal judgments of the individuals on its teaching staff, these judgments were finally dumped into the waste-basket, and the salary scales of the teachers were adjusted mainly on the basis of the preferences of the president who felt he was a better judge than the alumni. The validity of such a stand would be hard to prove or disprove, for it contains within itself a confusion of point of view that simply illustrates the necessity for a logical examination of the process of judging personality.

What fails to be objective and scientific when viewed from one logical standpoint may become so when viewed from another standpoint. Most scientific definitions of personality assume that personality exists outside of a social context (Allport, 1937, see Ch. 2). Such an assumption may be fruitful for many of the problems in this field, but it does not fit another assumption, that most phenomena relevant to the analysis of personality emerge as a consequence of social interaction (see Chapter 3 by Mowrer and Kluckhohn). One may abstract for study that aspect of a person concerned with his influence upon others. This influence appears to be the aspect of the individual popularly subsumed under the term personality. Personality has occasionally been defined in terms of this influence by men of science. An example is the conception of personality as the *social stimulus value* of the individual (May, 1932).

To limit the definition of personality to an individual's social stimulus value may be too narrow a view, for a man alone on a desert island would then have no personality because his gestures, speech, and other behavior could not be reflected in the conduct of others. Nevertheless, in many practical situations the aspect of the person in which one is interested is his social stimulus value. An individual is an effective salesman, for instance, not immediately because he has a certain blood pressure, a certain set of responses on the Rorschach, nor because he is energetic, vivacious, reliable, and/or punctual. He is an effective salesman because certain people react to him as they do. Likewise, a certain individual is an effective army officer, not because of what he really is, but because what he really is and does produces good morale and effective action from the individuals in his command. Occasionally one hears that the same salesman is effective with one sort of group but not with others, or that the same officer is effective with one command but not with another. This is the crux of the problem: A person's social stimulus value depends not only upon what he is and can do, but it depends also upon the attitudes and values of those who reflect his influence.

At the present stage of our knowledge it would be quite impossible to predict whether a given person would be effective in a given sort of situation with a given group of individuals from knowledge of his characteristics and capabilities and of the values and standards of the group. It is not surprising, therefore, that in everyday situations and again in the psychology of personality, men have turned to such subjective evaluations of the individual as written recommendations, ratings, and indices of popularity or status. These procedures, wisely managed, produce self-validating criteria. A man is tactful, generous, and capable of leadership if his acquaintances agree that he is (Garrett and Schneck, 1933, see Part II, p. 116). From a statistical point of view the reliability of measures of stimulus value is contingent upon the available sampling, its quality and numerical adequacy (see Newstetter, *et al.,* 1938). Moreover, in so far as the science of personality depends upon recommendations, ratings, and indices of popularity, the operational definition of a personality is its social stimulus value. Confusion frequently arises when one attempts to validate ratings against objective scores or vice versa, for subjective evaluations and objective measures belong to different systems of discourse. On the other hand, any objective records (e.g., of punctuality) may throw considerable light on the meaning of subjective evaluations.

The wise management of written recommendations, of ratings, and of indices of popularity depends on developing care and sincerity in judges, and also on empirical information. What one person will say about another will vary with the nature of the situation, with the relationship between the individuals, and on the data which are made available. Much of the fact finding of this field has been done with the aim of reducing the artistry involved, usually wisely, but sometimes resulting in a less complete analysis of the individual.

This brings us to the major dilemma of those who wish to characterize personalities, a dilemma which is bound up with the standard concepts of reliability and validity. We may, on the one hand, steer in the direction of accuracy and reliability of measurement, and those techniques which can be duplicated for verifiable data. This direction would seem to be in the path of objectivity. On the other hand, we may seek primarily a complete, truthful evaluation of a person, something which will be in the largest measure valid and convincing, including chance incidents or bits of conversation and the opinions of many kinds of people in varying situations. Most data of this kind could not be duplicated. Although most of the emphasis has been on the first point of view, we should not lose sight of the more uncontrolled final appraisals which are ultimately subjective. The final mark of a college student in a year course, based on papers, incidental gestures and comments, discussions, as well as examinations, is an illustration; the evaluation of an army officer as a leader of men is another illustration.

To attempt a synthesis of both kinds of emphasis, to be reliably accurate and also convincingly complete, is the primary burden of the modern student of personality diagnosis. How can we control the terminology and the setting of a subjective appraisal so that it will take on some of the aspects of objectivity, and yet leave expression free and final opinion untrammeled by narrowly conceived indices? Let us consider, therefore, the letter of recommendation, ratings of specific traits, measures of popularity and group-status, estimates of capacities of various sorts from interviews, and finally case studies.

Recommendations and Application Forms

A letter of recommendation or endorsement written by one person for another is usually discounted as an accurate indicator. Even more unreliable are forms or letters of application made out by a man applying for a job, in essence a self-recommendation. Hollingworth (1923) found almost no significance either in general reports of the "to whom it may concern" type, or in letters of application, as measured by agreement between consultants asked to review them. And yet some form of recommendation or more specific application is said to be used with initial sorting data by approximately 90% of employers. The question arises: Can such letters be improved so as to become more reliable?

Scientific development is often a matter of degree. An advance from complete unreliability to moderate accuracy is desirable from the practical standpoint.

Application blanks have been investigated by several observers who have devised a scheme of rating certain items usually found in them, on a positive or negative basis from the point of view of future salesmanship. For example, Moore (1939) records a system in which the age 30 to 40 received a plus 3, while before 22 and after 60 were given negative values. Marital status, clubs, previous experience, total amount of education up to 16 years, type of previous occupation (social *vs.* unsocial), a desire for a full time contract, and apparent confidence were all rated with positive values from 1 to 4. Such a scheme greatly facilitates the selection of good salesmen who stick on the job.

Burtt (1926) advocates a check list of items in every letter of application. It has the merit of comprehensiveness, but it is doubtful whether this would be satisfactory to most reviewers. Employers of all kinds like the free, spontaneous description of an applicant, just as they like to read full and natural letters of recommendation in preference to scanning the results of carefully collected ratings from a variety of sources. A high school principal who wants to hire a new teacher often looks for the letters written about her by two or three of her professors whose expression and judgment he trusts. He reads between the lines, he says, and "feels" that he can get to know his applicant because he values the sincerity of the man who writes the recommendation.

A few central offices, such as the Federal Civil Service and the T.V.A., have devised forms for recommendations of new applicants which are fairly discriminating as to specific areas of behavior. For example, among 10 or 12 questions will occur one or two covering the field of initiative, such as "Does the applicant carry on his own investigations effectively with the minimum of outside direction: Very well? Moderately well? Poorly?" Another type of question will be: "Is the applicant subject to moods of depression or irritation?" There is little published evidence concerning validity, but one would expect a man of some standing to be reasonably discriminating. Incidentally, the reliability of such a report is probably enhanced by asking for the signature, title, and actual position of the man writing the report. Recommendations vary in value according to their source and freedom from special bias.

Kornhauser (1927) investigated the validity of recommendations and statements about entering college students as judged by their later success in college. He found that the evaluations of family friends, lawyers, ministers, and others were of no significance, but that the judgments of employers and of teachers showed significant relation with school success (correlations of .35 and .26 respectively).

It is difficult to specify to what extent the endorsement of character by previous employers, teachers, and others can be relied on to interpret personality traits. In industry they are continually used in lieu of more adequate measures, particularly by bond houses and credit organizations. For the most part, however, these business houses are interested in checking on basic questions of veracity, such as "During what months was he employed with you?"

One method of improving recommendations, according to Moore (1939), is to avoid general statements, and to answer specific inquiries. Otherwise the majority of general letters of inquiry yield only the good points about a previous employee or associate. Many who read recommendations look only for negative statements or signs of disparagement. Examples of quite specific and objective questioning are the following: "Was he discharged, and if so, was it because of irresponsibility, or poor work, or lack of experience?" or "Did he have any work habits in your office to which you objected?" Provocative questions of this kind should obviously vary according to the job for which the candidate is being considered.

Kornhauser (1928) tried several different forms of reference in connection with the induction of freshmen at the University of Chicago. Ordinary short paragraphs were not as useful as some variety of rating. Moreover, ratings were improved by getting evidence from the rater about intellectual ability other than that required in the school room. He became convinced that such reference blanks and personal history forms from outsiders and the student himself gave considerable useful information about the industry and the initiative of the student not available in high school records.

It appears quite obvious that much can be done to improve the significance of the reference and recommendation blanks. Part of the problem appears to consist in selecting crucial and searching questions for the recommender to answer where objective criteria exist. Objectivity is to be preferred, but some traits are better assessed through a brief statement of attitude or by listing best and worst qualities. The consensus of opinion, according to Brogan (1930), among presidents and others concerned with the placement of teachers in teacher training institutions, is that a personnel office should collate recommendations and reference items regarding the candidate and interpret them adequately to principals and other employers.

In spite of the various attempts to be more specific, several indirect approaches suggest that considerable attention is being given, and probably will be given, to free, untrammeled expressions of opinions about people. The work of Murray (1938) and his associates is not conclusive, but the impression is clear to the writer that in the general conference, in the autobiography, and in other situations, free expression and discussion brought out important relevant facts about the men analyzed which would never have been elicited in more systematic tests and ratings. Similarly, one might expect that the free comment and discussion about a person, elicited in a carefully written recommendation or statement of character and personality traits, would present essential attributes relevant to the particular job under consideration. The value of such statements depends primarily on the motivation of the evaluators to be truthful and complete.

Among college faculties the most objective, and perhaps the most demanded, requirement concerns scholarly publication. According to Anna Reed (1935), however, college administrators tend to rate as very important many subjectively estimated items such as tolerance for the opinion of others. Some of these impressions about applicants are acquired principally through letters of reference.

In summary we can again point out that there are two schools of thought and emphasis regarding recommendations and letters of application. One school wishes to emphasize specific items for the purpose of reliability, the other prefers a more natural, free expression as more useful and valid. As previously suggested, one school implies scientific control, the other is more concerned with generalizations based on many subjective impressions.

The Appraisal of Traits in Interviews

The interview as a method of arriving at various personal characteristics has been reviewed by Bingham and Moore (1941) and others. In most cases studies have centered in the problem of selecting leaders, or in detecting people with special gifts (such as selling) or attitudes (e.g., motivation for study). Ordinarily one thinks of the interview as involving one interviewer and an interviewee, the latter alert to the purpose of the situation and anxious to put his best foot forward. However, because of biases in the single interviewer and the artificial preparedness of the subject interviewed, several modifications of the usual plan have been introduced: the controlled situation with specific questions, a conference of interviewers after meeting separately or together with the subject, and the formal or "framed" interview with particular test questions for detailed report.

In all types of interviewing studies the reviewer has difficulty in knowing how much credit can be given to a specific interview with its mutual give and take of gestures and language, and how much is based on supplementary data available for inspection. Clark (1926), comparing estimates of the ability of students and later grades, found correlations of .66 and .73 for two interviewers; but it is not clear how much other information was available for the inspection of the interviewers. If high school records, test scores, and outside hobbies were all at hand, perhaps the interview would add very little or even mislead the interviewer. An experienced interviewer is likely to treat the interview as an opportunity to summarize and synthesize a considerable array of data from different sources.

Several brief studies have centered in the problem of selecting leaders or of detecting special qualities (e.g., selling ability) or attitudes (e.g., desire to study). The consensus of opinion is that interviews of short duration and not supplemented by other data are nearly useless. Frequently there is some agreement between two judges at the same interview or in succeeding contacts, but both are likely to be over-influenced by superficial traits or attitudes in the individual. One can judge neatness of dress, spontaneity of conversation, and to some extent, ego expansiveness (through the number of times "I" is mentioned), but it is very easy to expand these specific tendencies into generalized traits such as "well poised," "intellectually alert," or damaging "egotism." In one college a slightly negative correlation was observed between the prognostic estimates of a borderline freshman by two personnel interviewers merely on the basis of brief conversations with them and the final average marks received at the end of the year. Even when intelligence tests and high school records were used in the appraisal, one of the interviewers tended to ignore such evidence in favor of a facile, pleasing front, neat dress, fluent speech, and a courteous manner. In any college personnel office one could cite several cases in which industrial employers have totally ignored the material available in the college office, and hired men merely on the basis of short interviews. Some of the older personnel men have, of course, used a phrenological system or other devices which they regard as more valid, and they do not wish to be muddled by other data.

Efforts to improve the interview have taken several tacks, few of which have been thoroughly tested.

1. O'Rourke (1929) put particular emphasis on training the interviewer to ask specific things and thereby to judge important reactions. He found that when this was done in civil service examinations, interviewers agreed better among themselves. O'Rourke also urges that specific situations be set up, so that correct evaluations can be made, e.g., presenting an office man with a disagreeable complaint letter to inquire what he would do about it.

2. Several investigators agree that nothing is more helpful to the interviewer than a very clear conception of the crucial parts of the job for which a person is applying, and of sampling behavior in the interview which would be pertinent for that job. For example, if speed of decision is necessary, this can be detected by actual problems. Receptionists should have good manners. If interviewers stick to areas of personality in which they have a right to make estimates, they are more accurate.

3. Finally, according to Moore (1939, p. 436ff) there is a tendency in many business offices to set up a controlled or standardized interview covering many specific questions concerning the previous work history of the applicant, his life aims and preferences as to type of work,

his fondness for dealing with people, his family and domestic problems. This method is said to have increased conspicuously the relation of interviewer's estimates to later production records.

Vernon (1935) attempted to evaluate total personality significance by having three investigators observe 25 students during the administration of several performance tests, and to write sketches about each. Ratings of intelligence, extroversion, quickness, and emotional stability showed quite remarkable consistency (corresponding to correlations of .72 between judges). Lester and Hewlett (1928) asked each of a number of girls 12 standard questions on the basis of which scores of extroversion and general optimism were indicated. The two investigators agreed closely in estimating extroversion, since the measure of extroversion was merely the amount of verbalization of the student in a social situation.

Asher and Gray (1940) found 15 items out of 30 originally used, which could be used in an interview to bolster predictions of college success. These items, e.g., "How many weeks did you lose on account of illness last year?" correlated .40 with college success, only .07 with intelligence. They were apparently mainly related to motivation.

A few experiments such as that of Spielman and Burt (1926) have been carried on with very brief interviews of a half minute each. This study of 16-year-olds showed high reliability correlations between two interviewers independently for some traits such as submissiveness (.85), self-confidence (.77), and energy (.64), but low reliabilities in other fields such as curiosity (.37). Nothing was done to test the validity of such evaluations. Allport (1937) feels there is an advantage in having some degree of similarity between the judge and the interviewee, superior intelligence and insight, some capacity for esthetic detachment and social intelligence.

Several studies have shown that slight changes in the form of questions used or differences in *rapport* before an interview starts are of great importance. Very little work seems to have been done in connection with gestures, autistic and otherwise, in evaluating personality, even though Krout (1935) found a remarkable consistency when individuals were presented with the same stimuli at different times. A word or situation which aroused a shrug of the shoulders once would have the same effect later. We may suspect that nervous, fidgety people would lack self-control in certain emotional situations, but the proof seems to be meagre.

All in all, it would seem that in judging personality we should be extremely modest in our claims for scientific interviewing. So much deceptive "front" is possible in the man interviewed, so many false judgments and prejudices prevail in the interviewer, that the resulting knowledge about a person is not likely to reach much higher validity than when one refers to a recommendation.

The Framed Interview with Test Questions.—Several interviewers have presented an extensive series of questions to determine reactions concerning a specific type of adjustment. These interviews may approach case studies in the detailed information sought, but the main emphasis is to secure judgments regarding a definite type of personality adjustment. For example, Carney Landis (1940) was interested in the appraisal of traits in women regarded as neurotic as compared with those in normal women. His associates presented problems and questions to 300 women individually, taking down detailed notes of their replies. Every effort was made to elicit honest and complete reports on delicate problems of sex adjustment, hence a special preparation of attitude was requisite to make individuals ready.

Some commercial companies have tried to frame situations for prospective candidates, to test out the normal emotional controls of each. For example, the question is raised suddenly, "What makes you think you are good enough for our company?" At least one objection to such a method is the ease with which knowledge of the technique might travel, so that future candidates would be forewarned.

It would seem that if a situation can be naturally presented to a candidate, the more controlled or framed, the better. It might be desirable to forewarn the interviewee regularly that certain kinds of questions will be asked, to distract him from other "test questions." This has been suggested by O'Rourke (1929) in civil service oral examinations.

Evaluations of Group Leadership.—Most of the thorough studies of leadership have veered away from objective tests, since character and personality factors are known to play such an important part. Simoneit (1933), the leader of the German military psychologists, insists that isolated measures of single abilities are useless. Only the combination of measures, intellectual, physical, and social, produce useful indices of leadership. In most fields of leadership one can, of course, analyze the previous accomplishments; in fact student leaders on a college campus are known mainly through positions attained in extracurricular fields. Among children, leadership is often evaluated by signs of aggressiveness and control of others. For older children and adults, however, samplings of behavior are too variable and difficult to collect; other devices are desirable to predict capacity for group management.

The study of Partridge (1934) on adolescent boys in scouting troops is one of the most comprehensive in America. In order to determine potential leaders, Partridge not only collected preference ratings of boys as a crude mean of group status, but determined the relation of age, intelligence, height, athletic ability, appearance, and dependability to proven scout leadership. Also, boys were actually tried out in leadership positions as patrol leaders. In one experiment he brought boys who were known leaders from one troop to a strange troop, and they were soon recognized as leaders, often by the voice alone when they were not seen. It appears that among boys 12 to 15 years of age there are several identifications of leadership ability, mainly associated with confidence in expression.

Group Interviews Followed by Discussion.—The interview, plus analysis of an individual, has frequently been followed up with discussions between two or more people. Several studies seem to indicate that under these conditions the results are usually more reliable. Thorndike (1938) found that when the factor of majority influence is present there is greater uniformity among individual estimates later, and also some increase in validity of the final total decision. Those who know more about a problem (e.g., selecting the more artistic of two pictures) communicate with greater confidence, and influence others toward the attitude that becomes generally accepted. However, in the college groups investigated by Thorndike the influence of discussion was not as great as some might expect. Often sides were taken and the most correct arguments strongly contested. Murphy and Newcomb (1937, pp. 715–739) have summarized several experiments suggesting that improved efficiency and correct thinking can flow from such joint airing of impressions because of mutual corrections and an increased number of items of information.

In certain colleges personnel placement officers have met with a group of instructors in a given department in order to talk over their graduating candidates for jobs. Some of these placement men feel that in this way they can get far truer, better balanced pictures of the men they must try to place. One person states his appraisal of a senior, which is often vigorously attacked by another member of the department, frequently with evidence that is convincing. On the other hand, the final appraisal of a candidate may be quite misleading when the only evidence available to the placement office is of this kind. A student may be seriously condemned because of the emotion of one individual, whereas individual ratings would have given him fairer analysis. The situation is particularly unfortunate with somewhat introverted personalities. If a boy seems diffident and one man is "sure" he will be unable to assume normal responsibility, the other instructors are likely to keep still because they do not know him well. Instead of a spread-out multiple picture of his personality which the personnel office receives through many ratings, grades, outside activity reports, and so forth, the consensus of judgment is likely to be steered by a single emphatic characterization.

Murray (1938) and his associates experimented extensively with a 45-minute interview, five judges who had discussed problems together being common observers who later discussed aspects of the interview. The agreement between total analysis on the basis of the interview and the total final conclusion regarding the person evaluated on the basis of all types of data was remarkably high. On the basis of different measurements the reliability correlation was in the neighborhood of .60 for the average of many variables analyzed. Murray felt that they had clear-cut evidence of an improvement in agreement between judges from one year to the next, but much of this was probably due to greater agreement on the meaning of terms.

The extensive work done by German military psychologists in assessing leadership necessary in officers has been excellently summarized by Ansbacher (1941), showing methods differing considerably from those common in this country. Skeptical of the inexhaustible variety of objective tests of intelligence, character, and personality, most of the German investigators have apparently veered in the direction of total mass judgments of individuals on the basis of many types of data, partly objective and partly quite subjective. Due to an immense reservoir of characterological studies, most of which seem to us statistically crude and biased, they have been brought up on a diet of types, racial traits, and innate endowments far more than would be convincing to us. However, a few psychologists have been interested in carefully controlling situations with varied types of judgment. In recent years the work of Simoneit has been especially extensive, his Wehrpsychologie (1933) becoming the bible for contemporary military psychologists.

The typical method of analysis of leaders was apparently to set up a board consisting of two officers, one physician, and three psychologists. The full testing program lasted for two full days, and included many individual tests as well as group performances, many of which were carried on in real life situations. Tests similar to Murray's (1938) thematic apperception test were used to get at the form and nature of free expression, but particular emphasis was given to "action analysis," in which they tried to evaluate power of sustained attention in the presence of distractions, uniformity of reaction, choice behavior, emotion, rate of learning, and fatigability. In some test situations, four candidates are examined simultaneously; in other situations common soldiers were trained to react under them in disconcerting ways. The prospective leader is analyzed from the standpoint of his instructional ability, his oratorical capacity in speaking to sustain morale, and in other respects. The primary result of the total program is an agreement of several examiners as to the leadership capacity of the applicant. The work is explicitly intended to be practical rather than scientific, in the sense of being easily verifiable.

It is significant that these German investigators are just as concerned in analyzing intelligence subjectively in military situations, as personality traits. They apparently have not been unduly impressed by the popularity of objective intelligence testing in this country. They have searched for every sort of measurable ability which would be an endorsement of leadership, including the ability to detect and resist enemy propaganda.

Many of these test results have not correlated well with each other. For example, there is little correlation between most of the tests and general motor performance.

There are no available records validating their results, for these involve divulging military secrets. Nevertheless, because of its evident promise, this work should provoke considerable thought and experimentation in this country. The usual evaluation of a college senior ready for work is, for example, an extremely flimsy affair. We recommend him for this or that position, saying, "Maybe he will work out," or "He has to get experience somewhere," with very little real consideration of his effectiveness. A mass voting by experts, all of whom have observed a man working in crucial test situations, is almost unheard of in this country. No wonder a large percentage of our officer material in the new army is proving to be inept in leadership.

Ratings of Personality

The term rating is used to cover an estimate of some aspect of a personality on a scale by an individual in lieu of more objective types of measurement. Ratings of personality may be made with name attached or anonymously, with careful consideration or as snap judgments of preference, on scales of from four to ten or more steps. We may also ask a person to rate himself. Early accounts of personality and character rating by Hollingworth (1923) were mainly disparaging of efforts to evaluate reliably the qualities of a person through ratings. Burtt (1926), in a more optimistic summary of experiments, proposed several safeguards for improved rating, which he feels are necessary in the evaluation of the many traits of a person which are not subject to testing by objective methods.

The various provisions for a rating blank have corresponded to different areas of research in the field, which may be classified as follows:

1. What particular form should the rating scale assume? Depending somewhat on the purpose intended for its use, there is general agreement that the dimensions on which a person is rated should be clearly specified, preferably with qualifying phrases or further descriptions of traits, at the extreme positions at least. There has been some tendency to change from earlier forms of numerical designations of quality, used in connection with handwriting, to graphic forms on which raters merely check estimates, as discussed by Freyd (1923) and defended by him as the form preferred most by raters.

As one aspect of the problem of form, the number of steps on a graphic scale has been widely discussed. Rugg (1922) and Symonds (1931) agree that the maximum number of steps for adequate reliability is seven, with some subjective traits, such as tact, limited to five steps. Not all recent investigators would wish every trait restricted to seven. It is generally agreed, however, that raters do not enjoy checking distinctions finer than they feel qualified to make, just as most professors prefer to mark papers on an *A, B, C, D,* or *F* basis rather than on a numerical scale.

2. Several refinements in the method of rating are suggested, that most frequently mentioned being the man-to-man scale devised by Walter Dill Scott for the personnel division of the U. S. Army. The main feature of this system was the stipulation that, before rating any officer, the rater should make up a preliminary card of concrete cases (actual individuals) to be regarded as Highest, High, Middle, Low, and Lowest for each of the traits, "physical qualities," "intelligence," "leadership," "personal qualities" of "industry," and "loyalty," each graded on the basis of 15 points, and also a final "general value to the service" graded on the basis of 40 points. There seemed to be considerable evidence, supported by Rugg (1921), and Scott and Clothier (1941), that such a method or a graphic modification thereof, insures greater reliability because of the time and care taken. The total score, on the scale of 100, showed for any one individual an average deviation of less than five points between pairs of raters. Although it is perhaps to the credit of this system that it still persists in the army in at least some branches, its adoption in industry and school systems is rare. The answer is patent to those formerly in the army who were asked to contribute ratings: they did not want to bother with man-to-man comparisons, and there is no way of enforcing such a scale every time a rating is made.

Some argue for a ranking device, instead of rating, in order to insure more thorough consideration of each person. Cattell (1910) asked each outstanding man in a scientific field to rank the abler men in his field, in this way evolving a starred or preferred list of eminent scientists. His method has been continued in later editions of *American Men of Science.* Hull (1928) gave a statistical formula for converting rank order values to sigma or other scale values.

The *American council scale,* described by Bradshaw (1930) and widely used among colleges, had an additional feature to insure greater care in rating, i.e., a request that the rater cite specific instances of behavior which were useful in determining the trait specified. How many professors can be persuaded to specify these bits of behavior for all students they rate is not mentioned. Further refinements are in order, not merely to insure greater care and accuracy in rating, but to inspire the rater to an interesting task. Too many ratings of personality become perfunctory. The judge is vague in his evaluations, and he hurries through his job.

3. Several have discussed training the rater or treating the judgments of careless and untrained raters. Rugg (1922) discovered that when personnel officers were sent around to instruct line officers in the exact method and care necessary for the man-to-man scale, the reliability of ratings as measured by correlations was greatly increased. The rater must be urged to spread out his ratings toward the extremes, and par-

ticularly not to ignore the low values, in order to avoid the errors of central tendency and overleniency common to all untrained raters. Several authors, including Burtt (1926) and Greene (1941), have suggested correction devices for the ratings of judges who stick to the middle of a scale, e.g., by using sigma values from a measure of central tendency for that particular judge. Since such statistical treatments are tedious it is much simpler and nearly as accurate to instruct judges in the various pitfalls. This has usually been found satisfactory.

4. The problem of *halo* effects, both negative and positive, has been repeatedly raised. Rugg noted that 10 out of 11 estimates for one trait were within one point of the rating given for another trait on a 5- or 7-point scale. Almost invariably one overrates a person in all traits if he likes him. Bradshaw (1930) found that the correlation between traits, when five or more judges' estimates were combined, was often as high as .80. Provisions to reduce halo are suggested by Greene (1941), who advocates a change in the order of the favorable side of a trait rating from left to right. Symonds (1925) measured this halo influence by partialing out of the correlations between traits the sum of the average judgments for that person. Intertrait correlations were reduced from over $+.4$ to under $+.2$. Knight (1922) pointed out that this error of halo is greatest among close acquaintances and can be reduced by warning individuals against the tendency.

Greene (1941) also refers to a *logical* error in rating, or the tendency to rate people as one would judge by generalizing from word cues rather than on the basis of observed behavior. For example, a person who stands up straight may be regarded as straightforward in his dealings with others. Newcomb (1931) found an average correlation of $+.49$ between estimated personality traits in boys, when records of observed behavior in the same traits showed intercorrelations of only $+.14$. This suggested a semantic factor in all ratings, i.e., a tendency to be led astray by words which have different meanings in different situations and in the minds of different raters. Sears (1936) found that we have no right to speak of a quality such as insight in general. Measuring insight on the basis of the discrepancy between self-ratings and ratings by others, he found that insight in regard to one trait (e.g., stinginess or obstinacy) did not correlate with insight in another trait.

5. The reliability of single ratings was considered by Hollingworth and Rugg, since each person's evaluations are based on unique personal relationships. The collation of ratings, to reach reliability, is almost entirely a problem of the number of cases. Cattell (1910) found that 12 leading scientists reached reliable averaged estimates of the status of their fellows. Investigators generally agree on the desirability of five to seven raters, to reach reliability correlations of around .8 or higher between one averaged rating and another average in the same trait from different raters. Carefulness in rating, and a clear description of the steps on a scale, all have the effect of increasing reliability.

Reliability is also connected with the terms or traits used. Hollingworth (1923) found that the relatively objective traits and those related to impersonal situations and tasks showed higher reliability than do traits referring to character and personal relationships. Allport (1937) summarizing several contributions confirms this. Hollingworth (1923) also found that in a long list of traits being rated, the terms used later in the series were less reliably rated than earlier terms. The attitude and perspective of the rater is hard to control but obviously is of great importance.

General all-around traits, such as "general value to the service," were found by Rugg (1922) in the army testing to be more reliably rated than more specific traits, but this generally confirmed result may be due mainly to the increased importance of halo in general factors. Some people, remarks Allport (1937), are easier to rate than others. Particularly, one expects the rating of extraverts and active types of people to be more reliable.

Kornhauser (1927) and others have found considerable unreliability of teachers' ratings of students in their classes. Students are known only narrowly by their professors. Even the ratings of the same students made in two different quarters of the same year by a single professor at Chicago correlated only +.60.

Adams (1936) believed it was desirable to measure the objectivity of a specific type of rating, i.e., a particular trait, term, or a particular situation. He devised a formula for objectivity, as the ratio of "group-consistency" to "self-consistency" in any set of duplicate ratings. Group-consistency is measured by the degree of agreement between different persons, and self-consistency, the agreement between different ratings of the same individual by the same person. In judging the sizes of circles, there was high objectivity, close to a ratio of 1.00, indicating no special individual bias; whereas, in estimating the character of people or their tact, there was high self-consistency, suggesting that individual biases and interpretations creep into judgments, lowering the objectivity ratio accordingly. For example, different individuals may judge tact by widely divergent indicators—quietness, neatness, use of English, etc. Each will be self-consistent but will not agree with the estimates of others.

6. Few writers have discussed the validity of ratings, largely, no doubt, because there are few criteria available which can be trusted to measure what rating scales are intended to measure. For example, one may correlate ratings of total personality with salary earned, but everyone recognizes that success is a much broader concept than personality. Even when attempts have been made to compare ratings of punctuality with actual measures of tardiness in keeping appointments, one can question whether the two are the same. Impressions concerning punctuality may include the tendency to be late at social engagements, which Dudycha (1936) found does not correlate closely with tardiness at

formal appointments. Or perhaps the person making the rating should not have made a guess at punctuality, as it lies beyond the scope of the usual observations of a person! The rater may be wrongly associating punctuality with precision in dress, etc.—logical error—for lack of other indicators.

One indication of validity is revealed in the general attitude of those who have used rating scales for some time when the values of ratings are observed in getting at problems of adjustment of students. Students whose marks are low, but whose intelligence test scores are high, almost invariably are rated quite low in industry or initiative by their professors. If they are not active on the campus they are similarly rated by fellow students. Considerable evidence of the utility of ratings is given in the American Council study of *Measurement and Guidance of College Students* (1933). Of 34 colleges using the blank in some respect or another, the majority were using the blank in connection with student interviews or to impart information to employers of graduates. Several comments indicated the great importance of the selection of judges and their motivation for careful rating. It is possible for the most assiduous raters, those judging more than their share of students, to be warped or narrow in their bases of evaluation.

Evaluations of Teaching Ability.—One of the most important contributions from rating scales is probably to be found in the field of teaching, because objective criteria of teaching efficiency are scarce, since this field is preeminently one of social interrelationships. More than ever it has been realized that any education which is unstimulating is a serious waste. Two techniques of rating are common. One is concerned with the evaluation by critics or inspectors of students preparing to be teachers. These critics are ordinarily practiced teachers, or high school principals. The other type of approach is of growing importance and it involves the direct evaluation of teachers by students.

In the forecasting of teaching efficiency almost every degree of relationship has been found, from zero or very low correlations between normal school marks or intelligence tests and teaching efficiency, found by Knight (1922), up to a .73 correlation between "normal school success" derived from grade average and "teaching success" as estimated by high school principals, reported by Somers (1923). This discrepancy suggests that the primary problem of evaluating teaching ability falls on the validity of a final criterion of success in the field, which is generally a rating by supervisors or school principals. Probably some of the higher correlations which have been reported are due to a spurious connection, the fact that many of the supervisors in some districts have access to the recommendations sent by normal school faculties for new teachers. Halo effects unquestionably play a leading role, arising from previous indications of leadership, or practice teaching comments, both of which contribute in final scores for effective "field teaching." If the majority of raters have an opportunity to observe most of these factors, intercorrelations are bound to be high. In general, the final ratings of teaching success do not check up closely with intelligence test scores, a fact which puts special emphasis on personality qualifications apart from intelligence.

The very careful work carried on at Toronto University on *Forecasting Teaching Ability* by Sandiford (1937) is deserving of special mention. Sandiford found that ordinary ratings of teacher critics correlated poorly with later teaching success. Improvement in the correlations resulted when the criterion of success was strengthened by comments, and when notes on young teachers by several raters taken at different times were pooled, on the basis of which additional inspectors made judgments of probable teaching success. In other words, the real criteria of success were ratings of ratings and other inspection notes made over a period of months during the early years of teaching. In this study actual teaching success correlated with practice teaching grades to the extent of only +.35, considerably higher, however, than with average grades in courses, +.24. Apparently social traits are more important than tested intelligence in determining field success. Jones and Southard (1937) found correlations between ratings of personality (attractiveness) and crude evaluations of the later success of men (+.40), many of whom were teachers, much higher than between success and school grades (+.24), outside activities (+.23), or intelligence tests (+.05).

Relatively low correlations between practice teaching estimates and apparent success in actual teaching do not invalidate ratings or marks in practice teaching. They do suggest that factors other than early demonstrations of teaching ability play an important role in later success. Such factors as willingness to work hard, loyalty, and interest in extracurricular affairs, probably play a part. Moreover, the marks and ratings of practice-teacher critics are perhaps still too academic. They may be based mainly on learned replies in examinations or on a particular formal technique of teaching, such as the outline. The high reliability correlations between the final ratings of inspectoral comments reviewed by two different men (from +.6 to over +.8 when three inspectors were matched against three others) was taken as suggesting the validity of these summarized ratings of teaching efficiency.

The studies concerned with the ratings of teaching efficiency by students are well reviewed by Roy Bryan (1937). This work begins with the study of Remmers (1929), who devised a special teacher rating blank which has been widely used in many colleges. The ten traits on which every student is asked to rate each teacher are: interest in his subject, sympathetic attitude toward students, liberal and progressive attitude, presentation of subject matter, sense of proportion and humor, self-reliance and confidence, personal peculiarities, personal appearance, and stimulating intellectual curiosity.

The rating is graphic and each trait is partially defined by supplementary remarks under a line, e.g.,

Interest in Subject

Always appears full of the subject	Seems mildly interested	Subject seems irksome to him

One of the most interesting results of this study was the discovery that most teachers did not mind it, and many apparently benefited by the results. The average correlation between the averaged ratings of a teacher in two different classes was +.74. Similar correlations, in which Remmers' or other scales were used, have run from .58 to .92.

Bryan's own study (1937) was carried out on junior and senior high school students who rated their teachers similarly on eleven different items. He found the correlation between chance halves of students as high as +.81 for the average of five traits of greatest significance (ability to explain clearly, sympathy, fairness in grading, pupil liking for teacher, and general teaching ability). The relation between estimates of students was much higher than the correlations between estimates by principal and assistant principal (+.52) or between pupils and the average of principal and assistant principal (+.55). Bryan believes reliability and validity are synonymous with such a rating instrument, if it is carefully managed and full cooperation is obtained from the students. With each of the traits rated, he could get reliability correlations over +.90 with 40 students. There was little difference between the results for junior and senior high schools, and there were no significant differences when ratings by superior students were compared with inferior students. The author suggests that the ordinary estimates of administrators of teachers are not very valid, since the amount of agreement between pupils and administrators varied directly with the amount of contact between the principal and the classroom situation. Furthermore, more halo effect is indicated on the part of the administrators, since they evaluate teachers more alike on various traits than do the pupils.

Several investigators have shown that students, either in college or high school, can be quickly taught to give fair and meaningful evaluations of teachers on a rating blank. Moreover, additional comments made by students are also useful. A careful study of terms used should be made for each population of students, since terms which yield high reliability and low intertrait correlations at one level of education may show quite different correlations at another educational level.

Self-Ratings.—In general, since the work of Hollingworth (1923), there has been almost universal condemnation of self-ratings. Self-ratings, however, may be found useful when compared with ratings by others, and if not taken at face value. A study of the discrepancies between self-ratings and ratings by others should at least be significant concerning "insight" (Sears, 1936). Apparently there is a certain amount of consistency, or split-half reliability, when people evaluate themselves, e.g., on extraversion. The correlation between self-ratings of extraversion (or other traits) and an average of five or more ratings made by others should be informative.

Adams (1930) found that a good judge of self tends to differ from a good judge of others in being rated by his colleagues as happier, more sympathetic, courageous, and generous. Vernon (1933), using an extensive set of tests and ratings on 48 college men, found that good self-raters were characterized as having a good sense of humor (both on the basis of a test and ratings), good insight, and high intelligence. Good raters of others, on the other hand, had a tendency toward introversion and esthetic appreciations. The psychoanalytical group would probably interpret these results as indicating a lack of inferiority complexes and absence of compensatory urges in the "good raters." Contrary to the usual expectation, that we rate ourselves favorably on complimentary traits, Allport (1937) points out that in a few fields self-ratings are above average even though uncomplimentary, particularly in introversion, radicalism, and emotionality. Allport interprets these unfavorable self-ratings as an implicit desire to suggest a rich inner life which is not exposed to others.

Summary on Ratings.—Personality ratings seem to have a number of valid uses, if and when they are well administered. Common sense should operate in determining the purposes of ratings and how they are to be used. For example, the ratings on personality traits by professors should not be expected to yield high correlations with similar ratings given by student leaders, particularly in such traits as initiative. This correlation (in one case .30) merely suggests that by initiative professors think of college work, whereas students mean leadership and individual expression in campus activities. It does not invalidate either rating, but does suggest that we should define more completely the type of initiative and the source from which ratings are secured. A particular averaged rating is self-validating, within limits prescribed by the number of cases and the quality, care, and sincerity of the raters.

More work on the validity of personal ratings should be carried on with still other kinds of traits which are clearly stated but which are not necessarily objectively measured. There is some question whether ratings should be presented merely as averages. Why should not the entire spread of ratings be given on a particular scale? This would show whether a person was a rather colorless, middle-of-the-road individual, or one capable of arousing strong likes and dislikes. A spread of ratings could also indicate whether ratings were made by different types of people, e.g., t for teachers, s for students, etc. The proper instruction and motivation of raters is a matter of the utmost importance. More research of a practical type is needed to indicate, for example, a method of inducing faculty members to rate their students carefully, at least in a few traits. Perhaps, however, they are in no position to rate personality except in a few superficial respects.

Popularity and Group Status

The rating methods we have just discussed have had to do with the reactions of single individuals to a number of specific traits in others. A certain amount of control, formality, and consequent artificiality results in such methods. We turn now to total reactions to people, which are more informal in nature. How do you like a person? How does he "rate"? These are questions often raised. Obviously much emotion is involved in such appraisals because comparisons are usually made between the rated person and the rater himself. In the broadest sense public and secret balloting for governmental purposes are illustrations. From Pericles to Franklin Roosevelt leadership has often been acquired and maintained through mass popularity voting, a measure of group status.

The work of Moreno (1934) and his associates is probably the oldest and most widely known controlled study in this field. The primary method consists in asking each member of a closed group of 20 or 30 to choose the individual person he likes best, the person with whom he would prefer to live, or the person with whom he would prefer to work. In order to avoid extraneous restraints in such choices, Moreno has insisted that the choices, in so far as possible, be functional in the sense that the chooser has an opportunity to live or work with his choices. In various groups the proportion of "isolates" (those not preferred by anyone) varied from 15% to 35%, even when each person was asked to name three choices. The percentage of mutual pairs (each member naming the other first) reached a maximum of 27% in the fifth grade of the school system, whereas more complex constellations such as triangles and chains are found among older children. Among a group of girls in a home-cottage assembly it was possible to determine and chart each person's "social atom," Moreno's term for a person's social attraction and repulsion. When individuals are allowed to choose those outside the group, Moreno considers that extensive preferences outside the group are indicative of extraversion in that group, and probably in the individuals so disposed.

Jennings (1937) used this technique with a colony of girls and found that it was possible to select a "leader nucleus" from the total group. Seven girls from one much larger group apparently cornered almost all the first and second choices. These girls were also strongly attached to one another. The actual "sociogram" could often be changed radically by altering the individuals in a group even a little, suggesting that popularity itself is not too stable.

Zeleny (1940) has suggested formulas for the measurement of social status, but he is not very explicit about measuring some of the terms. Social status ratio or S. R. is $\frac{N \times I}{T}$, where N stands for the number of acceptances of an individual, I for the intensity or strength of the acceptances, and T for the time or duration. A simpler statement of social status score is given by the formula: S. S. $= A$ plus C, where A is the algebraic sum of the acceptances and the rejections, and C the number of choices made of him by others.

One aspect of Moreno's study, referred to as spontaneity testing, has special significance for students of personality measurement. He introduced the factor of dislike as well as like into preference choices of a group of girls, and then persuaded certain girls to assume specific attitudes of affection, dominance, irritation, and the like toward others. Sociograms taken for the group after such attitudes were tried out showed very considerable change, as one would expect. It suggests not only a method of measuring group emotional atmosphere, but also changing it in the direction of better relationships and improved individual personalities.

Another study, by Newstetter, Feldstein and Newcomb (1938), covering experiments carried on for 10 years, is quite similar to that of Moreno in that the work was carried on in groups housed together. In this study the composite order of preference ratings collected for each boy in a colony was compared with samples of behavior ratings by counselors and other indicators. The average index or correlation between preference ratings and the "compresence" of an individual in groups of two to five members was $+.73$. The mean correlation between the group-status of an individual and the ratings by counselors was $+.76$. This study also indicated a consistent drop in reliability correlations between two different samples of group preference as the time interval between samples was increased. A further interesting aspect of this study was the lack of correlation between behaviors observed in each boy indicating cordialities received from others and cordialities given to others. The former correlated highly with group-status ($+.71$), but not the latter ($+.30$). This suggests to the authors that much covert activity, which is not now available for measurement, in the individual is responsible for his group-status as well as his "compresence" within small play groups.

The above two studies suggest an unlimited field of exploration in measuring group-status and the factors contributing to it. Preference ratings can be checked against all kinds of other data. The studies do suggest a continual change, or dynamic flow, in the building of group-status, varying from time to time, and from group to group. They support the conception that personality does not exist as a constant separated from the environment. Hunt and Solomon (1942) have carried preference analysis into a group of boys, six to nine years of age, in a summer camp. Asking each boy to name his first choice among the campers, a great deal of early instability in choices was found during the first weeks, but the number of changes in choices from one week to the next was not a linear function of the time interval. The proportion of the group changing choices dropped from nearly 60% the first week to 23% after the third week with little decrease thereafter. Young boys, as one might expect, showed more instability of choice than older boys. Group-status during the first week correlated most closely with athletic ability; but later, group-status became more clearly correlated with physical attractiveness, ordered activity, and generosity. The tendency to choose from inside one's cabin decreased during the first three weeks to 50% or to chance without much change thereafter.

On several college campuses the determinants of campus status or popularity have been investigated. From the diaries of students in co-educational colleges, Waller (1938) found that students could be placed in three strata, labeled A, B, and C. The A men were those in the more important campus positions. They usually possessed a combination of traits including leadership, wealth, and athletic ability. In contrast, the status of a woman was determined almost entirely by the men with whom she dated, and the frequency of these datings. Frequent dating with A men gave her a status at the A level.

Status rating and popularity are often considered equivalent, but we suspect an important distinction in a complex society. A professor may be recognized as a very superior scholar and teacher, but difficult, and therefore he may not be popular. Moreno's technique did not evaluate well those persons toward whom there existed an emotion of awe or mystery which would interfere with preference for mutual association. A college campus should furnish an excellent field for investigation of factors determining status and popularity.

Case Study of Personality

Case studies are variously described by different investigators. Some think of "cases" only as those in trouble, or as atypical; others refer to case studying as a technique coordinate with, but quite separate from, objective testing or other methods of investigation. Confusions and natural overlappings of psychological case studies occur with medical case histories, with social service case work, and with educational and industrial case studies. What is the province of case study in personality investigation? Probably it is limited only by the stretch of one's definition of personality and by the time one wishes to spend in collecting data. A complete and well-rounded case record is a biographical sketch plus almost every other conceivable type of material, including data regarding the family, the physical environment, education, legal entanglements, medical history, habits, attitudes, satisfactions, and needs. It may include extensive summaries of quite objective factual matter, even the results of intelligence or achievement tests. The main emphasis, however, in case reports is on unstandardized and unmeasurable data, leading to a final total appraisal of the individual and factors affecting his behavior.

In nearly all case studies so far reported there is a problem of adjustment, some form of asocial conduct or difficulty. Each case is generally treated by itself, and the incidents in the life history of the individual are interpreted by the case student in a causative linkage that depends largely on the disposition and theories of the investigator. If he is a strong Freudian adherent, an investigator will interpret incidents and make predictions accordingly. This leads to the dual fallacy brought against the usual array of cases. (1) The investigator tends to select only those cases for his report which he feels present a clear demonstration of his point of view. In other cases, selected at random, the evidence is not so clear, and they are therefore discarded. (2) The investigator almost invariably interprets those bits of behavior which he does select in terms of a general formula to which he is committed. For example, X is known to have collected stamps when he was young, or to have been denied the opportunity to build model airplanes. These may be interpreted as leading him to initiative in science or to some type of unsocial behavior in the future.

Case studies may be made for purely practical purposes, or for purposes of research. In developing the methodology of life histories, for research purposes, Dollard (1935) proposes a series of criteria which he views as indispensable—for example, "the subject must be viewed as a specimen in a cultural series." Other criteria have to do with watching the social relevance of organic factors, the continuous nature of experience from childhood through adulthood, the organized and social influences involved in actions. Dollard's proposals offer a valuable means of testing the thoroughness and quality of case studies, but one should regard them as hypotheses and subject to modification. Moreover, some of his criteria—for example, "the organic motors of action ascribed must be socially relevant"—leave the case student great leeway to interpret socially relevant material according to his own bent. The case student at best differs from the experimental scientist mainly in that he does not bring a person into a laboratory but follows his activities and the impressions he has made on others in a natural life setting.

Allport (1942) would not want to be restricted by Dollard's criteria. In his comprehensive survey of personal documents, he argues for the extension of idiographic knowledge as a necessary basis for a science of personality. Autobiographies, diaries, and other forms of projection can be broadly conceived of as types of case reports.

Case Studies as Science.—Sociologists have been preeminent in this field of scientific case studies. Nels Anderson's *Hobo* (1923) and Ruth Cavan's *Suicide* (1928) are illustrations of carefully followed groups of cases, with every apparent effort to be free from prejudice and to test out hypotheses as they emerged. Work of this kind does not support the conception of Symonds (1931) that the case study is not a research method but merely a practical device to help out those in difficulty. Lewin (1936) insists that only through a complete exposition of individual cases can non-Aristotelian science be evolved. Attending to deviates leads to new conceptions for further study. Williamson and Darley (1937) make a plea, not only for greater objectivity, but for longer case records among vocational counselors, in order to probe more thoroughly into vocational adjustments.

Psychologists have unquestionably been influenced by the great expansion of objective tests, and behavioristic experimentation in general, to select and condense data, so far as possible, into brief cumulative record folders as described in the American Council booklet on Guidance (1933). They tend to ignore enormous portions of relevant material. They would apparently rather record a neurotic inventory score taken from a test, even when they do not know what the test really measures, than to note that a boy was clumsy in his oral expression and that his nose kept twitching as he talked, data that may have obvious social implications.

The approach of Plant (1937) in studying asocial behavior as a key to personality problems in the culture of any community in general is a fine contribution to case study technique. By analyzing faithfully the dramatic incident which occurs (a suddenly developed truant or a man who flares up at his wife, leaving the house never to return), one is able to approach problems affecting many other individuals that are not quite serious enough to cause dramatic incidents. He notes as the basis of a study of the "casual breakdown" these conditions: (1) one must seek to study the individual as close to his "usual" environment as possible; (2) one must study the situation at a time when the individual's "relations" with that environment are thrown in high relief; and (3) one must accept the certainty of artifacts in the material collected.

The recognition of artifacts in the data of case work is an essential but often neglected point. Not only is some material inaccurately observed or recorded, but often the interpretation is wrong. For example, by more careful prolonged observation of case incidents the anthropologist B. Malinowski (1926) has corrected many of the impressions of former students of primitive life in the South Sea islands, particularly the general impression that there were very few who deviated from the mores of the primitive group. For a long time the common conception that primitive folk adhered very rigidly to the mores was an artifact influencing the reporting of nearly all investigators.

Schools of Thought.—In addition to inaccuracies of observation, case studies are necessarily colored by various philosophies and points of view. A strong eclectic psychologist focusing every possible light on the individual, as does Murphy et al. (1937), will be relatively unbiased, but others have more definite frames of reference. Goldstein (1938) attempts to combine psychoanalytical thinking and mechanistic conceptions far more than do those of the Freudian school. Robinson (1936) has used the will-therapy doctrine of Otto Rank in her exposition of the growth of the "professional self" of the case worker. Others suggest the definite use of psychoanalysis in the classroom, presenting case records of children thus treated.

The tendency in many child study laboratories has been in the direction of setting the stage for some kind of conduct, then observing and writing case reports accordingly. Sheffield (1937) in this way proposes to control his "situational" case studies, urging that each observer enter realistically into the actual situation through "participant observing." Out of this participation will come insight, through the cooperation of doctor, social worker, visiting teacher, and psychologist. This total or mass clinical approach is apparently being tried out in several hospitals and clinics. The main difficulty with such an approach for practical purposes is the time that is consumed with a single case by several experts. There have been several time-saving suggestions and at least a few experiments in group-psychiatry or group-observation in which one or more experts assemble with a small group to encourage discussion or play. On the basis of the performances observed, case records may be built. *Alcoholics Anonymous* (1939) proposes the method of group cooperative therapy, without "experts" in the treatment of chronic cases, indicating that the mutual liquidations of ideas and tensions assist each person to unbend and hold to his purposes. Usually, however, this also involves the aid of religion.

Short Contacts.—Many investigators or practical case workers are faced with the necessity of short contact relationships, in which the expert has not the time for extended background studies, and will probably not remember the subject at another meeting. The employment and vocational experts are more likely to be in such a position than is the social case worker with a restricted case load. The necessity of strictly differential treatment is indicated in such short-time relationships by Robert Wilson (1936), a limited focusing of pertinent questions for a single purpose. One may raise the question: Can this type of brief investigation be a worthwhile case study? It may become little more than an interview in which one informs or preaches to the subject, guessing perhaps concerning his various attitudes and difficulties.

Personality Analysis or Therapy Through Case Reports.—The use of case records for personality analysis is relatively new, since most social or medical workers place their attention on the environment or on physical factors. The "anecdotal behavior record" described by Jarvis and Ellingson (1940) is an illustration of the broader use of such records in an educational institution to help the student develop properly and to point out his strongest inclinations. In the Rochester Mechanics Institute these authors have instituted such a journal for each student, made up of comments by teachers and administrators of employment. A behavior journal is assembled, including impressions from many individuals, used in a clinical conference concerning the student. The dynamic trends in the personality and the "personal frame of reference" are sought, frequently requiring the personnel office to go back to early incidents in the family or grammar school training. One student was described by several reporters as being crude and generally unpopular, largely because she asked too many questions. After she had been notified of this habit, her journal showed considerable change in the tone of comments about her.

The authors prefer the free type of casual report to more systematic ratings, largely because it is a more natural form. They feel, however, that it takes special instruction of teachers and cooperation for the best comments, also considerable skill in the interpretation of data for conference purposes or in dealing directly with the student.

An interesting question concerns the degree to which personality, in the narrow sense as contrasted with character, can be brought into a relatively objective case record. One is more likely to record what a person does than how he does it. Cautious investigators may have impressions of attitude, but may avoid giving such impressions. The attractiveness of a person, his emotional poise, the forcefulness of his expression may be ignored in favor of money earned, marks, speed, dress, and actual conversation or misbehavior.

Reliability of the Case Method.—Can the case history be made a reliable indicator of personality traits? In the sense that one can duplicate the exact sequence of events in several cases and find reliability correlations, this is of course impossible. However, there is a type of control which the case worker can attend to. Reviewing several cases resulting in the same general behavior—for example, inability to stick to a job or poor adjustment in college—one can usually run into a few common types of disturbance which convince one of the causes of the difficulty. One might call this backward control, as it must be made after the incidents are completed. It can be carelessly done, by lumping cases together representing varied types of difficulty. However, if cases are fully described, including all the details which were accessible to the observer, each type of case becomes a pattern with familiar elements so delineated that, in spite of some errors of interpretation, one has a fair chance of hitting a correct hypothesis. Take the case of Mike Romano, reported by Sayles (1932), similar to other cases studied by her and others. He was a continual nuisance in the school, driving his teachers crazy, and was repeatedly reported to the juvenile court for various misdemeanors until the visiting teacher discovered a craving in his life denied him by an irascible father. When the boy was furnished a violin and treated with reasonable kindness, he changed into a normal personality. The background and detailed aspects of the study, in this case as in others, are necessary to furnish the total pattern of conduct and bring it verisimilitude as a thoroughly convincing situation.

Lazarsfeld (1940) has suggested a quantification of case studies of personality by summarizing all items favorable (+1) and unfavorable (−1) into a total to be divided by the total number of items mentioned. This, he argues, results in getting away from the dichotomy of good or bad, and can be extended to cover more than one area or trait of personality, depending on the extent of case material available. He does not give reliable correlations for the personality indices, as estimated by different judges. Better still would be correlations between estimates of different summarizers of different case studies for the same people. It must be admitted, however, that reliability is the weakness of the case study device. Since the ordinary statistical devices for testing reliability (depending on duplication of very similar results) are lacking, the chief test is the truthful and complete unfolding of pertinent data.

Supplementary Uses of the Case Method.—The case study is largely a device for therapeutic treatment and individual analysis; it is as much related to art as to science, since one must be ever sensitive to relief and background without clear-cut formulas. It is more useful to be truthful and thorough in every sense than to use technical terminology or loose generalizations. As Lewin (1936) suggests, the case study can become the starting point for more accurate investigations. One observes unusual patterns of behavior in response to a particular sequence of stimuli, and on this basis may construct highly controlled situations for more careful analysis and generalization. Case studies may also be used to instruct others in making more careful observations. Allen (1933), following the earlier work of Brewer (1926), has used the case conference method in secondary school guidance. He advocates group discussion conferences, not merely to give keener insight into the problems of guidance, but also so that curricula and methods of instruction may be reviewed with an eye to modification. Williamson (1936) presented cases, similarly, before the guidance officers of the University of Minnesota faculty. Young (1938) has applied the case study method extensively in the analysis of reading disabilities.

The case method may be used, as in medicine, in connection with a course of treatment to study changes in personalities from time to time as related to various environmental factors (see Chapter 34 by Appel). It is also used to justify treatments that have been made. Many possibilities of error are attendant on this use, since one may interpret changes to fit his theory. The records of supposed schizophrenics who have been treated with metrazol or camphor are good illustrations: in one report, nearly all are reported to have been benefited; in another report, perhaps a little more carefully controlled, few more are permanently benefited by the treatment than by mere rest.

What Is a Valid Case Study?—Bristol (1936) and others have described the nature of useful and significant case work. Above all, it must be true, and truth can be attained more accurately by trained investigators who are taught to observe certain kinds of causes and behavior on the basis of searching questions. Objectivity is always preferred to opinions, a relating of incidents to conjecture about attitudes and possible behavior. Case work records will obviously vary tremendously in respect to length, according to the use made of them. Often brevity and specific relevance to a problem are to be preferred. There is a possible danger in wandering around in the early life of the patient to discover causes of unemployment, or other maladjustment, when it is really not the individual's fault or when the cause is quite recent. The case work study, to be valid, should make proposals and then follow up the individual for further diagnosis. Perhaps the best test of the value of a case study is the degree to which specific treatment helps the adjustment of the case.

Conclusion.—In conclusion it appears that most of the work done in the field of subjective evaluations of personality has been primarily with practical ends in view. Most of it is an attempt to estimate leadership or attractiveness, or other traits for purposes of hiring or promotion. No one has been particularly confident on the side of the high reliability of specific items, yet many would argue that the results are relatively valid. It appears that the personality of teachers may be more beneficially judged by their students than students by teachers. The value of recommendations, interview comments, and case studies depends mainly on the thoroughness, integrity, and capacity of the reporter or investigator. A consideration of the German methods of investigating leadership and the experiences reported by Murray raises the question: Have we not paid too little attention in this country to the judgment of capacity on the basis of numerous behaviors and attitudes or dispositions in critical situations? The judge should observe the individual in real situations; he should judge ability for a purpose; and he should be thoroughly motivated for careful reporting.

BIBLIOGRAPHY

ADAMS, H. F. 1930a. An objectivity-subjectivity ratio for scales of measurement. *J. soc. Psychol., 1,* 122–135.
—— 1936b. Validity, reliability and objectivity. *Psychol. Monogr., 47,* No. 2, 329–350.
ALCOHOLICS ANONYMOUS. 1939. New York: Works Pub.
ALLEN, R. D. 1933. Case-conference problems in group guidance. New York: Inor Pub.
ALLPORT, G. 1937. Personality, a psychological interpretation. New York: Holt.
—— 1942. The use of personal documents in psychological science. *Soc. Sci. Res. Coun. Bull.* No. 49.
American Council on Education. 1933. Measurement and guidance of college students. Baltimore: Williams & Wilkins.
ANDERSON, NELS. 1923. The hobo; the sociology of the homeless man. Chicago: University Chicago Press.

ANSBACHER, H. L. 1941. German military psychology. *Psychol. Bull., 38,* 370–392.

ASHER, E. J., & GRAY, E. 1940. The relation of personal history data to college success. *J. educ. Psychol., 31,* 517–526.

BERNE, E. V. 1930. An experimental investigation of social behavior patterns in young children. *Univ. Ia Stud. Child Welf., 4,* No. 2.

BINGHAM, W. E., & MOORE, B. V. 1941. How to interview. (Rev. ed.) New York: Harper.

BRADSHAW, F. F. 1930. Rating scale; its reliability, validity, and use. Washington, D. C.: American Council on Education.

BREWER, J. M., *et al.* 1926. Case studies in educational and vocational guidance. Boston: Ginn.

BRISTOL, C. 1936. Handbook on social case recording. Chicago: University Chicago Press.

BROGAN, W. 1930. The work of placement offices in teacher training institutions. *Teach. Coll. Contr. Educ.,* No. 434.

BRYAN, R. 1937. Pupil rating of secondary school teachers. *Teach. Coll. Contr. Educ.,* No. 708.

BURTT, H. E. 1926. Principles of employment psychology. New York: Houghton-Mifflin.

CATTELL, J. McK. 1910. American men of science. (Supplement.) Lancaster, Pa.: Science Press.

CAVAN, R. S. 1928. Suicide. Chicago: University Chicago Press.

CLARK, E. L. 1926. Value of student interviews. *J. Person. Res., 5,* 204–207.

DOLLARD, J. 1935. Criteria for the life-history. New Haven: Yale University Press.

DUDYCHA, G. J. 1936. An objective study of punctuality in relation to personality and achievement. *Arch. Psychol., N. Y.,* No. 204.

FREYD, M. 1923. The graphic rating scale. *J. educ. Psychol., 14,* 83–102.

GARRETT, H. E., & SCHNECK, M. R. 1933. Psychological test methods and results. New York: Harper.

GOLDSTEIN, J. 1938. Mechanism and psychoanalytic theory. *Amer. J. Orthopsychiat., 8,* 192–213.

GREENE, E. B. 1941a. Measurements of human behavior. Boston: Odyssey Press.

—— 1941b. Students' appraisal of a college course. *J. higher Educ., 12,* 365–370.

HOLLINGWORTH, H. L. 1923. Judging human character. New York: Appleton-Century.

HULL, C. L. 1928. Aptitude testing. New York: World Book.

HUNT, J. McV., & SOLOMON, R. L. 1942. The stability and some correlates of group status in a summer camp group of young boys. *Amer. J. Psychol., 55,* 33–45.

JARVIS, L. L., & ELLINGSON, M. 1940. A handbook on the anectodal behavior journal. Chicago: University Chicago Press.

JENNINGS, H. 1937. Structure of leadership-development and sphere of influence. *Sociometry, 1,* 99–143.

JONES, E. S., & SOUTHARD, H. F. 1937. Employment of college graduates. *Univ. Buffalo Stud., 15,* 1–24.

KNIGHT, F. B. 1922. Qualities related to success in teaching. *Teach. Coll. Contr. Educ.,* No. 120.

KORNHAUSER, A. W. 1927a. A comparison of raters. *Person. J., 5,* 338–344.

—— 1928b. A study of four reference report forms. *Person. J., 6,* 38–46.

KROUT, M. H. 1935. Autistic gestures; an experimental study in symbolic movement. *Psychol. Monogr., 46,* No. 4.

LANDIS, C., *et al.* 1940. Sex in development. New York: Harper.

LAZARSFELD, P. F., & ROBINSON, W. S. 1940. The quantification of case studies. *J. appl. Psychol., 24,* 817–825.

LESTER, O., & HEWLETT, T. 1928. Measuring introversion and extroversion. *Person. J., 6,* 352–360.

LEWIN, K. 1936. Principles of topological psychology. New York: McGraw-Hill.

MALINOWSKI, B. 1926. Crime and custom in savage society. New York: Harcourt, Brace.

MAY, M. A. 1932. The foundations of personality. In Achilles, P. S., *Psychology at work*. New York: McGraw-Hill. Ch. 4.

MOORE, H. 1939. Psychology for business and industry. New York: McGraw-Hill.

MORENO, J. L. 1934. Who shall survive? *Nerv. ment. Dis. Monogr.*, No. 58.

MURPHY, G., MURPHY, L. B., & NEWCOMB, T. M. 1937. Experimental social psychology. New York: Harper.

MURRAY, H. A. 1938. Explorations in personality. New York: Oxford University Press.

NEWCOMB, T. M. 1931. An experiment designed to test the validity of a rating technique. *J. educ. Psychol.*, *22*, 279–289.

NEWSTETTER, W. I., FELDSTEIN, M. H., & NEWCOMB, T. M. 1938. Group adjustment—a study in experimental sociology. Cleveland: Western Reserve Univ.

O'ROURKE, L. J. 1929. Measuring judgment and resourcefulness in selecting prohibition service investigators. *Person. J.*, *7*, 427–440.

PARTRIDGE, E. DEA. 1934. Leadership among adolescent boys. *Teach. Coll. Contr. Educ.*, No. 608.

PLANT, J. S. 1937. Personality and the culture pattern. New York: Commonwealth Fund.

REED, A. Y. 1935. The effective and ineffective college teacher. New York: American Book.

REMMERS, H. H. 1929. The college professor as the student sees him. *Stud higher Educ., Purdue Univ.*, No. 11.

——— 1939. Appraisal of college teaching through rating of student opinion. In *Yearb. nat. Soc. Coll. Teach. Educ.*

ROBINSON, V. P. 1936. Supervision in social case work. Durham, N. C.: University North Carolina Press.

RUGG, H. 1922a. Is the rating of human character practicable? *J. Person. Res.*, *13*, 30–42, 81–93.

——— 1921b. Is the rating of human character practicable? *J. Person. Res.*, *12*, 425–438.

SANDIFORD, P., CAMERON, M. A., CANWAY, C. B., & LONG, J. A. 1937. Forecasting teaching ability. *Bull. Dep. educ. Res., Ontario Coll. Educ.*, No. 8.

SAYLES, M. B. 1925. The problem child in the school. New York: Commonwealth Fund.

SCOTT, W. D., CLOTHIER, R., *et al.* 1941. Personnel management. New York: McGraw-Hill.

SEARS, R. R. 1936. Experimental studies of projection. *J. soc. Psychol.*, *7*, 151–163.

SHEFFIELD, A. E. 1937. Social insight in case situations. New York: Appleton-Century.

SIMONEIT, M. 1933. Wehrpsychologie: ein Abriss ihrer Probleme und politischen Folgerungen. Berlin: Bernard & Graefe.

SOMERS, G. T. 1923. Pedagogical prognosis. Predicting the success of prospective teachers. *Teach. Coll. Contr. Educ.*, No. 140.

SPIELMAY, W., & BURT, C. 1926. In *Rep. Industr. Fatigue Res. B.*, *33*, 57–72.

SYMONDS, P. 1925a. Notes on rating. *J. appl. Psychol.*, *9*, 188–195.

——— 1931b. Diagnosing personality and conduct. New York: Appleton-Century.

THOMAS, W. I., & ZNONIECKI, F. 1927. Polish peasant in Europe and America. New York: Knopf.

THORNDIKE, R. L. 1938. The effect of discussion upon the correctness of group decisions when the factor of majority influence is allowed for. *J. soc. Psychol.*, *9*, 343–362.

VERNON, P. E. 1933a. Some characteristics of the good judge of personality. *J. soc. Psychol.*, *4*, 42–57.

——— 1935b. Can the "total personality" be studied objectively? *Character & Pers.*, *4*, 1–10.

WALLER, W. W. 1938. The family. New York: Cordon.

WILLIAMSON, E. G., 1936. Faculty counseling at Minnesota. *Occupations*, *14*, 426–433.

WILLIAMSON, E. G., & DARLEY, J. G. 1937. Student personnel work. New York: McGraw-Hill.

WILSON, R. 1936. The differential approach in case work treatment. New York: Family Welfare Assn.
YOUNG, R. A. 1938. Case studies in reading disability. *Amer. J. Orthopsychiat.*, 8, 230–254.
ZELENY, L. D. 1940. Measurement of social status. *Amer. J. Sociol.*, 45, 576–582.

Chapter 5

PERSONALITY TESTS

By J. B. MALLER, Ph.D.

FOR THE PURPOSE of this chapter personality is defined as the integration of innate dispositions and acquired patterns of behavior (for discussions of the history of the concept of personality, see Chapter 1 by MacKinnon; and Allport, 1937). Personality tests are objective psychometric devices which purport to measure tendencies, habits and a variety of distinctive characteristics other than those of physique and intellectual capacity. The assessment of personality implies a field of psychological inquiry involving various measuring devices and a diversity of approaches, but not a task to be performed by a single instrument.

In this sense no single test can possibly be diagnostic of the total personality, just as no simple examination could be diagnostic of all aspects of a person's health. Furthermore, since personality is not merely the sum of a series of static elements but the resultant of dynamic forces in action, even a battery of tests of many isolated elements of personality would fail to yield a picture of the total personality as it functions.

To refer to any questionnaire or inventory as a test of personality (Tiegs, Clark and Thorpe, 1941) represents either a narrow concept of personality or a market appeal to the uninformed in their eternal quest for cure-alls. This is particularly true when the test in question is of the self-report variety.

Classification of Personality Tests.—Personality tests may be classified according to the type of test material (pencil and paper tests and performance tests, verbal and nonverbal tests), according to the manner of presentation (written or oral), or on the basis of the general testing situation (classroom activities and out-of-school conduct). The tests may be grouped according to the method of approach (direct questions or disguised situations), or they may be classified on the basis of the qualities to be measured (honesty, suggestibility, poise, etc.), or according to the purpose the tests are to serve (personnel selection, vocational guidance, educational orientation, or clinical use, particularly in work with cases of behavior disorders).

Because of the elusive nature of personality and the variety of meanings ascribed to the term, the classification of available personality tests is more in the nature of an expedient than a logical nonoverlapping system. In this chapter, personality tests will be considered under four broad categories:

1. Measures of character—including knowledge of social standards and behavior in accordance with such principles.
2. Measures of temperament and adjustment—including performance tests as well as self-descriptions of a person's mode of behaving and emotional balance.
3. Measures of attitudes, opinions, and interest-values, including direct and indirect measures.
4. Miscellaneous testing devices.

The first group of tests reveals a person's goodness in the light of tradition and ethical principles, while the second group reveals his tempo, his ways of doing things, his idiosyncrasies and adjustment in the light of norms and standards of mental health. The third group reveals a person's motives, ideals, aspirations, and hierarchy of values. The present chapter will not deal with rating scales, projective methods, and environmental factors which contribute to personality and its articulation.[1]

Historical Background.—Though relatively new in scope and application, the quantitative evaluation of personality dates back to the earliest attempts at psychometrics, even antedating mental measurement. The ancient systems of classification of personality types may be considered as forerunners of measurement. For example, people were classified on the basis of both the tempo and the intensity of their reactions. As a result of this cross-classification, four major types were considered: (1) the sanguine, those whose reactions are generally fast and mild; (2) the phlegmatic, whose reactions are slow and mild; (3) the choleric, reactions fast and intense; (4) melancholic, those whose reactions are slow and intense (Roback, 1927).

James's distinction between the tender minded and tough minded, Jung's classifications of introverts and extraverts, and similar grouping of persons on the basis of subjectivity-objectivity, ascendance-submission, domination-compliance, inferiority-superiority, expansion-reclusion, and the like are not unrelated to early references to fundamental types. However, any dichotomous classification of people must be taken as referring to extreme cases. Psychological inquiry has established rather conclusively that individual differences in regard to practically any

---

[1] Rating scales and other measures of reputation are discussed in Chapter 4 on Subjective Evaluations of Personality by E. S. Jones, while such approaches as the Rorschach test, which yields an inclusive record of personality, Murray's Thematic Apperception Test and related projective devices for the evaluation of personality are considered in Chapter 6 on Interpretation of Verbal and Imaginal Activity by R. W. White.

human attribute are in the nature of a gradual and continuous scale. Except for the early attempts at classification, personality tests are definitely a modern product. The great majority of personality tests have been devised within the last two decades.[2]

Personality Tests Compared with Intelligence Tests.—Because of the numerous elements common to all psychometric devices in regard to construction and application and because of the extensive experience of psychologists with tests of mental ability, an analysis of the differences between intelligence tests and personality tests as well as their similarities will throw additional light on the nature of both fields of measurement. The comparison might also serve as a guide in forecasting future development in personality measurement.

SIMILARITIES.—Personality and intelligence tests are similar in that both are based upon a limited number of responses which are considered as representative of broader areas of behavior and that several different types of samples (subtests) may be combined for more adequate measurement. In both instances the measures are objective, not based upon the subjective judgment of the examiner; the procedure of administering and scoring is prescribed and some norms, based upon preliminary testing of representative groups, are usually available. With some exceptions, both groups of tests consist of pencil-and-paper work or conduct in classroom situations.

DIFFERENCES.—The differences between measures of intelligence and personality are more numerous and more fundamental. Differences in constancy, growth, linearity, and reliability will be considered.

(a) *Constancy.* The general and specific factors which constitute intelligence are relatively stable. While subject to marked changes under unusually favorable or unfavorable conditions, mental abilities have been shown to remain fairly constant under ordinary conditions. The elements of personality, on the other hand, seem to be more explosive and more susceptible to outside influences. Relatively speaking, intelligence is more innate while personality is more acquired.

Furthermore, not only are the persons tested more constant in regard to intellectual qualities as compared with those of personality, but the very qualities of the former are more stable and fixed than those of the latter. The correctness of answers to questions of intelligence may be demonstrated in terms of principles of natural science and mathematics while the answers to questions of personality tests are based primarily upon social usage and values, and prevailing concepts of goodness and normality.

There seem to be also greater individual differences in the relative

---

[2] Two notable exceptions of tests which antedated the general movement of personality testing are measures of moral knowledge and the free association tests.

constancy of the elements of personality than is true of mental abilities. In other words, some personalities are reasonably stable, well integrated, showing little fluctuation from one situation to another. Other personalities are more explosive, varying radically from one extreme to another in regard to any given quality. Thus, the question "Can personality be measured?" may be changed to "Whose personality can be measured?" since stable personalities, at any level, could be measured more reliably than those of lesser stability.

(b) *Growth.* While practically all mental abilities show a fairly definite curve of growth from early infancy to maturity, no such definite trend of development is observable in regard to many aspects of personality. Even where a trend toward maturity is observable, it is not always continuous or consistent or parallel to physiological development. The average adult is more capable, more intelligent than the average child but not necessarily more honest, more cooperative or more courageous.

The concept of the ratio of mental age to chronological age, which is one of the most basic and useful contributions of psychometrics, has practically no counterpart in personality measurement. The expression *personality quotient* is definitely inconsistent with our present knowledge of the nature of personality.

The qualities of personality are themselves not continuous or linear. Courage beyond a certain point may become recklessness, extreme caution may be cowardice, etc. From the point of view of desirability, such qualities may be considered as curvilinear in nature. This may be contrasted with mental abilities which are generally continuous and linear.

Personality tests, as compared with intelligence tests, may thus be considered less reliable, since a person's score may show considerable variations from time to time; less valid, since the personality qualities themselves may change in meaning and desirability; and less universal because of the differences in the pattern of social values. While intelligence tests deal with capacities, personality tests are concerned with dispositions, ways of behaving or ways of appearing to other people.

Because of the superficial similarity between tests of intelligence and personality and the danger that those with inadequate psychological training might use the latter in the same routine manner as the former, psychologists should repeatedly point out the special nature of personality tests and their practical limitations.

In some instances, test makers have unwillingly overemphasized the similarity between the two types of tests. In one instance, *Personality Quotient* is the designation of a test and the distinction reported between "the well known IQ" and the newly devised PQ is that the former indicates "what a person knows about things and people" while the latter reveals "what a person does about things and people." As the test in question is a self-description inventory, what it reveals is merely what a person says he does in answer to a series of direct questions. Neither in subject matter nor in method of obtaining score is the comparison with IQ justified.

PERSONALITY AND EDUCATION.—It should be added that while the relative unreliability of personality tests may appear unfortunate to the psychometrician, the basic fact of the dynamic nature of personality and its modifiability should be a challenge to the psychologist and educator. The potentialities of changing personality in a desired direction are the very essence of social progress and human betterment. While the possibilities of changing a person's intellectual level are limited in scope and involve great difficulties, changes in character and personality are almost of unlimited scope and may be brought about with relatively little difficulty. Inconstancy, the psychometrician's nightmare, may be considered the educator's paradise.

Tests of Character

The most extensive research in the objective measurement of character qualities was conducted by the Character Education Inquiry under the direction of Hartshorne and May and a number of associates. The investigation, which included the construction and validation of a large number of testing devices, extended over a period of five years, 1924–1929, and the reports on moral knowledge, honesty, cooperation, persistence, inhibition, and the organization of character appeared during the period 1927–1930. Unless otherwise indicated, the tests described in the present section are those which were devised by the Character Education Inquiry (Hartshorne, May, *et al.*, 1928, 1929, 1930) or those which grew out of that series of studies.

Tests of Moral Knowledge.—The objective measurement of familiarity with social standards began with the earliest attempts as psychometrics. Sharp (1898) and Fernald (1912) devised and used objective instruments for studying the development of moral judgment. The Stanford Revision of the Binet-Simon Intelligence Test (Terman, 1917) includes the following questions: "What ought you to say when someone asks your opinion about a person whom you do not know very well? What is the thing for you to do when you have broken something which belongs to someone else? What's the thing for you to do if a playmate hits you without meaning to do it?" Woodrow (1926) prepared a series of pictures for testing moral judgment while Schwartz (1932) devised some pictorial presentations of social and ethical situations for use in psychiatric interviews.

The Character Education Inquiry (Hartshorne, May, *et al.*, 1928, 1929, 1930) has experimented with a number of tests of moral knowledge. The Good Citizenship Test consists of a series of 50 problems of social situations each followed by four solutions. The examinee is to indicate his choice as to the most sensible, helpful, and useful solution.

The Information Test includes a test of knowledge of words that have moral significance (including an ethical vocabulary) and a test of foresight of consequences. The Attitudes and Opinions Tests consist of questions on attitudes toward misconduct, preferences, generalizations about moral conduct, duties and principles.

Careful studies with measures of moral knowledge have revealed their limitation as character tests. The scores on such tests were found to show high correlations with intelligence and extremely low correlations with actual behavior.

According to Hartshorne and May (1930) the correlation between moral knowledge and intelligence for pupils of grades 5 to 8 was on an average +.70. This correlation is as high as the average intercorrelation among different tests of moral knowledge or different intelligence tests. On the other hand, the correlation between moral knowledge and scores on tests of honesty, cooperation, inhibition, and similar behavior tests is extremely low (about +.25).

Tests of social information and comprehension similar to those included in the Social Intelligence Test by Moss and others (Hunt, 1928) may be of some value. Although such information may correlate with tests of abstract intelligence, there is some evidence that these scores differentiate between different social groups.

The shortcomings of the tests of moral knowledge could probably be reduced by more rigorous methods of test construction. Only such items should be included which are uncorrelated with intelligence and correlated with behavior. Such tests might be based on problems of conflicting principles. Instead of dealing with differences between right and wrong these problems would be concerned with conflicts between right and right or those between wrong and wrong. The correctness of the answers might be determined on the basis of the opinion of competent judges.

Behavior Tests of Character.—From the social standpoint this is the most significant of all groups of character tests. Included are measures of honesty, cooperation, persistence, inhibition, and the like. Most of the tests involve situations which, though controlled to some extent by the examiner, are natural life situations, as far as the subject is concerned.

The validity of the conduct test is to a large extent self-evident. The real problem is that of reliability and consistency of behavior under varying circumstances. Interesting as it may be to have a record of a child's behavior in a specific situation, the record has test value only if such behavior is found related to behavior in similar situations.

TESTS OF HONESTY.—Voelker (1921) conducted the first extensive experiment in the objective measurement of honesty and trustworthiness based on prearranged situations. The Character Education Inquiry (Hartshorne, May, *et al.*, 1928) devised a great variety of test situations, involving opportunities for honest or deceptive behavior. Among the most significant methods of testing honesty were the following:

(a) *Double Testing Technique*. A test is given and the subjects are allowed to score their own papers by means of a key. They are told that they must not copy the answers from the key. They are retested later under controlled conditions by means of equivalent tests. A difference between the scores on the two tests indicates that the examinee copied the answers from the key when he was entrusted with it to score his paper. Similarly the children are given a test to take home and to complete without accepting help. An equivalent test is given subsequently in the classroom. The difference in score indicates the extent to which the child did accept help at home.

(b) *Improbable Achievement Technique*. The subjects are presented with such difficult tasks as tracing complicated mazes with their eyes shut. Success on this test, which under careful control was found to be extremely difficult, indicates that the examinee did not comply with the directions and thus accepted credit unfairly.

(c) *Impossible Achievement Technique*. This consists of a test and a key which the examinees are to use to score their own papers. Some of the questions are of such nature that the examinees could not possibly have known the correct answers (some answers are actually fictitious). The number of such difficult questions answered is evidence of misusing the key. To avoid undue motivation to copy from the key, the tests usually include also a number of easy questions which are not considered in the honesty score. This method has been used in the Self-Marking Test (Maller, 1930).

(d) *Money Test*. Each member of the group to be tested is given a "game" involving the arrangement of a large number of coins in a certain pattern. Upon completion, the boxes including the coins are to be placed in a common cupboard. By means of an inconspicuous identification symbol, a record is secured of the coins retained by subject.

TESTS OF COOPERATION.—Five tests of cooperation and helpfulness were devised and used by the Character Education Inquiry (Hartshorne, May, *et al.*, 1929) :

(a) *The Self-group Test*. This test measures the degree of efficiency at which children work when engaged in a group project as compared with work under personal incentives. A contest of speed in simple additions is arranged between two groups. The children are told not to write their names on their papers, but to write the names of the respective groups, such as 7A, 8B, etc. The only incentive to work is evidently the desire to help one's group attain a high average score. On another set of material the children are to write their names and to work for themselves. Prizes are promised to those making high scores on the latter test material. This work for self and group is alternated several times. The difference in speed between work for self and for group was found to be a reliable and consistent measure of cooperativeness. Sixty-five per cent of the children tested worked faster under personal motivation than under group motivation, with considerable variation in the degree of cooperativeness.

(b) *The Free Choice Test.* This is part of the Self-group Test. On this test children are given an opportunity to contribute part of their work units toward the group score or to have this work count toward their own personal scores. The scores on these tests varied from zero, where a child took all units for himself, to 100%, where a child contributed all of his work to the group. The average child took 74% of the work for himself, and gave 26% of the work to the group (Maller, 1929).

(c) *A Vote Test.* In connection with the previously described tests, each classroom was promised a prize if it were to attain high standing in the contest. Before the prize was given the children of each classroom were given an opportunity to vote as to how the prize, if won, was to be disposed of. The alternatives were:

(1) Give all the money to the boy or girl scoring highest in the test.
(2) Buy something for our school, such as bats, balls, skipping ropes, or a picture.
(3) Buy something for the classroom, such as a picture, a globe of goldfish, a plant.
(4) Divide the money equally among the members of the class.
(5) Buy something for some hospital child or some family needing help, or some other philanthropy.

The five votes were ranked by a number of educators according to the degree of social-mindedness involved.

(d) *The Contribution Test.* Kits containing ten school articles each, such as drinking cup, pencil sharpener, and the like were given to each member of the class as a present from a friend of the school. An appeal was then made to send some of those articles to poor children who do not possess them. Each child was given the opportunity to give away in an inconspicuous manner any part, all, or none of the articles received. The amount given was identified without the child's knowledge.

(e) *The Helpfulness Test.* A letter was read to the class in which an appeal was made for pictures and jokes which were to be put in booklets for children in hospitals. Four envelopes were provided for each child for the collection of jokes, puzzles, stories, and pictures. The children were allowed ten days to bring in their contributions, during which period the teacher mentioned the matter three times. The great variety of things handed in were given score values from which a score of helpfulness was obtained.

INHIBITION TESTS.—Among these were several tests of distraction. One of these consisted of a series of tests of simple additions dispersed among numerous pictures and puzzles. The degree of distraction was measured by the decrease in speed. During another test, little boxes of candy were placed on the desk of each child at the beginning of an arithmetic test, but the directions were not to partake of the sweets before the completion of the test. The scores of several inhibition tests were combined into one composite (Hartshorne and May, 1929). Several measures of inhibition were employed by Crane (1923) in his study of race differences in this factor.

PERSISTENCE TESTS.—One measure of persistence was based on the level of speed when working for an hour at the monotonous task of simple additions.[3] Another test involved the reading of a story printed in run-in type, requiring a great deal of attention and effort. The child was allowed to stop work at will and the score was the length of time voluntarily devoted to this task. Similar measures involved the length of time devoted to attempts at solving a difficult puzzle (Hartshorne, May, et al., 1929).

Analysis of Character Test Scores.—

INTERCORRELATIONS.—The correlations among the four groups of character tests were obtained. These correlations reveal two significant facts concerning the relationship between different phases of character (see also Chapter 1 by MacKinnon). All the correlations are positive. Apparently such aspects of character as honesty, cooperation, inhibition, and persistence seem to go together to some extent. There was no evidence of negative relationships among character qualities.

The second observation is the consistently low magnitude of the correlations (average about .24). Correlations between different tests of the same character quality, though higher than the correlations between composite scores of different character qualities, were generally low, considerably lower than the correlations usually found among different measures of intelligence or educational skills. Apparently the various measures of a character quality contribute to the composite score without duplicating one another, and none of the elements could be eliminated without affecting the composite score. The short-cuts and brief tests so useful in intelligence tests do not apply to character measurement. To secure character scores of some value, one has to conduct an extensive testing program. In character education, the specific elements entering into any given quality require special attention, since these elements do not seem to be highly correlated with one another (Hartshorne and May, 1930).

---

[3] Persistence is one of those qualities which according to our method of classification might be grouped under character, e.g., persistence in a task of cooperation, or under personality. References to other persistence tests will therefore be found in a later section.

Application of factor analysis to those correlations reveals a pattern similar to that found among intercorrelations of mental tests. There is evidence of the existence of one factor common to these four phases of character (Maller, 1934). A score on each of the tests may be looked upon as composed of one element common to the responses to all the tests, plus a specific element varying from test to test.

RELATION TO INTELLIGENCE.—The scores on the above character tests were also correlated with measures of mental ability. Analysis of the resulting correlations indicates that the factor common to these behavior tests can in no way be identified with general intelligence. What, then, is this factor common to honesty, cooperation, persistence, and inhibition?

An examination of the situations constituting the four groups of character tests reveals that each of them involves some form of conflict between interests. In each case the "right" response, as scored by those who constructed the test, requires the subordination of the immediate interest to one that is remote but superior in nature. In the honesty tests there is the conflict between the desire to excel and the general gain resulting from fair play. The tests of cooperation involve a conflict between personal and social interests. In the tests of persistence and inhibition the conflict between the immediate stimulus and the remote goal is quite clear.

We may therefore say that the factor common to the various character tests, which may be referred to as factor C, is the readiness to forego an immediate gain for the sake of a remote but greater gain. The latter may be remote in time and greater in the sense of leading to other gains of greater magnitude, or it may be remote in being social rather than personal and greater in the sense of affecting a greater number of individuals.

The value of the general factor, common to these aspects of character, is seriously affected by the low magnitude of the intercorrelations. Though the general factor exists, it accounts for only a small segment of the total area of the character qualities measured, with specific elements constituting the major segments of those qualities. This, however, is partly due to the imperfection of the tests in their experimental forms. In other words, the so-called specificity of character elements is more apparent than real, being partly the result of errors of measurement. It is likely that in the light of the results of these tests other attempts will be made toward the construction of character tests of greater reliability and of more definite validity.

Tests of Temperament

The essential elements in temperament include characteristic moods and their changes, the tempo of reactions and movements, the integration of abilities and the person's relation to others. There are two basic approaches to the measurement of temperament: the observation of representative samples of behavior, and the person's replies to questions regarding his behavior in such situations. The first approach involves measures of actual conduct: speed and persistence of work; tasks revealing the degree of mental inertia; records of association of ideas; acts involving relations with other people; and conduct revealing caution, imagination, suggestibility, conflicts, and various aspects of emotional disturbance. The tests in this group are in the nature of prearranged, standardized situations in which the person's behavior is revealed and recorded.

The second method, obviously a substitute for actual behavior, is based upon a series of questions or described situations to which the subject indicates his responses.

To illustrate the two approaches: in order to measure a person's relative persistence in routine work, we may either give him a fairly monotonous task, such as simple additions, keep a record of work done during successive periods and thus secure a measure of persistence (Hartshorne and May, 1929); or we may have him answer such questions as "Do you tire easily in doing routine work?" "Do you usually stick to a monotonous task until you finish it?"

The two approaches are somewhat similar to the two major groups of character tests, those of moral behavior and those of knowledge thereof. In character, the behavioral tests are more valuable because social action is generally more significant than social knowledge; a person's statement as to what ought to be done or what he would do does not necessarily correspond to actual behavior. Similarly, in temperament the qualities which reveal themselves in actual behavior are of greater importance, since they may not be revealed in a person's testimony regarding his behavior in hypothetical situations. A person may not know his reactions, or he may wish to hide them. In the measurement of temperament, it is the psychologist's dilemma to choose between the standardized questionnaire which is broad in scope but of doubtful validity and the performance record which is obviously valid but of narrow scope.

Performance Tests of Temperament and Adjustment.—

THE WILL-TEMPERAMENT TEST devised by Downey (1923) was among the earliest of these objective tests. It constituted a new approach and for several years the test was considered of great promise.

By means of handwriting tasks the following factors are supposedly measured:

Speed of decision—the time taken for a series of brief self-ratings;
freedom from load—based on the speed of work under various degrees

of motivation; writing name at retarded speed; memory test; coordination of impulses; speed of movement; motor inhibition; volitional perseveration; interest in detail; motor impulsion; self-confidence; noncompliance; finality of judgment.

Two forms for use individually and as a group test are available. Ream's (1922a) adaptation of the test in abbreviated form employs a time limit measuring work done, instead of measuring the time taken for the completion of certain tasks. Richardson (1929) adapted the test for use in British schools. A nonlanguage modification of the test utilizing designs, drawings and pictures in place of handwriting was devised by Uhrbrock and Downey (1927).

It is interesting to note that though the Will-Temperament Test was applied extensively in numerous psychological studies in the United States and abroad, the instrument is now in complete disuse. In spite of its basic merits, the indiscriminate use of the test, the exorbitant claims and the resulting contradictory findings have completely discredited the instrument.

THE CROSS-OUT TEST.—Pressey's (1921) X-0 Test for investigating the emotions consists of a long list of words related to fear, suspicion, hypochondria, sex, complexes, offenses, etc. The subject is asked to cross out the words which are distasteful. The original form was devised more than two decades ago. Lundholm's Emotional Cross-Out Test is similar in character. It consists of 292 words and the subject is instructed to indicate after each word whether it suggests something pleasant, unpleasant or indifferent. Stagner (1940) has examined the possibilities of using the cross-out method in the analysis of public opinion.

The Presseys (1933) designed an Interest Attitude Test for the measurement of the maturity of interest. These include 90 items grouped in four subtests: things thought wrong, things worried about, things interested in and traits admired. The directions call for single and double checking of the items according to the intensity of feeling. Tendler's (1930) test of emotional stability consists of statements to be completed, i.e., "I get angry when . . ."

ASSOCIATION TESTS.—Jung's test of free association for the analysis of emotional complexes appeared in 1905. Standardized revisions were constructed by Kent and Rosanoff (1910). A similar list of key words for the analysis of free associations was prepared by Woodworth and Wells (1911). Schemes have been devised for scoring the responses on the basis of unusual associations as well as those revealing excessive fear, guilt, anxiety, and other factors. Crosland (1929) discussed the use of word associations as tests of deception and Fauquier (1939) used free association tests for measuring delinquent tendencies. Goodenough

(1942) has studied the application of free association in personality testing.

Tendler (1933) prepared a comprehensive analysis of the responses to the Kent-Rosanoff list. He suggests that associations of contrast, superordination and coordination are indicative of maturity, while associations of contiguity or noun-adjective relations are juvenile in character. Lorge and Thorndike (1941) found that responses in a free association test are of little value as indicators of personal traits.

On the basis of the findings of Johnson O'Connor (1928), Kent and Rosanoff (1927), and other reports of free association studies, the writer devised a Controlled Association Test (Maller, 1936b). Each key word is followed by a pair of words which represent a normal and an "abnormal" association. The subject is to indicate in each line the word which he considers more closely associated with the key word. The test was found to differentiate between a group of psychiatric patients and a comparable group of normal adults.

PERSEVERATION TESTS.—These tests measure mental inertia, sometimes referred to as secondary function, the tendency of mental processes to lag. This perseverative tendency is not to be confused with perseverance. The latter implies voluntary control of attention while perseveration is involuntary. Perseveration was first experimentally studied by Heymans and Wiersma (1906). Spearman (1927) and other British psychologists including Stephenson (1935), Lankes (1915), Pinard (1932), Cattell (1935), Wynn Jones (1929) have analyzed the manifestations of *perseveration* and its opposite, *oscillation*, and have devised tests for their measurement. Perseveration is usually measured by the reduction in speed and accuracy of work as a result of the shifting of attention from one task to another. In this country, several types of perseveration material have been employed in various studies. Biesheuvel (1938) suggested that individual differences in the threshold of flicker may be taken as a measure of perseveration since perseverators were found to have a significantly lower threshold for flicker than nonperseverators.

Maller and Elkin (1933) have standardized a test of perseveration based on three simple functions, each including two similar tasks: simple additions and subtractions, writing small and capital letters, and drawing horizontal and vertical lines. The subject's basic speed in each function is first obtained and the subsequent directions call for several types of alternating from one task to another. The reduction in efficiency resulting from alternations is taken as a measure of mental inertia or perseveration.

PERSISTENCE.—The extent to which subjects will continue working on given tasks has been measured by Crutcher (1934), by Clark (1935), by Cushing (1929), who called it a test of perseverative tendency, and by Decroly and Wauthier (1929). Morgan and Hull (1920) devised a measure of intellectual persistence in problem solving and Howells (1933) constructed a dynamometer device for measuring the ability to overcome fatigue. The Character Education Inquiry developed a series of behavior tests involving persistence in reading, problem solving, and routine work. Thornton (1939) applied the method of factor analysis to the results of a number of persistence tests. The validity of a series of persistence tests has been examined by Rethlingshafer (1940), who found that a test based upon meaningless material differentiated between normal and subnormal groups.

SUGGESTIBILITY.—Binet (1900) devised five tests of the judgment controlling type. These consisted of verbal suggestions aiming to influence a person's judgment regarding differences in weight, length of lines, and arrangement of material. Otis (1924) designed a Direction Test for measuring the effect of direct and indirect suggestions upon young children. For example, pointing to an ordinary ink blot the examiner asks the child whether the blot looks like a cat. An affirmative reply is taken as indicative of suggestibility. The tests designed by Avelling and Hargreaves (1921) include: illusion of warmth, progressive weights and lines, fidelity of report, suggestion of line length, contradictory suggestions, etc. Brown's (1916) tests include the suggestion of electric shock, least perceptible odors, change of brightness, size and pitch, recognition of form, memory for size and pictures, size-weight illusion, expressions of preference and interpretation of ink blots. White (1931) studied the effect of suggestion upon the interpretation of ink blots and Hull (1929) described objective methods of studying waking suggestions.

THE MAZE TEST.—The Porteus Maze (Porteus and Babcock, 1926) has been used by the author and others for the purpose of measuring impulsiveness, persistence, and suggestibility (Poull and Montgomery, 1929). Ball's (1929) test of emotional stability is based on the manner of learning a relief finger maze. The emotionally unstable were found to show an irregular learning curve. Snow (1926) designed a test of caution based on the subject's ability to trace with a stylus through a groove without touching the sides. Every contact with the metal sides closes the circuit and thus registers the subject's carelessness. The self-administrative maze of Wechsler (1926) has also been designed to measure impulsive or reckless tendencies.[4]

MISCELLANEOUS TESTS.—Burtt and Frey (1934) have suggested the use of laboratory situations for the measurement of recklessness. These

---

[4] An example of an approach to the study of temperament which for a while was held of great promise and later fell into disuse is that of the psychogalvanic reflex. In a review of that field, Landis mentions 247 titles of studies published between 1929 and 1932.

situations are based on such tasks as filling graduate containers to a designated level, balancing copper discs, the handling of Bunsen burners and the like. O'Rourke (1929) considered the measurement of resourcefulness and judgment. From indications of changes in visual and auditory thresholds during reverie, Travis (1926) arrived at a measure of introversion-extraversion. The apparatus included a tone generator, a key and buzzer circuit and a crystal to serve as an aid to imagination.

Performance in throwing darts at a target was used by Hausmann (1933) for the measurement of individual differences in psychobiological reactions to success and failure. Hoffman (1923) suggested a measure of self-assertion based on the subject's self-estimate on certain abilities compared with actual tests in those abilities, while Trow (1923) arrived at a measure of self-confidence based on the subject's expressed confidence in his performance on tests of length and weight discrimination, memory, educational achievement, and other tests. The subject indicates on a scale the degree of confidence in the correctness of his responses in the various tasks.

Luria's devices of combining the association technique with a measure of reaction time was employed by Runkel (1936) in measuring deception. Autonomic behavior in relation to personality has been studied by Darling (1940). Ratings on alertness, excitability, inhibition, ability to sustain attention, etc., were found related to pulse rate, blood pressure, galvanic skin resistance and the like.

The value of records of expressive movement for the measurement of personality has been examined by Allport and Vernon (1933) and the relation between certain expressive movements and feelings of dominance was studied by Eisenberg (1937). Expressive movements included handwriting, drawing, voice, gestures, gait, speed of work, and the like. He found some positive relationship between dominance scores on a self-description inventory and speed of work, talkativeness and other behavior involving expressive movement.

WORK ANALYSIS.—Extensive studies in the analysis of work patterns for the measurement of general qualities have been conducted by a number of German psychologists. Henning (1929) devised a series of partnership tests. The apparatus is so arranged that the work of each partner in a joint task is automatically recorded without the knowledge of the subjects. In some phases, the work of one partner is arranged to interfere with that of the other. Measures of initiative and dominance are obtained. Other situations are arranged to yield also an objective measure of honesty.

Kunze (1931) devised similar work situations for the measurement of cooperation, and related aspects of team work, and Luithlen (1931) experimented with work samples for the testing of initiative, leadership, persistence, dominance, imagination, and suggestibility.

Simoneit (1933, 1937) described the use of work analysis, tests and controlled observations in the selection of army officers and candidates for officers' training schools. Ansbacher (1941) has pointed out a number of striking similarities between the methods described by Simoneit and those developed by Murray (1938) in the study of personality. He lists five primary features common to both approaches in the study of the whole personality: (1) The rate and mode of learning a sensori-motor task, yielding symptoms of insecurity, introversion and emotionality. (2) Projective material including the interpretation of pictures of dramatic events. (3) Observations of attitude and conduct in situations of success, failure and frustration. (4) Conference of judges, initial impression and observation of gestures and behavior. (5) Autobiography, including complete life history and significant items of family relations.

The relative strength of incentive as revealed in work done under several types of motivation was measured in the Character Education Inquiry. Performance on jig-saw puzzles was employed by Vernon (1929) in a series of temperament tests while Cattell (1941) has experimented with a new approach to the measurement of temperament.

Self-Description Tests of Temperament.—In medical practice, a diagnosis is usually based upon overt symptoms supplemented by information given by the patient in reply to the doctor's questions. It is not surprising that in the study of behavior disorders and in the attempts to diagnose personality maladjustment the psychologist resorts to interrogating the subject on a variety of intimate questions. Questionnaires of such nature are often called personality inventories or psychoneurotic inventories.

In psychological and psychiatric literature numerous symptoms and expressions of personality disturbances are described. The questionnaires generally consist of a large number of questions regarding such symptoms and the subject is asked to indicate whether or not he has each of the symptoms mentioned. The questions range from those of a fairly factual nature, such as suffering from dizzy spells, or insomnia, or seeing black spots before one's eyes, to vague personal questions, such as whether the person is "glad to be alive," whether he considers himself peculiar or unlucky and the like.

Woodworth's (1917) Personal Data Sheet, the first applied inventory of symptoms of maladjustment, was devised during the First World War. It was constructed for the purpose of aiding in the selection of emotionally stable recruits for duty in the American Expeditionary Force. This inventory consisted of 200 neurotic symptoms found in the case histories of psychiatric patients.

In the early inventories the items were all phrased in the negative direction and were not grouped into categories. The score was simply the number of questions answered in the affirmative.

Bell's Adjustment Inventory (1934) and Maller's Character Sketches (1932) are among the tests in which questions are grouped into several subcategories dealing with more specific aspects of maladjustment. In Bernreuter's Personality Inventory (1933) several different scoring keys are provided which assign different weights to the various questions and thus yield scores for neurotic tendency, self-sufficiency, introversion-extraversion, and dominance-submission.

What the numerous inventories purport to measure can be seen from the names of tests and subtests. These include: mental health, personal adjustment, home adjustment, health adjustment, social adjustment, emotional adjustment, self-control, social initiative, self-sufficiency, self-determination, self-esteem, ascendance-submission, dominance-submission, cheerfulness-depression, introversion-extraversion, social introversion, depression-elation, cycloid tendency, neurotic tendency, mental instability, withdrawal attitude, personal inferiority, social inferiority, emotional maturity, happiness, anxiety, fears, frustrations, and many others.

EXTRAVERSION-INTROVERSION TESTS.—During the late Twenties there appeared a veritable outbreak of tests for measuring extraversion-introversion. These included inventories by Gilliland and Morgan (1931), Laird (1925), Marston (1924), MacNitt (1930), Neymann and Kohlstedt (1929), Root (1931), Whitman (1929), and many others. In a review of the subject, Guilford (1934) listed 115 reports of studies. Soon, however, those fell out of favor with psychologists, though now and then new inventories are devised for measuring this factor (Evans and McConnell, 1941). The trend seems to be in the direction of a comprehensive inventory or an omnibus of several groups of items pertaining to various aspects of temperament and adjustment.

GENERAL INVENTORIES.—The inventory of Humm and Wadsworth (1934) is based upon Rosanoff's theory of personality (1927). The scores are analyzed into five categories: normal, hysteroid, cycloid, schizoid, and epileptoid. This inventory has been used in very large numbers by several industrial concerns with some evidence of value in personnel selection and classification. Willoughby (1934) has constructed a brief inventory composed of the best 25 items of the Thurstone Schedule (1930).

Brown (1935) adopted an inventory for use with children age 9 to 14. It is very doubtful whether children of the Fourth Grade would comprehend the meaning of a number of items in that inventory. Rogers' (1931) test of adjustment is composed of few but apparently significant questions, based upon experience in a child guidance clinic. In Thompson's (1934) Personal History the items are arranged to form a continuous scale.

RESTRICTED INVENTORIES.—Questionnaires of more restricted phases of temperament include an inventory of items typical of schizophrenic behavior by Page (1934), self-estimate of happiness by Watson (1930), symptoms of mental instability by Ingle (1934), items dealing with persistence by Wang (1932), Cason's (1930) list of common annoyances, questions on depression-elation by Jasper (1930), items on negative or withdrawal attitudes by Lecky (Pallister, 1933), the psychosomatic inventory by McFarland and Seitz (1938), inventories for measuring inferiority feeling by Smith (1932) and by White and Fenton (1932), Maslow's (1940) test of dominance, and others.

RELIABILITY OF SELF-DESCRIPTION TESTS.—The statistical reliability of such instruments is usually determined on the basis of the correlation between odd and even items (split-half technique). These correlations are generally quite high and match the reliabilities of intelligence tests. The correlations between test and retest scores, a more dependable expression of reliability, is generally lower, indicating that while a person's responses to the various items of such a test are fairly consistent at any given time, they may fluctuate considerably from one period to another. The stability of adjustment scores on test and retest was studied by Van Wagenen (1935) and McNamara and Darley (1938).

VALIDITY.—The validity of self-description tests is usually determined on the basis of internal consistency—the correlation between individual items and the total score—or on correlations with other tests. In a few instances, however, the selection of items was based upon an outside criterion. Two extreme groups are selected on the basis of the factor which the test purports to measure and the answers to each item prevailing in the two divergent groups are compared. The items which differentiate the two groups are included in the test.

ADVANTAGES.—These tests are easily constructed, perhaps too easily, and they include a variety of personality characteristics. They are useful in classroom discussions of the nature of personality and its measurement, in the psychological clinic, if used by a competent psychologist, and as instruments of research for the study of central tendencies in personality and its component elements. They are conveniently administered to individuals and groups, easily scored and tabulated, and the results are readily subjected to statistical analysis.

LIMITATIONS.—Because of the mechanical simplicity, the inventory lends itself to indiscriminate use. Many of the questions are too complex to be answered by *yes* or *no*, and probably differ in meaning to different individuals. Furthermore, people are generally annoyed by personal questions and, in some instances, would be unable to answer such questions in any dependable manner (Spencer, 1938b). Since the answers can be faked by the examinee, the score can be made to vary at will from one extreme to another (Kelly, Cox and Terman, 1936). When applied in personnel selection or in admission to schools or when used by persons with inadequate psychological training, these tests are apt to do more harm than good. The results are dependent upon conditions under which the test is given, and it is rare that these are comparable to the conditions prevailing during the process of standardization.

Some of the most widely used tests have been constructed as by-products of teaching psychology. College students constitute a readily available group of willing subjects for the try-out of test material, and projects of test construction are easily integrated with advanced courses in psychology and psychometrics. The adverse effect of this situation upon the general applicability of such tests is obvious. Not only are college students a highly selected group, but the classroom situation and the prevailing attitude toward examinations are factors which should be considered before such tests are used with other age groups or in out-of-school situations.

Some techniques have been devised for detecting any attempts at faking answers to self-description questions, but no dependable method for correcting the scores is feasible, since the errors will vary with the situation, the person tested, and the type of question. In some aspects of personality there is a tendency to understate the number of symptoms of maladjustment while in other aspects the reverse holds true. Allport (1942) found, for example, that people tend to rate themselves as more introverted and more emotional than would appear from objective records.

The danger of indiscriminate usage has been sensed by the authors of some self-description tests. Thus in the Manual of Allport's Scale for Measuring Ascendance-Submission, it is urged that the test "be used primarily as a basis of future research in the measurement of personality rather than as a hard and fast criterion for social guidance." This contrasts with the claim by Beckman (1933) that his revision of Allport's test "may serve as a criterion for the selection of candidates for promotion or of applicants for executive and supervisory positions."

An example of inadequate precaution is found in Bell's Adjustment Inventory (1934) which claims to yield scores of home adjustment, health adjustment, social adjustment and emotional adjustment. In addition to the ambiguity of the four aspects of adjustment, the announcement regarding the test states bluntly "that no special training is necessary to administer or score the inventory or to interpret the results" and that the test is "designed primarily as a clinical tool rather than as a research instrument." In spite of its claim as a standardized test with recommended norms, the instructions in the Manual indicate that when examinees inquire about the purpose of the test "they should be answered frankly and honestly." No indication is given as to what such frank and honest answers might be. Surely, on a test where the subject may vary the answers at will, differences in the statement regarding the purpose of the test will destroy the comparability of obtained scores with any suggested "norms." In a special study of the attitude of subjects in personality testing, Vernon (1934) concluded that the true purpose of such tests should not be revealed to the subjects tested.

Bernreuter's Personality Inventory (1933) is another illustration of the intrinsic shortcomings of self-description as a means of personality measurement. Though based on previous tests—including 50 items from Thurstone's Schedule (1930) and 31 items from Allport's A-S Reaction Study (1928)—and processed by painstaking statistical methods, the test has failed to demonstrate its validity in any conclusive manner. Available evidence does not justify the claim that "the scales give highly reliable measures of the following traits: neurotic tendency; self-sufficiency; introversion-extraversion and dominance-submission." The extremely high correlation between the neurotic tendency score and the introversion score shows that they measure one and the same variable. Instead of saving time, the examiner wastes time in scoring the same test twice. The correlations with other self-description tests are spurious because of the large number of items common to those tests. In spite of its wide distribution—Super (1942) lists some 135 studies in which this inventory was used—this test has yielded contradictory claims and no convincing evidence of validity (Lorge, 1935; Landis, Zubin and Katz, 1935).

Some attempts have been made toward reducing the dependence upon the subject's cooperation (Adams, 1941), and eliminating the weaknesses inherent in the self-description approach. Instead of wording the statements as direct questions beginning with "Do you . . . ?" "Are you . . . ?" impersonal descriptive statements are presented and the subject is asked to indicate whether he is the same or different. Instead of requesting the subject to write his name, age, etc., before beginning the test, these questions are given at the end of the test in the hope of reducing a person's self-consciousness (Olson, 1936). These variations have been introduced in the writer's Character Sketches (1932). The variations also include a series of questions which aim to gauge a person's "readiness to confide" and willingness to talk to others about his personal affairs. It was thought that these items might give an additional clue to the interpretation of responses in the main parts of the test. A very high adjustment score accompanied by definite indication of unwillingness to confide would thus be considered as practically useless.

Another innovation was to put the various items of the Character Sketches on separate cards and ask the subject to sort out the cards into two sets—those in which he is the same and those in which he is different. Since there is some resistance to leaving a written record of one's shortcomings, it was thought that the process of card sorting would reduce that resistance and thus yield a more accurate record. This device, which is intended for use as an individual test, is called Personality Sketches (Maller, 1935). Rosenzweig (1938) has suggested a basis for other improvements in personality tests.

The two main shortcomings of the self-description approach are the susceptibility to faking under various degrees of motivation and the uncertainty of the meaning implied in both the questions and the answers

(Benton, 1935). Thus a soldier who wishes to simulate shell shock will readily achieve it by answering all questions in the direction of instability. A negative reply to such a question as "Are you troubled by shyness?" may imply that the person does not consider himself shy or that he is generally shy but not troubled by that condition. Similarly, a positive answer to the question "Do you consider yourself the dullest pupil in your class?" may be a sign of inferiority feeling if given by a pupil who is average or better in his class. But it has different meaning if given by a youngster who actually is the dullest in his class. In the latter case the affirmative answer is probably indicative of a willingness to face reality, a symptom of emotional stability. In a similar vein, an affirmative answer to the question "Are you usually even-tempered?" may imply that the person is consistently good humored or consistently ill-tempered.

The late Dr. Kuhlman has aptly summarized the weakness and dangers of the personality inventory from the point of view of sound psychology:

> In the personality inventory one may be asked to report reliably— or at least report—in a brief half-hour how he feels about his employer, when for years he has not been able to make up his mind about it; what his state of health is, although with the assistance of many physicians he has not to date been able to find out; what in all the world he would like most of all to do, when his actual experience is limited perhaps to half a dozen of the thousands of things there are to do in the world in any one of which he might have his chief interest if he had had the experience necessary to find out (from *Our Changing Fashions in Methods of Research,* a paper read before the Minnesota Chapter of Psi Chi, March 20, 1941).

The indictment applies to practically all self-description tests and questionnaires purporting to measure adjustment and other aspects of personality. Those devices often constitute a path of least resistance, a striving to substitute mechanical devices for psychological insight, the eternal quest for a simple short cut to the solving of complex human problems.

Tests of Attitudes and Interests

In some classifications of personality tests, measures of attitudes and opinion are grouped with character tests, while measures of interest and values are classified with temperament tests. However, the nature of available measures of these factors, their similarity in form and conduct, and the fact that they are not concerned with either knowledge or actual conduct justify their grouping into a special category.

Tests of Attitude and Opinion.—These tests include measures of opinion on national and international problems, attitudes toward institutions, groups, and various controversial issues. The scores on these attitude scales do not show as consistent a relationship with intelligence as do moral knowledge tests. However, the great number of tests in this field are subject to the basic inadequacies of all verbal responses. The overt expression on such tests may not at all correspond to the person's true opinion and attitude. Though showing high reliability coefficients, the tests lack validity. A person may be consistent in his replies, yet be unwilling or unable to reveal his true attitudes.

Furthermore, there is no conclusive evidence that these opinions and attitudes are stable and constant. The reliability of the tests is usually based upon the correlation between odd and even items or between test and immediate retest. When the interval between the test and retest is increased the correlation usually decreases. It is also likely that there are individual differences in the degree of constancy and stability of attitudes. Studies in integration of some phases of character (Hartshorne, May, *et al.*, 1930) tend to support this supposition. These shortcomings were particularly marked in the early forms of attitude scales where the subject was to indicate his choice of a number of well-differentiated formulations of attitudes.

An outstanding contribution to the measurement of attitudes has been made by Thurstone (1931b) and his students in the development of objective techniques and their application in the construction and standardization of a series of attitude scales. Each scale consists of some 20 statements and the subject is to indicate agreement or disagreement with the respective statements. Scales have been prepared for studying attitudes towards the Negro, the Chinese, the Germans, toward War, the Law, capital punishment, communism, censorship, patriotism, the Constitution of the United States, the Bible, divorce, public ownership, unions, freedom of speech, and the like. Some of the scales have two equivalent forms. The following is an example of items included in Scale of Attitude Toward Censorship:

> Censorship is absurd because no two people agree about morality.
> Human progress demands a free speech and a free press.

Remmers (1934) and his associates have prepared generalized attitude scales toward items of a given series, such as school subjects, persons or institutions. A brief but significant scale for the measurement of social distance has been constructed by Bogardus (1933) for testing attitudes toward a person or group of a different race, nation, religion or economic level. An extensive scale for the study of opinion has been devised by Rundquist and Sletto (1936).

An expanded attitude scale has been employed by Sweet (1929) to measure children's attitudes and ideals regarding home and school life. In regard to each item the child is to state whether he likes or dislikes it, whether he feels he ought to like it and whether the boys of his age group like it. The scores include: idea of the right, feeling of difference, self-criticism and criticism of others.

There are a few indirect measures of attitudes based upon methods other than direct questioning. The person's tendency to take an extreme attitude, the consistency or inconsistency of his replies, or the differences between the answers to different questions, rather than the answers themselves, constitute the basis for scoring. In Watson's (1925) test of "Public Opinion on Some Religious and Economic Issues" the score is based on the number of times the subject chooses the extremes of the given choices. The test is actually designed for measuring fairmindedness. Similarly, in the Social Orientation test by Maller and Tuttle (1936), the attitudes are measured indirecly by controlled word associations and other disguised approaches.

Examples of available measures of attitudes include tests of social and international attitudes by Neuman (1926), Harper (1931), Droba (1931), and others. Droba (1932) in his review of this field reports 125 studies dealing with the measurement of attitudes. Katz, Allport, and Jenness (1931) present a comprehensive report on measurement of students' attitudes.

Tests of Personal Interests.—Numerous measures of vocational, educational, and social interests have been devised. The old approach of asking a person to indicate the nature and intensity of his interest in a given subject or vocation on a graded scale or in descriptive terms has been practically discarded. Psychologists have come to recognize that the evaluation of one's own interest requires considerable insight, experience, and articulation. Furthermore, such overt expressions of interest may be superficial or untruthful and may not represent a person's true interest. Ratings by others are of value, provided the raters have sufficient opportunity of observation. But as a rule such ratings, as other measures of reputation, are subjective and lack validity. Objective tests of interest may be grouped under five categories:

1. Information. Assuming that a person is likely to be better informed on those subjects in which he is interested, the extent of information or word knowledge in a given field may be taken as a measure of interest.
2. Free or controlled association. In response to carefully chosen words, the nature and frequency of associative responses may reveal predominant patterns of interest.
3. Preferences, likes, and dislikes. Lists of items are arranged so that their purport is not obvious to the subject tested. These may include forms of recreation, specific tasks, subjects of study, types of people, books, and the like. The subject's expressed reactions yield a score of interest.
4. Time schedules. A record of the complete distribution of time devoted to various activities and forms of recreation may reveal types of interest.

5. Observation of behavior. Careful observation of an individual's conduct, types of reading, contacts with other persons, ease of distraction when working on given tasks are useful in the evaluation of interest.

Interest scores of children have been found to be of limited predictive value because of the instability of expressed early interest. On the college and adult level, however, interest is generally stable and when given under proper circumstances the scores have practical application.

The great number of interest tests are primarily concerned with discovering vocational preference, the relative order of a person's interest in a number of given vocations. They are used most often in educational and vocational counseling. The general procedure in the construction of these tests is to try out a large series of items of information and preference on groups representing several vocations. The answers predominant in each group are noted. After eliminating items on which different vocational groups show little or no difference, the final form is prepared with a separate scoring key for each vocation considered. When a given subject's record is scored with the several keys it is possible to determine in which vocation he scores highest, the vocation which his interests resemble most closely.

The application of such tests to vocational counseling is based on the assumption that, other things being equal, a person will be best adjusted in a group in which the prevailing pattern of interest is similar to that of his own. With the enormous expansion of vocational education, these measures serve as useful supplements to measures of intelligence and aptitude. One of the best known of these instruments is Strong's (1927, 1933) Vocational Interest Blank. Separate forms are available for men, women, and adolescents. The test consists of more than 400 items including lists of occupations, amusements, school subjects, activities, and peculiarities of people to be marked "liked," "disliked," or "indifferent." The subject is to indicate the order of preference and choice of activities. Norms are based on numerous occupational groups: personnel managers, farmers, advertisers, lawyers, teachers, chemists, ministers, and many other groups.

VOCATIONAL INTEREST TESTS.—The earlier tests of interest were more restricted in scope and the form of response was more complicated. Thus, the Carnegie Interest Inventory (Freyd, 1922) aimed at the differentiation between the socially and the mechanically inclined and Cowdery's (1930) Interest Inventory was designed to measure relative interest in law, engineering and medicine. The latter test includes questions on occupations, types of people, sports and amusements, pets, reading, school subjects, and miscellaneous activities. In Freyd's Occupational Interest Blank the subject is required to indicate his preferences on a 5-point scale.

The Specific Interest Test by Brainard (1932) aims to analyze tendencies which are essential to vocations (rather than vocational fitness). The questions deal with interests and various activities: physical, mechanical, leadership, social, literary, and aesthetic. Each group includes five questions regarding different phases of the activity.

The Oberlin Vocational Interest Inquiry (Fryer, 1931) includes a series of paired comparisons in which two items of opposite functions are given and the subject is to indicate his preference in each case. The major types of work represented include: creative activities, research and investigation of personal histories.

Hepner's (1931) Vocational Interest Quotient consists of a series of four booklets: professional occupations, business occupations, skilled trades and occupations for women. The material is self-administering and self-scoring. Wyman's (1929) Free Association Test of Interests consists of a list of 120 free association stimulus words of intellectual and social activities.

Some tests have been devised specifically for women. Manson's (1931) Occupational Interest Blank for Women includes scoring keys based on interests of stenographers, secretaries, bookkeepers, office managers, saleswomen, teachers and nurses. McHale's (1930) Vocational Interest Test for College Women is an information test of interest, and includes questions on law, business, medicine, home making, agriculture and education. The claim of validity is based on surprisingly high correlations between test scores and success estimates by employers. The permanence of interests among college women has been studied by Burgemeister (1940).

Other interest tests for students include the Purdue Interest Report Blank (Remmers, 1929) which has been found to differentiate between agriculture and engineering students, the Minnesota Interest Inventory (Paterson, et al., 1930), Gentry's (1940) Vocational Inventory, Lehman's (1927) Vocational Attitude Quiz, Garrison's (1938) study of the interests of college students, and the Interest Questionnaire for High School Students, by Garretson and Symonds (1930). The latter purports to differentiate between technical, commercial and academic inclinations of high school freshmen. The questions cover occupations, activities, school subjects, jobs and extra-curricular activities, prominent men, things to do and to own, magazines and other items of choice. Miner's (1926) Analysis of Work Interest Blank for high school and college students purports to measure fundamental personal interests, with suggestions on how to observe one's likes and dislikes. The test was used with students in law, engineering, teaching, and premedical courses and is intended for educational counseling.

Boys' Activity Interest Finder by Sonquist (1931) consists of 70 activity interests including sports, crafts and other recreational activities. Each item is marked for interest, participation and skill.

NONVOCATIONAL INTEREST TESTS.—Ream's (1922b) Test of Social Relations is an information test of the type and range of social interest. Parts of Moss' Test of Social Intelligence (Hunt, 1928) also measure social interest as revealed in information regarding social situations. The University of Iowa Assayer, which is a revision of Hart's (1923) test, aims to measure personal interest and attitudes. Shuttleworth (1924) has employed the test in studies of character in relation to scholastic success.

Fryer (1931) reports on the measurement of range or breadth of interest by means of a series of information questions while Conklin (1927) measured introversion-extraversion tendencies as revealed in expressions of interest in contrasted activities. Pressey's Interest-Attitude Test (1933) consists of a series of word groups, based on the cross-out method. Thorndike (1935) explored several approaches to the objective measurement of interest. The latter was found related to information and ability.

TESTS OF VALUES.—Measures of Values, an outgrowth of interest tests, are more general in purpose and method. Rather than measuring a person's relative interest in specific vocations or subjects of study, the value tests purport to delineate the predominant pattern of a person's hierarchy of generalized values.

Thurstone (1931a) analyzed the intercorrelations of interest scores for 18 occupations on Strong's (1927) Vocational Interest Blank and showed that nearly all of the relationships among these scores can be accounted for by assuming four primary factors of interest. Thurstone has tentatively named them: (1) interest in science, (2) interest in language, (3) interest in people, and (4) interest in business.

Allport and Vernon's (1931) Study of Values is based on Spranger's types and aims to measure the relative prominence of six basic interests or motives: aesthetic, economic, political, religious, social, and theoretical. The test (Vernon and Allport, 1931) consists of 45 situation problems, and the subject is to select (from paired comparisons or multiple choices) alternatives diagnostic of relative degrees of these six basic interests.

The political value was found to be highly correlated with the economic values. Thus, in the Inventory of Values by Van Dusen, Wimberly and Mosier (1939), the political value has been omitted. The authors of the latter Inventory found a high correlation between the religious and the social values and they suggested that the two values, social and religious, probably have some common factor which may be postulated as humanitarianism.

The weakness of Allport-Vernon's Study of Values and many of its adaptations is similar to that of personality inventories. The questions are direct and the intelligent subject can "see through" its purpose.

Furthermore, each problem includes alternatives representing some, not all, of the six basic values. An expressed preference in one set may not be comparable to a preference in a different set of values.

The Interest Values Inventory by Glaser and the writer (1940) has been designed to measure four of Spranger's values. The political and religious values were eliminated. It is based upon word-associations and questions, each of which includes four alternatives, corresponding to the four basic values. The test has been validated on clearly differentiated groups and only those items were included on which the four alternatives were chosen "correctly" by the respective groups.

The following is a description of the basic types as given by the authors of the Interest Values Inventory:

The *Theoretic* type of person is characterized by intellectual curiosity, responsiveness to ideas, and an interest in the discovery of truth. He characteristically tends to compare and contrast, to observe and probe, and to consider pros and cons. Whatever his field or walk of life, he is marked by a rational and analytic approach to problems, and an interest in ordering and systematizing his knowledge.

The *Aesthetic* type of person is appreciative and responsive to form, color, design, harmony, symmetry, and pleasing effects, to the beautiful in art and nature. The aesthetic attitude tends to be opposed to the economic or commercial and negatively related to it. The aesthetic individual is artistically appreciative, and under proper circumstances is likely to be creative.

The *Social* type of person is characterized by his concern for the welfare of others. He manifests a will to help and a spirit of self-sacrifice. Though gregariousness is common in this group, it is not essential, for the sympathetic interest of the social person in human betterment may be indicated without a concomitant disposition toward easy social contacts.

The *Economic* type of person tends to evaluate things in terms of tangible, practical utility. He generally thinks of himself as being realistic, sensible, and as having "his feet on the ground." He may be sympathetic toward ideas if they seem to him practical, concrete, or likely to be productive of tangible benefits. He tends to be gregarious, but not deeply concerned with human problems as such. His criteria for judging accomplishments are largely material success, power, and comfort; he is likely to confuse luxury with beauty; and his interest in art is proprietary rather than creative.

Mixed Types. The classification into types must be viewed only as a generalization in terms of predominant interest or an interest pattern in a given personality. Generally a person has all these interests, but their respective degrees of development and relative intensity will vary greatly from one person to another. Many individuals present mixed types with two or more primary interests well balanced in strength. It should be added that while interest value patterns have stability and pervasiveness under normal circumstances, their organization as well as the relative dominance of a given interest may be altered when significant changes occur in the individual or in environmental conditions affecting the individual. (Glaser and Maller, 1940, pp. 67–81)

INDIRECT MEASURES OF VALUES.—Free association, picture interpretations and other projective methods, such as Murray's Thematic Apperception Test (1938), offer opportunities for the expression of values. Similar information on the hierarchy of personal values may be inferred from evaluations of preferences for certain works of music and art, expressions of wishes, choice of rewards, choice of conflicting activities, readiness to forego certain gains for the sake of other gains, expressions of use-values (e.g., answers to such questions as "What is the most important use of the radio?"), analysis of leisure time activities and other observations of uncontrolled behavior (see Chapter 6 of this book by White).

Comprehensive reviews of studies employing measures of evaluative attitudes have been presented by Duffy (1940) and Raths (1940) while Thomson (1941) reported on the relationship between scores on a test of values and several other tests.

COMPARISON WITH OTHER GROUPS OF PERSONALITY TESTS.—The measurement of attitudes and interest is among the frontier problems in psychology. When based upon objective evidence, or samples of behavior, such measures are of unquestionable value. When based upon self-ratings—or ratings by others—or upon direct questions and self-descriptions, their validity is open to question.

Attitudes and interests have several elements in common. They are similar in their genetic development and their susceptibility to change with age, knowledge, and experience. Interests, however, are more specific and more readily subjected to quantification. They are also more closely related to skills and capacities for which objective tests are available. It has been found that information about any subject of study or vocation, which is an integral part of interest, is usually related to corresponding special abilities as well as to general intelligence.

Compared with self-description inventories of adjustment, tests of interest enjoy several marked advantages. Questions regarding interest are generally less personal and less provocative in nature and a person is more likely to give fairly accurate replies. The concepts of vocational, educational and social interests are relatively simple in meaning and the questions are less ambiguous than those dealing with adjustment, ascendancy, self-sufficiency, introversion, and the like. Though subject to change with changing conditions, interest is generally more stable and less explosive in nature than is the case with emotional elements. The scores which interest tests yield are more comparable, from person to person, and from one period to another and more readily interpreted and applied than those of personality inventories.

Tests of Miscellaneous Aspects of Personality.—

MEASURES OF MUSIC AND ART.—In his studies of musical ability, Seashore (1919, 1931) devised various tests of tonal memory, rhythm, time, pitch, loudness, and timbre. Other tests of musical aptitude include Kwalwasser's (1927) test of tonal memory, the Drake Music Tests (1940), the Lowery (1929) measure of cadence and a test developed at the University of California based upon rhythmic and melodic patterns, dissonant and consonant chords, and differentiation in pitch and intensity.

A technique for measuring music appreciation has been devised by Semeonoff (1940). A series of musical recordings is presented and the subject is to choose one of four alternate interpretations for each musical selection. The appreciation of music is also measured by Dykema's Tests of Melodic Taste and Tonal Movement. Miller (1938) described the use of standard tests in studies of dramatic talent.

Among the better known tests of art aptitude and appreciation are the McAdory (1930) Art Test, Burtt's test of artistic appreciation, and those devised by Meier and Seashore (1929, 1939), Lewerenz (1929), and Varnum (1939). The latter's Selective Art Aptitude Measure includes exercises on color memory, tone gradations, proportioning, rhythmic and static balance, feeling for geometric forms and creative imagination. Dewar (1938) compared the results of several tests of artistic apprecation and Kinter (1933) has summarized the various methods of measuring artistic ability. The relationship between musical, artistic, and mechanical abilities has been analyzed by Morrow (1938).

MEASURES OF SUPERSTITION.—The prevalence of unfounded ideas was always of interest to the psychologist and several forms for the testing of superstitions have been devised. Unfortunately, the tests do not distinguish between the acceptance of misinformation (in the belief that it is true) and a superstitious attitude of mind. The difference is not easily discernible but from the psychological point of view it is of fundamental significance. Thus, the belief that "our winters are milder than they were 50 years ago," though unfounded, may be the result of misinformation. On purely rational grounds the statement might have been correct. But the belief that "if you make a wish upon seeing a falling star, the wish will come true" is fundamentally irrational in character.

Caldwell (1934) and his associates demonstrated in a series of experimental studies that the acquisition and elimination of superstition follow the general principles of learning. Peatman and Greenspan (1936) have devised a test of superstitions.

Of particular interest to the student of personality is the relationship between superstition and other personal qualities. This has been studied by Maller and Lundeen (1934). Significant correlations were found between the number of superstitious beliefs and scores on tests of neurotic tendencies. An item analysis revealed consistent relationships between maladjustment and acceptance of items dealing with luck or omens of future events. Belief in such items was definitely associated with feelings of insecurity and insufficiency.

MEASUREMENT OF MISCELLANEOUS QUALITIES.—Noll (1934) devised a test of scientific thinking but the validity was questioned by Blair (1940) who administered the test to a number of recognized scientists. Of greater promise is the test of scientific aptitude by Zyve (1927) which is composed of exercises requiring a high degree of accuracy and attention to detail. Bender (1938) devised a visual-motor test for clinical use.

Tests of social adequacy (McCormick, 1933) and social proficiency (Jackson, 1940) and knowledge of manners and social usage (Strang, 1931) are of some value in the study of personality. In general, however, they lack validity, not being sufficiently related to actual behavior in social situations. The same applies to tests of information regarding health and safety.

The relationship between success in military training and personality factors has been studied by Forlano and Watson (1937). Page (1935) found that leadership at a military school was positively related to personal appearance but unrelated to academic achievement. May (1920) designed and used a questionnaire for the psychological study of the attitudes and background of conscientious objectors.

A test for the indirect measurement of the cultural background of the home was devised by Burdick (1929) and scales for the measurement of socio-economic status were designed by Chapin (1931) and Dubin (1940). Morale scales were devised by Miller (1942) and Whisler and Remmers (1937). The measurement of public opinion is described by Murphy and Likert (1938).

There are numerous specific elements of personality for which testing devices have been developed. These are not to be considered as score-yielding tests of personality, and the qualities themselves will need further clarification, but they contribute to the field of personality measurement. The following are examples of a number of qualities and the authors of the respective testing devices:

Accuracy	Hartman (1928)
Affective potency	Watson and Fisher (1941)
Annoyance	Cason (1930)
Aspiration	Lewin (1935); Frank (1935)
Confidence	Trow (1923)
Conflict	Spencer (1938a)
Consistency	Newcomb (1929); Trawick (1940)
Euphoria	Barry (1935)
Fantasies	Morgan and Murray (1935)
Frustration	Rosenzweig (1935)
Happiness	Watson (1930); Sailer (1931)

Humor	Bird (1925) ; Landis and Ross (1933) ; Stump (1939)
Imagination	McGeouch (1924) ; Andrews (1930)
Job satisfaction	Hoppock (1935)
Like mindedness	Zubin (1938)
Likes and dislikes	Thorndike (1935)
Masculinity—femininity	Terman and Miles (1936) ; Gilkinson (1937)
Maturity	Farnsworth (1938) ; Furfey (1931)
Morale	Whisler and Remmers (1937) ; Miller (1942)
Originality	McClatchy (1928)
Overstatement	Woodrow and Remmels (1927)
Punctuality	Dudycha (1936)
Readiness to confide	Maller (1932)
Sociability	Gilliland and Burke (1926) ; Stauber and Hunting (1933)
Social adjustment	Washburne (1940)
Social maturity	Doll (1936)
Speed	Bernstein (1924)
Susceptibility to monotony	Thompson (1929)

Batteries of Tests.—Since it is impossible to measure all of personality by a single test, several attempts have been made to assemble series or batteries of tests which together might evaluate several important aspects of personality. An example of a large number of tests prepared and administered to a representative population is the testing program of the Character Education Inquiry.

A series of tests to be used for the diagnosis of delinquent tendencies has been devised by Loufbourow and Keys (1933) and the authors report that the test battery yields significant differentiations between delinquents and nondelinquents. The writer's Case Inventory (1936) is composed of four tests: controlled association, adjustment inventory, self-scoring test (honesty) and ethical judgment.

Murray and associates (1938) devised a series of approaches for the intensive study of personality, and Gannon (1939) and Brogden (1940) reported the results of large numbers of character tests and the intercorrelations among those tests.

Personality tests have been devised and employed in the study of special groups including delinquents (Hawthorne, 1932; Daniel, 1932; Loufbourow and Keys, 1933; Brooks, 1940; Washburne, 1940), mentally retarded children (Pertsch, 1936), tubercular patients (Seidenfeld, 1940), and other atypical groups.

Evaluation of Personality Tests and Their Application

In a discussion of the difficulties of measurement in this field, Terman (1934) questions the use of the term "measure," when applied to the complex pattern of personality. In this connection, psychologists will recall the heated polemics of two decades ago regarding the feasibility of measuring intelligence. Although there are definite distinctions between the measurement of intelligence and personality, the difference is not so fundamental as to make the concept of measurement acceptable in one and untenable in the other. The measurement of general intelligence is predicated upon a definition of intelligence which emphasizes the measurable aspects of problem solving, while the less tangible elements, as creative thinking or particular insight, are considered as special mental abilities. For the purpose of measurement, personality may be similarly defined in terms of measurable knowledge of social standards, appropriate conduct, expressed interests and the pattern of behavior and adjustment, reserving the less tangible elements for special consideration.

Burks (1936) discusses the limitations of the concept of traits in the light of scientific studies, and recommends the use of other terms. She points out that the prediction of the intent of behavior is more valid than the prediction of specific acts. Allport (1937) examines the value and limitation of personality tests and cites divergent interpretations of test results in their bearing upon the structure of personality.

A number of studies were devoted to a reexamination of the validity of some widely used tests. Lorge (1935), Landis, Zubin and Katz (1935), Feder and Baer (1941), Harris and Dabelstein (1938), and others have questioned the validity of several personality inventories in the light of selected criteria.

Character tests, particularly measures of conduct, have made a distinct contribution to education. The test results have raised doubts about the claims of certain approaches to character development. Methods used in certain schools and those advocated by some character education agencies have been questioned. One national agency revised its program completely when tests revealed a negative relationship between length of membership and degree of honesty, that those who obtained most recognition were most apt to cheat.

Moral knowledge tests and measures of attitudes have demonstrated the effectiveness of education in the improvement of ethical judgment and the clarification of desirable attitudes. Reading, speeches, and environmental contacts have been shown to have marked effects upon attitudes. There is less unequivocal evidence of the effectiveness of education in the modification of behavior, as measured by conduct tests.

Personality tests fell short of expectation in the field of educational prognosis. It was hoped that the addition of measures of personality to those of intelligence would greately enhance the prediction of educational success and thus prevent or reduce the waste resulting from failure. Unfortunately, the abundant variety of personality tests includes none which show significant and consistent correlations with school achievement over and above the correlations with intelligence. Occasionally, personality tests might aid in the interpretation of educational disability. While unable to predict or prevent failure, these tests are of some help in explaining it and in preparing a remedial program.

In vocational orientation personality tests offer some help in determining trends of predominant interest. They may thus contribute to vocational education and, to a lesser degree, to vocational adjustment. Though it has not been demonstrated that the proper pattern of interest is positively related to vocational success, it probably does contribute to personal adjustment in appropriate jobs. In case of specialized work requiring particular qualities of temperament, tests might be helpful in personnel selection and training. In aviation, for example, tests might aid in selecting those who have a high degree of control of attention, who are not easily fatigued and distracted, and who show no marked perseverative tendencies.

In the fields of delinquency, probation, and crime prevention, personality tests have been applied but the results are inconclusive. Claims have been made for some tests of the ability to predict delinquent tendencies before they are expressed in overt behavior, but these claims await substantiation.

Personality tests have been employed in marital adjustment service, in studies of problems of adolescents and in work of guidance and counseling. They have been used also in studies of the handicapped, such as the mentally retarded, the deaf, blind, tubercular, diabetic, cardiac, and similar groups.

In clinical diagnosis, personality tests have proved moderately helpful. Disregarding the exorbitant claims made for particular instruments, it is possible to diagnose certain forms of personality maladjustment by means of tests. In therapy, the tests are sometimes useful in supplementing the clinical practice of uncontrolled expression and free talk. The latter reveals the general nature of the problems and a variety of specific information valuable for clinical treatment.

Some tests of personality have been found of value in the selection of military officers and candidates for officers' training schools. The testing program consists of a variety of devices, including free expressions and observations on the ability to overcome fatigue and distraction.

One of the most significant findings revealed by tests of character and personality is the consistency of individual differences. These differences are generally gradual and, in most instances, there was found a concentration of cases in the middle of the scale with decreasing numbers toward either extreme. The practical implications of this variability in all aspects of personality, similar to the individual differences in intellectual qualities, are not sufficiently recognized. Corroboration of those individual differences comes from the experience of social workers and clinicians who deal with personality problems.

The measurement of character and personality by means of objective tests has progressed considerably during the last two decades. Instruments have been devised which are of value in education, measuring the relative outcome of various methods and curricula, in vocational orientation and guidance, revealing the various shades of interest, in clinical diagnosis of certain types of problem cases and, above all, in the study of variability with regard to numerous aspects of character and personality.

Available testing devices are of particular value in the measurement of the cognitive aspects of character and personality. This holds true for the testing of moral knowledge, ethical discrimination and related areas of character as well as for measurement of social interaction and familiarity with the cultural symbolism which plays a significant part in personality adjustment. Equally valuable are testing techniques which are based upon samples of behavior and conduct symptomatic of desirable character and measures of qualities, of the tempo of work, of control of attention, of artistic aptitudes and art, and of related elements contributing to personality.

Of limited value are those testing techniques which purport to measure the more intimate elements of personality, the unresolved conflicts within the individual, the disturbance resulting from contradictions between personal interest and social standards and the manifold aspects of personality disorganization. The intrinsic complexity of the concepts involved, the semantic problem of avoiding vague and variedly interpreted words and phrases, and the difficulty of overcoming resentment toward personal questions introduce elements of uncertainty in the results of such tests.

The most dependable application of personality tests is in the study of groups and trends. They are less reliable when applied to one particular person. Attempts at the construction of an over-all test of personality, easily administered and rapidly scored, have been disappointing. In view of the extreme complexity of the nature of personality and its susceptibility to change, it is not likely that we shall ever have a reliable personality test yielding a Personality Quotient similar to the IQ.

In recent years there has been relatively little progress toward the improvement of personality tests and a noticeable scarcity of original approaches. In spite of the abundant productivity in this field, there is little evidence of originality of approach or of newer trends. The great number of reported studies were routine applications of ineffectual procedures.

There has been discernible progress in methods of scoring, tabulating, and analyzing the results of tests. The advent of a special machine for the automatic scoring of test papers (1935) and the improvement of instruments for card sorting and tabulating have aided in item analysis and in the application of factor analysis to the correlations among different measures of personality.

There is some indication that tests which have been used excessively will soon fall into disuse as a result of failure to demonstrate their practical or theoretical value. Test users are likely to become more critical toward instruments which make unjustified claims. More attention will be given to defining clearly the objectives of testing devices, to setting up dependable criteria based upon practical experience for adequate validation and to conducting long-range experiments to determine their value. Until that is accomplished, interest is likely to shift to more intensive methods of personality study by means of controlled observations, projective methods, and a complete analysis of personal history.

BIBLIOGRAPHY

The number of publications in the field of personality measurement during the last two decades was so large that a complete bibliography would include more than one thousand titles. The following bibliography is thus selective. An attempt was made to select those which seem to be of greater scientific and practical value. In areas where the number of publications was greatest the selection was more severe in terms of apparent quality and recency.

As a rule, the publications describing tests, rather than the tests themselves, are listed in the bibliography, except where no special publication dealing with a test was available. A number of general references should be mentioned: the *Mental Measurement Yearbook* edited by Buros (1940), *Hildreth's Bibliography of Mental Tests* (1939), and the writer's (1937) *Annotated Bibliography of Character and Personality Tests* include extensive lists of tests in this field.

The *Psychological Bulletin* carries a yearly review of character and personality tests as well as critical reviews of specific areas of character and personality. The latter include reviews of extraversion-introversion, social attitudes, interest, suggestion, persistence, humor, personality inventories and related areas of measurement. Frequent articles on tests appear in the quarterly issues of *Character and Personality*.

The reports of the Character Education Inquiry, published under the general title of *Studies in the Nature of Character* (Hartshorne, May, *et al.*, 1928, 1929, 1930), include a comprehensive account of the construction, validation, and application of a large number of objective tests of moral knowledge, honesty, cooperation, persistence, and inhibition. Descriptive accounts and critical discussions of testing techniques will be found in the treatises on personality by Symonds (1932, 1934) and by Allport (1937, 1942). The latter include discussions of the principles underlying the objective measurement of personality.

Extensive reviews of character and personality tests have been published in the *Review of Educational Research* since 1932. Watson's (1932) first summary is based on a review of some 1,000 studies in this field, published prior to 1931. Each of the reviews published in 1935, 1938, and 1941 cover the publications of the preceding three-year period. Of special interest are the following reviews: *Personality Measurement* by Watson (1938) and Kirkpatrick (1939); *Projective Methods* by Symonds and Samuel (1941); *Persistence* by Ryans (1939); *Current Construction and Evaluation of Personality and Character Tests* by Traxler (1938, 1941); *Personality Trait Tests* by Bernreuter (1940); *Trends in Measurement* by Stagner (1938); *Application of Tests* by Rothney and Roens (1941); *Interest Tests* by Flanagen (1939); *Aptitude Tests* by Segel (1941); *Social Adjustment* by Wright (1942); *Morale* by Child (1942); and a comparison between the American and German approach to the study of character by Maller (1933) and Vernon (1933).

ADAMS, C. R. 1941. A new measure of personality. *J. appl. Psychol., 25,* 141–151.

ALLPORT, G. W. 1928. A test for ascendance submission. *J. abnorm. soc. Psychol., 23,* 118–136.

—— 1937. Personality; a psychological interpretation. New York: Holt.

—— 1942. The use of personal documents in psychological science. *Soc. Sci. Res. Coun. Bull.,* No. 49.

ALLPORT, G. W., & VERNON, P. E. 1931. A study of values. Boston: Houghton Mifflin.

—— 1933. Studies in expressive movement. New York: Macmillan.

ANDREWS, E. S. 1930. The development of imagination in the pre-school child. *Univ. Ia Stud. Charact., 3,* No. 4.

ANSBACHER, H. L. 1941. Murray's and Simoneit's (German military) methods of personality study. *J. abnorm. soc. Psychol., 36,* 589–592.

AVELING, F., & HARGREAVES, H. L. 1921. Suggestibility with and without prestige in children. *Brit. J. Psychol., 12,* 53–75.

BAKER, H. S. 1931. The analysis of behavior problems. *Ohio St. Univ. Bull., 36,* No. 3, 125–152.

BALL, R. J. 1929. Objective measures of emotional stability. *J. appl. Psychol., 13,* 226 256.

BARRY, H., & BOUSFIELD, W. A. 1935. A quantitative determination of euphoria and its relation to sleep. *J. abnorm. soc. Psychol., 29,* 385–389.

BECKMAN, R. O. 1933. Ascendance submission test revised. *Person. J.,* 387–392.

BELL, H. M. 1934. The adjustment inventory. Stanford University: Stanford University Press.

BENDER, 1938. A visual motor gestalt test and its clinical use. *Res. Monogr. Amer. Orthopsychiat. Assn.,* No. 3.

BENTON, A. L. 1935. The interpretation of questionnaire items in a personality schedule. *Arch. Psychol., N. Y.,* No. 190.

BERNREUTER, R. G. 1933. The theory and construction of the personality inventory. *J. soc. Psychol., 4,* 387–405.

—— 1940. Present status of personality trait tests. *Educ. Rec. Suppl., 21,* 160–171.

BERNSTEIN, E. 1924. Quickness and intelligence. *Brit. J. Psychol., Monogr Suppl., 3,* No. 7.

BIESHEUVEL, S. 1938. The measurement of the threshold for flicker and its value as a perseveration test. *Brit. J. Psychol., 29,* 27–38.

BINET, A. 1900. La suggestibilité. Paris: Schleicher Frères.

BIRD, G. E. 1925. An objective humor test for children. *Psychol. Bull., 22,* 137–138.

BLAIR, G. M. 1940. The validity of the Noll test of scientific thinking. *J. educ. Psychol., 31,* 53–59.

BOGARDUS, E. S. 1933. A social distance scale. *Sociol. soc. Res., 17,* 265–271.

BRAINARD, P. P. 1928. Interest tests in vocational guidance. *Voc. Guid. Mag., 6,* 156–159.

BROGDEN, H. E. 1940. A factor analysis of forty character tests. *Psychol. Monogr., 52,* No. 3.

BROOKS, J. J. 1940. A technique for determining the degree of behavior maladjustment of prison inmates. *J. crim. Psychopath., 1,* 339–353.

BROWN, F. 1935. Personality inventory for children. New York: Psychological Corporation.

BROWN, W. 1916. Individual and sex differences in suggestibility. *Univ. Calif. Publ. Psychol., 2,* No. 6, 291–440.

BURDICK, E. M. 1929. A group test of home environment. *Arch. Psychol., N. Y.,* No. 101.

BURGEMEISTER, B. B. 1940. The permanence of interest of women college students. *Arch. Psychol., N. Y.,* No. 255.

BURKS, B. S. 1936. Personality theories in relation to measurement. *J. soc. Psychol., 7,* 140–150.

BUROS, O. K. 1941. The nineteen forty mental measurements yearbook. Highland Park, N. J.: Mental Measurements Yearbook Co.

BURTT, H. E., & FREY, O. C. 1934. Suggestions for measuring recklessness. *Person. J., 13,* 39–46.

CALDWELL, O. W., & LUNDEEN, G. E. 1934. Do you believe it? New York: Doubleday, Doran.

CASON, H. 1930. An annoyance test and some research problems. *J. abnorm. soc. Psychol., 25,* 224–236.

CATTELL, R. B. 1935. On the measurement of perseveration. *Brit. J. Educ. Psychol., 5,* 76–92.

—— 1941. An objective test of character temperament: I. *J. genet. Psychol., 25,* 59–73.

CHAPIN, F. S. 1931. Socio-economic status: some preliminary results of measurement. *Amer. J. Sociol., 37,* 581–587.

CHILD, I. L. 1941. Morale: a bibliographical review. *Psychol. Bull., 38,* 393–420.

CLARK, W. H. 1935. Two tests for perseverance. *J. educ. Psychol., 26,* 604–610.

CONKLIN, E. S. 1927. The determination of normal extravert-introvert interest differences. *Pedag. Sem., 34,* 28–37.

COWDERY, K. M. 1930. The interest inventory in college vocational guidance. *Psychol. Clin., 19,* 59–62.

CRANE, A. L. 1923. Race differences in inhibition. *Arch. Psychol., N. Y.,* No. 63.

CROSLAND, H. 1929. The psychological methods of word association and reaction time as tests of deception. *Univ. Ore. Publ., 1,* No. 1, 14.

CRUTCHER, R. 1934. An experimental study of persistence. *J. appl. Psychol., 18,* 409–417.

CUSHING, H. M. 1929. A perseverative tendency in pre-school children. *Arch. Psychol., N. Y.,* No. 108.

DANIEL, R. P. 1932. A psychological study of delinquent and non-delinquent Negro boys. *Teach. Coll. Contr. Educ.,* No. 546.

DARLING, R. P. 1940. Autonomic action in relation to personality traits of children. *J. abnorm. soc. Psychol., 35,* 246–260.

DECROLY, O., & WAUTHIER, M. L. 1929. Contribution à l'étude des tests du character. *J. Psychol. norm. path., 26,* 201–250.

DEWAR, H. 1938. A comparison of tests of artistic appreciation. *Brit. J. educ. Psychol., 8,* 29–40.

DOLL, A. 1936. The Vineland Social Maturity Scale; revised 1936. Vineland, N. J.: The Training School, Department of Research.

DOWNEY, J. E. 1923. The will temperament and its testing. Yonkers, N. Y.: World Book.

DRAKE, R. M. 1940. The relation of musical talent to intelligence and success in school. *J. Musicol., 2,* 38–44.

DROBA, D. D. 1931. A scale of militarism-pacifism. *J. educ. Psychol., 22,* 96–111.

—— 1932. Methods of measuring attitudes. *Psychol. Bull., 29,* 309–323.

DUBIN, R. 1940. Measurement of social status. *Amer. J. Sociol., 45,* 771–773.

DUDYCHA, G. J. 1936. An objective study of punctuality in relation to personality and achievement. *Arch. Psychol., N. Y.,* No. 204.

DUFFY, E. A. 1940. A critical review of investigations employing the Allport-Vernon study of values and other tests of evaluation attitudes. *Psychol. Bull., 37,* 597–612.

DUNLAP, J. W., & KROLL, A. 1939. Observations on the methodology in attitude scales. *J. soc. Psychol., 10,* 475–487.

EISENBERG, P. 1937. Expressive movements related to feelings of dominance. *Arch. Psychol., N. Y.,* No. 211.

EVANS, C., & McCONNELL, T. R. 1941. A new measure of introversion-extraversion. *J. Psychol., 12,* 111–124.

FARNSWORTH, R. 1938. The measurement of emotional maturity. *J. soc. Psychol., 9,* 235–237.

FAUQUIER, W. 1939. The measurement of attitudes of delinquent and normal boys by use of an association technique. *Child Develpm., 10,* 231–239.

FEDER, D. D., & BAER, L. O. 1941. A comparison of test records and clinical evaluations of personality adjustment. *J. educ. Psychol., 32,* 133–144.

FERNALD, G. G. 1912. The defective delinquent class. *Amer. J. Insan., 68,* 523–594.

FLANAGAN, J. C. 1939. Measuring interests. *Psychol. Bull., 36,* 529–530.

FORLANO, G., & WATSON, G. B. 1937. Relation between success in military training and intelligence, extraversion and adequacy. *J. soc. Psychol., 8,* 243–249.

FRANK, J. D. 1935. Individual differences in certain aspects of the level of aspiration. *Amer. J. Psychol., 47,* 119–128.

FREYD, M. 1922. A method for the study of vocational interests. *J. appl. Psychol., 6,* 243–254.

FRYER, D. 1931. The measurement of interests. New York: Holt.

FURFEY, P. H. 1931. A revised scale for measuring developmental age in boys. *Child Develpm., 2,* 102–114.

GANNON, J. T. 1939. A statistical study of certain diagnostic personality traits of college men. *Stud. Psychol. Psychiat. Catholic Univ. Amer.,* Vol. 4.

GARRETSON, O. K., & SYMONDS, P. M. 1931. Interest questionnaire for high school students. New York: Bureau of Publications, Teachers College, Columbia University.

GARRISON, K. C. 1938. A study of the interests of college students. *Psychol. Monogr., 50,* No. 5.

GENTRY, C. G. 1940. Vocational inventory. Minneapolis, Minn.: Educational Test Bureau.

GILKINSON, H. 1937. Masculine temperament and secondary sex characteristics, a study of the relationship between psychological and physical measures of masculinity. *Genet. Psychol. Monogr., 19,* No. 1, 115–154.

GILLILAND, A. R., & BURKE, R. S. 1926. Measurement of sociability. *J. appl. Psychol., 10,* 315–326.

GILLILAND, A. R., & MORGAN, J. J. B. 1931. An objective measure of introversion-extraversion. *J. abnorm. soc. Psychol., 26,* 296–303.

GLASER, E. A., & MALLER, J. B. 1940. The measurement of interest values. *Character & Pers., 9,* 67–81.

GOODENOUGH, F. L. 1942. The use of free association in the objective measurement of personality. In McNemar, Q., & Merrill, M. A., *Studies in personality.* New York: McGraw-Hill. Pp. 87–103.

GUILFORD, J. P. 1934. Introversion-extraversion. *Psychol. Bull., 31,* 331–354.

HARPER, H. 1931. What European and American students think on international problems. New York: International Institute, Teachers College, Columbia University.

HARRIS, D. B., & DABELSTEIN, D. H. 1938. A study of the Maller and Boynton personality inventories. *J. educ. Psychol., 29,* 279–286.

HART, H. 1923. A test of social attitudes and interests. *Univ. Ia Stud. Child Welf., 2,* No. 4.

HARTMAN, G. W. 1928. Precision and accuracy. *Arch. Psychol., N. Y.,* No. 100.

HARTSHORNE, H., & MAY, M. A. 1928. Studies in deceit. New York: Macmillan.

HARTSHORNE, H., MAY, M. A., & MALLER, J. B. 1929. Studies in service and self control. New York: Macmillan.

HARTSHORNE, H., MAY, M. A., & SHUTTLEWORTH, K. 1930. Studies in the organization of character. New York: Macmillan.

HAUSMAN, M. F. 1933. A test to evaluate some personality traits. *J. gen. Psychol., 9,* 179–189.

HAWTHORNE, J. W. 1932. A group test for the measurement of cruelty compassion: a proposed means of recognizing potential criminality. *J. soc. Psychol., 3,* 189–211.

HENNING, H. A. 1929. Ziele und Möglichkeiten der experimentellen Charakterprüfung. *Jb. Charact., 6,* 215–280.

HEPNER, H. W. 1931. Vocational interest quotients. New York: Psychological Corporation.

HEYMANS, G., & WIERSMA, E. 1906. Beiträge zur speziellen Psychologie auf Grund einer Massenuntersuchung. *Z. Psychol. Physiol. Sinnesorg., 42,* 81–127, 258–301.

HILDRETH, G. H. 1939. Bibliography of mental tests and rating scales. New York: Psychological Corporation.

HOFFMAN, G. J. 1924. The measurement of self-assertion. New York: Thesis, Columbia University.
HOPPOCK, R. 1935. Job satisfaction. New York: Harper.
HOWELLS, T. H. 1933. An experimental study of persistence. *J. abnorm. soc. Psychol., 28*, 14–29.
HULL, C. L. 1929. Quantitative methods of investigating waking suggestions. *J. abnorm. soc. Psychol., 24*, 153–169.
HUMM, D. G., & WADSWORTH, G. W. 1934. The Humm-Wadsworth temperament scale. *Person. J., 12*, 314–323.
HUNT, T. 1928. The measurement of social intelligence. *J. appl. Psychol., 12*, 317–334.
INGLE, D. J. 1934. A test of mental instability. *J. appl. Psychol., 18*, 252–266.
JACKSON, V. D. 1940. The measurement of social proficiency. *J. exp. Educ., 8*, 422–474.
JASPER, H. H. 1930. Measurement of depression-elation and its relation to a measure of extraversion-introversion. *J. abnorm. soc. Psychol., 25*, 307–318.
JUNG, C. G. 1910. The association method. *Amer. J. Psychol., 21*, 219–269. (The original presentation of this method was published in German in 1905.)
KATZ, D., ALLPORT, F. H., & JENNESS, M. D. 1931. Students' attitudes. Syracuse, N. Y.: Craftsman Press.
KELLY, E. L., MILES, C. C., & TERMAN, L. M. 1936. Ability to influence one's score on a typical pencil and paper test of personality. *Character & Pers., 4*, 206–215.
KINTER, M. 1933. Measurement of artistic abilities. New York: Psychological Corporation.
KIRKPATRICK, F. H. 1939. The measurement of personality. *Psychol. Rec., 3*, 211–224.
KUNZE, B. 1931. Proben für die Zusammenarbeit von Menschen und deren Wechselwirkung. *Industr. Psychotech., 8*, 147–159.
KWALLWASSER, J. 1927. Tests and measurement in music. Boston: C. C. Burchard.
LAIRD, D. A. 1925. Detecting abnormal behavior. *J. abnorm. soc. Psychol., 20*, 128–141.
LANDIS, C., & ROSS, W. H. 1933. Humor and its relation to other personality traits. *J. soc. Psychol., 4*, 156–175.
LANDIS, C., ZUBIN, J., & KATZ, S. E. 1935. Empirical evaluation of three personality adjustment inventories. *J. educ. Psychol., 26*, 321–330.
LANKES, W. 1915. Perseveration. *Brit. J. Psychol., 7*, 387–419.
LEHMAN, H. C., & WITTY, P. A. 1927. Psychology of play activities. New York: Barnes.
—— 1929. The constancy of vocational interests. *Person. J., 8*, 253–265.
LEWERENZ, A. S. 1929. Predicting ability in art. *J. educ. Psychol., 20*, 702–704.
LEWIN, K. 1935. A dynamic theory of personality. New York: McGraw-Hill.
LINK, H. C. 1936. A test of four personality traits of adolescents. *J. appl. Psychol., 20*, 527–534.
LORGE, I. 1935. Personality traits by fiat: 1. The analysis of the total trait scores and keys of the Bernreuter Personality Inventory. *J. educ. Psychol., 26*, 273–278.
LORGE, I., & THORNDIKE, E. L. 1941. The value of the responses in a free association test as indicators of personal traits. *J. appl. Psychol., 25*, 200–201.
LOUFBOUROW, G. C., & KEYS, N. 1933. A group test of problem behavior tendencies in junior high school boys. *J. educ. Psychol., 24*, 641–653.
LOWERY, H. 1929. Musical memory. *Brit. J. Psychol., 19*, 397–404.
LUITHLEN, W. F. 1931. Zur Psychologie der Initiative und der Führereigenschaften. *Z. pädag. Psychol., 39*, 56–122.
LUNDHOLM, H. Emotional cross-out test. Waverly, Mass.: Psychological Laboratory, McLean Hospital.
MACNITT, R. D. 1930. Introversion and extraversion in the high school. Boston: Badger.
MALLER, J. B. 1929. Cooperation and competition: an experimental study in motivation. New York: Bureau of Publications, Teachers College, Columbia University.

MALLER, J. B. 1930. Self-marking test (a group test of honesty). New York: Bureau of Publications, Teachers College, Columbia University.
—— 1932. Character sketches. New York: Bureau of Publications, Teachers College, Columbia University
—— 1933. Studies in character and personality in German psychological literature. *Psychol. Bull., 30,* 209–232.
—— 1934. General and specific factors in character. *J. soc. Psychol., 5,* 97–102.
—— 1935. Personality sketches: for individual diagnosis. Distributed by Psychological Corporation, New York.
—— 1936a. Case inventory for the measurement of four aspects of personality. New York: Bureau of Publications, Teachers College, Columbia University.
—— 1936b. Controlled association test. New York: Bureau of Publications, Teachers College, Columbia University.
—— 1937. Character and personality tests: a descriptive bibliography including measures of attitudes, interest, adjustment, appreciation, moral knowledge, behavior and rating scales. New York: Bureau of Publications, Teachers College, Columbia University.
MALLER, J. B., & ELKIN, J. 1933. Attention test, for the measurement of perseverative tendencies. New York: Bureau of Publications, Teachers College, Columbia University.
MALLER, J. B., & LUNDEEN, G. E. 1934. Superstition and emotional maladjustment. *J. educ. Res., 27,* 592–617.
MALLER, J. B,. & TUTTLE, H. S. 1936. Social orientation test. The authors.
MANSON, G. E. 1931. Occupational interests and personality requirements of women in business and professions. *Mich. Bus. Stud., 3,* No. 3, 281–347.
MARSTON, L. R. 1924. Emotions of young children. *Univ. Ia Stud. Child Welf.,* No. 2, 49–77.
MASLOW, A. H. 1940. A test for dominance feeling (self-esteem) in college women. *J. soc. Psychol., 12,* 255–270.
MAY, M. A. 1920. The psychological examination of conscientious objectors. *Amer. J. Psychol., 31,* 152–165.
McADORY, M. 1930. The construction and validation of an art test. *Teach. Coll., Contr. Educ.,* No. 383.
McCLATCHY, V. R. 1928. A theoretical and statistical study of the personality trait originality as herein defined. *J. abnorm. soc. Psychol., 23,* 379–382.
McCORMICK, M. J. 1933. Measuring social adequacy. *Ment. Hyg., N. Y., 17,* 100–108.
McFARLAND, R. A., & SEITZ, C. P. 1938. P-S experience blank. New York: Psychological Corporation.
McGEOCH, J. A. 1924. The relationship between three tests of imagination and their correlation with intelligence. *J. appl. Psychol., 8,* 439–443.
McHALE, K. 1930. Information test of interests. *Psychol. Clin., 19,* 53–58.
McNEMARA, W. J., & DARLEY, J. C. 1938. A factor analysis of test retest performance on attitude and adjustment tests. *J. educ. Psychol., 29,* 652–664.
MEIER, N. C. 1939. Factors in artistic aptitude: final summary of a ten-year study of a special ability. *Psychol. Monogr., 51,* No. 5, 140–158.
MEIER, N. C., & SEASHORE, C. E. 1929. Meier-Seashore art judgment test. Iowa City: Bureau of Educational Research and Service, State University Ia.
MILLER, C. H. 1938. Value of certain standard tests for a study of dramatic talent. *J. soc. Psychol., 9,* 437–449.
MILLER, D. C. 1942. National morale of American college students in 1941. *Amer. sociol. Rev., 7,* 194–213.
MINER, J. B. 1926. A method for evaluating a psychograph for vocational guidance. *J. educ. Psychol., 17,* 331–340.
MORGAN, C. D., & MURRAY, H. H. 1935. A method for investigating fantasies. *Arch. Neurol. Psychiat., Chicago, 34,* 289–306.
MORGAN, J. J. B., & HULL, H. L. 1920. The measurement of persistence. *J. appl. Psychol., 10,* 180–187.
MORROW, R. S. 1938. An analysis of the relation among tests of musical, artistic, and mechanical abilities. *J. Psychol., 5,* 253–263.
MURPHY, G., & LIKERT, R. 1938. Public opinion and the individual. New York: Harper.

MURRAY, H. A., *et al.* 1938. Explorations in personality. New York: Oxford University Press.

NEUMANN, G. B. 1926. A study of international attitudes of high school pupils. *Teach. Coll. Contr. Educ.*, No. 239.

NEWCOMB, T. M. 1929. Consistency of certain extravert-introvert behavior patterns in fifty-one problem boys. *Teach. Coll. Contr. Educ.*, No. 382.

NEYMAN, C. A., & KOHLSTEDT, K. D. 1929. A new diagnostic test for introversion-extraversion. *J. abnorm. soc. Psychol., 23*, 482–487.

NOLL, V. H. 1934. Measuring scientific thinking. *Teach. Coll. Rec., 35*, 685–693.

O'CONNOR, J. 1928. Born that way. Baltimore: Williams & Wilkins.

OLSON, W. C. 1936. The waiver of signature in personal reports. *J. appl. Psychol., 20*, 442–450.

O'ROURKE, L. F. 1929. Measuring judgment and resourcefulness. *Person. J., 7*, 427–440.

OTIS, M. A. 1924. A study of suggestibility in children. *Arch. Psychol., N. Y.*, No. 70.

PAGE, D. P. 1935. Measurement and prediction of leadership. *Amer. J. Sociol., 41*, 31–43.

PAGE, J. D., LANDIS, C., & KATZ, S. 1934. Schizophrenic traits in the functional psychoses and in normal individuals. *Amer. J. Psychiat., 13*, 1213–1225.

PALLISTER, H. 1933. The negative or withdrawal attitude: a study in personality organization. *Arch. Psychol., N. Y.*, No. 151.

PATERSON, D. G., *et al.* 1930. Minnesota mechanical ability tests. Minneapolis: Univ. Minnesota Press.

PEATMAN, J. G., & GREENSPAN, I. 1936. An analysis of results obtained from a questionnaire on superstitious beliefs of elementary school children. *J. abnorm. soc. Psychol., 30*, 502–507.

PERTSCH, C. F. 1936. A comparative study of the progress of subnormal pupils in the grades and in special classes. New York: Dissertation, Columbia University.

PINARD, J. W. 1932. Tests of perseveration: 1. Their relation to character. *Brit. J. Psychol., 23*, 5–19, 114–126.

PORTEUS, S. D., & BABCOCK, M. E. 1926. Temperament and race. Boston: Badger.

POULL, L. E., & MONTGOMERY, R. P. 1929. The Porteus Maze Test as a discriminative measure in delinquency. *J. appl. Psychol., 13*, 145–151.

PRESSEY, S. L. 1921. A group scale for investigating the emotions. *J. abnorm. soc. Psychol., 16*, 55–64.

PRESSEY, S. L., & PRESSEY, L. C. 1933. Development of the interest-attitude test. *J. appl. Psychol., 17*, 1–16.

RATHS, L. E. 1940. Approaches to the measurement of values. *Educ. Res. Bull., Ohio St. Univ., 19*, 275–282, 304.

REAM, M. J. 1922a. Group will-temperament tests. *J. educ. Psychol., 13*, 7–16.

—— 1922b. Social relations test. *J. appl. Psychol., 16*, 69–73.

REMMERS, H. H. 1929. The measurement of interest differences between students of engineering and agriculture. *J. appl. Psychol., 13*, 105–119.

REMMERS, H. H., & SILANCE, E. B. 1934. Generalized attitude scales. *J. soc. Psychol., 5*, 298–312.

RETHLINGSHAFER, D. 1940. A statistical evaluation of tests of persistence. *Psychol. Rec., 4*, 163–172.

RICHARDSON, C. A. 1929. The measurement of conative factors in children and their influence. *Brit. J. Psychol., 19*, 405–412.

ROBACK, A. A. 1927. The psychology of character. New York: Harcourt, Brace.

ROGERS, C. R. 1931. Measuring personality adjustment in children nine to thirteen years of age. *Teach. Coll. Contr. Educ.*, No. 548.

ROOT, A. R. 1931. A short test of introversion-extraversion. *Person. J., 10*, 250–253.

ROSANOFF, A. J. 1927. Manual of psychiatry. (Rev. ed.) New York: Wiley. Ch. 7.

ROSENZWEIG, S. 1935. A test for types of reaction to frustration. *Amer. J. Orthopsychiat., 5*, 395–403.

ROSENZWEIG, S. 1938. A basis for the improvement of personality tests with special reference to the M-F battery. *J. abnorm. soc. Psychol., 33,* 467–488.

ROTHNEY, J. W. M., & ROENS, B. A. 1941. Applications of personality and character measurement. *Rev. educ. Res., 11,* 94–108.

RUCH, F. L. 1942. A technique for detecting attempts to fake performance on the self-inventory type of personality test. In McNemar, Q., & Merrill, M. A., *Studies in personality.* New York: McGraw-Hill. Pp. 229–234.

RUNDQUIST, E. A., & SLETTO, R. F. 1936. Minnesota scale for the survey of opinions. Minneapolis: Univ. Minnesota Press.

RUNKEL, J. E. 1936. Luria's motor method and word association in the study of deception. *J. gen. Psychol., 15,* 23–37.

RYANS, D. G. 1939. The measurement of persistence: an historical review. *Psychol. Bull., 36,* 715–739.

SAILER, R. C. 1931. Happiness self estimates of young men. *Teach. Coll. Contr. Educ.,* No. 467.

SCHWARTZ, L. A. 1932. Social situation pictures in the psychiatric interview. *Amer. J. Orthopsychiat., 2,* 124–132.

SEASHORE, C. E. 1919. The psychology of musical talent. Boston: Silver, Burdett.

—— 1931. Psychology of musical skills. Chicago: University Chicago Press.

SEGEL, D. 1941. Measurement of aptitudes in specific fields. *Rev. educ. Res., 11,* No. 1, 42–56.

SEIDENFELD, M. A. 1940. A comparative study of the responses of tuberculous and non-tuberculous subjects on the Maller Personality Sketches. *J. Psychol., 9,* 247–258.

SEMEONOFF, B. 1940. A new approach to the testing of musical ability. *Brit. J. Psychol., 30,* 326–340.

SHARP, F. C. 1898. An objective study of some moral judgments. *Amer. J. Psychol., 9,* 198–234.

SHUTTLEWORTH, F. K. 1924. A new method of measuring character. *Sch. & Soc., 19,* 679–682.

SIMONEIT, M. 1933. Wehrpsychologie: ein Abriss ihrer Probleme und politischen Folgerungen. Berlin: Bernard & Graefe.

—— 1937. Psychologische Offiziersanwärter-eignunsprüfung. *Umschau, 41,* No. 11.

SMITH, R. B. 1932. Development of an inventory for the measurement of inferiority feelings at the high school level. *Arch. Psychol., N. Y.,* No. 144.

SNOW, A. J. 1926. Tests for transportation pilots. *J. appl. Psychol., 10,* 37–51.

SONQUIST, D. W. 1931. Interests of young men. New York: Association Press.

SPEARMAN, C. E. 1937. Abilities of man: their nature and measurement. New York: Macmillan.

SPENCER, D. 1938. Fulcra of conflict. A new approach to personality measurement. Yonkers, N. Y.: World Book.

—— 1938. The frankness of subjects on personality measures. *J. educ. Psychol., 29,* 26–35.

STAGNER, R. 1938. Current trends in research upon personality and character. *Character & Pers., 7,* 161–165.

—— 1940. The cross-out technique as a method in public opinion analysis. *J. soc. Psychol., 11,* 79–90.

STANLIER, J. J., & HUNTING, L. M. 1933. An acquaintanceship questionnaire as a test of sociability. *J. soc. Psychol., 4,* 377–380.

STEPHENSON, W. 1935. Perseveration and character. *Character & Pers., 4,* 44–52.

STRANG, R. 1931. Knowledge of social usage in junior and senior high school. *Sch. & Soc., 34,* 709–712.

STRONG, E. K., JR. 1927. A vocational interest test. *Educ. Rec., 8,* 107–121.

—— 1933. Interest maturity. *Person. J., 12,* 77–90.

STUMP, N. F. 1939. Sense of humor and its relationship to personality, scholastic aptitude, emotional maturity, height and weight. *J. genet. Psychol., 20,* 25–32.

SUPER, D. E. 1942. The Bernreuter Personality Inventory: a review of research. *Psychol. Bull., 39,* 94–125.

SWEET, L. 1929. Measurement of personal attitudes in younger boys. New York: Association Press.

SWINEFORD, F. 1938. The measurement of a personality trait. *J. educ. Psychol., 29*, 295–300.

SYMONDS, P. M. 1932. Diagnosing personality and conduct. New York: Appleton-Century.

—— 1934. Personality diagnosis in social adjustment. New York: American Book.

SYMONDS, P. M., & SAMUEL, E. A. 1941. Projective methods in the study of personality. *Rev. educ. Res., 9*, No. 1, 80–93.

TENDLER, A. D. 1930. A preliminary report on a test for emotional insight. *J. appl. Psychol., 14*, 122–136.

—— 1933. Associative tendencies in psychoneurotics. *Psychol. Clin., 22*, 108–116.

TERMAN, L. M. 1917. The Stanford revision of the Binet-Simon Intelligence Scale. Boston: Houghton Mifflin.

—— 1925. Genetic studies of genius, Vol. 1. Stanford University: Stanford University Press.

—— 1934. The measurement of personality. *Science, 80*, 605–608.

TERMAN, L. M., & MILES, C. C. 1936. Sex and personality. New York: McGraw-Hill.

THOMPSON, L. A. 1929. Measuring susceptibility to monotony. *Person. J.*, 172–195.

—— 1934. Personal history, intelligence and academic achievement. *J. soc. Psychol., 5*, 500–507.

THOMSON, W. A. 1941. An inventory for measuring socialization—self-seeking and its relationship to the Study of Values Test, the A. C. E. Psychological Examination, and the Strong Vocational Interest Blank. *J. appl. Psychol., 25*, 202–212.

THORNDIKE, E. L. 1935. Psychology of wants, interests and attitudes. New York: Appleton-Century.

THORNTON, G. R. 1939. A factor analysis of tests designed to measure persistence. *Psychol. Monogr., 51*, No. 3.

THURSTONE, L. L. 1931. A multiple factor study of vocational interests. *Person. J., 10*, 198–205.

—— 1931. The measurement of social attitudes. *J. abnorm. soc. Psychol., 26*, 249–269.

THURSTONE, L. L., & THURSTONE, T. G. 1930. A neurotic inventory. *J. soc. Psychol., 1*, 3–30.

TIEGS, E. W., CLARK, W. W., & THORPE, L. P. 1941. The California test of personality. *J. educ. Res., 35*, 102–108.

TRAVIS, R. C. 1926. The diagnosis of character types by visual and auditory thresholds. *Psychol. Monogr., 36*, No. 2.

TRAWICK, M. 1940. Trait consistency in personality: a differential investigation. *Arch. Psychol., N. Y.*, No. 248.

TRAXLER, A. E. 1938. The use of tests and rating devices in the appraisal of personality. *Educ. Rec. Bull.*, No. 23, 1–80.

—— 1941. Current construction and evaluation of personality and character tests. *Rev. educ. Res., 11*, No. 1, 57–79.

TROW, W. C. 1923. The psychology of confidence. *Arch. Psychol., N. Y.*, No. 67.

UHRBROCK, R. S. 1928. An analysis of the Downey Will-Temperament tests. *Teach. Coll. Contr. Educ.*, No. 296.

UHRBROCK, R. S., & DOWNEY, J. E. 1927. A non-verbal will-temperament test. *J. appl. Psychol., 11*, 95–105.

VANDUSEN, A. C., WIMBERLEY, S., & MOSIER, C. I. 1939. Standardization of a value inventory. *J. educ. Psychol., 30*, 53–62.

VAN WAGENER, N. B. 1935. The stability of self-description tests of personality adjustment. New York: Dissertation, Columbia University.

VARNUM, W. H. 1939. Selective art aptitude measures. Scranton, Pa.: International Textbook Co.

VERNON, P. E. 1929. Tests of temperament and personality. *Brit. J. Psychol.,* *20,* 97–117.

—— 1933. The American versus the German approach to the study of temperament and personality. *Brit. J. Psychol., 24,* 156–177.

—— 1934. The attitude of the subject in personality testing. *J. appl. Psychol., 18,* 165–177.

VERNON, P. E., & ALLPORT, G. W. 1931. A test for personal values. *J. abnorm. soc. Psychol., 26,* 231–248.

VOELKER, P. F. 1921. Function of ideals in social education. *Teach. Coll. Contr. Educ.,* No. 112.

WANG, C. K. A. 1932. A scale for measuring persistence. *J. soc. Psychol., 3,* 79–90.

WASHBURNE, J. H. 1940. Washburne social adjustment inventory. Yonkers, N. Y.: World Book.

WATSON, G. B. 1925. The measurement of fair-mindedness. *Teach. Coll. Contr. Educ.,* No. 176.

—— 1930. Happiness among adult students of education. *J. educ. Psychol., 21,* 79–109.

—— 1938. Personality and character measurement. *Rev. educ. Res., 8,* 269–291, 340–352.

—— 1932. Tests of personality and character. *Rev. educ. Res., 2,* 184–270.

WATSON, R. I., & FISHER, V. E. 1941. An inventory of affective potency. *J. Psychol., 12,* 139–148.

WECHSLER, D. 1926. Tests for taxicab drivers. *J. person. Res., 5,* 24–30.

WHISLER, L., & REMMERS, H. H. 1937. A scale for measuring individual and group morale. *J. Psychol., 4,* 161–165.

WHITE, R. R. 1931. Influence of suggestibility on responses in ink spot tests. *Child Develpm., 2,* 76–79.

WHITE, R. R., & FENTON, N. 1932. Item validation of a test of inferiority feeling. *J. juven. Res., 16,* 231–241.

WHITMAN, R. H. 1929. A short scale for measuring introversion and extraversion. *J. appl. Psychol., 13,* 499–504.

WIERSMA, E. 1906. Die Sekundarfunktion bei Psychosen. *J. Psychol. Neurol., Lpz., 8,* 1–24.

WILLOUGHBY, R. R. 1934. Forms for the Clark-Thurstone Inventory. *J. soc. Psychol., 5,* 91–97.

WOODROW, H. 1926. A picture preference character test. *J. educ. Psychol., 17,* 519–531.

WOODROW, H., & REMMELS, V. 1927. Overstatement as a test of general character in pre-school children. *J. educ. Psychol., 18,* 239–246.

WOODWORTH, R. S. 1917. Personal data sheet. Chicago: C. H. Stoelting.

WOODWORTH, R. S., & WELLS, F. L. 1911. Association tests. *Psychol. Monogr., 13,* No. 5.

WRIGHT, V. 1942. Summary of literature on social adjustment. *Amer. sociol. Rev., 7,* 407–422.

WYMAN, J. B. 1929. The measurement of interest. *Voc. Guid. Mag., 8,* 54–60.

WYNN-JONES, L. 1929. Individual differences in mental inertia. *J. nat. Inst. industr. Psychol., 4,* 282–294.

ZUBIN, J. 1938. A technique for measuring like-mindedness. *J. abnorm. soc. Psychol., 33,* 508–510.

ZYVE, D. L. 1927. A test of scientific attitude. *J. educ. Psychol., 18,* 525–546.

Chapter 6

INTERPRETATION OF IMAGINATIVE PRODUCTIONS

By ROBERT W. WHITE, Ph.D.

WHAT A PERSON SAYS or writes about himself, what he reveals in an interview or puts down on a questionnaire, by no means completes the account of his personality (see Chapter 5 by Maller). In recent years scientific psychology has begun to explore the hidden regions that intuition has so often recognized but so little remembered. The careful mapping of this territory belongs to the future, but we can give ourselves an initial sense of direction by marking off three rough zones. In the first place there are the things that a person knows about himself but will not tell. Here belong the secret wishes and daydreams, the weaknesses and humiliations, very likely also the triumphs and deepest joys, the disclosure of which would embarrass the subject beyond bearing. Even a patient who understands that his cure depends on telling everything may take several months to overcome his repugnance at mentioning certain topics of which he is fully aware. In the second place there are the things that a person cannot tell about himself because they are repressed: the imaginings and strivings which are inaccessible because their recognition would give rise to unbearable anxiety. Finally there are the things that a person cannot tell about himself because they work so silently and diffusely as to escape his notice and afford him no ground for comparison with others. In this zone belong his unrealized emotional dependencies, his habitual expectations as to how his fellows will treat him, his fundamental courage or despair, his deeply ingrained patterns of defense, and beyond these the perceptual preferences, intellectual peculiarities, and mood climates which lie at the boundary where personality shades off into temperament.

To draw the facts from these invisible regions it is necessary to use what seem like roundabout methods. The natural starting-point for a review of such studies is the method of free association, the technique devised by Freud to help his patients reveal themselves, and the analysis of dreams, which he once ventured to call the royal road to the unconscious. In adopting these methods Freud hoped to elude the defensive, socially patterned personality in order to hear from the less disciplined, less rational private world. When the constraints of everyday necessity could be somewhat relaxed, as happened in dreams spontaneously and in free association by a voluntary effort, it proved possible to heighten to the point of visibility the effects of the hidden regions on behavior. The first serious attempt to embody this principle in a convenient test was the word association method, first brought into scientific prominence by Bleuler and Jung shortly after 1900. Wells (1935) calls this method the first important effort of experimental psychology to study personality through a language medium. Attracting considerable attention for perhaps a decade after 1905, it gradually succumbed to the less laborious questionnaire. The next important step came in 1921 when Rorschach published his work with ink-blots and showed that perceptual and imaginative processes might be made the basis for a comprehensive diagnosis of personality. In the past 15 years psychologists, at last aware *1930* of the limitations of direct questioning, have turned with increasing excitement to man's playful and imaginative behavior which by its very nature is more influenced from within than by serious demands from without. In his play as a child, in his drawing and painting and story-telling at all ages, even in his perception of the people and objects around him, a person shows about himself what he cannot or will not tell.

Most of the procedures to be described in this chapter are included under the convenient but somewhat ambiguous term, "projective methods." The general idea behind these methods is to confront the subject with an unstructured, ambiguous situation—an ink-blot, paper and crayons, an incomplete story, or an array of toys—and ask him to do something with it. The subject is thus given several degrees of freedom to organize a plastic medium in his own way, and since little external aid is provided from conventional patterns he is all but obliged to give expression to the most readily available forces within himself. It is further characteristic of projective methods that the subject does not know what kind of inferences the experimenter intends to make; his attention is focused on the play or task in hand, and it is well-nigh impossible for him to guess at its more remote psychological meaning. Favorable conditions are thus created for unselfconscious revelation from the hidden regions of personality.

From the nature of the material sought and from the unavoidable indirectness of the seeking it is obvious that the interpretation of imaginative productions will offer great scientific difficulties. Even a short segment of imaginative behavior contains items, patterns, and trends in bewildering variety; intuition can seize upon clues, but it is no easy matter to establish reliability, observer agreement, and validity. This atmosphere of guesswork is highly uncongenial to the psychologist who prefers his science in relatively finished form. To a certain extent, however, it arises from the novelty of the problems and recency of the attack upon them; pathways to a greater certainty are, as we shall see, already beginning to show themselves. Notwithstanding their present crudeness, projective methods have been assigned a status of no little scientific dignity by L. K. Frank (1939) who likens them to indirect methods of analysis, for instance the use of X-rays, electrical currents, and polarized light, that have lately been developed in the older sciences. It is characteristic of such techniques that they reveal the components and internal organization of a substance without at the same time altering it, a circumstance that may well make them the methods of choice in future analytic work. There is at least a fair chance that projective methods may one day perform a similar feat for the internal organization of personality.

Free Association

Late in the last century Breuer and Freud (1895) discovered what appeared to be an amazingly simple and rapid way of curing nervous disorders. If a patient could be made, with the help of hypnosis, to remember the situation and the associative connections in which his symptoms first appeared, if above all he could experience the emotions aroused but not fully expressed at that time, his illness gradually disappeared. Imprisoned emotions connected with forgotten traumatic incidents lay at the root of neurosis, and the therapeutic task was to set this energy free.

The application of this new method, however, soon ran into baffling obstacles. Many patients could not be hypnotized, and many others could not seem to recall their experiences in the vivid way necessary for emotional catharsis. In his perplexed search for a technique more successful than hypnosis Freud fell back on what he called a "prejudice," the idea of determinism in mental processes. In its general form, of course, this idea was no novelty, but Freud gave it a quite special application. He believed that when a patient came for treatment the forgotten experiences which lay behind his illness would be of necessity a powerful determinant of his thoughts. In order to heighten this determination and suppress that of the conventional and rational habits which usually govern speech, Freud asked the patient to relax on a couch and abandon himself to the spontaneous associations that his mind produced, not trying to control or select them in the interests of decency or logical connection. This method, which is still the corner-stone of psychoanalytic technique, has ever since been known by the unfortunate name "free association." Whatever the nature of such streams of thought, no one has ever supposed that they were free. The association which results from obedient adherence to Freud's instructions is always "controlled by a given premise" (1920), started from a given point, or dominated by the situation and all that it implies. Free association would be useless for science if it were really free; its value depends on the possibility of discovering its determinants.

Instructions for free association do not follow any fixed formula. In general the patient is asked to report everything that occurs to him. He is warned against altering the sequence, excluding items, or being swayed by considerations of relevance, logic, or discretion. It is suggested that he "assume a passive attitude toward his own trains of thought," "eliminate all conscious control over his mental processes," and "drop the last vestige of a critical attitude toward what he finds" (Alexander, 1937; Freud, 1920). This technique tends to transfer the weight of determination to the hidden regions of personality; as Alexander puts it, "once the patient abandons the conscious control and direction of his ideas, the train of the free spontaneous associations is guided more by the repressed material than by conscious motives." The patient is, however, under obligation to exclude various types of mental process the nature of which has been suggested to him, and he must maintain a fairly high level of vigilance if he is to avoid slipping into the old familiar ways and inviting the physician's censure. Free association is thus in reality a particular kind of controlled association.

The most interesting fact about free association is the obstacles it quickly encounters. It was through a study of these obstacles—the silences, blockings, embarrassments and anxieties of the patient which came to be called resistance—that Freud built up his concept of repression. It is worth while to point out and expressly reject a common misunderstanding about free association, the idea that it opens a highway over which repressed memories and fantasies roll smoothly into consciousness. No such miracle takes place, and the maximum effect that can possibly be attributed to the free associative technique is a small reduction in the efficacy of habitual defenses, a weakening of the top layer of conscious control. Small as this change may be when thought of in terms of behavior dynamics, it is just enough to upset the delicate balance of personality organization in favor of the hidden regions. If repressed material starts to ooze upward there is now an appreciable interval before it is met by the customary defenses, a precious moment during which the physician, if not the patient himself, can catch a glimpse of both parties to the conflict. Reflective psychoanalysts such as Anna Freud (1937) now consider themselves as much, if not more, concerned with analyzing the defensive operations of the ego as with revealing unconscious impulses. It is at those moments when he fails to obey instructions that the patient reveals himself most fully.

In so far as a theory of free association has been formulated, it falls under the theory of autistic thinking introduced by Bleuler and developed by Jung (1916). Bleuler (1924) drew a distinction between realistic thought, best represented in the serious solution of problems, and autistic thought such as took place in daydreams. Varendonck (1921) in his study of daydreams enumerates the following characteristics of autistic thought: (1) a turning away from reality so that inner mental life assumes the dominant position, (2) spontaneous drift without the toil and fatigue which attends working for communication by means of speech, and (3) guidance of associations by some tendency or striving often of a pleasant kind. It will be noticed that free association belongs somewhere between the realistic and the autistic as thus conceived. The

constraints of reality are by no means abandoned, but the special situation created by psychotherapy definitely favors a predominance of inner
tendencies over external considerations.

Dreams

Man was probably interested in his dreams long before it occurred
to him to examine his waking thoughts. Dreams have been regarded as
real events, as prophecies, and as divine revelations, and their interpretation is one of the oldest of the psychological arts. Nineteenth century
science brought with it an interlude of complete scepticism, when dreams
were considered to be nothing but the "rumbling of brain molecules" or
"wind playing over the strings of the soul instrument," but it was not
long before Freud began his work designed to show that the dream is
"a perfectly valid, sensible, and valuable psychic act," and before Havelock Ellis declared that "dreams, rightly understood, may furnish us
with clues to the whole of life." It is possible to regard the dream as a
kind of spontaneous free association. The constraints of reality are
somewhat withdrawn during sleep, opening the way for projections from
the usually hidden regions of personality. Thus the dream can be looked
upon as a natural projective method capable of revealing much valuable
information if only the signs can be correctly read.

If dreams are to be fully understood it is desirable to find some way
of bringing them under experimental control. In this paragraph we
shall notice the available *methods,* postponing the results to their appropriate places in the review that follows. Probably the first experimental
study of dreams was that of Maury (1861) who looked into the effects
of external stimuli such as the odor of perfume, pinching the neck, or
tickling the face with a feather. The principle behind Maury's experiments has been followed in all subsequent studies, but each investigator
introduces into his subject's dream life the particular kind of stimuli
that he considers important. Thus Klein (1930) has used a wide variety
of physical stimuli; Malamud and Linder (1931) had their subjects look
at pictures and noticed what residues appeared in dreams the following
night; Arnold-Forster (1921) used autosuggestion to influence the contents of her night fantasies; while Prince (1939), Schrötter (1912), and
Roffenstein (1923) gave suggestions calling for dreams based on personal problems or on themes related to inferred unconscious tendencies.
Another major problem for the experimenter has been to find a way of
producing dreams when they are wanted rather than waiting for them to
appear spontaneously. Prince and Schrötter produced a few night
dreams by post-hypnotic suggestion, but other investigators report only
the rarest success with this method. Both Roffenstein and Klein found
it relatively easy to bring about dreams in hypnosis, the latter maintaining that such dreams are similar in every way to those of natural
sleep.

Freud's Theory of Dreams.—Before taking up the observations and experiments which constitute our present knowledge about the subject we shall briefly scan the most influential modern theory of dreams. This theory was offered to the world in 1900 in *The Interpretation of Dreams,* a book which many readers consider Freud's masterpiece and which Freud himself believed to contain "the most valuable of all the discoveries it has been my good fortune to make" (1900). To begin with, Freud drew a distinction between the *manifest content* of a dream, the procession of images and events that one experiences in sleep and remembers on waking, and the *latent content* or basic strivings and memories that set the dream in motion in the first place. To make his way from the manifest to the latent content he used the method of free association starting in turn from each item in the reported dream. Just as free association led from the meaningless symptoms and imaginings of neurotic patients to their tangled underlying strivings, so it formed a bridge from the absurd manifest content to the meaningful motives that lay behind dreams.

Freud first became convinced that dreams represent the fulfilment of wishes; later (1933), in order to allow for battle dreams and nightmares where fear was the reigning emotion, he modified this view and said that "the dream is an *attempted* wish-fulfilment; under certain conditions it can only achieve its end in a very incomplete way, or has to abandon it entirely." The biological function of the dream is to preserve sleep. The principal disturbers of sleep are unfulfilled wishes, and the dream attempts to ward off the disturbance by representing that the wish is fulfilled. If such fulfilment involves too great anxiety or if the wish is constantly reinforced from somatic sources the dream fails in its purpose and the sleeper awakens.

If the manifest content does not in the least resemble an attempted wish-fulfilment, or indeed any other intelligible process, it is because the wish in its passage to finished dream expression incurs a high degree of distortion. Working backwards over the chain of free associations, Freud developed his theory of the dream-work, the process by which latent impulses combine with available images to fashion the final product. "The dream-content appears to us as the translation of the dream-thoughts into another mode of expression, whose symbols and laws of composition we must learn by comparing the origin with the translation" (1900). One of the mechanisms of translation is *condensation,* the compressing of numerous thoughts into a small number of images, a process that Freud believed necessary to raise the images to sufficient intensity; related to it is *displacement,* which is said to occur when the importance or value of an idea in the latent content is removed to a wholly neutral idea in the manifest. Further distortion arises because the latent thoughts have to be represented in *concrete imagery,* as events actually taking place, so that logical relations are almost entirely lost. Dream-work is not able to create its own images; the wishes that seek expression have to combine with images lying ready in the mind, usually remnants from the previous day. Finally there occurs a *secondary elaboration,* an unwitting attempt to make better sense of the dream as one recalls it afterward. All of these distortions arise from the peculiar nature of the sleeping state, but they can furthermore be seized upon by forces making for repression.

In practice this statement of the theory is qualified by two additional propositions. Freud believed that in adults at any rate the only wishes having power enough to create dreams were the repressed infantile sexual wishes that he had shown to be so important in neurosis. Furthermore, he maintained that certain symbols, especially those having to do with infantile conceptions of the sex act, were so nearly universal that they could be interpreted without regard to their connotation for the individual dreamer. Only when the theory is topped off with these last two propositions does the dream become what Freud claimed it to be, the royal road to the unconscious.

Many parts of Freud's theory have been subjected to critical attack. His notion of fixed symbols is almost universally rejected: a hundred titles could probably be assembled on this question. The remaining objections can be gathered under two heads. (1) There has been much criticism of the restriction of effective dream stimuli to unconscious infantile motives. "What is there," Jung (1934) asks in his most recent discussion of the topic, "which the dream cannot on occasion embody?" (2) There has been a great deal of objection to Freud's use of free association to reach the latent content of dreams and his contention that the pathways thus opened were those originally traversed by the dream process. Freud (1900, p. 491) was somewhat aware of this difficulty, but his concessions have not satisfied other investigators who agree with Jung (1934) that however straight free association may lead to complexes it never unravels the tangled skein of the dream. The cogency of these criticisms forces us to look beyond Freud's own evidence, but certain features of his theory hold their place as enduring contributions to the understanding of dreams. It is generally agreed that the dream has something to tell about the personality of the dreamer, that it springs from an attempt to interpret and manage tensions which are likely to disturb sleep, and that it takes place in a language of concrete images and events which may distort and conceal a perfectly intelligible process. In what follows we shall distinguish for separate treatment the *form* of dreams, the characteristics of the mind in dreaming, and their *content,* the sources of excitation and the ideas and motives that enter.

Formal Characteristics of Dreams.—Perhaps the chief peculiarity of dreams is their faithful adherence to the present tense. They are thoughts turned into realities. The transition can easily be observed in the hypnagogic images that occur in drowsy states. A systematic attempt to observe this important borderland was made by Silberer

(1909) who forced himself to notice the contents of his mind as he dropped off to sleep and as he awakened. Thoughts sometimes of a quite abstract nature can in this way be observed in the very act of free translation into dream images. Arnold-Forster (1921) believes that much of the apparent confusion of dreams results from this process of translation, the stream of association being constantly deflected by the very vividness of the images. In the waking state a person might say of a rumbling sound that it resembled a train or a herd of running horses; in the dream he sees a train go by which turns into a herd of horses, the similes becoming immediate realities. In Gutheil's recent study (1939) there are numerous examples of the same process; for instance, a patient who fears inability to control certain impulses dreams that she is teaching school and cannot prevent the children from runing around. The language of the dream is present events, and all other thoughts, abstract, conditional, remote, and complex, must be translated or symbolized in this medium.

Two bold attempts have been made to study the formation of dream symbols in cases where repression was presumed to be at work. Schrötter (1912) suggested to his subjects in hypnosis that they would dream about some specified repugnant sexual topic. Occasionally such a suggestion was not rejected and the subject produced a hypnotic dream filled with symbols and disguises but still clearly related to the suggested content. Roffenstein (1923) found it necessary to state explicitly that the dream should be disguised; under these circumstances his subject, a relatively uneducated woman, produced in her hypnotic dreams an extraordinary array of symbols similar to those found in Freud's interpretations. These experiments, of course, are very difficult; the necessary controls are almost impossible to establish. All that can be claimed for them is a hint concerning the devious ways of symbolism and a hope that the topic will not resist investigation.

Content of Dreams.—Just as thought occurs in an attempt to understand and solve the problems of waking life, dreams take place in an attempt to interpret and manage the tensions that disturb the equilibrium of sleep. Such disturbance can conceivably arise from a great many sources, and we shall now review the observations that bear on the nature of these sources.

There is little doubt that external stimuli may act as disturbers of sleep and find their way into dreams. It is well known that the perception of such stimuli is exceedingly inaccurate; as Bergson remarked, "a gust of wind blowing down the chimney becomes the howl of a wild beast or a tuneful melody." The most thoroughgoing research on this subject is Klein's experiments (1930) with hypnotic dreams. Internal stimuli such as bladder distention act in a similar fashion; moreover, Grünbaum (1926) has shown that a tumor involving the auditory nerve fills the dream with auditory experience, while Hoff and Pötzl (1937) found numerous dreams of flying and falling in two patients with labyrinthine disturbances. The latter investigators produced falling dreams in hypnosis and in paraldehyde sleep by rotating their subjects, but Klein (1930) found them to result from "a passive and sudden downward shift of a bodily part as the sleeper alters his position on a yielding surface such as a mattress or pillow." There is evidently a connection, but a fairly loose one, between dreams and direct stimulation.

We may next turn our attention to the content of children's dreams, an indirect way of approaching the question of sources. The chief studies are those of Blanchard (1926) and of Foster and Anderson (1936). Blanchard found parents and animals the principal actors, and wish and fear fulfilments the principal motives, in the dreams of 300 children at a guidance clinic. Foster and Anderson gave special attention to unpleasant dreams, which were found to decrease with age and to be concerned at first mainly with animals, from 5 to 9 with bad people and impersonal dangers, and from 9 to 12 with difficulties surrounding the dreamers or their friends and pets. No attempt was made in these studies to go beyond the manifest content, but the evidence as it stands tends to underline the importance of current matters of interest in the dreams of children.

The part played by current emotional stresses has been investigated by Cason (1935) and Bagby (1930). Cason's study, which was confined to nightmares, led to this conclusion: "the nightmare dream always seems to be concerned with what is for the person at the time his most important personal problem." Bagby collected some dreams from both members of an engaged couple; analysis by free association allowed him to go behind the manifest symbols to a content which was nevertheless sufficiently explained by "current emotional stresses." In his experiments with suggested dreams Schrötter (1912) noticed that the dreamer sometimes wove the suggested contents into a plot centered on the transference relation. In spite of these evidences one must be cautious about the part played by current emotional problems; everyone must often have noticed that persistent problems which harass him during the day cut no figure whatsoever in his dream life.

The importance of repressed infantile motives has been pointed out again and again by Freud and his followers, but no experimental studies have been possible. Other students of personality who favor depth analysis find somewhat different roots beneath the dream. Adler (1929), for example, considers it a piece of anticipatory thinking in which various possible forward steps into the future are tested. Jung (1922) emphasizes the compensatory function of dreams: "those thoughts, propensities, and tendencies of a human personality, which in conscious life are too seldom recognized, come spontaneously into action in the sleeping state, when to a large extent the conscious process is disconnected." This compensatory function, the taking up of what was neglected or repressed during the day, was exemplified in some ingenious experiments by Malamud and Linder (1931). Patients with known strong emotional problems were shown a picture for 30 seconds, asked to describe it a few minutes later, and required to report their dreams of the following night. In a long series Malamud and Linder found 16 instances in which details omitted from the description appeared in dreams, these details being plainly related to important emotional problems.

Summary: the Theory of Dreams.—It is clear from the foregoing discussion that dreams are multiply determined. Whatever tends to disturb sleep, whether it be external or internal stimuli, perseverating matters of interest, emotional problems, the unfinished business of the day, or the neglected and repressed tendencies in personality, receives treatment in the peculiar and primitive language of the dream. The part played by external disturbances has been studied to the point of diminishing returns; they are but one of many determinants, and the dreaming mind makes of them about what it pleases. The part played by unconscious infantile motives cannot be further clarified without new techniques rather difficult to imagine. The most fruitful field for research would seem to be the attempt to show what contribution is made by activants experimentally inserted the evening before: for instance, completed and uncompleted tasks, pictures shown too briefly to be fully grasped, or problems instituted by hypnotic suggestion.

Word Association Test

Like so many ingenious ideas, the word association method began with Francis Galton (1885). Watching the first thing that came to his mind upon reading a given word, Galton quickly noticed the decidedly small range of responses he seemed able to give, the unexpected preponderance of childhood associations, and the clearly unfree, overdetermined character of what at first seemed like a lawless jump of fancy. As early as 1896 Kraepelin was interested in the diagnostic possibilities of the method, but it was not until the extensive studies of Jung and his associates about 1906 (Jung, 1918) that these possibilities were to any serious extent explored. Jung felt that word associations offered a convenient means of testing the hypotheses which underlay the free association technique; in the end he worked out a standard procedure for the rapid preliminary detection of "complexes." A rather different use of the method was developed by Kent and Rosanoff (1910) who showed that it can be used to distinguish the insane from the sane. In contrast to Jung, they chose words that were unlikely to call up personal problems, and their diagnosis was based entirely on the proportion between common and uncommon associations. The success of these initial studies has set off no little research designed to clarify the nature of the word association process and to evaluate its diagnostic significance. The magnitude of this undertaking can be gauged from the 91 titles which Symonds assembled in his review 10 years ago (1931, Chapter 10).

Nature of the Test.—To make the most of its possibilities the word association test must be given individually. The subject is told that on hearing the experimenter speak a word he is to reply "as quickly as possible with the first word that comes to his mind" (Symonds, 1931). The examiner writes down not only the response word but also the reaction time and whatever peculiarities of speech and behavior he may observe. Jung's list of 100 words (1918) is designed to touch on all the common emotional problems, while Kent and Rosanoff's (1910) is as free as possible from such connotations. The standard procedure can be varied and complicated in numberless ways. Many workers prefer to ask for a chain of associations rather than a single word, thereby approximating more closely the original free association method. Others have sought to enrich the test by adding direct measures of emotional upset. The first variation of this kind was reported by Peterson and Jung (1907) who used both the pneumograph and the "psychogalvanometer." Measures of respiration have since been favored in socalled "lie-detector" methods, but the galvanic skin response has achieved greater popularity in studies of emotional disturbance. Another variation is the combined motor method of Luria (1932), who makes his subjects respond simultaneously with a word and a downward thrust of the finger on a plunger. Emotional disturbance betrays itself in a disruption of what under normal circumstances is a simple and easily controlled action. Kohs (1914) surveyed a number of further variations such as the completion of stories, the guessing at words presented very briefly with the tachistoscope, and the interpretation of phrases dimly pronounced from a phonograph record. Kohs' paper serves to remind us that modern projective methods are direct descendants of the word association test.

The factors that determine a given word association must of necessity be very numerous. If one proposes to use the test as a means of detecting "complexes" or other material from the less accessible regions of personality one must be prepared to state the exact way in which such material displays itself. There have been a good many studies that brought out the effect of factors having nothing to do with individual feeling or experience. Symonds (1931), however, ends his careful review of these studies with the statement that "in the main one must look to the individual experience for an explanation of the precise word given." It is because of this relation to individuality that the word association test has proved useful as a method of diagnosis. Its most common use, with which we shall first be occupied, is the detection of "complexes," but it has also been employed to investigate various other aspects of personality.

Diagnosis of Centers of Emotional Disturbance.—When the word association test proceeds smoothly the subject answers with a fairly regular reaction time and with responses sensibly related to the given words. The sign that a "complex" or center of emotional disturbance has been touched is a disruption of this regular pattern. At one time or another 20 or more such signs or complex-indicators have been proposed, but the ones that Jung pointed out in the beginning can still be considered the most important. In Jung's opinion prolonged reaction time, a perfect analogue to the blocking found in free association, was the strongest indicator of a complex, though an unusually short time, well below the subject's average, might sometimes have the same significance. Peculiarities in the content provided the second group of clues, and here Jung mentioned repetition of the stimulus word, misunderstanding, and imperfect replies such as stammering, whispering, or answering with more than one word. Finally there were direct signs of upset: catching the breath, laughing, flushing, and so on. Concurrence of several signs strengthened the impression that emotion was getting in its disruptive work, and the meaning of the words so affected sometimes outlined with surprising clearness the pattern of a patient's troubles.

The major scientific problem of the word association test is that of validity. How can one establish with reasonable certainty the relation between disrupted word associations and centers of emotional disturbance?

1. CONCURRENCE OF COMPLEX-INDICATORS.—If it can be shown that the different complex-indicators are not distributed through the word list in random fashion, but instead are bunched together on certain words, evidence is established that they are at least related among themselves, whatever else they may signify. Hull and Lugoff (1921) found significant intercorrelations among three complex-indicators: repetition of stimulus word, misunderstanding, and long reaction time.

2. CORRELATION WITH OTHER MEASURES OF EMOTIONAL DISTURBANCE.—Peterson and Jung (1907) were the first to demonstrate a correlation between a complex-indicator, prolonged reaction time, and an independent sign of emotional disturbance, the galvanic skin reflex. A more extended investigation by Smith (1922) disclosed a correlation of .47 between galvanic deflections and association times. More recently Hunt and Landis (1935) made a similar study but found that only one of their 22 subjects gave a correlation as high as four times its probable error. Krause (1937) reports significant coefficients of association between prolonged reaction time (over 2.6 seconds) and motor disorganization measured by Luria's method.

3. CORRELATION WITH KNOWN COMPLEXES.—Jung (1918) made extended comparisons between the results of the word association test

and the known complexes of patients as revealed by psychoanalysis. This method of global validation is in one respect highly sound: it keeps faith with the total personality, seizing upon patterns both in the test and in the person which are large enough to include the obvious complexities of each. But unfortunately it is on all sides open to errors of judgment, selection of data, halo effects, and projection of favorite interpretations. With this in mind, investigators have sought a more limited kind of complex such as an embarrassing misdeed which the subject would be loath to confess. Crosland (1929), after reviewing the history of deception tests and working out 40 signs of guilt, gave the word association test to 55 college students, seven of whom were guilty of known but unconfessed misdemeanors. His 40 signs piled up such an impressive weight of evidence that six of the seven confessed.

4. Correlation with Experimentally Induced Complexes.—The perfect scientific check of the validity of the word association test would be to induce a complex artificially and measure its effect on the responses. The difficulty lies, of course, in the induction of a complex by artificial means, but Luria (1932) availed himself of hypnotic suggestion for this purpose. With the aid of deep hypnosis Luria found it occasionally possible to persuade a person that he had committed some crime, for instance that he had stolen a friend's money, beaten and injured an annoying child, or in the case of a medical student performed an illegal abortion and killed the patient. Acceptance of the suggestion went well beyond verbal compliance, occurring sometimes with genuine and stormy emotional disturbance. The discovery that such acceptance was possible led Luria to set up an ideal situation for validating both the word association test and his own motor method. Choosing a word list sprinkled with references to the complex, he tested his subjects before and after the hypnotic session and again after a second hypnosis during which the earlier suggestions were removed. Luria reported positive findings but did not give them in detail. The experiment has been successfully repeated by Huston, Shakow and Erickson (1934), whose results in respect to word association confirm Luria's report.

Diagnosis of Further Aspects of Personality.—Although its greatest success has been achieved in the detection of centers of emotional disturbance, the word association test has been requisitioned for various other diagnostic services. No little care has been bestowed on the suggestion of Kent and Rosanoff (1910) concerning the diagnostic importance of unusual associations. Kent and Rosanoff made a comparison between 1,000 normal persons and 247 psychotic patients and found that the former gave 91.7% common replies as against 70.7% for the latter. A common reply is one that is made by several people, and the figures mean simply that psychotics give three times as many unusual, individual associations as do normal people. This line of research has led no further; Kent and Rosanoff's original finding simply stands for what it is worth. Several workers have undertaken to classify the responses, in the hope that their categories would point to traits of personality (Galton, 1885; Jung, 1918). Others have tried to convert word associations into a method for diagnosing interests, attitudes, and social capacity. Vernon (1938), in reviewing studies of this kind, concludes that it is futile to use the test to examine aspects of personality which can be so much better exposed by other devices. The value of word associations in the study of attitudes would seem to be a secondary one, the eluding of a first line of defenses in order to secure an expression of feelings and sentiments not available to direct questioning. Meltzer (1935) successfully employed chain associations for this purpose in a study of children's attitudes toward their parents. For any more systematic diagnosis other techniques are to be preferred.

Clinical Value.—The word association test still has its place, in spite of rising competition, among the devices at the clinical psychologist's disposal for investigating the hidden regions of personality. At the end of his survey Symonds (1931) writes: "That the association method is a powerful tool in the diagnosis of conduct has been demonstrated without a doubt." Ebaugh (1936) finds the combined motor method particularly useful in examining and even treating patients who are more willing to accept a graphic record of their emotional disturbances than an interpretation by the doctor. Wells (1935) does not recommend the association test except in situations "where individuals of rather superior intellect must be intensively studied with some regard to limitations of time." Meier (1938), however, outlines a somewhat wider clinical function: (1) to convince patients who deny the existence of unconscious trends in themselves, (2) to give the physician a first approach to these trends when there are no spontaneous manifestations, (3) with severely inhibited patients, (4) with rigid schizophrenics, and (5) with patients who remain for a time unable to talk easily about themselves.[1]

Rorschach Test

The Rorschach test is a good example of that happy combination of genius and hard work which the study of personality sorely needs. The initial genius was provided by the psychiatrist Hermann Rorschach, who between 1911 and 1921 experimented with ink-blots as a means of stimulating and testing imagination. The choice of ink-blots was perhaps no more than a happy accident, and was certainly not original with Rorschach, but his claim to genius rests less on the instrument chosen than on the use made of it. In his hands, what started as a technique for studying imagination ended as a method of studying the whole personality; what began as a vague and uncertain instrument became at last

---

[1] For some results of the association method from psychotic subjects and an interpretation, see Chapter 32 by Hunt and Cofer.

a sharp diagnostic tool.] Rorschach acted on the principle that every performance of a person is an expression of his whole personality, the more visibly so if the performance is of an unusual nature so that conventional patterns cannot be produced to conceal individuality. It is this very scope and completeness which gives the test its present popularity and which constitutes both its strength and its weakness. Clinical workers, after struggling for years to reconstruct from test scores convincing pictures of their clients, have begun to turn almost recklessly to a technique which gives complete even if somewhat generalized portraits. Rorschach showed that in telling what he sees in ink-blots a person can be made to display certain large outlines of his personality.

This much we can justly call genius, but all further credit belongs to scientific patience. Rorschach himself initiated in his *Psychodiagnostik* (1921) the laborious work of validating his intuitions, and his footsteps have been followed in the 251 publications which at the last count (Krugman, 1940) constituted the Rorschach bibliography. It may seem surprising that so much energy has been put forth on a single test. Nothing short of this, however, can reasonably be expected to accomplish the testing and retesting, the patient pursuit of each detail, the running down of every clue and the squeezing out of every hint, which alone can give us satisfactory methods for investigating a subject so complex as personality. It is not unduly difficult to make up a personality test, but it is a gigantic undertaking to find out what it is worth.

Nature of the Test.—As in other projective methods the examiner's purpose is not disclosed to the subject. A plausible fabrication having been made to suit the circumstances, sometimes with an explanation of how symmetrical ink-blots are made, the subject is simply handed the first of the ten plates and asked to tell what he sees there. Rorschach workers are by no means fully agreed on the exact instruction (Klopfer, 1937; Beck, 1937), but the central idea is contained in Rorschach's own formula: "What does it look like? What could this be?" The number of responses given and the time taken with each card are left entirely to the subject.

Aspects of Personality Revealed.—The apparent simplicity of this procedure is in sharpest contrast to the wide range of information which the Rorschach test is claimed to yield. An inventory of this information has recently been drawn up by Klopfer (1940) who prefaces it with the general warning that "the Rorschach method does not reveal a behavior picture, but rather shows—like an X-ray picture—the underlying structure which makes behavior understandable." Klopfer's division between underlying structure and behavior may be likened to the distinction between mainly innate temperamental qualities or capacities and the specific patterns laid upon them by experience. The Rorschach test is most informative about the former, in contrast to the personal content with which this chapter is otherwise mainly concerned.

Klopfer's inventory is divided into three parts, the first of which is called *"basic personality configurations."* Under this heading belong two types of balance. In the first place there is the balance between spontaneity and control, ranging from a rigid constriction of all spontaneous tendencies to a completely disintegrated impulsiveness. If we wish to think of this as a linear variable it might be called the control factor or the impulsion-deliberation ratio (Murray, 1938), and it readily takes its place in a wider frame of reference when we remember Luria's (1932) studies of the "functional barrier" that controls the release of energy, a barrier the efficiency of which increases with age but breaks down under emotional stress. The second type of balance which the Rorschach test reveals is that between introversial and extraversial tendencies. This relation, called the *Erlebnistypus,* or experience-balance, was one of Rorschach's most original ideas; it has been carefully compared by Vernon (1933) with similar concepts, especially Jung's introversion-extraversion. Klopfer defines it as the relative dominance of inner and outer promptings in personality. These two types of balance constitute the basic configuration of personality in so far as the Rorschach test is able to disclose it. The second part of Klopfer's inventory deals with *intellectual aspects* and includes not only the amount but also the kind of intelligence that a person displays. It is possible to assess the mental approach to problems, the preference for inductive, deductive, or intuitive thinking, the degree of originality and common sense, the relation between imaginative and rational functions, and the possession of special gifts along theoretical or artistic lines. The third section of the inventory has to do with the *emotional aspects* of personality, the emotional ties with inner life on the one hand and with outer reality on the other. Information of this type is particularly useful for detecting the presence of neurotic or psychotic disturbances.

Method of Scoring.—About any given response to a Rorschach inkblot it is possible to say four things. First there is the *location* of the part chosen for interpretation, the options being the whole blot, a large and fairly obvious portion, a small detail, or some part of the white background. In the second place come the *determinants* of the response, the characteristics of the blot that make it seem as it does. The inkblots themselves offer three possibilities in this respect, their form or shape, their shading, and in five of the plates their color, but these external determinants may set off certain imaginative processes that cause the figures to be seen either as in motion or as in deep perspective, giving two additional determinants of a less purely objective kind. The *content* of the response provides the third step of the scoring, and here Rorschach workers have set up several common categories, such as people, animals, man-made objects, plants, and landscapes, without denying themselves the right to look for more personal meanings and even for "complex-indicators" in the fashion of the word association test. The fourth judgment that can be made on any response has to do with its *originality,* a matter that is handled statistically in a way analogous to Kent and Rosanoff's common and unusual associations. There are certain more general features of the test which appear in the scoring, for example the total number of responses, the average reaction time, the orderliness of procedure, and the signs of blocking, uncertainty, self-correction, and the like, but in the main the Rorschach psychogram is built from a tabulation of the four scores assigned to each response.

For convenience of exposition we shall have to act as if each scoring category reflected a certain trait or aspect of personality. One of the soundest features of the Rorschach method, however, is its avoidance of this much too simple notion and its power of keeping uppermost the patterned and organized nature of personality. The psychogram shows not only the number but also the proportion of responses belonging in each category, and this proportion is of great weight in reaching the final interpretation. Two or more responses indicative of strong uncontrolled emotion may be taken as a distinct danger signal in one record but looked upon as harmless in another where there are signs of balancing factors and constructive possibilities. The Rorschach test remains faithfully a method of diagnosing the total personality.

Detailed statements of the meaning of each scoring category can be found in publications by Beck (1937) and Klopfer (1939). We shall here notice some of the more important and less obvious relations. In general, the *location* responses have their chief importance in diagnosing the intellectual aspects of personality; the proportions among them yield what Rorschach called *Erfassungstypus* or preferred mode of apperception. Whole responses (W) show an emphasis on the general as opposed to the particular; combined with other signs of mental excellence, they occur frequently in people with abstract and theoretical ability. Common detail responses (D) imply by contrast an emphasis on the concrete, and appear with greatest frequency in people with practical, unoriginal minds. Rare detail response (Dr) signify an interest in the less obvious, occurring relatively often in people with precise, discriminating, and critical minds, but they may imply pedantic and obsessive tendencies or even a pathological concern for the trivial. By itself no one sign establishes an important diagnosis; what these perceptual preferences mean in the particular case must be deduced from a much larger pattern of findings.

The most original part of the test is the interpretation founded on the *determinants* of response: form, color, shading, and movement. The most common determinant is *form* (F) which is regarded by Beck (1937) as "an index to control over intellectual processes." If the form is sharply and accurately perceived ($F+$) it may be inferred that control is in good order, and nothing is more characteristic of schizophrenics than their way of playing fast and loose with the presented forms ($F-$) in favor of their own distorted imaginings. Responses determined by *color* give the most direct clue to the impulsive and emotional life. Color usually arouses some degree of affect, and it is of great interest to see how the subject uses this experience. He may suppress it altogether, or on the contrary he may throw out a hasty interpretation based solely on color with no regard to form (C), an exclamation such as "blood!" The degree to which a person allows his responses to be determined by color is taken as a rough measure of his emotional intensity, and the way in which he combines color with form shows the pattern of his control over this emotion. Thus form-color response (FC), in which the two determinants are fused into a meaningful whole, implies a refined control of impulse and has been found again and again to be an index of capacity for social rapport, while color-form (CF), in which the form is secondary though not neglected, goes with somewhat impulsive, unrestrained natures. The third characteristic inherent in the ink-blots is *shading*. This somewhat less striking determinant was apparently overlooked in Rorschach's early work but made its appearance in a posthumous paper edited by Oberholzer (Rorschach and Oberholzer, 1924). The shading category is one of the most confused issues among Rorschach workers, as may be judged from the extensive review by Hertz (1940), and it is not yet possible to say exactly what it means. *Movement,* on the other hand, has been from the start a prominent though somewhat elusive determinant. As Wells (1935) puts it: "The fundamental fact is that the subject sees not somebody moving but *something going on*; the fancy is playing upon the blot in a way absent when only something static is seen." Rorschach, however, assigned the movement score (M) only when there was evidence of empathy, a true experiencing of the movement, and this could be present only in human movements or human-like movements of animals. In present work with the test the M-response stands as an indicator of the "richness of the inner life, the creative powers, and the acceptance of one's inner promptings" (Klopfer, 1939).

It is from the *relation among determinants* that the basic configurations of personality can be inferred. The balance between form on the one hand and color, shading, and movement on the other establishes the relation between control and spontaneity. The second balance, the relative dominance of inner promptings and outer stimulation (Rorschach's *Erlebnistypus*), is calculated from the proportion of movement and color. Undoubtedly the determinants yield the most important information about personality; on their validity the Rorschach test stands or falls.

Accepting color as an index of affectivity, it is possible to make a lengthwise analysis of a Rorschach record in order to discover the sequence of reactions to color and the defense adopted against it. Rorschach pointed out a number of signs that color was producing emotional upset or *color shock*. These signs, which include disturbances of reaction time, exclamations, and peculiar replies as well as the proportion of responses on colored cards, remind us directly of the complex indicators used in the word association test. Color shock is considered by many workers a highly reliable diagnostic sign of neurosis, particularly useful in distinguishing it from schizophrenia in the incipient stages.

Relation of Scoring Categories to Personality: Validity of the Test.—It is incredible to most people that an ink-blot test can tell so much about personality. There are two things that create disbelief. In the first place, there is the relation between the scoring categories and the aspects of personality they are supposed to reveal, between color and emotion, movement and creativity, form and control. Is it true, for example, that the color responses have the affective significance which Rorschach workers assign them? In the second place, there is the still more far-reaching question, applicable even to those categories whose nature is beyond dispute, as to whether the Rorschach performance is a true and sufficient sample of a person's behavior. Rare detail responses may well signify an emphasis on the minute and unusual, but is this a general characteristic of the person showing itself throughout his intellectual and personal habits or is it merely a peculiarity of his behavior with ink-blots?

Friends of the test bring forward one argument that makes these dubious relationships more plausible. The unfamiliarity of the task, they point out, the impossibility of producing conventional replies, the difficulty of fathoming the examiner's purpose, indeed the whole relaxed, spontaneous attitude that must to some extent be reached if anything at all is to be seen on the plates, forces a person to fall back on the primitive tendencies which are peculiar to his own individual make-up. It is this that establishes the fundamental continuity between free association and the Rorschach test. In both cases the top layers of habit and self-concealment are peeled off, leaving the hidden regions at least a little exposed. But beyond this the similarity continues only a short way: Rorschach set for himself the larger goal of detecting the fundamental, mainly innate variables of personality.

As a first step in establishing the validity of the Rorschach test it is natural to ask what is known about its *reliability*. This question has lately been the subject of a careful historical and experimental study by Fosberg (1941) who summarizes in tabular form the work of previous investigators and reports new results of his own, concluding that the test-retest reliability of the Rorschach method is high.

The problem of validation presents far more baffling obstacles. Hertz (1935, 1941) has given two excellent discussions of this problem, to which she finds four general approaches, by no means mutually exclusive. She first mentions *direct experimentation*, the giving of the test under experimentally altered conditions such as hypnosis (Sarbin, 1939) or insulin shock treatment (Piotrowski, 1939); to date such work has but barely scratched the surface. A second method is the *comparison of Rorschach categories with independent objective criteria*; for example, the correlation between estimates of intelligence and Binet scores, reported by Vernon (1935) to be .78 ± .06. Apart from intelligence little progress has been made along this line because, as Wells (1935) observes, "for the personality traits involved there is hardly a criterion worthy of the name." A third method of validation, ideal but laborious, is the *comparison of Rorschach findings with extensive individual case studies*. A single instance, impressive for the agreement between psychogram and personality study, is reported by Murray (1938), but the systematic cooperative project outlined by Rosenzweig (1935) still remains to be carried out.

The fourth method of validation, the *comparison of groups with known differences of intelligence and personality picture*, was Rorschach's own method of choice. He resorted in the main to mental patients, who offered fairly well-attested extremes in one or another trait, but he also brought in artists, scholars, people of average gifts, and the feeble-minded. He began no doubt with certain guesses, but in the end his statement that *M*-responses, for example, represent the inner life and its creativity stands not on a guess but on the fact that artists and other gifted people give many such responses, average people only a few, and the feeble-minded none. Most of Rorschach's studies have been repeated with larger groups and more refined techniques; many of his findings have survived this test, though some have been overthrown. The present state of knowledge relative to clinical groups and to age may be summarized as follows.

SCHIZOPHRENIA.—The two most comprehensive studies are those of Rickers-Ovsiankina (1938) and Beck (1938); they have been reviewed and compared by Kelley and Klopfer (1939). According to Beck the most certain sign of schizophrenic tendencies is a large number of inaccurately perceived forms (F—); next to this he puts a low score on popular responses. These two scores reflect the bizarre and unrealistic nature of schizophrenic perception: the patient does not see what others see, and he distorts the realities before him. Fitting well with this is the finding that schizophrenics score low in common details (D), leaning either to crude W-responses or to unusual and often absurd details (Dr). FC-responses are characteristically low in relation to CF and C, but the total of color-responses runs low and there are signs of emotional blocking, for instance in refusal to interpret the blot at all.

DEPRESSION.—The leading studies are those of Guirdham (1936a, b), to which Varvel (1941) has made useful additions. The characteristic signs are slow reaction-time, low movement and color scores, low originality, and a high percentage of obvious replies. These signs reflect the retardation, affective repression, and constricting of thought into meticulous exactness which dominate the clinical picture of melancholia.

HYPOMANIC CONDITIONS.—Levy and Beck (1934) and Beck (1937) have given attention to the characteristic marks of hypomania. The number of responses tends to be high, color predominates over movement, and the proportion of $F+$ runs low. This arrangement of peculiarities accords well with the clinical picture of agile but superficially determined thought, the flight of ideas without relevance or real creativity, to which the diagnosis of hypomania is ordinarily attached.

NEUROSIS.—Miale and Harrower-Erickson (1940) list nine signs of neurosis, the presence of five being considered sufficient for diagnosis. The more important signs are as follows: reduced M (ave. 1.1), color shock, FC low or absent (ave. 0.6), $F\%$ over 50. One can see in this pattern the lack of social adaptability, the attempts at too rigid control, the thwarting of the spontaneous and original, and above all the anxiety that can be regarded as well-nigh universal features of neurosis. Rorschach worked out a number of ways in which different types of neurosis can be distinguished.

DISTURBANCES OF THE CENTRAL NERVOUS SYSTEM.—Of great interest is the attempt to find the effect of cerebral lesions on Rorschach psychograms. The lead in this recent line of research has been taken by Piotrowski (1936a, 1937a) who first reported on a group of 33 patients, 18 with organic conditions involving the cortex, 10 with subcortical disturbances, and 5 with conversion hysteria whose external behavior closely resembled the organic cases. Organic disturbances revealed themselves in 10 characteristic signs which included a very small number of responses, slow reaction-time, almost no M, low popular response, naming of colors, much $F-$, along with more direct signs such as perplexity and self-distrust. At the same time Piotrowski (1936b, 1937b) and Tallman and Klopfer (1936) began reporting on patients with lesions of the frontal lobes, and recently Harrower-Erickson (1940) has started a series on cerebral tumors.

CHILDREN.—Perhaps the leading authority on the application of the Rorschach test to children is Loosli-Usteri (1937), who believes it well adapted for use from nine years onward. Other workers extend its use downward several years: Sunne (1936), for instance, has prepared norms for children between four and seven, while Klopfer and Margulies (1941) begin their series with infants of two years. Both the latter paper and Loosli-Usteri's monograph discuss the administrative difficulties involved in work with children. Statistical studies of the trends from infancy through adolescence are still so incomplete that we shall not try to summarize them here; but mention should be made of the tables prepared by Davidson and Klopfer (1938) whose paper includes references to preceding work on the problem.

The diagnostic value of the test has become clear in the foregoing account. "Innumerable investigations," Hertz wrote in 1935, "testify to the clinical possibilities of the test," a statement which she supported with mention of 32 papers. Hunter (1939) reports enthusiastically on the value of Rorschach's method in a psychological clinic, and Krugman (1941), while reminding us that no important diagnosis should be based on the ink-blots alone, enumerates several services which the test can perform in a bureau for child guidance. Benjamin and Ebaugh (1938) tested a series of fifty patients and found the correlation between Rorschach diagnosis and the final clinical diagnosis "somewhere between 84.7 and 97.8 per cent." Perhaps the greatest ultimate service of the method will be its contribution to mental hygiene. Ominous trends can sometimes be detected before behavior difficulties have arisen, providing an invaluable lead for preventive therapy.

Related Tests.—Wells has developed a variant form of the Rorschach test using a larger series of smaller ink-blots. He believes that this variation yields at least three quarters as much information in one quarter of the time. Norms have not been reported and the "Gamma" ink-blots accordingly remain a somewhat tentative clinical tool. Stern (1937) proposed the use of cloud pictures, perhaps ultimately as a psychodiagnostic technique, but primarily as a means of investigating imagination. He considered that the Rorschach blots, with their sharp outlines and symmetrical forms, narrowly restricted freedom of imagination; the cloud pictures, by contrast, offered many enticing possibilities with their irregular spots of black and gray more or less shading into one another. Quite recently Rapaport (1941) has called attention to the Szondi test, a projection technique which uses pictures of faces as its stimulus material and which seems to have good diagnostic potentialities.

Thematic Apperception Test

In describing the Rorschach test we have given our attention mainly to its function of disclosing the structural or formal aspects of personality. The Thematic Apperception Test, introduced in 1935 by Morgan and Murray, is in contrast most useful in bringing to light what might be called the content of personality, the particular images, strivings, and sentiments which have been developed in the course of individual experience. The test material consists of a series of pictures which the subject is asked to use as a starting point for fantasy.

> The test is based upon the well-recognized fact that when a person interprets an ambiguous social situation he is apt to expose his own personality as much as the phenomenon to which he is attending. Absorbed in his attempt to explain the objective occurrence, he becomes naïvely unconscious of himself and of the scrutiny of others and, therefore, defensively less vigilant. To one with double hearing, however, he is disclosing certain inner tendencies and cathexes: wishes, fears, and traces of past experience. (Murray, 1938)

Originally the subject was told to guess the probable facts represented in the picture, but experience showed that much more of the personality was revealed by asking him to create a dramatic fiction. At present the instructions imply, in words that may be freely altered to suit the age and understanding of the subject, that the test offers an opportunity to use imagination. The subject is asked to make up a story which tells how the depicted scene came about, what is going on at the moment, what the characters are feeling, and what the outcome will be.

Interpretation of Results.—The stories that a subject tells can be analyzed in a great many ways depending upon the investigator's purpose. There are hundreds of possible elements or variables ranging all the way from grammatical peculiarities to dominant themes. The stories furnish clues to the subject's level of intelligence and to the range and type of his interests, but other tests are better designed to yield this kind of information. The unique service of the Thematic Apperception Test is to disclose how and what a person imagines: how he uses his mind on an imaginative task and what kind of situations and motives he imagines.

In considering how a subject uses his imagination Rotter (1940) takes note of the following points: whether the plots are happy, humorous, unhappy, or neutral, whether the plots are illogical and incoherent or the reverse, and whether the interpretation of the picture is probable or improbable. A somewhat different approach is made by Balken and Masserman (1940) who analyze in great detail the language used. They find it possible to differentiate by several linguistic criteria the stories produced by three groups of neurotic patients: conversion hysterics, anxiety hysterics, and obsessionals. Profit would seem to lie in the hitherto untried comparison between thematic apperception material and certain Rorschach indices such as originality, organization, and movement responses.

Dynamic Content.—By the dynamic content of a story is meant the human situations and human motives that the subject, prompted by the picture, has imagined. The test material is purposely somewhat equivocal so that the dynamic content can be regarded as at least to some extent a projection of the subject's own personality. The fundamental hypothesis on which the method stands is that the need is father to the fantasy, that from the needs and situations appearing in the stories one can infer important strivings in the narrator. It must be realized, however, that a great many extraneous factors influence the content of fantasies. Masserman and Balken (1938), reflecting on their use of the test with patients, call attention to several of these factors, permanent and temporary: "the rapport of the patient, the status of the therapy, the immediate surroundings, and the even more complex and less tangible factors of the education, intelligence, culture, experience, and special interests of the subject." Moreover, in performing the imaginative task assigned them, subjects are likely to avail themselves of plots already in existence.

Morgan and Murray (1935) used subsequent interviews to examine the sources of the stories they collected. Four main sources could be distinguished: (a) books and movies; (b) events in which a friend or relative participated; (c) the narrator's own experience, objective and subjective; and (d) conscious and unconscious fantasies. Morgan and Murray do not reject, as fortuitous, material from the first two sources, considering it always significant that the subject has remembered and selected a plot from what must always be a larger mass of experience to which he has been exposed, but they attach greater importance to those plots that seem relatively free from external determination, that come into the narrator's head from he knows not where, and that seem therefore to be the purer instances of projection.

The relation between thematic apperceptions and personality is thus exceedingly complex. Even when account has been taken of all possible extraneous factors the diagnostic problem is not solved. The inference that needs in the story correspond to important strivings in the narrator is most direct in the case of tendencies displayed by a character with whom the narrator appears to have identified himself. Qualifications must be added when it comes to the forces acting on the hero: these may stand for the way he perceives his environment, for things he wishes or fears might happen to him, or even for tendencies of his own that are in conflict with the rest of his personality. Further qualification becomes necessary when we recall the different levels from which projections may issue. Much of the content very likely springs from needs and perceptions that are perfectly conscious; it is only at certain moments that subjects "project their deepest fantasies," as Morgan and Murray put it, "and thereby reveal directional tensions of which they are quite unconscious."

Proposals for Scoring.—The problem of scoring the Thematic Apperception Test has not as yet been satisfactorily solved. Different investigators have adopted schemes in accordance with their own particular requirements. Morgan and Murray used a mode of analysis and summary in which "each of the subject's stories was read and diagnosed separately and then the attempt was ·made to find a unifying thema" (Murray, 1938). Similar to this was the procedure of Masserman and Balken (1939) who attempted to infer from the stories the latent dynamics of each patient, comparing their results with the psychiatric record. Similar also was Rotter's (1940) procedure in looking for frequent themes and unusual themes. For some purposes, and in the hands of careful and responsible workers, this method of free analysis may be satisfactory, but Sanford (1939) has worked out a more complete and less subjective scheme for assessing dynamic content. Sanford's method makes it possible to give a weighted count of the needs manifested by the hero and the forces (press) that act upon him. This scheme is most suitable when it is desired to make an exhaustive analysis or to compare one set of stories closely with another. Criticisms have been raised by Rotter (1940) who points out that it overlooks more complex formations such as attitudes and thematic trends. Thus far no middle ground has been discovered on which accuracy and adequacy both can stand.

Validity of the Test.—In so far as the test reveals directional tensions that are unconscious it can be validated only by data derived from some kind of depth analysis. Morgan and Murray (1935) reported on a patient whose thematic apperceptions "adumbrated all the chief trends which five months of analysis were able to reveal"; so far this remains the sole attempt at a crucial depth investigation. Validation of less elusive test findings was undertaken by Harrison (1940) who found that "biographical and personality information, including interests, attitudes, traits, problems, and conflicts, were analytically deducible from the stories of psychiatric patients with a high degree of validity (83%) when hospital case records were used as the validating criterion." Harrison showed further that "psychiatric diagnoses of mentally disordered patients were inferred with fair accuracy" from their thematic apperceptions, and Masserman and Balken (1939) found characteristic differences among the fantasies of patients consistent with the psychodynamic mechanisms underlying their illness.

Related Tests.—

STORY COMPLETIONS.—Story completion tests have been used here and there for some time. In the last decade Zawodsky made considerable progress in standardizing such a test with both American and Polish children, but the results were destroyed during the invasion of Poland. Thomas (1937) used story completions as a means of discovering hidden conflicts in children; best results were obtained with ages 5 to 10, and the method was surprisingly successful in bringing out aggressive fantasies and death wishes. The story completion technique lends itself readily to a multiple choice form of test which greatly facilitates scoring, but some investigators prefer to use it with the widest possible freedom. Haigis (1936) and Despert and Potter (1936) find free story-telling a valuable diagnostic method for use with children, and Wheeler (Murray, 1938) reports interesting results when college students were asked to write on the theme of Hawthorne's story "The Minister's Black Veil."

Various abbreviated completion tests have been worked out beginning with the Masselon Test in which three stimulus words are to be combined into a meaningful sentence or little story. Research on sentence completion tests is now going on in several places. Wheeler (Murray, 1938) used a similes test in which subjects were asked to give apt original similes using such adjectives as "pathetic," "dangerous," and "deceptive"; "in many cases this relatively simple test furnished a surprising amount of information."

VERBAL SUMMATOR.—Another device that can be used as a projection test is the verbal summator invented by Skinner (1936). This device consists of a phonograph record that delivers various series of vowel sounds; the subject is asked to listen closely while each set is repeated several times at low intensity, and to report as soon as a phrase pops into his head. Obviously the opportunities for a projection of favorite themes are numerous; when allowance is made for external stimuli and for perseveration, the occurrence of a response can be attributed to its special strength in the individual. Shakow and Rosenzweig (1940), who prefer to call the apparatus the "tautophone," have worked out an elaborate system of scoring which in many respects resembles the Rorschach system. Pickford (1938) suggests that the nonsense syllable, once considered the acme of scientific impersonality, may profitably be used to stimulate fantasy of the most personal sort.

Play

It is a part of the definition of play that the constraints of adult reality are to some extent laid aside. This fact at once puts play in the category of projective techniques for the diagnosis of hidden aspects of personality. Older writers seemed bent on catching a single formula to describe the nature of play, but modern students are fully aware that it is a complex and multiply determined activity. For instance, Wälder (1933) mentions the following determinants: a need for mastery, a need to express various wishes, a leave of absence from reality and from the super-ego, the opportunity to become active in dealing with things, and the need to assimilate overpowering experiences by repeating them on a small and manageable scale. Play was first used for diagnosis and therapy by psychoanalysts who were seeking some substitute for free association in their child patients. The analogy between play and free association has been pushed to its ultimate point by Klein (1932) who copies the pattern of adult analysis in her treatment of children, even to the point of symbolic interpretation and the communication of her findings to the young patient. Play analysis is used in a more cautious frame of reference by Anna Freud (1928) who recognizes differences between free association and play; and the variables specific to play, such as extension in actual space, have been the object of study by Erikson (1937, 1940). Play was first used as an adjunct of therapy, but it soon became apparent that it held certain curative properties in its own right. Modern play techniques, therefore, are framed for a two-fold purpose—to understand and to cure.

Play Techniques for Diagnosis and Therapy.—Play technique consists of introducing a child to a small world of toys and allowing him to use them freely while the observer or therapist looks on. Toys are chosen to represent all the common interests of childhood: dolls representing the family, animals, vehicles, blocks to build houses, furniture including kitchen and bathroom pieces, water, sand, etc. For therapeutic purposes the exact inventory is not of importance, but Erikson (1940) has worked out a standard setting in order to observe and compare the first reactions of large numbers of children. There are various ways in which the resulting play can be interpreted. Perhaps the most important sign is play disruption, described by Erikson as follows:

> Our small patients either show an anxious care in excluding this or that toy from their play or they work themselves toward a border-line where they themselves suddenly find their doings unsafe, not permissible, unworkable, or unsatisfactory to the point of extreme discomfort. They cannot go on playing in peace—a phenomenon which we shall call play disruption.

A striking similarity will be noticed between disruption in play and the signs of emotional disturbance in free association. When conflicts and anxieties push too near to the surface, signs of disruption occur, and the observer in this way gets his first clues as to the sources of difficulty. In addition to play disruption Erikson uses the formal or spatial characteristics of the child's play as a means of diagnosis. Spatial arrangements of toys and blocks may yield valuable clues to basic reaction tendencies as well as specific problems. Some children build far and wide, scattering the toys over the whole available space; others retire to a corner and make neat enclosed arrangements. Differences of this kind have been emphasized by Lowenfeld (1939) who deduces from play constructions the nature of the child's outlook on the world.

In the therapeutic use of play the part taken by the therapist is a matter of great importance. Two tendencies can be discerned, called passive and active techniques. The passive type is well represented in Rogerson's (1939) monograph which includes detailed case summaries. The therapist at first simply sits by, taking no particular part, while the child tries out various lines of conduct to find out what is permitted. As times goes on the doctor may allow himself to be drawn into the play and to offer simple interpretations, but the child is always allowed to keep the lead. The passive method is the one in most common use, but active play therapy has been considerably developed by Levy (1937), Solomon (1938, 1940), and Conn (1938). A restricted play situation is offered and the therapist begins the play, encouraging the child to join him. Levy, for example, when treating child patients whose central difficulty is sibling rivalry, uses a mother doll, a child doll, and a baby doll. He points out that the mother doll can be dismantled and that the baby doll is made of destructible material, puts the baby at the mother's breast, and asks the patient what the third doll is going to do. In such ways the child is encouraged to express in a crude and direct way the resentful feelings which suffer suppression at home.

In a recent paper Newell (1941) compares the results obtainable by the two methods. Of active treatment he writes as follows:

I know of no other method of examining and interviewing a child which offers quicker insight into mental mechanisms or which gives clues more rapidly regarding the child's unconscious. It is truly amazing how readily a child, hiding behind the anonymity of a doll, will tell of death wishes toward a parent or sibling, of Oedipus wishes, as well as about masturbatory activities, castration anxieties, and the many forms of primitive, infantile sex theories. This method is thus a short-cut to insight which eliminates the necessity of building up a transference. . . . No other method can so quickly desensitize a child to a specific fear.

Because of these characteristics, active play therapy should be the method of choice for specific symptoms of short duration and known antecedents. It is contraindicated, however, for neuroses of longer standing, for problems created by disturbed family relations, and in cases of severe inhibition with deeply repressed hostility. In such cases the more natural passive method, which gives time for the development of a transference and which allows for the expression of resistances, is both safer and more profitable.

Play technique is primarily adapted to children, but certain workers have tried the experiment of using play in the study of adult personality. Erikson (1937), for example, asked subjects of college age to construct a dramatic scene with toys; their preliminary fumblings were observed through a one-way screen and their remarks about the final construction were collected. There were numerous signs of play disruption and hints as to unconscious problems, these hints being verified from other sources of information. College students were asked by Dubin (1940) to make two constructions, one of the world as it is and another of the world as they would like it to be. From the resulting constructions judges were able to guess with considerable success ($r = +49$) each subject's answers to an opinion questionnaire on labor, government, and war. Adult schizophrenic patients in a state hospital were put in a typical play situation by Rosenzweig and Shakow (1937) who found characteristic differences between hebephrenics, paranoids, and a normal control group, and who report favorably on the individual diagnostic possibilities of the method.

Why Does Play Have Therapeutic Value?—Various writers have discussed the reasons for the curative value of play. Rogerson (1939) mentions several factors that account for a child's improvement. Fore·-most is the relation with the therapist, the essential aspect of which is the finding of confidence to express impulses and fantasies without fear of censure, punishment, or rejection. The play situation is detached from everyday life; in it the child builds up a unique relationship in which he learns to deal with jealousy and aggression and finds out that his fears and guilty feelings are not so terrifying as he had supposed. In some cases Rogerson finds "a limited amount of interpretation helpful," but generally the important things in making a difficulty vanish are "the expression of it and the reception of it with understanding and without hostile criticism." Newell (1941) lists three sources of benefit as follows: (1) relationship with an adult who trusts and accepts but does not threaten or frighten, (2) a chance to act out fantasies and become desensitized to their emotional impact, and (3) the education and insight which the doctor can give. Neither interpretation nor any particular type of play technique is considered important by Valentine (1938) who believes that "friendly treatment in a place removed from the source of their trouble" is the best way of helping problem children. On the other hand Tallman and Goldensohn (1941) consider interpretation at crucial moments invaluable in reducing the child's anxiety in connection with certain problems. It is important to consider also what happens simultaneously outside the therapeutic sessions, when the child returns to his home and the source of his problems. This point is not overlooked in the following summary of play therapy by Erikson.

> Modern play therapy is based on the observation that a child made ambivalent and insecure by a secret hate against or fear of the natural protectors of his play (family, neighborhood) seems able to use the protective sanction of an understanding adult, in professional elaboration the play therapist, to regain some play peace. The most obvious reason is that the child has the toys and the adult for himself; sibling rivalry, parental nagging, and routine interruptions do not disturb the unfolding of his play intentions, whatever they may be.
> The observing adult's "understanding" of such play, then, is a beneficial factor even where it finds only an intangible minimum of expression in the child's presence, while its value for an indirect use in advice and guidance can hardly be over-estimated. The peace provided by solitary play or by play in the presence of a sympathetic adult often radiates for some time, often long and intensively enough to meet the radiation of recognition and love from some source in the environment, a necessary factor in all psychological cures. The chances therefore seem better where the mother too has an opportunity to relieve in conversations her ambivalence toward the child and is prepared to respond to his improvement. (1940, p. 562)

The problems most frequently treated by play therapy are those of jealousy and hate. Ackerman (1937) chose play as the most suitable medium for a study of constructive and destructive tendencies in children, while Baruch (1941) points out that among preschool activities there is no more sensitive index of aggression than play with dolls representing the family. Levy's important studies (1937) are centered on sibling rivalry, and Rogerson's (1939) material abounds with jealousy, hate, and death wishes; sexual problems taking a clear second place. Other problems, to be sure, have been studied and successfully treated by play methods, but a suspicion may well remain that this technique is particularly adapted to the dynamics of childhood aggressiveness, giving opportunity in a safe medium to express and thus learn not to fear the most unmanageable of emotions.

The value of play therapy in clinical work with children is attested by many writers. Hopeful results with 40 problem children upon whom all other methods failed are reported by Gitelson (1938) ; the value of a playroom in a hospital for mentally ill children is described by Despert (1937) ; and the application of play technique to preschool children is set forth by Despert (1940) and Tallman and Goldensohn (1941). The last-named paper describes in some detail the training that is necessary before play therapy can be successfully practiced even under psychiatric guidance. The play therapist must have come to terms with his own problems if he is to achieve the happy balance of friendly interest and alert observance without which the method may be a waste of time.

Related Methods.—The best developed variant form of play technique is drama, originally introduced by Moreno (1934). The theory, applications, and place in research of Moreno's "psychodrama" are reviewed in a paper by Franz (1940), and the therapeutic rationale is discussed by Dubin (1940) who declares that the aim is "to produce a catharsis and release of tension, thus preparing the individual for an easier adjustment in the real situation." Curran (1939) encourages his patients to write and produce their own plays, intervening occasionally to secure an assignment of parts likely to be of therapeutic value to the actors concerned, a timid and too-gentle youth, for instance, being pushed into the role of a gangster.

Not unlike the drama method is the use of puppet shows first introduced by Bender and Woltmann (1936). Standard characters representing various instinctive tendencies perform in the shows, the children being invited to participate by saying what will happen next in critical situations. So free is this participation that the method works out much like the psychodrama. Bender and Woltmann (1937) have also investigated the use of plastic material as a psychiatric approach to children's emotional problems.

Drawing and Painting

In childhood, artistic expression is purely a form of play. The child with pencil or crayons is psychologically no different from the child with toys; it is only his medium of expression that has changed. The drawings and paintings of children are particularly useful to the psychologist because, unlike the fleeting patterns of play, they can be collected and retained for leisurely, minute analysis. Such material, like all that we have examined in this chapter, can be analyzed in two ways. It can be used to investigate the content of personality, the particular fantasies and preoccupations of the artist, to which use it has frequently been put by psychopathologists. On the other hand, it can be treated as expressive movement which gives clues to the formal aspects of personality; in Stern's words, "as soon as we look upon drawing as an expressive movement, its products become an important aid in diagnosis, disclosing under certain circumstances deep-seated qualities of the child's psychic dynamics." Prior to the present-day use of drawing and painting as projective techniques especially adapted to childhood there was considerable study of the art of the insane. We shall first consider the general results of these studies, afterwards describing different methods of prompted art expression as diagnostic and therapeutic adjuncts.

The Art of the Insane.—The literature on the artistic productions of mental patients has lately been surveyed by Anastasi and Foley (1941). In the history of this subject Prinzhorn's monograph (1923) is probably the outstanding work; a second noteworthy study is Baynes' (1939) investigation of unconscious processes through schizophrenic drawings. The main gleanings from this field of research have been summarized as follows by Mosse (1940) : (1) the paintings of psychotics show a marked similarity to the drawings of children and of primitive peoples; (2) there are typical pathological signs such as stereotypy, mannerisms, symbolism, "a strange inaccessibility and a kind of noiseful display of importance amalgamated with a complete emptiness of the picture"; (3) even in the attempt to reestablish relations with reality by making an intelligible picture there is failure to achieve anything like realistic representation; (4) the creative impulse appears to be a compensatory striving and an attempt to be cured; (5) the meaning of psychotic pictures can be discovered by translating them into latent content in a way analogous to the interpretation of dreams. This last point has been developed in detail by Lewis (1928).

It is clear that very different aspects of personality can be revealed by drawing and painting. Baynes (1939) centers his study on unconscious fantasy life, following in this respect the lead of several psychoanalytic writers. Reitman (1939), on the other hand, using simple line drawings of facial expressions, found differences that distinguished schizophrenic, hysteric, and depressed patients, an observation that should be compared with the Szondi test mentioned earlier. Color and movement were noted by Pfister (1934) to yield diagnostic differences, thus establishing a parallel to two aspects of the Rorschach test. An index of a different sort, but still similar to one of the Rorschach ratios, was chosen by Schube and Cowell (1939) in a study of the spontaneous uninstructed paintings of 168 hospital patients. From various clues furnished by productivity, design, imagery, and technique, each drawing was rated on a restraint-activity scale. The range for normal people was found to be from 40 to 60, but the patients with only three exceptions fell outside these limits. Excess of restraint was found in depressed patients and in all neurotics except conversion hysterics; excess of activity characterized the work of patients in the categories of dementia praecox, mania, paranoia, and psychopathic personality. The importance of the restraint-activity variable as a fundamental dimension of personality would be greatly enhanced if it could be shown to appear both in painting and in the perception of ink-blots.

The significant diagnostic criteria of the graphic arts have been listed as follows by Liss (1938): (1) size, which may give clues to the inner attitude toward dimension and physical stature, perhaps also to ego evaluation; (2) line and form, which permits judgment on a scale from open and free to closed and stereotyped; (3) color, which seems directly related to emotion; and (4) subject or symbol, which leads to the content of personality. The parallels to Rorschach categories, graphology, and other projective techniques suggest an exceedingly interesting line of research.

Prompted Art Expression for Diagnosis and Therapy.—To speed the difficult process of establishing confidence and at the same time starting diagnosis with young patients, Appel (1931) suggested drawing a picture of the home, family, and pets. The drawings alone were often of diagnostic value, and they served also as starting points for conversation. Mira (1940) requires subjects to draw lines in three directions, deducing therefrom various aspects of personality such as its cohesion, nervous equilibrium, and amount and direction of aggression. The diagnostic possibilities of free design of limited scope have been explored by Abel (1938) who assigned the task of drawing 19 straight lines and 6 curved lines in a given rectangle. Berger (1939) reports an application of the Sander test which calls for the completion in crayon of six barely suggested line drawings. The productions could be judged in terms of position, inclusion of content, coloring, integration, and various other characteristics. Bender (1938) finds diagnostic value in what is called a visual motor Gestalt test which calls for the copying of figures having various Gestalt properties. A rather complex procedure has been worked out by Harms (1941) who first asks children to draw lines representing some subjective experience like anger or joy, then tells them to paint one of a given list of feelings, then requires them to draw realistically what most occupied their minds during the second part of the procedure. "The result was astonishing," Harms declares, "even to the point of fear, because this suggestion of abstraction caused the children to create things of the most crude realism, unveiling experiences which the teachers had never supposed to exist in their pupils." Traube (1937) and Morgenstern (1939) examine the drawings of difficult and neurotic children as a means of hunting out basic emotional problems.

Considerable psychological interest has been aroused by the technique of finger painting invented by Shaw (1934). This unfamiliar process can be likened to the unfamiliar perceptual task of the Rorschach test, and there is the additional advantage that every tentative step can be noted by the examiner. Shaw makes various claims concerning the diagnostic and therapeutic value of the method, and Mosse (1940) and Flem-ing (1940) have applied it in the treatment of adult neurotic patients. Mosse brings the method close to free association by advising the patient "to draw without thinking whatever may pass through his mind"; regular phenomena of resistance make their appearance, but "the patient sees his own unconscious," and this is held to cut short the length of the treat-ment. Mosse's use of finger painting is similar to Jung's (1934) use of drawing, the purpose being to give the patient some direct experience of the forces and impulses within him that ordinarily lie neglected or repressed.

It can be seen from this review that the psychological study of draw-ing and painting suffers from no lack of ingenuity or stimulating ideas. The crying need is for validation. An experiment like Schube and Cowell's offers a kind of partial, indirect validation of the hypotheses on which it rests. Systematic validation requires more extensive methods, and except for two unpublished studies mentioned by Vernon (1936) the only research to report is that of Spoerl (1940). Using the methods of sorting according to authorship and matching with personality sketches, Spoerl was able to show that personality can be judged from drawings with a success reliably above chance.

BIBLIOGRAPHY

ABEL, T. M. 1938. Free design of limited scope as a personality index. *Charac-ter & Pers., 7, 50–62*

ACKERMAN, N. W. 1937. Constructive and destructive tendencies in children. *Amer. J. Orthopsychiat., 7, 301–319.*

ADLER, A. 1929. The practice and theory of individual psychology. (Trans. by P. Radin.) New York: Harcourt, Brace.

ALEXANDER, F. 1937. The medical value of psychoanalysis. (Rev. ed.) New York: Norton.

ANASTASI, A., & FOLEY, J. P. 1941. A survey of the literature on artistic be-havior in the abnormal: III. Spontaneous productions. *Psychol. Monogr., 52,* No. 237.

APPEL, K. E. 1931. Drawings by children as aids to personality studies. *Amer. J. Orthopsychiat., 1, 129–144.*

ARNOLD-FORSTER, M. 1921. Studies in dreams. New York: Macmillan.

BAGBY, E. 1930. Dreams during periods of emotional stress. *J. abnorm. soc. Psychol., 25, 289–292.*

BALKEN, E. R., & MASSERMAN, J. H. 1940. The language of phantasy: III. The language of the phantasies of patients with conversion hysteria, anxiety state, and obsessive-compulsive neuroses. *J. Psychol., 10, 75–86.*

BARUCH, D. 1941. Aggression during doll play in a preschool. *Amer. J. Ortho-psychiat., 11, 252–259.*

BAYNES, H. G. 1939. Mythology of the soul; a research into the unconscious from schizophrenic dreams and drawings. London: Ballière, Tindall & Cox.

BECK, S. J. 1937. Introduction to the Rorschach method: a manual of personality study. *Res. Monogr. Amer. Orthopsychiat. Assn.,* No. 1.

—— 1938. Personality structure in schizophrenia: a Rorschach investigation on 81 patients and 64 controls. *Nerv. ment. Dis. Monogr.,* No. 63.

BENDER, L. 1938. A visual motor Gestalt test and its clinical use. *Res. Monogr. Amer. Orthopsychiat. Assn.,* No. 3.

BENDER, L., & WOLTMANN, A. G. 1936. The use of puppet shows as a psycho-

therapeutic method for behavior problems in children. *Amer. J. Orthopsychiat.,* 6, 341–355.
—— 1937. The use of plastic material as a psychiatric approach to emotional problems in children. *Amer. J. Orthopsychiat., 7,* 283–300.
BENJAMIN, J. D., & EBAUGH, F. G. 1938. The diagnostic validity of the Rorschach test. *Amer. J. Psychiat., 94,* 1163–1178.
BERGER, E. 1939. Der Sandersche Phantasietest im Rahmen der psychologischen Eignungsuntersuchung Jugendlicher. *Arch. ges. Psychol., 103,* 499–543.
BLANCHARD, P. 1926. A study of subject matter and motivation of children's dreams. *J. abnorm. soc. Psychol., 21,* 24–37.
BLEULER, E. 1924. Textbook of psychiatry. (Trans. by A. A. Brill.) New York: Macmillan.
BREUER, J., & FREUD, S. 1895. Studien über Hysterie. Leipzig: Autick.
CASON, H. 1935. The nightmare dream. *Psychol. Monogr., 46,* No. 209.
CONN, J. H. 1938. A psychiatric study of car sickness in children. *Amer. J. Orthopsychiat., 8,* 130–141.
CROSLAND, H. R. 1929. The psychological methods of word-association and reaction time as tests of deception. *Univ. Oregon Publ., Psychol. Ser.,* No. 1.
CURRAN, F. J. 1939. The drama as a therapeutic measure in adolescents. *Amer. J. Orthopsychiat., 9,* 215–232.
DAVIDSON, H. H., & KLOPFER, B. 1938. Rorschach statistics: Part II. Normal children. *Rorschach Res. Exch., 3,* 37–43.
DESPERT, J. L. 1937. Technical approaches used in the study and treatment of emotional problems in children: Part V. The playroom. *Psychiat. Quart.,* 677–693.
—— 1940. A method for the study of personality reactions in preschool age children by means of analysis of their play. *J. Psychol., 9,* 17–29.
DESPERT, J. L., & POTTER, H. W. 1936. Technical approaches used in the study and treatment of emotional problems in children: Part I. The story, a form of directed fantasy. *Psychiat. Quart., 10,* 619–638.
DUBIN, S. S. 1940. Verbal attitude scores from responses obtained in the projective technique. *Sociometry, 3,* 24–48.
EBAUGH, F. G. 1936. Association-motor investigation in clinical psychiatry. *J. ment. Sci., 82,* 731–743.
ERIKSON, E. H. 1937. Configurations in play: clinical notes. *Psychoanal. Quart., 6,* 139–214.
—— 1940. Studies in the interpretation of play. *Genetic Psychol. Monogr., 22,* 557–671.
FLEMING, J. 1940. Observations on the use of finger painting in the treatment of adult patients with personality disorders. *Character & Pers., 8,* 301–310.
✓FOSBERG, I. A. 1941. An experimental study of the reliability of the Rorschach psychodiagnostic technique. *Rorschach Res. Exch., 5,* 72–84
FOSTER, J. C., & ANDERSON, J. E. 1936. Unpleasant dreams in childhood. *Child Develpm., 7,* 77–84.
FRANK, L. K. 1939. Projective methods for the study of personality. *J. Psychol., 8,* 389–413.
FRANZ, J. G. 1940. The place of the psychodrama in research. *Sociometry, 3,* 49–61.
FREUD, A. 1928. Introduction to the technique of child analysis. (Trans. by L. P. Clark.) *Nerv. ment. Dis. Monogr.,* No. 48.
—— 1937. The ego and the mechanisms of defense. (Trans. by C. Baines.) London: Hogarth.
FREUD, S. 1900. The interpretation of dreams. (Trans. & ed. by A. A. Brill.) In *The basic writings of Sigmund Freud.* New York: Modern Library, 1938.
—— 1920. A general introduction to psychoanalysis. New York: Boni & Liveright.
—— 1933. New introductory lectures on psychoanalysis. New York: Norton.
GALTON, F. 1885. Inquiries into human faculty and its development. London: Macmillan.
GITELSON, M. 1938. Clinical experience with play therapy. *Amer. J. Orthopsychiat., 8,* 466–478.
GRÜNBAUM, A. M. 1926. Die Erforschung der Träume als eine Methode der

topischen Diagnostik bei Grosshirnkrankungen. *Z. ges. Neurol. Psychiat., 93,* 416–420.

GUIRDHAM, A. 1936a. The diagnosis of depression by the Rorschach test. *Brit. J. med. Psychol., 16,* 130–145.

—— 1936b. Simple psychological data in melancholia. *J. ment. Sci., 82,* 649–653.

GUTHEIL, E. A. 1939. The language of the dream. New York: Macmillan.

HAIGIS, E. 1936. Das bio-mythische Bewusstsein in der freien Märchenproduktion. *Z. Psychol., 138,* 249–292.

HARMS, E. 1941. Child art as aid in the diagnosis of juvenile neuroses. *Amer. J. Orthopsychiat., 11,* 191–209.

HARRISON, R. 1940. Studies in the use and validity of the thematic apperception test with mentally disordered patients: II. A quantitative validity study. III. Validation by the method of "blind analysis." *Character & Pers., 9,* 122–138.

HARROWER-ERICKSON, M. R. 1940. Personality changes accompanying cerebral lesions: I. Rorschach studies of patients with cerebral tumors. *Arch. Neurol. Psychiat., Chicago, 43,* 859–890.

HERTZ, M. R. 1935. The Rorschach ink-blot test: historic summary. *Psychol. Bull., 32,* 33–66.

—— 1940. The shading response in the Rorschach ink-blot test: a review of its scoring and interpretation. *J. gen. Psychol., 23,* 123–167.

—— 1941. Validity of the Rorschach method. *Amer. J. Orthopsychiat., 11,* 512–519.

HOFF, H., & PÖTZL, O. 1937. Über die labyrinthären Beziehungen von Flugsensationen und Flugträumen. *Mschr. Psychiat. Neurol., 97,* 193–211.

HULL, C. L., & LUGOFF, L. S. 1921. Complex signs in diagnostic free association. *J. exp. Psychol., 4,* 111–136.

HUNT, W. A., & LANDIS, C. 1935. Word-association reaction time and the magnitude of the galvanic skin response. *Amer. J. Psychol., 47,* 143–145.

HUNTER, M. 1939. The practical value of the Rorschach test in a psychological clinic. *Amer. J. Orthopsychiat., 9,* 287–295.

HUSTON, P. E., SHAKOW, D., & ERICKSON, M. H. 1934. A study of hypnotically induced complexes by means of the Luria technique. *J. gen. Psychol., 11,* 65–97.

JUNG, C. G. 1916. Psychology of the unconscious. (Trans. by B. M. Hinkle.) New York: Dodd, Mead.

—— 1918. Studies in word-association. (Trans. by M. D. Eder.) London: Heinemann.

—— 1922. Collected papers on analytic psychology. (Trans. by C. E. Long.) London: Ballière, Tindall & Cox.

—— 1934. Modern man in search of a soul. (Trans. by W. S. Dell & C. F. Baynes.) New York: Harcourt, Brace.

KELLEY, D. M., & KLOPFER, B. 1939. Application of the Rorschach method to research in schizophrenia. *Rorschach Res. Exch., 3,* 55–66.

KENT, G. H., & ROSANOFF, A. J. 1910. A study of association in insanity. *Amer. J. Insan., 67,* 37–96, 317–390.

KLEIN, D. B. 1930. The experimental production of dreams during hypnosis. *Univ. Texas Bull.,* No. 3009.

KLEIN, M. 1932. The psychoanalysis of children. New York: Norton.

KLOPFER, B. 1937. The technique of the Rorschach performance. *Rorschach Res. Exch., 2,* 1–14.

—— 1939. Theory and technique of Rorschach interpretation. *Rorschach Res. Exch., 3,* 152–194.

—— 1940. Personality aspects revealed by the Rorschach method. *Rorschach Res. Exch., 4,* 26–29.

KLOPFER, B., & MARGULIES, H. 1941. Rorschach reactions in early childhood. *Rorschach Res. Exch., 5,* 1–23.

KOHS, C. H. 1914. The association method and its relation to the complex and complex indicators. *Amer. J. Psychol., 25,* 544–594.

KRAUSE, L. S. 1937. Relation of voluntary motor pressure disorganization (Luria) to two other alleged complex indicators. *J. exp. Psychol., 21,* 653–661.

KRUGMAN, M. 1940. Out of the inkwell: the Rorschach method. *Character & Pers., 9,* 91–110.

KRUGMAN, M. 1941. Rorschach examination in a child guidance clinic. *Amer. J. Orthopsychiat., 11,* 503–511.

LEVY, D. M. 1937. Studies in sibling rivalry. *Res. Monogr. Amer. Orthopsychiat. Assn.,* No. 2.

LEVY, D. M., & BECK, S. J. 1934. The Rorschach test in manic-depressive psychosis. *Amer. J. Orthopsychiat., 4,* 31–42.

LEWIS, N. D. C. 1928. Graphic art productions in schizophrenia. *Proc. Assn. Res. nerv. ment. Dis., 5,* 344–368.

LISS, E. 1938. The graphic arts. *Amer. J. Orthopsychiat., 8,* 95–99.

LOOSLI-USTERI, M. 1937. Le diagnostic individuel chez l'enfant au moyen du test de Rorschach. Paris: Hermann.

LOWENFELD, M. 1939. The world pictures of children. A method of recording and studying them. *Brit. J. med. Psychol., 18,* 65–101.

LURIA, A. R. 1932. The nature of human conflicts. (Trans. by W. H. Gantt.) New York: Liveright.

MALAMUD, W., & LINDER, F. E. 1931. Dreams and their relationship to recent impressions. *Arch. Neurol. Psychiat., Chicago, 25,* 1081–1099.

MASSERMAN, J. H., & BALKEN, E. R. 1938. The clinical application of phantasy studies. *J. Psychol., 6,* 81–88.

—— 1939. The psychoanalytic and psychiatric significance of phantasy. *Psychoanal. Rev., 26,* 343–379, 535–549.

MAURY, A. 1861. Le sommeil et les rêves, études psychologiques. Paris: Librairie Academique et Cie.

MEIER, C. A. 1938. Über die Bedeutung des Jungschen Assoziationsexperiments für die Psychotherapie. *Zbl. ges. Neurol. Psychiat., 87,* 703.

MELTZER, H. 1935. Children's attitudes to parents. *Amer. J. Orthopsychiat., 5,* 244.

MIALE, F. R., & HARROWER-ERICKSON, M. R. 1940. Personality structure in the psychoneuroses. *Rorschach Res. Exch., 4,* 71–74.

MIRA, E. 1940. Myokinetic psychodiagnosis: a new technique for exploring the conative trends of personality. *Proc. R. Soc. Med., 33,* 9–30.

MORENO, J. L. 1934. Who shall survive? *Nerv. ment. Dis. Monogr.,* No. 58.

MORGAN, C. D., & MURRAY, H. A. 1935. A method for investigating fantasies: the thematic apperception test. *Arch. Neurol. Psychiat., Chicago, 34,* 289–306.

MORGENSTERN, S. 1939. Le symbolisme et la valeur psychoanalytique des dessins infantiles. *Rev. franç. Psychanal., 11,* 39–48.

MOSSE, E. P. 1940. Painting-analysis in the treatment of neuroses. *Psychoanal. Rev., 27,* 68–82.

MURRAY, H. A. 1938. Explorations in personality. New York: Oxford University Press.

NEWELL, H. W. 1941. Play therapy in child psychiatry. *Amer. J. Orthopsychiat., 11,* 245–251.

PETERSON, F., & JUNG, C. G. 1907. Psychological investigation with the galvanometer and pneumograph in normal and insane individuals. *Brain, 30,* 153–218.

PFISTER, H. O. 1934. Farbe und Bewegung in der Zeichnung Geisteskranker. *Schweiz. Arch. Neurol. Psychiat., 34,* 325–365.

PICKFORD, R. W. 1938. Imagination and the nonsense syllable: a clinical approach. *Character & Pers., 7,* 19–40.

PIOTROWSKI, Z. 1936a. On the Rorschach method and its application in organic disturbances of the central nervous system. *Rorschach Res. Exch., 1,* 23–40.

—— 1936b. Personality studies of cases with lesions of the frontal lobes: II. Rorschach study of a Pick's disease case. *Rorschach Res. Exch., 1,* 65–77.

—— 1937a. The Rorschach inkblot method in organic disturbances of the central nervous system. *J. nerv. ment. Dis., 86,* 525–537.

—— 1937b. Rorschach studies of cases with lesions of the frontal lobes. *Brit. J. med. Psychol., 17,* 105–118.

—— 1939. Rorschach manifestations of improvement in insulin treated schizophrenics. *Psychosom. Med., 1,* 508–526.

PRINCE, M. 1939. Clinical and experimental studies in personality. (Ed. by A. A. Roback.) Cambridge: Sci-Art.

PRINZHORN, H. 1923. Bildnerei der Geisteskranken. Berlin: Springer.

RAPAPORT, D. 1941. The Szondi test. *Bull. Menninger Clin., 5,* 33–39.

REITMAN, F. 1939. Facial expression in schizophrenic drawings. *J. ment. Sci., 85,* 264–272.

RICKERS-OVSIANKINA, M. 1938. The Rorschach test as applied to normal and schizophrenic subjects. *Brit. J. med. Psychol., 17,* 227–257.

ROFFENSTEIN, G. 1923. Experimentelle Symbolträume. *Z. ges. Neurol. Psychiat., 87,* 362–371.

ROGERSON, C. H. 1939. Play therapy in childhood. New York: Oxford University Press.

RORSCHACH, H. 1937. Psychodiagnostik. Methodik und Ergebnisse eines wahrnehmungsdiagnostischen Experiments. (3rd ed.) Berlin: Huber.

RORSCHACH, H., & OBERHOLZER, E. 1924. The application of the interpretation of form to psychoanalysis. *J. nerv. ment. Dis., 60,* 225–248, 359–379.

ROSENZWEIG, S. 1935. Outline of a cooperative project for validating the Rorschach test. *Amer. J. Orthopsychiat., 7,* 32–47.

ROSENZWEIG, S., & SHAKOW, D. 1937. Play technique in schizophrenia and other psychoses. *Amer. J. Orthopsychiat., 7,* 32–47.

ROTTER, J. B. 1940. Studies in the use and validity of the thematic apperception test with mentally disordered patients: I. Method of analysis and clinical problems. *Character & Pers., 9,* 18–34.

SANFORD, R. N. 1939. Procedure for scoring the thematic apperception test. Cambridge: Harvard Psychological Clinic. (Privately printed)

SARBIN, T. R. 1939. Rorschach patterns under hypnosis. *Amer. J. Orthopsychiat., 9,* 315–319.

SCHRÖTTER, K. 1912. Experimentelle Träume. *Zbl. Psychoanal., 2,* 638–646.

SCHUBE, K., & COWELL, J. 1939. Art of psychotic persons. *Arch. Neurol. Psychiat., Chicago, 41,* 709–720.

SHAKOW, D., & ROSENZWEIG, S. 1940. The use of the tautophone ("verbal summator") as an auditory apperceptive test for the study of personality. *Character & Pers., 8,* 216–226.

SHAW, R. F. 1934. Finger painting. Boston: Little, Brown.

SILBERER, H. 1909. Bericht über eine Methode, gewisse symbolische Halluzinations-erscheinungen hervorzurufen und zu beobachten. *Jb. psychoanal. psychopath. Forsch., 1,* 513–525.

SKINNER, B. F. 1936. The verbal summator and a method for the study of latent speech. *J. Psychol., 2,* 71–107.

SMITH, W. W. 1922. The measurement of emotion. New York: Harcourt, Brace.

SOLOMON, J. C. 1938. Active play therapy. *Amer. J. Orthopsychiat., 8,* 479–498.

—— 1940. Active play therapy: further experiences. *Amer. J. Orthopsychiat., 10,* 763–781.

SPOERL, D. T. 1940. Personality and drawing in retarded children. *Character & Pers., 8,* 227–239.

STERN, W. 1937. Cloud pictures: a new method for testing imagination. *Character & Pers., 6,* 132–146.

SUNNE, D. 1936. Rorschach test norms of young children. *Child Develpm., 7,* 304–313.

SYMONDS, P. M. 1931. Diagnosing personality and conduct. New York: Century.

TALLMAN, F. F., & GOLDENSOHN, L. N. 1941. Play technique. *Amer. J. Orthopsychiat., 11,* 551–561.

TALLMAN, G., & KLOPFER, B. 1936. Personality studies of cases with lesions of the frontal lobes: III. Rorschach study of bilateral lobectomy case. *Rorschach Res. Exch., 1,* 77–89.

THOMAS, M. 1937. Méthodes des histoires à complèter pour le dépistage des complexes et des conflits affectifs de l'enfant. *Arch. Psychol., Genève, 26,* 209–284.

TRAUBE, T. 1937. La valeur diagnostique des dessins des enfants difficiles. *Arch. Psychol., Genève, 26,* 285–309.

VALENTINE, C. W. 1938. A study of the beginnings and significance of play in infancy: II. *Brit. J. educ. Psychol., 8,* 285–306.

VARENDONCK, J. 1921. The psychology of daydreams. London: Allen & Unwin.

VARVEL, W. A. 1941. The Rorschach test in psychotic and neurotic depressions. *Bull. Menninger Clin., 5,* 5–12.

VERNON, P. E. 1933. The Rorschach ink-blot test. *Brit. J. med. Psychol., 13,* 89–118, 179–205, 271–295.

—— 1935. Recent work on the Rorschach test. *J. ment. Sci., 81,* 894–920.

—— 1936. The matching method applied to investigations of personality. *Psychol. Bull., 33,* 149–177.

—— 1938. The assessment of psychological qualities by verbal methods. London: H. M. Stationery Office.

WÄLDER, R. 1933. The psychoanalytic theory of play. *Psychoanal. Quart., 2,* 208–224.

WELLS, F. L. 1935. Rorschach and the free association test. *J. gen. Psychol., 13,* 413–433.

PART III

BEHAVIOR DYNAMICS, EXPERIMENTAL BEHAVIOR DISORDERS, AND HYPNOTISM

Chapter 7

CLINICAL APPROACH TO THE DYNAMICS OF BEHAVIOR

By Thomas M. French, M.D.

HUMAN BEHAVIOR IS EXCEEDINGLY complex. If we wish to gain an understanding of it, there are in general two methods open to us. We may create artificial, highly simplified situations. We may investigate experimentally, for example, whether one can train an individual to react with a knee jerk to the sound of an electric bell. In so doing we are attempting to follow a sound experimental principle. We attempt to simplify our problem by isolating the separate dynamic elements and investigating them one at a time. With this purpose in view, for example, we disregard the fact that our experimental subject is a struggling young professional man who is having the greatest difficulty in earning enough money to support his wife and three children. For the purpose of this investigation we regard this fact as irrelevant. For the present we are interested only in whether we can condition his knee jerk to respond to a new stimulus.

But the disadvantages of such a procedure are also evident. In the first place we cannot be entirely sure that the emotional difficulties of our experimental subject are really irrelevant in relationship to the conditioning of his knee jerks. In the second place we may not be entirely sure that the problem we have set ourselves is the one that is most likely to throw light upon the dynamics of behavior. We should probably be able to proceed more wisely in the choice of questions to investigate if we first made some attempt to get an orientation as to the problems presented by behavior when studied as a whole.

In the clinical approach to the study of behavior we have the advantage that we are compelled to see a person's behavior in its proper perspective. Thus we avoid the danger of studying some isolated detail of an individual's reaction entirely out of its usual context. On the other hand, we have the disadvantage that a clinical approach compels us to study behavior in all of its complexity. We are in danger, therefore, of being completely bewildered by the intricate patterns of interacting motives with which the everyday activity of any individual confronts us.

Ordinarily the attempt to understand human behavior by direct observation meets with another difficulty. People usually do not wish to tell us about the matters which touch them most deeply. Often the matters that are most important in an individual's life are a cause of some disturbance to him and are closely guarded as a secret from all except his closest friends. There is one situation, however, which may call forth a motive strong enough to overcome this natural reticence. The patient who consults a physician for treatment of a psychoneurotic illness can often be induced to talk freely about disturbing and intimate matters which he would otherwise keep to himself. It is for this reason that attempts to understand human behavior by direct observation have been so closely associated with the development of psychotherapy.

Psychoanalysis as a Method of Scientific Investigation

It is usual to discuss the psychoanalytic method as a method of therapy rather than as a method of scientific investigation. Discussion of psychoanalysis as a scientific contribution, on the other hand, very often starts with psychoanalytic theory. This approach to psychoanalysis has led to some confusion. Plunging immediately into the theoretical conclusions at which psychoanalysts have arrived, one gains the impression that psychoanalysis is a body of scientific doctrines based in very considerable part upon rather unrestrained speculation. Quite the contrary is the case. The most important scientific contribution of psychoanalysis has been not its conclusions but its method. It therefore seems appropriate in this chapter to discuss psychoanalysis as a method of scientific investigation, as a clinical approach to the study of the dynamics of behavior.

As a scientific method, psychoanalysis is indeed influenced by the fact that it is not only a method of scientific investigation, but also a method of therapy (see Alexander, 1936). In other words, the method is a clinical one and must always keep in mind the therapeutic interests of the patient. For this reason the first objective of a psychoanalytic investigation must be to understand the individual case in order to know how to handle the therapeutic problem. The most important complication that the therapeutic requirements introduce into the task of scientific investigation is the fact that in some cases it is necessary, in the interests of therapy, to make a quick diagnosis of a situation and to act upon conclusions that are in the nature of guesses and not yet definitely proved. This would be indeed a complication if these guesses were accepted as final scientific formulations instead of for what they are—tentative hypotheses that are to be tested and either proved or disproved by subsequent evidence. If this tentative attitude toward the interpretation of the patient's material is maintained, however, it is surprising to what degree the interests of therapy and the requirements of scientific investigation coincide.

The Fundamental Principle of Psychoanalytic Interpretation.— Psychoanalysis as a scientific method is based upon a single, very simple principle. If we do not understand a person's behavior, we seek to make it intelligible by finding its emotional context. To cite a very trivial example, if we see a man strike himself violently in the face, his behavior is likely to seem peculiar to us, but if we discover that he was killing a mosquito, we are no longer perplexed. If a man behaves as though he is angry, we try to learn more about the circumstances until we find something that seems adequate to account for his anger. If we learn that someone has made an insulting remark to him, we shall then find his anger quite "natural."

This method of attempting to understand human behavior was not invented by psychoanalysis. It is the method of the common-sense psychology of everyday life. It is essentially an intuitive method based upon the psychological knowledge, for the most part unformulated, that makes one person's behavior seem "natural" to us whereas another person's behavior seems "strange" and "unaccountable." Psychoanalysis has merely extended the range of application of this method and has succeeded in demonstrating that even the most irrational behavior becomes "natural" and "understandable" to us if we succeed, after long search, in finding its proper emotional context in the life history of the individual concerned.

Psychoanalytic literature is full of examples of the application of this method to the more perplexing types of behavior that are clinically known as psychoneuroses and psychoses. In order to make our discussion concrete, let us cite as illustration a brief analysis of a single life history.

A married woman with one child has an extramarital affair while her husband is in prison. She becomes pregnant. The husband is released from prison before the second child is born, but a divorce is secured and the patient wishes now to marry her lover. The lover, however, becomes evasive and is extremely reluctant to marry her, but the patient is insistent that the lover shall marry her, openly calls the children by his name, and wishes to get legal help in compelling him to marry her.

So far, perhaps, her behavior sounds not so very irrational. She has the two children to take care of, and it seems natural that she should wish to get the support of the man who is responsible for her last pregnancy. In the light of other facts, however, this appearance of rationality disappears. She admits confidentially to her therapist that she had deliberately allowed herself to become pregnant while she was still married to her husband in the hope that she might compel her lover to marry her. Moreover, it is not difficult to convince her that the marriage will almost certainly turn out badly, inasmuch as the lover is so utterly reluctant to assume any responsibility for her. Nevertheless she is determined to force through the marriage, even though she suspects she may want to divorce the man afterwards, and she gives as her motive for this determination that she wishes to legitimatize the child.

The question arises at once as to why the child needs to be legitimatized. Both children were conceived while she was still married, and the most practical way of avoiding unpleasant comment would be to say nothing about the paternity of the second child and to let it be tacitly assumed that the children are the children of her husband. Nevertheless, as we have seen, the patient's behavior is exactly contrary to these rational motives of social discretion. She has openly called the children by the lover's name and now insists upon giving the second child a legitimatization that by any practical standard he would not have needed, by forcing through a marriage that she herself realizes can result only in unhappiness. This behavior is obviously not intelligible in terms of the context of what we know about her present situation.

We get some light upon this patient's motivations, however, when we learn something about her early history. The patient was one of several children, but her parents separated very soon after her birth. All the other children remained with the father, but the patient was put in an orphan asylum. She was later taken into a foster home where she was well cared for until the foster father died. After a time economic difficulties forced the foster mother to place her with the foster mother's own parents, who were unsympathetic and frequently raised the question as to why her own father had not kept her. After she was grown, she looked up her parents and learned that her mother had been sexually promiscuous. The father was very cold to her and expressed doubt as to whether he was really her father.

In the light of this story, the patient's behavior with reference to her lover and to her own illegitimate child becomes much more understandable. The patient has evidently brooded a great deal about the circumstances concerning her own birth. Why did the father reject her alone when he took all the other children to live with him? This is a question about which she probably would have been curious anyhow, but her foster grandparents undoubtedly made the question all the more important to her by constantly reproaching her with it. Finally she learned the explanation that her mother was promiscuous in her sexual relations and that the reason for her father's rejection was that he believed her to be the child of an extramarital relationship. It will be noticed that the patient in her own behavior has identified very closely with her mother. It looks indeed as though she were under some compulsion to live through again the problems created by her mother's behavior. She, too, has one child from her marriage and now gets another one in an extramarital relationship. Now she is concerned with the problem of legitimatizing the child. It seems plain that her utterly impractical plan to legitimatize a child that she need not have had and that in any case could have passed as the child of her marriage is really based upon a need to legitimatize herself. She is under compulsion to do for her own illegitimate child what she feels her mother should have done for her. Her mother should have married her real father and given her a legitimate home instead of abandoning her to an orphan asylum while her

supposed father kept the other children with him. Thus in her relationship to her lover and his child, the patient is not really guided by the
rational requirements of her present situation at all, but by a compulsive
urge to set right, as it were by proxy, the wrong that was done to her
as an illegitimate child.

Interpretation and Analysis.—It will be seen from this example that
the psychoanalytic method, when properly practiced, really involves no
theoretical preconceptions whatsoever, other than the quite unformulated
psychological assumptions that guide us in our everyday relations with
other human beings and for the validity of which our everyday contacts with our fellow men offer us constantly repeated, empirical tests.
This common-sense psychology, however, is an unformulated psychology.
When we have succeeded by this method in "understanding" a person's
behavior, we have not yet in most cases formulated the reasons for the
patient's behavior in scientific terms. What we have done is first of all to
enlarge our knowledge of the emotional context of the patient's behavior.
After we have done this we may have little more than an intuitive sense
that this person's feelings and actions are quite "natural." Nevertheless
—and with justice—we speak of this kind of insight into a person's behavior as a "psychological understanding" of his reactions.

We must next inquire what must be added to this sort of "psychological understanding" in order to make use of it in arriving at valid
scientific formulations. Our task will be to analyze our "psychological
understanding," to attempt to reconstruct in detail the steps by which
different events in the life history of the patient have contributed to his
present behavior, and to separate out the component causes that have
contributed to it. In other words, it is useful to distinguish two successive steps in the scientific utilization of our clinical studies. We start first
with the interpretation, with the attempt to find the emotional context
that will make the patient's behavior seem "natural" to us. After the
interpretation, we proceed next to a more precise analysis. It is with
this scientific analysis of behavior that has already been "psychologically
understood" that the scientific formulation of our psychoanalytic observations properly begins.

It is imperative that the two steps should not be confused or condensed. As every teacher of psychoanalysis knows, there is no surer
way to inhibit a student's capacity for true psychological insight than
to allow him to proceed immediately to formulate his patient's material
in terms of universal clichés which he has learned from his reading of
psychoanalytic literature. The same principle holds true for any attempt
at analysis and formulation of the extremely rich observational material
that has resulted from psychoanalytic study of many different kinds of
"peculiar" behavior. In order to remain upon sound scientific ground,
therefore, it is important to distinguish carefully between psychoanalytic
interpretation and the scientific analysis of interpreted material.

The psychoanalytic interpretation must come first. It must find in the life history and present circumstances of the patient the proper emotional context for his apparently irrational behavior so that his behavior becomes quite "natural" and understandable to us. Upon this "psychological understanding" rests the whole objectivity of our procedure. Until we have an adequate "psychological understanding," any attempts at more precise formulation can only lead us astray, for they will certainly have nothing to do with psychological reality. The "psychological understanding" must, therefore, come first and should preferably be formulated in the language of everyday life with as few theoretical implications as possible. One of the chief dangers of going astray in our investigation of psychodynamic relationships arises from the loose habit of formulating our psychological observations in terms of one or another theory that happens to be popular at the moment. Just the opposite rule should guide our dynamic interpretations of behavior. Our interpretations should aim to express as simply and accurately as possible the dynamic relations implied by fitting the patient's behavior into its total emotional context and should endeavor to avoid further implications based on prevailing theories.

Once we have grasped the true sense and meaning of a patient's behavior, however, we are then ready to subject our imperfectly formulated "psychological understanding" to more careful analysis. A first step in this process will be to subject our interpretations to critical examination and analysis. When we have arrived at an interpretation we must next inquire how completely it "explains" the available facts. In most cases we find that our interpretations when thus critically examined leave a number of questions still unanswered. Usually there are a number of facts that are still not adequately accounted for. This leads to a search for a still wider emotional context in order to answer the questions arising successively out of each interpretation. It was in this way that Freud, in seeking for a "psychological understanding" of the neuroses, was led farther and farther back into the life histories of his patients.

Reconstruction of Life Histories.—Thus a critical application of the interpretative method leads us inevitably into the task which has been such a central preoccupation in the psychoanalytic literature, that of dynamic reconstruction of the life histories of individuals. Usually we find that a particular bit of "peculiar" behavior has been influenced by a considerable number of events both present and past. We seek, therefore, to study the dynamic interrelations between these events and to reconstruct the steps by which they contributed and cooperated in the chain of causation of which the patient's behavior was the result.

We have already illustrated the method that should be followed in such an analysis. We first examine the patient's behavior in relation to the patient's real situation at the time. Perhaps when we have gained a sufficient orientation into the patient's real situation, his behavior will seem quite intelligible. In many cases, however, careful examination of our "psychological understanding" in relation to the present situation will only raise new problems. In the case cited, for example, we attempted to explain the patient's behavior in terms of her desire to legitimatize the child of her extramarital relationship. Upon closer examination this could not explain why she had deliberately allowed herself to be impregnated or why she could not allow the fact that she was married at the time to be a sufficient legitimatization of the child. We then turned to the patient's previous history and found an explanation in the patient's brooding over the circumstances of her own birth. In this case we found the explanation for her irrational need to legitimatize the child in her own need to legitimatize herself. The fact of her own illegitimate birth and particularly the reproaches about it that she heard from her foster grandparents threw a great deal of light upon her subsequent need to legitimatize the child. We might, however, raise still further questions. This patient no longer lives with the foster grandparents and, so far as we know, no one reproaches her any more because of the circumstances of her birth. Why then can she not forget about the whole matter and accept whatever satisfactions life is able to offer her at present? In attempting to answer this question we should have to learn still more about her life history and her reactions to it and seek for a still wider emotional context.

Thus, as a rule, when we have once succeeded in finding an explanation for "irrational" behavior, closer examination of our interpretation will usually disclose still other problems that can be solved only by searching farther and farther back into the patient's life history for the wider emotional context that is necessary to explain each new discrepancy. In this way we arrive at more and more complete reconstructions of the psychological sense of the patient's life history.

Generalizations from Psychoanalytic Data

Psychodynamic Mechanisms.—The goal of science is not merely to find explanations for particular cases, but rather to formulate generalizations that are valid for many different cases. In this task of formulating valid generalizations we start again with "common-sense psychology." We have based our interpretations upon the psychological assumptions that guide us in our everyday relations with other people. These assumptions already imply generalizations about human behavior, but these generalizations are for the most part unformulated. Our first task is to formulate them, to make them explicit.

In this task we are aided by the fact that psychoanalysis has succeeded in extending the application of these assumptions to behavior that at first sight seemed quite peculiar. The elucidation of "peculiar" behavior has the advantage that it throws into relief relationships which we might otherwise take for granted. When a machine is running smoothly, there is often little incentive to study its mechanisms, but when it gets out of order, our attention is called to those mechanisms responsible for its failure to function. For this reason, as Freud has often pointed out, the study of psychopathology has been of enormous service in contributing to our knowledge of the "normal" psychology of everyday life. By studying the psychological contexts that throw light upon the symptoms of mental illness, we are able to see in isolated and exaggerated form dynamic relationships that can easily be overlooked and taken quite for granted in our everyday "understanding" of more usual behavior. Making use of these highlights which psychopathology can throw upon the dynamic mechanisms of normal behavior, psychoanalysis has already made considerable progress in the task of formulating scientific generalizations.

A first step was the description of psychodynamic mechanisms that are encountered over and over again in our patients' material. It will perhaps be of interest to discuss a few of the more important of these psychodynamic mechanisms.

The first mechanism to be described was the mechanism of repression. In their first studies of hysteria by means of hypnosis, Breuer and Freud discovered that many hysterical symptoms could be traced back to the memory of a disturbing experience that had been pushed out of consciousness and forgotten. Under hypnosis patients could be induced to bring such memories back to consciousness and to relive and discharge the disturbing emotions. The pushing of the disturbing memory out of consciousness, Freud called repression; and the discharge of the repressed affects that took place (in these cases under hypnosis), he called abreaction. After such recall of a repressed memory and the abreaction of the accompanying affects, the associated hysterical symptom often disappeared.

Thus repression was first defined in subjective terms as the exclusion from consciousness of psychic impulses or other psychic content which nevertheless continue to exert a dynamic influence upon behavior. Inasmuch as the repressed impulse is still active, it will usually be replaced in consciousness and in the patient's overt behavior by some substitute. This is the mechanism of substitution or displacement. To cite one of Freud's examples (Freud, 1893), "a highly intelligent man assists while his brother's ankylosed hip is straightened under an anaesthetic. At the instant when the joint gives way with a crack he feels a violent pain in his own hip joint which lasts for almost a year." Indeed hysterical symptoms are quite regularly to be understood as substitute manifestations for some repressed impulse or affect.

By studying such substitute phenomena in relation to the more complete emotional context, it is frequently possible to infer the memory or other content that has undergone repression. Freud's patient Dora, for example (Freud, 1905), told him once how Mr. K had suddenly embraced and kissed her. She pulled herself loose and ran away with feelings of disgust. Afterwards she could not bear to go near any man whom she saw talking tenderly or earnestly to a woman. Besides this she often experienced as a hallucinatory sensation the pressure of Mr. K's embrace about the upper part of her body. Piecing these facts together, Freud inferred that Dora's disgust and flight had been a reaction to her awareness of sexual excitement upon Mr. K's part, which, however, she had repressed. The hallucinatory sensations about her chest, Freud suspected, owed their persistence to a displacement of this perception and of her own sexual excitement. Frequently such inferences are confirmed after a shorter or longer period by the patient's recovery of the actual memory.

Very many of the psychodynamic mechanisms may be regarded as special cases of substitution. When a repressed impulse is replaced by another impulse of character opposite or antagonistic to it, we speak of reaction formation. Dora's disgust in the instance just cited is a good example of this mechanism.

The mechanism of projection may be defined as a tendency to react to dynamic tendencies within one's own personality as though the tendency in question belonged to someone else instead of to oneself. A classical example is the mechanism of the paranoid patient who reacts to his own unconscious recognition of homosexual impulses in himself by imagining that others are accusing him of homosexuality. This is the mechanism that plays a predominant role in cases of paranoia and paranoid schizophrenia; it is also encountered in less virulent forms in many other types of neurotic illness and may even play a role in the behavior of relatively normal persons.

A converse mechanism of introjection has also been described, according to which one reacts to someone else's wishes or tendencies as though they were one's own. This is a mechanism encountered with especial frequency in cases of melancholia. A beautiful example is cited by Helene Deutsch (1932). A woman who had been living alone with her little dog developed a severe melancholia when the dog ran away. So trivial a cause can obviously not offer a complete explanation for the development of a severe psychotic reaction. This patient's psychosis becomes much more understandable to us when we learn that this woman had devoted her whole life to a younger sister and that this sister a few years before had married and moved away to a distant country, leaving the patient to live a lonely life with no other companion than this little dog. The central theme of the patient's psychosis was her delusion that she was to be abandoned naked on the street to die a terrible death. Analysis disclosed that the source of this delusion was the patient's unconscious bitter reproach against the sister who had deserted her after accepting her love and care for so many years. It is not difficult to understand that this woman, who has been left all alone by the sister to whom she had devoted most of her life, should now feel in her bitterness that such a sister deserves to be cruelly deprived of all the love and care that she had received by being put out naked upon the street to die a terrible death. In the psychosis, however, the patient turned this reproach back upon herself. In her delusion it was she and not the sister who was to receive this punishment. The murderously bitter reproach against the sister has been "introjected."

Two other mechanisms of very general importance are fixation and regression. Traumatic experiences or difficulties in adjustment which cannot be faced and worked out regularly result in an arrest of emotional development at this point. Freud calls this fixation. As an example we may cite fixation upon the conflicts induced by the training of the infant in cleanliness, which is regularly found in cases of obsessional neurosis. In such patients impulses to play with dirt and energetic reaction formations, such as washing compulsions and other forms of obsessive cleanliness, may persist throughout life. In milder cases, however, this conflict may recede into the background but, after some frustration, such as disappointment in a love affair, may appear again later in life and give rise to an obsessional neurosis. Such return to a conflict belonging to an earlier period of development, Freud calls regression.

Other Generalizations from Psychoanalytic Data—Typical Life Histories.

—By reconstructing and comparing many life histories, psychoanalysis has also been able to reconstruct certain typical conflict situations which occur with a somewhat restricted number of variations in the life history of every individual. Conflicts over weaning, toilet training, rivalry with brothers and sisters, sexual investigation beginning early in childhood and leading to sexual interest in parents, brothers, or sisters, and often to intense jealousy based upon these sexual attachments—these are some of the earliest conflict situations whose importance had been very little realized until psychoanalysis was able to call attention to them. Other conflicts belonging to later periods and especially the relations of these later conflicts to the earlier ones have also had much light thrown upon them by psychoanalytic investigation.

Very considerable progress has been made also in describing features that are characteristic of the life history of individuals suffering from particular types of disorders. We know, for example (Freud, 1913), that severe childhood conflicts over toilet training are regularly found in the life history of patients who later suffer from compulsion neuroses. Depressive reactions (Freud, 1917) are particularly likely to occur in reaction to the loss of a loved object toward whom the patient has also entertained strong but repressed feelings of hostility. Paranoia, as Freud (1911) pointed out in his analysis of the Schreber case, seems quite typically to be associated with strong homosexual impulses which the patient is usually unable to avow and which he therefore attempts to handle by the mechanism of projection, either attributing the homosexual impulses themselves to others or thinking of himself as falsely accused by others. These are but a few examples of the generalizations that psycho-analysis has been able to establish concerning the psychogenic history of well-known clinical syndromes.

Studies of this kind are of course only first steps toward the solution of what Freud has called the problem of "choice of neurosis." We should like of course to be able to predict from the previous history of an individual under just what circumstances behavior disorders would develop and just what would be the nature of the pathological behavior to be expected. At the present time, indeed, psychoanalysts of experience are often able to make some shrewd guesses of this sort, but the factors involved are still too complex to admit of any high degree of certainty in such predictions. The problems of "choice of neurosis" still require much future investigation for their final solution.

Important for such future investigations will probably be a much more minute and detailed study of the voluminous data that are available whenever an analysis is carefully recorded. Indeed, we encounter the problem of "choice of neurosis" again in miniature if we make the attempt, for example, to compare the different dreams of a single patient and to account in detail for their similarities and differences by studying the previous life history and the events that have occurred in the intervals between them. Such studies aim to account for the recurrent patterns that run through a patient's life and dreams in terms of the frustrating and facilitating events of his life history. Upon this background the progressive influence of the analysis can be traced as a sort of emotional learning process correcting the earlier patterns. Studies of this kind are being made especially by Rado (as yet unpublished) and by the writer (French, 1936, 1937a, 1937b, 1939, and unpublished studies).

Clinical Data as Orientation for Experimental Studies

As will be seen in the following chapters, the extremely rich clinical material that has been accumulated by the psychoanalytic method of observation now offers us an orientation that should be extremely valuable in guiding us to problems that can be profitably investigated by experimental methods.

It should be emphasized, however, that the problems suitable for clinical and for experimental investigation are not always the same. Those who wish to make use of the insights that have resulted from psychoanalytic investigation should, therefore, not content themselves with summarizing psychoanalytic concepts and theories, but should rather familiarize themselves sufficiently with the fundamental psychoanalytic method of interpreting behavior by searching for its emotional context so that they will be able to evaluate clinical data upon their own merits. Too often attempts to "validate" psychoanalytic conclusions by experiment lead to evidence much less conclusive than the original clinical data upon which the conclusions were based. Experimental data must also be interpreted, and the interpretations of such data can often be less carefully controlled than our clinical data which take so much more careful account of the whole psychological context.

It is quite futile, for example, to try to test by experiment whether there is such a thing as repression of disturbing mental content. In this case the clinical evidence is quite incontrovertible and the experimental evidence not very conclusive. Equally incontrovertible is the accompanying evidence of displaced gratification of repressed impulses. Experimental studies of substitution (see Chapter 9 by Sears) have indeed yielded results that are interesting and significant in themselves but can hardly be regarded as a test of the validity of the clinical observations. Probably the clinical and the experimental observations are dealing with data that are not altogether comparable. The laws that govern the displacement of repressed impulses and affects probably differ considerably from those that prevail in the less traumatic situations that result from the artificial interruption of activities. A study of these differences, however, might offer a starting point for a very promising investigation.

In general, a much more fruitful kind of cooperation between clinical and experimental approaches is to use the clinical observations as cues to point to problems that are in need of much more detailed investigation. Every psychoanalyst whose eyes are open to the scientific as well as to the therapeutic implications of his work is aware of many such problems which the exigencies of the therapeutic situation or the complexity of the clinical data do not permit him to follow further but which might be quite suitable for experimental analysis. The psychoanalytic mechanisms, for example, are phenomena isolated enough to be quite suitable topics for experimental investigation. As one example out of very many, I might cite the question as to what conditions determine whether projection or introjection shall be used as a defense. A good example of the kind of attempted synthesis of clinical and experimental studies that I have in mind is Dr. Sears's analysis (Chapter 9) of the concepts of fixation and regression in the light of a long series of experimental studies. Very interesting and significant also are attempts like those of J. McV. Hunt (1941) and D. M. Levy (1934 and 1938) to subject animals to experimental procedures similar to some of the common traumata of childhood in order to reproduce and subject to experimental analysis the disorders that are encountered clinically in persons who have histories of similar childhood traumata. It is along lines such as these that clinical and experimental methods will best be able to supplement each other.

BIBLIOGRAPHY

The following list is not intended as a complete bibliography. Such a bibliography would cover almost the entire psychoanalytic literature. It is intended rather as a selected reading list for those who wish to make themselves .nore familiar with psychoanalysis as a method of scientific investigation. I have therefore included in it a number of Freud's own descriptions of the development of his method and also a considerable amount of illustrative case material, and have added a few papers on mechanisms of particular neuroses and on experimental studies of problems suggested by clinical observations.

PSYCHOANALYTIC METHOD

ALEXANDER, F. 1936. Medical value of psychoanalysis. (2nd ed.) New York: Norton.

FREUD, A. 1937. The ego and the mechanisms of defense. London: Hogarth.

FREUD, S. 1893. On the psychical mechanism of hysterical phenomena. In *Collected papers*. Vol. 1. London: International Psycho-analytical Press, 1924. Pp. 24–42.

—— 1904. Freud's psychoanalytic method. In *Collected papers*. Vol. 1. London: International Psycho-analytical Press, 1924. Pp. 264–272.

—— 1912. The dynamics of the transference. In *Collected papers*. Vol. 2. London: Hogarth, 1924. Pp. 312–323.

—— 1914. Further recommendations in the technique of psycho-analysis. Recollection, repetition and working through. In *Collected papers*. Vol. 2. London: Hogarth, 1924. Pp. 366–376.

—— 1920. Introductory lectures on psycho-analysis. London: Allen & Unwin, 1936.

ILLUSTRATIVE CASE MATERIAL

ALEXANDER, F., & HEALY, W. 1935. Roots of crime. New York: Knopf.

DEUTSCH, H. 1932. Psycho-analysis of the neuroses. London: Hogarth.

FREUD, S. 1900. The interpretation of dreams. In *The basic writings of Sigmund Freud*. New York: Modern Library, 1938.

—— 1904. Psychopathology of everyday life. London: Fisher & Unwin, 1914.

—— 1905. Fragment of an analysis of a case of hysteria. In *Collected papers*. Vol. 3. London: Hogarth, 1925. Pp. 13–146.

—— 1905. Wit and its relation to the unconscious. In *The basic writings of Sigmund Freud*. New York: Modern Library, 1938.

—— 1909. Notes upon a case of obsessional neurosis. In *Collected papers*. Vol. 3. London: Hogarth, 1925. Pp. 296–383.

—— 1911. Psychoanalytic notes upon an autobiographical account of a case of paranoia. In *Collected papers*. Vol. 3. London: Hogarth, 1925. Pp. 390–470.

ADDITIONAL PAPERS ON MECHANISMS OF PARTICULAR NEUROSES

FREUD, S. 1913. A predisposition to obsessional neurosis. In *Collected papers*. Vol. 2. London: Hogarth, 1924. Pp. 122–133.

—— 1917. Mourning and melancholia. In *Collected papers*. Vol. 4. London: Hogarth, 1925. Pp. 152–173.

—— 1922. Certain neurotic mechanisms in jealousy, paranoia and homosexuality. In *Collected papers*. Vol. 2. London: Hogarth, 1924. Pp. 232–244.

MICROSCOPIC AND COMPARATIVE DREAM STUDIES

FRENCH, T. M. 1936. A clinical study of learning in the course of a psychoanalytic treatment. *Psychoanal. Quart.*, 5, 148–194.

—— 1937a. Reality testing in dreams. *Psychoanal. Quart.*, 6, 62–77.

—— 1937b. Reality and the unconscious. *Psychoanal. Quart.*, 6, 23–61.

—— 1939. Insight and distortion in dreams. *Int. J. Psycho-Anal.*, 20, 287–298.

EXPERIMENTAL STUDIES

HUNT, J. McV. 1941. The effects of infant feeding-frustration upon adult hoarding in the albino rat. *J. abnorm. soc. Psychol., 36,* 338–360.

HUNT, J. McV., & WILLOUGHBY, R. R. 1939. The effect of frustration on hoarding in rats. *Psychosom. Med., 1,* 309–310.

LEVY, D. M. 1934. Experiments on the sucking reflex and social behavior in dogs. *Amer. J. Orthopsychiat., 4,* 203–224.

—— 1938. On instinct satiation; an experiment on the pecking behavior of chickens. *J. genet. Psychol., 18,* 327–348.

Chapter 8

PHYSIOLOGICAL EFFECTS OF EMOTIONAL TENSION

By Leon J. Saul, M.D.*

THIS CHAPTER WILL DEAL primarily with the newer developments in a field which has come to be known as *psychosomatic relations.* (Dunbar, 1938; Alexander, 1939; Saul, 1941). Although perhaps not immediately apparent, these developments are of central importance for an understanding of the fundamentals of personality and behavior disorders because they deal directly with the biological forces which motivate the human organism, producing thoughts and emotions, behavior, and symptoms. The mental and emotional life with its loves, hates, fears is a reflection of the biological driving forces of our lives. Hence the mental life cannot be fully understood without understanding its relationships to these forces. The field of psychosomatic relations is concerned primarily with the biological aspects and basis of psychology. Psychosomatic symptoms are one of the modes of expression of the emotional life, especially of the unconscious emotional life—one of its languages, like dreams, slips of the tongue, and neurotic behavior—and as such, of direct concern to the student of the mental life.

The triumphs of modern medicine have been based chiefly upon the concept of the body as a machine—a machine built of cells. When groups of cells are in some way damaged, the physiological functioning of the organism is impaired and symptoms of disease result. But there is another aspect to the biological organism, namely its internally motivated functioning in relation to its environment. What physiology and cellular pathology have been to modern mechanistic medicine, biology and motivation are to psychosomatic medicine. The achievements of the former, particularly in reducing the infectious diseases, have brought the "biological functional" disorders to the center among the medical problems of today.

The organism functions as a unit from its very beginning as an egg cell. It is not a static reflex apparatus, like a switchboard, but from the start is dynamically motivated from within by biological (physico-chemical) forces (Child, 1924; Tracy, 1926; Coghill, 1929). As the cells multiply and the complex organs and tissues differentiate, the coordinating organ par excellence is the nervous system, the highest integrating center

* The writer is indebted to Agnes Plenk, Librarian of the Institute for Psychoanalysis, for her valuable assistance in the preparation of the bibliographies for the various sections of this chapter.

of which is the brain. Consciousness is a function of the brain, and is like a sense organ (Freud, 1910, 1922). Through it we perceive the biological forces which motivate us. Our "subjective" perceptions of these forces and derivatives of them we call "emotions" (Whitehorn, 1939). Our accustomed mode of handling them in relation to the environment (particularly to other persons) we call the "personality." "Thought" and "ideas" probably arise from these forces as highly developed adaptations of them to the environment. The "conscience" and "ideals" arise largely from the training or "conditioning" (Pavlov, 1927) in one way or another of these forces (French, 1933; Freud, 1933; Kubie, 1934). Life consists essentially in satisfying these forces (needs, urges, responses) in the environment, in accordance with the conscience and ideals (see Chapter 3 by Mowrer and Kluckhohn; Chapter 7 by French; Chapter 20 by Ribble). This is difficult despite the wonders of memory, judgment and thought. Stresses and strains develop. Tensions accumulate. If they affect the highest levels of the brain, they cause disturbances of thought and behavior (neuroses, psychoses). In so far as they affect lower levels of the nervous system and are mediated through them, they cause disturbances in the body physiology (organ neuroses). There is no sharp distinction. All tensions, for example, anger, are probably reflected throughout the body physiology. Why the emphasis falls now on this organ, now on that, will be seen to some extent later. We shall be concerned with "functional" symptoms, that is disturbances resulting in an intact mechanism because of stresses in its functioning. The same symptoms arise from other causes also—for example, from structural damage (see Chapter 18 by Cobb; Chapter 19 by Shock)—but these will not concern us.

History.—Psychosomatic knowledge reflects the maturation of a trend which is evident in many phases of human endeavor, a development beyond static, mechanistic, atomic thinking toward a more unified dynamic concept of psycho-socio-biological functioning. This is evident from the review of representative studies in closely related fields, which appears in Dunbar (1938). These include general biology, comparative anatomy, physiology, psychology, psychoanalysis, anthropology, clinical medicine, and other disciplines, all of which have contributed to psychosomatic knowledge. The various biases of these approaches as well as certain problems of measurement are discussed, thus providing an excellent introductory orientation.

A comprehensive history of the development of our knowledge of the physiological effects of emotions remains to be written. That the emotions and physiology are interrelated has been known since the days of tribal medicine men (Whitwell, 1936; Bromberg, 1937; Lewis, 1941; Zilboorg and Henry, 1941) and has been discussed by Hippocrates, the father of modern medicine, and later by great physicians, such as Paracelsus (trans. 1894). It was a special concern of the philosophers (Aristotle, trans. 1913). Attempts were made in antiquity and down through the middle ages to establish certain specific interrelationships. These are reflected in our language and folklore. Love and generosity are linked with the heart, hatred with the spleen, courage with the gut, and so on. But psychosomatic medicine is only now emerging as a demarcated field. It has developed from several scientific currents. It derives in part from French neurology, via Charcot and his illumination of emotional factors in producing hysterical symptoms (see Chapter 15 by Jenness). It was through Charcot and also Bernheim and his work on hypnosis that Freud found the inspiration and guidance which led to his studies of hysteria—the emotional basis of physical symptoms—which laid the groundwork for his entire biological approach to psychology and medicine. Meanwhile deriving from Kraepelinian psychiatry, Bleuler was developing his ideas of psychobiological parallelism and Adolf Meyer in this country was contributing his psychobiology to psychiatric thought. In physiology, Cannon (1936a) was conducting his famous researches on the physiological effects of acute emotion. The whole field of general medicine was becoming ripe for psychosomatic investigations, for with the triumphs of bacteriology and cellular pathology, the functional disorders have come more and more to the forefront of medical problems (Cannon, 1936b). Psychosomatic research today is carried on not only by individuals, but by certain groups whose clinical training includes neurology, psychiatry, and psychoanalysis. The largest and most active of these groups are those at the Columbia University Presbyterian Hospital center in New York City, the Harvard Medical School and the Massachusetts General Hospital and also the Beth Israel Hospital in Boston, the Menninger Sanitarium in Topeka, Kansas, Temple University in Philadelphia, and the Chicago Institute for Psychoanalysis.

Extensive reviews such as Wittkower's (1935) and Dunbar's (1938) show that until recently the bulk of the work of the past has described the general fact that emotions affect the physiology and play a role in producing the symptoms. Psychosomatic medicine is just entering an epoch of "specificity" that is an investigation of the specific emotional constellations which produce specific physiological disturbances. These studies have received great impetus from Freudian psychoanalysis which provides a sort of clinical microscope, a systematic method beyond individual common sense or intuition for the more detailed and precise observation and description of mental and emotional states (see Chapter 7 by French).

Methodology.—There are various methods of studying these problems—for example physiologically by such animal experiments as Cannon's (1939) and Bard's (1939), by experimental neuroses of animals as in the work of Liddell (see Chapter 12) and Gantt (1943) and clinically by experimental situations, such as the startle pattern of Landis and Hunt (1939), and by laboratory and statistical studies. We shall here report only on direct clinical studies of the specific emotional factors related to specific physiological disturbances. We shall therefore deal largely with psychoanalytic findings. This approach has the disadvantage of having to make essentially descriptive observations upon the experiments of nature with relatively little control of the environmental situation. However, this is compensated for by the fact that here the clinician can observe in the most direct possible fashion the central object of his study—the human mental and emotional life (see Chapter 7 by French). Moreover, the psychoanalytic situation is in reality an experimental situation, a laboratory sample as it were, of the analysand's emotional relationships toward other persons, as these develop toward the analyst and are influenced by making conscious the unconscious or unappreciated elements. Secondly, the subject, unlike the animals, has available a special instrument for communicating mental phenomena, namely, human speech. And in addition, it is probably only in such a therapeutic situation that the subject can communicate his true motivations freely, because it is only for relief from mental suffering that a person can fully reveal himself to another or even to himself (Saul, 1939).[1]

Specific Correlations

The emotions and the physiology are of course intimately interrelated. Tensions activate physiological responses in at least three ways: (1) Indirect or factitious, as when sore gums develop from teeth-grinding during sleep, or when excoriations of the skin result from scratching (Saul, 1935). (2) Hysterical, in which subtle ideational processes are an important link in the mechanism, for example dramatization of an idea—guilt over a "false step" sexually, leading to a limp (Freud, 1905); identification—as when a boarding school girl has hysterics on receiving an unhappy love letter and, when the other girls learn of it they also have hysterics (Freud, 1922); suggestion—as seen in various complex ideational hypnotic effects. (3) Organ neurosis, "psychosomatic," in which the physiological effects are direct, mostly vegetative nervous system responses to emotional tensions, which, as in the other two types, are not fully conscious or appreciated by the patient. It is with this latter type of situation that this review will be primarily concerned. In all three, however, the basis is in biological needs, urges, responses.

Gastro-Intestinal Disturbances

Among the first symptoms to be studied for specific psychological relationships are the functional gastro-intestinal disturbances. Of these, peptic ulcer and nervous diarrhea and constipation have been further

---

[1] In evaluating criticism of psychoanalytic findings it must be borne in mind (1) that this approach has been chiefly in the hands of practitioners and not research workers, and (2) that it takes at least five years' experience in conducting analyses after one's own basic training, in which the personal analysis is only the first step, before the average student is sufficiently oriented in this difficult field to make valid scientific criticism of it. Lack of this experience is like a reading knowledge of microscopic anatomy without experience in the laboratory use of the microscope, a training which would not enable one to evaluate microscopic findings.

elucidated than the others. An excellent review has been made by Alexander (1941). The following is largely based upon it. The reader is also referred to the general reviews by Jones, *et al.* (1938) and by Brush (1939).

There are normal psychic influences upon the gastro-intestinal tract, such as the thought or sight of food, "psychic secretion" (Pavlov, 1927). There are acute disturbances of it, as by rage or fear. When a disturbance is of a chronic or recurrent nature, it is spoken of as a gastro-intestinal neurosis (Menninger, 1937).

Psychology of Imbibitional Processes.—It is well established that almost from birth eating is closely associated with the emotions, especially receiving food with receiving love (see Chapter 20 by Ribble, and Chapter 3 by Mowrer and Kluckhohn). This is largely because in the nursing situation imbibition is directly associated with maternal love and care. Taking food may become associated with taking and possessing other things, impulses which, when strong enough, lead to greed, envy, possessiveness. Moreover, biting is a primitive means of hostile aggression. Thus, besides needs for love, hostile and grasping impulses and guilt because of them are prominent in the motivation of eating disturbances. The association of eating with these emotional impulses may follow the lines described by Pavlov (1927) for "conditioning" (see Chapter 12 by Liddell).

DISTURBANCES OF APPETITE AND EATING—*Bulimia.* Most people do not eat only to live. Eating can afford a satisfaction beyond calories alone. Sometimes this leads to pathologically excessive appetite, known medically as "bulimia." We have seen that eating often becomes associated with desires for care, attention, love. It has been found that eating can serve as a substitute satisfaction for such desires. Aggressive biting can also play a role (Coriat, 1921; Wulff, 1932; Benedek, 1936; Schmied, 1936; Benedek and Rubenstein, 1941). The following case is typical:

A young woman complained of obesity due to irresistible desires for food. These desires were displacements to food of intense frustrated desires for love (Saul, 1941; Benedek and Rubenstein, 1941). She had been deprived and exploited in childhood by her father and stepmother. At about twelve she left home and found a job. With her first week's salary her debauch consisted in buying all the ice cream she could eat. When especially lonely and frustrated she would console herself by orgies of eating. She was pitifully poor and was frigid sexually. Her only free satisfaction was eating. When she saw a well-laden table she literally quivered with excitement and could hardly restrain herself. Sometimes when expectations —especially those of a sexual nature—were disappointed, she would enter a restaurant in a daze, and a little while later realize that she had eaten inordinately. Benedek and Rubenstein (1941) have traced a relationship between the ovarian hormonal level and bulimic cravings.

Pertinent to the psychology of bulimia are the findings of Bruch and Touraine (1940) who made a careful study of the families of 40 obese children. Their central psychological finding (apart from possible hereditary and endocrine factors) was the consistency with which these children were found to have mothers who overprotected them and restricted their activities excessively, so that they could not indulge in normal activities of exercise and play. On the other hand, these mothers regularly overemphasized eating. Thus, they not only blocked these children in the enjoyment of normal activities (conditioned the children against them) but at the same time they encouraged eating and passivity as the only forms of pleasure. In this way the mothers drove them to eating and passivity as their main enjoyments.

Anorexia Nervosa. Exaggerations of appetite are sometimes seen to alternate with loss of appetite in the same individual. This is often seen in the manic-depressive psychoses. In the depressed phase food may be entirely refused. Some persons do not show the dramatic fluctuations of mood which mark the manic-depressive states, but they show alternations of appetite of such proportions that they gain or lose 50 to 100 pounds in six months. Bulimia sometimes precedes a loss of appetite severe enough to threaten life, which is part of a neurotic condition known as "anorexia nervosa" (Lasegue, 1873; Gull, 1874; Sheldon, 1937; Farquharson and Hyland, 1938; Rahman, Richardson, and Ripley, 1939; Richardson, 1939). In these cases it has been found that certain impulses which are rejected by the rest of the personality as intolerable because of guilt and shame are so closely associated with eating that food cannot be taken. In many cases these rejected impulses are of a sexual nature, for example, unconscious impulses to fellatio or cunnilingus (Freud, 1905; Abraham, 1924) or wishes for pregnancy (Rahman, Richardson, and Ripley, 1939). A typical case (Waller, Kaufman and Deutsch, 1940) is that of a girl in a strong conflict situation with her mother, whose sexual life is blocked by the prohibitions of the parents, by internal inhibition, or by both, who has ideas of being impregnated through eating, who at first displaces her sexual wishes onto cravings for food and eats gluttonously and then develops a revulsion for food similar to her revulsion against sex. Cessation of menstruation is a usual feature.

In other cases not libidinal but aggressive impulses are in the foreground—grasping, envious, attacking desires. These are unconscious and are associated with biting and eating, which are inhibited because of guilt and shame. It may be recalled that fasting is an ancient method of atonement and that hunger strikes make deep impressions on the public. A simple case illustration (Alexander, 1941) is a girl of eight who refused practically all food. She had a two-year-old sister who was fed by the nurse in the presence of the mother, at the same time as the patient. A few interviews showed the intensity of (1) her wishes for love and attention for herself, which she forced by her symptom; (2) her resentment against the little sister as an intruder and against the parents; and (3) her guilt for these selfish and aggressive impulses. A few interviews plus having the patient eat as a little grownup with the parents instead of with the baby sister promptly relieved the symptom.

The not uncommon cases in which there is fear of eating which appears only in certain situations, for example, in public restaurants but not at home, are known as eating phobias. They occur on a similar emotional basis.

Nervous Vomiting. Emotional upsets can cause not only loss of appetite but actual vomiting. The reasons for the difference are not well worked out. Probably the more active rejection of certain impulses is important and perhaps in some cases impulses of restitution. Various rejected impulses have been reported, including sexual urges, wishes for pregnancy, and aggressive, grasping desires. These are rejected chiefly because of shame and guilt (Ferenczi, 1919; Levine, 1934; Bond, 1938; Masserman, 1941). For example, a girl saw her suitor several times clandestinely against the commands of her mother, and each time reacted with vomiting. In some cases hysterical mechanisms are prominent, for example a girl's identification with a pregnant friend's "morning sickness," because of her own rejected wish to be pregnant; or the fantasy of having incorporated something which must be ejected or restored.

Oesophageal Neuroses. Oesophageal neuroses are probably still another form of the same general conflict situation. In these the emotional tension causes a constriction of the oesophageal muscles (Faulkner, 1940) either at the entrance to the stomach (cardiospasm), in which case there is difficulty in swallowing (Winkelstein, 1931; Moschcowitz, 1935), or in the upper part, in which case a lump is felt in the throat (Globus hystericus) (Ferenczi, 1919a).

In all of these cases of imbibitional disturbances we see overindulgence, inhibition, or reversal of function, because, respectively, of the substitute gratification, the inhibition, or active rejection of emotional impulses which become connected with eating.

DISTURBANCES OF DIGESTION.—*Stomach Neuroses.* It is common knowledge that emotional tensions affect the stomach. They do so in many ways, causing symptoms which range from slight distress to severe pains and intractable vomiting. The physiological bases are equally varied, including disturbances of secretion and motility. No systematic studies of the specific psychological connections have yet appeared. But on the basis of closely related work it seems that in gastric neuroses of all sorts the main pertinent emotional trends include wishes to be passive, dependent, receptive, possessive, helped, loved. The symptoms appear when this trend is frustrated, either through external disappointment or internally through the individual rejecting such childhood wishes, and striving with excessive energy and independence. Granet (1940), for example, observed total spasm of the stomach in a patient whose emotional dynamics were precisely those described by Alexander, *et al.* (1934) for ulcer cases. It is common to see such cases as that of a successful commercial artist in a big city, whose stomach pains ceased completely when he left his highly competitive, strenuous, metropolitan existence for teaching and painting in a small western town. These dynamics are illustrated by studies of patients with peptic ulcers.

Peptic Ulcers. It is so well known that excessive drive, worry, and nervous tension are of importance in peptic ulcer that this condition has been referred to as "Wall Street stomach," and the *Chicago Daily News* has stated that the strain of national defense problems may give many business executives ulcers (*Time,* Sept. 15, 1941). There is general scientific agreement that emotions can play a role in ulcer formation (Davies and Wilson, 1937), and some authorities consider peptic ulcers to be an end result of a long standing functional stomach neurosis (Bergman, 1913; Westphal, 1914).

As to the nature of this neurosis, clinicians find that peptic ulcers are most apt to occur in ambitious, hard-driving business men (Alvarez, 1929) who are constantly meeting obstacles which they feel driven to overcome (Hartman, 1933). Hartman considers peptic ulcer to be a disease of the striving and ambitious men of Western civilization. Draper and Touraine (1932) have reached a similar conclusion. They found that their ulcer patients rejected unconscious passive receptive feminine tendencies, and reacted against these with activity and masculine protest. These findings have also been emphasized on the basis of anthropometric studies by Daniels (1934), who found the ulcer type to be the slender asthenic longitudinal type.

These findings have been confirmed and extended by the studies of Alexander, *et al.* (1934). These show that the essential point is the close association of stomach function with cravings for care, support, dependence, love, so that these cravings stimulate the stomach to secretion and motility just as desires for food do. The situation is similar to, perhaps identical with, the conditioned reflex (Pavlov, 1927; see also Chapter 12 by Liddell). These cravings, if constantly frustrated, act as constant stimuli to the stomach which eventually breaks down in ulcer formation. The usual psychological constellation is an ambitious driving individual who does not permit himself the satisfactions of these cravings because he is ashamed of them. Indeed, his overambition is usually in large part a denial of them. He must be the big giving "he-man" in order to deny that underneath the surface he craves to be a little boy cared for by an indulgent parent. But the frustration is not always due to such conflict in his own personality. It may be due to external circumstances. The important point is that these cravings are frustrated and affect the functioning of the stomach. The following case illustrates this point: A 46-year-old man had been overindulged in childhood by his mother. He married a superior woman, expecting that she would indulge him, but she devoted herself to her own career with such success that the patient felt impelled, out of self-respect, at least to equal his wife's position and earnings. It was when he drove himself to business activity that his postprandial stomach pains and chronic hyperacidity developed. After eighteen years this eventuated in an ulcer, with a hemorrhage two years later. After the hemorrhage he established a relationship with a soft, unambitious, indulgent, motherly type of woman and his symptoms disappeared. Unlike this patient, the majority of ulcer cases studied had an inner drive to responsibility and activity, which in large part they accepted and enjoyed, protesting against it only unconsciously. But this example is given here because it "shows that it is the thwarting of receptive cravings and not a certain personality type that is of primary importance. Here the specific external situation in which the patient lived created a conflict through external deprivation similar to the one which in the majority of cases is produced by internal deprivation as a result of an inner conflict" (Alexander, 1934).

The evidence for psychogenic factors in peptic ulcer is based not only upon psychological observation, but also upon data from physiology and pathology, of which van der Heide (1941) reviews the following. Pavlov's (1927) experiments demonstrated "psychic" secretion and von Bergmann (1936) pointed out the factor of local ischemia and neural influence in addition to the role of hyperacidity and hypermotility. Cushing (1931) pointed out the frequent occurrence of peptic ulcers after parasympathetic stimulation caused by operative irritation of the midbrain, and Light (1931) reported the experimental production of gastric ulcers by injecting pilocarpine into the brain. Watts and Fulton (1935) and Hoff and Sheehan (1935) succeeded in causing multiple and hemorrhagic lesions in the gastric mucosa of monkeys through hypothalamic injuries. Keller (1936) showed that cerebral lesions do not cause bleeding in the stomach wall if the sympathetic chain is removed beforehand, thus showing the importance of the autonomic nervous innervation. A fusion of the evidence from these various sources suggests that the following causal chain (Alexander, 1934; van der Heide, 1941) operates as at least one factor in certain cases: emotional stimulus related to the function of the particular organ (frustrated wishes for love, care, dependence) ⟶ stimulation of subcortical centers ⟶ disturbance of the autonomic innervation of the organ ⟶ dysfunction of the organ ⟶ hypersecretion, hypermotility, alterations in blood supply ⟶ chronicity and structural damage. Of course it may well be that in other cases the psychogenic element is of no importance and that the ulcers are caused by other mechanisms.

Disturbances of the Eliminative Functions

Psychology of the Excremental Functions.—For the infant, whose life is largely vegetative, the eliminative functions, their care and training, are second only to eating in emotional importance. Yet their psychological importance has not been appreciated. That such a connection exists is a matter of folk knowledge. Fear is known to cause involuntary bowel movements, and the courageous man is spoken of as having "guts" or "intestinal fortitude." Studies of these emotional connections have shown that elimination becomes associated early in life with feelings of possessiveness, pride in accomplishment, and giving, and also with impulses to attack, soil, disparage (Freud, 1905, 1915, 1916, 1918; Jones, 1913; Abraham, 1921, 1924; Alexander, 1936). Alexander (1941) summarizes the probable development of this connection, and the subject is treated by Ribble in Chapter 18. It is probable that thwarting of the pleasures connected with suckling and sucking stimulate the child's discovery of certain pleasure sensations from the rectal region. Although in these the child is more independent, bowel training interferes, requiring that stools be parted with only in certain places and at certain times. In this situation of parental concern the child's naïve interest in excrements becomes associated with a sense of possession and accomplishment, as well as with disgust and depreciation. The disgust is probably not only a result of training alone, for it is seen in young untrained animals. The excremental function thus becomes connected with the feeling of accomplishment, of giving, and of attacking, soiling, and depreciating, and becomes the first symbol of possession. These infantile emotional associations are largely repressed in normal adult life, but often appear in normal dreams, neurotic symptoms, and psychotic behavior.

Chronic Diarrhea, Spastic Colitis, Mucous Colitis, Ulcerative Colitis.—That emotional tensions can cause diarrhea and colitis has long been known to medicine. In a recent investigation and review of the problem White, Cobb, and Jones (1939) conclude that mucous colitis is a physiological disorder of the colon brought about through the action of the parasympathetic nervous system and that the commonest source of the parasympathetic overstimulation is emotional tension. Emotional tension was obviously present in 92% of the psychogenic cases in the series of 60 cases. Certain specific characteristics of the personality—overconscientiousness, dependence upon the opinions of others, and sensitivity—appear to predispose to the development of these tensions as do anthropological habitus, allergy, fatigue, and other factors.

Even ulcerative colitis is considered by many authors to develop in certain cases as a result of emotional tensions (Sullivan and Chandler, 1932; Wittkower, 1938). Murray (1930) found that in twelve cases these usually concerned marital relationships. Bell (1933) describes a woman in whom guilt feeling toward her divorced husband was the central emotional feature.

Psychoanalytic studies of diarrhea and colitis cases show that the symptoms are stimulated chiefly by impulses to make restitution to others for grasping, demanding, receptive attitudes toward them, and also by impulses of hostility, depreciation, and soiling. The peptic ulcer patient usually compensates for his wish to be passive and dependent by real work, activity, exertion, accomplishment, and independence—often exaggerated in order to deny the opposite. But the diarrhea patient only makes the gestures. The schema in these cases is that these urges are not acted out in life, but stimulate the autonomic nervous system, causing increased peristaltic activity of the bowels instead. This becomes a substitute activity—a symbolic substitute for genuine accomplishment and giving (Alexander, 1934; Wilson, 1934). An example (author's case) is a young physician, an only child, who had been overly protected by his parents and enjoyed his extreme dependence upon them. When he graduated from medical school and faced the responsibilities of his interneship he developed anxiety and diarrhea. He did not dare withdraw, however, because he felt that he must make restitution for all his parents had given him and sacrificed for him. The same constellation repeated itself when he stepped out into practice. He resented the new responsibilities and demands and regularly, if he were settled down for a quiet evening and received a call to go out, he would feel glad to have the practice but resentful of leaving his comfort for exertion and responsibility and would react with diarrhea. The connection of defecation with hostile impulses needs no special demonstration. One need only think of the vulgar words for this function and their use in all manner of obscene and aggressive idioms.

In women, conflicts over giving and receiving often center around pregnancy, which is to be expected, since this is the most creative, giving, active, responsible function of the female organism. Where child-bearing is feared and rejected, diarrhea is seen in some cases to serve as an emotional and symbolic substitute (Nacht and Eliet, 1938; Daniels, 1940). A review of 30 patients by Brown, Preu, and Sullivan (1938) corroborates the detailed psychoanalytic findings, in that prominent features of the series were lack of output of drive and tendencies to avoid responsibility and to give up easily in the face of difficulty.

Chronic Psychogenic Constipation.—Chronic psychogenic constipation can be distinguished from the intermittent constipation which often occurs in colitis. It results from a typical psychological constellation, in which there are usually feelings of being rejected and unloved, distrust, especially regarding dependence upon others, and a pessimistic outlook. An exaggeration of feelings of being rejected is seen in melancholia, and of distrust in paranoia; and constipation is more common in paranoia and melancholia than in control groups (Menninger and Alexander, 1936). The emotional logic of this constipation is "I cannot expect anything from anyone and therefore I must hold on to what I have; I need not give." The emotional attitude is acted out, as it were, by the bowel, as though the excrement were a possession, as it is often regarded by the young child, and, unconsciously, by the adult. In line with the hostile soiling meaning of defecation, another factor in psychogenic constipation is the inhibition of these aggressive impulses; i.e., defecation becomes so closely associated with inhibited hostile, soiling impulses that it, too, is inhibited. (Compare with the mechanism of the inhibition in anorexia nervosa.)

This survey of the influence of emotional tensions upon the functioning of the gastro-intestinal tract reemphasizes the fact that it is not the personality type which is related to the symptoms, but certain emotional tensions and constellations which may arise in persons of very different personality make-ups. These tensions and constellations may of course be important trends in the personalities which would then be similar to the extent to which they have these in common.

On the basis of findings in the gastro-intestinal study, Alexander .(1935) developed the concept of "vectors," that is of noting the similarity in both the physiological and psychological data—of the *directions* of the impulses. These are grouped as (1) toward the individual, centripetal, intaking, incorporative; (2) centrifugal, eliminative; (3) retentive. As an example of the intaking vector, a young man is parasitic and demanding with many dreams of getting something for nothing, especially food. Physiologically he is a gourmand and alcoholic, with chronic hyperacidity and epigastric pains. Illustrative of the centrifugal vector is a man who, when he felt he should pay out money, developed diarrhea (Freud, 1918). The retentive vector is exemplified by a constipated woman who dreamt of a cat sitting on a pile of ham, to which she associated her stubborn refusal to give a friend some money. It has proved useful to reduce further the three major vectors as follows: intaking, as passive receiving and aggressive taking; retaining, as upbuilding and spiteful withholding; eliminating, as giving and attacking. As examples, diarrhea usually expresses in some proportion giving impulses and also soiling attacking impulses; and constipation expresses retentive impulses and may also result from inhibition of sadistic soiling impulses.

It is evident that on the physiological side this concept of vectors is most easily applicable to organ systems such as the gastro-intestinal, which have orifices at the body surface and very clearly serve intaking, retentive, and eliminative functions. These functions are fundamental to life and we are well acquainted with them from the field of metabolism. An interesting methodological·application of the vector concept has been made by Alexander and Wilson (1935). In an effort to reach quantitative estimates of balances of emotional forces in a series of gastro-intestinal patients, they analyzed all the dreams recorded during the psychoanalyses and recorded the tendencies found in accordance with the vector classification. They thus obtained a statistical representation of the frequency of appearance of these tendencies in the gastro-intestinal cases and compared them with the findings in a control series.

Cardiovascular Disturbances

Expressions in all languages link the heart to emotion—big-hearted. soft-hearted, broken-hearted, etc. The heart has also been called the organ of anxiety (Wolfe, 1934). The great anatomist, John Hunter, is reputed to have said concerning his angina pectoris, "My life is at the mercy of any rascal who can make me angry."

Essential Hypertension.—A recent symposium shows the present status of the problem of essential hypertension (Anderson, Parmenter, and Liddell, 1939; Katz and Leiter, 1939; Solomon, Darrow, and Blaurock, 1939; Alexander, 1939, 1939a; Saul, 1939; Miller, 1939). The following is drawn chiefly from this source.

By essential hypertension is meant elevated blood pressure without evidence of related kidney, vascular, or other disease. Weiss (1939) points out in his review that essential hypertension is "the gravest problem of middle adult life, not even excepting cancer (Hedley, 1935). . . . It is a disorder largely confined to occidental civilization. Studies of African natives (Donnison, 1929), the Chinese (Cadbury, 1922), the Buddhist priests in Ceylon (Gunwardene, 1935), and Egyptians of the laboring classes (Ismail, 1928), all indicate that hypertension is very rare among these peoples. The blood pressure of foreigners living in China (Foster, 1927) and the tropics (Roddis and Cooper, 1926) are lower than when they are living in a temperate zone." Hypertension has not been found in the Negroes in Africa, yet "Schulz and Schwab (1936) found the incidence of hypertension in the American southern Negro two and a half times greater than that of the southern whites," and the disease runs a more severe course in the Negro. The findings to be reported below suggest that the psychological position of the Negro in this country, in contrast with his life in Africa, may be a factor in this. However, authorities are substantially in agreement that constitutional and hereditary factors are important in the etiology of hypertension and other factors must also be considered.

Elevated blood pressure is popularly connected with anger, as evidenced by such expressions as "Don't get your blood pressure up." That anger can raise the blood pressure is demonstrable experimentally. Elevation of the blood pressure is "one constant of a complex physiological syndrome characteristic for the emotional state of rage and fear" (Cannon, 1929, 1936).

The medical literature shows general agreement that emotional factors play a role in essential hypertension, and detailed psychoanalytic studies of individual cases agree as to the importance of hostile, resentful feelings (Hill, 1935; Alexander, 1939; Saul, 1939; Schwartz, 1940). Wolfe (1936) and Dunbar (1939) find in the hypertensives a "tenseness, which is of both skeletal and smooth muscles, and which is part of the attempt to inhibit, and a defense against, both action and fantasy relative to their chronic rage" (Dunbar, 1939). The dreams of hypertensives show aggressive impulses, usually in the form of life-threatening situations (Wolfe, 1934).

The blood pressure of a patient of Alexander (1939), taken before and after 201 analytic sessions, averaged 160/111 for the "disturbed" interviews, 141/99 for the "calm" interviews.

Seven hypertensives and later three others were accepted for analyses at the Chicago Institute and were studied by cardiologists before and during analysis. Blood pressures were taken before and after each analytic hour under standard conditions. Although the series is small, the results are suggestive because of the consistency of the findings. The essence of these is (1) that the patient is caught in a conflict situation with which he struggles without adequate solution or escape and (2) that he sustains a chronic repressed rage.

A typical case was the following:

> Mr. A. came with a complaint of anxiety. He was in his forties, with a hypertension fluctuating from 160 to 200 systolic over 110 to 130 diastolic, which had been increasing for the preceding ten years. He was the only patient of the series with marked arteriosclerosis and somewhat impaired renal function. He was one of a number of children, and had been spoiled and dominated by his mother who also dominated the physically strong father. His mother made him work from the age of six to contribute to the family who lost their money at that time. He reacted with lifelong bitterness to being thus prematurely forced to work after the earlier extreme spoiling. She forbade sports as dangerous, and later forbade the patient to see girls other than those of his own faith. He obeyed despite his envy of the boys who engaged in athletics and in sexual play with girls. She set him the ideal of wealth, inspired him with excessive ambitions and great expectations, and forced him into marriage against his will with a girl of her choosing. Thus his whole life, his work, his religion, his marriage, came to mean submission to the mother—"bending the knee," as he put it—and also being forced out of the earlier situation of maternal spoiling and protection into excessive ambitious activity. He tried in vain for many years to escape or rebel against this unconscious attachment to the mother. Finally he actually got a divorce and tried to indulge in sexual promiscuity and alcoholism. He even took a girl to the Orient in an effort to escape his fears and be free sexually. But the anxiety was too great and he was forced to give up the rebellion. The patient's hypertension always increased during these periods in which anxiety frustrated his attempts at heterosexuality. Apparently in an effort to escape the conflict with his dominating mother, this patient turned to his father. But although on the surface his relations with men were less acutely disturbing, the dependence and submissiveness toward them was even more intolerable than toward women. Again the patient rebelled, using unconscious hostility as his defense. This was most clear toward his boss to whom again he would not "bend the knee." Besides his hostility from rebellion against his dependence and submissiveness, he would rage at not getting the passive receptive satisfaction he demanded, i.e., at not being able to be dependent on others, but being forced to ambitious independent exertion and responsibility. But his rage from rebellion and from frustration was never directly expressed. He was quiet and gentlemanly with all. (Saul, 1939)

The emotional make-up of this patient was to a remarkable degree similar to that of the patient reported by Alexander (1939).

> Both of these patients were chronically pessimistic, anxious, and mildly depressed. They tried to escape by recourse to alcohol and

promiscuity, although they were really very inhibited sexually. Drinking and promiscuity were to them symbols of defying conventions, and means of escaping from dependence and submissiveness, and resulted in feelings of deep guilt and anxiety. When in the country, away from women, bosses, and obligations both were much relieved. A number of their early dreams were almost identical, namely dreams of being in a sexual situation with a woman and being seen by a man with consequent anxiety. (Saul, 1939)

This type of dream was found to occur in four analyzed male patients with well-established hypertension. It was not found in an early mild fluctuating case. Elevations of pressure correlated with dreams of this type in which the patient was caught in an unsolved conflict, while low points of the blood pressure correlated with dreams of leaving the conflict for some passive situation, such as a pleasant vacation (Saul, 1940).

Eight cases with no hypertension but with similar conflicts to the hypertensives were selected as controls. These patients all had some way of avoiding, escaping, or relieving the conflict and emotional tensions. Some accepted the submissiveness instead of rebelling, others avoided submissive situations, as was done by one young man who could never tolerate a boss and so did free-lance work. Or, in other cases, the rebellion and hostility found adequate release in neurosis or otherwise.

Hence, it seems that not the conflict and hostilities themselves, but their particular *status* is the important factor for the hypertension. The following was the status of the hostilities in the cases studied: The hostility was (1) intense and (2) chronic. However gentle the exterior, the analyses revealed that these individuals were chronically boiling with rage. One of the patients, Mr. A., told the following dream: "I heard the hissing of steam all around me and then realized it was within myself. I became tense and trembling with the pressure. An elderly woman called me 'the boss.' But I said: 'No, that man is the boss.' " In his associations the patient brought out his envy of, and his rebellion against, his boss and the analyst, and to *the steam* associated a machine trembling with the pressure of steam within. This pressure was his hostility against the boss and the analyst, chronic and unvented. (3) The hostility was in all these cases the central issue of the analysis, the pathogenetic element so to speak. (4) The hostility was close to consciousness. There is reason to suspect that the crucial point here may be the proximity of the hostilities to motility. (5) The hostility was in all cases very inhibited. On the surface these individuals were nonhostile and even overly gentle, but did not lack energy. They worked, in fact overworked, and succeeded, while protesting against doing so. The hostility found no adequate outlet in behavior in life, through drainage by sexual activity (which often discharges unconscious sadistic impulses) or even in dreams or fantasies. (6) Although inhibited, the hostility in these cases was not adequately bound in an organized chronic neurosis, for example, paranoia, compulsion neurosis, chronic alcoholism, etc.

Cases have been reported by Draper (1935) in which the hypertension disappeared when the patient developed neurotic symptoms. The hostility was never adequately expressed but never relinquished. The regressive wishes to give up the struggle and accept a passive dependent emotional situation were also not accepted. Both were blocked.

A common feature in this small series was conflict with a dominating parent.

> Two main reactions were seen. The one was a submissiveness to the parent, against which the patient was in constant but unsuccessful hostile rebellion, (unable) to accept either the submission and dependence which hurt the pride or the hostile rebellion which caused anxiety. (By contrast, a control patient refused a better paying executive position because he did not wish to relinquish his dependence upon his boss which he freely acknowledged.) The other main reaction was the dependent attachment chiefly to the mother, which formed part of the submissiveness and was rebelled against, but which, when not satisfied, due to both external thwarting and internal inhibition (guilt, pride, ambition, and self-love) led to chronic rage at the frustration. The unsatisfied dependent wishes with consequent anger were conspicuous in the material in all the cases. This checks with K. Menninger's (1938) statement that it is common to find in the histories of essential hypertensives that in childhood they have been thrust prematurely into situations of self-reliance. (Saul, 1939)

Other similarities were anxiety about heterosexuality, but with more or less indulgence despite this; and the fact that in all cases the problem was a very deeply ingrained and repressed one, intimately organized into the whole personality.

Weiss (1940) has stressed the importance of these repressed emotional tensions in precipitating cerebral hemorrhage, coronary occlusion, pulmonary edema, and similar vascular accidents in cases of essential hypertension.

In order to test the role of inhibited hostilities in hypertension, Miller (1939) interviewed 193 psychotic patients, paranoias, depressions, and passive regressed schizophrenics. He divided them into three groups according to the intensity and status of their hostilities and found a correspondence between these groups and the blood pressure levels.

The psychological findings in hypertension support the hypothesis that hypertension is a disease of civilization in so far as civilized society generates much hostility and conflict of this nature but also demands a high degree of repression of the hostility which therefore persists and accumulates (Alexander, 1939).

Cardiovascular Neuroses.—The term "cardiac neurosis" signifies symptoms relative to the heart, such as pains, palpitations, tachycardia (rapid beat), irregularities of beat as extrasystoles (a skipped beat and then a fast one), and so on, which are not caused by structural damage, but by emotional tensions. Caughey (1939) in his review finds that their importance is apparently increasing, a fact which has been attributed to the stresses of modern life. He quotes certain characteristics which have been noted. For example, whereas patients with organic heart disease usually resent limitation of physical activities, those with cardiac neuroses usually acquiesce readily and show a marked lack of endurance and of capacity for effort. In the angina group, a higher percentage of neurosis was found in cases with cardiac pain than in those without it (Bourne, Scott, and Wittkower, 1937). The physician may do actual harm if he regards the patient as no more than an isolated mechanical unit, and if he does not recognize that "sustained and disabling physiological abnormalities may occur in the absence of any organic disease" (Willius, 1937; Caughey, 1939).

Dunbar (1939) on the basis of a survey of 1300 patients found that a

> comparison of cardiac patients with the fracture group brought out marked differences both in reaction type and in history. Ninety per cent of the latter (about one hundred and fifty cases) gave a history of stern parents (or foster parents) both of whom lived into the patient's adolescence, and of strict religious upbringing. Of this group of cardiacs on the other hand (same number of cases), although brutality on the part of one parent or the other was often reported (forty per cent) only two per cent reported strictness on the part of both father and mother, and interestingly enough, in only three more cases was the mother strict or violent with the children.
>
> Usually there was a very marked attachment to the mother on the part of both males and females, accompanied by fear of the father, or absence of the father as a result of death or divorce.

Despite the extreme frequency of functional cardiac disorders, and the compendious literature on this subject, the specific factors have not been thoroughly worked out. The few short studies available indicate that as in essential hypertension, hostile aggressive impulses are central and further that competitiveness and hostile identification may play a role. Thus the Menningers (1936) report three cases in which they found chest pains in the region of the heart to be connected with strongly aggressive tendencies which were totally repressed. These were men who were more or less hostile to their mothers, and whose strong attachment to their fathers obliterated the deeply buried hostilities to them. Moreover, the fathers had heart symptoms. (This identification with an individual toward whom one has unconscious hostility is called "hostile identification." It is motivated largely by guilt. Hostile feelings to the loved father are intolerable and hence repressed from consciousness, but they lead to the feeling: you deserve to suffer in the same way he does.) Dunbar from her survey (1939), states that

> Patients with coronary disease and pseudo-angina present a complex picture in which vascular and muscle spasm related to repressed hostility is marked. They show also a prominent sense of guilt and tendency to self-punishment; they are the only group of patients with cardiovascular disease that seemed to show any considerable

tendency to have accidents prior to the onset of illness except perhaps the hypertensives, who resemble them.

Identification with the cardiac illness of a parent was also found in four cases of palpitation and extrasystoles reported by Miller and McLean (1941). They observed that the symptoms occurred when aggressive, hostile, competitive impulses were mobilized and near to consciousness but repressed. They stress the motive of competitiveness in these cases. Gunther and Menninger (1939) observed the development of extrasystoles in a woman when she was about to be examined gynecologically and recorded them on the electrocardiogram at the time. This patient suffered from severe anxiety concerning sexuality. The emotional states which cause palpitations and extrasystoles are probably not very individual or restricted since increased heart rate occurs in everyone in situations of emotional tension and irregularities of beat are also extremely common.

Respiratory Disturbances

Asthma.—The importance of psychogenic factors in bronchial asthma has been known since antiquity, but studies of them have diminished since about 1915 following the discovery of the part played by anaphylaxis (allergic hypersensitivity to specific substances). A renewed interest is evident, however, in the recent literature owing probably in part to the fact that the allergic approach (finding the allergens and eliminating them or desensitizing the patient) is by no means uniformly successful. Thus, McDermott and Cobb (1939) found 37 of their 50 cases to have an emotional component in their asthma attacks, and the 13 "nonemotional" patients were predominantly young males who might have hidden the emotional component from shame. Most authors agree that the emotional and allergic factors are probably not in opposition but in some way supplementary to each other.

Extensive reviews are available (Wittkower, 1935; Dunbar, 1938), and French in a recent detailed study (French and Alexander, et al., 1941) has made a critical survey of most of the literature on the subject up to the present. From this, especially from the work of Rogerson, Hardcastle, and Duguid (1935), and of Weiss (1922), it appears that the outstanding personality traits of asthmatics are overanxiety, lack of self-confidence, and a deep-seated clinging dependence upon the parents which is often a reaction to parental oversolicitude. The asthma attacks themselves are precipitated by sudden intense emotions (fright by a dog, sudden suppressed anger), by sexual conflicts (guilty illicit affair, unexpected kiss), by identification (sight of mother gasping for breath), and by threats to dependence and security (birth of sibling). They bear a relationship to anxiety and to crying (weeping changing to wheezing).

A monograph presents the results of the psychoanalytic study of 24 asthmatics, eight of whom were children (French and Alexander, et al., 1941). On the basis of the literature, especially Weiss (1922), and of these studies it is well established that the core of the emotional factor in asthma is a deep dependence upon the mother, of a type which appears in the dreams and fantasies as a wish, not to be fed, as in the gastro-intestinal cases, but rather as a wish for shelter, protection, security, symbolically represented as intra-uterine fantasies. The asthma attack occurs when this dependence is threatened. The threat is often a temptation—to behave in some way, sexual, aggressive, or otherwise—which will estrange the mother or mother substitute. The asthma often has an emergency character, as though the person is too suddenly overwhelmed with anxiety to be able to behave in some way to relieve it other than by the asthma attack. The attack is then equivalent to a repressed cry of helplessness for the mother, the prototype of which is possibly the cry of the newborn because of separation from the mother (Weiss, 1922). In many instances asthma attacks terminated with crying, and in others permanent relief from asthma followed the ability to cry, in persons who had previously been unable to do so, when in emotional situations which had previously precipitated asthma attacks. The diverse personalities of asthmatics reflect different psychological defenses against the central fear of separation from the mother whether physically or psychologically through estrangement or loss of love. The common features in their otherwise diverse personalities arise from the common task of dealing in one way or another with fear of separation (or estrangement) from the mother.

There is no question of the importance of this conflict situation in precipitating asthma attacks as testified by case histories and observations, by the precipitation of attacks when the analyses were interrupted or when the defenses were weakened, and by the relief often afforded by the mere beginning of an analysis.

The chief method used in this study was the detailed investigation of the psychological situations in which the attacks occurred. The common feature in these situations was consistently the sudden danger of separation or estrangement from the mother or mother substitute. Thus one patient's asthma began when he married against his mother's wishes. After his analysis he had an attack in the winter, although his asthma was seasonal and had never occurred in winter, precipitated by meeting a former girl friend who tried to seduce him. He fled to his wife, but found he could not confess the sexual part of the meeting despite a strong urge to do so. He suffered from asthma on and off for two months and was relieved when he realized its connection with the incident which had made him guilty.

A frequent finding in the childhood situation is an overprotective mother who makes the child overly dependent upon her, but then strongly rejects any signs of sexual interest. Pregnancy of the mother and the birth of siblings are also important in precipitating asthma in childhood. Such situations are also important in adult life. One patient developed asthma when a married woman with whom he was having an affair became pregnant. Sexual factors are not the only precipitants. A young man suffered a severe attack when, facing disgrace, he struggled with the idea of leaving his town and family.

The asthma attack seems to be "a reaction of acute helplessness. At the moment of temptation the dependence upon the mother is so great that the threat of losing her completely overpowers the patient. The mechanism is similar to that postulated by Freud for acute anxiety. The asthma attack occurs only when the patient is overpowered by a mass of excitation which the ego is powerless to master" (French, 1939).

The wishes for maternal protection appear in the dreams and fantasies, and in the play of the children in the form of being in enclosed places, symbolic of being in the womb. A statistical study by Alexander (French, Alexander, et al., 1941) showed an average of 18% of such "intra-uterine" dreams in the group of 12 asthmatics, compared with a 7% average in the control group. Water is also symbolic of the mother, and the relationship of the asthmatic to water, first noted by Deutsch (1922) and confirmed by McDermott and Cobb (1939), is in all probability an expression of this same deep dependence on the mother.

Concerning the relationship between allergy and emotions in asthma certain findings are significant. A patient with marked hypersensitivity to cat hair dreamed frequently of cats as symbolizing temptations. A woman with violent conscious resentment of children who displaced most of her maternal interest on to cats showed an extreme reaction to cat hair on skin tests. In many cases the analytic treatment markedly relieved the asthma and in some of these cases the asthma was replaced by crying. A patient with clinical as well as skin test sensitivity to horse dander was able to ride horseback without asthma after her analysis. These observations support the supposition of a supplementary relationship between the allergic and emotional factors. Stokes and Beerman (1940) conclude from their review of the literature on emotional factors in allergy that there is a slow accumulation of evidence that psychogenic factors are capable of modifying allergic sensitivity, particularly of the skin. The importance of the longing for the mother in allergic conditions, not only in asthma but also in hay fever and urticaria, suggests that this longing bears some relationship to allergic sensitivity (Saul, 1941).

Dunbar (1939) has made a comparison of certain psychosomatic conditions which is of interest at this point in connection with asthma, hay fever, hypertension, and cardiovascular disturbances. Her conclusions are based on 1300 patients of whom representative groups were studied psychoanalytically. Oriented in terms of the inhibitory influence of the cortex upon the instincts (Sherrington, 1933) and in terms of muscle tension as a defense against instinct, Dunbar (1939) finds that: "fracture patients (especially those with the accident habit) seem to have the greatest tendency to impulsive action and the least psychic elaboration in fantasy; then come asthma patients with their constant oscillation between action and its inhibition combined with a rich fantasy life; hypertensive patients show little tendency to impulsive action and relatively little psychic elaboration; patients with arthritis have little tendency to impulsive action but have a rich fantasy life." These of course are merely general statements. There are examples of the opposite type in each group depending on the degree of overcompensation and the reaction-formations developed.

Hay Fever.—Compared with asthma, few studies of specific psychogenic factors in hay fever are available. Many of the patients in the asthma study of French, Alexander, *et al.*, (1941) had hay fever and in some cases marked therapeutic results were achieved by the psychoanalyses, but the material has not been worked up in this connection. Dunbar (1938a), reporting the analyses of three patients with both asthma and hay fever, has remarked their interest in the sense of smell, and their sexualization of the respiratory function. Wilson (1941) has made a systematic study of seven analyzed patients in regard to the role of olfaction in hay fever. He concludes that strong visual sexual curiosity is repressed, thus stimulating and intensifying olfactory sexual curiosity, which in turn affects the nasal mucosa and determines this site for the symptom of hay fever.

Laryngitis, Common Cold.—Wilson (1934) found an acute transient laryngitis to be due to inhibition of a wish to attack verbally by using obscene words of anal connotation. Thus the mechanism of the aphonia was the same as of the type of constipation which is due to inhibited hostility (see Gastro-Intestinal section above).

Menninger (1934) reported emotional factors in a case of common cold which occurred during analysis, and Saul (1938) observed during eight analyses that colds developed when the patients repressed rage from receptive frustration, as when the analyst had to leave a very dependent patient for two weeks or when a patient who wanted a vacation had to work. As with all symptoms reviewed in this chapter, the fact that the emotional factors operate in certain cases by no means excludes other factors, such as infection, susceptibility to which may perhaps be influenced by the effect of the emotional state on the general resistance and on the local conditions of the membranes.

Skin Disturbances

That the emotions affect the skin is generally known. Flushing with anger or embarrassment or blanching with fear are well recognized, and popular expressions connect itching with impatience. The literature leaves little doubt that emotional tensions can influence the physiology of the skin sufficiently to produce symptoms (Stokes, Kulchar, and Pillsbury, 1935; Stokes and Beerman, 1940). However, few detailed studies of the specific factors are available.

Ackerman (1939) found a neurodermite to be related to hate of others, with self-marring by the patient of her own skin to make herself repulsive, as a self-punishment.

In two cases of inflammatory skin lesions Pearson (1940) found self-injury to the skin as a form of childish autoerotism and fear of the super-ego, to be prominent features.

Observations in the analytic literature connect chronic urticaria (hives) chiefly with masochism, prolonged unsatisfied sexual excitement, and rejection of responsibility and effort (Oberndorf, 1912; Lorand, 1930; Graf-Best, 1932; Menninger and Kemp, 1935). Although allergens are usually found as causative agents in acute urticarias, they are found in only 10% of the chronic urticarias (Sulzberger, 1940). Only one study of an analyzed case is available. Saul (1941) found that in this case the twelve attacks during analysis all occurred when intense longings for love, of a dependent nature but with a strong although repressed sexual coloring, were aroused but frustrated. This same frustration situation appeared in the eight dreams of this patient which were associated with urticaria, typified by the patient's repetitive dream of reaching for her mother (who died when the patient was one and a half) but having her just slip away from her grasp. Weeping was an alternative to urticaria and her attacks often terminated when she began to weep. This is of special interest in connection with the role of crying in asthma (see French and Alexander, 1941, mentioned above). Skin erotization appears to be of importance. These findings were confirmed by a second analyzed case and by five others seen in interviews. This same patient was one of those in the endocrine series of Benedek and Rubenstein (1941) (see section on Endocrine Disturbances). At the times when she was especially frustrated and the urticaria developed, her hormone level fell, suggesting an endocrine factor in the mechanism, as has long been suspected (Sulzberger, 1940).

Endocrine Disturbances

The interrelationships between the endocrine system and emotional tensions are intimate, complex, and of great psychosomatic significance, and understanding of endocrine function is widely expected to contribute much to psychological and biological understanding (Freud, 1933; Hoskins, 1933, 1941; Benedek, 1934; Lurie, 1935; Levy, 1936; in this book, see Chapter 19 by Shock). Confining ourselves to a single aspect of the whole complex problém, there is ample evidence that emotional states influence endocrine function and play a part in certain endocrine disturbances (Menninger, 1935; Carmichael, 1938; Dunbar, 1938). Anxiety and hostility have been implicated in hyperthyroidism (Benedek, 1934); Lorand and Moschcowitz, 1934) and emotional factors can probably be of importance in certain cases of diabetes mellitus (Menninger, 1935a, 1935b; Daniels, 1939). Anxiety and deep oral cravings were found by Daniels (1936) in an analyzed case, and Meyer's (1938) formulation of the significant emotional constellation in his analyzed case is that deep oral dependent cravings were frustrated causing intense hostility with consequent anxiety. Extensive investigations of the specific emotional factors in endocrine disturbances have not yet been made.

Our purpose is to review representative studies of physiological effects of emotion, but a recent study of the converse relationship is so illuminating that its inclusion is indicated. This study (Benedek and Rubenstein, 1939, 1941) deals with an aspect of the physiological and biological tensions, perceived as emotions, which arise from the relatively automatic endocrine changes which take place in women during the menstrual cycle. In fifteen cases the endocrine level during the menstrual cycles (determined by the vaginal smear method of Papanicolaou, 1935) was correlated with the emotional attitudes as observed during psychoanalysis. It was found that whereas the details of the cycle vary greatly from case to case, the basic normal pattern is, in somewhat oversimplified form, about as follows: Following menstruation there is a gradual increase for ten days to two weeks of the oestrogenic or follicular hormones, and paralleling this, psychologically, an outward emotional orientation, marked by interest in the opposite sex. Thus, as in the lower animals, the oestrogenic hormones stimulate sexual interest and activity (Hoskins, 1941). Then ovulation occurs and the effects of the oestrogenic hormones are masked by the increase of the corpus-luteum hormone, progesterone. With this, the psychological material shows a brief period of flighty irritability, followed by a decrease in the interest in men, and in emotional orientation to the outside world, and an increased interest in the woman herself, in her bodily welfare, in pregnancy, and children. Thus the concern of the organism for pregnancy, stimulated by the hormone of the corpus-luteum, is reflected psychologically in the emotional life. A few days before the menstrual period, the progesterone level falls, and feelings of frustration and irritability become more prominent in the psychological material. This work provides an illustration of the fundamental psychoanalytic and psychosomatic concept described in the introduction, of the mental and emotional life as a reflection of the biological forces which motivate the organism.

Not only do the hormones thus influence sexual and maternal interest, but conversely, the hormonal level is affected by the emotional state. It is common knowledge that emotional disturbance can suppress menstruation. The sexual repression of one of the patients was so great that throughout her analysis she had not a single frank dream dealing with sexuality or pregnancy—she dared not even dream of these topics. This led Benedek to predict an infantile uterus and an abnormally low hormone level, both of which were found. This raises the possibility that the psychological effect of sexual repression was so severe that it inhibited the anatomical sexual development and also the hormone production. Thus the hormone production influences the emotional state and the emotional state influences the hormone production. The method used in this study was the independent charting of the hormonal levels and time of ovulation, by the physiologist from the vaginal smears and by the psychoanalyst from the psychological data. The results were compared and found to be almost identical.

Epilepsy

(See Chapter 31 by Lennox.) There is evidence from psychoanalytic observation of epileptics (Kardiner, 1932; Bartemeier, 1934; Jelliffe, 1935) that psychogenic attacks are essentially mass discharges of hostility. It is as though the hostility arising from subcortical centers stimulates the cortex to activity (Head, 1921; Lennox and Cobb, 1928; see also Chapter 33 by Lindsley). But to discharge this rage in life would mean murderous attack. It is therefore repressed, but not sufficiently to avoid episodic undirected diffuse mass discharges. In Dostoievsky's *The Brothers Karamazov* it is the epileptic son who murders the father, whereas the other two sons only *wished* to do so. In hysterical attacks erotic and exhibitionistic tendencies are also prominent.

Hendrick (1940) has reported that aurae in two of his cases of epileptiform convulsions were conscious vestiges of repressed, neurotic anxiety attacks which antedated the seizures. In one case the aura was apparently the persistence of the reflection from a vase observed by the patient when his mother appeared, and intense anxiety-provoking feelings were aroused but repressed, and the memory displaced from the mother to the incidental reflection from the vase.

Headache

Although it is common knowledge that distressing situations can be "enough to give one a headache," the specific emotional determinants, if any, have not been well worked out. Feminine identification in a male patient (Abraham, 1910) and heterosexual, homosexual, and aggressive factors in a female case (Gutheil, 1934) have been reported in connection with headaches. Touraine and Draper (1934) consider that migraine is a neurotic symptom which occurs in persons of a special constitutional type (acromegaloid skulls, outstanding intelligence and retarded emotional development). They find a struggle against dependence on the mother to be a specific emotional factor, with migraine precipitated by threats of separation from her. This similarity to the psychological factors in asthma is especially interesting because of the generally recognized association of migraine with allergic conditions. Recent observations implicate anger as the emotion most directly related to the symptom (Knopf, 1935; Slight, 1936; Fromm-Reichman, 1937). These authors also agree in describing these patients as sensitive, reserved and repressed.

Genito-Urinary Disturbances

It is common knowledge that urination can be stimulated by sudden emotions, such as fear, anger and even intense laughter, and also that it can be connected with sexual feelings (as would be expected from the anatomic and physiologic relationships). Urination often has the meaning of masculinity in common symbols and folklore (Christoffel, 1935).

A study of enuresis by Gerard (1939) presents an orderly approach to this subject which is dealt with in a voluminous and rather confusing literature. Her results are based upon a review of the literature and upon 72 cases observed over seven years. Etiological factors of an emotional nature were present in the majority of cases. The author classifies the causes as: (1) physical disorders of the nervous system or bladder; (2) faulty training; (3) episodes of regression of the total personality such as those precipitated by jealousy of a new sibling; (4) revenge cases; (5) hysterical identification; and (6) true enuresis nocturna.

Bed Wetting (Enuresis Nocturna).—True enuresis nocturna is distinguished from other types of wetting in that it occurs during unconsciousness, that is, during sleep.

> In these cases the enuresis was one symptom of a syndrome which presented a clear-cut neurotic pattern of behavior and neurotic mechanism development. These disclosed a common etiology, fear of harm from persons of the opposite sex. This fear, in turn, probably developed as a result of three factors working together: destructive wishes toward the rival parent, traumatic sexual experiences or information and experiences of parental seduction or rejection, depending upon the sex of the patient. Of importance in terms of treatment of the case, this group proved resistant to therapy of a superficial nature because the emotional conflict was deeply repressed and partially solved by unhealthy defense mechanisms. (Gerard, 1939)

URGENCY AND FREQUENCY.—Freud, who began his psychological studies with hysterical patients, and so pointed out many specific emotional determinants of physical symptoms, reported a case of fear of having to urinate when out socially. This was a prudish young woman, the basis of whose phobia was the repression of sexual feelings which were transferred to urination so that when erotic sensations were aroused they led to a desire to micturate (Freud, 1894). Freud (1908) also pointed out that urethral erotism (pleasurable interest in urinating) often appeared in connection with ambition and competitiveness.

In his study of pollakiuria (undue frequency of urination) van der Heide (1941) finds general agreement in the nonpsychoanalytic literature that it can be purely psychogenic (Schwartz, 1926; Wobus, 1922; Leshnew, 1928). More recent studies support this finding (Sleeper and Jellinek, 1936; Miller, 1936), but in these the frequency was apparently secondary to psychogenically exaggerated thirst (polydipsia) which resulted in polyuria (excessive amount of urine). Sadger (1910) and Jelliffe (1930) found erotic sensations central in their cases of pollakiuria. Campbell (1918) found that in two female cases it was connected with hostility to men, and Alexander (1933) mentions a transient pollakiuria which signified a denial of self-castrative wishes. Van der Heide (1941) found a number of determinants for the urinary frequency in his case, a 23-year-old girl. The central one was envy, competition and ambition, which appeared prominently in childhood urinary play and observations, and served as an unconscious aggressive defense against sexual wishes, and also against a tendency to oral regression (undue needs for love and dependence upon others). Besides the aggressive competitive impulses, wishes to give in the positive sense also found unconscious expression in the symptom, which in addition provided an exhibitionistic satisfaction although in a masochistic way (i.e., fraught with suffering, occasioned in this case by the embarrassment and inconvenience). These emotional factors are somewhat similar in certain respects to those found in colitis, but in pollakiuria the ambitious and sexual elements seem to be more prominent.

Genital Function.—Emotional tensions influence genital functioning just as they do other physiological activities. As a single example, aggressive impulses often become associated with sexuality and intensify it, while in other cases they are inhibited and the inhibition affects the sexuality also—mechanisms similar to those we have seen in bulimia and anorexia, and in diarrhea and constipation, where the function is intensified or inhibited. But the interrelationships of sexuality with motivation and the emotional life are so complex, and the literature is so voluminous, that this subject is beyond the scope of the present survey. For the emotional aspects the reader is referred especially to Freud (1905, 1914, 1920, 1933); Ferenczi (1922); Alexander (1937, 1940).

Neurophysiological Mechanisms

Motivation and cause must be distinguished from physiological mechanisms of mediation; but a complete picture requires an understanding of both and of their interrelationships. A few attempts have already been made to integrate available knowledge of psychobiological functioning with the facts of physiology. There is emerging the following tentative and preliminary formulation, presented in an oversimplified and schematic form.

This chapter has dealt chiefly with physiological disturbances which result from emotional tensions mediated via the autonomic nervous system. In so far as the central nervous system and cortex are directly affected, there result hysterical tremors and certain other hysterical symptoms, epileptiform phenomena, and various disturbances of thought and behavior which carry beyond our present purpose and are dealt with in other chapters. It must suffice here to state that a considerable recent literature, in addition to the classic facts of brain anatomy and physiology, supports the concept of biological urges and responses (Cannon, 1936, 1939; Bard, 1939) mediated through the hypothalamus (Masserman,

1941) transmitted to, and integrated, discriminated, transformed and controlled by the cortex (Grinker, 1939; Stone, 1939) which is involved in education and conditioning (French, 1933; Kubie, 1934; Jelliffe, 1936; Sherrington, 1941). If unrelieved through the normal pathways of thought and behavior, the tensions accumulate, stimulate the autonomic nervous system and produce psychosomatic symptoms. This neurophysiological formulation corresponds roughly to Freud's (1922, 1927, 1933) psychological formulation of the Id (biological needs, urges, responses), Ego (consciousness, will, memory, intellect, judgment) and Super-Ego (conscience, ideals, training, conditioning). Alexander (1939) has pointed out that aggressive, progressive, emotional impulses tend to affect chiefly the sympathetic pathways as in essential hypertension where the individual carries on the struggle; while regressive impulses tend to stimulate the parasympathetics as when dependent longings affect the stomach. Why the emotional tensions result in some cases chiefly in psychosomatic symptoms and in others in neurosis, psychosis, criminality, character disorders, and all manner of psychological and sociological phenomena is a question toward whose answer only a beginning has been made.

Summary and Discussion

Emotional tensions are reflections of the biological forces which motivate the organism. When not adequately relieved they accumulate and affect the cortex to produce disturbances of thought and behavior, and, mostly via the autonomic nervous system, affect the physiology to produce symptoms. There are certain specific determinants in the relationships between emotional constellations and symptoms. This survey of some representative studies yields the following tentative preliminary formulations: Reviewing disturbances of imbibition there emerges a common underlying dynamic situation for all of them. A variety of emotional impulses become closely associated with eating. These impulses include wishes for love, care or dependence, sexual wishes sometimes in the form of fellatio, wishes for impregnation, aggressive grasping desires, hostile biting reactions, coprophilic impulses, and possibly others. The common features is that these variegated impulses become connected with eating in certain ways which produce the symptoms: (1) They may act to reinforce normal eating, which then becomes more than a process of nutrition and serves as a means of gratifying these emotional impulses (bulimia). (2a) Because of the intimate connection of eating with these impulses, eating takes on their emotional meaning to such an extent that when the impulse is inhibited because it is unacceptable to the rest of the personality (usually because of guilt and shame), then the eating is inhibited also (anorexia); (2b) and when the inhibition consists of active rejection of a situation (as an unwanted pregnancy or of intolerable guilty or shameful impulses), then reverse peristalsis occurs and the food is regurgitated (nervous vomiting). Thus various impulses through association with eating and biting cause intensifications, inhibitions, and reversals of function.

In the gastric ulcer cases the impulses involved are apparently less various, and consist more specifically of frustrated desires for love, care, dependence, and the like; these have become so intimately associated with the functioning of the stomach, that cravings for them cause the stomach to behave physiologically just as though it were expecting food.

In psychogenic diarrhea certain types of active impulses become associated with bowel activity and stimulate it. These are usually: (1) hostile impulses which are inhibited in expression through physical attack and find a pathway to activity via the bowel instead; (2) urges to give, produce, make restitution, which are unaccepted and for which bowel activity is substituted; and (3) eliminating, rejecting reactions, wishes to be rid of disagreeable situations or impulses. All these are seen typically in the person who, when faced with a responsible, demanding task (course of study, business responsibility, pregnancy, etc.) becomes angry, wants to be rid of it, and when he forces himself to do it, develops diarrhea.

The relationship of diarrhea to constipation is similar to that of bulimia to anorexia. In diarrhea and bulimia the original impulses, inadequately satisfied in other ways in life, find substitute satisfaction and relief by activating the respective parts of the gastro-intestinal tract. In constipation, as in anorexia, it is the inhibitory forces and not the original impulses which are effective. It is refusal to give and inhibition of hostile aggression which cause the constipation. This too is not unrecognized generally, for one sometimes hears of a cruel miser "looking constipated."

In the cardiovascular disturbances, hostility is thus far the chief emotion to be implicated. It has been found in connection with essential hypertension, anginal pains and disorders of heart beat. Some hostility is in everyone, and its status is what appears to be important for these conditions. In essential hypertension it is intense, chronic, and near to consciousness, but sufficiently inhibited that these patients are generally very pleasant. The hostility was not relieved in life nor adequately bound in an organized neurosis. It is not clear whether or not the sources of the hostility are important. In the cases studied it arose most frequently from rebelliousness against domination, from protest against activity and responsibility, and from constant struggles with an emotional conflict situation with neither solution nor retreat. This unremitting struggle with an unsolved conflict may be of special importance.

The emotional factors in asthma have been worked out in considerable detail. These patients defend themselves against a fear of separation or estrangement from the mother or mother substitute. They feel that such a situation would be terrifying, intolerable, overwhelming. If they feel threatened by it too suddenly to handle it, they react with a cry (of the child for its mother) which is repressed and which comes to expression as the asthma attack.

Various other psychogenic symptoms have been studied, but not in such detail and often not by a number of different workers. The following relationships are therefore either less specific or more preliminary or both.

In palpitations and extrasystoles, which are extremely common, hostility near to consciousness, competitiveness, and identification with a parent with heart disease have been reported. Preliminary study of chest pains suggests possible connections with very deeply repressed hostilities and with identification with the heart disease of a parent.

In hay fever, repressed olfactory sexual curiosity has been reported. Acute transient laryngitis has been observed when hostile verbal attack was inhibited, a mechanism similar to that in constipation. Common colds are reported to have been precipitated by frustration of wishes for love and dependence with consequent repressed rage. Chronic urticaria has been seen in connection with intense longings for love when these were aroused and frustrated. A review of the findings in asthma, hay fever, and urticaria, suggests that dependent longings for the mother bear a relationship to allergy.

Specific emotional factors in skin disorders have not been established, but exhibitionism, tendencies to self-punishment (especially by marring the skin) and heightened skin erotism have been noted.

The interrelationships of psychology and endocrinology are especially intimate. Not only do the emotions effect endocrine function, as seen in thyroid disturbances and in diabetes, but the converse relationship has been observed in women. After menstruation, oesterone production increases, sexual interest heightens, and after ovulation, with progesterone production, interest turns from men to become more self-directed and maternal.

Epileptic attacks in certain instances appear to be explosive discharges of hostile impulses. There is evidence that hostility is a factor in headaches.

Enuresis nocturna has been found to result typically from fears of the parent of the opposite sex, these fears being generated by hostile feelings and traumatic sexual experiences of seductive or rejecting nature. In urinary urgency and frequency aggressive competitive and ambitious impulses have been reported as central.

It must be clear from this survey that these specific emotional factors (in psychosomatic conditions) do not consist in a naïve one to one relationship of a certain emotion to a particular physiological disturbance. Rather, the specificity comprises such factors as the kind, quality, and intensities of the emotional forces, their status, possible paths of discharge, time relations (such as chronicity or emergency nature of reaction), and the *constellations* in which they are more or less organized. As these specific factors are worked out, they cast light upon interrelationships between emotional tensions and physiological disturbances; they help us to understand psychosomatic symptoms as part of the language of expression of the emotional life; and thus they deepen our understanding of the mental and emotional life itself.

The present survey is representative and not exhaustive. It makes no claim to completeness and apology must be made for not including other interesting and important contributions. The aim has been to present sufficient representative work to give some acquaintance with this approach via clinical study of specific psychological determinants of the various physiological effects.

BIBLIOGRAPHY

INTRODUCTION, HISTORY, AND METHODOLOGY

ALEXANDER, F. 1939. Psychological aspects of medicine. *Psychosom. Med., 1,* 1–18.
ARISTOTLE. 1913. Physiognomica. In Whitwell, S. R., *Historical notes on psychiatry.* London: Lewis, 1936.
BARD, P. 1939. Central nervous mechanisms for emotional behavior patterns in animals. *Res. Publ. Assn. nerv. ment. Dis., 19,* 190–218.
BROMBERG, W. 1937. The mind of men. New York: Harper.
CANNON, W. B. 1936a. Bodily changes in pain, hunger, fear and rage. (2nd ed.) New York: Appleton-Century.
—— 1936b. The role of emotion in disease. *Ann. intern. Med., 9,* 1453–1465.
—— 1939. The wisdom of the body. New York: Norton.
CHILD, C. M. 1924. The physiological foundation of behavior. New York: Macmillan.
COGHILL, G. E. 1929. Anatomy and the problem of behavior. Cambridge: Harvard University Press.
DUNBAR, H. F. 1938. Emotions and bodily changes. (2nd ed.) New York: Columbia University Press.
FRENCH, T. M. 1933. The interrelations between psychoanalysis and the experimental work of Pavlov. *Amer. J. Psychiat., 12,* 1165–1195.
FREUD, S. 1900. The interpretation of dreams. In *The basic writings of Sigmund Freud.* (Trans. & ed. by A. A. Brill.) New York: Modern Library, 1938.
—— 1922. Beyond the pleasure principle. London: Hogarth.
—— 1933. New introductory lectures on psychoanalysis. (Trans. by W. J. H. Sprott.) New York: Norton.
GANTT, W. H. 1943. The origin and development of behavior disorders in dogs. *Psychosom. Med. Monogr.* (In press)
KUBIE, L. 1934. Relation of the conditioned reflex to psychoanalytic technique. *Arch. Neurol. Psychiat., Chicago, 32,* 1137–1142.
LANDIS, C., & HUNT, W. A. 1939. The startle pattern. New York: Farrar & Rinehart.
LEWIS, N. D. C. 1941. A short history of psychiatric achievement. New York: Norton.
PARACELSUS. 1894. The hermetic and alchemical writings of Phillipus Aurelius Theophrastus Bombastus Paracelsus von Hohenheim, now for the first time faithfully translated into English. London: Elliott.
PAVLOV, I. P. 1927. Conditioned reflexes. New York: Oxford University Press.
SAUL, L. J. 1939. The physiological effects of psychoanalytic therapy. *Res. Publ. Assn. nerv. ment. Dis., 19,* 305–317.
—— 1941. Psychosomatic knowledge in case work. *Family, 22,* 219–226.
TRACY, H. C. 1926. The development of motility and behavior reactions in the toad fish. *J. comp. Neurol., 40,* 253–369.
WHITEHORN, J. C. 1939. Physiological changes in emotional states. *Res. Publ. Assn. nerv. ment. Dis., 19,* 256–270.
WHITWELL, S. R. 1936. Historical notes on psychiatry. London: Lewis.
WITTKOWER, E. 1935. Studies on the influence of emotions on the functions of the organs. *J. ment. Sci., 81,* 533–682.

ZILBOORG, G., & HENRY, G. W. 1941. A history of medical psychology. New York: Norton.

GASTRO-INTESTINAL

ABRAHAM, K. 1921. Contribution to the theory of the anal character. In *Selected papers*. London: Hogarth, 1927. Pp. 370–392.
—— 1924. A short study of the development of the libido viewed in the light of mental disorders. In *Selected papers*. London: Hogarth, 1927. Pp. 418–501.
ALEXANDER, F. 1935. The logic of emotions and its dynamic background. *Int. J. Psycho-Anal., 16*, 399–413.
—— 1936. The medical value of psychoanalysis. (2nd ed.) New York: Norton.
—— 1941. Gastro-intestinal neuroses. In Portis, S. A., *Diseases of the digestive system*. Philadelphia: Lea & Febiger. Pp. 206–223.
ALEXANDER, F., BACON, C., LEVEY, H. B., LEVINE, M., & WILSON, G. W. 1934. The influence of psychologic factors upon gastro-intestinal disturbances: a symposium. *Psychoanal. Quart., 3*, 501–588.
ALEXANDER, F., & WILSON, G. W. 1935. Quantitative dream studies. *Psychoanal. Quart., 4*, 371–407.
ALVAREZ, W. C. 1929. Ways in which emotions can affect the digestive tract. *J. Amer. med. Assn., 92*, 1231–1237.
BELL, A. 1933. Colitis—psychogenically motivated; report of a case. *J. nerv. ment. Dis., 77*, 587–593.
BENEDEK, T. 1936. Dominant ideas and their relation to morbid cravings. *Int. J. Psycho-Anal., 17*, 40–56.
BENEDEK, T., & RUBENSTEIN, B. B. 1942. The sexual cycle in women; the relation between ovarian function and psychodynamic processes. *Psychosom. Med. Monogr., 3*, Nos. 1 & 2.
BERGMAN, G. VON. 1913. Ulcus duodeni und vegetatives Nervensystem. *Berl. klin. Wschr., 50*, 2374–2379.
—— 1936. Funktionelle Pathologie. (2te Aufl.) Berlin: Springer.
BOND, E. 1938. Psychiatric contributions to the study of the gastro-intestinal system. *Amer. J. digest. Dis., 5*, 482–486.
BROWN, W., PREU, W., & SULLIVAN, A. 1938. Ulcerative colitis and the personality. *Amer. J. Psychiat., 95*, 407–420.
BRUCH, H., & TOURAINE, G. 1940. Obesity in childhood: V. The family frame of obese children. *Psychosom. Med., 2*, 141–206.
BRUSH, L. A. 1939. Recent literature relative to the psychiatric aspects of gastro-intestinal disorders—a review. *Psychosom. Med., 1*, 423–428.
CORIAT, I. H. 1921. Sex and hunger. *Psychoanal. Rev., 8*, 375–381.
CUSHING, H. 1931. The possible relation of the central (vegetative) nervous system to peptic ulcers. *New Engl. J. Med., 205*, 979.
DANIELS, G. F. 1934. Neuroses associated with the gastro-intestinal tract. *Amer. J. Psychiat., 91*, 529–540.
—— 1940. Treatment of a case of ulcerative colitis associated with hysterical depression. *Psychosom. Med., 2*, 276–285.
DAVIES, D. T., & WILSON, A. T. 1937. Observations on the life history of chronic peptic ulcer. *Lancet*, Part 2, 1353–1360.
DRAPER, G., & TOURAINE, G. 1932. The main environment unit and peptic ulcer. *Arch. intern. Med., 49*, 616–662.
FARQUHARSON, H., & HYLAND, H. H. 1938. Anorexia nervosa; metabolic disorder of psychologic origin. *J. Amer. med. Assn., 111*, 1085–1092.
FAULKNER, W. B. 1940. Severe esophageal spasm. *Psychosom. Med., 2*, 139–140.
FERENCZI, S. 1919a. Disgust for breakfast. In *Further contributions to the theory and technique of psychoanalysis*. London: Hogarth, 1926.
—— 1919b. The phenomena of hysterical materialization. In *Further contributions to the theory and technique of psychoanalysis*. London: Hogarth, 1926.
FREUD, S. 1905. Three contributions to the theory of sex. In *The basic writings of Sigmund Freud*. New York: Modern Library, 1938.
—— 1915. Instincts and their vicissitudes. In *Collected papers*. Vol. 4. London: Hogarth, 1925.
—— 1916. On the transformation of instincts with special reference to anal erotism. In *Collected papers*. Vol. 2. London: Hogarth, 1924.

—— 1918. From the history of an infantile neurosis. In *Collected papers.* Vol. 3. London: Hogarth, 1925.

—— 1922. Group psychology and the analysis of the ego. London: Hogarth.

GRANET, E. 1940. Total gastrospasm. Psychological factors involved in etiology —case report. *Psychosom. Med., 2,* 17–21.

GULL, W. 1874. Anorexia nervosa. *Trans. clin. Soc. Lond., 7, 22.*

HARTMAN, H. R. 1933. Neurogenic factors in peptic ulcer. *Med. Clin. N. Amer. 16,* 1357–1369.

HOFF, E. C., & SHEEHAN, D. 1935. Experimental gastric erosions following hypothalamic lesions in monkeys. *Amer. J. Path., 11,* 789–802.

JONES, C., URAY, T., BENEDICT, E., CLIFFORD, M., & WHITE, B. 1938. Progress in internal medicine; gastroenterology; review of literature from January 1937 to June 1938. *Arch. intern. Med., 62,* 652–718.

JONES, E. 1913. Papers on psychoanalysis. (4th ed.) Baltimore: William Wood.

KELLER, A. D. 1936. Protection by peripheral nerve section of the gastro-intestinal tract from ulceration following hypothalamic lesions, with preliminary observations on ulcerations in the gastro-intestinal tract of dog following vagotomy. *Arch. Path. Lab. Med., 21,* 165–184.

LASEGUE, 1873. On hysterical anorexia. *Med. Times, Lond., 2,* 265.

LEVINE, M. 1934. Pregenital trends in a case of chronic diarrhea and vomiting. *Psychoanal. Quart., 3,* 583–588.

LIGHT, R. N. 1931. Experimental observations on the production of ulcers by pilocarpine. *New Engl. J. Med., 205,* 980.

MASSERMAN, J. H. 1941. Psychodynamism in anorexia nervosa and neurotic vomiting. *Psychoanal. Quart., 10,* 211–243.

MENNINGER, W. C. 1937. Functional disorders of the gastro-intestinal tract. "The gastro-intestinal neuroses." *Amer. J. digest. Dis. Nutrit., 4,* 447–453.

MENNINGER, W. C., & ALEXANDER, F. 1936. Relation of persecutory delusions to the functioning of the gastro-intestinal tract. *J. nerv. ment. Dis., 84,* 541–554.

MOSCHCOWITZ, E. 1935. The psychogenic origin of organic disease. *New Engl. J. Med., 212,* 603–611.

MURRAY, C. 1930. Psychogenic factors in the etiology of ulcerative colitis and bloody diarrhea. *Amer. J. med. Sci., 180,* 239–248.

NACHT, S., & ELIET, J. 1938. Remarques sur la guerison par le traitment psychoanalytique d'une nevrose organique. *Rev. franç. Psychoanal., 10,* 76–86.

RAHMAN, L., RICHARDSON, H., & RIPLEY, H. S. 1939. Anorexia nervosa with psychiatric observations. *Psychosom. Med., 1,* 333–365.

RICHARDSON, H. B. 1939. Simmonds disease and anorexia nervosa. *Arch. intern. Med., 63,* 1–28.

SAUL, L. J. 1935. A note on the psychogenesis of organic symptoms. *Psychoanal. Quart., 4,* 476–483.

—— 1941. The emotional settings of some attacks of urticaria. *Psychosom. Med., 3,* 349–369.

SCHMIED, M. 1936. Erstoerung und Verstimmung vor dem dritten Lebensjahr. *Z. psychoanal. Pädag., 10,* 241–250.

SHELDON, J. H. 1937. Anorexia nervosa with especial reference to physical constitution. *Lancet, Part 1,* 369–373.

SULLIVAN, A. J., & CHANDLER, C. A. 1932. Ulcerative colitis of psychogenic origin. *Yale J. Biol. Med., 4,* 779–796.

VAN DER HEIDE, C. 1941b. A study of mechanisms in two cases of peptic ulcer. *Psychosom. Med., 2,* 398–410.

WALLER, J., KAUFMAN, M., & DEUTSCH, F. 1940. Anorexia nervosa; a psychosomatic entity. *Psychosom. Med., 2,* 1–16.

WATTS, J., & FULTON, J. 1935. The effect of lesions of the hypothalamus upon the gastro-intestinal tract and heart in monkeys. *Ann. Surg., 101,* 363–372.

WESTPHAL, K. 1914. Untersuchungen zur Frage der nervoesen Entstehung peptischer ulcera. *Dtsch. Arch. klin. Med., 114,* 327–395.

WHITE, B., COBB, S., & JONES, C. 1939. Mucous colitis. A psychological medical study of 60 cases. *Psychosom. Med. Monogr., 1,* No. 1.

WILSON, C. W. 1934. Typical personality trends and conflicts in cases of spastic colitis. *Psychoanal. Quart., 3,* 558–573.

WINKELSTEIN, A. 1931. Psychogenic factors in cardiospasm. *Amer. J. Surg., 12,* 135–138.

WITTKOWER, E. 1938. Ulcerative colitis; personality studies. *Brit. Med. J., Part 2*, 1356–1360.

WULFF, M. 1932. Über einen interessanten oralen Symptomenkomplex und seine Beziehung zur Sucht. *Int. Z. Psychoanal., 18*, 281–302.

CARDIOVASCULAR

ALEXANDER, F. 1939. Psychoanalytic study of a case of essential hypertension. *Psychosom. Med., 1*, 139–152.

—— 1939a. Emotional factors in essential hypertension. *Psychosom. Med., 1*, 173–179.

ANDERSON, O., PARMENTER, R., & LIDDELL, H. 1939. Some cardiovascular manifestations of the experimental neurosis in sheep. *Psychosom. Med., 1*, 93–100.

BOURNE, G., SCOTT, R., & WITTKOWER, E. 1937. The psychological factor in cardiac pain. *Lancet, Part 2*, 609–625.

CADBURY, W. 1922. The blood pressure of Kantonese students. *Arch. intern. Med., 30*, 362–377.

CANNON, W. B. 1929. Bodily changes in pain, hunger, fear and rage. An account of recent researches into the function of emotional excitement. New York: Appleton-Century.

—— 1936. The role of emotion in disease. *Ann. intern. Med., 9*, 1453–1465.

CAUGHEY, J. 1939. Cardiovascular neurosis—a review. *Psychosom. Med., 1*, 311–324.

DONNISON, C. P. 1929. Bloodpressure in African natives; its bearing upon aetiology of hyperpiesia and arteriosclerosis. *Lancet, 216*, 6–7.

DUNBAR, H. F. 1939. Character and symptom formation; some preliminary notes with special reference to patients with hypertensive, rheumatic and coronary disease. *Psychoanal. Quart., 8*, 18–46.

FOSTER, J. H. 1927. Bloodpressure of foreigners in China. *Arch. Surg., 15*, 129 ff. and 298 ff.

GUNTHER, L., & MENNINGER, K. 1939. Intermittent extrasystole directly associated with emotional conflict; a case report. *Bull. Menninger Clin., 3*, 164–176.

GUNWARDENE. 1935. High blood pressure. London: Ballière, Tindall & Cox.

HEDLEY, O. F. 1935. Study of 450 fatal cases of heart disease occurring in Washington (D. C.) hospital during 1932 with special reference to etiology, race and sex. *Publ. Hlth Rep., Wash., 50*, 1127–1153.

HILL, L. B. 1935. Psychoanalytic observation on essential hypertension. *Psychoanal. Rev., 22*, 60–64.

ISMAIL, ABD-EL-AZIZ. 1928. Aetiology of hyperpiesis in Egyptians. *Lancet, Part 2*, 275–277.

KATZ, L. N., & LEITER, L. 1939. Present conception of "essential hypertension." *Psychosom. Med., 1*, 101–117.

MENNINGER, K. A., & MENNINGER, W. C. 1936. Psychoanalytic observations in cardiac disorders. *Amer. Heart J., 11*, 10–21.

MILLER, M. L. 1939. Blood pressure findings in relation to inhibited aggressions in psychotics. *Psychosom. Med., 1*, 162–172.

MILLER, M. L., & McLEAN, H. V. 1941. Status of emotions in palpitation and extrasystoles with note on "effort syndrome." *Psychoanal. Quart., 10*, 545–560.

RODDIS, L., & COOPER, G. 1926. Effect of climate on bloodpressure. *J. Amer. med. Assn., 87*, 2053–2055.

SAUL, L. J. 1939. Hostility in cases of essential hypertension. *Psychosom. Med., 1*, 153–161.

—— 1940. Utilization of early current dreams in formulating psychoanalytic cases. *Psychoanal. Quart., 9*, 453–469.

SCHULZ, V. E., & SCHWAB, E. H. 1936. Arteriolar hypertension in the American Negro. *Amer. Heart J., 11*, 66–74.

SCHWARTZ, A. 1940. An analyzed case of essential hypertension. *Psychosom. Med., 2*, 468–486.

SOLOMON, A. P., DARROW, C. W., & BLAUROCK, M. 1939. Blood pressure and palmar sweat (galvanic) responses of psychotic patients before and after insulin and metrazol therapy. *Psychosom. Med., 1*, 118–138.

WEISS, E. 1939. Recent advances in pathogenesis and treatment of hypertension; a review. *Psychosom. Med., 1*, 180–198.

—— 1940. Cardiovascular lesions of probable psychosomatic origin in arterial hypertension. *Psychosom. Med., 2*, 248-264.

Willius, F. A. 1937. Cardiac clinics. Cardiac neurosis. *Proc. Mayo Clin., 12,* 683–687.

Wolfe, T. P. 1934. Dynamic aspects of cardiovascular symptomatology. *Amer. J. Psychiat., 91,* 503–514.

—— 1936. Emotions and organic heart disease. *Amer. J. Psychiat., 93,* 681–691.

RESPIRATORY

Deutsch, F. 1922. The production of somatic disease by emotional disturbance. (Trans. in: *Res. Publ. Assn. Res. nerv. ment. Dis., 1939, 19,* 271–292.

Dunbar, H. F. 1938. Emotions and bodily changes. (2nd ed.) New York: Columbia University Press.

—— 1938a. Psychoanalytic notes relating to syndromes of asthma and hay fever. *Psychoanal. Quart., 7,* 25–68.

—— 1939. Character and symptom formation. *Psychoanal. Quart., 8,* 18–47.

French, T. M. 1939. Psychogenic factors in asthma. *Amer. J. Psychiat., 96,* 87–98.

French, T. M., & Alexander, F., & others. 1941. Psychogenic factors in bronchial asthma. Parts I & II. *Psychosom. Med. Monogr., 1,* No. 4; 2, Nos. 1 & 2.

McDermott, N. T., & Cobb, S. 1939. A psychiatric survey of 50 cases of bronchial asthma. *Psychosom. Med., 1,* 201–244.

Menninger, K. 1934. Some unconscious psychological factors associated with the common cold. *Psychoanal. Rev., 21,* 201–207.

Rogerson, C. H., Hardcastle, D. H., & Duguid, K. 1935. A psychological approach to the problem of asthma and the asthma-eczema-prurigo syndrome. *Guy's Hosp. Rep., 85,* 289.

Saul, L. J. 1938. Psychogenic factors in the etiology of the common cold and related symptoms. *Int. J. Psycho-Anal., 19,* 451–470.

—— 1941. Some observations on the relations of emotions and allergy. *Psychosom. Med., 3,* 66–71.

Sherrington, C. 1933. The brain and its mechanism. Cambridge: The University Press.

Stokes, J. H., & Beerman, H. 1940. Psychosomatic correlations in allergic conditions; a review of problems and literature. *Psychosom. Med., 2,* 438–458.

Weiss, E. 1922. Psychoanalyse eines Falles von nervösem Asthma. *Int. Z. Psychoanal., 8,* 440–455.

Wilson, G. W. 1934. Report of a case of acute laryngitis occurring as a conversion symptom during analysis. *Psychoanal. Rev., 21,* 408–414.

—— 1941. A study of structural and instinctual conflicts in cases of hay fever. *Psychosom. Med., 3,* 51–65.

Wittkower, E. 1935. Studies on the influence of emotions on the functioning of organs including observations in normals and neurotics. *J. ment. Sci., 81,* 533–682.

SKIN

Ackerman, N. W. 1939. Personality factor in neurodermite. *Psychosom. Med., 1,* 366–375.

Graf-Best, A. M. 1932. Psychische Behandlung einer Urtikaria. *Psychoanal. Prax., 2,* 40–44.

Lorand, S. 1930. The psychogenic factors in a case of angioneurotic edema. *J. Mt Sinai Hosp., N. Y., 2,* No. 5.

Menninger, W. C. & Kemp, J. 1935. Psychogenic urticaria. *J. Allergy, 6,* 467–473.

Oberndorf, C. P. 1912. Disappearance of angioneurotic edema after appendectomy. *J. Amer. med. Assn., 59,* 623.

Pearson, G. H. 1940. Some psychological aspects of inflammatory skin lesions. *Psychosom. Med., 2,* 22–33.

Saul, L. J. 1941. The emotional settings in some attacks of urticaria. *Psychosom. Med., 3,* 349–369.

Stokes, J. H., Kulchar, G. V., & Pillsbury, D. M. 1935. Effect on the skin of emotional and nervous states; etiological background of urticaria with special reference to the psychoneurogenous factor. *Arch. Derm. Syph., Chicago, 31,* 470–499.

Sulzberger, M. 1940. Dermatologic allergy. Springfield, Ill.: Thomas.

ENDOCRINE

BENEDEK, T. 1934. Mental processes in thyrotoxic states. *Psychoanal. Quart., 3,* 153–172.

BENEDEK, T., & RUBENSTEIN, B. B. 1939. The correlations between ovarian activity and psychodynamic processes: I. The ovulative phase: II. The menstrual phase. *Psychosom. Med., 1,* 245–270, 461–485.

—— 1942. The sexual cycle in women; the relation between ovarian function and psychodynamic processes. *Psychosom. Med. Monogr., 3,* Nos. 1 & 2.

CARMICHAEL, H. T. 1938. The role of the endocrines in mental disorders. *J. abnorm. soc. Psychol., 33,* 205–216.

DANIELS, G. E. 1936. Analysis of a case of neurosis with diabetes mellitus. *Psychoanal. Quart., 5,* 513–547.

—— 1939. Present trends in the evaluation of psychic factors in diabetes. A critical review of experimental, general medical and psychiatric literature of the last five years. *Psychosom. Med., 2,* 527–553.

DUNBAR, H. F. 1938. Emotions and bodily changes. (2nd ed.) New York: Columbia University Press.

FREUD, S. 1933. New introductory lectures on psychoanalysis. New York: Norton.

HOSKINS, R. G. 1933. The tides of life. New York: Norton.

—— 1941. Endocrinology. The glands and their function. New York: Norton.

LEVY, D. M. 1936. Aggressive-submissive behavior and the Froehlich syndrome. *Arch. Neurol. Psychiat., Chicago, 36,* 991–1020.

LORAND, A., & MOSCHCOWITZ, E. 1934. A psychoanalytic interpretation of the constitution in Grave's syndrome. *J. nerv. ment. Dis., 79,* 136–152.

LURIE, L. A. 1935. Endocrinology and behavior disorders in children. *Amer. J. Orthopsychiat., 5,* 141–154.

MENNINGER, W. C. 1935. The relations between the endocrine system and the personality. *J. Kans. med. Soc., 36,* 353–363.

—— 1935a. The interrelationship of mental disorders and diabetes mellitus. *J. ment. Sci., 81,* 332–357.

—— 1935b. Psychological factors in the etiology of diabetes. *J. nerv. ment. Dis., 81,* 1–13.

MEYER, A. 1938. Correlations between emotions and changes in carbohydrate metabolism in a case of diabetes mellitus. Papers read before the Chicago Psychoanalytic Society, June 5th, 1938.

PAPANICALAOU, G. 1935. The sexual cycle in the human female as revealed by vaginal smears. *Amer. J. Anat., 52,* 519–637.

EPILEPSY

BARTEMEIER, L. H. 1932. Some observations on convulsive disorders in children. *Amer. J. Orthopsychiat., 2,* 260–267.

HEAD, H. 1921. The release of function in the nervous system. Croonian lectures. *Proc. roy. Soc.,* B 92.

HENDRICK, I. 1940. Psychoanalytic observations on the aurae of two cases with convulsions. *Psychosom. Med., 1,* 43–52.

JELLIFFE, S. E. 1935. Dynamic concepts and the epileptic attack. *Amer. J. Psychiat., 92,* 565–574.

KARDINER, A. 1932. The bio-analysis of the epileptic reaction. Albany: Psychoanalytic Quarterly Press.

LENNOX, W. G., & COBB, S. 1928. Epilepsy. Baltimore: Williams & Wilkins.

HEADACHE

ABRAHAM, K. 1910. Hysterical dream states. In *Selected Papers.* London: Hogarth, 1927.

FROMM-REICHMAN, F. 1937. Contributions to the psychogenesis of migraine. *Psychoanal. Rev., 24,* 26–33.

GUTHEIL, E. 1934. Analysis of a case of migraine. *Psychoanal. Rev., 21,* 272–299.

KNOPF, O. 1935. Preliminary report on personality studies in 30 migraine patients. *J. nerv. ment. Dis., 82,* 270–286, 400–415.

SLIGHT, D. 1936. Migraine. *Canad. med. Assn. J., 35*, 268–273.
TOURAINE, G. A., & DRAPER, G. 1934. The migrainous patient. *J. nerv. ment. Dis., 80*, 1–23, 183–204.

GENITO-URINARY

ALEXANDER, F. 1933. The relation of structural to instinctual conflicts. *Psychoanal. Quart., 2*, 181–207.
CAMPBELL, C. M. 1918. A case of childhood conflicts with prominent reference to the urinary system; with some general considerations of urinary symptoms in the psychoneuroses and psychoses. *Psychoanal. Rev., 5*, 269–290.
CHRISTOFFEL, H. 1935. Harntriebaeusserungen insbesondere Enuresis, Urophilie und Uropolemie. *Int. Z. Psychoanal., 21*, 374–388.
FREUD, S. 1894. The defense neuropsychoses. In *Collected papers*. Vol. 1. London: Hogarth, 1924. Pp. 59–75.
—— 1908. Character and anal erotism. In *Collected papers*. Vol. 2. London: Hogarth, 1924. Pp. 45–50.
GERARD, M. W. 1939. Enuresis; a study in etiology. *Amer. J. Orthopsychiat., 9*, 48–58.
JELLIFFE, S. E. 1930. What price healing. *J. Amer. med. Assn., 94*, 1393–1395.
LESHNEW, N. F. 1928. Psychogene Erkrankungen in der Urologie. *Z. Urol., 22*, 921–929.
MILLER, W. R. 1936. Psychogenic factors in the polyuria of schizophrenia. *J. nerv. ment. Dis., 84*, 418–426.
SADGER, J. 1910. Über Urethralerotik. *Jb. psychoanal. Forsch., 2*, 409–450.
SCHWARTZ, O. Handbuch der Urologie. Berlin: Springer.
SLEEPER, F. H., & JELLINEK, E. M. 1936. A comparative physiologic, psychologic and psychiatric study of polyuric and nonpolyuric schizophrenic patients. *J. nerv. ment. Dis., 83*, 557–563.
VAN DER HEIDE, C. 1941. A case of pollakiuria nervosa. *Psychoanal. Quart., 10*, 267–283.
WOBUS, R. E. 1922. Notes on the psychic influence on bladder diseases in women. *J. Mo. med. Assn., 19*, 111–113.

GENITAL FUNCTION

ALEXANDER, F. 1937. Psychoanalytic aspects of mental hygiene and the environment. *Ment Hyg., N. Y., 21*, 187–197.
—— 1940. Psychoanalysis revised. *Psychoanal. Quart., 9*, 1–37.
FERENCZI, S. 1922. Thalassa: a theory of genitality. (Trans. by H. A. Bunker.) Albany: Psychoanalytic Quarterly Press, 1938.
FREUD, S. 1905. Three contributions to the theory of sex. In *The basic writings of Sigmund Freud*. New York: Modern Library, 1938.
—— 1914. On narcissism: an introduction. In *Collected papers*. Vol. 4. London: Hogarth, 1925. Pp. 30–59.
—— 1920. Introductory lectures on psychoanalysis. New York: Liveright.
—— 1933. New introductory lectures on psychoanalysis. New York: Norton.

NEUROPHYSIOLOGICAL MECHANISMS

ALEXANDER, F. 1939. Further contributions concerning specific emotional factors in different organ neuroses. Paper read before the American Psychoanalytic Assn., Chicago, May 1939.
BARD, P. 1939. Central nervous mechanisms for emotional behavior patterns in animals. *Res. Publ. Assn. nerv. ment. Dis., 19*, 190–218.
CANNON, W. B. 1936. Bodily changes in pain, hunger, fear and rage. (2nd ed.) New York: Appleton-Century.
—— 1939. The wisdom of the body. New York: Norton.
FRENCH, T. M. 1933. The interrelationship between psychoanalysis and the experimental work of Pavlov. *Amer. J. Psychiat., 12*, 1165–1195.
FREUD, S. 1921. Group psychology and the analysis of the ego. New York: Liveright.
—— 1927. The ego and the id. London: Hogarth.
—— 1933. New introductory lectures on psychoanalysis. New York: Norton.
GRINKER, R. R. 1939. Hypothalamic functions in psychosomatic interrelations. *Psychosom. Med., 1*, 19–47.

JELLIFFE, S. E. 1936. The bodily organs and psychopathology. *Amer. J. Psychiat.*, *92*, 1051–1076.

KUBIE, L. 1934. Relation of the conditioned reflex to psychoanalytic technique. *Arch. Neurol. Psychiat., Chicago*, *32*, 1137–1142.

MASSERMAN, J. 1941. Is the hypothalamus a center of emotion? *Psychosom. Med.*, *3*, 3–25.

SHERRINGTON, C. S. 1941. Man on his nature. London: Cambridge University Press; New York: Macmillan.

STONE, L. 1939. Concerning the psychogenesis of somatic disease: physiological and neurological correlations with the psychological theory. *Int. J. Psycho-Anal.*, *19*, 63–76.

Chapter 9

EXPERIMENTAL ANALYSIS OF PSYCHOANALYTIC PHENOMENA

By Robert R. Sears, Ph.D.

Nineteenth century psychology, whether lay or academic, was a psychology of consciousness. Inevitably it influenced the choice of anyone who wished to think psychologically. If Freud had learned his academic prejudices a quarter century later than he did, if Pavlov, Bekhterev, McDougall, and Watson could have influenced him, psychoanalytic theory might have had a very different systematic texture. But by the time the stirrings of behavioral science had led to reexamination of subjectivism, Freud had long since conceptualized his psychiatric observations in terms of conscious and unconscious processes.

In spite of this, the psychoanalytic way of looking at man's motives, defenses, and personality structure has been so invigorating to psychological thought that experimentalists have been reluctant to let it remain unincorporated in the general science of psychology. The subjective character of the system has proved a difficulty, however, since it does not permit of the conventional scientific tests of proof and disproof, and it prevents assimilation of psychoanalytic concepts and principles with those from other disciplines that impinge upon it. Attempts have been made, therefore, to examine psychoanalytic notions by more conventional scientific logic, and in order to do this they have been translated into behavioral psychological terms.

The procedure has led to considerable difficulty. Descriptions of such processes as regression, repression, and projection are clear while embedded in the structure of psychoanalysis but lose their definitive character when removed. Further, after such a translation has been made, the conditions it presupposes are often difficult to establish artificially. In the original formulation of repression, for example, the "unpleasant experience" can be readily understood as a factor in the life history, but such an event is hard to produce safely and effectively in the laboratory. Psychoanalysis deals heavily in the more potent emotions and motives, and if society is hard put to it to control sex, aggression, anxiety, pride, idealism, and unreason, it is little wonder the experimentalist shies away from unleashing them in his laboratory.

306

The consequence of these difficulties is that experimentation has gone forward hesitantly, has made many errors, and as with the processes of *projection* and *sublimation* has more often than not tried to find ways of measuring what has already happened to a subject in real life. There are many lacunae in the efforts; there is much that has not been examined. Indeed, the materials for this chapter constitute a series of investigations whose fraternity is often discernible only in the communality of their psychoanalytic paternity.[1]

A Fixation and Regression

The concepts of fixation and regression were first presented by Freud in connection with the libido theory. Many neurotic patients, he observed, seemed to suffer a reactivation of their childhood affections under certain conditions. This return naturally created difficulties for the otherwise mature adult, and if the earlier forms of behavior or objects of affection were ones that adult standards find unacceptable, there was an inevitable strain to suppress the unwanted impulses and ignore the ignoble objects.

The notion of regression was based quite specifically on the theory of the sexual instinct and therefore its details are a function of the nature of that theory. Briefly, the sexual instinct is conceived of as combining impetus, aim, object, and source (Freud, 1915a). The process of loving involves a physiological *source* of stimulation that instigates behavior toward the loved *object*. The *aim* of the behavior is the elimination of this stimulation. The loved object is determined by experience rather than by instinct and normally changes from one developmental period to the next.

These developmental periods themselves, however, represent stages of growth during which the instinct has different sources of stimulation (Freud, 1905). The earliest source is oral, the next is anal, and the final one is genital. Naturally, both objects and techniques of removing the source of stimulation must change from one period to the next.

Regression from a later stage to an earlier one is a function of two factors, *fixation* and *frustration* (Freud, 1920). By *fixation* Freud (1915a) means "a particularly close attachment of the instinct to its object," and by *frustration* is meant the prevention of satisfaction for the instinct. Hence if a person were strongly attached to a particular libidinal object and if for some reason he relinquished it in favor of some other object, regression to the primary object might occur if he were frustrated in his efforts to gain gratification from the new one. This may be called *object regression*. Freud (1920) distinguishes a second kind of regression, however, that is quite different—the "return of the entire sexual organization to an earlier stage of development." The person may return

---

[1] In preparing this chapter the writer has drawn heavily from a more extensive appraisal of the problems and experimental literature relating to psychoanalytic theory prepared for the Social Science Research Council (Sears, 1943).

from the genital stage to the oral, adopting not only older objects but older ways of gaining gratification. This implies a return to older sources of stimulation as well, and represents what may be called *drive regression*.

Neither of these kinds of regression has been subjected to experimental investigation, the latter for obvious social reasons, but Freud's formulations have led directly to the discovery and analysis of a third type by students of animal learning. This has been called, variously, retrogression, habit regression, and instrumental act regression. In any behavior sequence, whether it be instinctive or habitual in origin, there can be distinguished (1) the original instigator or drive, (2) the goal response, (3) the object necessary for the performance of the goal response, and (4) the specific instrumental acts that put the organism in such context with the object that the goal response may be performed. It is entirely possible for the drive, the goal response, and the object to remain the same, in the face of a frustration, but for the instrumental acts to revert to a kind that had been relinquished at an earlier time. For example, an older child may seek attention from busy parents by whimpering, crying, and baby talk, or a lover may try to recapture a lapsing love by repeating the special attentions he found effective in the first instance. If the strength of attachment to an object is important in determining a later object regression, it seems probable that the strength of the instrumental act sequence would be equally important in determining a later instrumental act regression. Attention must therefore be given first to experimental data that indicate the factors with which this type of habit strength varies.

Instrumental Act Fixation.—Investigation of the conditions under which learning takes place has revealed a number of factors that determine the strength of instrumental acts. It must be emphasized that while Freud (1920) has spoken of fixation as if it were a unique qualitative event, all such matters of *strength* can be considered only from the standpoint of quantitative continua; i.e., the variables isolated here must be viewed as correlates of strength, and fixation, defined as great strength, will be the consequence of a certain amount or degree of each variable.

The most meaningful measure of the strength of a habit is its resistance to change, either by extinction or by retraining. This measure has been used in all the studies cited below to document the factors listed as determiners of habit strength. It is essentially the criterion used clinically to diagnose fixation; a person is fixated if he fails to relinquish an obsolete love object under normal social pressure.

AMOUNT OF REINFORCEMENT.—The first variable to be examined with explicit reference to the problem of fixation was the amount of reinforcement. Krechevsky and Honzik (1932) trained three groups of rats to run along the stem of an *F*-shaped pathway and turn into the shorter of the two alleys in order to get food. The groups were given different amounts of training and then the two alleys at the head of the *F* were reversed so that where the short (rewarding) one had been before, the long one now was. The problem for the animals was to change the timing of their turn in order to get food. The difficulty in making this change was a function of the amount of practice the rats had had on the previous habits; i.e., the group that had the most practice on the original habit took longest to unlearn it in favor of the new habit.

In this experiment the original instrumental act was running down the stem and turning into the shorter alley. This behavior was first learned because the rat was hungry, i.e., he was motivated by the hunger drive, and he received food (the goal object) after performing the instrumental act. He then ate the food (the goal response); this put an end to his running for the moment and strengthened the habit of turning where he did for food. The measure of strength of the instrumental act (the turning) was the resistance to changing its occurrence from one position to the other.

This experimental situation is intended to be comparable to a real-life one in which, for example, a child is given extra affection when he cries. The extension of the principle here demonstrated would be that the more frequently the child's crying (instrumental act) was rewarded, the harder it would be to train him not to cry when he wanted affection.

Evidence confirmatory of this principle has been obtained by Youtz (1938) and Williams (1938). They used resistance to extinction instead of resistance to retraining as a measure of instrumental act strength; the learned act was a simple Thorndikian response with which a rat could obtain food simply by pressing down on a small brass horizontal bar jutting out from the wall of a box in which he was enclosed. Each time the bar was pressed, a pellet of food would drop into a trough beneath. In this case pressing the bar was the instrumental act that was reinforced by the goal response of eating the food pellet (the goal object). Youtz permitted one group of rats to practice the habit 10 times and another group 40 times. Then he broke the electrical circuit that released the pellet and henceforth the rat received no food for his efforts. Eventually the bar-pressing habit was extinguished in all the rats, but it was much more resistant to extinction in those rats that had had 40 trials than in those that had had but 10. Williams, in the course of securing other information, verified these findings with four groups of rats that were allowed, respectively, 5, 10, 30, and 90 reinforcements. The differences, based on unusually large groups, were extremely reliable.

It seems safe to conclude that the more practice a person or animal has at performing a particular instrumental act, the more resistant that act will be to either change or extinction.

STRENGTH OF DRIVE AT TIME OF LEARNING.—Evidence has been obtained by Finan (1940) that instrumental acts are more strongly established by a given number of reinforcements when the drive is strong than when it is weak. The technical details of this and subsequent experiments are so similar to those described above that little would be gained from their description. Throughout these studies resistance to change has been the customary method of measuring strength of habit.

AMOUNT OF REWARD.—In view of the above findings, it might be supposed that a habit would be more strongly established with a large reward than with a small one. Unfortunately no data are available to give a direct test of this hypothesis, but such studies as those of Grindley (1929) and Fletcher (1940) have demonstrated that a higher degree of performance can be achieved with a large than with a small reward.

INTERVAL BETWEEN INSTRUMENTAL ACT AND GOAL RESPONSE.— Skinner (1936) has shown with the bar-pressing technique that when a delay is introduced between the rat's act of pressing down the bar and the actual delivery of the food pellet, there is a reduction in the act's later resistance to extinction. The amount of weakening was found to be roughly proportional to the length of delay. It can be concluded, then, that one factor that conduces to fixation is the promptness with which an instrumental act originally leads to the performance of the goal response.

PUNISHMENT.—If punishment is administered immediately after the performance of an act, that act is normally supposed to undergo a certain weakening. If punishment occurs during the progress of the act, however, there is evidence from the work of Hamilton and Krechevsky (1933), Everall (1935), Fairlie (1937), and Martin (1940) that behavior becomes more stereotyped. For example, Hamilton and Krechevsky found that when rats were learning to go to the opposite branch of a single-unit T-maze from the branch they had originally preferred, they became very fixed in their choices if shock were regularly administered just before the choice-point. The direction of the stereotyped behavior was not consistently either toward or away from the shortest of two alleys nor was it consistently in the direction of the previous training.

SUBGOAL REINFORCEMENT.—When an instrumental act leads to a goal response consistently and continuously, it eventually achieves the properties of a goal response itself; i.e., it can serve to reinforce a new instrumental act and it becomes the final act in a conative or striving series (Anderson, 1941; Wolfe, 1936). Likewise, if an otherwise neutral object is presented simultaneously with a primary reward (goal object), the neutral object will take on reward value (Wolfe, 1936; Fletcher, 1940). It would be expected, therefore, that if an instrumental act is accompanied by the continued presentation of such an object during the extinction process, i.e., when the primary reward is no longer being presented, there would be greater resistance to extinction than if there were no such subgoal reinforcement. Bugelski (1938), using the bar-pressing technique, has shown that such is the case. Instrumental acts are stronger if subgoals as well as primary ones are reached than if there are no subgoal reinforcements.

GENERALIZATION.—Williams (1941a) has shown that when two rather similar habits are learned there is a transfer of strength from one to the other in such a way that either habit is more resistant to extinction than it would be if the other habit had not been learned. This effect has been found with relatively weak habits only, however, and may have limited significance for the problem of fixation.

EFFECT OF PREVIOUS EXTINCTIONS.—Although it is possible to eliminate an instrumental act by preventing the occurrence of the goal response, a period of elapsed time will permit a spontaneous recovery of the act. Youtz (1938) and Williams (1938), in the studies described on page 309 above in connection with amount of reinforcement, have shown that these spontaneously recovered habits are much less resistant to extinction than the original not-previously-extinguished habit. Ellson (1938) and Youtz (1939) have shown, further, that previous extinctions of similar responses in the same stimulus situation have virtually the same effect as previous extinctions of the tested response itself.

STRENGTH OF DRIVE AT TIME OF EXTINCTION.—Sackett (1939) and Heathers and Arakelian (1941) have found that although a habit is stronger when the drive is stronger, any extinction carried out under strong drive is more effective than under weak drive, i.e., a habit is more severely weakened by partial extinction under the former condition than under the latter.

COMMENT.—Various other factors are known to influence the resistance of a habit to extinction or retraining but they are either unimportant or irrelevant to the problem of fixation. It is clear that these investigations of animal learning have contributed an extraordinarily useful series of principles that can be used coordinately with psychoanalytic principles.

Instrumental Act Regression.—When an animal's ongoing activity is blocked, that is, when it is frustrated, the animal is faced with the necessity of performing some different instrumental act, and the new act may be either a previously discarded one or a completely novel combination of habit segments. If it is the former, instrumental act regression is said to have occurred. In any case, the act that occurs will be the one that has the largest net residue of "strength" accruing, not only from the several factors described above as determiners of instrumental act fixation, but in all probability from other as yet unascertained sources of strength as well.

The first experimental work done on this process was that of Hamilton and Krechevsky (1933). They trained rats to choose the shorter of the two alleys in a single-unit T-maze and then reversed the sides. A control group merely learned the new position, but the experimental group was always shocked at the choice point after the new learning had definitely started. More than half these animals suddenly reverted to the former direction of turning although it now led them through the longer alley to the food reward. The authors interpreted this as a form of regression to a previously learned habit but suggested it might be reversion to original position habits. A second experimental group, treated somewhat differently from the first, gave support to the latter interpretation.

Further data concerning the relative ease with which regression to native position habits and to purely learned habits occurred were secured by Sanders (1937). As would be expected, regression occurred more readily to the response that secured extra strength from being native.

Sanders tested also for the effects of *generalization* of the effect of shock by shocking the animals in another box and then putting them in the discrimination unit to test for regression. There was no evidence of regression. Mowrer (1940) has suggested that the shock was not a sufficient frustration to produce regression except when it was presented during the actual response sequence where it could interfere with the important anticipatory or expectancy reactions. Mowrer's own demonstration of regression relied on shock as the frustrating agent but it served to produce frustration not simply by being painful but by interfering with well-established escape-from-other-shock behavior. One group of five rats was permitted to learn by trial and error that the electric shock in the grill on which they stood could be turned off by pressing a foot pedal. Another group was given shocks for an approximately equal amount of time but had no pedal to press. These latter rats learned to sit up on their hind legs to escape the shock. When this had been well learned they were permitted to learn how to use the foot pedal. Then both groups were frustrated by having shock introduced to this foot pedal, so that when they tried to turn off the floor shock they got a shock from the instrument of salvation. The rats that had originally learned to escape by standing on their hind legs almost immediately regressed to that habit while the other rats continued to press the pedal. A third group of rats that suffered shock on the pedal from the very beginning of their training at escape from floor shock "voted" four out of five to use the pedal rather than the hind leg standing as a method of avoiding punishment. These results seem to indicate that regression can occur to a response that is not "primary" in the rat's choice.

Final evidence that regression is a function of strength comes from a recent investigation by Martin (1940, Experiment II), who trained three groups of rats in a *T*-unit to make a choice congruent with their original position habits. They were then reversed, trained to make the opposite response. The three groups were differentiated by the relative amount of training given on the two habits, i.e., the ratios of the strengths were varied. When shock was administered at the choice point during the operation of the second habit, regression occurred to some degree in all three groups, but the number of rats that regressed in each group was a function of the relative strength of the first habit. O'Kelly

(1940a, 1940b) has secured results with a somewhat different technique that support Martin's findings.

These experiments have relied on electric shock as the frustrating agent, but removal of reward can be equally efficacious. Hull (1934) trained rats to run along a straight 40-foot alley to get food. The speed of running through consecutive 5-foot sections was measured and it was found that a clear speed gradient existed during the early trials; the rats started slowly but speeded up as they neared the goal and then slowed again just at the end. This gradient virtually disappeared after several days of practice, but reappeared almost at once when the food was removed from the goal and the animals were no longer rewarded. Another group of rats was trained in the same way but the alley was only 20 feet long. Removal of reward produced the same effects. These rats were then trained on the full 40-foot alley. At first there was a considerable slowing up at the 20-foot point where the gradient had ended before, but this soon disappeared and the time scores for consecutive sections of the alley were very like those of the other group after lengthy training, i.e., the gradient in speed-of-locomotion had disappeared. When these rats were frustrated, however, they regressed to the "hump" pattern of the gradient; they were evidently regressing to the behavior learned in the original series of trials on the 20-foot alley. Miller and Miles (1936), using a maze, obtained somewhat similar consequences from removal of reward.

Even satiation can serve as a method of reducing the strength of a response and thus permit the occurrence of a previously relinquished response. O'Kelly (1940b) trained a group of eight rats to run in one direction and when that habit was well learned he reversed the direction. When this new habit had been learned the rats were satiated and tested again. All eight rats regressed to the previously learned response. On the following day, with the customary motivation, they again performed the second habit.

These various demonstrations of the reactivation of earlier learned-and-discarded habit patterns suggest that the problem of *instrumental act regression* is primarily one of *instrumental act strength.* Frustration is significant only in so far as it serves, first, to give rise to a situation in which a *change of response* is necessary or possible, and second, to reduce the strength of actions that have immediately preceded it. The detailed implications of these two frustration effects have been discussed at some length by Sears (1943). In any case, it is apparent that regression is a purely descriptive term. It alone does not indicate the dynamics lying beneath the phenomena it describes. These dynamics relate, as has been shown, to the complex interaction of various sources of instigation and inhibition; fundamentally they are the dynamics of the learning process. Both data and logic support Freud's statement that regression is a function of fixation—habit strength—but it is a function of frustration in a secondary way only, and what effect frustration has is primarily in the direction of influencing the strength of instrumental act sequences.

Primitivation.—Freud used *regression* as a purely descriptive term, and thereby led to some confusion as to just what regressive behavior is from a systematic standpoint. Some investigators have emphasized the reactivation of older habits, as described above, while others (Lewin, 1937; Barker, Dembo, and Lewin, 1941) have concerned themselves with the deteriorative effects of frustration. In essence, this second type of regression is a frustration-induced *primitivation of action*, i.e., behavior becomes relatively disorganized, vague rather than specific, scanty in detail, restricted as to area of activities and interest, and decreasingly realistic. This is an adequate description, in reverse, of the changes in method of playing with toys that a child displays as he gets older; his play becomes more organized, contains more elaborate phantasies, and involves larger and more differentiated units of action (see Wells, 1935). Barker, Dembo, and Lewin evolved a scale for the measurement of these age changes, using months as the unit of scoring.

For the investigation of regression they established a free play situation for 30 preschool children. All were above average in intelligence. In the experiment each child was allowed to play alone with some toys, without assistance or interference, for a half-hour. The next day he was brought in again and this time allowed to play first with some much more desirable toys. After 15 minutes the experimenter, without explanation, returned the child to the other end of the room, where he had played the previous day, and allowed him to play with the original, much less attractive, toys for a half-hour. During this period the fine toys were in constant view of the child through a wire net that had been lowered between him and the toys.

This permitted a measure of the constructiveness of play with the original toys after frustration, while the first day gave a prefrustration control measure. It was found not only that primitivation occurred following frustration, as measured by number of months reduction produced on the constructiveness-of-play scale, but that those children who showed the most extensive signs of frustration also showed the greatest primitivation.

Schizophrenia.—Since many of the symptoms of the schizophrenias seem to represent a kind of childishness, it is not surprising that the disorder has itself been called a disorder of regression. Experimentation has not justified this hypothesis, although studies of schizophrenic thinking do fit the description of primitivation to some extent.

Cameron (1938a, 1938b) examined schizophrenics' methods of reasoning in completing such sentences as "A man fell down in the road because . . ." and "A boy threw a stone at me because . . ." Piaget has shown that *cause and effect* explanations (". . . in the road because he stumbled") rarely occur before age seven, but are characteristic of 95% of normal adults. *Logical justification* ("That animal is not dead because it is moving") is somewhat less mature, and *psychological motivation* (". . . stone at me because he wanted to hit me") is the predominant form in young children. Schizophrenics proved to be different from adults but there was no similarity to the distribution of types of explanation found in children. A further comparison of the relative frequency of these types among patients clinically diagnosed as mild, moderate, and severe in their disorganization showed an actual superiority of the severe ones with respect to cause and effect explanations. When the schizophrenics were compared with seven- to nine-year-old children on the frequency of adequate answers to incomplete sentences that suggested either cause and effect or psychological motivation completions, the patients did more poorly on both than the children but the deficiency was even greater with the motivation than with cause and effect sentence. A fourth comparison is of interest; Piaget found that the notion of exception as implied in "although" is of later development than causation ("because"). Again grouping his schizophrenics as mild, moderate, and severe, Cameron found that there was a decreasing frequency of adequate answers to "because" sentences but no difference between the groups with respect to "although" sentences. From these various data Cameron was forced to conclude that schizophrenia did not represent a regression to childhood forms of thinking and that adult forms were, if anything, less disturbed than the childhood forms. His analysis of the exact nature of schizophrenic thinking is too complex for consideration here.

DuBois and Forbes (1934) measured the frequency with which catatonics adopted a foetal position during sleep. The assumption was that this might represent a regression to that stage. Only 9% of the total number of postures and 6% of the total sleeping time represented foetal position. One normal man on one night showed 7% and 4% respectively. The control data are inadequate but the patients showed a minimal amount of foetal return in any case.

These two studies fail to support a theory that schizophrenia is a regression of thought or postural processes, but they are not relevant to the question of whether it is an affective regression (see also Chapter 32).

Aggression

A somewhat more direct effect of frustration, according to Freud (1917), is aggression. In *Mourning and Melancholia* the view was presented that the "primordial" reaction to interference with pleasure-seeking is an aggressive attack on, or a feeling of hostility toward, the source of the frustration. This qualitative statement has been supplemented by an analysis of the quantitative aspects of the frustration-aggression relationship by Dollard, *et al.* (1939).

Neither Freud nor the authors of *Frustration and Aggression* suggested that aggression was the only response to frustration (Miller, 1941; Sears, 1941); regression, substitution, and sublimation, for example, are important alternatives. Considerable experimental evidence has accumulated, however, that aggression is a *frequent* consequence of frustration and Rosenzweig has emphasized its importance in ego defense (see Chapter 11).

Sources of Frustration.—Aggression has been obtained as a response to interference with various kinds of activity, and while the particular circumstances of each frustration determine whether aggression will occur or whether some other response will override it, there seems to be some support for the belief that frustration of any response sequence can be the antecedent condition for aggression.

Interference with eating has caused angry crying in young babies (Sears and Sears, 1940) and an increase in snapping and biting behavior in rats (Miller and Stevenson, 1936; Hull, 1934). Interference with normal desires to go to sleep have produced a great variety of aggressive actions, as Sears, Hovland, and Miller (1940) have shown in their summary of the relevant literature.

At a somewhat more complex motivational level, where ego drives and social activities are involved, similar phenomena have been observed. Lippitt (1940) established children's play groups in some of which the experimenter, serving as leader, was very strict in his domination and control of the children. These groups evidenced more aggression when they were released from supervision than did groups whose leader was less dominating. Barker, Dembo, and Lewin (1941), in the study described above, found that when a wire net was lowered between a child and his toys, there was more kicking and knocking than there had been in a control period during which the toys were not visible. This study gives emphasis to the fact that a frustration can be produced not only by interfering with the activity in progress but by keeping an unreachable goal within the person's range of perception.

Quantitative Relationships.—

STRENGTH OF INSTIGATION TO AGGRESSION.—The basic factor determining the strength of instigation to aggression is the amount of frustration. Two variables have been shown to influence this: the strength of the frustrated response and the amount of interference with it. Sears and Sears (1940) varied the point during bottle-feeding of a six-months-old baby at which the nipple was withdrawn from the mouth. They found that the quickness with which crying started was related to the degree of the child's hunger; if he had had little milk the crying started almost instantly but if he had had nearly a full ration there was a longer latency to the reaction. Doob and Sears (1939) obtained evidence of this same principle in a study of the recall of real-life frustrations. Subjects were asked to report what their behavior had been the last time each of a series of commonly-occurring frustrations had happened to them. The frequency with which overt aggression was reported varied directly with strength of motivation as reported on a rating scale accompanying the description of each frustrating situation. Supporting data are contributed, too, by Barker, Dembo, and Lewin (1941). Ten of their subjects who were relatively unfrustrated by the interrupted play technique showed somewhat less aggressive behavior than did the more highly frustrated ones.

The importance of amount of interference with motivated activity has been somewhat demonstrated by Hovland and Sears (1940), who found that in fourteen Southern states the annual frequency of Negro lynchings correlated — .70 with the annual farm-value of cotton from 1882 to 1930. It was reasoned that the lower the farm-value of cotton in these states, the greater was the interference with the normal activities of people living at a marginal economic level. Such evidence as this is merely illustrative; it can hardly be conclusive.

INHIBITION OF AGGRESSION.—Doob and Sears (1939) have shown that the degree to which a given strength of instigation to aggression is actually translated into action of an aggressive nature is a function of the amount of punishment anticipated for such action. In the questionnaire mentioned above there was opportunity for a subject to indicate, on a 4-point rating scale, the amount of punishment or injury he had expected if he acted in certain aggressive ways. Some of these were overt and some were nonovert forms of aggression. A similar scale indicated the amount of satisfaction he expected from the action. It was found that when anticipated satisfaction exceeded anticipated punishment the overt aggression most frequently occurred, but when the opposite situation obtained there was a greater tendency to have nonovert, unexpressed aggression.

A vivid example of this process was described by Lewin, Lippitt, and White (1939) in their study of aggressive behavior in autocratic and democratic atmospheres. Under autocracy, in four of the six cases, there was an extremely low level of aggression, much lower than in any of the democratic or laissez-faire atmosphere groups. That this was not a result of nonfrustration was demonstrated when the leader left the room. With his repressive influence gone aggression flared up to ten times its previous level. Again, when these apathetic groups were changed over to another atmosphere under a new leader, there was a sudden tremendous outburst of aggression. It appeared that when the strict disciplinarian, the autocrat, was present, there was a general inhibition of aggressive action, but once that inhibitor was removed the aggression flared forth.

Direction of Aggression.—Since the original instigation to aggression exists even under the most severe inhibition, some inquiry has been made into its fate. Freud has suggested that if all expression of aggression toward the external sources of frustration is prevented, aggression may be turned toward the self or displaced on relatively blameless objects.

DISPLACEMENT.—This is a mechanism whereby an affective response normally to be directed at one object is diverted to another because of fear of punishment for directing it at the former. An example of this was found in the study of social atmospheres. In one of the autocratic groups (inhibited aggression) the aggression of four of the five members was twice focussed on the remaining youngster to such a degree that in both instances the scapegoat left the group. After this release there was a brief reduction in the total amount of group aggression; the displaced emotion had served as a catharsis.

From the standpoint of learning theory, Miller (1939) has shown that this process can be derived from the principle of generalization. When aggression, love, or anxiety has been instigated by one object, other objects that are similar to it will, in reduced degree, serve to elicit the response if the original object is not present. To demonstrate this, Miller trained pairs of white rats to fight with each other by putting them in a box with an electrified floor and turning off the current only when they had assumed a belligerent posture. On subsequent occasions a small white celluloid doll was introduced into the box with the pair of rats, but they ignored it in order to adopt their fighting postures. If only *one* rat was placed in the box with the doll, however, that rat would start to fight with the doll. This is a simple generalization of stimuli.

In order to secure displacement it would be necessary to punish the animal for assuming the fighting posture toward the other rat. The animal would subsequently avoid that behavior and this nonfighting action would generalize to the same series of stimuli, including the doll, to which the positive response had generalized. Brown (1940) has shown, however, that the generalization of such avoidance responses is narrower, i.e., extends to fewer objects, and decreases more steeply as it moves out from the original object, than the positive generalization. As a consequence there is a point on the similarity dimension at which the two gradients cross and the positive (generalized) response is stronger than the negative (generalized) response. According to this theory, it should be possible to punish the rats for fighting to such an extent that they would no longer do so but would nevertheless make fighting responses (generalized) to the doll.[3]

CHANGE OF FORM.—A study performed by Fredericksen (1942) demonstrates another possible consequence of the inhibition. He secured the cooperation of nursery school teachers in establishing frustrated and nonfrustrated groups of children in terms of the amount of restriction and dominating control exerted in the school room by the teachers. There was no increase in overt aggression in the frustrated group, even toward other children, but there was a reliable increase in the amount of "submissive negativism" (crying, drawing away, running away, etc.). Here, as with the Iowa social atmosphere studies, it would seem that the very nature of the frustrating situation was such that it contained a repressive influence against the free expression of aggression. In the Fredericksen subjects, however, there was no evidence of displacement toward other children as there was in the case of the scapegoat behavior under autocracy. On the other hand, Fredericksen suggests that the sub-

---

[3] The writer is indebted to Dr. Neal E. Miller for this theoretical analysis.

missive negativism may represent a modified aggression directed toward the frustrating agent—the adult. This modified aggression belongs to the classification called *nonovert* by Doob and Sears (1939).

None of these studies is complete and unequivocal in its demonstration of the theoretical points it has been described to illustrate. Taken in bulk, however, they do present a small backlog of support of the theoretical relationship between frustration and aggression as it was originally stated by Freud and has been more recently reviewed and supplemented by Dollard, Doob, Miller, Mowrer, and Sears (1939).

Substitution

To return to frustration: Freud (1920, Ch. 23) has pointed to still another of its consequences, namely, the securing of alternative or substitute gratifications for those which must be relinquished. This refers primarily to situations in which pregenital sexuality has been suppressed and neurotic symptoms or sublimations are formed to reduce the tension of such frustration. Again, as with regression and aggression, there is considerable disparity between the kinds of behavior to which the theory originally applied and those with which experiments have been performed.

Alternative Tasks.—The strength of instigation to a frustrated activity can sometimes be reduced if a certain other action is performed. This substitute action must have certain similarities to the frustrated one, however, if it is to have this effect, and experimental research on the problem of substitution has been largely directed at the discovery of the properties of tasks possessing substitute value.

In order to have a quantitative measure of the effectiveness of different tasks as substitutes, Ovsiankina (1928) used the frequency with which an interrupted task was resumed. Thus if 75% of a group of subjects resumed an interrupted task after having performed one interpolated task while only 25% resumed after another task, the latter would be said to have greater substitute value, i.e., it reduced the strength of instigation to the original task more (greater catharsis) as measured by the lesser tendency to resumption.

The details of the various experiments are unimportant here. H. H. Nowlis has summarized the significant variables as follows:

> 1. The nature of the original activity: resumption is more frequent with a task which has a definite goal than with one which lacks an objective goal and is more or less continuous (Ovsiankina, 1928; Zeigarnik, 1927).
> 2. The point at which interruption occurs in the progress of the original activity: interruption at points immediately after the instructions have been given and just before the completion of the task produces the highest frequency of resumption (Katz, 1938; Ovsiankina, 1928; Zeigarnik, 1927).

3. The nature of the interruption: "accidental" interruptions produce more frequent resumption than do those which are clearly intentional on the part of the experimenter (Lissner, 1933).

4. The intensity of the primary action tendency: resumption is less frequent when the original task has been performed to satiation (Sliosberg, 1934).

5. Four characteristics of the period following the interruption: (a) the degree of similarity between the interrupted and the second activity (Lissner, 1933); (b) the degree of difficulty of the second activity relative to the first (Lissner, 1933); (c) the degree of contact between the tension systems involved in the two tasks (Lissner, 1933); and (d) the degree of reality of the second activity (Sliosberg, 1934; Mahler, 1933). (1941, p. 307)

Over and above these various attributes of the tasks, however, there is an additional factor that can influence the occurrence of substitute responses. Nowlis (1941) has shown that when the substitute activity itself leads to gratification, via artificially induced feelings of success, there is greater probability of a resumption of the previously frustrated activity than if the substitution is accompanied by an induced feeling of failure. It is as if the achievement of substitute gratification raised hope that the original goal might be reached after all. The limits of this principle are badly in need of further elucidation, since it appears that here experimental psychology may have something authoritative to say that would assist the analytic therapist.

Sublimation.—A special form of substitution is sublimation. When pregenital or genital impulses do not undergo repression they may be transformed into impulses to perform acts having supposedly "higher" cultural value than direct libidinally instigated activity. Freud (1905) acknowledged that the causes of such behavior were obscure, and more recently the theory has been criticized on various grounds (Levey, 1940).

The empirical evidence is sharply against the theory. Taylor (1933) investigated the sources of sexual gratification of 40 brilliant, healthy, esthetically refined young men and discovered that, although all were unmarried, all habitually obtained direct genital gratification by means of either autoerotic or illicit heterosexual activity. The men's characters and their achievements were of an order to make them clear cases of sublimation, but no such agenitality existed.

This factual consideration together with the logical difficulties discussed by Levey force a rejection of Freud's early formulation of the process.

Repression

Anxiety holds a position of great importance in psychoanalytic theory, an importance at least as great as that of frustration. Its significance lies in its dual roles as signal or indicator of conflict and as reinforcing agent (Mowrer, 1939) for repression, reaction-formation, and projection. Indeed, all the defense mechanisms (see Frenkel-Brunswik, 1939), antagonistic to reality as they appear to be, depend for their existence on the fact that they reduce the strength of anxiety.

Repression is closely related to anxiety in two ways: first, anxiety serves as the signal of danger that activates a defense through repression, and second, the reduction of anxiety by this defense operates as a direct reinforcement for that process. This is best understood in terms of the genesis of *primal repression.*

According to Freud (1915b, 1915c), an instinctual impulse may produce behavior that results in severe punishment. On subsequent occasions the arousal of that impulse will be followed by feelings of anxiety, i.e., it serves as a stimulus to anticipation of pain. The ego then rejects all ideational representation of the impulse in order to prevent the carrying through of the behavior and the expected occurrence of punishment. To be distinguished from this primal repression is repression proper, or *after-expulsion;* any ideas that come into associative contact with the repressed ideational representation of the impulse are also subject to repression.

This skeletonized description gives no indication of the extraordinary richness and detail of Freud's theoretical formulation. There are a number of important quantitative aspects to the theory that, for their investigation, await only a satisfactory method of measuring repression, but to date this problem is unsolved. The refined techniques adapted from the experimental psychology of memory have led, it seems, only to futile efforts to relate feeling and memory to each other. Unhappily, as Sears (1936a, pp. 255–257) has shown in detail, P and U qualities have no relevance to repression theory.

Measurement of Existent Repressions.—

RECALL OF EXPERIENCES.—Of some importance to the theory, however, is the group of studies designed to measure recall of real life experiences. Wohlgemuth (1923), Meltzer (1930), Jersild (1931), Stagner (1931), and Waters and Leeper (1936) secured descriptions of children's or adults' pleasant and unpleasant experiences and then compared the two kinds of memory for obliviscence after various lengths of time from two days to several months. With the exception of Wohlgemuth, all these investigations demonstrated in varying degree a greater recall for the pleasant than for the unpleasant (see Moore, 1935), and Waters and Leeper found further that the effectiveness of recall was directly related to the strength of affect attached to the experience.

Stagner (1931) secured a much finer measure of recall by having his subjects write out a series of "redintegrative items," e.g., odors, objects, feelings, that were associated with each experience. After three weeks the subjects were reminded of the original description of the experiences and asked to recall the redintegrative items. The difference was clearly in favor of better recall for those associated with pleasant experiences.

It is not certain that all or even a majority of the experiences reported by the subjects of these experiments were of the type to which the repression theory applies. Koch (1930), on the other hand, selected the material to be recalled with special consideration for its relevance to the theory. College students were given a series of ten-minute quizzes; these were graded and returned to the students, who then rated the grade on a scale of 1 to 5 to indicate their satisfaction or dissatisfaction with it. The papers were collected again and five weeks after the last quiz the students were asked to recall all ten grades. The "1" grades were best recalled, and whether the "2" or "5" grades were next best seemed to depend on whether the "5" grades represented truly dangerous threats to passing the course. These results are clearly in support of the repression hypothesis, but they indicate too that such other factors as a requirement for immediate adjustment to a threatening environment are also very important in determining this kind of recall behavior.

ASSOCIATIVE REPRESSION (AFTER-EXPULSION).—Another technique for securing a measure of real-life repressions is that used by Sharp (1930) and Flanagan (1930). Sharp constructed lists of paired nonsense words that made religious or profane meanings when pronounced together. The learning and recall of these was compared with that of control lists with neutral meanings. Flanagan used a similar technique with paired associates that gave a sexual meaning. His control list gave rural meanings. Both Sharp and Flanagan found a much better recall for the control material than for the experimental. The assumption was that religious, profane, and sexual words tapped already existent repressions and by after-expulsion these specific words, too, became repressed. The only criticism of these studies is that under the described experimental conditions it is not certain that the differential recall may not have been a result of sheer conscious embarrassment at speaking forbidden words.

Sharp (1938) developed another quite ingenious method; from the case histories of a group of neurotics she secured two lists of words that related respectively to serious emotional problems in their lives and to sources of gratification. These were then structured into two lists of paired associates and used as learning material for these same neurotic patients. Although the lists were of virtually equal difficulty in learning, the list relating to gratifications was better recalled after two days and after three weeks.

Sharp was able to secure similar results with the same lists of words from a group of normal adults. Presumably the words referred to sources of anxiety or gratification that are fairly universal in American society. On this assumption Heathers and Sears (1943) attempted to repeat Sharp's results with a group of subjects similar to those used by Sharp in her normal group. Neither with this group nor with college students was the same difference in recall between the two lists obtained. A number of variations in procedure were tried but were ineffective in influencing these negative results. It seems probable that rather intangible aspects of the experimental situation may have been responsible and these results suggest that in general the tapping of existent repressions by the relatively crude laboratory methods of the conventional learning experiments is difficult and not reliable.

Experimental Induction of Repression.—Two principal techniques have been employed for the artificial induction of repression: one through the forming of complexes under hypnosis, with suggestion of amnesia, and the other through experimental production of feelings of failure at competitive activities. The significance of the former type of experiment is still too unclear and too intimately dependent upon what interpretation is placed on hypnotic amnesia to be of great importance. Results from such experiments as those of Huston, Shakow, and Erickson (1934), however, may eventually serve to clarify the processes by which nonconscious activities influence conscious ones.

The use of failure as a means of creating anxiety by punishment of ego-striving was first used in connection with repression by Rosenzweig and Mason (1934). They presented a series of simple jig-saw puzzles to young children, permitting each child to complete only half the puzzles. Afterward the children, who had seen a picture of each puzzle at the time it was attempted, were asked to recall the names of as many of the puzzles as possible. It was found that children who were rated low in pride recalled more uncompleted tasks, a simple Zeigarnik effect, but that those whom their teachers looked upon as having a good deal of pride recalled more of the completed ones. The children who were *capable* of being punished by these failures, in other words, showed a repressive defense.

In order to test this conclusion in another way, Rosenzweig (1941) presented similar puzzles under the same conditions to two groups of Harvard students. One group was told that it was a mental test situation and the other group that the properties of the puzzles, not the subjects, were being studied; the first group felt on trial, the second group did not. A comparison of the relative number of names of completed and uncompleted tasks recalled demonstrated that the group that felt on trial recalled a much larger proportion of the completed tasks and the other group recalled more uncompleted ones. This clearly confirmed the results of the earlier experiment.

These various efforts to subject the repression hypothesis to measurement and test in the laboratory have induced the collection of many kinds of interesting data. To what degree they are relevant is still an open question. In nearly every instance, as Sears (1936a, pp. 238–263) has emphasized in an extensive critical appraisal of both the theory and the experimental literature, some aspect of the experimental situation invalidates a rigorous interpretation in terms of the Freudian theory. On the other hand, despite methodological confusion, there is a growing pile of evidence that some kind of process does operate to produce a differential recallability of painful and gratifying ideas. The mechanics of this difference have yet to be investigated.

Projection

Of all the technical terms of psychoanalysis, none has been so inadequately defined as *projection*. Behavior so described has varied from the philosophical category of differentiating the self from the outer world to the psychopathological phenomena of phobias, delusions, and hallucinations. In effect, several rather different types of reactive or perceptual relationships between the person and his environment can be distinguished but only one can be interpreted as a *defense mechanism* in the sense of Freud's original usage (1911).

Motivationally Determined Perception.—The so-called "projective techniques" for measurement of personality are based on the assumption that what is perceived is in part a function of the motivational structure of the personality. As a general statement about perception this scarcely needs documentation, but the details of the relation between motive and percept have been little considered. Murray (1933) has reasoned that several different principles must be involved. He found that five little girls attributed a good deal more maliciousness to the photographs of some unfamiliar people after having played an exciting game of *murder* than before. This was inexplicable on the basis of a simple projection theory, according to Murray, and required the presumption that some preferential perception occurred as well. Sanford (1936, 1937) measured the frequency with which food was mentioned in speculation about the missing parts of incomplete pictures and found that the frequency varied roughly with degree of hunger. This is a quantitative principle of some importance.

Both these investigations pave the way for further analysis of the conditions under which motives produce congruent perceptions (wishful thinking, etc.), but neither, in itself, represents the operation of a projective defense mechanism.

Objectification.—A somewhat similar process is that by which objects in the outer world, or ideas relating to them, become imbued with new meanings. For example, in an ingenious series of experiments with young boys, Mierke (1933) induced a reversal of color-preference for little sticks with which a laboratory task was performed; this was done by providing that failure should accompany the use of the preferred color and success the nonpreferred. In a crude way this is the production of cathexis and anti-cathexis, the development of like and dislike, the investment of objects with libido. Other experiments of this type have been reported, the technique of artificial induction of success and failure having proved particularly effective in studies by Rosenzweig (personal communication) and Nowlis (1941).

Somewhat more elaborate emotional responses were evoked by Thurstone (1931a, 1931b) and Peterson and Thurstone (1932) in the service of changing attitudes by showing emotion-provoking motion pictures. In the first study, expressed attitudes toward the Chinese were shifted in different directions by the use of different kinds of movies. Condemnation of gambling and friendliness toward Germans were increased by the pictures used in the other two studies. The luncheon technique of Razran (1938a, 1938b) has served to modify preferences for modern music and for photographs of faces. In each instance the change was produced by presenting the stimulus object in association with a free meal.

There is small excuse for calling these projection, however; the actual mechanics of change are as much a function of outer as of inner events and the whole process can more usefully be considered in connection with the learning process than with defense mechanisms.

Attribution of Traits.—Projection as a defense against anxiety (Freud, 1911) is a quite different matter. In such instance analytic experience has shown that anxiety is reduced when the patient is able to cast the blame for a shameful circumstance into the outer world, leaving himself guiltless or even victimized.

In an attempt to measure such behavior, Sears (1936b) secured character trait ratings of themselves and each other from nearly a hundred college fraternity men. The ratings related to stinginess, obstinacy, disorderliness, and bashfulness. A comparison of the degree of a given trait attributed *to* others with the amount attributed to the individual *by* others indicated that there was no simple relationship between these two variables. When a rough measure of *insight* was taken into consideration, however, it was found that those men who possessed more than the average amount of a trait tended to attribute more than average amount to others, provided insight was lacking, i.e., provided their self-ratings deviated markedly from the ratings attributed to them by others. In essence this means that projection of these character traits appeared to be a function of lack of insight (repression).

The source of such repression might be the feelings of guilt for possessing a socially undesirable trait oneself. Sears found, however, that such projection occurred at each end of the dimension of ratings, i.e., with generosity as well as with stinginess, etc.

In contrast with this measurement of already existing tendencies to projection, Wright (1940) has actually created the conditions necessary for guilt feelings and has found that only when such conditions are present does the projection occur. Eight-year-old children were given pairs of toys, one a preferred toy and one nonpreferred, and then asked to give one toy to a friend to play with. Immediately afterward they were asked which toy the friend would have given away. The proportion of times that the friend was considered generous (giving away the preferred toy) was much less after the conflict situation, in which the child himself was forced to give away a toy, than it was after a control situation in which the child did not have to give away a toy. Posner concludes from this that stinginess is projected when the person feels guilty about his own stinginess.

There is evidence from these two studies that projection, as a defense mechanism, accompanies a lack of insight into one's own qualities and that guilt concerning a particular kind of action can initiate the projection.

Ideas of Reference.—A special form of attributing one's own ideas to others is ideas of reference. According to Healy, Bronner, and Bowers (1930) these represent a projection of feeings of self-criticism and there is some experimental evidence that if such is not the case there is at least a close relation between them.

Coover (1913) conducted an experiment in which he measured the accuracy with which blind-folded subjects could tell whether or not they were being stared at from behind. From the subjects' introspections he concluded that the belief in being able to tell when one is being stared at comes chiefly from "attributing an objective validity to commonly experienced subjective impressions in the form of imagery, sensations and impulses." One girl, for example, made a "yes" judgment when she had a "feeling of being criticized," or a "feeling of nearness to the experimenter," and a "no" judgment when she had a "feeling of being alone."

In an effort to subject both ideas of reference and feelings of self-criticism to objective and quantitative measure, Sears (1937a) constructed a questionnaire-type test for each. In three hundred college men the correlation between the two scales was $+ .82$ when corrected for attenuation. Clear-cut evidence was also obtained, from friends of the experimental subjects, that the ideas of reference were in no way justified by the realistic aspects of their social relationships.

Both these studies support the view that ideas of reference and feelings of self-criticism are intimately related, but Sears has questioned whether the relationship is one of *projection*. Such an interpretation assumes that the self-criticism is temporarily prior to the ideas of reference in the individual's life history and such has not yet been established.

Paranoia and Homosexuality.—These experiments have, of course, taken projection out of its original clinical setting. The theory of paranoia (Freud, 1911) represented the first formal statement of the relation between projection and a recognizable behavioral consequent. Briefly, it was hypothesized that a person suffering from inadequate repression of homosexual impulses first denied his homosexuality through reaction-formation ("I hate him") and then, when that proved still inadequate, through projection ("He hates me"). This theory has suggested still another approach to the complex problem of projection, therefore: the measurement of the empirical relationship between paranoia and homosexuality.

Gardner (1931) examined 120 consecutive admissions diagnosed as paranoid dementia precox and paranoid condition, and recorded the presence of direct homosexuality and homosexual symbolism. Sex differences were slight, and of the total group almost 47% showed some clear-cut evidence of homosexuality. No comparative data were given for the rest of the hospital population.

A similar trend was found by Page and Warkentin (1938), who gave the Terman and Miles Masculinity-Femininity Test to 50 paranoid patients. These were selected so as to be fairly equivalent to the "normal adult" group of Terman and Miles' original standardization. In general, the paranoids' scores resembled those of passive homosexuals more than those of either the normal male population or the active homosexuals.

In a group of 50 college men, Sears (1937a) found no relation between either ideas of reference or feelings of self-criticism and the Masculinity-Femininity score, but it is doubtful whether such ideas of reference can be considered as very closely related to paranoid symptomatology.

The measurements of Gardner and of Page and Warkentin seem to verify the clinical observations concerning *a* relation between homosexuality and paranoid condition, but whether the relation is mediated by the projection mechanism or not is yet to be determined.

The Psychoanalytic Interview

Curiously enough, although the researches surveyed here have covered the past twenty years (perhaps rather thinly), little attention has been given to the actual process of psychoanalysis itself—the discovery of the factual substructure on which the psychoanalytic theory rests. Of major interest, therefore, are the few attempts to discover something concerning the effects of the therapeutic process.

From the standpoint of emotional action, the analytic interview serves as a constant instigator to anxiety, hostility, love, shame, and other more delicately differentiated reactions. That these are genuine and deep-seated can scarcely be called in question, but the investigations by Lasswell (1935), Alexander (1939), and Mittelmann and Wolff (1939) substantiate the clinical observations with measures of sharp physiological changes accompanying manifest emotional reactions in the interview. Mittelmann and Wolff measured skin temperature of the fingers before and after a patient's discussion of certain anxiety-inducing experiences and found a drop of 13.2° C. Alexander measured the blood pressure of a patient before and after each of 201 analytic sessions and compared the direction of change in pressure with the kind of material produced during the session. He found that distressing sessions were accompanied by increased pressure.

Lasswell performed a somewhat more extensive investigation of physiological accompaniments of the analytic process. He reasoned that since, during an interview, emotion could be conscious and active in its expression or could be interfered with by unconscious resistances, there might be some correlate of this difference in the associated physiological reactions. In order to have an objective index both of active emotion and of unconscious tension (or resistance), he measured the patient's rate of talking and counted the number of references he made to the analyst. The *rate* was assumed to vary inversely with unconscious tension and the *number of references* to vary directly with the amount of active emotion. Skin resistance and pulse rate were also measured. Complete data are given for but one of the subjects; the other subjects are said to have substantiated the conclusions derived from the first. In general there was a positive relation between pulse rate and number of references to the analyst (conscious affect) and an inverse relation between skin conductivity and rate of talking (unconscious tension). While there may be some question of the usefulness of this interpretation of conscious and unconscious in the analytic situation, there seems little doubt that the deeper physiological reactions associated with emotion bear some direct relationship to the kind of affective behavior displayed at a verbal level.

Kovsharova (1937) has demonstrated another effect of the interview by use of a so-called conditioned reflex technique. Patients were taught a moderately complex discrimination problem before and after the analytic hour and the strength of the response was measured in terms of its vigor; a bulb-squeezing response was used. The data are meager but in general it appears that analytic hours resulting in catharsis of anxiety were followed by an increased vigor and those resulting in a revelation of depressing thoughts produced a lessened vigor. Measures of inhibition in the learning process were inversely related to the measures of vigor.

In none of these studies is it entirely clear what the psychological correlates of the motor or physiological phenomena are. Neither the "conscious affect" and "unconscious tension" of Lasswell's study, nor the "catharsis" and "revelation of depressing thoughts" of Kovsharova's are clearly definable in the systematic terms of psychoanalytic theory. Thus it is not easy to decide just what light is cast on psychoanalytic theory by the studies. From a practical standpoint, however, Lasswell (1936) has obtained a modicum of evidence that the direction of change in his indices during the first ten analytic sessions may be used as a prognosticator of success or failure in the therapeutic process. The report is preliminary, however, and the data are too scanty to be a sure guide.

So far, it must be concluded, the complicated interplay of psychological forces in the analytic interview, i.e., in the fact-finding situation (see Chapter 7 by French), remains a fascinating tangle for the experimental psychologist. The problems of resistance, transference, anxiety, catharsis, and the total reeducative aspects of the therapeutic process will have to be carefully formulated in objective terms, probably those of learning theory, before the *process of psychoanalysis itself* can be subjected to realistic and insightful investigation.

Conclusion

In casting up these accounts one is driven to the conclusion that experimental psychology has not yet made a major contribution to these problems. This is not to say that no contribution has been made to the dynamics of personality. Quite the contrary; where experimentation has gone forward with little attention to the specific forms of psychoanalytic theories it has made important strides. Instrumental act fixation and regression are examples in point; virtually none of the work on habit strength was instigated by analytic concepts. To a slightly lesser extent this appears to have been true of substitution as well. It is a pure happenstance that habit strength is closely related to fixation and that these studies, therefore, can be brought into service here. But the studies of aggression, displacement, repression, and projection serve no more than to give crude confirmation of phenomena that do not require it.

It seems doubtful whether the sheer testing of psychoanalytic theory is an appropriate task for experimental psychology. Its general method is estimable but its available techniques are clumsy. Instead of trying to ride on the tail of a kite that was never meant to carry such a load, experimentalists would probably be wise to get all the hunches, intuitions, and experience possible from psychoanalysis and then, for themselves, start the laborious task of constructing a systematic psychology of personality, but a system based on behavioral rather than experiential data.

BIBLIOGRAPHY

ALEXANDER, F. 1939. Psychoanalytic study of a case of essential hypertension. *Psychosom. Med., 1,* 139–152.

ANDERSON, E. E. 1941. The externalization of drive: IV. The effect of prefeeding on the maze performance of hungry non-rewarded rats. *J. comp. Psychol., 31,* 349–352.

BARKER, R., DEMBO, T., & LEWIN, K. 1941. Frustration and regression: an experiment with young children. *Univ. Ia Stud. Child Welf., 18,* No. 1, 1–314.

BROWN, J. S. 1940. Generalized approach and avoidance responses in relation to conflict behavior. New Haven: Dissertation, Yale University.

BUGELSKI, R. 1938. Extinction with and without sub-goal reinforcement. *J. comp. Psychol., 26,* 121–133.

CAMERON, N. 1938a. Reasoning, regression and communication in schizophrenics. *Psychol. Monogr., 50,* No. 1.

—— 1938b. A study of thinking in senile deterioration and schizophrenic disorganization. *Amer. J. Psychol., 51,* 650–664.

COOVER, J. E. 1913. "The feeling of being stared at"—experimental. *Amer. J. Psychol., 24,* 570–575.

DOLLARD, J., DOOB, L. W., MILLER, N. E., MOWRER, O. H., & SEARS, R. R. 1939. Frustration and aggression. New Haven: Yale University Press.

DOOB, L. W., & SEARS, R. R. 1939. Factors determining substitute behavior and the overt expression of aggression. *J. abnorm. soc. Psychol., 34,* 293–313.

DUBOIS, P. H., & FORBES, T. W. 1934. Studies of catatonia: III. Bodily postures assumed while sleeping. *Psychiat. Quart., 8,* 546–552.

ELLSON, D. G. 1938. Quantitative studies of the interaction of simple habits: I. Recovery from specific and generalized effects of extinction. *J. exp. Psychol.,* 23, 339–358.

EVERALL, E. E. 1935. Perseveration in the rat. *J. comp. Psychol., 19,* 343–369.

FAIRLIE, C. W. 1937. The effect of shock at the "moment of choice" on the formation of a visual discrimination habit. *J. exp. Psychol., 21,* 662–669.

FINAN, J. L. 1940. Quantitative studies in motivation: I. Strength of conditioning in rats under varying degrees of hunger. *J. comp. Psychol., 29,* 119–134.

FLANAGAN, D. 1930. The influence of emotional inhibition on learning and recall. Chicago: Thesis, University Chicago.

FLETCHER, F. M. 1940. Effects of quantitative variation of food-incentive on the performance of physical work by chimpanzees. *Comp. Psychol. Monogr., 16,* No. 82, 46.

FREDERIKSEN, N. 1942. The effects of frustration on negativistic behavior of young children. *J. genet. Psychol., 61,* 203–226.

FRENKEL-BRUNSWIK, E. 1939. Mechanisms of self-deception. *J. soc. Psychol., 10,* 409–420.

FREUD, S. 1905. Three contributions to the theory of sex. In *The basic writings of Sigmund Freud.* New York: Modern Library, 1938.

—— 1911. Psycho-analytic notes upon an autobiographical account of a case of paranoia (dementia paranoides). In *Collected papers.* Vol. 3. London: Hogarth, 1925. Pp. 387–470.

—— 1915a. Instincts and their vicissitudes. In *Collected papers.* Vol. 4. London: Hogarth, 1925. Pp. 60–83.

—— 1915b. Repression. In *Collected papers.* Vol. 4. London: Hogarth, 1925. Pp. 84–97.

—— 1915c. The unconscious. In *Collected papers.* Vol. 4. London: Hogarth, 1925. Pp. 98–136.

—— 1917. Mourning and melancholia. In *Collected papers.* Vol. 4. London: Hogarth, 1925. Pp. 152–170.

—— 1920. General introduction to psychoanalysis. New York: Liveright.

GARDNER, G. E. 1931. Evidences of homosexuality in 120 unanalyzed cases with paranoid content. *Psychoanal. Rev., 18,* 57–62.

GRINDLEY, G. C. 1929. Experiments on the influence of the amount of reward on learning in young chickens. *Brit. J. Psychol., 20,* 173–180.

HAMILTON, J. A., & KRECHEVSKY, I. 1933. Studies in the effect of shock upon behavior plasticity in the rat. *J. comp. Psychol., 16,* 237–253.

HEALY, W., BRONNER, A., & BOWERS, A. M. 1930. The structure and meaning of psychoanalysis. New York: Knopf.

HEATHERS, G. L., & ARAKELIAN, P. 1941. The relation between strength of drive and rate of extinction of a bar-pressing reaction in the rat. *J. gen. Psychol., 24,* 243–258.

HEATHERS, L. B., & SEARS, R. R. 1944. Experiments on repression: II. The Sharp technique. (To be published)

HOVLAND, C. I., & SEARS, R. R. 1940. Minor studies of aggression: VI. Correlation of lynchings with economic indices. *J. Psychol., 9,* 301–310.

HULL, C. L. 1934. The rat's speed-of-locomotion gradient in the approach to food. *J. comp. Psychol., 17,* 393–422.

HUSTON, P. E., SHAKOW, D., & ERICKSON, M. H. 1934. A study of hypnotically induced complexes by means of the Luria technique. *J. gen. Psychol., 11,* 65–97.

JERSILD, A. 1931. Memory for the pleasant as compared with the unpleasant. *J. exp. Psychol., 14,* 284–288.

KATZ, E. 1938. Some factors affecting resumption of interrupted activities by preschool children. *Univ. Minn. Child Welf. Monogr. Ser., 16,* 1–52.

KOCH, H. L. 1930. The influence of some affective factors upon recall. *J. gen. Psychol., 4,* 171–190.

KOVSHAROVA, T. V. 1937. An attempt at an experimental investigation of psychoanalytic therapy. *Psychoanal. Quart., 6,* 426–452.

KRECHEVSKY, I., & HONZIK, C. H. 1932. Fixation in the rat. *Univ. Calif. Publ. Psychol., 6,* 13–26.

LASSWELL, H. D. 1935. Verbal references and physiological changes during the psychoanalytic interview: a preliminary communication. *Psychoanal. Rev., 22,* 10–24.

——— 1936. Certain prognostic changes during trial (psychoanalytic) interviews. *Psychoanal. Rev., 23,* 241–247.

LEVEY, H. B. 1940. A theory concerning free creation in the inventive arts. *Psychiatry, 3,* 229–293.

LEWIN, K. 1937. Psychoanalysis and topological psychology. *Bull. Menninger Clin., 1,* 202–211.

LEWIN, K., LIPPITT, R., & WHITE, R. K. 1939. Patterns of aggressive behavior in experimentally created "social climates." *J. soc. Psychol., 10,* 271–299.

LIPPITT, R. 1940. An experimental study of the effect of democratic and authoritarian group atmospheres. *Univ. Ia Stud. Child Welf., 16,* No. 3, 43–195.

LISSNER, K. 1933. Die Entspannung von Bedürfnissen durch Ersatzhandlungen. *Psychol. Forsch., 18,* 218–250.

MAHLER, W. 1933. Ersatzhandlungen verschiedenen Realitätsgrades. *Psychol. Forsch., 18,* 27–89.

MARTIN, R. F. 1940. "Native" traits and regression in rats. *J. comp. psychol., 30,* 1–16.

MELTZER, H. 1930. Individual differences in forgetting pleasant and unpleasant experiences. *J. educ. Psychol., 21,* 399–409.

MIERKE, K. 1933. Über die Objectionsfähigkeit und ihre Bedeutung für die Typenlehre. *Arch. ges. Psychol., 89,* 1–108.

MILLER, N. E. 1939. Experiments relating Freudian displacement to generalization conditioning. *Psychol. Bull., 36,* 516–517.

——— 1941. The frustration-aggression hypothesis. *Psychol. Rev., 48,* 337–342.

MILLER, N. E., & MILES, W. R. 1936. Alcohol and removal of reward. *J. comp. Psychol., 21,* 179–204.

MILLER, N. E., & STEVENSON, S. S. 1936. Agitated behavior of rats during experimental extinction and a curve of spontaneous recovery. *J. comp. Psychol., 21,* 205–231.

MITTELMANN, B., & WOLFF, H. G. 1939. Affective states and skin temperature: experimental study of subjects with "cold hands" and Raynaud's syndrome. *Psychosom. Med., 1,* 271–292.

MOORE, E. H. 1935. A note on the recall of the pleasant vs. the unpleasant. *Psychol. Rev., 42,* 214–215.

MOWRER, O. H. 1939. A stimulus-response analysis of anxiety and its role as a reinforcing agent. *Psychol. Rev., 46,* 553–565.

——— 1940. An experimental analogue of "regression" with incidental observations on "reaction-formation." *J. abnorm. soc. Psychol., 35,* 56–87.

MURRAY, H. A., JR. 1933. The effect of fear upon estimates of the maliciousness of other personalities. *J. soc. Psychol., 4,* 310–329.

NOWLIS, H. H. 1941. The influence of success and failure on the resumption of an interrupted task. *J. exp. Psychol., 28,* 304–325.

O'KELLY, L. I. 1940a. An experimental study of regression: I. Behavioral characteristics of the regressive response. *J. comp. Psychol., 30,* 41–53.

——— 1940b. An experimental study of regression: II. Some motivational determinants of regression and perseveration. *J. comp. Psychol., 30,* 55–95.

OVSIANKINA, M. 1928. Die Wiederaufnahme unterbrochener Handlungen. *Psychol. Forsch., 11,* 302–379.

PAGE, J., & WARKENTIN, J. 1938. Masculinity and paranoia. *J. abnorm. soc. Psychol., 33,* 527–531.

PETERSON, R. C., & THURSTONE, L. L. 1932. The effect of a motion picture film on children's attitudes toward Germans. *J. educ. Psychol., 23,* 241–246.

RAZRAN, G. H. S. 1938a. Conditioning away social bias by the luncheon technique. *Psychol. Bull., 35,* 693.

——— 1938b. Music, art, and the conditioned response. Paper, Eastern Psychological Assn., April 1–2.

ROSENZWEIG, S. 1938. The experimental study of repression. In Murray, H. A., *Explorations in personality.* New York: Oxford University Press. Pp. 472–490.

——— 1941. Need-persistive and ego-defensive reactions to frustration as demonstrated by an experiment on repression. *Psychol. Rev., 48,* 347–349.

ROSENZWEIG, S., & MASON, G. 1934. An experimental study of memory in relation to the theory of repression. *Brit. J. Psychol., 24,* 247–265.

SACKETT, R. S. 1939. The effect of strength of drive at the time of extinction upon resistance to extinction in rats. *J. comp. Psychol., 27,* 411–431.

SANDERS, M. J. 1937. An experimental demonstration of regression in the rat. *J. exp. Psychol., 21,* 493–510.

SANFORD, R. N. 1936. The effects of abstinence from food upon imaginal processes: a preliminary experiment. *J. Psychol., 2,* 129–136.

—— 1937. The effects of abstinence from food upon imaginal processes: a further experiment. *J. Psychol., 3,* 145–159.

SEARS, R. R. 1936a. Functional abnormalities of memory with special reference to amnesia. *Psychol. Bull., 33,* 229–274.

—— 1936b. Experimental studies of projection: I. Attribution of traits. *J. soc. Psychol., 7,* 151–163.

—— 1937a. Experimental studies of projection: II. Ideas of reference. *J. soc. Psychol., 8,* 389–400.

—— 1937b. Initiation of the repression sequence by experienced failure. *J. exp. Psychol., 20,* 570–580.

—— 1941. Non-aggressive reactions to frustration. *Psychol. Rev., 48,* 343–346.

—— 1943. Survey of objective studies of psychoanalytic concepts. *Soc. Sci. Res. Coun. Bull.,* No. 51.

SEARS, R. R., HOVLAND, C. I., & MILLER, N. E. 1940. Minor studies of aggression: I. Measurement of aggressive behavior. *J. Psychol., 9,* 275–295.

SEARS, R. R., & SEARS, P. S. 1940. Minor studies of aggression: V. Strength of frustration-reaction as a function of strength of drive. *J. Psychol., 9,* 297–300.

SHARP, A. A. 1930. The influence of certain emotional inhibitions on learning and recall. Chicago: Thesis, University Chicago.

—— 1938. An experimental test of Freud's doctrine of the relation of hedonic tone to memory revival. *J. exp. Psychol., 22,* 395–418.

SKINNER, B. F. 1936. The effect on the amount of conditioning of an interval of time before reinforcement. *J. gen. Psychol., 14,* 279–295.

SLIOSBERG, S. 1934. Zur Dynamik des Ersatzes in Spiel- und Ernstsituationen. *Psychol. Forsch., 19,* 122–181.

STAGNER, R. 1931. The redintegration of pleasant and unpleasant experiences. *Amer. J. Psychol., 43,* 463–468.

TAYLOR, W. S. 1933. A critique of sublimation in males: a study of forty superior single men. *Genet. Psychol. Monogr., 13,* No. 1, 115.

THURSTONE, L. L. 1931a. The measurement of change in social attitude. *J. soc. Psychol., 2,* 230–235.

—— 1931b. Influence of motion pictures on children's attitudes. *J. soc. Psychol., 2,* 291–305.

WATERS, R. H., & LEEPER, R. 1936. The relation of affective tone to the retention of experiences of daily life. *J. exp. Psychol., 19,* 203–215.

WELLS, F. L. 1935. Social maladjustments: adaptive regression. In Murchison, C., *Handbook of social psychology.* Worcester, Mass.: Clark University Press.

WILLIAMS, S. B. 1938. Resistance to extinction as a function of the number of reinforcements. *J. exp. Psychol., 23,* 506–522.

—— 1941a. Transfer of extinction effects in the rat as a function of habit strength. *J. comp. Psychol., 31,* 263–280.

—— 1941b. Transfer of reinforcement in the rat as a function of habit strength. *J. comp. Psychol., 31,* 281–296.

WOHLGEMUTH, A. 1923. The influence of feeling on memory. *Brit. J. Psychol., 13,* 405–416.

WOLFE, J. B. 1936. Effectiveness of token-rewards for chimpanzees. *Comp. Psychol. Monogr., 12,* No. 60, 1–72.

WRIGHT, B. P. 1940. Selfishness, guilt feelings, and social distance. Iowa City: Thesis, State University Iowa.

YOUTZ, R. E. P. 1938. Reinforcement, extinction, and spontaneous recovery in a non-Pavlovian reaction. *J. exp. Psychol., 22,* 305–318.

—— 1939. The weakening of one Thorndikian response following the extinction of another. *J. exp. Psychol., 24,* 294–304.

ZEIGARNIK, B. 1927. Über das Behalten von erledigten und unerledigten Handlungen. *Psychol. Forsch., 9,* 1–85.

Chapter 10

LEVEL OF ASPIRATION

By Kurt Lewin, Ph.D., Tamara Dembo, Ph.D., Leon Festinger, Ph.D., and
Pauline Snedden Sears, Ph.D.

Almost any set of psychological problems, especially those in the
fields of motivation and personality, inevitably involves goals and goal-
directed behavior. The importance of setting up goals for behavior is
especially accentuated in a culture with as strong a competitive emphasis
as ours. Until recently, however, little formal attempt has been made to
study goals as phenomena in themselves and the effects of attainment or
nonattainment of goals on the behavior of the individual.

The concept of "level of aspiration," introduced by Dembo (published
in 1931), made explicit the possibility of observing goal levels occurring
in the course of a relatively specific activity, designating some of the
factors associated with fluctuation of such goals and linking the experimentally observed manifestations of goal-striving to the individual's
behavior in other situations. The experimental results stemming from
her observations and those of Hoppe (1930), who performed the first
experiment directed toward analysis of the aspiration phenomena, have
mounted until at the present time there is a considerable body of data
bearing on the problems of that goal-striving behavior which occurs
within a range of difficulty, i.e., *level of aspiration.* Gradually also seem
to be emerging the common factors which establish the level of aspiration phenomena with reference to other fields and problems of psychology, notably to social standards and forces, conflict and decision,
personality characteristics, value phenomena, success and failure, developmental aspects of personality. This is, then, an appropriate time to
look backward at the trends of the last decade and forward to the future
directions in which research may profitably be directed. A review of the
relevant literature up to 1941 may be found in Frank (1941), and Rotter
(1942) has examined critically the material which seeks to evaluate the
methodological aspects of level of aspiration.

What Is the Level of Aspiration?

A Typical Sequence of Events.—In discussing the many problems
and aspects of the level of aspiration, it may be helpful to consider a
sequence of events which is typical for the situations concerned. A person has scored 6 in shooting at a target with ring 10 at the center. He

decides the next time to try for 8. He attains 5, is much disappointed, and decides to try the next time to reach 6 once more.

Within such a sequence we can distinguish the following main points (Figure 1):

1. The (last) past performance (in our example: "has scored 6").
2. The setting of the level of aspiration, e.g., deciding how high to set the goal for the next performance ("try for 8").
3. The execution of action, e.g., the new performance ("attains 5").
4. The reaction to the level of attainment, such as feeling of success or failure ("disappointment"), leaving the activity altogether, or continuing with the new level of aspiration ("try again for 6").

Each of these four points can be discussed in relation to one another. In case an individual begins a new activity, no past performance would appear within the sequence, although he might have had experience with similar activities.

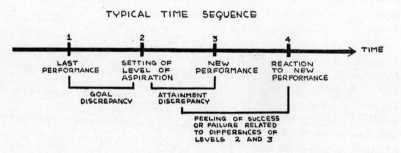

TYPICAL TIME SEQUENCE

Figure 1

Four main points are distinguished in a typical sequence of events in a level of aspiration situation: last performance, setting of level of aspiration for the next performance, new performance, and the psychological reaction to the new performance. The difference between the level of the last performance and the level of the new goal is called goal discrepancy; the difference between the goal level and that of the new performance is called attainment discrepancy. This difference is one of the bases of the reaction at the point 4.

Each point within the time sequence represents a situation that has characteristic problems. For the dynamics of the level of aspiration, point 2 (setting of the level of aspiration) and point 4 (reaction to achievement) are particularly significant. Two problems arise immediately, then, out of consideration of this sequence: (a) What determines a level of aspiration? (b) What are the reactions to achieving or not achieving the level of aspiration?

Description of Terms Involved in the Sequence.—Some of the terms and factors involved may well be identified before proceeding to discussion of the experimental data.

Action goal—ideal goal; inner discrepancy; confidence level. We have mentioned before that the level of aspiration presupposes a goal which has an inner structure. In our example the individual will not merely shoot, but tries to hit the target and even a certain area of the target. What he would really like to do is hit center. This is his "ideal goal." Knowing that this is "too difficult" for him, at least at the present, he sets his goal at 8 for the next action. This we will call his "action goal." It is the level of the action goal which is usually taken as the criterion for the level of aspiration for an individual at a given time. Frank, one of the early investigators in this field, defines the level of aspiration as "the level of future performance in a familiar task which an individual, knowing his level of past performance in that task, explicitly undertakes to reach" (1935a, p. 119).

Setting the action goal at point 2 of the time sequence (Figure 1) does not mean that the individual has given up his ideal goal. In order to understand this behavior, we must consider the action goal as within the whole goal structure of the individual. This may include quite a number of more or less realistic goal levels. Goal levels within one goal structure may include a high dream goal, a somewhat more realistic wish goal, the level which the person expects to reach when he tries to judge the situation objectively, and a low level he might hit if luck were against him. Somewhere on that scale will be what can be described as the action goal, e.g., what the person "tries for" at that time; somewhere his ideal goal will be located. Sometimes the individual comes closer to his ideal goal, sometimes the distance between the ideal goal and the action goal becomes wider. This is called "inner discrepancy."

Another characteristic of the goal structure is the discrepancy between the level of the action goal and the level of the expected performance. This difference might be characterized directly as the "goal-expectation discrepancy." This discrepancy will depend in part on the "subjective degree of probability" which the individual holds with reference to his chances of reaching his action goal. One expression of the subjective probability is the confidence level.

Past performance—goal; goal discrepancy. One can compare the level of aspiration, e.g., the level of the action goal at point 2 in our time sequence (Figure 1), with the level of the past performance (point 1 of our time sequence). The difference between the two levels has been called "discrepancy score." Since there are other discrepancies important for the level of aspiration, we will call this one "goal discrepancy." The goal discrepancy is said to be positive if the level of the goal lies above that of the past performance; otherwise, it is called a negative goal discrepancy.

Level of aspiration and attainment; attainment score; success, failure. The individual has set his level of aspiration and then has acted with this goal in mind (point 3 of the time sequence, Figure 1). The level of this performance can be called "attainment or performance score." The difference between the level of aspiration and the attainment score may be

called "attainment discrepancy." It is said to be positive if the attainment is higher than the level of aspiration. It is called negative if the
attainment falls short of the level of aspiration.

The direction and size of the attainment discrepancy are two of the
major factors for the feeling of success or failure. The term "success"
or "failure" will be used to indicate the psychological factor of feeling
success or failure and not as indicating the difference between the level of
aspiration and the achievement. Everyday language speaks of success
and failure in both meanings, sometimes referring to the difference between points 2 (level of aspiration) and 3 (new performance) of our
time sequence, sometimes referring to point 4. The difference between
points 2 and 3 is called "attainment discrepancy." The success and
failure indicate a reaction to this discrepancy (point 4 of the time
sequence).

Operational definitions: verbal goal and true goal. How the different
goal levels and performance levels can be measured or defined operationally is a technical question which frequently has to be answered differently in different experimental settings. To observe or measure the level
of performances (points 1 and 3 of the time sequence) is frequently not
difficult if one uses proper activities.

More difficult is a direct measurement of the level of aspiration or
other points of the psychological goal structure, such as the ideal goal
or the level of expectation. Once the laws of the level of aspiration are
known it will be possible to use a number of reactions for an indirect
determination. Today one of the best methods of determining the level
of aspiration, the ideal goal or the level of expectation is, as a rule, the
direct expression of the subject. Of course, there is the danger that the
verbal or written statement of the individual may actually not reveal his
"true" action goal, his "true" ideal goal, or "true" expectation. It would
not be a safe procedure to ask an individual after the performance,
e.g., at point 4 of our time sequence, what his level of aspiration had been
at point 2, because after failure his verbal expression might easily be a
rationalization. It is important to have the verbal expression given during that situation to which it refers. In case the social atmosphere is
sufficiently free, the direct expression of the individual is at present for
many settings the best approximation and, therefore, the best operational
definition of the various goal levels. For the action goal, the actual behavior of the individual in a choice among tasks on various levels of
difficulties can be used as a behavioral measure.

The problem of the determination of true and/or verbal level of
aspiration has proved a difficult one for many of the earlier investigators
in this field. Hoppe (1930) employed various lines of evidence in in-
ferring a given subject's momentary level. Since later investigators have
preferred to use more definite behavior for the inference of aspiration
level, the breadth of the operations studied has been to a certain extent
restricted in the interests of methodological precision. Gardner (1940b)
has clarified the theoretical situation resulting from the attempts to im-

prove on Hoppe's methods of measurement without making entirely specific the consequences of the methodological changes.

Size of goal units. An individual may throw a ring over a stake. He may or may not reach his goal. In another case his goal might be to throw a series of five rings over a stake. How good his achievement is (nothing missed, three missed) can be stated in this case only after all five rings are thrown. His reaction to this achievement with the feeling of success or failure will be related to the achievement as a whole rather than to each ring separately.

The size of the units of activity to which a goal refers is an important point to be considered in the discussion of the level of aspiration. The maximum size and the complication of units to which a goal might refer are important characteristics of certain maturity levels in children. To avoid misunderstandings one will always have to keep in mind the size and character of the activity unit to which the goal refers.

What Determines the Level of Aspiration?

Reference Scales.—Experimental work on the level of aspiration has brought out the variety of influences which are present for a single decision as to action goal. Some of these influences are probably rather stable and permanent in their effects; i.e., their value will be much the same for all individuals of a given culture in a variety of competitive situations. It has been found, for example, that nearly all individuals of western culture, when first exposed to a level of aspiration situation, give initially a level of aspiration which is above the previous performance score, and under most conditions tend to keep the goal discrepancy positive. The effects of cultural pressures toward improvement in performance, and the value which positive discrepancies have for many individuals in stimulating them to greater endeavor, have been brought out by a number of investigators in this field (e.g., Gould, 1939). Such influences may be conceived of as frames, involving a scale of values, within which the individual makes his decision as to a goal. The relative dominance or potency of each scale of reference is a function (a) of more temporary situational factors and (b) of general cultural factors. For either of these the momentary level of aspiration can be regarded as determined (a) by the individual's perception of his position on each reference scale which is relevant to his present situation, and (b) by the forces which act upon him in these positions. This point of view will be developed more extensively in the summary. Here will be considered the experimental data relevant to understanding the various phenomena.

Temporary Situational Factors.—

Success and Failure Within a Series.—The statement can be made that generally the level of aspiration will be raised and lowered respectively as the performance (attainment) reaches or does not reach the level of aspiration. In speaking of shifts in the level of aspiration which rigidly adhere to the above principle, Jucknat (1937) has introduced the term "typical" cases. The existence of "atypical" cases will be discussed later. This experimenter used two series of ten mazes in a range of difficulty, one series in which the mazes were solvable and one in which they were not. With thirty children as subjects, the following results were obtained: In the solvable series the level of aspiration rose from a beginning level of 5.6 to an end level of 7.5. Of the observed shifts in level of aspiration, 76% were upward and 24% downward. In the nonsolvable series the level of aspiration fell from a beginning level of 6.5 to an end level of 3.6. Of the observed shifts, 84% were downward and 16% upward. Thus, under one condition 76% and under the other 84% of the shifts were "typical" ones, and the general trend followed the "typical" pattern.

Festinger (1942a), analyzing data specifically for this purpose, obtained the following results. After attainment of the level of aspiration there were 51% raisings, 41% staying on the same level, and 8% lowerings of the level of aspiration. After nonattainment of the level of aspiration these figures are 7%, 29%, and 64%, respectively. There were 219 shifts after attainment and 156 shifts after nonattainment.

Jucknat has carried this type of analysis one step further with a rating of the *reaction* to the attainment or nonattainment, i.e., the strength of success or failure judged to be experienced by the subject. Table I gives these results.

TABLE I

FREQUENCY OF RAISING OR LOWERING OF THE LEVEL OF ASPIRATION AFTER DIFFERENT INTENSITIES OF SUCCESS AND FAILURE

	Shifts after Success				Shifts after Failure		
	S!!	S!	S	DS	F	F!	F!!
Number of cases	24	45	29	34	36	41	17
Percentage raising	96	80	55	56	22	19.5	12
Percentage lowering ...	4	20	45	44	78	80.5	88

(Taken from Tables 3a and 3b, Jucknat, 1937, p. 99)

S!! Very good success
S!   Good success
S   Just successful solution without evidence of distinct success
DS   Solution with considerable effort

F   Weak failure without evidence of serious feelings
F!   Strong failure
F!! Very strong failure

From this it appears that the stronger the success the greater will be the percentage of raising the level of aspiration, and the stronger the failure the greater the per cent of lowering the level of aspiration.

Thus we find that there is a high degree of agreement not only as to the direction which the shift in level of aspiration will take after success and failure, but even as to the percentage of such changes which will occur.

TRANSFER.—Jucknat (1937) continued her work by investigating the effects of success or failure in one task on the level of aspiration for a subsequent task. Using the same two series of pencil and paper mazes, on one of which the subjects always get success and the other on which they always get failure, she finds that the reactions to the series given first affect the level of aspiration behavior in the other series of tasks, the extent of the effect depending upon the extent to which the second series is regarded as a continuation of the first series. When the success series follows the failure series, the beginning level of aspiration for the second is lower than it was for the first series. When the failure series follows the success series, the reverse is true. If the success and failure series are made to look more different than previously, the effects are less marked although in the same direction as described above.

This indicates that less transfer of reactions to attainment of the level of aspiration occurs when the two series do not appear to constitute a single task. Thus the beginning level of aspiration for the second series is always put somewhere between the beginning and end levels of the first series. When the two series appear contiguous, the beginning level of the second series is nearer the end level, but when the two series appear different, the beginning level of aspiration for the second is nearer to the beginning level of aspiration of the first. The effect of one series on the other is then a partial one, the amount depending upon the similarity between the tasks.

Frank (1935b) finds that the level of aspiration on a "normal" task differs according to whether it followed an easy activity or a hard one. The average height of the beginning level of aspiration is higher when the normal task follows the easy activity than when it follows a hard one.

RANGE OF LEVEL OF ASPIRATION.—It is important to answer various further questions: within what absolute levels of difficulty will the person set his goal level; within what ranges of performance will feelings of success and failure be experienced; and when will the person cease setting up aspiration levels for a given task?

There are some indications. An adult usually does not set any level of aspiration in connection with buttoning his overcoat nor does he set one in connection with physically impossible accomplishments. When faced with a difficulty continuum, the individual will set up goals near the boundaries of his ability. Experimental verification of this may be found in Hoppe (1930). Using a task which was ordinarily performed in about 88 seconds by the subjects, Hoppe found it impossible to produce feelings of success by setting a goal of 120 seconds or more nor could he produce failure by imposing a goal of 60 seconds or less. Under these circumstances the individual set up his own goals. Success and failure were experienced only when the goals ranged from 65 to 110 seconds.[1]

---

[1] There are two cases out of 124 which did feel success when a goal of 150 seconds was imposed. The rest fall within the limits mentioned.

This tendency against setting up levels of aspiration in regions of activity which are either "too" easy or "too" difficult is also reflected on those occasions of stopping activity after a series of trials. Data on such cessation of activity is reported by Hoppe (1930) and Jucknat (1937). Hoppe (p. 20) reports that out of 42 cases of spontaneous stopping, ten stopped after a complete success "when raising the level of aspiration seems impossible either because the limits of personal ability have been reached or because the nature of the task or the instructions hinders such raising." Twenty-three cases stopped after complete failure "when the last possibility of getting a success is exhausted." Eight cases stopped after a single success following a series of failures when the previous failures had demonstrated the unlikeliness of a success with a higher level of aspiration. One case stopped after a single failure. Jucknat (p. 103) reports that of those subjects stopping after successes, 42% stopped on reaching the maximum possible achievement, 50% stopped after insufficient success, and 8% stopped before the maximum in spite of good successes.

From the above reported data it seems that in general there is a tendency to stop when the possibilities of achieving further success are not good. R. R. Sears (1942) found, furthermore, that subjects under failure conditions needed significantly more reminding than did subjects working under a success condition in order to have them state the level of aspiration. Here no stopping was permitted, but the failure subjects were able to a certain extent to withdraw themselves from the situation by not making the verbal statement of their goals.

General Cultural Factors.—

STANDARDS OF ONE'S OWN GROUP.—The level of aspiration situation may involve certain clearly defined reference scales, i.e., the individual's performance is judged on a reference scale of another individual or the group to which he belongs. Anderson and Brandt's (1939) experiment illustrates the effects of this procedure. Their subjects (fifth-grade children) were given a series of six cancellation tests spaced a half-week apart. The relative performance scores of the subjects were posted on a graph so that each subject could see how he stood in relation to the group but could not identify the position of any other child. Before each succeeding test the subjects were asked to write down privately the score they thought they could make on the succeeding trial. The graphs showing the relative standing were kept up to date throughout the experiment. Grouping the subjects according to performance quartiles gives clear-cut trends showing the effectiveness of the knowledge of group standing. For the upper quartile (those scoring highest in the group) the level of aspiration was, on the average, 5.8 points below the performance level. For the second quartile the level of aspiration was, on the average, 1.9 points above the performance level. For the third quartile the level of aspiration was 2.1 points above the performance level. For the fourth, or lowest, quartile the level of aspiration was 13.6 points above the performance level. In short, we find a consistent trend in which those subjects who find themselves above the average of the group tend to have a negative discrepancy score, those finding themselves close to the average of the group tend to have a slightly positive discrepancy score, while those finding themselves below the mean of the group tend to have a very large positive discrepancy score. The correlation between discrepancy score and position of performance with respect to the group mean, taking positive and negative discrepancies into account, was —.46, i.e., the lower the performance relative to that of the group, the larger the discrepancy. The same result was found for college students, working in small groups, by Hilgard, Sait, and Magaret (1940). Here public announcement of the performance scores was made, while the levels of aspiration were recorded privately. These workers also performed a second experiment (1940) in which the ranking of the subjects in the group was experimentally controlled by giving some of the subjects hard problems, others problems of medium difficulty, and others easy problems. These three groups form the low, medium, and high performance groups. In this experiment the effect of the position in the group on the level of aspiration is more marked than when the natural performance was allowed to have its effect. Whereas all three groups start off with approximately the same amount of positive discrepancy score, by the last four trials the group that had easy materials has a discrepancy score of —3.4; the group that had medium materials has a discrepancy score of +1.0; and the group that had the difficult problems has a discrepancy score of +4.2. These experiments give reason to assume the existence of a frame of reference in which the individual's performance is placed on the scale formed *by the performances of his group*. Gardner's (1939) technique of reporting performance scores in terms of prearranged percentile values has the effect, similarly, of placing the subject's score with reference to that of others, and his finding that the goal discrepancies were higher at the lower portions of the performance curve than vice versa is consistent with the other findings.

STANDARDS OF OTHER GROUPS.—The fact that the level of aspiration is subject to regular and consistent influence by the subject's knowledge of his own standing relative to that of his group suggests the possibility that knowledge of performances of other groups, identifiable as more or less prestigeful or superior than the subject's own, may have a similar effect. The scale of values defined by the "own group" may, in effect, be extended upward and downward with knowledge about other groups. Chapman and Volkman (1939) made the first attack on this problem. By giving groups of college students comparison scores of (a) literary critics, (b) students, (c) WPA workers, for a test of "literary ability," they were able to manipulate the level of aspiration in a clear-cut way. The comparison scores were actually all equal but this fact was not known to the subjects. The heights of the aspiration levels for the various groups followed this order, from lowest to highest: (a) comparison with experts (critics), (b) no comparison, (c) comparison with own group (students), (d) comparison with inferiors (WPA). The subjects giving these results had not taken the test and they were therefore ignorant of their own performance scores, although they knew the maximum possible score and the score obtainable by chance. Gould and Lewis (1940) and Festinger (1942a) followed this experiment with others which offer corroborative evidence for the influence of group standards of varying prestigefulness. The latter investigator used as the chief experimental measure the *change* in goal discrepancy score from a condition in which the subject had no scores but his own previous ones with which to compare his present performance, to an experimental condition in which his score was made to appear either above or below one of three groups: (a) high school, (b) college, and (c) graduate students. The subjects, themselves, were college students. The trends which the results show are illustrated in Figure 2, which gives the change in size

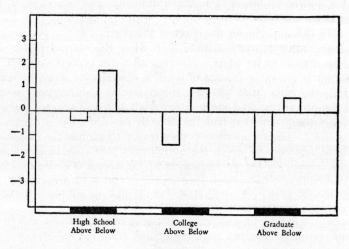

Figure 2

Changes in discrepancy score for college students compared to groups of low, medium, or high prestige.

and direction of goal discrepancy scores when the subjects believed that their performances were either inferior to (below) or superior to (above) those of one of the comparison groups. Here we have a reference scale with a gradient of positive valence related to the prestige of the comparison group. This scale of values is analogous to that reported in the previous section in which the individual was placed with reference to his own group, but in the present case the individual is placed with reference to other groups which are conceptualized in a definitely valuative way. This frame of reference will be identified as that embodying comparisons with *other groups* of varying prestige.

ASPIRATIONS OF GROUP.—The individual may orient himself with respect to others' aspirations as well as to their performances. Hertzman and Festinger (1940) have explored this problem. After the average discrepancy scores for the subjects in a first experimental session had been determined, the subjects were given a second experimental session a week later at which they were told the average score and average level of aspiration of a group of other people of their own scholastic standing. The scores attributed to the group were arranged so that the individual's performance was equal, on the average, to the performance of the group. The positive or negative sign of the group goal discrepancy, however, was reported as opposite to that of the subject. The results showed that the level of aspiration changed significantly from the first to the second session in the direction of conforming to the group, i.e., the changes observed in level of aspiration were changes in the direction of the group level of aspiration. Changes from the first to the second session were statistically significant. Interviews with the subjects indicated that the conscious effect of such conforming to the group was very slight, or even nonexistent. The subjects' main conscious set was toward the scores (performances) of the group rather than toward the levels of aspiration. This would make one tend to suspect that although such conforming to group atmospheres exists, its effect in most cases is weak as compared to the effect of the performance of the group. It is, however, a frame of reference which may exert considerable influence under some conditions.

PSYCHOLOGICAL EFFECTS OF SOCIO-ECONOMIC BACKGROUND.—A study by Gould (1941) gives evidence that goal discrepancies are related to various factors in the background of the subjects. Those individuals giving relatively low (negative or low positive) discrepancy scores, when compared to those giving predominantly high positive scores, are found to be also in a relatively more favorable social and economic position. Indices as: more college training and income of the subjects' fathers, extent to which the students are not required to work their way through school, birth of the parents in this country, and expectancy of larger salaries in the future are found on the side of those subjects showing lower discrepancy scores. This reference scale and the one to be discussed in the next section represent attitudes toward endeavor and aspiration which have been determined before the subject comes to the experiment. Their effects are apparently similar to those in which an external standard is set by the experimenter on the foundation of internalized attitudes and values.

HABITUAL SUCCESS AND FAILURE.—Jucknat (1937) has evidence of the effect of another background factor on level of aspiration. When her experimental group of 500 children is divided into those who have been consistently good, medium, or poor students in their school work, differences in the height of the first level of aspiration are found between the groups. Faced with mazes placed in an ascending order of difficulty from 1 to 10, the group of good students set an initial level of aspiration rather high in the scale, between 7 and 10. The medium students' average was in the middle ranges, between 5 and 6. The poor students tended to set the aspiration level either low or high, between 1 and 4 on the one hand or between 7 and 10 on the other.

P. S. Sears (1940) selected small groups of children who had had clearly different school experience over a period of time with respect to success and failure. Those of the past failure group showed a higher goal discrepancy on the average than those of the past success group. More pronounced, however, was the wide variability among subjects of the failure group, such that the range of discrepancies was from very high positive to negative scores. The variability among subjects of the success group was much less, with discrepancies almost entirely within the small positive range.

Reality Levels.—When a subject is asked to state his goal verbally he may interpret this question in many different ways and the stated goal will differ according to the particular interpretation made. Gould (1939) showed this to be the case when she asked her subjects the question "What will you do next time?" Some subjects took the question to mean what they thought they really would get. Others interpreted the question as meaning what they hoped to get and responded accordingly. Gould distinguished three general groups in regard to interpretation of the experimental question: (a) those who set their level of aspiration at a minimum which the individual undertakes to overreach; (b) those who set it at a maximum which represents a mark they hope to come close to (actually being prepared not to reach it); (c) those who set their stated level of aspiration at about the average of their performance.

Thus a variety of attitudes on the part of the subjects will influence the nature of the results obtained through statements of aspiration levels. The stated action goal may represent, as Gould says, an incentive in one case and in another a protection against possible failure. The desire to come as close as possible to the level of aspiration, or to "guess accurately," may be a factor in some cases. Frank (1936) used comparison questions for eliciting the level of aspiration and finds that subjects who were asked "What do you think you will do?" were more likely to adopt a goal of trying to come close to their "guesses" than subjects who were asked "What do you intend to do?"

Festinger (1942a) found that subjects who were asked "What score would you like to get next time?" had a significantly higher discrepancy score (2.19) than subjects who were asked "What score do you expect to get next time?" (—.10). The former group was also significantly more variable than the latter in its goal discrepancy score. This result is completely corroborated in a study by Irwin and Mintzer (1942). Different attitudes, such as those occasioned by the two questions used by Festinger, may be interpreted as possessing different degrees of reality. The subject who tells what he expects to get seems to be realistic and keeps his level of aspiration close to his performance. The subject who tells what he hopes or what he likes, seems to become wishful and unrealistic and raises his goal far above his performance level.

There is some evidence favoring this type of interpretation. Frank (1935c), reasoning that a play situation is less bound to reality than a serious situation, finds that the discrepancy scores for a task like quoit-throwing which has a playful character are greater than for tasks of more serious nature such as printing. Sears (1940) finds that the subjects with a low positive discrepancy score (realistic subjects) show more flexibility in the level of aspiration than those with a high positive discrepancy score (irrealistic subjects), i.e., they are more sensitive to changes in the performance. Corroborating this is the finding by Irwin and Mintzer (1942) that their "realistic" group showed a significantly greater number of changes of the level of aspiration than did the other group. Festinger (1942a) found that when compared to the performance of other groups, the unrealistic subjects behaved so as to avoid failure to a greater extent than did the realistic subjects by refusing to be influenced by an unpleasant external standard.

We may summarize these experimental findings as follows: The realistic attitude will produce a small discrepancy score with a level of aspiration that is flexible and responsive to changes in performance. The unrealistic attitude will produce a large discrepancy score with level of aspiration which is unresponsive to reality influence, and may reflect a wishful attitude toward the attainment of the action or stated goal.

In an attempt to control more adequately the attitude of the subject, Preston and Bayton (1941) asked their subjects to state three levels of aspiration; namely, the least they expected to do, the most they hoped to do, and what they actually thought they would do. Their results show that while the least estimates are unrelated to either of the other two estimates, there is a high correlation between the actual and the maximum estimates. In addition, the actual estimates are always closer to the maximum than to the least estimates. This suggests that even a statement involving a supposedly objective ("actual") estimate will, in the absence of external factors designed to control the subjects' attitudes, tend in the upward rather than the downward direction. The actual as well as the maximum estimate thus appears to be more influenced by wishful considerations than does the least estimate. The latter may be regarded by the subject as a performance which he *might* (but hopes he will not) sink to if conditions are especially adverse.

Individual Differences

Previous sections have shown that numerous factors tend to influence the level of aspiration in certain rather consistent ways. Application of the principles resulting from the previous discussion to the prediction of a specific individual's behavior involves an additional problem, viz., to what extent are the experimentally observed behavior patterns samples of behavior which may occur in more than one goal-striving situation? This is the problem of generality of the behavior pattern, whether the generality be that involved in setting levels of aspiration for two motor tasks or that involved in estimating one's score on a golf game and on an important examination. The generality is measured by the correlation of the behavior in two different situations. Whether the operations measured in these situations are the subject's own verbal statements involving explicit goals or are nonverbal behaviors interpreted by another person, the relations obtained are representative of the extent to which the same reference scales and other dynamic factors are involved in both. Viewed in this way, the problem of generality is one of determining within what limits the same factors will be found playing a significant role in different situations.

Closely allied to the study of generality by correlation of specific aspiration level scores, is the analysis of the relation between experimentally obtained scores and other personality variables. Not all of these variables are conceptually relevant to goal-setting, but because most of them have been first observed clinically in the goal-setting situation, the majority are closely related to that aspect of behavior. Both generality and the establishment of relationships with other variables involve comparison of individuals in two or more situations.

A third problem is that of the variability of behavior within a single situation. Instead of asking whether one individual maintains, in different situations and on various measures, the same relative position with respect to other members of the group, we may inquire as to the extent of difference between individuals on a single measure under specified conditions. For example, one might ask whether there is greater variability in a highly structured situation than in one in which various individual interpretations are possible, and if so, what the conditions are for structuralization of goal situations. This problem has so far received little attention in the literature, but there is evidence that, in a gross way, the heterogeneity of behavior is important for understanding the behavior in such situations. Once the factors determining the individual's behavior in one experimental situation have been established, the analysis may be continued, as described above, in terms of the generality of his position on various tasks and operations which may be significant for generalizing about his behavior.

The literature in this field falls naturally into several groups. First, the most experimental work has been directed toward ascertaining the extent of generality of the *goal discrepancy score* in various tasks, and this will be first discussed. Second, many workers have felt the inadequacy of thus depending on a single measure culled from the wealth of material which the level of aspiration situation yields, and have attempted to utilize measures other than the goal discrepancy. Two types of study have appeared so far: (a) those of the statistical generality of the secondary measures, and (b) those attempting an analysis of the "course of events" or patterning of the level of aspiration behavior. Third, the relationship of aspiration responses to factors beyond the confines of the experimental level of aspiration situation has been investigated. Although this problem is commonly referred to as that of correlated "personality traits," it is, as has been shown, that of more broadly conceived generality of goal behavior combined with exploration of relations to other, possibly independent, variables. Fourth, there is the examination of variability within a group of persons put under various experimental conditions.

Generality of the Goal Discrepancy Score.—Hoppe (1930) was aware of the broad problem of generality and devoted some time to demonstrating the consistency of the behavior of different individuals. The first specific study of generality of the discrepancy was performed by Frank (1935a). Correlating the discrepancy scores for two different sessions on the same task he finds correlations ranging from .57 to .75 for two of his tasks. For the third task the correlations are .26 and .63. From these data he concludes that the level of aspiration behavior is consistent and explains the low correlation for the third task (quoits) by the fact that it was more of a play (irreal) situation, and therefore the individual's reactions to it are less bound by realistic factors which tend to stabilize the behavior in the other situation. Correlations within the same session of the discrepancy scores between his first two tasks, printing and spatial relations, also yield fairly large coefficients, ranging from .50 to .65. Correlations involving the quoits were mostly either zero or slightly positive. Gould (1939), using six different tasks, three given in one session and three in another, finds intercorrelations among the tasks on the discrepancy score ranging from .44 to .04 with a median intercorrelation of .29. When the correlations were calculated separately for those tasks given in the same session and for those given in different sessions, the median intercorrelation for the discrepancy score on tasks given in the same session goes up to .46 while the median intercorrelation for discrepancy score on tasks given in different sessions stays at .30. Gould's correlations, although lower than those obtained by Frank, still indicate some tendency toward consistency. The fact that the correlations were higher for tasks in the same session leads Gould to make the interpretation that the individuals respond more to the situation than to the task itself.

The difference between the results of Gould and Frank is perhaps due to the greater diversity of tasks used by Gould and the lesser amount of control over the subjects' attitudes in the Gould experiment.[2] Gardner (1939), more adequately controlling the latter factor, obtains gen-

---

[2] The two tasks for which Frank obtained relatively high correlations were rather similar in nature, and it will be remembered, for the quoits, which were quite different from his other tasks, the correlations were lower. In addition, the question used by Gould, "What will you do next time?" probably allows more fluctuation of attitude than the question of "What do you intend to do?" used by Frank. Gardner asked the subject where he "expected to stand" in relation to a group of students.

erality correlations close to Frank's. Gardner's technique involves arranging the situation so that all subjects have the same scores. The series of scores present in one place a rising curve of performance (successful experience), in another place a falling curve (failure experience), with occasional reversals in order. Four tasks were used and generality correlation coefficients were calculated for the discrepancy scores at different places along the performance curve. The mean correlation for the beginning level of aspiration was .37. A mean correlation of .37 was also obtained for the average of three consecutive discrepancy scores in that part of the curve where the performance remained on the same level. In the middle portion of the curve the performance rapidly increases for three trials and then after a single reversal increases for another two trials. The mean correlation coefficient for the average of the discrepancy scores for the five increasing performances was .55. After this rising portion, the performance curve slowly but regularly falls for five performances. The mean intercorrelation for the average discrepancy scores of these five trials was .61. The intercorrelations of the average discrepancy scores over the whole series of performances with the exception of the first two and last two trials yields a mean of .57.

Conflicting results on the question of generality are to a large extent reconciled in the results obtained by Heathers (1942). With the idea that the amount of generality observed will depend to a large extent on the similarities of the different situations, Heathers varied three factors of the objective situation to determine their influence on the degree of generality: the scale or units in which the performance scores were presented to the subject, the shape of the curve which the series of performance scores followed, and the motivation of the subjects. Prearranged performance scores were used and the subject was asked to tell what score he was "going to try to make on the next trial," or what his goal was.

When the scale of units in which the scores were reported to the subjects and the shape of the performance curve are both the same in two tasks, the correlation of the discrepancy scores for these tasks is .87. When the curves are the same but the scale in which the scores are reported is different for the two tasks, this correlation drops to .67. The difference between these two correlations is statistically significant, indicating that the difference in scale is enough of a difference in similarity between the two situations to reduce significantly the degree of generality. No significant differences were found between correlations for the group having both scale and curve constant and the group for which the scale was constant but the curve was varied. Generality in both instances is very high, with correlations ranging from .74 to .86. There is evidence that variation in shape of curve will produce differences in generality if, as the author concludes, "the contours of the curve are different enough to provide the subject with different interpretations concerning the amount and rate of his improvement" (p. 403). In the present case the average amount of increase for all the curves was about the same from beginning to end, and therefore the total success and failure experience is presumably roughly equivalent. Reliable differences in generality are obtained when the curves are split so that amounts of improvement, with consequent changes in amount of success stimulation, are varied. These results indicate how important it is to distinguish in detail the specific success and failure conditions for any measure of generality.

When both the shape of the curve and the scale are varied, the results are significantly different from the case where they were both held constant. For the latter group the correlations range from .93 to .79 while for the former group they vary from .35 to .74.

In another group of subjects the motivation to perform well on the tasks was varied by making the task an intelligence test and offering prizes for good performances for one group. The generality correlation coefficient for the group that was highly motivated to do well was .93 for the two tasks in the first experimental session. The comparable correlation for the group which was not highly motivated to do well was .84. This difference is significant statistically. Significant differences do not appear, however, in the correlations obtained from a second session at which it appeared that the high level of motivation arranged for the experimental group had considerably declined.

It is interesting to note that the average intercorrelation for tasks during the same experimental session is .81 while the average intercorrelation for tasks in different experimental sessions is .62. This latter value of .62 agrees rather well with the average intercorrelation of .57 reported by Gardner (1940). The relatively greater constancy of the subjects' attitudes and moods within the same experimental session undoubtedly makes for a greater similarity between tasks on the same day as compared with tasks on different days.

One can also look at the question of generality by investigating the extent to which experience of success or failure in one situation will affect the level of aspiration in another situation. This might be called a "transfer effect." Jucknat's and Frank's findings on this problem have been reported already. The transfer effect of success and failure is greatest when the subject finds the two tasks to be similar or two parts of one larger activity.

Generality of Other Measures Related to the Level of Aspiration. —Rotter (1942b), calculating test-retest generality after a period of one month, found the following correlations on a motor performance task in a situation where the subject was rewarded for correct estimates and penalized for incorrect. For the number of times the subject reached or exceeded his estimate, the coefficient is .46; for the shifts up and down, respectively, following such "success" or "failure" to reach the estimate, .56; frequency of shifts, .70. All the coefficients are statistically significant and indicate a certain stability of measures of aspiration behavior other than discrepancy.

Patterning of discrepancy scores and other measures related to level of aspiration has been observed by many investigators and rough attempts at formulation of such patterns are described by Sears (1940), working with school children, and Rotter (unpublished) for adults.

In the case of neither investigation is it found that patterns are rigidly marked off from one another; rather, these combinations of factors are described as rough approximations of constellations which may prove to have psychological significance.

Both workers find that there is a pattern represented by (a) the "low positive discrepancy score," utilized in a realistic way with adequate adjustment to both success and failure. Responsiveness of the level of aspiration up or down following changes of similar direction in performance score is rather high; flexibility (shifts) of the level of aspiration is average, (b) the "low negative discrepancy score" pattern is chiefly characterized by a protectively low action goal, which is ordinarily kept below the level of performance. Slightly less responsiveness and flexibility are found to be associated with this kind of response than with the preceding.

Sears gives data on two more patterns, the "high positive discrepancy" pattern, with very low flexibility and responsiveness, and the "mixed" pattern in which responses are irregular and highly variable throughout the successive trials of one task. Rotter distinguishes seven more types of pattern: the "medium high positive discrepancy" associated with responsiveness to success and failure and a realistic attitude; the pattern of "achievement following" in which the level of aspiration is constantly changed to conform as exactly as possible to the level of the previous performance; the "step" pattern, characterized by shifts in an upward direction only; the "very high positive" pattern, with responses largely of a phantasy nature; the "high negative" pattern; the "rigid" pattern, showing an absence of shifts regardless of achievement, and the "confused" or "breakdown" pattern.

Hilgard and Sait (1941) asked subjects to estimate their past as well as their future performance, and thus obtained two discrepancies in addition to the usual goal discrepancy: (a) estimate of past performance minus (true) past performance, and (b) estimate of future performance minus (true) future performance. The third difference used was the familiar goal discrepancy. Odd-even reliabilities for all three discrepancies are satisfactory, and generality coefficients between two motor tasks fairly high. The authors conclude that subjective distortion enters into estimates made of both past and future performance, i.e., goal strivings are not only oriented toward the future, but also influence an individual's perception of his past. These influences are not consistent in direction for different individuals, but do show considerable generality, i.e., for the same individual, the direction of the distortion appears rather consistent from task to task.

Preston and Bayton (1941) further vary the standard technique in asking subjects (a) what they actually expect to get, (b) the least they would be likely to get, and (c) the most they would hope to get. Generality of these estimates from task to task is rather high. In a second paper (1942), correlations between the various estimates are presented. Those between the least and the actual estimates and between least and maximum are all negligible, while correlations between the actual and the maximum estimates are appreciable (range from .45 to .84).

Personality Characteristics. All workers in this field are agreed that the level of aspiration situation is a favorable milieu in which to observe individual traits relating to the competitive and goal behavior of the subject. So far, however, objective demonstration of relationships has proceeded but slowly.

The problem basic for personality characteristics as determinants of the level of aspiration behavior is the evaluation of relative weights which different reference scales have for a given individual. For example, social standards may play a relatively greater role for one subject than for another in the same objective situation; failure may be more decisive than success and a wishful attitude may be more characteristic of a given subject in a certain situation than is a more realistic attitude.

Hoppe (1930), Jucknat (1937), and Frank (1935c) describe types of personality traits which are deduced from the level of aspiration situation and which are regarded as influential in determining the behavior in that situation, e.g., ambition, prudence, courage to face reality. Independent measures of the personality factors were not obtained by these investigators.

Gould and Kaplan (1940) and Gardner (1940) have made correlational studies relating certain broad personality variables to goal discrepancy scores. The former investigators found only insignificant relationships between discrepancy scores and scores (a) for dominance-feeling (Maslow inventory) and (b) extraversion-introversion (Guilford). Gardner obtained ratings for his subjects on a number of broad traits culled from the observations of Hoppe, Jucknat, and Frank. These also show low correlations with discrepancy scores, although in each case the findings were in the same direction as the hypotheses of the previous investigators would suggest.

Frank (1938) reports correlations obtained in connection with Murray's personality studies. Size of goal discrepancy is positively correlated (.20 or higher) with personality variables involving, according to Frank's analysis, the following factors: "(1) the wish to do well (often unaccompanied by the will to do well), (2) a subjective attitude, and (3) the ability to dismiss failures." Evidently some slight relationships make their appearance through such correlational techniques, but the evidence is far too slim to provide a solid basis for future thinking in this area. The variables so far investigated are probably too broad and generalized to be usefully isolated as correlatives or determinants of specific level of aspiration scores such as the goal discrepancy.

More fruitful than correlational studies has been analysis of factors associated with "high," "medium," and "low," or "negative" discrepancy scores. Results showing differences in security of socio-economic and academic status between groups of subjects which show chiefly one of these types of scores have been discussed in a previous section. Gardner's "high" and "low" discrepancy groups give results which are confirmatory though based on small numbers of subjects and statistically not highly significant. In his experiment, the ten subjects having the highest average (positive) discrepancy scores were also rated highest on (a) *dissatisfaction with status* and (b) *importance attached to intellectual achievement*. The ten subjects having the lowest discrepancy scores were rated lowest on (a) *subjective achievement level,* (b) *general sense of security,* (c) *tendency to face failure frankly,* (d) *realism,* and (e) *motivation,* and were rated highest on *fear of failure.* These ratings were made outside of the experimental situation by raters who were thoroughly acquainted with the subjects.

Sears (1941) has made clinical studies of selected small groups of children who were highly motivated for good school work and had been either (a) highly successful or (b) unsuccessful at obtaining good school status over a period of several years. When these subjects were divided according to size of discrepancy scores for experimental school type tasks, certain related factors emerged as also differentiating these groups. Children using predominantly a "high" discrepancy pattern are poorer in school achievement than the other groups and are rated as showing an attitude of low self-confidence accompanied by rather free admission of their incompetence. Here is an example of a specific relationship between goal setting for success and self-confidence. The correlation holds between behavior in the experimental level of aspiration (for school tasks) area and the aspirations (also for school tasks) observed in the schoolroom and clinical situations. Those children showing characteristically the "low positive" discrepancy ("realistic") reaction are, on the other hand, rated as highly confident, successful and comfortable in their achievement. Behavior problems and unfavorable personality traits (rated by the teacher) appear less frequently in them than in the other groups. A third group, called in this study the "negative discrepancy" group, is equivalent to Gould's and Gardner's "low" groups. These children fall in between the other two in confidence and academic success, but are differentiated from both others in terms of high ratings for self-consciousness, socially- rather than self-oriented motivation, defensiveness and self-protection in their attitudes toward failure. It is of some interest with respect to generality of aspiration that when in this study the subjects rated themselves on a paper and pencil questionnaire with reference to a number of diverse life activities, their averages for the ratings "how good I am at" and "how good I wish I were at" followed the course to be predicted on the basis of the aspiration level classification if the "how good I am at" rating is conceived as analogous to a performance score and the "how good I wish I were at" rating analogous to a level of aspiration score. The high postive discrepancy group showed the

greatest difference between perceived and wished-for skills, the low positive group the next difference, and the negative discrepancy group the
least difference.

Similar findings are reported by Rotter (unpublished) who has amplified and elaborated the discrepancy patterns as previously described.
Three patterns of response, the low positive, low (slightly) negative,
and medium high discrepancy score patterns are designated arbitrarily
as "socially acceptable" methods of solution for the self-evaluation problem presented in the level of aspiration situation.[3] Six other patterns,
including the very high positive and high negative discrepancies, step,
rigid, confused, and achievement-following patterns, are designated as
"socially unacceptable." Prison inmates were classified, in terms of past
history and present behavior in situations involving self-evaluation, into
(a) a "normal" group, in which goals had in actual behavior been held
fairly close to the experiences of achievement, (b) a "defeated" group,
whose behavior was characterized by lack of confidence, strong fear of
failure, and protection against failure by setting very low explicit goals,
(c) a "conflict-tension" group characterized by inability to reach a
decision in problem situations. The "normal" group of prisoners showed
in the level of aspiration situation a preponderance of the "socially acceptable" patterns over the "unacceptable," while acceptable and unacceptable were approximately evenly balanced in the "defeated" and "conflict-tension" groups. Of the other subjects employed, college cripples
as compared to college normals had a relatively high percentage in the
protective high negative discrepancy score pattern. College students
showed higher percentages of "achievement-following" and "step patterns" than did the hospital employees, but were not up to them or to
the "normal" prison group in terms of percentage of acceptable patterns
used.

Yacorzynski (1942) has studied the relation between degree of effort
expended on a task and the direction of the aspiration level. An inverse
relation appears between these two variables; i.e., an increasing degree
of effort is associated with a decreasing number of predictions that the
scores will improve. *Confidence* in one's own ability, he feels, may increase predictions of improved scores on successive trials and also
decrease the amount of effort shown.

Variability Within a Group.—A given attitude permits according
to its nature greater or smaller individual differences. Thus as we have
seen before, the realistic attitude binding the subject to his performance
will not permit so much deviation from this point as appears in the wide
range of irreality or wishful thinking. The distribution of individual
scores according to these attitudes can be measured by the variability of
the group.

Festinger (1942) finds that a group forced to a realistic attitude is

---

[3] In this case a premium was put on exact estimation of performance by spe-
cially designed instructions similar to those of Hausmann (1933).

less variable than one for which the instructions permitted various degrees of realism. McGehee (1940) devised an experiment in which the future of performance was estimated by an observer while the person performing set a level of aspiration. The levels of aspiration were regularly more variable than the estimates of the other person, though in this case the differences do not reach complete reliability.

Sears (1940) found reliable differences in spread of scores (group variability) between groups whose past school experience of the task had been either successful or unsuccessful. The success subjects showed on the average lower discrepancies than did the failure subjects and appeared more realistically oriented to their levels of aspiration, but the most marked differences between groups were those of the variability of the scores. The failure group showed a spread of discrepancies varying from negative to high positive, while the success group scores were concentrated within the low positive range. Further, those subjects of the failure group who utilize the high positive discrepancy maintain their discrepancies rigidly, without the responsiveness to performance and attention to the performance scores which seem to be related to a realistic attitude.

Another kind of variability is that shown by the individual subject in the generality of his behavior on different tasks. Gould (1939) finds a correlation of .33 between variability of this kind and height of discrepancy. That is, there is a tendency for those having low or negative discrepancies to respond more to the situation as a whole than to the specific task, while those with high discrepancy scores on some tasks tend to vary more in their responses from task to task.

The Development of the Level of Aspiration

The age level at which a level of aspiration can be said to exist depends upon a number of considerations. Observational evidence suggests the existence of a "rudimentary" level of aspiration in very young children. Repeated efforts toward a difficult accomplishment are observed in the very young child, e.g., in his attempts to walk independently, to pull off an article of clothing, or to sit down upon a chair. However, before these behaviors can be regarded as precursors of the level of aspiration phenomena previously discussed, it is necessary to postulate the development of the child's thought processes to a level which permits cognition, comparison, and choice of psychological values in general and specifically of that value continuum or scale called "overcoming of difficulties."

Steps preceding the Fully Developed Level of Aspiration.— Fales (1937) considered the child's wanting to do something by himself rather than with someone's help as a stage preceding the full development of the level of aspiration. This type of behavior may be called "rudimentary aspiration." The level of aspiration differs from "rudimentary aspiration" by being the stage at which achievement *levels* can be distinguished.

The strivings for "independence" as a rule occur only in a situation where moderate difficulties exist. Thus the child tries to become independent in his marginal areas of ability.

Fales studied two- and three-year-old children in a nursery school performing the activity of putting on and taking off wraps. The percentage of refusal of help was taken as a measure of "rudimentary aspiration." This was found to exist already at the two-year-old level.

Fales next trained one group of children in taking off their wraps and compared this group before and after training with a group which was not trained. The comparison observations were made in putting on the wraps. The group which received the training, that is, the group which became more skilful and more secure in its performance, increased considerably in percents of refusal of help as compared with the group which did not receive training.

In another experiment Fales praised one group of children for their endeavors. They were compared with a group which was not praised. The praised group increased in "independence" considerably more than the control group and even exceeded the trained group mentioned above. It may be concluded that training the child to become more skilful and rewarding the independent behavior by praise promotes "rudimentary aspiration."

Anderson (1940) used a ring-throwing task with three groups of children averaging about three years, five and a half years, and eight years of age, respectively. This investigator distinguishes four aspects of behavior, each of which shows different developmental steps. They are: (1) *Manner of throwing*, i.e., the child can get the rings on by actually placing them, by dropping them, or by throwing the rings from a distance. The developmental steps follow this order. (2) *Rethrowing of rings*. Rings which were missed may or may not be rethrown by the child. The latter indicates a higher developmental stage. When rings are rethrown they may be rethrown immediately or after a whole series has been thrown. The latter is again a higher developmental step. (3) *Size of unit*. Of those subjects who threw the rings, some regarded each ring as a unit while others regarded the series of five rings as a unit. The latter is considered a higher developmental step. (4) *Amount of failure*. The willingness of the subject to risk missing rings was also taken as an indication of a higher development of level of aspiration behavior.

Taking the above described factors into consideration, Anderson attempted to determine the "maturity" of the level of aspiration. The highest possible maturity score is 9. The mean maturity scores for the oldest, middle, and youngest groups are 8.54, 6.34, and 2.13, respectively. The differences among all these groups are statistically significant. The maturity scores for the groups on each of the separate factors making up the total score follow the same pattern. Thus we find the maturity of the level of aspiration, in terms of adult standards, increased with age.

Anderson's experiments show that in his experimental set-up all components of the level of aspiration observed in adults in a similar situation can be found in the eight-year-olds. Jucknat's (1937) findings are consistent with these results. She finds no differences in the level of aspiration behavior in regard to beginning and end levels in a group of children between the ages of 11 and 12 and a group of adults. The tasks she used were solvable and unsolvable mazes.

There are conditions under which the level of aspiraton behavior of the child can appear less mature than it actually is under optimal conditions. Such a condition exists when the "means to a goal" character of the task is emphasized. Anderson reduced the emphasis on performance *per se* by giving a reward for getting many rings on the stick. The mean maturity scores for the oldest, middle, and youngest groups were reduced to 7.34, 5.03, and 1.03, respectively. The differences between the reward and nonreward situations are significant for each group, the maturity score being uniformly lower in the reward situation.

A regression to a lower developmental level with respect to the maturity of the level of aspiration probably could be produced in children in a frustration situation. This can be expected because frustration experiments in adults (Dembo) showed that subjects, performing the ring-throwing task, would start to rethrow rings and, instead of throwing them from the distance, place them on the stick when severely frustrated.

For further research it would be important to investigate the development in respect to different reference scales (see pp. 337 to 353, and pp. 368 to 371) of the level of aspiration.

Summary and Theoretical Considerations

The studies of the level of aspiration have grown from empirical findings and have been influenced by various considerations. Some studies have tried to determine the factors which influence the raising and lowering of the level of aspiration and to understand the conditions of success and failure; others concern themselves with the question of the degree to which personality traits play a role. A theoretical survey and summary may help to clarify a situation which is at present a bit chaotic, and to give orientation to further experimentation. No attempt will be made in this summary to take in all the results. Essentially we will follow the "resultant valence theory" which has been presented by Escalona (1940) and elaborated by Festinger (1942b). Gould and Lewin (unpublished manuscript) have brought this theory into a wider setting by linking it to various "frames of reference."

Level of Aspiration as a Choice Situation; Valences and Probability.—A basic problem of the level of aspiration can be formulated as an apparent discrepancy between the tendency to set up higher and higher goals (that is, a willingness to enter difficult undertakings) and the customary notion that life is governed by the tendency to avoid unnecessary effort (parsimony). Have we to assume an innate tendency to "strive for higher things" to explain the fact that the individual prefers the difficult task or prefers doing certain activities himself rather than using the easy way of being helped by someone else (page 355)?

According to Escalona this problem can be solved if one considers the psychological situation as it exists at the time when the individual makes up his mind about the next goal; that is, the point 2 of our sequence (page 334).

The psychological situation at that moment can be characterized as a choice situation (Figure 3). The person has to decide whether he will choose a more difficult, an equally difficult, or an easier level; for

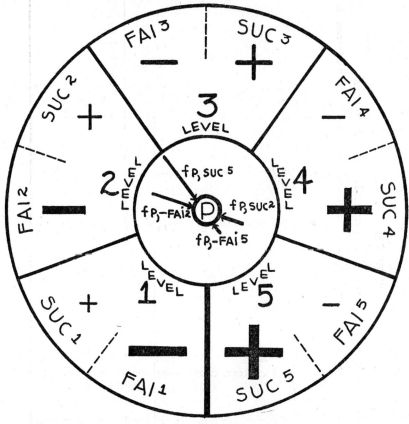

Figure 3

The difference in the attractiveness of the various difficulty levels 1 to 5 of the activity is determined by the valence of future success (SUC) and failure (FAI) at that level. The valence of success increases, that of failure decreases with increasing difficulty level. Correspondingly the force toward success, for instance, f_{P,Suc^5} is greater than the force f_{P,Suc^2} on level 2. The force away from failure $f_{P,-Fai^5}$ is smaller than $f_{P,-Fai^2}$. Therefore, the total valence of the more difficult level is higher than the easier level.

TABLE II

EXAMPLES OF REFERENCE SCALES UNDERLYING A LEVEL OF ASPIRATION

TABLE IIa

1	2 Valences of	3 Valences of	4 Subjective Probability	5 Subjective Probability	6 Weighted Valence of	7 Weighted Valence of	8 Resultant Weighted Valence	Resultant Weighted valence when group standard has potency = .3
Levels of Possible Objective	Fut. Suc.	Fut. Fai.	Succeeding	Failing	Fut. Suc.	Fut. Fai.		
15	10	0	0	100	0	0	0	0
14	10	0	0	100	0	0	0	0
13	10	0	0	100	0	0	0	0
12	10	0	0	100	0	0	0	0
11	10	0	5	95	50	0	50	47
10	9	0	10	90	90	0	90	*63* Level of aspiration
9	7	−1	25	75	175	−75	100	−35
8	6	−2	40	60	240	−120	*120* Level of aspiration *g ds = 1*	−24 *g ds = 3*
7	5	−3	50	50	250	−150	100	−50
6	3	−5	60	40	180	−200	−20	−98
5	2	−7	75	25	150	−175	−25	−93
4	1	−9	90	10	90	−90	0	−30
3	0	−10	95	5	0	−50	−50	−50
2	0	−10	100	0	0	0	0	0
1	0	−10	100	0	0	0	0	0

Too difficult → levels 15–12

Too Easy → levels 2–1

Level of past performance and of expectation (column 8, levels 6–1)

NOTES ON TABLE II

Column 1 indicates the possible objectives. The "too difficult" and "too easy" levels correspond to the areas where the subjective probability of failing (column 5) and of succeeding (column 4) are 100% or close to 100%. Columns 2 and 3 give valences of future success and failure on each level; they vary between 0 and 10. Columns 6 and 7 represent the weighted valences, e.g., valence times probability, according to formulae (5a) and (5b). Column 8 gives the resultant valence according to formula (6) (see p. 364).

In this schematic example the level of past performance is assumed to have been on the level 7. The individual expects his next performance to lie on the same level, perhaps because he has found it difficult to reach that level. This "level of expectation" corresponds to the 50–50 level of subjective probability. The level of aspiration according to formula (6) is determined by the maximum value of the resultant weighted valence, that is, in our example the value of 120 corresponding to difficulty level 8. The goal discrepancy score ($g\,ds$), that is, the level of aspiration minus the level of past performance, equals 1.

NOTES ON TABLE IIa

Table IIa represents the resultant weighted valence in a case where the valences of future success and failure are based on two reference scales: the one is the scale related to group standards as expressed in columns 2 and 3 of Table V; the other scale of reference might have the same distribution of values as that in columns 2 and 3 of Table II. This distribution of values might be an expression, for instance, of the valences based on one's own past performance.

The relative weight or "potency" of these two frames of references might be 3 (group standard) to 7. In such cases the valence of future success or failure would be determined by the sum of the corresponding values on the two frames of reference multiplied by that fraction which represents the relative potency of that scale. For instance, the valence of future success on the level 7 would be $5 \times .7 + 2 \times .3$; that of future failure would be $-3 \times .7 - 10 \times .3$. These values would have to be weighted by the subjective probability of success and failure as usual.

Our example shows that the poor student in our case would set his level of aspiration less high if he is not exclusively influenced by the reference scale of the group standard: the goal discrepancy equals 3 instead of 4 as in Table V.

instance, whether he will try to finish the job on hand in 10 minutes, or only in 12 or 15 minutes. (Actually, he could also "stop" entirely, which means a change to a different activity. We will consider this aspect of the choice later.)

One can state analytically for this as for any other choice situation that that action is chosen as a goal for which the sum of attractiveness (position valence) minus the sum of disagreeableness (negative valence) is a maximum. To determine this maximum one should know the factors which bring about the positive or negative valences of these different actions. We will discuss some of these factors in a step-by-step order, going from the general to the specific.

The choice in the case of the level of aspiration involves the relative valences of variations in the *same* activity; in dealing with a choice between different tasks, e.g., target shooting, multiplying two-place numbers, and solving puzzles, a great many factors enter into the valences or attractiveness. Prediction is more difficult in this case since wide individual differences result. In level of aspiration situations analysis of the choice is somewhat simplified by the fact that the general character of the activity is constant. The choice is determined by the different valences which different degrees of difficulties within the same activity have for the person.

The individual faces the possibility of succeeding or failing and the positive or negative valence of such a future success or failure on the various levels is one of the basic elements for the decision. To determine the valence (Va) of each level (n) of activity $[Va(A^n)]$ we have to consider the negative valence that future failure has on that level $[Va(Fai_A{}^n)]$ and the positive valence of success on that level $[Va(Suc_A{}^n)]$.

$$(1) \qquad Va(A^n) = Va(Suc_A{}^n) + Va(Fai_A{}^n).\text{[4]}$$

The valences of future success and failure on various levels may be illustrated by the example of doing twenty simple additions in a given time. To the adult subject, achievement on a very easy level, such as finishing the twenty simple additions in one hour, would not bring any appreciable feeling of success. This is "child's play." The valence of success on this level 1 (Table II, columns 2 and 3) is approximately zero. The valence of success on levels of greater difficulty, such as finishing these additions in 50 minutes, 40 minutes, and so on, continues to be zero until the tasks cease to be altogether "too easy." Then the valence of achievement starts to be perceptibly positive although at first very small. In our example (Table II) we assume that at the difficulty level 4, the valence of success will equal 1.

With increased difficulty the valence of success also increases. Finally, we reach the level of difficulty that taxes the person's ability to capacity.

---

[4] As the valence of failure is usually negative (neg Va) and the valence of success is usually positive (pos Va) formula (1) means that usually the former is subtracted from the latter: $Va(A^n) = \text{pos } Va(Suc_A{}^n) - \text{neg } Va (Fai_A{}^n)$.

There the valence is likely to be at a maximum (arbitrarily indicated by 10). Still more difficult levels beyond the boundary zone of ability will probably have the same high positive valence.

Higher on the scale there are degrees of difficulty which seem "entirely out of reach of the individual," for instance, solving the twenty additions in 20 seconds (level 14), and levels above this which are "humanly impossible," for instance, finishing the task in 5 seconds. Such levels are usually not even considered and one might leave these values blank on the scales. The greater the degree of difficulty, therefore, the higher the valence of success, within the boundary zone of ability.

The absolute value of the negative valence of failure usually changes in the opposite direction. On levels of extreme difficulty the negative valence of failure would be negligible. Even on the level of very difficult performance, failure might have no negative valence. The negative valence increases until it reaches a maximum in the area of relatively easy tasks. There it remains close to a maximum and finally drops out of consideration somewhere in the area of "too easy" tasks.

Within the crucial range of difficulty we can say that:

$$(2) \qquad\qquad \text{pos } Va(Suc_A{}^{high}) > \text{pos } Va(Suc_A{}^{low})$$

$$(3) \qquad\qquad \text{neg } Va(Fai_A{}^{high}) < \text{neg } Va(Fai_A{}^{low})$$

The total valence of the level according to formula (1) is the algebraic sum of these valences. As the positive valence of success increases with difficulty and the negative valence of failure decreases we can conclude, from formulae (2) and (3), that the total valence on the high level should always be greater than the total valence on the lower level because

$$(4) \quad Va(A^{high}) = Va(Suc_A{}^{high}) + Va(Fai_A{}^{high}) > Va(Suc_A{}^{low}) + Va(Fai_A{}^{low}) = Va(A^{low})$$

The analytical considerations lead therefore to the conclusion that, given the valence of success and failure which is predominant in our culture, there is nothing paradoxical in the fact that people reach out for difficult tasks. We rather have now to explain why it is not always the most difficult task which is chosen.

Probability of Future Success; the Basic Theoretical Assumption.—The answer is that we have to deal here with a *future* success and failure. The individual is, therefore, not only influenced by the attractiveness of such an event but also by the probability of its occurrence as this is seen by him (Figure 4).

Columns 4 and 5 (Tables II and III) give values for subjective probability of succeeding or failing. The probability of success increases from zero to 100% with decreasing difficulty and the probability of failure changes in the opposite direction.

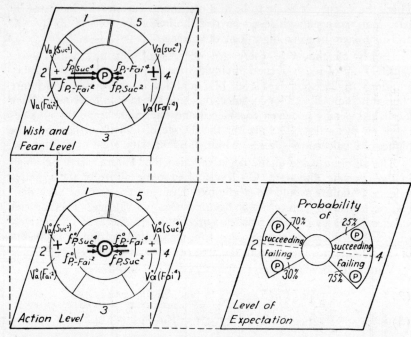

Figure 4

Figure 3 takes into account the valences of success and failure but not the probability of the succeeding or failing at the various degrees of difficulty. Such a situation corresponds psychologically to a constellation which may exist on the "wish and fear level." The constellation of forces on the "action level" depends, in addition, on the individual's perception of the future, that is, the structure of the "level of expectation." Notice the difference in the direction of the resultant forces on the wish and on the action level.

1, 2, . . . , 5 tasks of increasing degrees of difficulty;
$Va(Suc^2)$ valence of success in task 2⎫
$Va(Fai^2)$ valence of failure in task 2⎬ on wish and fear level.
$V^oa(Suc^2)$ weighted valence of success in task 2⎫
$V^oa(Fai^2)$ weighted valence of failure in task 2⎬ on action level.
f_{P,Suc^2} force toward success in task 2.
$f_{P,-Fai^2}$ force away from failure in task 2.
f^o_{P,Suc^2} weighted force toward success in task 2.

Escalona sets forth the "resultant valence theory" according to which the choice is determined, not by the valence of future success or failure as such, but rather by these valences modified by the probability of the occurrence of these events. The most simple assumption is that this "weighted" valence of success $[^oVa(Suc_{a^n})]$ is the product of the valence and of the probability of success.

(5a) $^oVa(Suc_{a^n}) = Va(Suc_{a^n}) \cdot \text{Prob.}(Suc_{a^n})$

The corresponding formula for failure is:

(5b) $^oVa(Fai_{a^n}) = Va(Fai_{a^n}) \cdot \text{Prob.}(Fai_{a^n})$

NOTES ON TABLE III

Table III shows the same level of past performance and the same distribution of valences of success and failure as Table II. However, the 50–50 level of subjective probability, corresponding to the expectation for the next performance, lies one level higher. As a result, the maximum resultant weighted valence is raised so that the goal discrepancy score ($g\,ds$) is now 3.

The level of new performance is 8. The attainment discrepancy ($att\,ds$) is, therefore, −2 and would usually lead to the feeling of failure. In our case the individual consoles himself by setting up a "post-factum" goal line on the level of his past performance, in this way creating a "satisfactory" post-factum attainment score of +1.

TABLE III

EXAMPLE OF REFERENCE SCALES UNDERLYING A LEVEL OF ASPIRATION

1	2	3	4	5	6	7	8
Possible Objective	Valences of		Subjective Probability		Weighted Valence of		Resultant Weighted Valence
	Fut. Suc.	Fut. Fai.	Succeeding	Failing	Fut. Suc.	Fut. Fai.	
15	10	0	0	100	0	0	0
14	10	0	0	100	0	0	0
13	10	0	0	100	0	0	0
12	10	0	5	95	50	0	50
11	10	0	10	90	100	0	100
10	9	0	25	75	225	0	225
9	7	− 1	40	60	280	− 60	220
8	6	− 2	50	50	300	−100	200
7	5	− 3	60	40	300	−120	150
6	3	− 5	75	25	300	−125	175
5	2	− 7	90	10	180	− 70	110
4	1	− 9	95	5	95	− 45	50
3	0	−10	100	0	0	0	0
2	0	−10	100	0	0	0	0
1	0	−10	100	0	0	0	0

Level of Aspiration

$att\,ds = -2$

Level of New Performance

$g\,ds = 3$

Level of Past Performance

← "Post-Factum Goal Line"

Columns 6 and 7 in Tables II and III give the values of the weighted valences of future success and failure. The sum of these valences will be called "resultant weighted valence" [$°Va(A^n)$].

(6)   Level of aspiration $= n$ if $°Va(A^n) =$ maximum

Column 8 gives the values for these "resultant weighted valences." In Table II the maximum of the resultant weighted valence lies on level 8 of the scale of possible objectives. It means that under the given conditions the individual will choose the objective 8 as his goal. We can represent that by indicating a "goal line" across the diagram. The curve of resultant weighted valence shows a decrease from the level of maximum toward both the levels of greater and of smaller difficulties.

Mathematically the 50–50 level of probability of failure and success is indentical with the "most probable achievement." That level of achievement which is subjectively the most probable is usually meant when one speaks of one's expectation. In other words, the level of expectation is identical with the subjective 50–50 probability of failure and success.

Table III shows the same distribution of valences of success and failure, but in this example we assume that the individual expects to show a better performance next time. This rise of his expectation from level 7 to level 8 raises the position of the maximum resultant valence from level 8 to level 10.

In case of realistic judgment the individual will place his expectation somewhere within the boundary zone of his ability. Given a distribution of valences like that in Table II or III, the goal line will tend to lie relatively close to the subjective 50–50 level of probability. It can be concluded, therefore, that the level of aspiration should tend to lie close to the boundary zone of ability of the person at that time. Indeed, the experiments show that, on the whole, the probability scale has sufficient weight to keep the level of aspiration close to that zone. A young child will not generally try to lift a weight as heavy as his father can, although he might try to reach the level of aspiration of his older sibling. The factors which tend to move the goal line outside the boundary zone of ability will be discussed presently.

The theory thus far explains several groups of experimentally established facts:

(a) The tendency to seek a relatively high level of aspiration.
(b) The tendency of the level of aspiration to go up only to certain limits.
(c) The tendency of the level of aspiration to stay out of an area too difficult and too easy.

It is probably safe to assume that the subjective *probability* of success is, for the same person, more or less inverse to the probability of failure, that is, probability of success plus the probability of failure equals 100.

TABLE IV

Example of Reference Scales Underlying a Level of Aspiration

1	2	3	4	5	6	7	8
Possible Objective	Valences of Fut. Suc.	Fut. Fai.	Subjective Probability Succeeding	Failing	Weighted Valence of Fut. Suc.	Fut. Fai.	Resultant Weighted Valence
15	10	0	0	100	0	0	0
14	10	0	0	100	0	0	0
13	10	0	0	100	0	0	0
12	10	0	0	100	0	0	0
11	10	0	5	95	50	0	50
10	9	0	10	90	90	0	90
9	7	-2	25	75	175	-150	25
8	6	-4	40	60	240	-240	0
7	5	-6	50	50	250	-300	-50
6	3	-10	60	40	180	-400	-220
5	2	-14	75	25	150	-350	-200
4	1	-18	90	10	90	-180	-90
3	0	-20	95	5	0	-100	-100
2	0	-20	100	0	0	0	0
1	0	-20	100	0	0	0	0

$g\ ds = 3$

NOTES ON TABLE IV

The values on the scale of valence of future success and on the scales of subjective probability are the same as in Table II. The negative valences on the failure scale are doubled, expressing the great weight which failure has for the individual. It is obvious that, as a rule, the greater negative values on column 3 would tend to lower the position of the resultant weighted valence. In our example the greater fear for failure actually raises the level of the resultant valence in an atypical way from the level 8 to the level 10. Such atypical cases where fear of failure leads to a high level of aspiration and a high goal discrepancy score (equals 3) are frequently observed. They are one of the reasons why a group of individuals who fail show a great scattering of discrepancy scores.

However, it would be incorrect to assume that the *valence* of success and the valence of failure are always inverse. Great differences exist among people in regard to the degree to which they are ruled by the tendency to avoid failure or by the tendency to seek success. Some people appear very much afraid of failure and to them the possibility of failure is uppermost in their minds. These people would show high negative valences on column 3 (see Table IV). In general this lowers the level on which the maximum weighted valence lies. That this derivation is well in line with the experimental findings relative to the effect of fear of failure on the discrepancy score (page 352) will become clearer if we consider in more detail the factors which determine the distribution of values on the scales of valences and on the scales of subjective probability.

We are now going to discuss factors underlying the distribution of values in columns 2, 3, 4, and 5, Tables II to IV.

Scales of Reference.—

Factors Determining the Values on the Scale of Probability.—*Past Experience.* A main factor which determines the subjective probability of future success and failure is the past experience of the individual in regard to his ability to reach certain objectives.

In case an individual has had *much experience* in this particular activity, he will know pretty well what level he can expect to reach or not to reach. That means that his 50–50 level of probability of succeeding or failing will be well defined and the gradient of values on the probability scale will be steep; the steepness will be the greater the less the performance of the individual in this particular task fluctuates. Thus, the experiments about transfer (page 339) shows that success or failure in one area influence the level of aspiration in a second area less if the person is well at home in the second area than if this area is new to him.

At the other extreme are cases where the subjective probability is practically undetermined. Here the observations are also in line with the theory. In fields of activity which a person *tries* for the first time in his life and where he is unable to judge his probable performance, the individual frequently does not spontaneously set himself a definite level of aspiration. Instead he goes into the action without definite goal level; in popular terms he merely "tries it out."

It is not only the average past performance which determines the subjective probability. If, for instance, the *sequence* of achievements follows an order such that the later trial is better than the previous one, the individual will feel that he "is steadily improving." He is then likely to expect that he has not yet reached the end of the learning process and will place the 50–50 level of probability higher than his last achievement. This will tend to lead to a rise in the level of aspiration (Table III).

One would expect that the *last* success and failure will have a particularly great influence on the subject's expectation of the future achievement level because of the greater psychological weight of the more recent experience. The fact that all the experiments find that much of lowering and raising is dependent upon the quality of the last performance proves in general the correctness of this statement.

However, it would be erroneous to treat the effect of past experiences only as a result of their recency. A given sequence of achievements will set up certain *"subjective* hypotheses" which the subject uses to predict his achievement. In the case of a nonachievement which is linked, for instance, to outside disturbances, the subject is not likely to lower his level of aspiration in the way he would if he believed that the nonachievement represented a genuine decrement in his performance ability. Each trial may be regarded by the subject as an additional datum to be added to what he already knows about the activity and may change his ideas about probability of achievement. Therefore, if the previous performance has been accompanied by feelings of success, the level of aspiration should tend to rise in most cases (page 338) ; if the previous performance has by its less good quality engendered failure reactions, the level of aspiration should tend to go down (page 338). It is well in line with this derivation that after "barely reached successes" as well as after "weak failures" the level of aspiration tends to remain unchanged (page 338).

In studying individual differences we have become more and more aware that individual constancies (for instance, in regard to the discrepancy score) are much less if the sequence pattern is not kept constant (page 348). Future investigations will do well to be still more careful on this point.

Goal Structure of Activity. Aside from past experience, certain cognitive settings influence the expectation of future success and failure. If, for instance, the series of levels to be chosen from has a definite upper and lower limit (page 340), the probability of reaching what is in that setting "top performance" may appear less probable. The tendency to make higher and higher records in some sports seems to be related to a goal structure which appears to have no upper limit. The effect of using large or small numbers (page 348) when the experimenter indicates success or failure seems to be based on similar factors.

Wish, Fear, and Expectation. The judgment of the probability of success or failure on a given level is not only determined by past experience and "realistic" considerations, but also by wishes and fears, i.e., by the valence of future success and failure. This is proved by the fact, for instance, that knowledge of group standards influences our level of expectation (page 341). In other words, the various parts of the life space are an interdependent field: the realistic expectancy is based mainly on past experiences. The structure of the psychological past affects the structure of the psychological future. However, the expectancy or reality level of the psychological future is also affected by the wish and fear (irreality) level of the psychological future.

SCALES OF REFERENCE UNDERLYING THE VALENCES OF FUTURE SUCCESS AND FAILURE.—The numerical values for the valences along the scale of future success or failure follow the general observation that the valence of success, within limits, is an increasing function of the difficulty of the objective, and the valence of failure a decreasing function of difficulty. This is usually correct in our culture, but only as a first approximation. It is the result of a composite picture, some of the constituents of which we will discuss briefly.

Group Standards. Individuals belonging to a certain group are usually deeply affected by the "standards" of this group. In matters of level of aspiration, such a standard means that a frame of reference exists on which the standard level is particularly significant.

In some cases, for instance, in case of the ideology underlying the college term "Gentleman *C*," the group standard is equivalent to the maximum valence on the scale of success: to be either above or below this standard is considered less desirable than the standard (Table V). The fashion, particularly in democratic countries, frequently follows a similar pattern of an optimum rather than a maximum of elegance as the most desirable level.

In other cases, the group standard merely indicates a level at which the valence gradient is particularly steep: there is little success valence and much negative valence of failure immediately below the group standard, and much success and little failure valence directly above group standard.

For Table V, which is an example of the first type, the resultant valences are figured for an individual who has his achievement score (50–50 probability) definitely below the group standard, for one whose achievement lies at the group level, and for one individual above that level. One can see that, independent of the level of probable achievement, the maximum resultant valence (and therefore the goal line) should lie close to the group standard. The experimental results (page 342) show that this is true. They also show, as one would expect, that these phenomena are the more striking the greater the relative weight of such a frame of reference. (Compare Table V and Table IIa.)

In extreme cases of regard for such standards the most able person should tend to keep his level of aspiration low and may even show a negative discrepancy score; the least able person should keep up a high level of aspiration even at the price of a great positive discrepancy score. It is obvious that such a constellation might lead to a level of aspiration well above or below the "boundary zone of ability." This is illustrated by experimental data previously cited (page 340).

Standards set from outside do not need to come from a definitely structured group, such as the school class or an age group. Frequently they are related to another individual, for instance, the father, the friends, the wife, or they are based on certain requirements of law or society. As a rule, there are, coexisting, quite a number of such scales of reference which include certain standards.

TABLE V

EXAMPLE OF THE EFFECT OF A GROUP STANDARD. COMPARISON OF AN INDIVIDUAL WITH LOW, MEDIUM, AND HIGH PERFORMANCE LEVEL

Possible Objective	Valence		Subj. prob. of success for a person with			Resultant weighted valence for a person with		
	Suc.	Fai.	low perf.	medium perf.	high perf.	low perf.	medium perf.	high perf.
15	6	0	0	0	10	0	0	60
14	6	0	0	0	25	0	0	150
13	6	0	0	5	40	0	30	240
12	6	0	0	10	*50* Last	0	60	300
11	8	0	5	25	60	*40*	200	400
10	9	−1	10	40	75	0	*300*	650
9	10	−8	25	*50*	90 Last	−350	100	820
8	6	−10	40	60	95	−360	−40	520
7	2	−10	*50*	75	100 Last	−400	−100	200
6	0	−10	60	90	100	−400	−100	0
5	0	−10	75	95	100	−250	−50	0
4	0	−10	90	100	100	−100	0	0
3	0	−10	95	100	100	−50	0	0
2	0	−10	100	100	100	0	0	0
1	0	−10	100	100	100	0	0	0

Group Standard (objectives 11, 10, 9)

performance (low) — performance (medium) — performance (high)

$g \, ds = 4$ $g \, ds = 1$ $g \, ds = -3$

NOTES ON TABLE V

In this example the group standard lies on the position of the maximum valence of success and on a steep gradient of the valence scale of failure. Columns 3, 4, and 5 indicate the subjective probability of success for three individuals whose performance is below the group standard, on the group standard and above the group standards, for instance, a poor, medium, and good student in a class. To condense the table we are not presenting the scale of probable failure which is the converse of that of success. It is assumed in our example that our three individuals are rather realistic and that their level of expectation, that is, the 50–50 level of probable success, lies on the level of their past performance.

If the group standards were the only scale deter-mining the valence of success and failure the level of aspiration of all three individuals would lie on or above the group standard; this would mean that the poor student would have a high positive goal discrepancy score ($g\,ds = 4$); the best students, a negative discrepancy score ($g\,ds = -3$). In our example the level of aspiration of the poor students would be even higher than that of the good one.

This example illustrates why the level of aspiration might be kept above or below one's own ability.

As a rule, of course, the scale related to the group standards is only one of several reference scales underlying the valence of future success and failure. Table IIa gives the result of a combination with another reference scale.

Past Achievements; the Space of Free Movement.—Certain standards may result from the fact that the individual "competes with himself." In this case his "past achievements" not only determine the probability of future achievements; they also provide certain standards for future goals (Table IIa).

One factor which seems to be important for the striving toward the more difficult is the desire to reach beyond the area which has been accessible until then to the person. The totality of accessible areas of activities is called "space of free movement." A person's space of free movement is limited partly by the rules of society and the power of other persons, partly by his own ability or what is called the nature of things. The growth of the space of free movement is a fundamental factor of development, and the reaching out for the yet unreached is a powerful desire of the child and of many adults in many fields of activity. One can view the tendency to raise the level of aspiration as due partly to these desires.

In summing up we might state: a multitude of coexistent frames of reference may underlie the probability scale and the scale of valences of future success and failure. They can technically be recombined to these main scales if one attributes to each of the underlying frame of reference scales (uRS) the relative weight or potency with which it influences the individual; for instance, we would have three reference scales indicated by uRS^1, uRS^2, and uRS^3, underlying the valence of success. If uRS^1 were twice as influential as a motive for this individual as the reference scales uRS^2 and uRS^3, the value of the valence of success and failure on a given level would be calculated by referring to the corresponding levels on the underlying reference scale according to the formula $uRS^1 \times .5 - uRS^2 \times .25 - uRS^3 \times .25$. Table IIa presents an example. *Differences of "culture" as well as differences of "personality" might then be represented as a number of frames of reference and a pattern of relative weight.*

The Discrepancy Score and the Relative Potency of the Various Frames of Reference.—The recent studies of the level of aspiration have expressed their results frequently in terms of goal discrepancy score, that is, of the difference between level of aspiration and past achievement (page 335). Although the discrepancy score in itself is an important aspect of the problems of the level of aspiration, most workers in the field agree that it has been somewhat overstressed. It is recognized that the discrepancy score is a resultant of many factors and that it is important to find out what are the particular factors behind a certain discrepancy score in a given case.

Discrepancy Score, Level of Expectation, and the Discrepancy between Expectation and Past Performance. If a person were entirely realistic, his expectation would on the average coincide roughly with his future performance. That means that the discrepancy score between past performance and expectation should be the same as the difference between his past and his new performance. As a rule, it would be zero or slightly positive.

Actually our "expectation" is not entirely independent of our wishes and fears. However, this dependency is less close than that between these wishes and fears and the level of aspiration. From this follows that the discrepancy between the level of expectation and past performance should be less than the discrepancy between level of aspiration and past performance (discrepancy score). Experiments (page 344) show the correctness of this conclusion.

They also show that the variability of the discrepancy is less in regard to expectation than in regard to the level of aspiration. This follows theoretically from the fact that the variability of the level of aspiration depends not only on the variability of the values on the probability scale but in addition on the variability of values on the valence scales.

The Effect of the Structure of the Reference Scales and of their Relative Potency. The example of discrepancy scores in Tables II to V may suffice to show that the size and direction of the discrepancy score depend upon the level of the last achievement, upon the distribution of values along each of the reference scales, and upon the relative potency of each reference scale. It is, therefore, impossible to predict a discrepancy score accurately without knowing these data for the particular case. It is, however, possible to make certain general statements about the effect on the discrepancy score of a change in the relative potency of various reference scales, if the numerical values along these scales are kept constant and if we refer to situations where the learning improvement is not important.

Realism.—Realism in matters of the level of aspiration refers to one or both of two factors: (1) it refers to the probability scale and means closeness of expectation and "reality"; that is, closeness of the 50–50 level of "subjective" and of the "objective" probability. Such a correctness of judgment about one's own future action may be measured by the discrepancy between expectation and new performance. (2) Realism refers to a tendency to keep the maximum resultant weighted valence close to the 50–50 level of subjective probability. This implies that the individual chooses a distribution of values on the valence scales in such a way that this closeness of expectation and action goal results. We have previously spoken about the fact that the subjective probability scale is not entirely independent of the valence scale. Realism implies that, inversely, the distribution of the valence scale is not entirely independent of the probability scale.

It follows from this consideration that the absolute size of the goal discrepancy score would be the smaller the more realistic the person is. This is borne out by a number of findings:

(a) Realism is obviously greater in case the subject is asked what he "expects" than what he would "like to get." Indeed, the discrepancy score is smaller in the first case (page 344).

(b) The "realistic" attitude is greater in work than in play situations or activities. Correspondingly, the discrepancy score is smaller in the former (page 345).

(c) Realism should be greater for "realistic" than for "irrealistic" persons. The experiments bear out the derivations (page 352).

(d) Success, if not given in too strong doses, should make for a less tense emotional situation than failure, particularly in cases of repeated failure. Emotionality makes for an irrealistic attitude. We should expect, therefore, the absolute size of the discrepancy score to be greater in case of a chronic failure situation than in continued success. This derivation is again borne out by several experiments (page 352).

The Values on the Success Valence Scale Relative to the Values on the Failure Valence Scale.—The discrepancy score should be the more positive the higher the values on the success scales are, relative to the absolute values of the failure scale on the same level, provided that the gradient on each scale is not changed. This is borne out by a number of findings.

THE READINESS TO TAKE RISKS.—Lowering the values of the failure scale means psychologically being less afraid of failure. This would tend to move the resultant valence and therefore the goal line up relative to the achievement, resulting in high positive discrepancy scores. In other words, the relative weight of the success and failure scale determines what is usually called the readiness of the individual "to take risks" or to be cautious.

The findings about individual differences are in line with this conclusion (page 351).

BEING INSIDE OR OUTSIDE THE FAILURE REGION.—The tendency to avoid future failure, or the force on the person away from failure

$(f_{P,-Fai})$ is a function of the present position of the person, particularly whether he sees himself at present in the region of "being successful" or "failing." It seems that the force $f_{P,-Fai}$ is usually greater and, therefore, the values on the failure scale higher if the person is at present in the region of failing (Fai) than if he is in a region of not failing $(NFai)$. This holds at least as long as the person does not "accept" being a failure. Accepting failure frequently creates a "don't care" attitude which is equivalent to the diminishing of the valence of failure. Usually, however, it holds:

$$(7) \qquad\qquad f_{Fai,-Fai} > f_{NFai,-Fai}$$

From this assumption we can derive a number of conclusions which are all borne out by experiments.

1. A recent failure should tend to lower the level of aspiration. This is one of the major findings in the field. The "atypical" cases of raising the level of aspiration after failure (occurring in from 10% to 20% of

the cases) would follow from a decrease in the realism of the situation or from acceptance of "being a failure."

2. The level of aspiration should decrease more after strong failure than after a weak failure. It should, of course, increase after success (page 338).

3. Due to the cumulative effects of the above mentioned factors the person who fails habitually should have a lower discrepancy score than the person who usually succeeds. Atypical cases of high positive discrepancy score after habitual failure would again be understandable as a result of the factors mentioned in paragraph 1 (page 344).

4. There should be a tendency to avoid finishing a series of trials with a failure since this means letting oneself remain relatively permanently in the area of failure (page 340).

THE VARIABILITY OF DISCREPANCY SCORE AND THE EASE OF CHANGING THE LEVEL OF ASPIRATION.—The ease with which the level of aspiration can be changed, that is, the width of change by a small additional force, depends on the flatness of the curve of the resultant weighted valence near its maximum. Obviously, the same factor would determine the variability of the discrepancy score.

The gradient toward the more easy task in Table III, column 8, for instance, is less steep than in Table II, column 8. The steepness of the resultant valence curve depends on the steepness of the gradient on the various reference scales, their relative position to each other, and their potency.

For instance, if group standards play a great role and if the distribution of values along that scale shows as steep a gradient as in columns 2 and 3, Table V, a lowering of the potency of that scale and an increase of the potency of other reference scales (which have the distribution, for instance, of columns 2 and 3, Table II), would flatten out the curve of the resultant valences and make the individual more ready to change. Table IIa is an example of such a combination resulting in a small gradient on the resultant valence curve.

In cases where the probable achievement is quite precisely known and where the individual is realistic the gradient should be relatively steep.

Reaction to Achieving or Not Achieving the Level of Aspiration.—After the person has set his level of aspiration and then acted, he reacts to his achieving or not achieving his goals (point 4 in Figure 1). The main types of reactions are the following:

FEELING OF SUCCESS AND FAILURE.—The experiments show that the feeling of success and failure does not depend on an absolute level of achievement. What for one person means success means failure for another person, and even for the same person the same achievement will lead sometimes to the feeling of failure and sometimes to the feeling of success.

What counts is the level of achievement relative to certain standards, in particular to the level of aspiration (goal line) : if the achievement lies on or above the goal line, the subject will probably have a feeling of success; if it lies below the goal line he will probably feel failure, depending on the size of this difference and the ease with which the achievement has been reached.

RATIONALIZATION, AVOIDANCE OF FEELING OF FAILURE.—The forces $f_{P,suc}$ and $f_{P,-Fai}$, that is, tendencies to seek success and avoid failure are one of the bases for the level of aspiration. They also influence strongly the events at the point 4 of our sequence. The tendency to stay out of the failure region can lead to what is called rationalization.

There are two ways in which an individual after failing to achieve his level of aspiration still may avoid the feeling of failure.

1. He might change his goal line *post factum*, for instance, after a person has tried for level 10 (Table III) but reached only 8 he might then say, "Well, that is still better than any previous achievement" (or better than the average of previous achievement, or better than another person). In other words, he might switch his standard in a way which amounts to a sufficient lowering of his goal line afterwards (see notes on Table III).

2. Severing the relation between achievement and the individual himself as a "responsible" person is another means of avoiding failure. Only if the result of the action is "attributed" to the person as actor and not attributed to other persons or to "nature" can we speak psychologically of an "achievement" of this person. There is a tendency after failure to link the poor result to a faulty instrument, to sickness, or to any event "outside the power" of the individual involved (see Gould and Hoppe). The fact that such severing of the link between the result and the individual is more frequent after poor than after good achievement shows that it can be due to the force of avoiding failure.

CONTINUING THE ACTIVITY WITH A NEW TRIAL OR STOPPING.—As a result of his achievement, the individual might decide to attempt a new trial in the same activity or to stop.

Whether a person will continue or stop depends on a great number of factors, such as, the hope of doing better, his being on the whole successful or unsuccessful, his involvement in the particular activity, the alternative he would have in regard to other activities, and so on. Finally, however, the stopping or not stopping depends upon whether the force $f_{P,A}$ is smaller or greater than zero (where A means the activity on hand).

(8)	Stopping occurs if $f_{P,A} < 0$

In case no outside pressure is exerted on the individual to continue, the individual will stop if the maximum value on the resultant valence curve is still negative, or more correctly if this value is smaller than the valences of an alternative activity. In line with this theory, Escalona

(1940) found that patients in a mental hospital who disliked going back to the ward were less ready to stop than those who wanted mainly to be left alone.

One factor which tends to lower the values of the resultant weighted valence curves is a general decrease of the probability of success. This explains why and when after a series of failures the person will stop.

The values for the person with low, medium, and high performance in Table V are an example of how the decrease in the probability of success leads to a higher negative resultant valence. Whereas for the successful person all values on the scale of resultant valences are positive, indicating an attractiveness of the activity as a whole, most of the values for the unsuccessful person are strongly negative. This indicates a negative valence for the task as a whole and the individual should stop if the only remaining positive value on the level 11 should disappear.

In case of pressure, the individual will continue as long as the force away from the activity $f_{P, -A}$ is smaller than the pressure exerted.

In case the individual chooses to continue with the same activity, his level of aspiration will be determined by the factors we have discussed.

General Conclusion

These theoretical considerations show that most of the qualitative and quantitative results related to the level of aspiration can be linked with three factors, namely, the seeking of success ($f_{P, Suc}$), the avoiding of failure ($f_{P, -Fai}$), and the cognitive factor of a probability judgment. These forces operate in a setting which has to be characterized as a choice for a future objective. The strength of these forces and the values corresponding to the subjective probability depend on many aspects of the life space of the individual at that time, particularly on the way he sees his past experience and on the scales of reference which are characteristic for his culture and his personality.

On the whole, the study of the level of aspiration has reached a point where the nature of the problems and their relations to other fields is sufficiently clear to be useful as a guide for future research. Within the field of "goal behavior" one can distinguish problems of "goal striving" and problems of "goal setting." Goal striving is a "directed" behavior toward existing goals and is closely related to problems of locomotion toward a goal, of frustration, reaching a goal and consummatory behavior. Goal setting is related to the question of what goal will emerge or become dominant after another goal has been reached or not reached. Within this field lie, for instance, the problems of psychological satiation and a major part of the problems of level of aspiration. The latter, however, are closely interwoven with all aspects of goal behavior.

Future research can, it appears, be conducted along two general lines.

1. One can try to understand more fully the general laws of the level of aspiration. The analysis is far enough along at present to encourage an attempt to determine quantitatively the values on the various scales

Chapter 11

AN OUTLINE OF FRUSTRATION THEORY

By Saul Rosenzweig, Ph.D.

FRUSTRATION THEORY IS AN ATTEMPT to give concrete expression to the organismic point of view in psychobiology. It also provides a reformulation of psychoanalytic concepts in keeping with experimental possibilities. The theory is a natural outcome of work in experimental psychoanalysis (Rosenzweig, 1938c, 1938d; Maslow, 1941; Barker, 1941; see also Chapter 9 by Sears).

Levels of Psychobiological Defense

While the unity-of-the-organism has now for many years been cherished by both psychologists and biologists, little beyond the purely declarative attitude seems to have been achieved. One impediment is apparently the danger of adopting concepts which, while bridging the gaps among the various aspects of the organism, at the same time suggest the bugbear of analogy. Impartially considered, however, analogy in some guise is intrinsic to the organismic standpoint since that standpoint assumes similar principles to be involved throughout the activity of the living individual. If anything is to be doubted, it would rather seem to the artificial segmentation of the individual into various parts which then makes necessary a reunion of them by some *tour de force*.

One possible way of giving concreteness to the unity-of-the-organism is to consider the various levels of vital defense. Conceived schematically these are threefold. There is in the first place a *cellular* or *immunological* level primarily concerned in the protection of the body against infectious disease. Skin, phagocytes and antibodies here come into play. A second level may be called the *autonomic* or *emergency*, in keeping with Cannon's conception, and concerns the defense of the total organism against gross bodily injuries. Such reactions are psychologically heralded by pain, fear and rage; physiologically they are mediated by an increase in free adrenin and related alterations of function. Finally, representing a still higher organic integration, is the *cortical* or *ego-defense* level which guards the inviolacy of the personality from psychological insults. This level will be considered in detail below. What is to be noted at this point is that in the mere possibility of formulating these three levels of

379

defense the unity of the organism is already implied and that in the interrelationships of them, particularly as demonstrated in recent psychosomatic medicine, may lie the solution to many baffling problems.[1]

As an illustration of such problems, that of anxiety may be mentioned. In the present setting pain may be regarded as peculiar to the first and second of the defense levels, fear to the second and third, and anxiety mainly to the third. For a salient feature of anxiety is its anticipatory character and by this token it is recognized as representing a probably cortical function. Pain registers injury already inflicted; fear recognizes present danger, while anxiety anticipates the possibility of harm. The series, pain-fear-anxiety, thus parallels the levels of defense.

This arrangement of defense levels not only reflects the unity of the organism but also provides a new orientation to the theory of disease. That is to say, frustration theory in its broadest form would include not only phenomena on the ego-defense level but would also embrace the autonomic and the cellular levels of defense. It may therefore be seen that frustration theory, however limited in other respects, is broad in scope as regards abnormalities of adjustment. Frustration theory falls naturally into the following main subdivisions: (1) definition; (2) types of stress; (3) reactions to frustration; (4) frustration tolerance.

Definition of Frustration

The general denotative definition of frustration which may be adopted is as follows: *frustration* occurs whenever the organism meets a more or less insurmountable obstacle or obstruction in its route to the satisfaction of any vital need. The stimulus-situation representing such an impediment may be termed a *stress* and the corresponding distress of the organism may be conceived as an augmentation of *tension*.

A distinction is made between primary and secondary frustration. *Primary frustration* involves the sheer existence of an active need. It is characterized by tension and subjective dissatisfaction due to the absence of the end-situation necessary for quiescence. Another name for primary frustration is *privation*. An obvious example is the state of hunger occasioned by a long elapsed time since the last meal. *Secondary frustration* more strictly embraces the definition given above, emphasis being placed upon supervenient obstacles or obstructions in the path to the goal of the active need. Thus, for example, a hungry individual would experience secondary frustration if he were prevented from reaching his meal by the breakdown of his automobile or through being detained by an unexpected visitor. For the most part studies in the field of frustration theory have tended and will probably continue to orient themselves mainly toward secondary frustration with the hope that a knowledge of primary frustration will follow.

---

[1] A fourth level, concerned with the defense reactions of social groups, is not discussed here but is necessary to a complete picture.

While it is not possible in the present state of psychobiology to provide an adequate classification of needs—perhaps because the criteria for such a classification have not yet been discovered—it may be indicated that whatever be the eventual catalogue adopted, the needs will doubtless extend along the following continuum: needs concerned with protection against loss or impairment of structures or functions; needs dealing with the maintenance of the individual's growth level; needs concerned with the reproduction of the organism and thus involving a certain degree of self-expansion; and, finally, needs in which such expansion is carried to creative as well as procreative activities and involves symbolical as well as concrete biological behavior. It will at once be recognized that the preceding discussion of defense levels is directed chiefly toward the first of these four groups and that in this respect these defense needs have a special relationship to frustration. Where they are concerned certain contentual as well as formal characteristics of reaction are explicitly taken into account. The other needs are for the most part considered only formally in frustration theory, becoming particularly significant for it when the defensive needs of the organism regarding integration are called into play by the frustrating obstruction.

It may be observed that in anticipation of a final system of needs, frustration theory affords the possibility of managing without it temporarily and may even lead in part to its eventual establishment. For provided that frustrating experiences, including the apparent content of the implicated needs, are described operationally, the nature of the elementary needs—and even more likely the criteria by which they can profitably be classified—are apt to be revealed from a study of the general principles of frustration.

Types of Stress

The nature of the obstacle provides a basis for dividing frustrating or stress situations into certain operationally convenient groups. An obstruction may be either passive or active in character. If *passive* it represents impassibility without being itself threatening; e.g., a locked door to a room containing food when the hungry individual has no key. *Active* obstacles not only have the impassible character of the passive but are in addition dangerous of themselves; e.g., a policeman who bars the way of a hungry and destitute man to an area containing food is an obstacle not merely by virtue of his bulk but because of the weapons and authority he could bring to bear. In other words, whereas passive obstructions entail only the need which is frustrated, active ones invoke additional needs pertaining to the immediate security of the organism. This distinction serves to indicate that frustration includes situations both of dissatisfaction and of danger. Because of the close relationship between danger and dissatisfaction and their essential identity in biological terms, the concept of defense is again seen to be central in frustration theory.

382   PERSONALITY AND THE BEHAVIOR DISORDERS   [11

Obstacles may differ not only in respect to passivity or activity but also by being external or internal, i.e., they may be present either outside or within the individual. By combination four types of stress result. The passive external obstacle has been illustrated above by reference to the locked door. Similarly, the active external obstacle has been exemplified by the policeman. Passive internal obstacles imply incapacities of the individual, as abundantly illustrated in Adlerian psychology.

Active internal obstacles embrace the situations of intrapsychic *conflict* emphasized in Freudian psychoanalytic theory; e.g., the case of the man who is sexually attracted to a woman but is inhibited by moral scruples or other sources of anxiety, conscious or unconscious. In so far as the obstruction which impedes approach to the goal is, as in this example, itself dangerous to integrated personality functioning, the new needs which arise tend to shift the behavior away from its original end. True conflict results when the original and the fresh needs thus brought together are of nearly equal strength though opposite in direction. Thus conceived, conflict is a special type of frustrating or stress situation in which the obstacle to satisfaction consists in contravalent needs (see also Chapter 14 by Miller).

In the further classification of frustrating or stress situations various points of view may be adopted. The content of needs would represent one of these. From such a standpoint the relevance of various other disciplines, including medicine, economics, sociology, and anthropology, would be great since from them must come the detailed knowledge of particular kinds of frustrating experience—disease, hunger, sexual and vocational dissatisfaction. However, this type of information is not, as has already been indicated, the chief business of frustration theory which directs itself to the more general characteristics of frustration reaction.

Of greater theoretical relevance is the importance of developmental factors. Thus the relationship between precipitating and predisposing experiences of frustration is highly significant since, from present indications, it would appear that earlier frustrations are not only apt to implant patterns of reaction to later situations, but may also modify the individual's capacity to respond subsequently in an adequate fashion. The relevance of a possible *psychic anaphylaxis* is strongly suggested in this connection since, as in physical anaphylaxis, an earlier minor sensitizing experience is often crucial in the production of disruptive reactions at a later time. Similarly significant is the phenomenon of *deprivation* which, following a period of satisfaction, introduces factors not encountered in other types of frustration or in privation.

Reactions to Frustration

The chief distinction in reactions to frustration is concerned with the economy of the needs frustrated. Reactions are here classified according to whether the fate of the frustrated segmental need or the fate of the personality as a whole is considered. The former type is designated *need-*

persistive and may be conceived to occur invariably after frustration. The latter, which is designated *ego-defensive,* is conceived to occur only under special conditions of ego-threat. The distinction thus corresponds roughly to that between passive and active obstacles in stress situations. Most behavior incident to frustration includes both types of reaction but cases of each alone are found and the distinction is useful theoretically.

The discussion of ego-defensive reactions to frustration may be amplified on the basis of considerable existing data (Rosenzweig, 1935, 1938b; Dollard, 1939). A threefold division has been attempted (Rosenzweig, 1934).

(a) *Extrapunitive* responses are those in which the individual aggressively attributes the frustration to external persons or things. The associated emotions are anger and resentment. The cognate psychoanalytic mechanism is projection. It should, however, be noted that the extrapunitive response is not always projective. When it proceeds from anger directly it has a very different character from that found when aggression is first inhibited and then only indirectly finds expression in extrapunitive projection. Fulfilling the latter conditions are paranoid psychotic reactions. These well exemplify pathological extrapunitiveness.

(b) *Intropunitive* responses are those in which the individual aggressively attributes the frustration to himself. The inturning of aggression is perhaps a consequence of the inhibition of its outward expression. Associated emotions are guilt and remorse. The related psychoanalytic mechanisms are displacement and isolation. Abnormal instances of this type of response are found in the psychasthenic neuroses, especially obsessional conditions.

(c) *Impunitive* responses differ from both the extrapunitive and intropunitive in that aggression does not apparently supply the motivating force; more socially directed or "erotic" drives are at work. Here the attempt is made to avoid blame altogether, whether of others or of oneself, and to gloss over the frustrating situation as though with a conciliatory objective. The cognate psychoanalytic mechanism is repression, exemplified pathologically in certain forms of hysteria.

It is probable that the above defined ego-defensive reactions to frustration have a characteristic order of genetic emergence. From such data as exist it would appear that the extrapunitive response is earliest; the intropunitive follows in consequence of the inhibition of the extrapunitive; and both occur earlier than the impunitive reaction.

Need-persistive reactions are more limited in their aim than are ego-defensive ones. They serve to fulfill the specific frustrated needs by one method or another as if to restore a disturbed energy equilibrium. Their nature may be clarified by recalling the psychoanalytic concepts of sublimation, as in artistic production, and symptomatic gratification as exemplified in hysterical conversion. The needs of the individual in such cases presumably achieve satisfaction despite present obstacles even when devious routes and disguised expressions have to be adopted.

It may thus be seen that reactions may differ formally in the extent of their *directness*. While some responses are patterned closely after the frustrating situation in a straightforward fashion, others are to a greater or less degree substitutive in character and may even extend into the realm of symbolism. Factors which make for the inhibition of the direct response at a given time prepare the ground for these substitutions, and it is thus easy to appreciate that many inadequate modes of response—which are in a certain sense substitutes for adequate ones that are not possible—will have an indirect character. But it is not to be overlooked that many adequate reactions are also substitutive.

From the biological standpoint all modes of response—direct or indirect, adequate or inadequate—are adjustive in aim. They represent the best of which the organism is capable under the total existing conditions. Presumably an attempt is being made in every case to preserve integrated functioning by the restoration of equilibrium. Claude Bernard's famous generalization regarding the tendency of the organism to keep the conditions of the internal physiological environment constant is relevant here and may be extended to the psychological field. Just as the body in its resistance to infectious disease adopts non-disruptive protective reactions as long as possible but eventually resorts to defense reactions which, as symptoms of the illness, seriously interfere with the patient's normal behavior; so when psychological constancy cannot be achieved in more adequate ways, less adequate ones are inevitably adopted.

Differences in the adequacy of reactions to frustration are thus only extrinsic and reduce essentially to grades of efficiency. While a definitive criterion of adequacy is not yet possible, an approximate one can in theory be given. This centers attention upon the individual's behavior in time. According to it reactions are adequate in so far as they represent progressive rather than retrogressive trends of the personality. Responses which tend to bind the subject to his past unduly or interfere with reactions in later situations because of such binding are less adequate than those which leave the individual free to meet new situations as they arise. In practice this temporal criterion is difficult to employ. Its applicability will probably increase with additional knowledge regarding what is appropriate or inappropriate in contemporaneous response—the common-sense criterion of adequacy.

The adequacy of need-persistive and ego-defensive responses may be specified in somewhat greater detail. Need-persistive behavior which continues fixedly toward the goal in spite of obstacles is considered adequate and is termed *adjustive persistence*. If repeated indefinitely and fatuously, however, such behavior is designated *non-adjustive persistence* (Hamilton, 1916; 1925) and is regarded as inadequate. The critical point which separates adequate from inadequate persistence must be conceived to be a mobile one in a continuum of which only the extremes are recognized without difficulty. Ego-defensive reactions may vary in like manner. Any one of the three types is adequate when warranted by the existing conditions, e.g., a man blames himself for failing in an undertaking to which his ability was not equal. A response is inadequate when similarly unwarranted, e.g., a man blames himself for failure due to the mistakes of another. Consistent adherence to one or more of the reaction types marks an individual as having a particular trait of frustration reaction and would appear to imply some weakness of the personality structure demanding special defense.

Frustration Tolerance

Frustration tolerance may be defined as an individual's capacity to withstand frustration without failure of psychobiological adjustment, i.e., without resorting to inadequate modes of response. In its broadest implications the concept is related to resistance in the medical sense. This relationship is well shown in the recent work of Seleye (1938) who conceives of the organism as possessing a certain amount of "adaptation energy" for meeting all dangerous or painful situations. In so far as such energy is being employed to combat one type of attack, less is available for resisting others.

More psychologically pertinent is the psychoanalytic distinction between the pleasure and reality principles (Freud, 1911). The former involves immediate gratification of every impulse and is characteristic of the very young infant. In the course of education reality comes to be recognized as demanding certain restrictions of gratification and behavior is accordingly guided by possible future consequences as well as by immediate pleasure. In this formulation the essential notion is, therefore, the capacity of the individual to delay gratification. This same capacity is implied in the concept of frustration tolerance.

The pleasure principle is psychoanalytically considered to be operative when inadequate ego-defense reactions are adopted since the latter are modes of protecting the personality from the unpleasantness connected with frustration. Inasmuch as only a weak ego needs to defend itself by such inadequate methods, the analytic concept of *ego weakness* is seen to be also relevant at this point.

As compared to the alternative psychoanalytic formulations, the present one, while sharing much with them, has the advantage of possible quantification. Unlike the pleasure and reality principles which represent a dichotomy, and ego strength which is too vague for specific measurement, frustration tolerance, implying a continuum, instantly suggests quantitative investigation.

Moreover, the concept holds out the theoretical advantage of assuming that individuals differ in respect to certain frustration tolerance thresholds. Within a specifiable range of stressfulness, the responses of a given individual would be adequate. Below it they would be lacking in adequacy because insufficiently motivated to initiate appropriate behavior. Above it their inadequacy would result from the disorganization of excessive stress.

Differences in the degree of frustration tolerance in the various aspects of the same personality may also be conceived. Thus, circumscribed areas of low frustration tolerance would correspond to Freudian "complexes." Neurotics could be characterized as having one or more such areas. In similar terms the psychotic would be depicted as having many, perhaps overlapping, low areas while the normal healthy individual would be credited with a fairly general high frustration tolerance.

The capacity to delay gratification implies some type of inhibitory process. Since, as was observed above, frustration is accompanied by an increase of tension while satisfaction results from a discharge of tension, the inhibition in question may consist in a capacity to sustain tension and to withhold discharge.

While thus far emphasis has been placed on the purely motivational aspects of frustration tolerance, its implications as to intellectual functioning must now be considered. This approach to the thought processes may be made through the concept of inhibition. Just as in its motivational application frustration tolerance implies the capacity to delay gratification, so on the intellectual side it signifies some form of "delayed reaction" (Hunter, 1913). Hunter postulates that symbolic thinking (in the behavioristic sense) involves the capacity of the organism to retain impressions after the stimulus has been removed and to respond later in selective fashion. Abstract symbolic thought could on this basis be considered a form of delayed reaction prerequisite to the delay of gratification previously discussed. For in both instances it is necessary that certain specific residues of stimulation persist beyond the moment. If a response occurs immediately on the reception of the stimulus, there is no possibility either for the accumulation of concrete content necessary to abstract thinking or for gratification delay of a providential kind. And unless the capacity to retain symbolic processes is present, the experiential nucleus for a delay of gratification is obviously lacking. Since, moreover, both these capacities for delay appear to increase with maturation (Hunter, 1913; Rosenzweig, 1933), they are included together in the concept of frustration tolerance.

In this context the psychopathological work of Goldstein (1940) is relevant. He has shown that one of the striking defects of patients with brain injuries is their incapacity to think abstractly. He characterizes them as in danger of getting involved in *catastrophic* situations which would extend beyond their capacities to respond adequately—or, in the present terms, beyond their frustration tolerance. Goldstein finds that these patients adopt various protective devices of avoiding or coping with such situations and that the concreteness of their thinking is a reflection of such adjustment. It may be added that concrete symbolic (as opposed to abstract symbolic) thinking, usually termed fantasy, together with inadequate modes of ego-defense is similarly found in states of low frustration tolerance independent of organic injury.

The determinants of frustration tolerance are still largely unknown. One possibility looks to differences in innate endowment as manifested in nervous, glandular, or other somatic functions. It is not improbable that in these terms the long mooted question of heredity in mental disorder may eventually be answered. As related to such congenital physiological factors, certain transient conditions like fatigue and physical illness are worthy of consideration.

In the psychological realm early educational influences, both informal and formal, undoubtedly play a part. While such influences cannot be exactly specified, it is consistent with available information to suppose that insufficient frustration "spoils" the individual so that he is later unable to withstand frustration adequately. Excessive frustration, on the other hand, may create areas of low tolerance because the immature child, unable to assimilate these inroads, is forced to react by adopting inadequate ego-defenses that impede later development. The previous mentioned frustration tolerance thresholds have here a genetic correlate.

The application of the concept of frustration tolerance to psychotherapy (Rosenzweig, 1938a) deserves brief mention. Psychoanalysis may be regarded from this standpoint as a form of reeducation which corrects the individual's previous experience in so far as this has entailed either too little or too much frustration. The analysand who in daily psychoanalytic sessions follows the rule that nothing, however humiliating or unpleasant, must be left unsaid is being exposed to repeated small doses of frustration. In this way frustration tolerance is gradually built up until the inadequate modes of ego-defense underlying the neurotic symptoms are rendered unnecessary. Psychotherapy thus conceived as *defrustration* may be compared with active immunization against infectious disease since in both methods of treatment resistance is increased through repeated small doses of the injurious agent till the natural defenses of the organism are adequate for dealing with unforeseeable encounters.

What must in conclusion be clearly borne in mind is the heuristic character of the preceding outline. The indications for frustration theory from experimental psychoanalysis, studies of "neuroses" in animals, psychosomatic medicine and other sources are numerous. The establishment of detailed principles is, however, a matter of future research for which the above discussion may be taken as a schematic plan (Rosenzweig, 1943).

BIBLIOGRAPHY

BARKER, R., DEMBO, T., & LEWIN, K. 1941. Frustration and regression: an experiment with young children. *Univ. Ia Stud. Child Welf., 18,* No. 1.

DOLLARD, J., DOOB, L. W., *et al.* 1939. Frustration and aggression. New Haven: Yale University Press.

FREUD, S. 1911. Formulations regarding the two principles in mental functioning. In *Collected papers.* Vol. 4. London: Hogarth, 1925.

GOLDSTEIN, K. 1940. Human nature in the light of psychopathology. Cambridge: Harvard University Press.

HAMILTON, G. V. 1916. A study of perseverance reactions in primates and rodents. *Behav. Monogr., 3,* No. 2.

—— 1925. An introduction to objective psychopathology. St. Louis: Mosby.

HUNTER, W. S. 1913. The delayed reaction in animals and children. *Behav. Monogr., 2,* No. 1.

MASLOW, A. H., MILLER, N. E., SEARS, R. R., *et al.* 1941. Symposium on effects of frustration. *Psychol. Rev., 48,* 337–366.

ROSENZWEIG, S. 1933. Preferences in the repetition of successful and unsuccessful activities as a function of age and personality. *J. genet. Psychol., 42,* 423–441.

—— 1934. Types of reaction to frustration: an heuristic classification. *J. abnorm. soc. Psychol., 29,* 298–300.

—— 1935. A test for types of reaction to frustration. *Amer. J. Orthopsychiat., 4,* 395–403.

—— 1938a. A dynamic interpretation of psychotherapy oriented towards research. *Psychiatry, 1,* 521–526.

—— 1938b. The experimental measurement of types of reaction to frustration. In MURRAY, H. A., *et al., Explorations in personality.* New York: Oxford Univ. Press. Pp. 585–599.

—— 1938c. The experimental study of repression. In MURRAY, H. A., *et al., Explorations in personality.* New York: Oxford University Press. Pp. 472–490.

ROSENZWEIG, S., MOWRER, O. H., *et al.* 1938d. Frustration as an experimental problem. *Character & Pers., 7,* 126–160.

ROSENZWEIG, S. 1943. Human frustration. (Unpublished.)

SELEYE, H. 1938. Experimental evidence supporting the concept of "adaptation energy." *Amer. J. Physiol., 123,* 758–765.

Chapter 12

CONDITIONED REFLEX METHOD AND
EXPERIMENTAL NEUROSIS*

By H. S. LIDDELL, Ph.D.

DURING THE OPENING YEARS of the present century Professor I. P. Pavlov (1902) had reached a turning point in his classical investigation of the influence of the central nervous system on the work of the digestive glands. Having thoroughly explored the reflex mechanisms of gastric and salivary secretion, he felt compelled to give an account in physiological terms of the psychical or anticipatory secretion of these digestive juices; of saliva in particular, because of the ease with which it could be collected and the rate of its secretion determined.

In planning an experimental strategy for this purpose he found it unnecessary to depart from his previous well-standardized laboratory procedures. His dogs had been trained to stand quietly for long periods of time in a special frame, with loose loops under the limbs, while gastric juice or saliva was being collected. With the aid of simple arrangements for automatically presenting small portions of food to the dog and for recording its salivary secretion at a distance, Pavlov was able to train his dogs to secrete saliva in anticipation of food when certain signals regularly preceded feeding. When distractions were eliminated and a given signal, such as a tone, regularly preceded the coming of food, Pavlov (1928) discovered that anticipatory or psychical secretion of saliva could be confidently predicted.

Upon the basis of such observations he found it necessary, for scientific clarity, to think of the dog's behavior exclusively within the framework of reflex action. He now regarded all instances of psychical secretion as conditioned reflexes established upon the basis of the unconditioned secretory reflex evoked by the presence of food or noxious substances in the mouth. Through the many ensuing years Pavlov resolutely continued these investigations in the belief that behavior so studied lay within the province of the physiologist.

However, during the training of one of the dogs in the conditioned reflex laboratory, a dramatic incident occurred and Pavlov's description of this unexpected event now has considerable historical interest.

---

* The substance of this chapter was presented in two lectures at the California Institute of Technology on May 13 and 15, 1941.

A projection of a luminous circle onto a screen in front of the animal was repeatedly accompanied by feeding. After the reflex had become well established a differentiation between the circle and an ellipse with a ratio of the semi-axes 2:1, of the same luminosity and the same surface area, was obtained by the usual method of contrast. A complete and constant differentiation was obtained comparatively quickly. The shape of the ellipse was now approximated by stages to that of the circle (ratios of the semi-axes of 3:2, 4:3 and so on) and the development of differentiation continued through successive ellipses. The differentiation proceeded with some fluctuations, progressing at first more and more quickly, and then again slower until an ellipse with ratio of semi-axes 9:8 was reached. In this case, although a considerable degree of discrimination did develop, it was far from being complete. After three weeks of work upon this differentiation not only did the discrimination fail to improve, but it became considerably worse, and finally disappeared altogether. At the same time the behavior of the animal underwent an abrupt change. The hitherto quiet dog began to squeal in its stand, kept wriggling about, tore off with its teeth the apparatus for mechanical stimulation of the skin, and bit through the tubes connecting the animal's room with the observer, a behavior which never happened before. On being taken into the experimental room the dog now barked violently, which was also contrary to its usual custom; in short it presented all the symptoms of a condition of acute neurosis. On testing the cruder differentiations they also were found to be destroyed, even the one with the ratio of the semi-axes 2:1. . . . After these experiments we paid considerable attention to pathological disturbances in the cortical activity and began to study them in detail. (1927, pp. 290–292)

The strong impression which the abnormal behavior of this dog made upon Pavlov and his clear intuition as to the importance of what another might have regarded as a trivial and annoying incident in the program of experimentation led him inevitably to a reorganization of his whole plan of attack upon the analysis of behavior by the method of the conditioned reflex. This reorganization of investigation in his laboratories is reflected in the subject matter of his last fifteen lectures, recently translated and edited by W. Horsley Gantt under the title *Conditioned Reflexes and Psychiatry* (see Pavlov, 1941).

Our own interest in the experimental neurosis began as the result of an accident in the laboratory similar to that described by Pavlov. In attempting to determine the effect of thyroidectomy on the behavior of the sheep and goat I had employed the maze method and was disappointed to discover that, except for frequent long pauses in traversing the maze, the thyroidectomized animals equalled the learning scores of their normal twins, even where the problem was made too difficult for either sheep or goat to solve, as for example, in the three-alley maze, reversing the position of the blind alley at every trial.

It seemed paradoxical that, whereas pronounced changes in the functioning of separate physiological systems, such as neuromuscular and

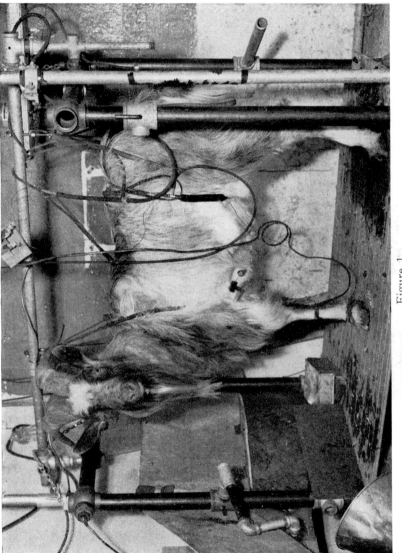

Figure 1

A goat undergoing its daily test in the conditioned reflex laboratory. This experiment does not differ fundamentally from Pavlov's experiments on salivary conditioning in the dog. In this case, however, a mild electric shock is applied to the animal's left foreleg. The goat learns to anticipate this mild shock when it hears the ticking of a telegraph sounder which has always preceded the shock.

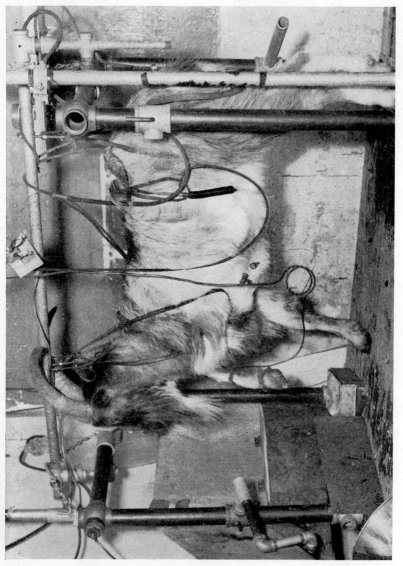

Figure 2

Here the goat is lifting its left foreleg at the clicking of the telegraph sounder. The leg is lifted in a deliberate and methodical manner. No emotional upset results from such simple experiments. The experiments with mild electric shock have been performed on sheep, goat, pig, and dog.

cardiovascular, were affected by thyroidectomy, a corresponding effect upon the behavior of the animal could not be shown. The impossibility of demonstrating reliable differences in learning scores between a normal, alert, and active sheep and its undersized, weak, lethargic twin suggested a fundamental defect in the method of maze learning as a precise test of adaptive behavior.

The decision having been made to continue the investigation, it seemed necessary to find some method for studying behavior which would prove comparable in reliability to the procedures being employed in studying the effects of thyroidectomy on the separate organ systems. The selection of Pavlov's method of the conditioned reflex was an obvious choice since Pavlov's writings had convinced us that this method was a physiological method. Having constructed a small conditioned reflex laboratory and prepared to establish conditioned salivary reflexes in sheep and goat, we soon discovered that the continuous secretion from the parotid gland was a serious obstacle to the study of salivary conditioned reflexes in these species. However, since both sheep and goats adapted themselves easily and quickly to the Pavlov frame, we proceeded with the study of conditioned motor reflexes based upon the defensive reaction of the foreleg to a mild electric shock (Figures 1 and 2).

In our first experiments concerning the effect of thyroidectomy on the conditioned reflex a sudden increase in the number of daily tests led to a state of persistent agitation in a normal sheep which rendered it useless to us for further conditioning experiments. From Pavlov's clear description of experimental neurosis in the dog we were convinced that our sheep was exhibiting a similar abnormality of behavior (Liddell and Bayne, 1935).

Although for a time we continued our study of the effects of thyroidectomy on conditioning, we became increasingly preoccupied with the experimental neurosis itself. Since the first sheep to exhibit this condition had been trained for some years in the maze with no sign of behavioral disturbance we were led to believe that Pavlov's classical method of the conditioned reflex was not an impersonal observational procedure, but a traumatizing procedure.[1] We believed that, as a method of training, it might exert upon the nervous system effects essentially similar to the traumatic influence of certain cultural factors in human life (Liddell, et al., 1934; Anderson, et al., 1935).

As our study continued the need for an intimate understanding of the conditioning method appeared more and more urgent and in my own case led to a lessened interest in testing or attempting to modify Pavlov's theory of conditioned reflex action. During the course of our study of conditioned reflexes, from 1927 to the present, I came to believe that Pavlov's method of the conditioned reflex could be accurately characterized as a method for producing the experimental neurosis. In the

---

[1] See Miller's discussion of conflict in the discrimination situation in Chapter 14. (Editor)

present chapter, therefore, a careful analysis of the method itself will take precedence over the detailed consideration of the many manifestations of experimental neurosis in the animal species in which it has been clearly recognized.

The Conditioned Reflex Method

Perhaps the most significant feature of the conditioned reflex method is to be found in its monotonous and unsatisfying repetitiveness. The animal, having become accustomed to standing in the Pavlov frame, does so willingly and quietly and, during the experimental period, is subjected to trivial and repeated stimuli. Having learned to assume an attitude of alert quiet during the daily test, it is roused to brief conditioned and unconditioned activity by signals which indicate that food or no food, shock or no shock, is about to follow. The extremely mild electric shock applied to the animal's foreleg or the very small amounts of food given following the signals can have but little import for the animal's well-being. The reinforcing agents, shock or food, cannot be thought of as important goals polarizing the animal's behavior. Observation of the responses to these routine unconditioned stimuli (food or shock) give us scarcely more insight into the consequences of a long-continued regimen of training in the laboratory than do punctuation marks in helping us to understand the written page.

In the course of months or years of training in the conditioned reflex laboratory a progressive change in the animal's behavior is observed and in our experience this behavior moves toward the pathological terminus which we call the experimental neurosis. This *terminus ad quem* of monotonously repeated conditioned activity within the environment of the laboratory room must be accepted as an essential element in the definition of the conditioned reflex method.

Another fundamental characteristic of the method is the intimacy which develops during training between animal and experimenter (Anderson and Parmenter, 1941; Gantt, 1942, 1943). In the course of months or years this intimate relationship alters infallibly, first in the direction of dependence and solicitation, but later toward avoidance or hostility. We believe that this feature of Pavlov's method differentiates the study of conditioned reflex action from investigations in essential physiology. In chronic physiological experiments of long duration the cooperation of the animal must be secured; but, within the limits which the physiologist imposes upon his thinking, intimacy between animal subject and investigator is taken for granted and does not enter into the appraisal of the results of the experiment.

Among our case histories of sheep, two cover periods of 5 years, three of 10 years, and three others of 8, 13, and 14 years (Anderson and Parmenter, 1941). Daily observations extending over such periods reveal, even in so simple an animal, an unexpectedly complex pattern of adjustment to barnyard and laboratory environment.

Anyone interested in observing this pattern of the farm animal's life from day to day will find himself insensibly minimizing the differences and emphasizing similarities to the human social situation. The domesticated sheep establishes most complex relations in its dependence upon caretaker and experimenter, and a like complexity can be observed in its relations with the sheep and goats in the barn. Differences in species, age, sex, dominance or submissiveness, must all be carefully analyzed in their effect upon the individual experimental sheep.

In the early part of our investigation we failed to appreciate the scientific importance of the complex barnyard scene just sketched. We centered our attention upon the brief periods during which the sheep stood in the Pavlov frame and responded to signals associated with electric shock applied to its foreleg. In the course of experiments during which the animal came to be unable to discriminate between signals for shock and for no shock, a state of agitation similar to one form of the experimental neurosis was observed. Because of laboratory training and bias we concentrated upon the physiological analysis of this abnormal state of the sheep and, not sensing the importance of the animal's daily life experience outside of the laboratory, failed to see what was there. The sheep had to be caught and led to the laboratory, and so we were forced to notice that, after the onset of the experimental neurosis, it resisted capture and was reluctant to enter the laboratory room.

The situation, as we now view it, appears as follows. Domestication itself imposes upon the animal restrictions and pressures, a hierarchy of them, beginning with the simple physical restraints imposed by the fenced-in area within which the animal lives. It must be recognized that its food is not sought after but is supplied at stated times. It is forced to associate with other animals of its own species and of other species. Crises involving self-defense, reproduction, and food arise from time to time. Then again, the animal assumes a submissive relation to the attendant and experimenter. From this account it can be seen that the perplexing problems which face the animal in the conditioned reflex laboratory represent restraints and pressures situated at the apex of a pyramid. Progressive restriction of liberty and correlative increase in pressures (similar to those exerted by society on the human individual) extend from the wild state, through domestication, to the too refined training of the laboratory.

To illustrate the progressive change in the pattern of conditioned behavior following the monotonous repetition of daily training let us begin with an untrained sheep or goat and consider samples of the behavior recorded during a long-continued regimen of motor conditioning. The animal is placed in the Pavlov frame with loops under the limbs which allow of considerable movement but prevent locomotion (see Figure 1). The brief induction shocks applied to the forelimb are startling but not painful. For example, equally vigorous attempts to escape from the harness are elicited by the shock to the forelimb of the untrained animal or by a sudden movement of the experimenter when standing near its head.

The following samples of activity routinely appear in our tracings: movements of head and forelimb, respiratory movements, and heart beat amplified by the cardiotachometer, together with records of conditioned signal, shock, and time in seconds (Figure 3).

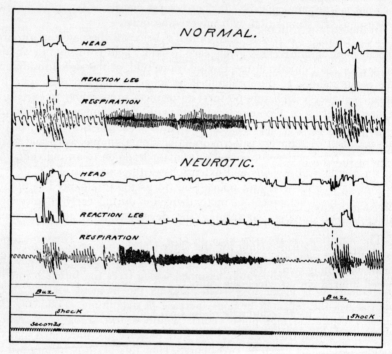

Figure 3

A composite tracing contrasting the conditioned reactions of a normal sheep with a sheep exhibiting signs of experimental neurosis. The lowest three lines indicate two buzzer signals followed by shock, with a 5-minute rest interval between. As seen in the last line, indicating time in seconds, the kymograph has been slowed during the rest interval between the first and second door buzzer signals. Samples of behavior recorded for each animal include head movement, flexion of the left forelimb (to which the shock is applied at the end of the 10-second conditioned signal), and respiration recorded by means of a mask placed over the snout. The abnormalities of the neurotic sheep in the Pavlov frame are well displayed. Especially characteristic of the animal's mild agitation are the repeated movements of the head, the small twitch-like movements of the left forelimb during the rest interval, and the rapid and irregular respiration. The characteristic overreaction to the sound of the buzzer is also well shown in this tracing. (From the experiments of O. D. Anderson)

In a tracing of the conditioned motor reflex of a sheep shortly after the beginning of training, the movements of the head may show the same spikes as do movements of the forelimb. Here the animal attempts to run during the signal and these running movements, with bobbing of the head, are abruptly terminated by the shock. At this stage of training the heart may show alternating periods of acceleration and slowing not correlated with activity or respiration.

Early in training the animal is unable to repress bursts of activity not associated with signal or shock. It is not possible to decide without reference to the record of signal and shock whether the movements are conditioned or spontaneous. Behavior in the conditioning environment has not yet become episodic. It does not yet consist of bursts of activity in response to stimulation with intervening quiet.

As training progresses the animal's behavior becomes more predictable and impulsiveness gives place to skill. That is to say, the animal comes to stand quietly in the Pavlov frame and, at the signal intimating the coming shock to the forelimb, it no longer struggles to escape. Instead, it makes a deliberate postural adjustment preparatory to executing a precise series of flexion movements with the member to which the shock is about to be applied. As in Coghill's (1929) description of the development of behavior patterns in amblystoma, in our sheep and goats the initial total pattern of escaping behavior leads on to an individuation of the rhythmical flexions and extensions of the single forelimb. It was Professor Coghill who first pointed out to us the pronounced similarity between this development of motor behavior during early conditioning and his own findings concerning the development of the embryonic behavior pattern.

The physiological setting for the skilled performance of the forelimb has also altered with the progress of training. At the signal preceding shock a posture is deliberately assumed which frees the forelimb for the movements it is about to execute, and as the moment for the shock approaches the repeated flexions increase in magnitude. Following the shock, respiration and pulse return within a few seconds to resting tempo. In a well-trained animal the state of quiet just illustrated may be maintained for as much as two hours. That this poise is maintained at a cost is shown when the experimenter enters the room to release the animal from the harness at the end of the daily test. The increase in heart rate at this moment is prompt and prolonged.

When a level of habitual quiet and skilled response has been achieved the animal comes willingly to the laboratory. Among our goats those which are in training customarily separate themselves from the other animals at testing time so that there is no difficulty in selecting the animal desired for the hour's experiment.

What has just been said concerning the gradual modification of behavior during defensive conditioning applies to alimentary conditioning as well.

The daily period of self-imposed restraint to which the animal is subjected in the conditioning laboratory, together with its relinquishment of initiative and spontaneity within the testing period, we now believe, lays the foundation for the pathological outcome of long-continued training. Yet this self-imposed restraint is not of itself sufficient to lead to

disturbed behavior. Something more is needed for a pathological outcome, and that something more is, in the simplest case, provided by the
monotonous repetition of a specific pattern of stimulation involving the
trivial but inevitable reinforcement mentioned above.

Recent experiments with the goat illustrate this point. The animal,
after preliminary conditioning, was subjected to an unvarying schedule
of tests in which a telegraph sounder clicking once a second for 10 seconds was followed by shock to the forelimb and, after a 2-minute rest,
this 10-second conditioned stimulus was repeated with shock. The day's
schedule consisted of ten conditioned signals of 10 seconds' duration,
always followed by shock, and always separated by rest periods of
exactly 2 minutes. During the early days of the experiment the goat
gave repeated precise flexions of the forelimb in response to the clicking
of the telegraph sounder (Figure 2), with a single, brief flexion in response to the mild shock applied to the forelimb. This reaction pattern
soon gave place, however, to a deliberate single flexion of the forelimb,
delayed until about 8 seconds after the beginning of the clicking. This
phase of delayed and deliberate flexion was followed by a stiffening of
the forelimb with flexion of the stiffened limb from the shoulder.

Training was discontinued at the stage where the animal could barely
raise the stiffened limb from the platform. Now a 6-week rest period
intervened. With the resumption of training the animal reverted to its
former pattern of brisk and repeated flexions, but by the second day of
testing it had recapitulated the previous sequence of phases and now
showed a rapid, brisk extension of the forelimb followed by a delayed
and deliberate flexion movement. In other words, the animal's progress
toward motor incapacity through the rigid immobility of the limb was
interrupted by a rest period and at the first test following the rest
period the animal reverted to an earlier and more normal mode of
response. But now, with continued testing, it more rapidly approached
the state of complete immobility of the reacting member. At the very
time, however, that the animal was showing increasing difficulty in raising its foot from the platform, it was also showing the greatest willingness in coming to the laboratory and was exhibiting unusual quiet in
the Pavlov frame between conditioning tests. However, as incapacity
approached, the forelimb gave increasing signs of sensitivity. First a
brisk knock with the side of the hand on the goat's forefoot caused a
brief, precise flexion movement; but later, as the rigid stiffening phase
supervened, a light touch of the finger on the forefoot was followed by an
extremely rapid, small tic-like flexion of the limb.

We have already observed a number of sheep in which the rigidity of
the reaction limb persisted for years and in which evidences of conditioning were to be obtained only from records of head movement, breathing, or heart rate (Liddell, James, and Anderson, 1934; Anderson and
Parmenter, 1941). This leg-stiffening phase may be regarded as an inhibitory type of experimental neurosis. In the sheep, however, the outcome of long-continued and monotonous conditioning leads more often

Figure 4

Tantrum behavior of a pig without adequate training in restraint when an electric shock is applied to its left foreleg.

Figure 5

Behavior of the pig shown in Fig. 4 after its struggles following the shock have ceased. It maintains this resistant posture when not struggling.

Figure 6

The behavior of a pig five weeks old at the first attempt to lead it on leash.

Figure 7

A trained pig on leash.

to the persistent and intractible agitation observed in our first sheep with experimental neurosis.

Our investigation suggests, then, that there are at least two traumatic factors characteristic of Pavlov's method. First, the monotonous repetition of conditioned stimuli inevitably followed by trivial reinforcements, mild shocks, or small bits of food; and second, the tensions developed by the animal's self-imposed restraint within the Pavlov frame. The tensions resulting from self-imposed restraint are particularly well shown in attempts to habituate the pig to the Pavlov frame for purposes of motor or salivary conditioning.

In some early experiments we attempted to build up conditioned motor reflexes in the pig by force (Liddell, James, and Anderson, 1934). Three of us were required to secure the pig in the Pavlov frame and during several days of testing it never once discontinued its tantrum behavior. Discrimination was established between signals for shock and for no shock only in the sense that the animal's reaction at the signal for shock was extremely violent struggling, while during the negative signal it maintained a rigid crouching posture (Figures 4 and 5). I discovered, in discussing our work with Pavlov, that he too had experienced like difficulty in attempting to use the pig in his experiments on sham feeding.[2]

However, it eventually proved relatively simple, although time-consuming, to habituate the pig to the Pavlov frame in the same sense that sheep, goat, or dog is habituated. Seven years ago Sutherland and I began training a litter of four pigs shortly after weaning, following a predetermined procedure aimed at a gradual encroachment upon their freedom.[3] First they were trained to run on leash and, after an initial period of resistance, they all capitulated and willingly went for a daily walk (Figures 6 and 7). Then they were introduced singly and sometimes in pairs into a small laboratory room and coaxed to open a food box in order to secure pieces of apple. Then a door buzzer signaled the delivery of apple into the box while a door bell was a signal that no apple was to be obtained. Now a small pen was fenced off with the food box at one end, provided with an arrangement for delivering pieces of apple into the box from an adjoining room.

By this time the pigs readily approached and opened the box at the sound of the buzzer, but not of the bell. The next encroachment on the pigs' freedom was to reduce the dimensions of the training pen and

---

[2] "From those pigs from which I wished to obtain gastric juice _ obtained nothing. As soon as such a pig was lifted onto the stand it squealed at the top of its voice and all work in the laboratory was impossible. All complained and do what we might—try to soothe it—nothing came of it. Thus we spent almost a month on it without obtaining any results, and at last had to give it up." (From the record of Pavlov's seminar, April 25, 1934)

[3] The account of the conditioning of pigs which follows is the summary of an investigation extending from 1935 to 1938. In 1936 Quin F. Curtis, a National Research Fellow, joined with us in the investigation, and later G. B. Davis became a collaborator.

finally to tether the pig in the pen where formerly it had run freely. The reaction to collar and chain within the training pen was two-fold. Attempts to escape being unsuccessful, the pig reacted to the added restraint by lying at the back of the pen with eyes closed, although it might grunt and rock back and forth at the sound of the buzzer (Figure 8). This stage of resistance past, the pig readily submitted to the straps of the Pavlov frame and was prepared to open the cover of the box at a signal for food, light or buzzer, clearly discriminating it from the bell which had been a signal for no apple (Figure 9).

At this stage of the experiment the aim was to discover whether the animal, now accustomed to stand in the Pavlov frame without resistance, could restrain tantrum behavior if an electric shock were applied to the forelimb. The ringing of the door bell, the former signal for no apple, was now followed by shock. The animal, ignoring the bell, flexed the leg at the shock but at the same time opened the cover of the food box (Figure 10). There was no outcry and no sign of excitement at the shock itself even when increased in strength. However, when this same pig was taken to a strange laboratory room and placed in the Pavlov frame, one ringing of the bell followed by shock precipitated the persistent tantrum behavior which we had encountered in our earlier experiment, although when it was returned to the familiar room on the same day it continued to ignore the bell and to react to the shock by combined leg flexion and box opening without emotional expression.

Since it seemed reasonable to assume that the pig regarded its familiar laboratory room as a place in which to be fed, and that its interpretation of changes or signals occurring within this familiar environment centered about preoccupations with food, it occurred to Sutherland that it might be possible systematically to alter the pig's interpretation of its laboratory environment as a whole.

Without supplying complete details of this experiment, the general plan was to follow on every day the same regimen of training as to number of signals and time intervals between them. An audio-oscillator supplied a constant musical tone of moderate intensity and, when this tone was discontinued for 10 seconds, the period of silence constituted the conditioned signal. A lower tone characterized feeding day and a higher tone, shocking day, and these days alternated. The pig soon fell into the habit of distinguishing between the two days according to whether food or shock followed the first period of silence, and during the subsequent periods of silence on shocking day it would squeal and shake the foreleg (Figure 11), while during the corresponding 10 seconds of silence on feeding day it typically held open the cover of the food box with the snout and waited for the falling of the piece of apple (Figure 12).

At this point a still further curtailment of liberty was imposed on the pig. If it opened the cover of the food box at any time other than when a signal for food was given, it received an electric shock. This additional restriction was followed by the development of the following abnormal behavior. The pig now disregarded the signal and opened the cover only when the apple fell into the box.

In attempting to reestablish conditioned box opening, shocking days were discontinued and the conditioned signal (or period of silence) on feeding day was continued until the pig made the appropriate reaction of opening the cover of the food box. It delayed longer and longer in doing so, however, and during a single experimental period it might delay box opening for an hour. Its behavior was now definitely abnormal in that it would attack the food box. Standing quietly with eyes closed during the signal, it began to grunt and squeal and then, with a sudden lunge, charged upon the box, thrusting up the cover with its snout and rapidly sweeping the interior, sometimes missing the piece of apple. Finally, it no longer opened the box at all and, with the cover open and pieces of apple dropped in the box following each signal, the pig allowed them to accumulate until the experimenter entered the room to release it, when it would rouse itself and begin rapidly to eat the accumulated food.

As in the cases of experimental neurosis observed in the dog and sheep, the animal's behavior in the living quarters showed a marked change from friendliness to irascibility, so that it was no longer to be trusted.

Having demonstrated the possibility of habituating the pig to the Pavlov frame, Sutherland proceeded to prepare a salivary fistula in one of the animals and was able to form typical positive and negative salivary conditioned reflexes to auditory stimuli.

Recently, a new study was undertaken in our laboratory by Marcuse and Moore (1942) with three young pigs for the purpose of establishing salivary conditioned reflexes as in the dog.

It was found possible to curtail greatly the laborious procedure formerly adopted. The animal was led almost directly from training on leash into the Pavlov frame (see Figure 13) and no serious difficulties were encountered in establishing a salivary conditioned reflex comparable in every way to that exhibited by Pavlov's dogs (see Figure 14). Although the pig is much more vocal than the dog while being prepared for the experiment, it is quiet and cooperative, but the potentialities for violent behavior lurking beneath its calm exterior may easily be demonstrated. In order to see whether the chain about the neck of one of the pigs might be impeding the salivary flow it was unfastened. An immediate outburst of tantrum ensued, which persisted steadily during a number of days. This is another illustration of the compression-chamber-like character of the Pavlov conditioning situation, where pent-up tension will escape through any leak provided.

Let us imagine the morphology of the animal's psychological environment as it stands in the Pavlov frame. There is evidence, we believe, of a definite structuring of its psychological space. This structuring may be thought of as a series of concentric shells encapsulating the animal. Proceeding inward each shell imposes increased tension with decreased freedom. Proceeding outward, each boundary passed means lessened tension with increased freedom. In the salivary conditioning situation the sensitized head and neck are enclosed in the innermost shell, while in the motor conditioning context it is the highly reactive leg which is separately encapsulated.

Evidence for such a picture has been independently furnished by Gantt (1943) at Hopkins, Dworkin (1939) at McGill, and our own group. An experimentally neurotic sheep best illustrates what happens when proceeding inward from pasture to Pavlov frame. The sheep avoids the experimenter in the pasture. It resists being led to the laboratory and seeks to avoid entering the door. It struggles when the harness is being adjusted. It may urinate or defecate when the shaving brush is applied to the skin in preparing to attach the tachometer electrodes. It again flinches when the leg is touched and is further disturbed when the experimenter leaves it to begin the tests.

Other illustrations given earlier in this chapter will be remembered; for example, cardiac acceleration when the experimenter enters the room to release the animal after its daily test (for clinical examples of such phenomena in human beings, see Chapter 8 by Saul).

In order to place the study of conditioned reflex action in its proper relationship to physiology, the following question may be asked: Where do these reflexes, conditioned and unconditioned, come from? In attempting to answer this question it is possible to arrive at a composite formulation derived from certain generally accepted principles of physiology.

It should be pointed out, however, that physiologists have never been crippled by the rigidity of their accepted principles. Sherrington (1933) speaks of the nervous system as thinking in terms of movements rather than of muscles and envisages the animal's head encased in a shell of its own futurity. Cannon (1929), too, has considered the shell of futurity surrounding the animal in studying the mechanisms which it employs in preparing to meet an emergency. The principles derived from research in essential physiology concern an abstract organism, not an individual. They play their part in helping us to understand human behavior by giving us specifications or blueprints of standard mammalian functioning.

In order to maintain a living system it is necessary that certain materials be incorporated and others extruded. In this general sense we recognize "tissue needs" which must be supplied. According to Cannon's (1932) formulation, the constancy of the internal environment is maintained by two interlocking mechanisms of behavior. Interofective mechanisms are inwardly directed toward the maintenance of a constant fluid environment bathing the living cells. The exterofective mechanisms are outwardly directed and seek to bring the animal in contact with optimum conditions within its ever-changing external surroundings. Richter's (1941) experiments on the selection by the rat of a proper diet or of a proper nest to compensate for disequilibria imposed by adrenalectomy, thyroidectomy, or parathyroidectomy, demonstrate the refined integrations which obtain between mechanisms for outwardly directed behavior and inwardly directed behavior. The phenomena of conditioned reflex action described by Pavlov illustrate the complex and fragile exterofective behavioral mechanisms which can come into being under laboratory conditions when an animal's bodily needs are standardized.

These examples, however, go beyond the mere formulation of principles of standard mammalian functioning. They focus attention upon a particular animal as an individual and where, as in Pavlov's experiments, years may be devoted to the fabrication of a pattern of behavior in a certain dog, that dog assumes the same scientific status as does a patient under the care of a physician. In the investigation of conditioned reflex action the experimenter probes an individual animal's possibilities for complex adjustment to its surroundings. In doing so he courts the occurrence of a pathological outcome to his regimen of training.

No impassable barriers are encountered when we proceed from a recognition of tissue needs in a living system to the mechanisms of interofective and exterofective action for meeting these needs. Nor is any barrier encountered when we proceed from the physiologist's standard mammal to the individual dog undergoing a carefully planned routine of conditioning. And, finally, we need not be blocked in our logical thought progression in proceeding from a study of the dog which has successfully adjusted itself to its conditioning routine to the same dog which has arrived at another adjustment, namely, an experimental neurosis.

The study of animal behavior by Pavlov's classical method of the conditioned reflex may be regarded as a separate field of experimental medicine. The student of conditioned reflex action in animals depends upon the results of basic research in essential physiology in devising techniques for sampling the various physiological functions in his conditioned animals, and his relation to clinical medicine, including psychiatry, is an equally close and dependent one.

Pavlov, in attempting to bring all data concerning behavior within the framework of reflex action, was preoccupied with measuring the responses of a single effector organ, the salivary gland, but investigators of the conditioned reflex now seek to follow changes in the patterning of many physiological functions as a consequence of conditioning, and must depend upon the researches in essential physiology for the appraisal of this aspect of their behavioral data. At present we emphasize, perhaps more than Pavlov did, the importance of the case history of the individual animal, particularly since we regard the development of the experimental neurosis as a logical consequence of the fundamental characteristics of Pavlov's conditioning method, the use of which leads to this pathological state. Our close relations with clinical medicine and psychiatry are inevitable when we give due weight to the special intimacy which develops between animal subject and experimenter in the course of months and years of observation. This intimacy appears to be similar in fundamental respects to the rapport between patient and psychotherapist.

The case for conditioned reflex study as a separate branch of experimental medicine rests too upon a careful consideration of the experimental neurosis. In this abnormal state not only are the animal's physiological functions (cardiovascular, respiratory, gastrointestinal) disturbed, but the relations between the animal and experimenter and the animal and its companions in the living quarters are disturbed also.

The experimenter devises apparatus and techniques for making things happen. In so doing he multiplies opportunities for observation, not only for himself, but for others who use his methods. The medical importance of studies of conditioned reflex action and experimental neurosis lies, not in a theory or a doctrine to account for mental life and mental disorder, but rather in a carefully tested method for analyzing patterns of behavior so complex and unstable that most biologists have heretofore been content to relinquish completely the study of them to the sociologist or psychiatrist.

Manifestations of the Experimental Neurosis in the Dog, Cat, Sheep, and Pig [4]

In the previous discussion Pavlov's classical method of the conditioned reflex was characterized as a method for precipitating the experimental neurosis. Adherence to a rigid time schedule in conducting conditioning tests, together with never-failing reinforcement, was described as the simplest means of producing disturbances of behavior through training in the laboratory. Many other maneuvers are available to the experimenter in effecting the animal's breakdown. The procedures most commonly used in Pavlov's laboratories for precipitating the experimental neurosis are the following: demanding of the animal progressively finer discriminations, establishing progressively longer delayed conditioned reflexes, sudden reversal of long familiar positive and negative conditioned stimuli, all positive signals becoming negative and all negative signals positive. A procedure recently introduced at the Cornell Behavior Farm consists of repeating the same conditioned signal four times in succession, keeping the duration of the signal and the interval between signals constant and failing to reinforce every other signal.

In the course of an extensive investigation of pitch discrimination Dworkin trained cats to open the lid of a food container in response to tones of carefully controlled pitch and intensity. He found that complex disturbances of behavior, enduring for as much as two and a half years, resulted when the animals were "trained to listen for tones at or near the actual loudness threshold. As long as the tone-stimuli were distinctly audible (40 to 15 decibels above the actual threshold) the behavior was smooth and even, but when the signals approached the range of doubtful audibility, there was always a tendency to behavioral disturbance. The immediate cause of the altered behavior was the fine discrimination required between presence and absence of a stimulus" (Dworkin, et al., 1942, p. 75).

---

[4] For the manifestations in the rat, see Chapter 13 by Finger.

Figure 8

The pig reacts to being tethered in the enclosure by lying with eyes closed.

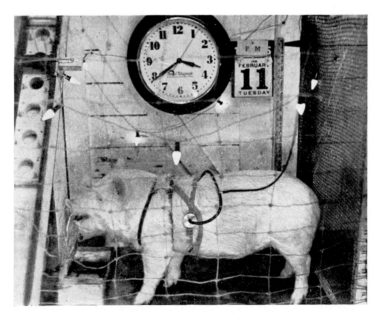

Figure 9

The pig bites the lid of the food box when the lights overhead are turned on. The lights have been associated with the dropping of a piece of apple into the box from the food carrier shown at the left.

Figure 10

The pig trained to expect apple when placed in the harness reacts to the application of a series of strong electric shocks to its left foreleg by kneeling and opening the lid of the food box without squealing or grunting.

Figure 11

Typical behavior on shocking day. The signal for shock has been given and the pig flexes the foreleg to which the shock will shortly be applied.

A simpler method for speedily inducing experimental neurosis in cats has recently been described by Masserman. Cats trained to lift the lid of a box to secure food in response to some signal such as sound or light were, without warning, subjected to a harmless air blast blown across the box at the moment of food taking. One or two repetitions of this procedure resulted in an experimental neurosis. It was found, however, that "if the animal were fed outside the cage before being put into the experimental situation, its neurotic reactions to the feeding signal and to space constriction were less marked than those that occurred when its hunger was intense" (Masserman, 1942). Moreover, once the neurosis was overcome by retraining, constriction, or other therapeutic means, the air blast might even act as a conditioned food signal leading the cat to open the cover of the box.[5]

Then, too, animals develop long-lasting disturbances of behavior in consequence of threatening situations outside of the laboratory. Pavlov describes experimental neurosis resulting from a flood in Leningrad during which the dogs narrowly escaped drowning in their kennels. Some years ago I observed the development of an experimental neurosis in my three-year-old dog. The animal was trapped on a railway trestle by the approach of a fast passenger train and saved its life only by crouching between the rails as the train passed over him. He suffered no injury other than an abrasion and his immediate reaction to the incident was a precipitate flight from the scene. However, he exhibited thereafter a radical change of disposition, from a well-balanced, friendly dog to an aggressive and even dangerous one. His quarrelsomeness and frequent attacks upon people coming to the house or even passing by increased particularly during the third year after the accident and made it necessary for him to be killed.

Where the experimental neurosis has developed in the dog as the result of laboratory conditioning a pronounced change in its disposition is noted, but in such cases the dog directs its resentment toward the experimenter. Gantt's neurotic dog, Nick, snubbed or conspicuously avoided him and behaved in an overly friendly manner to strangers in his presence. Gantt describes Nick's behavior when he was sent to the country for a vacation.

> On first arriving in the country he showed in a marked degree his antipathy to people who had been associated with him in the experimental environment. To these he reacted as he had to a neutral stimulus, such as a light, which had occurred simultaneously with the tone [the conditioned signal associated with the development of

---

[5] Since this chapter went to press, Masserman (1943) has described his work on experimental neuroses in greater detail in a book. In this new book, he also presents an extended critique of the Pavlovian method and of conditioned reflex principles. Masserman bases his own interpretation of experimental neuroses on dynamic principles derived from comparative psychobiology and psychoanalytic theory. He also discusses their relation to the results of experiments on motivation, frustration and conflict and to the phenomena of "social interaction" as observed clinically, and describes their clinical and psychotherapeutic applications.

the experimental neurosis]. Thus when I met him at the station and led him up the road . . . he paid absolutely no attention to my calling him and other friendly gestures but even turned his head in the opposite direction and attempted to pull away from me. Toward strangers he was much more friendly. (1943)[6]

Anderson has described a more aggressive form of hostility exhibited toward him by one of his experimentally neurotic dogs (personal communication). When he entered the experimental room the dog standing in the Pavlov frame would bare its teeth and growl at him and, if too closely approached, would snap.

Before attempting to outline the manifestations of the experimental neurosis some comment upon Pavlov's designation of deviations from normal behavior as experimental neurosis is desirable. It is regrettable that this designation has become imbedded in the literature. However, Pavlov was the first to systematize and to put upon an experimental basis our knowledge of abnormal behavior in animals, and therefore for the present at least the term "experimental neurosis" should probably be retained for the purpose of clearly referring new observations of experimentally produced behavioral abnormality in animals to Pavlov's systematic writings upon this subject. The disturbed state of the dogs following the Leningrad flood was referred to by Pavlov as experimental neurosis because these animals, when tested in the laboratory, showed abnormalities of conditioned reflex action in no way different from abnormalities shown by the dogs whose breakdown resulted from a difficult regimen of conditioning.

The signs of experimental neurosis in the mammals listed above, although diversified, are reducible to a fairly simple common plan. Experimentally neurotic behavior is stereotyped and varies from somnolence, inertness, and immobility to hypersensitivity and overactivity, carried in some instances to the point of manic excitement. One definitely harmful result from the use of the term "experimental neurosis" to describe these devient behaviors is that neurosis suggests specific reference to the clinical manifestations of human nervous and mental disorders. In a field such as ours, in which extensive pioneering is still in progress, the investigator gains little by referring his fragmentary observations on behavioral abnormalities in animals to the thoroughly explored and highly systematized field of human psychopathology. The experienced clinician, casually observing the experimentally neurotic animal, will be reminded of closely similar instances of disordered human behavior. Gantt (1943), describing the behavior of a dog with experimental neurosis which he observed over a period of eight years, says, "If Nick had been a patient his symptoms would have been referred to as anxiety neurosis, merer-

[6] This and the following quotations from Gantt are reproduced with his kind permission from the manuscript of his monograph, "The origin and development of behavior disorders in dogs," forthcoming in the *Psychosomatic Medicine Monographs*.

gasia, phobias, functional tachycardia, palpitation, asthmatic breathing, enuresis, ejaculatio praecox, gastric neurosis."

In discussing his recent investigation of experimental neurosis in the cat Masserman comments on the comparison of "neurotic" behavior patterns in animals and man as follows:

> Specifically, the patterns will differ in efficiency, tempo, duration, lateral or temporal spread, finesse, and complexity of adaptation, depending upon the sensory, perceptive, integrative and motor capacities of the species and of the individual animal under study. For example, from the standpoint of behaviour potentialities, a cat has within its repertoire only a few and relatively primitive patterns even of "normal" behaviour; it eats, drinks, copulates, explores, purrs, chases objects or fights; its "neurosis" can therefore consist only of correspondingly simple deviations in the form of self-starvation, sensory hyperaesthesias, rudimentary phobias, compulsions, regressions, fixations, and other relatively elemental behavioural aberrations. Although the pattern of these phenomena are highly suggestive of their more complex symbolic and persistent counterparts in the human, nevertheless, no cat that I have observed thus far has had the imagery to solve its anxiety by, let us say, strutting, growling, or dressing like Mussolini in overreaction to feline feelings of frustration and inferiority. Similarly, a cat will show experimental behaviour abnormalities only if a relatively elemental drive, such as hunger, be frustrated or made internally conflictful. (1942, p. 346)

When the state of the disturbed animal is systematically examined from the onset of its experimental neurosis, the abnormalities of its physiological functions are observed to pursue a fluctuating course. The "neurotic" manifestations never seem to reach a steady state. The deviations from normal functioning may be briefly summarized.

Neuromuscular manifestations of the experimental neurosis vary according to the surroundings of the animal. When allowed freedom of locomotion within the testing situation its abnormalities of behavior are patent. Moreover, description in teleological terms seems to be a direct and natural procedure. For example, Masserman, in describing the neurotic behavior of his cats in the conflictful feeding situation writes as follows:

> 1. *Chronic "anxiety" in or out of the experimental situation.* This was manifested by restlessness, trembling, crouching, hiding, marked startle responses to minor sensory stimuli, and recurrent or chronic disturbances of pulse and respiration.
>
> 2. *The development of "phobic" responses to stimuli symbolic of the emotionally conflictful stimulation.* The neurotic animal, despite its hunger, now reacted to the formerly welcomed feeding signal with marked accentuation of the symptoms of anxiety and with immediate attempts to escape from the vicinity of the food box. Some animals actually starved themselves into severe cachexia with the food openly displayed and readily available, whereas others accepted only small amounts of food from the hand of the experimenter pro-

vided even then that it differed materially from that used in the conflict situation.[7]

3. *"Regressive" and defensive phenomena.* During their neurosis many cats indulged in kittenish vocalization and behavior, licked and cleaned themselves excessively, became sullen, or courted an unusual amount of fondling by the experimenter and often reacted aggressively toward other animals. "Fixation" of reaction patterns was also observed; e.g., once an animal learned a specific method of escaping from the vicinity of the food it persisted in this pattern, no matter how difficult or apparently painful, even when much easier avenues of escape were made available. "Compulsive" acts likewise appeared; for instance, one animal would hide its head in the food box at the food signal, but would not take the food despite days of starvation. (Masserman, 1942, p. 344)

Gantt also has observed a fixation of reaction pattern in his neurotic dog.

On this day we also noted an important characteristic of Nick's behavior—that he reacted to the past rather than to the present reality. Thus when a tone was sounded Nick began to whine as he had before, and instead of looking toward the source of the tone he looked fixedly in the opposite direction, in that corner of the room whence the tone had previously come and *backed away from the old location of the tone but actually toward its present location.* (1943)

Two further quotations from Gantt's case history of the same dog clearly refer the neuromuscular abnormalities in the experimentally neurotic animal to their site of origin in the conditioning laboratory room.

At times (December 1, 3, 1932 *et seq.*) various steps in the preparation for the experiment seemed to have a summating influence in bringing out the defense reaction. Before the experiment he ate readily outside the camera, and ate first 6 biscuits inside, and even 1 biscuit after the collar was attached to the leash, another biscuit hesitatingly after the salivary disc was applied and even some biscuit afterwards until the conditioned stimuli were given and he started whimpering, crying and refusing food. Conversely, on removing the attachments at a certain stage he began to eat. . . . Thus on December 3, after the experiment he would not eat after the salivary disc was removed, nor when he was taken out of the straps nor when the pneumograph was taken off, but only after the collar was removed, when he jumped on the floor and quickly ate 700 grams of dry dog biscuit.

On January 13, 1933 Nick exhibited a type of restless behavior which was often seen thereafter. When he was released from the apparatus, he jumped off the table, gobbled up his biscuit which he had dropped from his mouth on the floor, dashed in and out of the

[7] Gantt's dog Nick would not eat, even in his kennel, the biscuit (Spratt's Ovals) which had been fed him during the tests leading to his neurosis, but would accept another brand of biscuit (Purina Checkers).

camera, sniffing under the table, jumping on the table a number of times, barking at the biscuits on the table without eating them. Though he would look into the food box, he turned sharply away refusing the food he saw there. Previously he would dash in and out of the camera, but the pattern which appeared on this date in defense form was often repeated thereafter for years. When on the table he shook himself violently, as he had often previously done when in harness to rid himself of the salivary disc. (1943)

When the spontaneous activity of the neurotic sheep is continuously recorded in the living quarters restlessness during the night hours is pronounced in the disturbed animal, although its total activity during the 24-hour period does not differ significantly from that of its normal companions (Anderson and Parmenter, 1941). In the dog, however, Gantt has observed that the neurotic animal is definitely hyperactive for the 24-hour period and the record of its activity from hour to hour shows little or no correspondence with the records of its normal kennel mates.

The observations of the neuromuscular action of the neurotic sheep in the conditioning frame have already been reviewed. In the pig, during the period just preceding the onset of the experimental neurosis, behavior was observed which suggests hallucinatory phenomena. The animal, during an interval between conditioned signals, suddenly began to shake the foreleg to which the shock was routinely applied, squealing as it did so and in every respect suggesting the usual reaction to the conditioned signal. Later, these false reactions disappeared and were replaced by complete immobility in the conditioning pen as has been previously described. Such false reactions have never been observed in the sheep.[8] Pavlov (1941) frequently observed instances of immobility of the dog in the conditioning frame, and Anderson and Parmenter (1941) have recently described the behavior of a neurotic dog which showed pseudo-decerebrate reactions. The limbs could be passively placed in abnormal positions and these positions were maintained for nearly half an hour. Both limbs and neck were rigid and resisted passive flexion and extension. Later this animal developed the excitatory form of experimental neurosis.

Respiratory abnormalities are prominently exhibited in the conditioning frame by the neurotic sheep, dog, and pig and these abnormalities are manifested, though perhaps to a less striking degree, in the living quarters. In the sheep, Anderson describes rapid and shallow respiration and a slower pattern in which apnoeic pauses are frequent (Anderson and Parmenter, 1941). He has recorded similar bizarre patterns in the neurotic sheep when it was standing in the barn with the flock. Gantt (1943) lists four abnormal types of respiration in the neurotic dog, including rapid respiration (150–250 maintained for as long as 10–15 minutes) and a second stereotyped, asthma-like pattern which first ap-

---

[8] Unpublished experiments of Marvin Goldmann, from our laboratory, include records of such false reactions in the goat.

peared in Nick several years after his original conflict. It differed from asthma in that there was no evidence of bronchial spasm. This noisy, raucous breathing, slow and labored, was audible for several hundred feet and was exhibited by him not only in the conditioning laboratory but also when he was taken to the elevator on his way to the experimental room.

Cardiovascular manifestations of the experimental neurosis have so far proved to be substantially the same in sheep and dog (Anderson and Parmenter, 1941). Premonitory signs of the experimental neurosis in the sheep include a gradually rising pulse rate as recorded by the cardiotachometer while the animal is standing quietly in the Pavlov frame. The cardiac disorder which invariably accompanies the experimental neurosis is shown by rapid and irregular pulse and by the extreme sensitivity of the heart's action to conditioned and other stimulation. Mildly startling stimuli induce rapid increases of pulse rate and wide spontaneous variations of rate are observed both in the living quarters and in the laboratory. The conditioned stimulus produces an abnormally long-continued tachycardia with frequent occurrence of premature beats. Gantt has observed in his neurotic dogs that marked increases of pulse rate occur in response to isolated elements of the conditioning situation, particularly to the approach of the experimenter. He (1943) says: "The notable increase in Nick's heart rates to the situation of conflict over the rates to the presence of real danger (growling bull dog, clawing cat) is evidence of the greater effect of the former, the highest heart rate observed in the camera was 205, to the bull dog only 140."

The *gastrointestinal* and *urinary* manifestations of the experimental neurosis have as yet been little explored. In the sheep the frequent defecation and micturition of the neurotic animal in the Pavlov frame are regularly observed and Dworkin, *et al.,* (1942) has reported micturition and vomiting in his neurotic cats when confined to the conditioning box. Refusal of food, sometimes carried to the point of extreme self-starvation, has been noted in the cat in association with the onset of the experimental neurosis (Masserman, 1942) and negativism toward food, together with failure of the salivary conditioned responses, has been reported both by Pavlov (1941) and Gantt (1943). From the examination of samples of gastric juice Gantt has reported the presence of persistent hyperacidity in the neurotic dog. During conditioning tests on certain dogs, when they were subjected to the stress of difficult differentiations, a fecal odor could be detected in the experimental room. In Gantt's dog Nick, pollakiuria was a prominent manifestation of his experimental neurosis. In describing this abnormal behavior Gantt says:

> Working with a large number of normal dogs for 15 years, though they might be kept on the experimental stand for 7 or 8 hours at a time, I do not recall a single instance of micturition during experimentation with a normal animal. . . . During the year prior to experimentation in Nick no instance of micturition in the camera or antecamera was observed. It is of especial interest that the polla-

Figure 12

Typical behavior on feeding day. The pig stands quietly with the lid of the food box held open. The signal for food has been given and a piece of apple will fall into the box in a few seconds.

Figure 13

Experimental arrangement for the study of salivary conditioned reflexes in the pig. The pig is waiting for the signal indicating the presence of food in the box at the foot of the platform. The pig has, through training, learned to suppress its tantrum behavior and to submit to the mild restraint provided by the loose harness shown in the picture.

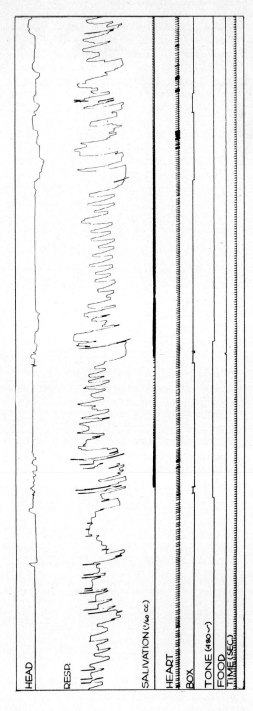

Figure 14

Conditioned salivary reflex from the pig shown in Fig. 13. Reading from the top, the following samples of behavior are recorded: (1) movements of the head. (2) respiration. (3) saliva from the left parotid gland in 1/60 cc. units. (4) heart as recorded electrically by the cardiotachometer. (5) opening of the cover of the food box. The upstroke on the third line from the bottom indicates the sounding of a tone of 480 cycles, the downstroke indicates its cessation. The upstroke on the second line from the bottom indicates the delivery of a small dog biscuit down a chute into the food box. The bottom line gives time in seconds.

kiuria did not begin during the period of excessive strain (1933) but after he had been absent two years or more from the active work of the laboratory, when he was returned to the laboratory in 1936— nearly three years after the period of stress. The pollakiuria became prominent about the time that the dog in estrus was first brought into the camera with Nick, and has persisted until the present, appearing whenever he is brought into the experimental environment, or when *elements* of this environment are present, such as when H.S. approached him even when Nick was on the farm. The severity of this symptom after 1936 was in general parallel to other symptoms of the disturbance. The worst period was 1936 and 1937 before he was taken to the farm. The record was about 30 times in 25 minutes (1937) while running free in the antecamera. Punishment was entirely without effect; after whipping he would run to another part of the room and urinate immediately. Pollakiuria began even in the elevator and the corridors when H.S. was bringing him *toward* the experimental environment. (1943)

Sexual manifestations of the experimental neurosis have not been observed in the sheep. Only castrated males and females have been conditioned to the point of experimental neurosis and in the ewes sexual behavior was normal in all cases, as was their maternal behavior. In the dog, Anderson reports that among his neurotic animals only one excessively shy male showed a possible sexual abnormality. He paid no attention to a bitch in heat placed in the same pen with him although this female was normally receptive. In Gantt's prolonged study of Nick he observed a complex and long-continued sequence of pathological sexual reactions, as the following account shows:

The abnormal sexual erections elicited specifically by the environment of conflict came considerably later than the other pathological reactions. At first were the general definite changes in activity, inhibition of the food conditioned reflexes (as early as 1933), then appeared the stereotyped respiration; the pollakiuria (1935, 1936) and finally in 1937 the pathological sexual erections—first recorded on 20 May 1937 to the sound of the metronome. At first infrequently, later the erections appeared oftener, and not only when the dog was taken into the experimental camera and to the auditory stimuli used there but to isolated elements of this environment. Thus while on the farm in 1939 the presentation to Nick of the kind of food which had been used in the camera resulted more than once in immediate micturition on the food, and sometimes erection with ejaculation. Also the social factors—the presence of those who worked with him, particularly H.S., but also W.H.G., even in a remote environment as on the farm —repeatedly evoked erections with ejaculations. It is remarkable to note that these reactions were elicited by close blood relations of the people who worked with Nick, the son and other close relatives of W.H.G., just as he had shown negativism to the brother of H.S. As the erections were never noted to any other people, there is a possibility that olfactory resemblances exist for the dog with members of the same family. (1943)

In view of our present fragmentary knowledge of the conditions surrounding the onset of the experimental neurosis and of the complex interrelationships of the various manifestations of this condition, little benefit can be derived from an exhaustive account of the therapeutic procedures which have been employed by various investigators. No procedure yet employed has led to the complete disappearance of the neurotic manifestations. A vacation from the laboratory for periods up to three years has proved most efficacious both in sheep and dog, although the establishment of friendly relations between animal and experimenter and reassurance of the animal by the experimenter in the laboratory have proven somewhat effective in the cat and dog. Even in the case of the sheep, however, it has been noticed over a period of many years that the presence of the experimenter in the laboratory room with the neurotic sheep exerts a quieting influence on the animal, which effect disappears when the experimenter enters the adjoining room to begin the tests. Anderson reports the case of an aged sheep in which all manifestations of the experimental neurosis disappeared, although another neurotic sheep at the Cornell Behavior Farm showed the usual manifestations of this disorder up to the time of its death at 13½ years of age. Evanescent benefits are observed from the use of sedatives in the cat (Masserman, 1942), dog (Gantt, 1943), and sheep, and from injections of extract of the adrenal cortex in the sheep (Anderson and Parmenter, 1941).

At present such therapeutic procedures are of value principally as tools which the experimenter may employ in controlling the degree of severity of the neurotic manifestations, the better to understand the causes for the usual waxing and waning of this disturbed state.

Because of their possible theoretical importance two further instances of pathological generalization should be noted. Some time after the development of Nick's experimental neurosis, the tone to which he had formerly reacted by salivating and then promptly eating the proffered biscuit now aroused a definite defensive reaction. When a flashing light was combined with this tone which it preceded by a few seconds, after only 15 tests with the combined stimuli the flashing light alone regularly aroused the abnormal defensive reaction formerly evoked by the tone. The rapid establishment of this new conditioned reflex illustrates the readiness with which neurotic reactions may come to be aroused by trivial or accidental features of the place of origin of the experimental neurosis. A recent experiment [9] still in progress at the Cornell Behavior Farm showed that a sheep, trained in one laboratory room and then transferred to another room where a difficult conditioning procedure precipitated an experimental neurosis, behaved in a normal manner when immediately returned to the room in which it was first conditioned. After the lapse of several days, however, it exhibited the usual signs of the experimental neurosis in both rooms. As we know from previous

---

[9] Unpublished observations of H. S. Liddell and A. Freedman.

observations sheep with experimental neurosis of long standing exhibit the neurotic signs in any laboratory room and in the pasture and barn as well.

Theoretical Considerations.—Although the manifestations of the experimental neurosis just described must be referred for eventual explanation to the operations of the mammalian nervous system their experimental analysis does not as yet fall within the province of the neurophysiologist. Recent advances in the techniques for the direct examination of the functioning of nervous tissue and in refined procedures for the simultaneous recording of the various physiological functions involved in conditioned reflex action give promise of an early fusion of these two experimental disciplines. When it is possible, in the same animal, directly to examine the functioning of its nervous tissue and the changing patterns of effector action resulting from conditioning, a comprehensive theory to account for the experimental neurosis in terms of central nervous action and of effector patterning will be profitable. Meanwhile, the experimenter in the field of animal behavior must remain a peripheralist. His theoretical formulations must be derived from the data of interofective and exterofective action. In this sense, both internist and psychiatrist are peripheralists and, like them, the behaviorist is chiefly concerned with the organization and disorganization of behavior. The behavior of the well adjusted animal subjected to laboratory conditioning differs from that of the experimentally neurotic animal in the many specific details described above. Masserman characterizes the behavior of the neurotic animal as deviant, vacillating, ambivalent, excessively substitutive or symbolic, and biologically inefficient (Masserman, 1942).

In other words, the neurotic pattern exhibits disorganization. To arrive at a working hypothesis as an aid to further laboratory investigation of the experimental neurosis the investigator must explore the spread and temporal course of this disorganization in quantitative detail, not only the instances of neuromuscular maladaptation but also the full particulars concerning autonomic imbalance and endocrine involvement.

BIBLIOGRAPHY

ANDERSON, O. D., & LIDDELL, H. S. 1935. Observations on experimental neurosis in sheep. *Arch. Neurol. Psychiat., Chicago, 34,* 330–354.
ANDERSON, O. D., & PARMENTER, R. 1941. A long-term study of the experimental neurosis in the sheep and dog, with nine case histories. *Psychosom. Med. Monogr., 2,* Nos. 3, 4.
CANNON, W. B. 1929. Bodily changes in pain, hunger, fear and rage. New York: Appleton-Century.
—— 1932. The wisdom of the body. New York: Norton.
COGHILL, G. E. 1929. Anatomy and the problem of behavior. Cambridge: Cambridge University Press.
DWORKIN, S. 1939. Conditioning neuroses in dog and cat. *Psychosom. Med., 1,* 388–396.
DWORKIN, S., BAXT, J. O., & DWORKIN, E. 1942. Behavioral disturbances of vomiting and micturition in conditioned cats. *Psychosom. Med., 4,* 75–81.

GANTT, W. H. 1942. The origin and development of nervous disturbances experimentally produced. *Amer. J. Psychiat., 98,* 475–481.

—— 1943. The origin and development of behavior disorders in dogs. *Psychosom. Med. Monogr.* (In press.)

LIDDELL, H. S., & BAYNE, T. L. 1927. The development of "experimental neurasthenia" in the sheep during the formation of difficult conditioned reflexes. *Amer. J. Physiol., 81,* 494.

LIDDELL, H. S., JAMES, W. T., & ANDERSON, O. D. 1934. The comparative physiology of the conditioned motor reflex, based on experiments with the pig, dog, sheep, goat and rabbit. *Comp. Psychol. Monogr., 11.*

MARCUSE, F., & MOORE, A. U. 1942. Conditioned reflexes in the pig. *Bull. Canad. psychol. Assn., 2,* 13–14.

MASSERMAN, J. H. 1942. Psychobiologic dynamisms in behavior. *Psychiatry, 5,* 341–348.

—— 1943. Behavior and neurosis: an experimental psychoanalytic approach to psychobiologic principles. Chicago: University of Chicago Press.

PAVLOV, I. P. 1902. The work of the digestive glands. (Trans. by W. H. Thompson.) London: Charles Griffin.

—— 1927. Conditioned reflexes. (Trans. by G. V. Anrep.) London: Oxford University Press.

—— 1928. Lectures on conditioned reflexes. (Trans. by W. H. Gantt.) New York: International Publishers.

—— 1941. Conditioned reflexes and psychiatry. (Trans. by W. H. Gantt.) New York: International Publishers.

RICHTER, C. P. 1941. Biology of drives. *Psychosom. Med., 3,* 105–110.

SHERRINGTON, C. S. 1933. The brain and its mechanism. (The Rede Lecture delivered before the University of Cambridge). Cambridge: Cambridge University Press.

SUTHERLAND, G. F., CURTIS, Q. F., DAVIS, G. B., & LIDDELL, H. S. 1943. Conditioned reflexes and experimental neurosis in the pig. (Unpublished)

Chapter 13

EXPERIMENTAL BEHAVIOR DISORDERS IN THE RAT

By Frank W. Finger, Ph.D.

THE USE OF ANIMAL EXPERIMENTATION as an adjunct to the investigation of human behavior disorders has been a recognized psychological field since Pavlov's original account of experimental neurosis in the dog (see Chapter 12 by Liddell). For the most part, however, the early research made use of such experimental subjects as dogs, sheep, and pigs, which were unavailable to the average laboratory worker. The possibility of substituting the rat in these studies has been an inviting prospect, for the extreme convenience in the use of this species makes it an almost standard fixture in the psychological laboratory. The maintenance of a rat colony requires relatively little of space, expense, or attention; the rat adapts itself readily to handling and responds well to training; it is remarkably resistant to infection; its fertility and short life cycle facilitate genetic studies; its critical developmental periods are well marked and bring about changes paralleling the growth sequence in man. It is to be expected that the psychopathologist will eventually receive much suggestive information from studies of the behavior of this animal.

During the period from 1937 to 1940, there was a rather widespread effort to establish experimental neuroses in the rat with conflict as the precipitating factor. Very few of the published studies reported success, however, and it is reasonable to assume that many failures never reached print. Cook (1939) used a situation involving restraint and the method of conditioning to induce conflict, and obtained patterns of disordered behavior in three rats. The individual constellations of symptoms were not uniform, but each animal showed both a disruption of the learned habit of response in the experimental situation and a qualitative change in behavior outside this situation. These two behavior changes seemed to him to justify classification as "experimental neurosis."

Taking their cue from Liddell's (1938) report that the diurnal distribution of activity in sheep was modified in the experimental neurosis, a group of investigators obtained continuous activity records from rats before, during, and after experimental conflict sessions. Hunt and Schlosberg (1944), and Evans and Hunt (1942) found small but statistically significant reductions in the rat's activity as a result of conflict in a discrimination box, with motivation provided by shock. Finger

(1941b) found a slight decrement in activity after sessions involving punished discrimination errors in a Lashley jumping situation. (These activity decrements in the rat contrast with the increases in activity accompanying experimental neurosis in the sheep.) The reduction in the rats' activity lasted, however, for less than 24 hours. It is possible that this capacity for rapid recovery prevents the accumulation of the effects of conflict, and thereby accounts for the difficulty of establishing "experimental neurosis" in the white rat with the procedures ordinarily effective in other mammals.

The fact that several forms of "neurotic" behavior appeared in one experiment where the rats were kept continuously in conflict tends to confirm this hypothesis. Hunt and Schlosberg (1944) electrified the water supply of animals living in metal activity cages. The resulting forms of "neurotic" behavior included large decrements in activity, behavior reminiscent of that associated with hallucinations in human beings, and acute fits of violent activity. The "hallucinatory" behavior occurred during short periods when the electrification of the water supply was discontinued. On several such occasions the rat approached the now-harmless tube with considerable hesitation, drank ravenously for a few seconds, and then suddenly withdrew from the tube, shaking head and nose rapidly as if shocked. The pattern was strikingly similar to that regularly seen in a thirsty rat drinking from the electrified water-tube. The "fits" appeared in only three animals. These were precipitated either by presenting the tube of a test-bottle and withdrawing it or by shaking a few drops of water onto the nose of these animals. Even these "fits" were quite temporary, disappearing whenever the current to the water supply was discontinued for a few days. It would appear from this study that the rat becomes disturbed only when the most primitive of drives are in conflict. Hunt and Schlosberg have suggested the possibility that the capacity for symbolic behavior is too undeveloped in the rat "to allow it to carry its troubles about."

In spite of the failure to establish relatively permanent and severe disorders in the rat, many workers have observed such temporary disturbances as aggressive behavior, flight, huddling, and incontinence. But the rats showing these disturbances appeared quite normal as soon as they were removed from the experimental situation. Such disturbances of behavior also have been noted in the course of numerous learning and discrimination experiments (e.g., Fields, 1931; Hall, 1933; Carmichael, 1938; Turner, 1941; Witkin, 1942). These disturbances are important as analogues of certain human functional disorders, but at present the observations are too uncertain and fragmentary to allow their meaningful integration.

The effort to utilize the rat in experimental psychopathology led in 1938 to the rediscovery of an extremely atypical pattern of response. First classified as an "experimental neurosis" (Maier and Glaser), this strikingly aberrant pattern quickly became the center of considerable controversy, from which the conclusion has gradually evolved that the pattern occurs as a relatively reflex reaction to direct sensory stimulation (primarily of an auditory nature), and has little immediate significance for the study of "conflict." The etiology of this abnormal behavior has been emphasized by the wide acceptance of the designation "audiogenic seizure" (Morgan and Waldman, 1941), while its remarkable objective similarity to human epileptic episodes has been recognized in such terms as "audio-epileptic seizure" (Smith, 1941).[1] But the necessary reinterpretation of the phenomenon has not deprived it of its fascination for the research worker. If it is irrelevant to the problem of human neurosis, its possible implications for the convulsive disorders (see Chapter 31 by Lennox) are thereby increased, and its fundamental potentialities for the more general field of neurophysiology and the specific sector of neuromuscular coordination is in no way lessened. The continued interest in the audiogenic seizure is evidenced by the appearance of some two-score experimental reports in the three and one-half years since its first public demonstration. The complex interrelationships among the various factors of the inducing situation have provided a fertile field for experimental ingenuity. But perhaps most challenging to the researcher is the realization that order has been brought to only a portion of the field, and that the final organization awaits still more systematic and concentrated experimental effort.

In 1938, Maier and Glaser presented a striking photographic record of the abnormal pattern. While forcing rats, with blasts of air, to respond in a discrimination situation for which no appropriate response was available, the experimenters observed several subjects leap from the apparatus and dash violently about the room in an apparently undirected and somewhat uncoordinated manner (Maier and Glaser, 1938; Maier, 1939). After a few seconds an animal might fall into a convulsive state, exhibiting tonic and clonic spasms of varying magnitude and degree of specificity. Following this active period occurred a passive phase, during which resistance to handling was virtually abolished and the animal could be "molded" into practically any position. Behavior very similar to this had been reported before (e.g., in mice, Dice, 1935; possibly in rats, Donaldson, 1924, p. 134), but because in Maier's demonstration the pattern seemed so clearly dependent upon the conflict situation, it was seized upon as having great significance for "neurotic behavior in human beings" (report of the committee on award of the AAAS prize; see *Science,* 1939, 89, p. 93). It was soon pointed out, however, that the same response could be elicited in completely untrained rats by a few seconds of simple auditory stimulation (Morgan and Morgan, 1939). Further, it was noted (Morgan, 1940; Morgan and Waldman, 1941) that this same explanation was applicable to the "neurotic" pattern of Maier's rats: in no instance had seizures occurred

---

[1] This same pattern has also been characterized by the phrases "epileptoid convulsive reaction" (Auer and Smith, 1940), "noise-induced seizure" (Humphrey, 1941), "convulsive seizure" (Patton, 1941; Griffiths, 1942b), and "noise-fright convulsion" (Stainbrook, 1942).

without the use of the air blast which "made a fairly loud noise" (Maier, 1939, p. 9), while in several cases the pattern had been obtained by auditory stimulation alone, while the rat was outside the discrimination situation. Other reports corroborated both the description of the attacks and the fact that intense auditory stimulation, rather than conflict, was the invariable antecedent of the behavior (Humphrey and Marcuse, 1939; Auer and Smith, 1940; Hall and Martin, 1940). Since conflict induced by training was not the prime causal factor, since the latency of many attacks was probably too short to allow the building up of appreciable "psychological tension," and since generalized after-effects of significant duration were not apparent (Finger and Schlosberg, 1941), the consensus of opinion was that this abnormal response pattern did not fit into the classical category of "experimental neurosis" described by Pavlov (1927) and Liddell (1938).[2]

As has been noted, the banishment of the phenomenon from the realm of the neuroses did not extinguish interest in its experimental study. In addition to the detailed analysis of the behavior pattern itself, the principal trends of research have been toward the determination of the external factors affecting seizure-behavior and the clarification of the intrinsic characteristics of the organism that influence susceptibility to attack. Because of the great number of variables that apparently have significance in this respect, some of the studies have not been as well controlled as might be desired. As a result, the data of the various investigators are not always in obvious agreement. An examination of some of the studies may, however, suggest certain tentative conclusions and indicate the directions which future research can profitably take.

The Abnormal Behavior Pattern

Considering the extreme atypicality of the audiogenic behavior pattern and the wide variety of conditions under which it has been elicited, it is perhaps surprising that there is such close agreement among the descriptions emanating from the different laboratories. There are, to be sure, a few discrepancies regarding certain details, but the majority of these may be understood in terms of the nonuniformity of experimental conditions. In general, the outlines of the salient features are sufficiently parallel to justify the assumption that the several investigators are considering the same phenomenon.

---

[2] Some writers (e.g., Kreezer, 1942, p. 240) would classify as experimental neurosis any behavior, produced experimentally, which resembles abnormal states in man. Such a definition allows the inclusion under this heading of these audiogenic attacks, as well as, presumably, seizures induced by metrazol injection, electroshock, and dietary deficiency, and any abnormal behavior produced by surgical means which resembles an "abnormal state in man." Without attempting to decide just what behavior of a rat may resemble human behavior it would seem that such a definition strains the meaning of the term confusingly beyond the limits of its original connotation.

Overt Reaction.—For the sake of analysis, the complete audiogenic seizure may be divided into three parts: the fore-period, the active phase, and the passive phase. In the strictest sense, perhaps, only the active phase should be included as the seizure proper, for it is commonly regarded as the distinguishing characteristic of the behavior pattern. In the interest of ultimate explanation, however, the complete sequence should be examined.

The fore-period is more than an interval of inactive latency. After the initial startle response to the onset of the auditory stimulation, a variety of behavior may be observed, much of it symptomatic of later reaction. Sometimes the animal crouches low, or attempts to burrow beneath the floor covering or his fellow subjects. A state of heightened sensitivity (particularly to additional auditory stimuli) is frequently apparent. "Substitute behavior" (nose rubbing, ear scratching, digging movements, chattering of the teeth, cleaning, and yawning) is observed, particularly in trials that do not culminate in a seizure. Usually before the beginning of the active phase characteristic activity of a "premonitory" nature occurs—pivoting movements of head or body, brief backward scurrying, jerky sidling steps, short quick runs. Smith (1941) reports that this "motor aura" is followed in 80% of instances by a clear-cut seizure.

After a latency varying between 2 seconds (or less) and 2 or 3 minutes of stimulation (average 30–40 sec.), the active phase begins with an explosive burst of running. To the casual observer the extreme speed and disorientation of this activity place it in a category outside the normal range of behavior, and quantitative stabilimeter recordings confirm this judgment (Auer and Smith, 1940; Smith, 1941). The animal in this stage seems to make no effort to avoid running into obstacles. If the rat is confined in a cage, his behavior is frequently interpreted as an attempt to escape. The running aspect of the pattern may be interrupted by a quiet period, but usually it leads directly into the tonic-clonic phase. This segment of the pattern is marked first by either extreme tonicity or very rapid clonic beating of the limbs, during which the animal is prone or lying on his side. More distinct clonic twitches gradually begin to be differentiated from the gross contractive state, increasing in amplitude and decreasing in frequency until a period of spasmodic jumping (one jump every 1–6 sec.) is reached. This may continue for the duration of stimulation, or the animal may pass into a state of relative immobility. During the active phase incontinence, ejaculation, squealing, and cyanosis are sometimes observed, and in a very small percentage of young animals this phase terminates in death. (More complete descriptions, including variations, may be found in the accounts of Maier, 1939; Smith, 1941; and Stainbrook, 1942.)

The final, passive phase may take either of two forms. In a few cases (particularly following a brief seizure) the animal is hypersensitive to sound or tactual stimulation (Hall and Martin, 1940), although for the greater part motionless in the absence of such stimuli. In most instances, however, there is a coma-like condition, during which reaction to external stimulation is greatly decreased. Reflexes are depressed to varying degrees: placing, pinna, tactual, and even corneal responses may fail to appear. Spontaneous activity is entirely lacking; the animal is nonresistant to handling and maintains any imposed position. Most investigators (e.g., Maier, 1939, p. 64) report failure of the righting reflex after a complete seizure, and unpublished data of the present writer indicate a marked diminution of righting even after a brief running attack. On the other hand, Stainbrook states that immediately following the convulsion "the righting reflexes can be demonstrated" (1942, p. 339). The comatose condition may continue for as long as 10 minutes (although seldom lasting longer than 2–3 min.), with gradual recovery to a near-normal condition. A recovering animal seems extremely fatigued, and activity records demonstrate that the frequency of movement is subnormal for about 12 hours (Finger and Schlosberg, 1941).

Criterion of a Seizure.—The generalized description given above refers only to a complete seizure. Many times one or more components fail to appear but the behavior is nevertheless so definitely atypical that it can be classified as an audiogenic seizure. Maier uses as his usual criterion the violent running aspect (Maier and Sacks, 1941). Humphrey and Marcuse (1941), and Snee, Terrence, and Crowley (1942) require that the passive phase as well as the running occur before the reaction is placed in the seizure category. It would seem that unless there is an unmistakable period of running or convulsion, definite evidence in such form as the lack of righting response should be a requisite for classification as audiogenic seizure. The question of what constitutes an attack has only an arbitrary answer. It is probable that there exists in reality a continuum of severity and consistency of attack, ranging from premonitory behavior or a few mild jumps to the total constellation of symptoms. The data of a particular experiment will of course have meaning only in relation to the specific criterion adopted.

Electrical Activity.—As a supplement to the observation of overt seizure behavior, Lindsley, Finger, and Henry (1942) recorded the rat's electroencephalogram and electrocardiogram before, during, and after seizures. By means of the electrical records it was sometimes possible to predict the imminence of a seizure before any externally observable sign appeared. The EEG pattern during attacks exhibited many features in common with the EEG in human subjects during epileptic seizures or in convulsions induced by metrazol injection or electro-shock. The character of the abnormal electrical activity varied with the phase of the overt attack: "large slow waves or spike-and-slow waves of two to four per second were associated with clonic phases; series of spikes or fast low amplitude waves were found during tonic periods; during comatose periods there was a tendency toward absence of all electro-cortical activity at first, but with a gradual return of the EEG to a normal prestimulation level as the animal recovered from the coma. . . . There was no evidence of subclinical attacks, i.e., abnormal EEG patterns of convulsive character without overt signs of seizure" (p. 187ff).

The heart rate of susceptible animals, especially those about to have a seizure, showed a marked change following the onset of stimulation. Most frequently there was an increase of considerable magnitude, followed by a slowing just before the attack. In some rats (particularly those with an initially high heart rate) the beginning of auditory stimulation led to an immediate and sharp drop, with an increase usually intervening before the attack. The EKG of a few animals exhibited alternate accelerations and decelerations, with an overall increase predominating. During the active phase of the seizure the heart rate was usually elevated. The passive phase was marked by an extreme decline in heart action, often reaching a level as low as 100–200 beats per minute (prestimulation level of 400–440 per min.). Frequent irregularities were observed, and in two animals the QRS or ventricular component of the EKG was omitted. [Marcuse and Moore (1941) also report variability of heart rate, as well as of respiration, during the comatose stage.] As recovery was noted in the overt behavior picture, the heart action returned gradually to normal.

Incidence.—Not all rats respond with the aberrant pattern to auditory stimulation. Some exhibit only substitute behavior, or make no noticeable response. The percentage of susceptible animals, as well as the consistency with which a given animal will respond positively, varies with the experimental sample and with a variety of extrinsic and intrinsic factors. The early paper of Morgan and Morgan (1939) reported less than 10% of susceptible subjects, but later experiments with larger groups have yielded higher figures. Smith (1941) found 33% of 1309 rats responding; Farris and Yeakel (1942), 38% of 76 rats; Hall and Martin (1940), 43% of 51 rats; and Morgan (1941), 44% of a group of 160. The results of test trials spread over several months of the animal's life suggest that a total incidence of responding rats as high as 65–72% may be expected in an unselected population (Finger, 1943).

Factors Influencing Susceptibility

Few, if any, rats will respond overtly every time the standard stimulus is given. A brief discussion of the effect on susceptibility of the factors in the objective situation and within the organism itself will indicate the difficulty of predicting the response in an individual instance.

Extrinsic Factors.—

THE PRECIPITATING STIMULUS.—The early controversy of "neurotic pattern" *vs.* "audiogenic seizure" centered primarily around the question of the stimulus agent required to precipitate the abnormal behavior. Maier (1939) held that the conflict engendered by an intolerable problem situation was the factor producing the response. But Morgan and Morgan asserted (1939), and Humphrey and Marcuse (1939) and Hall and Martin (1940) confirmed, that only an auditory stimulus of certain characteristics was necessary to produce the reaction. Maier and Glaser later concurred to the extent of stating that "auditory stimuli are basic in the production of abnormal behavior" (1940a, p. 29) and experimentally comparing the relative effectiveness of several stimulus situations.

Among the auditory stimuli that have been used in the elicitation of the pattern are the hiss of air or air blast (Maier and Glaser, 1938; Bayroff, 1940; Martin and Hall, 1941), the high-pitched tones of a Galton whistle (Auer and Smith, 1940; Morgan, 1941; Finger and Schlosberg, 1941), the ringing of a bell (Humphrey and Marcuse, 1939; Bernhardt, et al., 1941; Griffiths, 1942b; Sisk, 1942), the sound of a buzzer (Patton and Karn, 1941; Stainbrook, 1942), the jingling of keys (Maier and Glaser, 1940a; Donaldson, 1924), the combined sound of buzzer and Galton whistle (Snee, et al., 1942), and the tones of an oscillator (Morgan and Gould, 1941). The degree of effectiveness varies with the stimulus agent employed, and Maier and Glaser (1940a) state that the quality, rather than the intensity of the sound, is the significant determining variable. For example, they report that the jingling of keys is less loud (to the human ear) than the sound of the Galton whistle, and yet it provokes more attacks. Morgan and Gould's results, however, indicate a clear-cut positive relationship between intensity and number of attacks, with sound frequency constant; and a similar relationship between percentage of attacks and frequency of the stimulating sound, with intensity constant (1941). It may be, then, that the jingling keys precipitated the greater number of attacks because the particularly effective high-pitched tones (inaudible to the human ear) were of greater intensity with this form of stimulation than when the whistle was used. Morgan and Galambos (1943) make this stimulus-response relationship still more explicit: the effectiveness of stimulation depends not upon absolute intensity level, but upon sensation level (i.e., decibels above threshold). The fact that high-pitched tones produce more attacks than lower tones of the same objective intensity is thus dependent upon the rat's lower threshold for tones of high frequency. It may be concluded, then, that the likelihood of aberrant response to auditory stimulation becomes greater as the intensity of the particular stimulus is raised further above the animal's threshold.

In the light of this relationship, it is not surprising that the percentage of responses varies with the type of chamber in which the rat is stimulated. Thus, close to the sound source and within a closed box, the rat is stimulated more intensely than when one side of the box is open or the sound source is more remote. It would seem reasonable to require that the changed physical aspects of the stimulation be considered before variation in response is attributed to the more subtle variable of conflict (see Maier and Glaser, 1940a).

The possibility that other forms of stimulation may induce the seizure pattern must be examined. Dice reports (see Maier, 1939, p. 1) that blowing smoke at the "epileptic" mouse will in some instances result in an attack. Chick, El Sadr, and Warden describe "epileptiform fits" similar to the audiogenic seizure in rats suffering from long-term vitamin B_6 deficiency: "the slightest external stimulus seemed to precipitate them" (1940, p. 597). This perhaps means that because of the chronic nutritional subnormality the rats were extremely sensitive to sounds not loud enough normally to cause the aberrant reaction. But, further, the fits occasionally followed merely the stroking of the rat or the pricking of the tail. Also to be considered are the fits appearing in vitamin-deprived pigs, with no mention by the experimenters of a precipitating stimulus (Chick, Macrae, Martin, and Martin, 1938). The implications of these studies must be checked experimentally before the conclusion is reached that the seizure pattern can result only from intense auditory stimulation.[3]

RESTRAINT.—Maier emphasized in his early reports (1939; Maier and Glaser, 1940a) that "psychological restraint," in the form of reduced possibilities for response, was a determining factor of the "neurotic pattern." That such procedures as partially or wholly enclosing the animal in a small chamber do increase the frequency of attack is not controverted, but the first explanation that must be considered is the possibility that the stimulation value of the sound reaching the animal is changed thereby. It is quite possible, on the other hand, that the restrictions imposed on the animal bring about a physiological (emotional) alteration which, as pointed out below, might be expected to effect a temporary elevation of the susceptibility level.

The more severe mechanical restraint of binding the rat seems to have the opposite effect on susceptibility. Griffiths (1942) reports that this procedure at least "alleviates" the seizures, while the data of Humphrey (1941) and Lindsley, et al. (1942) suggest that the num-

---

[3] Page (1941) has produced seizures in the rat by passing a brief electric current through the cortex. These seizures lack the running stage characteristic of the audiogenic seizure, but include strikingly similar tonic-clonic aspects. Stainbrook (1942) has by means of less intense electrical stimulation precipitated attacks which further resemble audiogenic seizures in their inclusion of a running phase. Hamilton (1942) has described a convulsive seizure in certain strains of rats which usually appears in response to tactile or auditory stimulation. In a few instances the behavior has been observed when "there was no known precipitating factor." This pattern differs from the typical audiogenic seizure in several respects but principally in the absence of the running component of the attack. Since this chapter went to press, Griffiths (1942a) has described an experiment in which 10% of the animals had seizures in response to a conflict situation without auditory stimulation. Providing a shelter into which the animals might run when stimulated reduced the incidence of seizures by 58%. Such findings have led Griffiths to reject the audiogenic theory and to argue that fear is the basic factor producing the seizures.

ber of seizures decreases with increasing degrees of restraint. The latter report suggests that the lack of overt and electrical manifestations of the abnormal pattern under conditions of extreme restriction may be due to the draining off of nervous energy through the continuous isometric contractions against the restraining bonds. Obviously the final interpretation of this point waits upon further research.

GROUP FACTORS.—According to Hall and Martin (1940), the results of group testing are the same as for individual testing. No specific evidence is cited in support of this statement, and it is not impossible that more complete investigation will reveal that at least certain "social" situations do affect response. That the noisy reactions of one animal will reinforce the clonic spasms of another is a definite observation of the present writer. To the extent that such auditory stimulation may be regarded as "social," it is legitimate to state that the behavior pattern can be altered by social or group factors.

Intrinsic Factors.—When all external experimental conditions are held constant, wide ranges of intra-group and intra-individual variability are observed. This residual variation in susceptibility must be ascribed to certain organic characteristics of the individual, both transitory (e.g., physiological state) and more or less permanent in nature (structure). Enough experimental evidence is available to allow a discussion of several of these intrinsic factors.

HEREDITY.—Incidental observations early suggested that the predisposition to audiogenic seizure is to some degree heritable. The "epileptic" pattern in mice was reported by Dice (1935) and Watson (1939) to be transmitted as a Mendelian recessive trait. An experimental test of the hereditary factor in the rat was made by Maier and Glaser (1940b). The parent generation was tested with jingling keys on five successive days; any form of attack appearing at any time was construed to indicate susceptibility. The offspring ($N = 78$) were tested similarly at the age of 12 weeks. 74.3% of the offspring of five susceptible-susceptible crosses, 52% of four susceptible-normal crosses, and 0% of three normal-normal matings, were classified as susceptible. On the basis of these results the experimenters concluded that the abnormal reaction tendency is inherited, and that "the evidence suggests that it is transmitted as a dominant trait and that the trait is unitary" (p. 418).

Later experiments indicate that this conclusion may be too simple (Finger, 1943). Using a greater number of cases and testing the filial generation repeatedly over the first ten months of life, it was found that 73% of the animals resulting from the susceptible-normal crosses exhibited the abnormal response, and 68% of the offspring of apparently normal parents gave positive reactions to the stimulus (Galton whistle). No clear-cut conclusion may be drawn from these figures, for the parents were tested over a relatively limited period of their life-span; some of the apparently nonsusceptibles might have reacted positively if tested at a different age. It would seem safe to assume, however, particularly in view of individual gradations in degree of response, that the hereditary determination of the response pattern is somewhat more complex than in a unitary Mendelian trait. Further investigation is required to settle the question, with long-term testing of each generation, and with a systematic variation of the other pertinent factors.

SEX.—Little experimental evidence exists concerning sex differences in susceptibility. Morgan (1941) found no significant inter-sex difference in latency of attack, but reported nothing regarding percentages of responding animals. Some data point toward appreciably greater susceptibility in the male: unpublished figures of the writer show 50 of 268 unselected males (18.7%) responding in a series of four test-sessions, while only 13 of 112 females (11.6%) exhibited the abnormal response. These incidental results are, however, little more than suggestive, and fail to find definite confirmation in other experiments (e.g., Finger, 1943). Females may be expected because of physiological factors to show greater variability of response than males (e.g., greater susceptibility during lactation (Patton, 1941), decreased susceptibility during the oestral period of increased general activity). But it is premature at this juncture to impute to either sex the greater overall tendency to audiogenic seizure.

AGE.—The influence of age on susceptibility has frequently been disregarded when the seizure-producing effects of various experimental conditions have been compared. The importance of controlling this factor becomes clear when it is demonstrated that the susceptibility of an animal changes as a function of his age, that the percentage of susceptible rats in a group will depend in part upon the age of the individuals composing the group. Conclusions regarding the relative effectiveness of the various stimulus situations may be distorted unless the age differentials of the groups are taken into account. A group which, at one month, includes 20% of responding animals may be expected to have a different susceptibility index two or twelve months later; long-range studies of diet, for example, are necessarily complicated by this fact.

The relationship between age and susceptibility is not a simple one. Smith (1941) reports that 32% of six- to seven-week-old rats exhibited seizures, while in a group of eight-month-old animals the percentage was 38 (although the attacks in the older rats tended to be less severe). Farris and Yeakel (1942) compared the proportion of susceptible animals in three groups: 32% in rats 21–26 days old, 15% in rats 289–442 days old, and 6% in rats 589–632 days old. The data of these two studies are not directly comparable, inasmuch as certain other relevant conditions were dissimilar. They may be combined tentatively, however, to suggest that increasing age may first bring about an increase, and then a decrease in percentage of attacks. The curve of susceptibility as a function of age may be multi-modal (Finger, 1943), fluctuating with the numerous physiological and receptor changes that normally mark the successive stages of an animal's life. The frequency figures characterizing the different ages will undoubtedly vary from experiment to experiment, depending upon the genetic background of the groups, as well as upon dietary factors and the objective conditions of testing. It would appear, certainly, that in the design of a satisfactory experiment the possible significance of the age factor must be recognized.

PREVIOUS SEIZURES.—It is generally accepted that immediately after a complete audiogenic seizure the susceptibility of the rat is greatly reduced, so that it is seldom possible to elicit promptly a second full attack. But the conclusions of the several studies investigating this problem of adaptation over longer periods (e.g., 24 hours) are not in agreement. The experiments of Morgan (1941), Smith (1941), Billingslea (1941), and Humphrey and Marcuse (1941) indicate that as the testing of the rat continues, his susceptibility decreases in successive trials. On the other hand, Patton and Karn (1941) and Parker (1941) report that little or no decrease in number of attacks was observed even when daily testing was continued systematically for four weeks. Adaptation took place when Maier and Glaser used the air blast as stimulus, but little decrease in frequency of attacks occurred when the jingling of keys provided the stimulation (1940a). These apparently contradictory results may partially be reconciled by reference to other variables affecting susceptibility, if it is assumed that there is an individual susceptibility threshold that is temporarily raised following a seizure. If sufficient time elapses before the next trial to allow the return of the threshold to its original level, response is again possible; if the interval has been too short to permit recovery, adaptation is apparent. This is consistent with the finding that rats regularly responding when tested at 24-hour intervals exhibit the adaptation phenomenon (i.e., fail to respond) when stimulated at shorter intervals (Finger, 1942). Further, if the threshold has not yet returned to normal, response may still occur if the stimulus is sufficiently intense: the high-pitched components of Maier and Glaser's jingling keys were louder than the corresponding frequencies of the air blast. In short, the probability of response depends upon the interval since previous response, the individual rat's rate of recovery, and the intensity of stimulation, as well as upon the factors of genetic constitution, age, and physiological condition. That the effect of an attack on this threshold may be attributable to the resultant fatigue is suggested by Humphrey and Marcuse's report that exercise in an activity wheel prior to stimulation decreases the likelihood of seizure.

DIETARY DETERMINANTS.—The nutritional state, temporary or chronic, is a potent determiner of susceptibility. After a 12- to 24-hour period of total food and/or water deprivation, the number of rats responding abnormally to auditory stimulation increases markedly (Finger,

1942; Patton, Karn, and King, 1942).[4] A long period of restricted rations, even when supplemented by vitamin feeding, also increases susceptibility. Patton, *et al.*, have found further that a temporary rise in sensitivity to the precipitating stimulus is brought about by the restoration of an *ad lib.* diet following 72-hour deprivation.

The effects of vitamin B deficiency have been studied intensively by Patton and his collaborators. It is well established that deprivation of food normally supplying these elements increases the susceptibility to attack, while supra-normal feeding of the vitamins (and particularly of the B_1 component—thiamin) provides a significant degree of protection against the seizures (King, Karn, and Patton, 1941). However, vitamin deficiency plus restricted caloric intake may in extreme cases actually decrease the susceptibility to attack (Patton, *et al.*, 1941). In each of a group of rats given basal diets containing carbohydrate in the form of sucrose or raw starch, and in addition deprived of vitamin B_6, a condition was produced by Chick, *et al.* (1940), in which minimal stimulation precipitated attacks. Since injection of vitamin B_6 improved or cured the condition, it may be concluded that the vitamin deficiency was an important predisposing factor in the situation. On the other hand, Smith found that in six-weeks-old rats, deprived of the normal amount of vitamin D for the first four weeks of life, there was no higher proportion of susceptible animals than in a normally fed group (1941).

These studies demonstrate that the nutritional basis of susceptibility to seizures is a complex matter the interrelationships of which can be determined only by experiment. They indicate clearly, however, that the sensitivity to auditory stimulation is closely dependent upon the physiological state of the organism.

DRUGS.—The dependence of the susceptibility threshold upon physiological condition has been confirmed by studies involving the administration of certain drugs. Subconvulsive injections of metrazol temporarily increase the frequency of aberrant response to sound; rats never responding in their normal condition to auditory stimulation may react positively after small doses of the drug, and the consistency of susceptible animals' responses may in the same manner be increased. The audiogenic response pattern induced in the metrazol state is unusually severe (Karn, Lodowski, and Patton, 1941), but it nevertheless includes the typical components of the auditory seizure (Maier, Sacks and Glaser, 1941).

Injections of strychnine sulphate and of caffeine sodium benzoate predispose the rat to audiogenic seizure to an even greater extent; the tonic and clonic stages of these attacks are especially pronounced (Snee, *et al.*, 1942). Eserine and nicotine also increase the frequency of attacks

---

[4] Longer deprivation may lead to an irregular decrease in susceptibility, according to Patton, Karn, and King; this drop in response level may be due in part, however, to the adaptation factor, for their test trials were spaced at only 6-hour intervals.

(Humphrey, 1941, 1942a, 1942b). On the other hand, atropine decreases susceptibility (Humphrey), and a similar effect may follow injections of curare (Lindsley, *et al.*, 1942), of dilantin, and of adrenal cortex extract (Griffiths, 1942b).[5] The mode of operation of these drug effects is still obscure. Presumably the alteration of the internal environment brings about some change in the level of neural (probably autonomic) excitability. The solution of this problem may have great therapeutic implications for the human convulsive disorders.

CONFLICT AND EMOTIONALITY.—It would seem quite clear that experimentally induced conflict is not the essential condition for the elicitation of the aberrant behavior. Such a fact does not, however, preclude the possibility that conflict may increase the susceptibility of rats to audiogenic seizure, as Maier and Glaser have asserted (1940a). It has been demonstrated above that the tendency to respond abnormally is in part a function of physiological condition. One of the ways in which the physiological condition of an organism can be altered is the precipitation of an intense emotional state; by changing the emotional level of the rat, conflict could thus increase the likelihood of response to auditory stimulation. Bernhardt, Tobin, and Signori (1941) have demonstrated that although forcing the animals by means of electric shock to respond in a discrimination-jumping situation does not cause convulsive behavior, the conflict-trained animals are more susceptible to seizure when the auditory stimulation is finally applied. The role that emotion can play in the determination of susceptibility is illustrated in this experiment, as well as in Humphrey and Marcuse's early report on the effect of chronic disturbances (1939) and in their later finding that 62% of a group of untamed rats, in contrast to only 8% of a tamed group, exhibited audiogenic seizures (1941). That the development of fixations and abortive jumping may decrease the number of convulsive attacks (Maier, 1940; Maier and Klee, 1941) is perhaps to be ascribed to the emotion-relieving character of these "escape" reactions. But even though conflict and escape from conflict can change the frequency of attack in response to auditory stimulation, the seizure is attributable to conflict only to the same extent as to any other factor (e.g., feeding deprivation or drug injection) that significantly alters the physiological state of the organism.

Chronic emotionality of an hereditary nature has also been related to susceptibility. Billingslea (1941) and Martin and Hall (1941) have shown that rats found by the open field technique to be extremely "emotional" (see Hall, 1934) are less prone to convulsive attacks than are "nonemotional" rats. Their postulation that the excitability (i.e., high activity level) of the emotional rats serves as a safety valve for the noise-induced "emotional tension" is indirectly confirmed by the report of

---

[5] Griffiths' results are inconclusive, for his drug-test sessions occurred only 20 minutes after a previous seizure. This is too short an interval to allow the return of the susceptibility threshold to normal, and so a greatly decreased frequency of attack would be expected, even without the drug treatment.

Humphrey and Marcuse (1941) that neuromuscular activity before and during auditory stimulation decreases the percentage of seizures.

OTHER FACTORS. The sensitivity to nonseizure-producing sounds may prove to be a pertinent factor. Turner (1941) has found that rats susceptible to seizures have a more pronounced startle response to sudden sounds, and probably respond more actively to an increased general noise level, than do nonsusceptible animals. Whether this relationship depends upon sensory acuity or is of a more central nature is not clear.

Some fragmentary data indicate tentatively that extirpation of the frontal pole of the cortex abolishes the convulsive response (Smith, 1941). It may also be that section of the vagus nerves decreases (Humphrey, 1941) or eliminates (Lindsley, et al., 1942) the appearance of the attacks. The use of the operative technique—cortical and subcortical destruction, severing of the auditory and vestibular nerves, cochlear damage, limiting of effector innervation—holds exceptionally great promise for the determination of the neurophysiological bases of audiogenic seizures.

Theoretical Implications

This survey of the experimental phenomena of the convulsive disorder points to the conclusion that the aberrant pattern is the result of direct sensory stimulation, and not of conflict. Since intense auditory stimulation is the only invariable antecedent of the behavior that has been demonstrated,[6] it would seem logical to assign the primary "cause" of the behavior to this factor. Little progress has been made in the determination of the underlying physiological mechanisms, perhaps because the complexity of the predisposing background has not been sufficiently recognized. The records of electrical activity suggest that increased autonomic discharge and an abnormal building up of a cortical excitatory state precede the seizures (Lindsley, et al., 1942). It is not clear, however, why these effects result from auditory stimulation, or why they should culminate in the violent overt attack. The need is apparent for an integrated program of investigation which will make particular use of electrical and operative techniques and employ controlled and systematic variation of single isolated factors in the situation.

It is difficult to evaluate the ultimate significance of these investigations for problems of human behavior disorders. The resemblance of the audiogenic seizure to certain forms of human epilepsy cannot be overlooked; our understanding of the human disturbance may eventually be advanced through the study of the rat's abnormal reaction. Moreover, the findings of these animal experiments may contribute appreciably to

---

[6] By auditory stimulation is meant stimulation by air vibrations of a frequency within the rat's normal audibility range. The mediation by the associated vestibular apparatus cannot be ruled out at this point. A possible exception to the rule of auditory stimulation is found in Chick's dietary studies in which the precipitating stimulus is not clearly designated (1938, 1940).

the theory and practice of shock therapy. In any instance, the revelation of the nature of the audiogenic seizure will do much to further our general knowledge of the principles of normal and atypical neuro-muscular reaction.

BIBLIOGRAPHY

AUER, E. T., & SMITH, K. U. 1940. Characteristics of epileptoid convulsive reactions produced in rats by auditory stimulation. *J. comp. Psychol., 30,* 255–259.

BAYROFF, A. G. 1940. Air blasts as substitutes for electric shock in discrimination learning of white rats. *J. comp. Psychol., 29,* 109–118.

BERNHARDT, K. S., TOBIN, F. J., & SIGNORI, E. 1941. Exploratory studies of abnormal behavior in the rat. *J. comp. Psychol., 32,* 575–582.

BILLINGSLEA, F. Y. 1941. The relationship between emotionality and various salients of behavior in the rat. *J. comp. Psychol., 31,* 69–77.

CARMICHAEL, L. 1938. Learning which modifies an animal's subsequent capacity for learning. *J. genet. Psychol., 52,* 159–163.

CHICK, H., EL SADR, M. M., & WARDEN, A. N. 1940. The occurrence of fits of an epileptiform nature in rats maintained for long periods on a diet deprived of vitamin B_6. *Biochem. J. 34,* 595–600.

CHICK, H., MACRAE, T. F., MARTIN, A. J. P., & MARTIN, C. J. 1938. The water-soluble B-vitamins other than aneurin (vitamin B_1), riboflavin and nicotinic acid required by the pig. *Biochem. J., 32,* 2207–2224.

COOK, S. W. 1939. The production of "experimental neurosis" in the white rat. *Psychosom. Med., 1,* 293–308.

DICE, L. R. 1935. Inheritance of waltzing and of epilepsy in mice of the genus *Peromyscus. J. Mammol., 16,* 25–35.

DONALDSON, H. H. 1924. The rat: data and reference tables. (2nd ed.) Philadelphia: Wistar Institute.

EVANS, J. T., & HUNT, J. McV. 1942. The "emotionality" of rats. *Amer. J. Psychol., 55,* 528–545.

FARRIS, E. J., & YEAKEL, E. 1942. The effect of age upon susceptibility to audiogenic seizures in albino rats. *J. comp. Psychol., 33,* 249–251.

FIELDS, P. E. 1931. Contributions to visual discrimination in the white rat: II. *J. comp. Psychol., 11,* 349–366.

FINGER, F. W. 1941a. Quantitative studies of "conflict": I. Variations in latency and strength of the rat's response in a discrimination-jumping situation. *J. comp. Psychol., 31,* 97–127.

—— 1941b. Quantitative studies of "conflict": II. The effect of "conflict" upon the general activity of the white rat. *J. comp. Psychol., 32,* 139–152.

—— 1942. Factors influencing audiogenic seizures in the rat: repeated stimulation and deprivation of food and drink. *Amer. J. Psychol., 55,* 68–76.

—— 1943. Factors influencing audiogenic seizures in the rat: heredity and age. *J. comp. Psychol., 35,* 227–232.

FINGER, F. W., & SCHLOSBERG, H. 1941. The effect of audiogenic seizures on general activity of the white rat. *Amer. J. Psychol., 54,* 518–527.

GRIFFITHS, W. J., JR. 1942a. The production of convulsions in the white rat. *Comp. Psychol. Monogr., 17,* No. 8. P. 29.

—— 1942b. The effects of dilantin on convulsive seizures in the white rat. *J. comp. Psychol., 33,* 291–296.

HALL, C. S. 1933. A comparative psychologist's approach to problems in abnormal psychology. *J. abnorm. soc. Psychol., 28,* 1–5

—— 1934. Emotional behavior in the rat: I. Defecation and urination as measures of individual differences in emotionality. *J. comp. Psychol., 18,* 385–403.

HALL, C. S., & MARTIN, R. F. 1940. A standard experimental situation for the study of abnormal behavior in the rat. *J. Psychol., 10,* 207–210.

HAMILTON, J. R. 1942. Epileptiform convulsions in rats: I. Description of the phenomena and a comparison with symptomatology of human epilepsy. *J. comp. Psychol., 33,* 297–303.

HUMPHREY, G. 1941. Experiments on the physiological mechanism of noise-induced seizures in the albino rat. *Bull. Canad. psychol. Assn.. 1,* 39–41.

HUMPHREY, G. 1942a. Experiments on the physiological mechanism of noise-induced seizures in the albino rat: I. The action of parasympathetic drugs. *J. comp. Psychol., 33,* 315–323.

—— 1942b. Experiments on the physiological mechanism of noise-induced seizures in the albino rat: II. The site of action of the parasympathetic drugs. *J. comp. Psychol., 33,* 325–342.

HUMPHREY, G., & MARCUSE, F. 1939. New methods of obtaining neurotic behavior in rats. *Amer. J. Psychol., 52,* 616–619.

—— 1941. Factors influencing the susceptibility of albino rats to convulsive attacks under intense auditory stimulation. *J. comp. Psychol., 32,* 285–306.

HUNT, J. McV., & SCHLOSBERG, H. S. 1944. The behavior of rats kept continuously in conflict. *J. comp. Psychol.* (To be published)

KARN, H. W., LODOWSKI, C. H., & PATTON, R. A. 1941. The effect of metrazol on the susceptibility of rats to sound-induced seizures. *J. comp. Psychol., 32,* 563–567.

KING, C. G., KARN, H. W., & PATTON, R. A. 1941. Nutritional deficiency as a factor in the abnormal behavior of experimental animals. *Science, 94,* 186–187.

KREEZER, G. L. 1942. Technics for the investigation of psychological phenomena in the rat. In Griffith, J. Q., & Farris, E. J., *The rat in laboratory investigation.* Philadelphia: Lippincott. Pp. 199–273.

LIDDELL, H. S. 1938. The experimental neurosis and the problem of mental disorder. *Amer. J. Psychiat., 94,* 1035–1041.

LINDSLEY, D. B., FINGER, F. W., & HENRY, C. E. 1942. Some physiological aspects of audiogenic seizures in rats. *J. Neurophysiol., 5,* 185–198.

MAIER, N. R. F. 1939. Studies of abnormal behavior in the rat: the neurotic pattern and an analysis of the situation which produces it. New York: Harper.

—— 1940. Studies of abnormal behavior in the rat: IV. Abortive behavior and its relation to the neurotic attack. *J. exp. Psychol., 27,* 369–393.

MAIER, N. R. F., & GLASER, N. M. 1938. Experimentally produced neurotic behavior in the rat. (Film.) Bethlehem: Psychological Cinema Register.

—— 1940a. Studies of abnormal behavior in the rat: II. Comparison of some convulsion-producing situations. *Comp. Psychol. Monogr., 16.* P. 30.

—— 1940b. Studies of abnormal behavior in the rat: V. The inheritance of the "neurotic pattern." *J. comp. Psychol., 30,* 413–418.

MAIER, N. R. F., & KLEE, J. B. 1941. Studies of abnormal behavior in the rat: VII. The permanent nature of abnormal fixations and their relation to convulsive tendencies. *J. exp. Psychol., 29,* 380–389.

MAIER, N. R. F., & SACKS, J. 1941. Studies of abnormal behavior in the rat: VI. Patterns of convulsive reactions to metrazol. *J. comp. Psychol., 32,* 489–502.

MAIER, N. R. F., SACKS, J., & GLASER, N. M. 1941. Studies of abnormal behavior in the rat: VIII. The influence of metrazol on seizures occurring during auditory stimulation. *J. comp. Psychol., 32,* 379–388.

MARCUSE, F., & MOORE, A. U. 1941. Heart rate and respiration preceding and following audiogenic seizures in the white rat. *Proc. Soc. exp. Biol., N. Y., 48,* 201–202.

MARTIN, R. F., & HALL, C. S. 1941. Emotional behavior in the rat: V. The incidence of behavior derangements resulting from air-blast stimulation in emotional and non-emotional strains of rats. *J. comp. Psychol., 32,* 191–204.

MORGAN, C. T. 1940. Review of N. R. F. Maier's *Studies of abnormal behavior in the rat. J. gen. Psychol., 23,* 227–233.

—— 1941. The latency of audiogenic seizures. *J. comp. Psychol., 32,* 267–284.

MORGAN, C. T., & GALAMBOS, R. 1942. Production of audiogenic seizures by tones of low frequency. *Amer. J. Psychol., 55,* 555–559.

MORGAN, C. T., & GOULD, J. 1941. Acoustical determinants of the "neurotic pattern" in rats. *Psychol. Rec., 4,* 258–268.

MORGAN, C. T., & MORGAN, J. D. 1939. Auditory induction of an abnormal pattern of behavior in rats. *J. comp. Psychol., 27,* 505–508.

MORGAN, C. T., & WALDMAN, H. 1941. "Conflict" and audiogenic seizures. *J. comp. Psychol., 31,* 1–11.

PAGE, J. D. 1941. Studies in electrically induced convulsions in animals. *J. comp. Psychol., 31,* 181–194.

PARKER, M. M. 1941. Some fundamental characteristics of convulsions in rats. *Psychol. Bull., 38,* 579.

PATTON, R. A. 1941. The effect of vitamins on convulsive seizures in rats subjected to auditory stimulation. *J. comp. Psychol., 31,* 215–221.

PATTON, R. A., & KARN, H. W. 1941. Abnormal behavior in rats subjected to repeated auditory stimulation. *J. comp. Psychol., 31,* 43–46.

PATTON, R. A., KARN, H. W., & KING, C. G. 1941. Studies on the nutritional basis of abnormal behavior in albino rats: I. The effect of vitamin B₁ and vitamin B-complex deficiency on convulsive seizures. *J. comp. Psychol., 32,* 543–550.

—— 1942. Studies on the nutritional basis of abnormal behavior in albino rats: II. Further analysis of the effects of inanition and vitamin B₁ on convulsive seizures. *J. comp. Psychol., 33,* 253–258.

PAVLOV, I. P. 1927. Conditioned reflexes. (Trans. by G. V. Anrep.) London: Oxford University Press.

SISK, H. L. 1942. The effect of experimentally induced audiogenic seizures upon relearning in the white rat. *J. Psychol., 14,* 85–88.

SMITH, K. U. 1941. Quantitative analysis of the pattern of activity in audio-epileptic seizures in rats. *J. comp. Psychol., 32,* 311–328.

SNEE, T. J., TERRENCE, C. F., & CROWLEY, M. E. 1942. Drug facilitation of the audiogenic seizure. *J. Psychol., 13,* 223–227.

STAINBROOK, E. J. 1942. A note on induced convulsions in the rat. *J. Psychol., 13,* 337–342.

TURNER, R. H. 1941. An approach to the problem of neurosis through the study of respiration, activity, and startle in the white rat as influenced by the difficulty of visual size discrimination. *J. comp. Psychol., 32,* 389–405.

WATSON, M. L. 1939. The inheritance of epilepsy and of waltzing in *Peromyscus. Contr. Lab. vertebr. Genet., Univ. Mich.,* No. 11. P. 24.

WITKIN, H. A. 1942. Restriction as a factor in adjustment to conflict situations. *J. comp. Psychol., 33,* 41–74.

Chapter 14

EXPERIMENTAL STUDIES OF CONFLICT

By Neal E. Miller, Ph.D. *

CONFLICTS CAN DISTRACT, DELAY, AND FATIGUE the individual and force him to make maladaptive compromise responses. In fact, clinical studies demonstrate that severe conflict is one of the crucial factors in functional disorders of personality.[1] These observations receive additional support from experiments demonstrating that difficult discriminations and other situations creating intense conflict can cause animals to break down into a so-called experimental neurosis. Many laboratory studies of conflict have been attempts to produce these states seemingly analogous to human mental disorders. They have been summarized in Chapter 12 by Liddell. The present chapter does not deal with the problem of producing such abnormal states; it is concerned with the principles or laws of conflict behavior.

Conflict is produced by competition between incompatible responses. But not all situations tending to elicit such responses produce that hesitancy, tension, vacillation, or complete blocking, which are ordinarily considered to be conflict behavior. Almost every situation tends to elicit a variety of responses which cannot all be made at once; nevertheless, first one and then another of these responses usually becomes dominant so that behavior ripples smoothly on. What are the factors which make some choices easy and others so difficult?

Some Fundamental Distinctions.—Smith and Guthrie (1921, pp. 126–127) have pointed out that some types of competition are much more likely than others to produce a stalemate. They make the useful distinction between states of stable and unstable equilibrium.

In *unstable equilibrium*, as soon as one response gets started it produces effects which either increase its own strength or decrease that of its competitors. Therefore, the first response to get started continues to increase in relative strength and becomes completely dominant. The situation is like that in which a pencil, balanced on a razor-sharp point, starts

---

* The author is grateful to Mr. Fred D. Sheffield for helping with references, drawing the diagrams and criticizing parts of the theory and manuscript.

[1] See Chapters 28 and 29 of this book, Freud (1920, p. 302), Guthrie (1938, pp. 29, 171), Janet (1925, Vol. I, p. 450), McDougall (1926, pp. 217–220), Prince (1921, pp. 448–528), Rivers (1923, p. 144), and Strecker and Ebaugh (1940, p. 34).

to fall one way or the other and always topples completely over in that direction. Though incompatible, the responses do not continue to inhibit each other.

In *stable equilibrium* the dynamics are reversed: as soon as any response gets started, it produces effects which either reduce its strength or increase that of its competitors. Thus, unless the first response is very strong to begin with, it is likely to lose its dominance before it is completed. The situation is like that of a ball, suspended on a string, always tending to return to a point of balance. Incompatible responses continue to inhibit each other unless there is a great difference in their relative strengths.

A basic type of situation producing stable equilibrium is one in which the subject has strong tendencies both to approach and to avoid the same goal. For example, a timid person, urged to demand a higher salary but fearing to do so, has tendencies both to approach and to avoid the chief's office. This type of situation is likely to produce conflict behavior. It will be refered to as an *approach-avoidance* competition.

A second type of situation likely to produce stable equilibrium, and hence conflict behavior, is one in which the individual is hemmed in by stimuli all of which elicit only avoidance. This is proverbially called being placed between the devil and the deep blue sea, but will be more drably described as an *avoidance-avoidance* competition.

Both of these situations are to be contrasted with a third type, one in which the competition is between tendencies to approach two or more desirable goals. Such situations produce a state of unstable equilibrium unless concealed tendencies to avoid are also involved. As soon as the response of approaching one goal gets started, it becomes completely dominant and choice is easy. The behavior actually observed is in striking contrast to the mythical plight of Buridan's ass starving in conflict between two equally desirable stacks of hay. This type of situation will be referred to as an *approach-approach* competition.

Lewin (1931) has made a penetrating analysis of these three types of conflict situation. His analysis is in terms of spatial diagrams of so-called field forces. The important thing about Lewin's analysis is that it indicates clearly the reasons why the first two types of situation tend to produce stable equilibrium with indecision, while the third leads to unstable equilibrium in which no conflict is expected. Hull (1938) has translated this analysis into the terminology of the goal-gradient and Miller (1937) has elaborated upon it. A considerable body of experimental work has grown out of this analysis. These experiments have started with simple situations involving spatial approach or avoidance and led toward a better understanding of some of the more complicated conflicts met in the clinic.

Plan of the Chapter.—This discussion will first list the principles most essential to an understanding of conflicts involving approach and avoidance. It will describe a series of experiments aimed directly at verifying these principles. Then it will deal with their application to relatively simple approach-avoidance, approach-approach, and avoidance-avoidance situations. The logic of the deductions leading from the simple principles to the details of behavior to be expected in these different situations will be outlined and the experimental evidence testing these deductions will be summarized.

Having dealt with these relatively simple types of situations, the analysis will progress to more complicated ones. It will show that under certain conditions, avoidance tendencies will be expected to appear in choices between desirable goals. Where such latent avoidance lurks, it changes the choice from a pure approach-approach competition not producing any conflict, into a double approach-avoidance one which, as will be shown, may produce serious conflict.

Next the analysis will show how difficult discriminations can produce approach or avoidance competitions. It will describe the chief conditions determining which type of competition is produced, and hence what type of behavior is to be expected.

After the basic types of approach and avoidance conflict have been delineated, other factors which can produce stable and unstable equilibrium will be briefly considered. As soon as the discussion departs from responses, such as approach and avoidance, which are obviously mutually exclusive, it will be necessary to give at least a passing bow to the problem of incompatibility. Then a few data from experiments on dynamogenesis and transfer of training will be considered. Since the logic in a condensed panorama of this kind cannot even pretend to be rigorously systematic, from time to time certain additional assumptions, not considered as thoroughly as the rest, will have to be introduced. This will be especially true of the latter portions of the chapter.

In conclusion, the analysis will deal with the way in which compromise responses are produced and the manner in which conflicts spread from one situation to another.

Four Fundamental Principles

A theoretical analysis verified by experimental work indicates that four simple assumptions are fundamental to an understanding of conflicts between tendencies to approach and to avoid:

1. The tendency to approach a goal is stronger the nearer the subject is to it. This will be called the *approach gradient*.
2. The tendency to go away from a place or object avoided is stronger the nearer the subject is to it. This will be called the *avoidance gradient*.
3. The strength of avoidance increases more rapidly with nearness than does that of approach. In other words, it may be said that the avoidance gradient is *steeper* than the approach gradient.

4. The strength of the tendencies to approach or avoid varies with the strength of the drive upon which they are based. Thus, an increased drive may be said to raise the *height* of the entire gradient.[2]

These assumptions are closely related to the still more basic idea of *a gradient of reinforcement* and to other general principles of learning which have been found useful in explaining a wide range of human behavior.[3]

Independent Verification of Assumptions.—Each of the four fundamental assumptions has been investigated separately in a series of studies by Brown (1940). His tests all involve one additional assumption, namely, that the stronger the subject's tendency to respond, the harder he will pull against a temporary restraint.

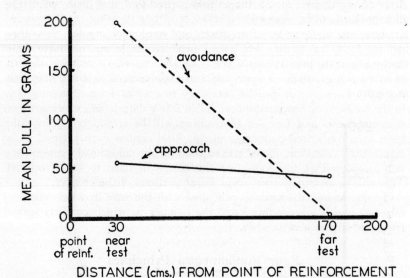

Figure 1. Gradients of Approach and Avoidance

The approach gradient represents the force with which rats under a 48-hour hunger drive pulled against a restraining harness at different distances from the point at which they had been fed. The avoidance gradient shows the force with which rats pulled away from the point at which they had received a strong shock on the previous trial. It should be noted that in this and succeeding diagrams the only reason why the test points are joined by a straight line is because that helps the clarity of the exposition; assuming a curvilinear function would not change the essential deductions.

---

[2] For equivalent assumptions stated in terms of so-called field forces see Lewin (1931) or (1935.)

[3] For a simple exposition of the broader scope of learning theory and a more detailed discussion of some of the more general concepts referred to in this chapter, see Miller & Dollard (1941); for a rigorous technical exposition, see Hull (1943).

In the study of the approach gradient Brown trained a group of hungry albino rats to run down an alley to secure food at a point made distinctive by the presence of a light. During these trials, the animals wore a little harness attached to a cord which moved so easily that it was not a hindrance. After they had learned to run down the alley to approach food, some of the animals were restrained for one second at a point near the goal and others at a point far from the goal. During this restraint, they pulled against a calibrated spring attached to a marker tracing on a polygraph so that the average force of their pull could be computed. The results are represented by the solid line in Figure 1. It was found that the animals restrained near the goal of food pulled reliably harder than those restrained farther away. This test verified the first assumption, that of an approach gradient.

In an investigation of the avoidance gradient Brown gave a different group of animals a brief electric shock at the same end of the alley. After receiving two shocks the animals, when placed in that end of the alley *without shock*, showed a marked tendency to avoid it. Brown restrained half of them near the place they were avoiding and the other half far from this place. The rats pulled harder when restrained near than when restrained far, thus verifying the second assumption, that of an avoidance gradient. These results are represented by the dotted line in Figure 1.

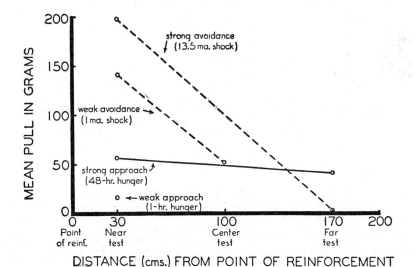

Figure 2.   Effect of Strength of Drive upon Height of Gradient

The two avoidance gradients represent the strength of pull on near and far nonshock tests of two groups of rats that had received shocks of different strengths. The approach gradient represents the strength of pull at near and far points of animals tested after 48 hours of food deprivation; weak approach represents a single test at the near point of another group of animals with one hour of food deprivation.

A comparison of the separate measurements of approach and avoidance tendencies indicates that the strength of avoidance increases more rapidly with nearness than does that of approach. This verifies the third assumption, the greater steepness of the avoidance gradient. Since the two gradients actually cross each other in these tests, this verification depends only on the assumption that stronger tendencies produce stronger pulls; it does not involve any assumption that this relationship is linear.

In his final experiments Brown demonstrated that a reduction in the strength of either hunger or shock produced a reduction in the strength of pull. Thus he verified the assumption that the heights of the gradients vary with the strengths of the drives involved. These results, verifying the fourth assumption, are presented in Figure 2.

Approach-Avoidance Competition

Approach and avoidance have been studied separately; what happens when they are both present at the same time? An analysis of the situation in which the individual has strong tendencies both to approach and to avoid the same goal is fundamental to an understanding of human conflict. The young swain who is hard smitten but very bashful vacillates helplessly at a distance from the object of his affection. Why is he unable to go resolutely either forward to get her or away to forget?

From the principles verified in the separate studies of approach and avoidance, one can predict what behavior to expect when these two tendencies are in conflict with each other. The first deductions arise from the fact that the avoidance gradient is steeper than the approach, so that the two may cross. Under the conditions represented in Figure 2 (strong approach and avoidance) it can be seen that at a distance from the goal the approach tendency is stronger than avoidance. Whenever the subject is in this region, he should advance toward the goal. As he gets nearer, however, the strength of avoidance increases more rapidly than that of approach. Thus, he eventually reaches a point at which the strength of avoidance equals that of approach; the two gradients cross. At this point he should stop. Similarly, whenever the subject is too near to the goal, he should retreat with the strength of avoidance falling off more rapidly than that of approach till he reaches the point at which the two are equal, and consequently is stopped. Thus it can be seen that the subject (like the timid man wanting to demand a higher salary, or the bashful lover) should tend to remain trapped at an intermediate point of stable equilibrium where the two gradients cross.[4]

---

[4] The pattern of going part way and then stopping can be predicted only on the assumption that the gradient of avoidance is steeper than that of approach. If the two gradients were parallel, the relative strengths of the two tendencies would not change with distance; there would be nothing to cause the subject to stop. If the approach gradient were steeper than the avoidance, the subject would tend to move away from the point at which they crossed so that whatever difference there was would be not reduced but increased. This would produce easily resolved, unstable equilibrium.

The location of this point will, as can be seen in Figure 2, vary with the relative heights of the two gradients. As avoidance is lowered or approach is raised, the intersection will shift toward the goal. If either of these changes is carried far enough, it is obvious that the two gradients may not cross at all, so that the subject will be expected to reach the goal.

Verification of Simple Deductions.—These deductions have been tested in experiments by Miller, Brown, and Lipofsky (1943). They studied the behavior of albino rats in situations in which tendencies to approach and avoid were in conflict. First the experimenters trained hungry rats to run the length of an alley to secure food at a point made distinctive by the presence of a small light. Then they established tendencies to avoid this point by giving the animals a brief electric shock there while eating. Finally the animals received test trials without shock; the experimenters placed them at the start of the alley and observed their conflict behavior. During both training and tests a light cord attached to a little harness on the animals operated a device which recorded their locomotion without restraining it.

To determine the effects of different strengths of avoidance the experimenters divided the animals into groups, each of which received a different strength of shock during training. To determine the effects of different strengths of approach, they further divided each of these groups into halves, one of which was tested with a strong, and the other with a weak, hunger drive.

The results confirm the deductions. The characteristic behavior was to approach part way and then stop. The place at which the animals stopped was determined by the relative strength of the two drives. Stronger hunger or weaker shock caused the animals to come nearer to the goal before stopping.

Vacillation.—Thus far we have been concerned with the fact that the subject should stop, and not with the manner in which he will stop. If we assume that the opposing tendencies add up in something resembling algebraic summation, we can deduce that as the subject approaches the point where the gradients cross, he will be expected to become increasingly hesitant. If stimulation from the external situation were all that is involved, the subject would be expected to stop exactly at the point of intersection. But in making the responses of going forward, he produces additional stimulation from anticipatory goal responses and from the proprioceptors in his muscles. This internal stimulation should add to the tendency to continue advancing and thus function like a psychological momentum. It should carry the subject forward beyond the point of intersection, so that by the time he is stopped (and this stimulation disappears) avoidance is considerably stronger than approach. Furthermore, as soon as he starts retreating, his responses should produce additional cues helping to elicit a still more hasty withdrawal. Thus, after slowing down and eventually stopping, the subject will be expected to retreat rapidly. Similarly, when the additional stimulation produced by retreating carries him too far beyond the point of intersection, he will be expected to slow down again and start another advance. In short, the subject will be expected to oscillate in the region in which the gradients cross.

While the reinforcement of securing food has been most immediately associated with the internal stimuli from the last steps of approach, that of escaping shock has coincided with those from the first ones of retreat. Thus, according to the gradient of reinforcement, stronger tendencies should be elicited by the internal stimuli from later steps of approach and the first of retreat than by those from the first of approach and later ones of retreat. Therefore, shifting from approach to avoidance should produce a greater effect than from avoidance to approach; the subject should move faster during the first part of retreat than the first part of approach.

These deductions are in general borne out by the records secured in the experiments. The animals showed a definite tendency to vacillate in the conflict situation. In some cases the form of the oscillations was in the exact pattern predicted by the theory. An increasingly hesitant approach was followed by an abrupt retreat which was far more rapid than the approach. In some records a succession of such oscillations, all in the same pattern, occurred with a consistency that can scarcely be attributed to chance. Rasmussen (1940) has also observed similar behavior without recording it.

In other records, however, a different pattern was observed. The animal would move forward, hesitate, stop for a while, then abruptly move forward, hesitate, and stop again. The repetition of this performance gave his record the appearance of a series of steps, ending in either a plateau or a retreat. Why these animals merely stopped instead of retreating is not known. It would be interesting if further experiments should demonstrate that such animals are ones whose initial reaction to the original shock was crouching. It seems probable that the tendency for these animals to move forward after a period of time can be explained by the progressive extinction of their fear responses and that the abruptness of the shifts from one type of behavior to another is to be attributed to the momentum-like effects of response-produced stimulation.

With many other animals the form of the oscillations was so irregular that no consistent pattern could be detected.

Strengths of the Competing Tendencies.—From the theoretical analysis it is obvious that if the relative strength of the approach tendencies is strong enough so that the two gradients do not cross, the animals will be expected to go completely to the goal and not show any vacillating behavior.[5] Conversely, if the relative strength of the avoidance tendencies is so strong that the point of intersection lies outside of the alley, the

---

[5] Furthermore, once they have reached the goal, approach will be strengthened by reward, and avoidance weakened by extinction, so that the relative difference between the two will be further increased and vacillation will become progressively less likely.

animals will be expected to remain against the far end without vacillation. The experimental results confirmed these deductions. The maximum amount of vacillating behavior occurred at an intermediate strength
of shock. As would be expected, the amount of shock producing the
maximum amount of vacillation was stronger for the animals with a
strong drive than for those with a weak one. Presumably maximum
oscillation occurred when the two tendencies were relatively equal near
to the goal.

The records also showed that competition between strong tendencies
produced more oscillation than competition between weak ones.

A still further analysis of the effects to be deduced from changes in the
relative strengths of the competing tendencies leads inexorably to two
rather unexpected conclusions of interesting clinical significance. The
immediately preceding discussion has dealt with conditions in which
on the one hand the subject was able to go completely up to the goal
because the relative strength of approach was so great that the two
gradients did not cross, or on the other hand, the subject was unable to
complete the retreat elicited by strong avoidance because of the physical
limitation of the end of the alley. The following discussion deals with
different circumstances; it applies only to conditions of approach-avoidance conflict in which the subject has enough time and space to retreat
without physical restraint and in which avoidance is strong enough to
intersect approach and prevent the subject from completely reaching the
goal. Such conditions are frequently met in the life situation.

Under the conditions just specified, increases in the strength of approach will, as has already been demonstrated, cause the subject to move
nearer to the goal. But at this closer distance to the dangerous goal,
stronger avoidance tendencies will be elicited. The situation is illustrated
graphically in Figure 3A in which it will be noted that when the approach
gradient is raised, the point of intersection not only is shifted nearer to
the goal, but also occurs at a higher point on the avoidance gradient.
Conversely, if tendencies to approach are absent or quite weak, the subject will be expected to remain far enough away from the dangerous
goal so that little if any avoidance will actually be elicited. Therefore,
as long as the gradients intersect and the subject has had time and space
for free movement, the strength of avoidance aroused (usually accompanied by fear) should be a function of the strength of approach present.[6]

This deduction from stimulus-response principles affords a plausible
basis for a Freudian contention which superficially seems paradoxical if
not deliberately perverse: namely, that evidence of strong fear or with-

---

[6] On the basis of the stimulus function of anticipatory responses Hull (1930),
Miller and Dollard (1941, pp. 54–90), it can be deduced that a certain amount of
increased fear may be expected with increases in the approach tendencies even
if the subject is restrained from moving nearer to the dangerous goal. Furthermore, it seems possible that anxiety may become conditioned directly to the drive
stimulus itself.

drawal may often be taken as a sign that strong tendencies to approach are present.

Similar paradoxical effects may be deduced when the attractiveness of the goal is held constant and its repulsiveness varied within limits allowing the two gradients to cross. As the strength of avoidance at the goal is weakened, the subject will be expected to move forward. But as he moves forward, the strength of approach increases so that stronger avoidance must be aroused before his advance is stopped. The fact that the subject moves nearer to the dangerous goal more than compensates

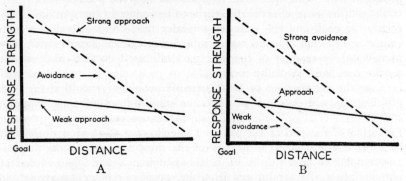

Figure 3. Paradoxical Effects of Changes in Strength

Diagram A demonstrates that with an increase in the strength of approach tendencies the intersection is not only moved nearer to the goal but also occurs at a higher point on the avoidance gradient. Diagram B demonstrates that within the limits in which the two gradients cross, decreasing the strength of avoidance increases the height of the point of intersection. Thus in both cases the amount of avoidance actually aroused will be increased.

for its reduction in unattractiveness. This is illustrated in Figure 3B in which it can be seen that the intersection with the approach gradient is higher for weak than for strong avoidance. Since this effect depends on the slope of the relatively flat approach gradient, it will be less marked than the one illustrated in Figure 3A.

Conversely, if the strength of avoidance is increased to the point where it drives the subject to a distance at which little if any approach is elicited, there will be almost no conflict; the subject will no longer be tempted to go near enough to experience appreciable fear.

These last deductions afford a possible basis for the unfavorable reaction which patients sometimes show after a therapist has taken steps to reduce a strong fear associated with one of their goals. Of course, if the fear can be reduced to the point where the two gradients no longer intersect, the subject should go completely to the goal so that this paradoxical increase in anxiety will no longer be expected with further decreases in the dangerousness of the goal.

Position of the Source of Avoidance.—In the situations just analyzed the source of avoidance was at the goal; Miller and Davis (1943) have performed experiments in which the source of avoidance did not coincide with the goal. After having learned to run the length of the alley to secure food, one group of hungry rats received a brief electric shock when they reached a point half-way to the goal, another immediately before reaching the goal, and a third 5 seconds after reaching it. Trials in which the animals received shock were alternated with nonshock trials, during which their conflict behavior was recorded. On successive shock trials the strength of current was increased.

From the gradient principles it will be expected that shocks, as a means of preventing the subjects from reaching the goal on subsequent trials, will be more effective the earlier they occur in the sequence leading to the goal, and less effective the later they occur after it has been reached. The experimental results afforded a little evidence (statistically unreliable) in support of the first part of this deduction, and reliable evidence in support of the second.

Varying the position of the source of avoidance should change the effectiveness with which it prevents the subject from reaching the goal; it should not change the general form of the approach-avoidance conflict behavior to be expected except under one set of conditions: namely, that in which a shock too weak to prevent the subject from reaching the goal is administered part way to it. In this situation a new type of behavior should appear. As the subject nears the source of danger, avoidance will increase at a faster rate than approach and will conflict with it. Thus the subject should slow down. But as soon as he passes the source of danger, the conflict will cease; both tendencies will be operating in the same direction. Therefore an increasingly hesitant approach should be followed by a sudden dash forward. This is exactly the type of behavior that was recorded in the nonshock trials of the experiment by Miller and Davis.

From the mechanism of anticipation [7] it may be deduced that the response of suddenly dashing forward should tend to occur before the place where the shock has been received. This deduction was also confirmed by the experimental records.

Nonspatial Situations.—Deductions of the details of approach-avoidance conflict behavior have been verified in simple experiments in which the responses involved produced forward or backward movement through space. The more complicated situations met in life often involve sequences which are partly nonspatial, for example, the series of responses leading toward or away from a fateful decision, an open act of aggression, or a sexual adjustment. It seems probable that the same principles will also be found useful in analyzing these situations. One step in this direction would be a series of experiments determining whether or not the temporal gradient of reinforcement is steeper for responses of avoidance than for those of approach.

[7] See Hull (1929), or Miller & Dollard (1941, pp. 49–52).

Difference Between Approach and Avoidance Choices

Approach-Approach Competition.—Figure 4 may be used to represent the situation in which the individual is confronted with a choice between two equally desirable alternatives, both eliciting *only* tendencies to approach. It can be seen that if the subject is not exactly at the center, the tendency to approach the nearest goal will be the strongest, so that the subject will move toward it. The nearer he goes to this goal the greater becomes the relative difference favoring continuing to approach it. Thus the situation is one of unstable equilibrium, like the pencil balanced on its point which, as soon as it starts, has an ever-increasing tendency to continue falling, and hence never reverses its direction. Since it is extremely unlikely that the two alternatives will be perfectly balanced, and since even in such cases a slight distraction will be likely to upset the equilibrium, choices between purely desirable alternatives will be expected to be made quickly without vacillation.

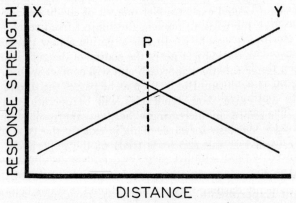

Figure 4.   Difference Between Approach and Avoidance Choices

This is a schematic diagram of the gradient to approach (or to avoid) two stimulus objects, X and Y. If the two objects elicit only approach, the individual started at P will be expected to go directly to X; if they elicit only avoidance, he will be expected to go away from X until he passes the point at which the gradients cross, and then to turn back.

Avoidance-Avoidance Competition.—Quite the opposite is to be expected when the individual is forced to choose one of two undesirable alternatives. In this case he will be expected to go away from the nearest evil. But as he retreats farther the tendency to avoid that evil will become weaker, while that to avoid the other will become stronger. Thus the situation is one of stable equilibrium, like a pendulum suspended so that the farther it is pushed off center the stronger is its tendency to return. Provided that there is no third way out, the individual will remain vacillating in conflict, trapped between the two sources of avoidance.

If one of the alternatives elicits much stronger avoidance than the other, it is obvious that the intersection of the gradients, and hence the region in which the subject will remain trapped, will be farther away from that alternative. If the difference is too great, the gradients will not cross and the subject will be driven past the weaker source of avoidance and out of the situation. From the diagram it can be seen that with shorter distances between the two sources of avoidance, less difference will be required to produce this effect.

Going Out of the Field.—In the preceding deductions it has been assumed that the conditions are such that the subject must go toward either one or the other of the sources of avoidance. Frequently he is not limited in this way. Perhaps the clearest illustration is the case of a free subject in an open space between two point sources of avoidance, for example, a man in a field between two nasty dogs. In originally learning to avoid dangerous objects, each person has tried many different responses. The ones resulting in motion directly away from the object have been rewarded most immediately and frequently by escape from pain and fear. Movement away at a less direct angle has also been rewarded but less immediately and frequently. This should establish a hierarchy of avoidance habits, with strengths varying as the directness of the line of avoidance. It can be seen that as soon as the subject in a direct line between the two nasty dogs starts moving to one side or the other, continuing on is a more direct avoidance than turning back. Thus the tendency to continue should be stronger than that to go in the opposite direction. The farther the subject moves, the greater the difference becomes between continuing the same line of retreat and reversing it. Therefore, the situation is one of unstable equilibrium which should be easily resolved without conflict behavior. Unless hemmed in, the subject should escape.

Relevant Experiments.—Results from a considerable number of experiments are relevant to these deductions. Though most of the experiments did not deal with pure cases in which tendencies to approach or avoid were uncomplicated by other factors, they clearly indicate that being forced to select one of two alternatives elicits much more vacillation and blocking when they are predominantly sources of avoidance instead of approach. They also indicate that the more difference there is between the strengths of the two competing tendencies, the less likely conflict behavior is to appear. When the subject is not hemmed in, avoidance-avoidance competition is unstable, producing strong responses of lateral escape.

Hovland and Sears (1938) had human subjects sit at a table on which was exposed a surface of paper six inches square, framed by brass strips. In the middle of the side toward the subject was a nick in which he rested his pencil at the beginning of each trial. At the two corners away from the subjects were lights. One group of subjects was instructed to draw a diagonal line as quickly as possible directly to whichever light was turned on. Another group was instructed to draw a line diagonally forward to the corner opposite the flashing light, that is, they were to go to the corner at which the bulb was not lighted. After giving the subjects 20 practice trials, the experimenters created a conflict by flashing on both lights at once.

Only 9% of the subjects instructed to go directly to the light were blocked in the conflict test; 46% of those instructed to go to the corner away from the light were blocked. This difference is in line with theoretical expectations. That it was not still greater may perhaps be explained by assuming that instructions to go to the opposite corner established in some cases tendencies to approach this corner rather than to avoid the light flashed.[8] It is also possible that when the subjects instructed to go toward the light were tested for conflict, they did not want to be fooled into making a wrong response, and hence were not in a pure approach-approach choice. Hovland and Sears point out that many choices encountered in life produce mixed, or double approach-avoidance conflicts.

In other similar experiments, Sears and Hovland (1941) demonstrated that avoidance-avoidance choices are less likely to produce conflict the greater the difference in the strengths of the competing tendencies. This occurred when the different strengths were produced by different amounts of training and also when they were the results of different amounts of motivation from electric shock.

Barker (1942) required ten-year-old boys to choose which of two liquids they were going to drink. In some cases the subjects were confronted with a choice between small glasses containing liquids they liked (i.e., orange vs. pineapple juice), in other cases liquids they disliked (i.e., vinegar vs. a saturated salt solution), and in still other cases relatively neutral liquids. Each boy indicated his choice by moving a lever toward the glass he decided to drink. Movements were timed by a concealed device attached to the lever. When confronted with neutral or pleasant choices the subjects exhibited little conflict behavior. When confronted with unpleasant alternatives they required much longer and shifted the lever back and forth more times. The greater the difference in the desirability of the alternatives, the more rapid the choice and the fewer the vacillations.

Barker points out that the avoidance conflict, when the subjects were confronted with bad-tasting solutions, was complicated by the tendency to select some alternative and thus move toward the goal of finishing the task and getting paid for the experiment. The rise in the strength of this factor with increasing delay was presumably what caused the subjects eventually to resolve the conflict.

Klebanoff (1939) trained hungry rats to secure food by approaching whichever end of an alley was distinguished by a light and a buzzer. Then he placed them in an approach-approach competition by turning

---

[8] Hovland and Sears report in a footnote that when the incompatible responses were made to two lights directly opposite each other instead of at the opposite corners of a V, they secured a larger percentage of blocking.

on the lights and buzzers at both ends of the alley. He found that, if the animals were started some distance away from the center, they always went directly to the nearest goal. If started at the center, they went quickly to one goal or the other with little tendency to vacillate.

He trained another group of animals to escape an electric shock by running away from whichever end of the alley was distinguished by a light and buzzer, and then placed them in an avoidance-avoidance conflict by turning on the lights and buzzers at both ends of the alley. When released a considerable distance away from the center, all of the animals started by avoiding the nearest light. After running in one direction these animals stopped and turned back, remaining in conflict between the two lights. When released at the center, they started more slowly than the approach-approach animals, vacillated much more, and remained nearer the starting point. In the avoidance-avoidance conflicts, the animals showed a definite tendency to try to escape to the side and up out of the alley.

Hunt (1943) placed rats in a starting chamber from which they could move forward into either of two separate compartments. Five seconds after the appearance of a light in either of the two compartments a grid on the floor of the starting chamber was electrified. One group of animals could escape shock only by going to the lighted compartment, another only by going to the dark compartment. After the animals had learned this discrimination they were given tests in which both compartments were lighted. Those trained to approach the light showed no more hesitancy or vacillation than during preceding training trials; those trained to go to the dark compartment (and presumably to avoid the light) did not move forward into either compartment, but made frantic efforts to claw their way out of the starting chamber.

According to our theoretical analysis, the subject who is not completely hemmed in tends to escape from avoidance-avoidance conflicts by lateral compromise responses because of the fact that he has learned not only the single habit of going directly away, but also a whole hierarchy of other habits of moving away at various indirect angles. Hovland and Sears (1944) have secured evidence supporting this interpretation by demonstrating that the frequency of compromise responses is indeed dependent upon the previous training of the subject. They had men hold a vertical lever mounted on a universal joint below which a recording mechanism was concealed. Signal lights were mounted off to each side of the pivot point. All subjects started from a central position and practiced moving the lever arm directly away from whichever light flashed. One control group received only this training. Another control group was trained to go directly to the position of the right-hand light whenever a buzzer was sounded. Experimental groups learned the habit of moving the lever off at various angles whenever the buzzer was sounded. Then all subjects were presented test trials in which both lights were flashed at once.

The subjects who had learned the habit of moving the lever off at various angles exhibited more compromise responses than either of the two control groups. Those who had learned to move the lever at right angles to the line of the lights made more such responses than those who had learned to move it at 30° or 60° angles. This study would have been more realistic and should have shown still greater differences between the experimental and control groups if the responses of moving off at an angle had been attached directly to the lights during part of the previous training instead of being attached to the buzzer and generalized to the lights.

Double Approach-Avoidance Competition

According to the theoretical analysis, choices between goals which elicit *only* tendencies to approach should be made rapidly with no signs of conflict; those between undesirable alternatives should produce continuous conflict. Two experiments on animals and two on people have afforded evidence supporting this analysis in that far more signs of conflict were produced when the alternatives were undesirable than when they were desirable. Though the difference was definite, and in the direction demanded by the theory, a slight amount of oscillation was produced in choices between desirable goals. Furthermore, such choices sometimes produce definite signs of conflict in life situations. The question thus arises: is the theory wrong in demanding that choices involving only approach tendencies should produce neither blocking nor vacillation, or are some factors entering to induce avoidance even though both goals are desirable?

In some cases, of course, the goals may not be completely desirable, so that tendencies to avoid (concealed by still stronger tendencies to approach) are brought into the choice situation. In other cases certain factors in the choice situation itself may induce avoidance and hence conflict. Godbeer (1940) has studied the influence of such factors. First she made observations on a group of adolescent girls in social situations. She found that choices between desirable alternatives were often complicated by the necessity of relinquishing one goal in order to achieve the other. Often an unwillingness to relinquish either goal seemed to induce a tendency to avoid a definite commitment to one of them. The subject had tendencies both to approach and avoid each goal.

The dynamics of such a double approach-avoidance conflict are represented in Figure 5. It can be seen that the greater steepness of avoidance leads to a situation in which the net tendencies to approach a given goal are weaker the nearer the subject gets to it. Thus the distant goal seems more attractive, and he is likely to turn back toward it. In such a situation the subject should remain in conflict indefinitely unless the stable equilibrium is disturbed by other factors. With sophisticated subjects the disturbing factor is likely to be a desire to come to a decision. This may be produced by the fact that the state of conflict is uncomfortable, or by the fact that the subject has in the past been punished for waiting too long by losing both goals.

From the diagram it can be seen that if the net approach to one of the goals is strengthened (i.e., the gradient raised), the point of inter-section will be moved toward that goal and the difference between the two gradients at the goal decreased. Thus it will be easier for any factor

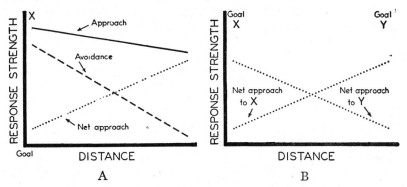

Figure 5. Double Approach-Avoidance Competition

In A is represented a single approach-avoidance situation. Subtracting the strength of the avoidance from that of the approach results in a net approach tendency which becomes weaker nearer the goal. In B the two net tendencies are represented in a double approach-avoidance situation. As the individual moves toward either of the two goals, X or Y, the net tendency to approach that goal becomes weaker, and to approach the other, stronger. This should produce vacilla-tion.

which builds up an avoidance of the central point of indecision to force the subject up to that goal. The more unequal the net approaches, the easier it should be to resolve the conflict.

Experimental Tests of Factors Inducing Conflict.—After the pre-liminary observations in social situations Godbeer devised an experiment to test for the effects of having to relinquish one goal when selecting the other. A child was seated at a table directly in front of a vertical board into which two windows were cut. These were covered by sliding plates of glass and tin shutters. Candy was exposed on the shelf behind one of the windows when the experimenter lifted its shutter. The child was instructed to secure the candy as quickly as possible by pushing a handle attached to a lever diagonally forward so that it hit a button under the window where the candy was exposed. As soon as he did this the experi-menter lifted the glass so that the child could secure the candy.

After the children had learned to secure candy in this way the effects of three conditions were tested in a balanced order:

1. Only one window containing candy was exposed. This was a control trial to determine the behavior when there was no competition between incompatible responses.

2. The children were told that they could get the presents which
would be exposed behind both windows. Since they could not
move toward both at once, competition between incompatible
responses occurred, but was not complicated by the necessity
of relinquishing one of the goals.

3. The children were told that as soon as they selected the present
in one window the shutter on the other would close. Thus
the competition between incompatible responses was complicated by the fact that choosing one goal meant relinquishing
the other.

During these tests movements of the lever toward the windows were
recorded by a concealed pantograph, and electrically timed. The child's
eye movements were counted as he looked back and forth between the
two windows.

Under the first two conditions the children behaved the same. When
the choice of the present in one window did not mean that the present
in the other had to be relinquished, the exposure of presents in both
windows did not increase the choice time nor the number of eye movements made during the choice, and did not affect the path over which
the subject moved the lever toward the window first approached.[9] Thus
a pure approach-approach choice produced no conflict behavior.

Tests under the third condition produced different results. The subjects took longer to choose, made more eye movements back and forth
from one window to the other, and the path over which they moved the
lever to the window chosen was reliably deflected somewhat in the direction of the other window. The necessity of relinquishing one present
when selecting the other induced conflict behavior.

In her preliminary study of girls in social situations, Godbeer noticed
that when the goals were qualitatively dissimilar the choices seemed to be
more difficult. Apparently the more dissimiliar the goals, the less one
of them was a substitute for the other; hence the girls were more reluctant to renounce either of them by making a definite choice.

In order to determine the effects of qualitative dissimilarity, another
group of subjects was given tests similar to those just described, except
that the choice was between qualitatively different types of reward instead of between two highly similar pieces of candy. The present exposed
in one window was a large gumdrop, that exposed in the other was a
group of little tin soldiers. For each child an attempt was made to determine the number of tin soldiers which he considered equally desirable to
a large gumdrop, so that the choice would be between equally attractive
goals. These tests demonstrated that confronting the subjects with qualitatively dissimilar goals increased the choice time, the number of eye

---

[9] A control group demonstrated that this lack of difference was not produced
by the fact that the children got more candy when both windows were exposed under
condition 2.

movements, and the deflection of the path in the direction of the other window. Some increases were produced even when selecting one goal first did not mean that the other had to be relinquished. Greater increases were produced when selecting one goal meant giving up the other.

The effects of inequality of reward were determined as a control on the results in the preceding experiment. After the soldiers had been equated with the candy, one group was tested as before in a choice between a piece of candy and a number of soldiers stated to be of a value equal to it. Another group was tested in a choice between goals of unequal value. For half of these the value of the soldiers presented exceeded that of the candy; for the other half it was less. The subjects choosing between rewards of unequal value chose more quickly, made fewer eye movements, and went in a more normal path than those choosing between equal rewards. Thus in the previous experiment any effects of failing perfectly to equate the value of the qualitatively dissimilar rewards could only have served to work against the results actually secured.

In her observations of behavior of girls in social situations it seemed to Godbeer that yet another factor frequently induced latent avoidance tendencies strong enough to increase the amount of conflict behavior. This was the factor of uncertainty. When a girl was not sure whether or not she would have a good time at either of two parties, the choice between them was more difficult. This type of situation, of course, is one in which the subject's reactions to the goals are somewhat ambivalent, even before the necessity of a choice appears.

She tested for the influence of the factor of uncertainty by exposing, instead of candies directly, two small metal boxes either of which might or might not contain candy. Under these conditions evidence of conflict appeared in a longer reaction time, more eye movements, and a deflection of the path.

Greater Steepness of the Avoidance Gradient

The deductions concerning the type of behavior to be expected in both single and double approach-avoidance situations hinge on the assumption that the gradient of avoidance is steeper than that of approach. The experimental results have demonstrated that this assumption is applicable to some situtaions. A deeper analysis of the reason for this greater steepness is desirable as a means of determining whether similar results will be expected in all situations or only under certain definite conditions. A complete analysis has not yet been made and tested. It seems plausible, however, that at least two factors are relevant to the relative steepness of the two gradients.

Constant Elements.—Both tendencies to approach and those to avoid are in part directly dependent upon external cues present in the environment. Cues nearer the goal will be expected to elicit stronger responses because they are more immediately associated with the event of reinforcement and because they are more similar to those present during reinforcement. But in both cases the external stimuli are only a part of the pattern; the responses of approaching and avoiding are also dependent upon the drive stimulus. In the case of the avoidance used in the non-shock trials of the experiment this was an acquired drive, fear, which was elicited by the external cues, and hence would be expected to be stronger the nearer the animal is to the point of reinforcement.[10] In the case of approach a primary drive, hunger, was present, which was dependent upon internal conditions and would not be expected to vary with distance from the goal. This greater constancy of the hunger drive as a stimulus element common to the near and far situations will be expected to make the gradient of approach flatter than that of avoidance. Unpublished exploratory work by Miller and Brown has indicated that if a constant stimulus from the primary drive of pain is supplied by having the whole length of the grid electrified during the test trials, the slope of the avoidance gradient becomes much flatter.

Past Experience.—If the individual is consistently rewarded for approaching near goals but not far ones, he should learn to discriminate on the basis of cues indicating distance and cease attempting to approach far goals. Such learning actually seems to occur in the case of adults, who will not attempt to reach through small openings for objects obviously more than an arm's length away. In these situations learning produces an approach gradient which falls off very steeply, in an almost step-wise manner at about the limit of the subject's reach. Similarly, the principles of learning, backed up by casual observation, indicate that the steepness of the avoidance gradient should be subject to modification. If this analysis is correct, the relative slopes of the two gradients will depend upon whether or not the conditions of learning have been the same for both. In many situations approach is almost as likely to be reinforced when the subject is at a distance as when he is nearby;[11] avoidance is not. Wherever such conditions are found they should tend to increase the relative steepness of the avoidance gradient.

It seems probable that in the experiments described, as well as in many life situations, both of these factors operate to produce greater steepness of the avoidance gradient. Further analysis of these and other factors influencing the slopes should enable the investigator to delimit more exactly the types of situations to which he can legitimately apply deductions dependent upon the greater steepness of the avoidance gradient.

---

[10] For a more detailed discussion of the mechanism of acquired drives see Ch. 4 of Miller and Dollard (1941).

[11] The gradient of reinforcement will, of course, weaken somewhat the effectiveness of rewards for starting distant approaches so that the resulting gradient of approach will not be expected to be absolutely flat.

Contrast Between Types of Choice Situations

The results of theoretical analysis verified by experimental evidence may be briefly summarized to bring out more clearly the contrast between different types of situations:

1. *Approach-approach* competition should be resolved quickly without vacillation unless contaminated by latent avoidance.

2. *Avoidance-avoidance* competition should be characterized by compromise resolutions; the individual should escape both evils unless restrained by physical limitations or additional sources of avoidance. When lateral escape is impossible, vacillation and blocking should occur.

3. In *approach-avoidance* competition no barriers will be needed to hold the subject in the conflict situation; the approach tendency will bring him into it. As long as the gradients cross, the subject should remain trapped part way to the goal, unable either to achieve or leave it.

4. In double *approach-avoidance* competition no barriers are needed to hold the subject in the situation. Choices between goals toward which the subject is ambivalent may elicit vacillation and blocking even though the avoidance tendencies are too weak to prevent approach when the subject is confronted with each goal separately. Furthermore, additional avoidance may be aroused by the necessity of renouncing one of the goals in making the choice.

5. In each of the three preceding types of competition, conflict behavior does not appear if the opposing tendencies are so unequal that the gradients do not intersect.

The Relation Between Anxiety and Conflict

In the preceding analysis it will be noticed that pure approach-approach choices are easily resolved; conflict only appears when avoidance is present. This suggests that whenever unexplained indecision and conflict appear, it may be wise to look for concealed sources of avoidance. Since fear is one of the strongest sources of avoidance, one may often profitably ask: What is feared?

The relationship also works the other way. As has been suggested, the subject who is not physically restrained will soon escape from most fear-producing situations unless he is prevented by conflicts arising from other sources of avoidance keeping him away from the avenues of escape or unsatisfied drives stimulating him to approach goals in the region of the danger. Therefore, when unexplained anxieties persist, one should ask: What conflicting tendencies prevent the subject from escaping the fear-provoking stimuli? [12, 13]

---

[12] In addition to physical limitations and conflict, two other conditions may prevent escape: the anxiety may be conditioned to internal stimuli, such as primary drives over which the subject has no control; or it may be attached to stimuli which are ubiquitous.

[13] Mowrer (1941) has clearly called attention to the relationship between conflict and anxiety, though tending to emphasize a different type of explanation.

Discrimination Conflict

According to the principle of generalization, after a response has been connected to a given stimulus there is a tendency for similar stimuli to elicit the same response; the more similar the stimuli, the stronger the tendency. Spence (1936) and Gulliksen and Wolfle (1938) have pointed out that this principle affords an explanation of why the discrimination between similar stimuli is more difficult to learn than that between dissimilar ones. When the two stimuli are more similar, the greater tendency for the response attached to each of them to transfer to the other interferes with the learning of differential responses; thus discrimination is more difficult.

Brown (1942b) has collaborated with Miller in further applying the principle of generalization to the analysis of the type of conflict behavior

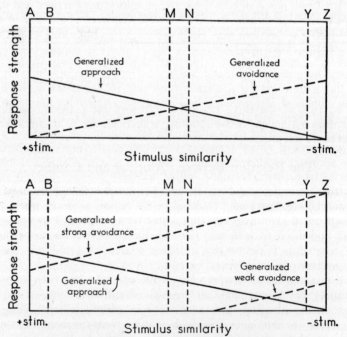

Figure 6. Analysis of Discrimination Conflicts

The upper diagram represents the situation in which the subject has been rewarded for approaching the bright light, *A*, and punished for approaching the dim light, *Z*. It is assumed that these two stimuli are so dissimilar that almost no generalization occurs from one to the other. Then, a discrimination between the two similar bright lights *A* and *B* produces an approach-approach competition; the intermediate lights, *M* and *L*, produce a double approach-avoidance conflict, and the two dim lights, *Y* and *Z*, produce an avoidance-avoidance conflict.

The lower diagram shows that increasing the strength of punishment shifts all discriminations toward the avoidance-avoidance type; weakening its strength shifts them toward the approach-approach type.

which difficult discriminations should produce. Let us assume that a subject has been trained to approach a positive stimulus, A, and to avoid a negative one, Z. These may be thought of as a very bright and a very dim light, respectively. It is assumed that the two are so different that but little of the tendency to approach A generalizes to Z, and but little of the tendency to avoid Z generalizes to A. These assumptions are represented diagrammatically in the upper part of Figure 6.

It can be seen that when the subject is confronted with the two dissimilar stimuli, there is a strong tendency to approach A and to avoid Z, so no conflict behavior will be expected. If, instead of this easy discrimination, the subject is now confronted with a choice between A, the positive cue, and B, another similar stimulus, it is apparent that the situation will be predominantly one of approach-approach. In this type of choice, as has already been shown, the subject will be expected to go directly to that goal toward which he happens to start. Since A elicits the stronger approach, he should be more likely to start in that direction. But as the similarity between the two stimuli is increased, the tendencies to approach them will become more nearly equal, so that it will be easier for chance factors to get the subject started in the other direction. This will be an error. Under these conditions difficult discriminations should be disrupted by indiscriminate approaches.

In like manner, if the subject is presented with a choice between two similar stimuli of intermediate brightness, say K and L, it can be seen that each of them will elicit generalized tendencies of both approach and avoidance, and that the more similar the two stimuli are, the more nearly equal amounts of either tendency they will elicit. Since the effects of double approach-avoidance conflicts have already been analyzed and are known to be greater the more evenly matched the two goals, it can be predicted that under these conditions difficult discriminations should be disrupted by vacillation and blocking in the region of the choice point.

Finally, if the difficult discrimination is between stimuli resembling the original negative stimulus, for example between two dim lights, Y and Z, the subject will be in a situation which is predominantly avoidance-avoidance, and hence will be expected to withdraw from the choice point if possible, and if not, to remain blocked.

In short, the types of conflict situation produced by difficult discriminations should range on a continuum from pure approach-approach at one extreme, through intermediate degrees of double approach-avoidance, to pure avoidance-avoidance. The kinds of behavior expected to characterize the different points in this continuum are respectively: indiscriminate approach, blocking and vacillation at the choice point, and withdrawal from the choice point.

The behavior should be shifted toward the approach-approach type the more the stimuli being discriminated resemble the one that was originally positive, and toward avoidance-avoidance the more they resemble the one that was originally negative.

From the lower part of Figure 6, it can be seen that a shift toward the approach-approach type of behavior should also be produced by any change, such as an increase in the strength of the hunger drive, that raises the height of the entire gradient of generalized approach. Similarly, any change, such as an increase in the strength of punishment, increasing the relative height of generalized avoidance, should produce a shift toward the avoidance-avoidance end of the continuum.

Experimental Verification.—These deductions have been verified in a series of experiments by Brown. First (1942a) he studied separately the fundamental assumptions involved. He demonstrated the gradient of generalization by showing that if hungry rats are trained to approach a light of a given brightness for food they will approach lights of other brightness, and if restrained will pull harder the more similar the illumination is to that used in the original training. He also verified the assumption that increases in the strength of drive raise the whole gradient of generalization by demonstrating that increased hunger caused the animal to pull harder to both similar and dissimilar stimuli.[14]

After having studied generalization of responses to a single light varying in brightness, Brown (1942b) investigated the behavior of animals trained to discriminate between two lights of different intensities. He measured approach responses by electric contact recorders on the platforms leading to each of the stimuli, determined the strength of withdrawal by measuring the force that animals exerted when they were temporarily restrained in a retreat from the choice point, and secured an index of vacillation by counting the number of head movements, first to one side and then the other.

He found that as the discrimination was made more difficult, differential behavior was disrupted. The type of disruption depended upon the conditions in the manner demanded by our deductions. The difficult discrimination was more likely to be disrupted by indiscriminate approaches, the stronger the hunger drive, the weaker the punishment for making wrong choices, or the more the stimuli resembled the one that had originally been positive. Conversely, the difficult discrimination was more likely to be disrupted by withdrawal from the choice point, the weaker the hunger drive, the stronger the punishment, or the more the stimuli resembled the one that had originally been negative. Conditions between the two extremes produced vacillation.

It should be noted that when the discrimination is easy, both of the stimuli are still somewhat similar to those involved in difficult discrimination. Furthermore, the general features of the choice situation remain unaltered. Therefore, it would be expected that the habits involved in indiscriminate reactions to a difficult comparison should tend to generalize to subsequent easy ones. Brown also verified this deduction. After the

[14] The principle of a gradient of generalization has, of course, been verified by many other studies. See Hilgard and Marquis (1940), Ch. 8. The dependence of the height of the whole gradient upon the strength of drive had not previously been studied.

choice reactions had been broken down by too fine a discrimination, there was a definite tendency for the same type of disruption to appear in subsequent coarser ones. This, of course, is in line with the work described in more detail by Liddell in Chapter 12.

Throughout this analysis the conflict was between tendencies to approach or avoid a region in space. In other types of discrimination the reactions may vary in their temporal nearness to a goal or point of reinforcement. It remains for further work to indicate whether or not an analysis in terms of approach and avoidance can be made relevant to all such instances.

In all cases, however, it seems probable that the principle of generalization will be found relevant, and that the discrimination will be more likely to break down the more similar the stimuli. Thus, in psychophysical investigations, the choice time increases when the stimuli being compared are more similar (Kellogg, 1931).[15] Furthermore, Gibson (1940) has successfully used an analysis in terms of generalization to explain the type of interference commonly called retroactive inhibition. She has shown (1941) that learning a new set of responses causes more blocking and errors in the performance of previously learned habits the more similar the stimuli eliciting the old and new responses.

Other Factors Influencing Type of Equilibrium

As has been shown, gradients in the strength of approach and avoidance tendencies are very important in determining whether the situation will be one of stable or unstable equilibrium. They are not, however, the only factors which can be involved.

Any crucial changes which the responses produce in the stimulus situation will influence the type of equilibrium. If the response creates additional stimulation which facilitates it, unstable equilibrium will be produced. Similar results will be produced if the response removes sources of stimulation supporting its competitors. In most approach-approach situations, starting for one of the goals involves turning toward it and away from its competitor. This increases stimulation from the chosen goal and decreases that from the competitor. Therefore it strengthens the tendency to continue and summates with the effect of the approach gradient in producing easily resolved, unstable equilibrium.

If the response tends to remove its own stimulus, or to produce stimuli facilitating its competitors, opposite results will be produced. Thus, when the subject is between two sources of avoidance without opportunity for lateral escape, turning away from one evil and toward

---

[15] If the subject is not limited to two responses, but instructed to make judgments of "equal" also, then there will actually be two discriminations involved: the difference between the stimulus of *A* greater than *B* and that of *A* equal to *B*, and the difference between the latter and *A* less than *B*. As Cartwright (1941b) has shown, the longest choice times will then appear at the points at which each of these discriminations is difficult. His theoretical interpretation of this phenomenon is couched in Lewinian terms (Cartwright, 1941a).

the other will tend to cause him to turn back even before he has gone far enough for the gradients to have much effect.

These effects are not limited to external stimulation in spatial situations. Proprioceptive stimulation facilitating the response producing it —as in the previously discussed example of psychological momentum— tends to produce unstable equilibrium. On the other hand, stable equilibrium is produced in postural reflexes by the fact that the response of leaning forward stretches the muscles down the rear of the leg and stimulates them to reflex contraction pulling the body back up.

Finally, in addition to changes in the stimulus situation, other factors such as refractory phase, fatigue, and experimental extinction, which weaken whatever response is occurring, tend to produce that vacillation and blocking which is characteristic of conflict situations.

Types of Incompatibility

Conflict occurs only when responses are incompatible. Thus far the discussion has, for the most part, dealt with responses, such as approach and avoidance, which are obviously mutually exclusive. In other cases, however, it is not always immediately apparent that the responses will be incompatible; they may be neutral or even mutually facilitating. Although the problem of incompatibility has not yet received thorough analysis, it seems probable that there are a number of different kinds. These may be sketched briefly.

Mechanical.—The most superficial type of incompatibility is that based on the physical structure of the body: for example, the flexion and extension of the arm. The characteristics of competition at this overt, mechanical level are that it involves fatiguing muscular tension and that the opposing responses subtract from each other, *pari pasu*, in a rough approximation of algebraic summation.

Neural.—In most cases overt mechanical incompatibility is paralleled by a more central neural incompatibility which Sherrington (1906) has called *reciprocal innervation*. Thus the spinal cord functions in such a way that if the muscles operating to flex a limb are reflexly excited to contract, those operating to extend it relax. This central resolution of competition prevents a wasteful physical cancellation of opposing muscular contractions. It is when this mechanism fails, so that competition is fought out on the mechanical level, that the individual most obviously manifests conflict.

Responses which are not obviously mechanically incompatible may be physiologically antagonistic through reciprocal innervation. Thus reflex flexion of one leg tends to inhibit the flexion of the contralateral one. Similarly, gripping hard with one hand tends to interfere somewhat with exerting the maximum grip with the other. In general, the more strongly the reflexes are excited the more likely they are not to be neutral, but either facilitating or inhibiting. When reciprocal inhibition is uncomplicated by other mechanisms, responses summate algebraically.[16]

The problem of neural incompatibility is complicated by the fact that contractions of the same pair of muscles may be incompatible responses when mediated through one center and not when mediated through another. Thus the extensors relax when the flexors are excited by a spinal reflex, but both may contract at once if the impulses come from higher, "voluntary" centers.

Chemical.—A few internal secretions are known to have opposite effects on certain responses (Goodman and Gilman, 1941). Acetylcholine increases the frequency and amplitude of intestinal peristalsis, epinephrine reduces it. Epinephrine is released by fear and its persistence in the blood stream accounts for an interference with digestion which continues for a period after the fear stimulus has been withdrawn and direct sympathetic neural activity has ceased. It may be that chemical effects of this type are involved in antagonisms between certain drives, as, for example, a tendency for fear to interfere with hunger.

Perceptual.—Two responses may be incompatible because the performance of one removes the stimulus which elicits the other. In the simplest examples, the performance of the responses may depend upon two mechanically incompatible orientations of a sense organ, such as the eye. Reversible illusions, ambiguous figures, and limitations of the span of attention seem to involve more central types of incompatibility. The mechanism of these is not well understood, but it may be ventured that the competition between mutually exclusive central cue-producing responses is involved.

In some cases of sensory interference, for example, Heyman's law (1899), the summation is roughly algebraic; in others, such as reversible illusions, it seems to be all-or-none. Sometimes alternations occur, as in retinal rivalry. In peripheral examples, like the orientation of the eye, the kind of summation depends on the type of equilibrium of the competing cue-producing responses. A situation involving unstable equilibrium between antagonistic eye movements tends to produce all-or-none summation; stable equilibrium is likely to produce algebraic summation. Similar factors may be involved in central conflicts.

Acquired.—Responses which are originally compatible may acquire a certain amount of incompatibility. Very young children often manifest little conflict over expressing love and hate more or less simultaneously, and none at all over logical inconsistencies. By the time they become adults, either contrasting expressions of emotion or logically contradictory ideas may generate conflicts. Innately compatible responses seem to acquire incompatibility in situations in which responding with either

---

[16] Actually, of course, the ultimate units of nerve conduction obey the all-or-none law; progressive effects of facilitation or inhibition are produced by the activation of more and more units.

one or the other is rewarded, but responding with both is punished or extinguished. Since making both responses together may be punished in some situations but not in others, the same two responses may under some conditions be incompatible, and under others not. Acquired incompatibilities tend to reflect the culture patterns of the social group in which the individual has been reared. Unfortunately, acquired incompatibility has not yet been studied experimentally. A stimulus-response analysis suggests that it can be produced by several different mechanisms. These are diagrammed in Figure 7.

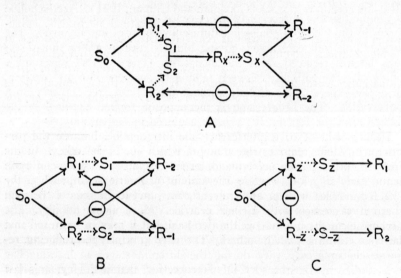

A

B   C

Figure 7.   Types of Acquired Incompatibility

S_0 is the stimulus situation eliciting two responses R_1 and R_2, which originally were compatible. These responses produce the proprioceptive stimuli S_1 and S_2. In A the pattern of S_1 and S_2 appearing together elicits the anxiety response R_x, producing the anxiety stimulus S_x. This stimulus elicits the responses R_{-1} and R_{-2} incompatible with R_1 and R_2 respectively. In B the responses inhibiting R_1 and R_2 are attached directly to the stimuli produced by R_1 and R_2, respectively. In C the two original compatible responses R_1 and R_2 are dependent upon mutually incompatible cue-producing responses, R_z and R_{-z}. To the extent that these mediating responses are mutually exclusive, R_1 and R_2 will not appear simultaneously.

(a) Two responses, such as putting bread into the mouth with one hand and meat with the other, are originally compatible. Then the individual learns to respond with anxiety to the pattern produced by simultaneous stimulation from both responses. This anxiety motivates the subject not to perform both of the responses at once.

(b) Two responses are originally compatible, but the subject learns to react directly to the stimuli produced by each of them with a response incompatible with the other.

(c) Originally both of the responses are elicited directly by external cues and are compatible. Later both are elicited indirectly by internal cues from stimulus-producing responses which are incompatible with each other. Since the stimulus-producing responses are mutually exclusive, the responses elicited by them do not appear simultaneously.

Interference of Complex Habits

Sometimes habits interfere with each other at one stage of learning but not at another. When a person is first learning to drive, handling the car and carrying on a conversation interfere with each other; the experienced driver can do both at once. In such cases it seems plausible to assume that the difference in interference at various stages of learning is due to the fact that somewhat different responses are involved. The novice thinks out each move, giving himself cues by rehearsing directions he has received from the instructor. These verbal links are a source of incompatibility between talking to someone else and driving. Since the expert reacts directly without them, he is free to carry on a conversation. The progression is the opposite to that outlined in the discussion of the last, or (c) type of acquired incompatibility.

Studies of associative interference and retroactive inhibition (Melton and Irwin, 1940) demonstrate that practicing one habit tends to interfere with other habits involving different responses to similar stimuli. In the early stages of learning the amount of interference produced by a habit increases with practice; eventually, however, a point is reached where it decreases with further practice. Here again the stimulus-response elements involved in the two habits may overlap more in some stages of learning than in others. The way in which the range of response elements may vary during the different stages of learning has been studied by Beritov (1924). He observed that if dogs are trained to lift a paw to a stimulus which precedes shock, the conditioned response during early trials will be relatively generalized, involving movements of almost all parts of the body. As training proceeds the scope of the reaction gradually becomes more limited, until finally only the specific muscles essential to paw raising are involved. Girden's observations (1938) indicate that this narrowing may be produced by trial and error. Experiments on stimulus generalization (Pavlov, 1927) suggest a trend of initial widening, followed by gradual narrowing. In many habits a greater specificity may be produced by non-reinforcement of responses to irrelevant stimuli. Whenever the range of stimulus and response generalization becomes narrower with thorough practice, fewer different stimuli and responses are involved in an overlearned habit. Thus two such habits are less likely to involve units incompatible with each other.

Sometimes in a complex habit two or more responses are being learned at the same time but at different rates. If one of these facilitates while another interferes with some other habit, it is easy to see that the net effect will be different at different stages in learning. This is illustrated in Figure 8. An experiment by Jackson (1932) is an excellent example in point. He gave different groups of rats different amounts of training in a maze of one pattern and then tested the rate at which they learned a different maze. He found positive transfer during certain stages of learning, and negative during others.

Similarly, Bunch (1939) has shown that complex habits may be mutually interfering at one stage of forgetting and facilitating at another. He explains this by assuming that components which interact differently are being forgotten at different rates.

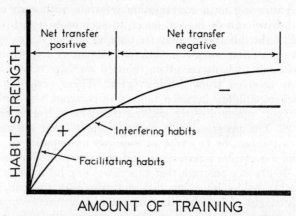

AMOUNT OF TRAINING

Figure 8.   Reversal of Net Transfer Effect with Additional Training

This diagram represents the situation in which two different types of habit are being learned at two different rates in the same situation. One set of habits will facilitate correct behavior in subsequent tests in a new situation; the other will interfere. If the learning curve for the first set is rapid with a low asymptote while that for the second is slow with a high asymptote, the net effect of small amounts of training in the original situation will be positive transfer, and that of large amounts negative transfer.

Experiments on dynamogenesis have demonstrated that the way in which complex responses interact may also depend on their relative strengths. A typical experiment, Courts' (1939), tested the influence of requiring the subject to grip a dynamometer upon his performance in learning a list of nonsense syllables. It was found that the response of weakly gripping the dynamometer facilitated performance, while gripping strongly interfered with it. Similar results have been found for responses to sound and other types of distraction.

In some cases the different effects of distractions may partly be explained by physiological factors. For example, if each response is made up of a series of action units whose thresholds vary in a normal distribution, the cumulative curve will form an ogive. If the responses involved in the task which the subject is performing are moderately excited, while the muscles antagonistic to these responses are at a low level of excitation, a slight increase produced by dynamogenesis will be expected to add more to the responses in the task than to their antagonists. A much stronger general increase in excitation may raise the already excited responses involved in the performance of the task to the flat portion of the ogive, where relatively little additional effect can be produced, while the reactions antagonistic to these responses are raised to the steep portions of the ogive, where many additional units are thrown into action so that the net result of further increases will be interference.

In many cases, it seems plausible to assume that psychological factors play an important role. The individual may have learned to compensate for distractions by exerting additional effort. If a weak distraction produces effort appropriate to a stronger one, the net result will be facilitation. If the distraction is strong enough, the conflicting responses which it elicits may override the effects of the habit of exerting additional effort.

Compromise Responses

One kind of compromise response has already been discussed: the lateral escape in a simple spatial situation of avoidance-avoidance conflict. The deduction of this response hinged on the proposition that each of the competing avoidances is composed of a whole hierarchy of habits. Responses of direct withdrawal from each of the stimuli are incompatible and tend to inhibit each other; responses of lateral escape are compatible and tend to summate. Similarly, many nonspatial responses are actually not simple but composed of a large number of subunits. Some of these may be elements which are present as parts of the overt, complete response. Others may be alternative modes of reaction which were originally used in earlier stages of trial-and-error learning, but later lost their dominance to other, more strongly rewarded reactions. Still others may always have been latent tendencies produced by the mechanism of response generalization. It seems reasonable to suppose that when two complex response hierarchies arc in conflict, those elements which are not incompatible will tend to summate so that the one whose combined strength from both hierarchies is the greatest will tend to appear as a compromise response.

In an attempt to study this problem, Miller (1943) trained subjects to depress both of their hands to one stimulus and to depress the left hand and raise the right to another. Then both stimuli were given simultaneously. The apparatus was designed to measure the latency and force of the movements of each hand. He found that the depression on the left hand (i.e., the part of the patterns which was not incompatible) was stronger than the response of either depressing or raising the right, but that it was much weaker than that occurring on nonconflict trials. This apparent spread of the conflict to the compatible elements of each pattern suggests that each pattern was facilitated or mediated as a whole by a different central cue-producing response. To the extent that these were crucial, conflict between them would be expected to affect the whole pattern as a unit. It should be noted that, according to Freudian theory, displaced and other compromise responses are more likely to occur when the conflict is not on a conscious level—i.e., when it is not mediated by verbal, or other cue-producing responses.

When a newly introduced reaction conflicts with the dominant response but is compatible with some weaker member of the hierarchy which was a part of earlier trial-and-error learning, the resultant reappearance of this response is called regression. Experimental evidence (Mowrer, 1940) indicates that such responses do reappear as compromise resultants of conflict situations.

In addition to the mechanisms just described, it seems likely that the conflict itself, as Miller and Stevenson (1936) have suggested, may produce strong stimulation. Thus, any response terminating the conflict will be rewarded by a reduction in the strength of this stimulation. In this way the subject may learn responses which take him out of the situation. That conflict can produce strong stimulation tends to be confirmed by Finger's (1941) finding that the force with which rats jump across a gap from the starting platform to the stimulus card is increased when the animals are placed in a discrimination conflict.

Spread of Conflict

Clinicians often observe that one situation seems to be the focus of a conflict which spreads to invade other areas of the patient's life. It has been shown that the generalization of responses from one stimulus to another can induce conflict in situations demanding fine discriminations. It can also induce an apparent spread of conflict. This is illustrated in a simple experiment which the author has performed for a class demonstration.

Hungry albino rats were trained to secure food in three different situations. The first was a flat board, two feet square, surrounded by celluloid walls, and placed on top of a table. In the center of the board was a food cup elevated by a small metal peg. The second was a smooth, long, fairly broad, elevated path leading to a similar food cup, and the third, also leading to a similar food cup, was a relatively short, narrow, elevated strip of quarter-inch wire screen. After the animals had learned to secure food in the three situations, the experimenter placed them on the flat board and just as they were commencing to eat gave them an electric shock through a grid of fine wires wrapped around the board. After a few trials of this kind the animals showed obvious conflict, remaining well away from the food cup, tentatively approaching and then hastily withdrawing, first from one side and then from another.

The animals also showed definite vacillation when tested in the other two situations in which they had never been shocked. The fear generalized on the basis of the similar food cups and created new conflicts in both of these situations. On the first trial the animals approached very near to the food cup, started to stand up to reach for the food, then vacillated back and forth several times and suddenly withdrew. Apparently the generalized fear and withdrawal was quite specific to reaching up toward the cup. On successive trials the conflict behavior appeared at progressively earlier points in the path leading to the cup. The fear and withdrawal originally elicited by the stimulus of standing up and seeing the cup became conditioned to the other cues which had preceded that stimulus. In a description of phobias, Fenichel (1934, pp. 53–54) gives a description of human cases in which a similar enlargement of the area of conflict seems to be occurring by a process of progressively higher order conditioning.[17]

In a more formal experiment Miller (1935) has observed that avoidance, and hence conflict, can generalize from a device in which animals are fed when hungry to a somewhat similar device in which they drink when thirsty. He also observed that anticipatory goal responses can mediate a type of generalization which would ordinarily be described as foresightful. In all of these cases, of course, it is not the conflict itself which spreads; one or more of the competing tendencies responsible for the original conflict generalizes to new situations and creates new conflict there.

The experiments cited have shown that a simple approach situation can be changed to an approach-avoidance conflict by generalized fear. Similar generalization will also be expected to occur in more complex situations originally involving a choice between two goals. If avoidance generalizes to each of the goals, it will be expected to change the situation from an easily resolved approach-approach competition into a double approach-avoidance conflict. Thus, when the fears producing a severe conflict generalize, they tend to make all choices more difficult. Furthermore, it seems possible that the act of making a decision may produce stimuli which are relatively similar in different choice situations, so that after an individual has been severely punished for the immediate consequences of one decision, he may have anxiety about making others. These interpretations contrast with Janet's (1925) view that a severe conflict makes other choices harder by depleting the store of mental energy needed to make decisions.

Studies of experimental neuroses (see Chapter 12 by Liddell) have demonstrated that after an animal's behavior has been seriously disrupted by an attempt to force a discrimination between stimuli that are too similar, responses conditioned to other stimuli may also be disrupted. On the basis of generalization one would expect the habits involving stimuli most similar to those in the original conflict to be the ones most disrupted. But, can the effects of generalization account for all the disturbance observed, or must one also assume some more fundamental upset or damage? No one has yet aimed an experiment at deciding this issue.

---

[17] From this description it seems probable that a more complicated mechanism may also be at work. Anxiety may be conditioned to the stimuli produced by certain anticipatory goal responses. As the drive motivating these anticipatory responses mounts, they generalize to more and more stimuli in the environment, carrying with them the anxiety which they mediate.

BIBLIOGRAPHY

BARKER, R. G. 1942. An experimental study of the resolution of conflict by children; time elapsing and amount of vicarious trial-and-error behavior occurring. In McNemar, Q., & Merrill, M. A., *Studies in personality*. New York: McGraw-Hill.

BERITOFF, J. S. 1924. On the fundamental nervous processes in the cortex of the cerebral hemispheres: I. The principal stages of the development of the individual reflex: its generalization and differentiation. *Brain, 47*, 109–148.

BROWN, J. S. 1940. Generalized approach and avoidance responses in relation to conflict behavior. New Haven: Dissertation, Yale University. (Unpublished)[18]

—— 1942a. The generalization of approach responses as a function of stimulus intensity and strength of motivation. *J. comp. Psychol., 33*, 209–226.

—— 1942b. Factors determining conflict reactions in difficult discriminations. *J. exp. Psychol., 31*, 272–292.

BUNCH, M. E. 1939. Transfer of training in the mastery of an antagonistic habit after varying intervals of time. *J. comp. Psychol., 28*, 189–200.

CARTWRIGHT, D. 1941a. Decision-time in relation to the differentiation of the phenomenal field. *Psychol. Rev., 48*, 425–442.

—— 1941b. Relation of decision-time to the categories of response. *Amer. J. Psychol., 54*, 174–196.

COURTS, F. A. 1939. Relations between experimentally induced muscular tension and memorization. *J. exp. Psychol., 25*, 235–356.

FENICHEL, O. 1934. Outline of clinical psychoanalysis. (Trans. by B. D. Lewin & G. Zilboorg.) Albany, N. Y.: Psychoanalytic Quarterly Press.

FINGER, F. W. 1941. Quantitative studies of "conflict": I. Variations in latency and strength of the rat's response in a discrimination-jumping situation. *J. comp. Psychol., 31*, 97–127.

FREUD, S. 1920. A general introduction to psychoanalysis. New York: Boni & Liveright.

GIBSON, E. J. 1940. A systematic application of the concepts of generalization and differentiation of verbal learning. *Psychol. Rev., 47*, 196–229.

—— 1940. Retroactive inhibition as a function of degree of generalization between tasks. *J. exp. Psychol., 28*, 93–115.

GIRDEN, E. 1938. Conditioning and problem-solving behavior. *Amer. J. Psychol., 51*, 677–686.

GODBEER, E. 1940. Factors introducing conflict in the choice behavior of children. New Haven: Dissertation, Yale University.[18]

GOODMAN, L., & GILMAN, A. 1941. The pharmacological basis of therapeutics. New York: Macmillan.

GULLIKSEN, H., & WOLFE, D. L. 1938. A theory of learning and transfer: I. *Psychometrika, 3*, 127–149.

GUTHRIE, E. R. 1938. The psychology of human conflict. New York: Harper.

HEYMANS, G. 1899. Untersuchungen über psychische Hemmung. *Z. Psychol. Physiol. Sinnesorg., 21*, 321–359.

HILGARD, E. R., & MARQUIS, D. G. 1940. Conditioning and learning. New York: Appleton-Century.

HOVLAND, C. I., & SEARS, R. R. 1938. Experiments on motor conflict: I. Types of conflict and their modes of resolution. *J. exp. Psychol., 23*, 477–493.

—— 1944. Experiments on motor conflict: III. The influence of previous training upon mode of resolution. (Unpublished)

HULL, C. L. 1929. A functional interpretation of the conditioned reflex. *Psychol. Rev., 36*, 498–511.

—— 1930. Knowledge and purpose as habit mechanisms. *Psychol. Rev., 37*, 511–525.

—— 1938. The goal-gradient hypothesis applied to some "field-force" problems in the behavior of young children. *Psychol. Rev., 45*, 271–299.

---

[18] Originally planned as one of a series of related studies to be published as a book. Because of the war, these will probably be published as separate members of a series under the general title: *A Theoretical and Experimental Analysis of Conflict Behavior.*

HULL, C. L. 1943. Principles of behavior. New York: Appleton-Century.

HUNT, J. McV. 1944. Motor behavior of rats in a conflict situation. *J. comp. Psychol.* (To be published)

JACKSON, T. A. 1932. General factors in the transfer of training in the white rat. *Genet. Psychol. Monogr., 11,* 1–59.

JANET, P. M. F. 1925. Psychological healing. (Trans. by Eden & Cedar Paul.) (2 vols.) London: Allen & Unwin; New York: Macmillan.

KELLOGG, W. N. 1931. The time of judgment in psychometric measures. *Amer. J. Psychol., 43,* 65–86.

KLEBANOFF, S. G. 1939. An experimental analysis of approach-approach and avoidance-avoidance conflict. New Haven: Dissertation, Yale University.[18]

LEWIN, K. 1931. Environmental forces in child behavior and development. In Murchison, C., *A handbook of child psychology.* Worcester, Mass.: Clark University Press.

—— 1935. A dynamic theory of personality. New York: McGraw-Hill.

McDOUGALL, W. 1926. Outline of abnormal psychology. New York: Scribners.

MELTON, A. W., & IRWIN, J. M. 1940. The influence of degree of interpolated learning on retroactive inhibition and the overt transfer of specific responses. *Amer. J. Psychol., 53,* 173–203.

MILLER, N. E. 1935. A reply to "Sign-Gestalt or conditioned reflex?" *Psychol. Rev., 42,* 280–292.

—— 1937. Analysis of the form of conflict reactions. *Psychol. Bull., 34,* 720.[18]

—— 1943. The influence of conflict upon the compatible and incompatible sub-units of two competing response patterns. (Unpublished)[18]

MILLER, N. E., BROWN, J. S., & LIPOFSKY, H. 1943. A theoretical and experimental analysis of conflict behavior: III. Approach-avoidance conflict as a function of strength of drive and strength of shock. (Unpublished)[18]

MILLER, N. E., & DAVIS, M. 1943. A theoretical and experimental analysis of conflict behavior: IV. The influence of the positions of reward and punishment in the response sequence. (Unpublished)[18]

MILLER, N. E., & DOLLARD, J. 1941. Social learning and imitation. New Haven: Yale University Press.

MILLER, N. E., & STEVENSON, S. S. 1936. Agitated behavior of rats during experimental extinction and a curve of spontaneous recovery. *J. comp. Psychol., 21,* 205–231.

MOWRER, O. H. 1940. An experimental analogue of "regression" with incidental observations on "reaction-formation." *J. abnorm. soc. Psychol., 35,* 56–87.

—— 1941. The Freudian theories of anxiety: a reconciliation. Address given before Monday Night Group of the Institute of Human Relations, March 3, 1941. (Mimeographed.) New Haven: Institute of Human Relations, Yale University.

PAVLOV, I. P. 1927. Conditioned reflexes. London: Oxford University Press.

PRINCE, M. 1921. The unconscious, the fundamentals of human personality, normal and abnormal (2nd ed., rev. 1924). New York: Macmillan.

RASMUSSEN, E. W. 1940. The shock method as a measure of hunger and of the intensity of a conflict. *Acta psychol., Hague, 5,* 63–78.

RIVERS, W. H. R. 1923. Conflict and dream. London: Kegan Paul; New York: Harcourt, Brace.

SEARS, R. R., & HOVLAND, C. I. 1941. Experiments on motor conflict: II. Determination of mode or resolution by comparative strengths of conflicting responses. *J. exp. Psychol., 28,* 280–286.

SHERRINGTON, C. S. 1906. The integrative action of the nervous system. New Haven: Yale University Press.

SMITH, S., & GUTHRIE, E. E. 1921. General psychology in terms of behavior. New York: Appleton-Century.

SPENCE, K. W. 1936. The nature of discrimination learning in animals. *Psychol. Rev., 43,* 427–449.

STRECKER, E. A., & EBAUGH, F. G. 1940. Practical clinical psychiatry. (5th ed.) Philadelphia: Blakiston.

Chapter 15

HYPNOTISM

By ARTHUR JENNESS, Ph.D.

"HYPNOTISM MUST BE A VERY INTRIGUING FIELD," a young woman said to the writer not long ago. Probably she meant that it was an interesting subject, or attention-compelling, as the term "intriguing" is sometimes naïvely employed, but in this case the phrase was more apt than its user knew. Hypnotism is literally a "tricky, cheating, or complicated" field of knowledge and research, even when one disregards the uses to which hypnosis has been put by exhibitionists and charlatans. Probably no psychological phenomenon has been the subject of so much investigation and is at the same time so little understood as hypnosis. Yet hypnotism still holds forth the promise of yielding a better understanding of human behavior; it engages the attention of many sober physicians and psychologists, much as it is deprecated by others. The outlook for research in hypnotism has been described by Clark L. Hull:

> . . . to enter seriously on a program of investigation in this field is a little like tempting fate; it is almost to court scientific disaster. Small wonder that orthodox scientists have usually avoided the subject! Yet each generation may be expected in the future, as in the past, to produce a very few rash souls who will not only risk the dangers of making scientific errors but will also have the courage to brave the semi-superstitious fears of the general public and the uneasy suspicions of their orthodox scientific brethren. (1933, p. 403)

Definitions

While the technical terms of hypnotism are few and generally understood, it is well to specify their manner of use in this chapter.

The term *hypnosis* is defined in Warren's Dictionary of Psychology as follows: "an artificially induced state, usually (though not always) resembling sleep, but physiologically distinct from it, which is characterized by heightened suggestibility, as a result of which certain sensory, motor, and memory abnormalities may be induced more readily than in the normal state." While this definition is inadequate in some respects, it is the best one known to the writer and it will serve as a point of departure for the discussion which is to follow. *Hypnotism* refers to knowledge about hypnosis, including theories regarding hypnotic phenomena and the history of investigations of hypnosis. A *hypnotist* is one who induces hypnosis in another person. The verb *hypnotize* designates what the hypnotist does in inducing hypnosis. When we say that a person is *hypnotized*, we shall mean that he is in a state of hypnosis. So far, no one has invented a satisfactory technical term to designate the person who is being hypnotized; psychologists usually fall back on the convenient term *subject*, and medical practitioners use the term *patient*, in order to designate the person who is being hypnotized.

Although it is difficult to arrive at a satisfactory verbal definition of hypnosis, many investigators and practitioners agree on the essential characteristics of hypnosis. Instead of attempting to define hypnosis concisely, they describe the procedure of inducing hypnosis and specify the criteria which they employ in deciding whether a person is hypnotized. Thus, in effect, they define hypnosis operationally, even though the precision of the definition leaves much to be desired.

The Technique of Hypnotizing

While no brief description can do justice to the technique of hypnotizing, the following outline of the elements of hypnotic procedure will perhaps clarify the definitions given above.[1] Probably no two hypnotists proceed in exactly the same manner, and each hypnotist adapts his methods to the particular subject with whom he is dealing. Some hypnotists, after obtaining the confidence of the subject in any way they deem best, seat the subject in a comfortable chair or have him recline on a couch. Others prefer to begin by using a test of suggestibility, which serves the dual function of discovering how well the subject responds to verbal suggestion and establishing a set to respond positively to the directions of the hypnotist. One such device is the postural sway technique mentioned on page 471. Another is to have the subject extend his arms straight before him, with the hands clasped tightly, and to suggest that at a given signal, say the count of ten, he will not be able to unclasp them. Then the hypnotist may count from one to ten slowly, interspersing the words, "tight, tight, tight" between the counts and repeating the suggestion that at "ten," the hands will remain clasped tightly.[2] A similar procedure may be employed with the eyelids, the

---

[1] This description is not intended as sufficient instruction to enable one to begin the practice of hypnotizing. Hypnotizing is an art which requires a thorough background of knowledge of human behavior. Skill in hypnotizing may be developed by practice, but this practice should preferably be based on instruction and supervision from a competent hypnotist. The beginner may accomplish results in the case of some subjects without adequate instruction, but the undesirability of such a procedure will be evident from later sections of this chapter. Some persons may be lightly hypnotized merely by relaxing and listening to a phonograph, such as the one described by Estabrooks (1930).

[2] When the subject clasps his hands tightly and continues to do so for a while, it is difficult for him to unclasp them, simply because a muscular set has been established and because the knuckles are larger than the bones of the fingers; even when the hands are relaxed, it requires some effort to pull them apart. If the subject does pull his hands apart, the hypnotist may call attention to the fact that they did not come apart easily, without explaining the reason.

subject being told to close his eyes as tightly as he can until the count of ten, at which time he will be unable to open them. If the subject is sitting or reclining, the hypnotist may have him fixate a small object with his eyes, with the suggestion that as he stares at it, his eyes will become fatigued and finally close.

After the subject is in a comfortable position, the hypnotist asks him to imagine how it would feel to go into a deep sleep, and describes as vividly as possible the warm, drowsy sensation of sleep coming over his whole body. Suggestions regarding the relaxation of muscles are helpful. Often, stroking the arms and legs very lightly, accompanied by such phrases as "heavy and drowsy," "relaxed and comfortable," "fast asleep," is effective. If it is desired to hypnotize the subject deeply, the hypnotist may direct the subject to carry out various activities which facilitate the hypnosis and serve as indicators of its depth. He may suggest that when he has counted to ten, the subject's arm will be stiff and rigid and that he cannot bend it. Stroking the arm and repeating "stiff and rigid" between counts aids in bringing on contractures of the arm muscles. Similarly, it may be suggested that an arm or leg will be relaxed and paralyzed, with the subject unable to move it. Furthermore, it may be suggested that one of the subject's hands will lose all sensation (become anesthetic) or that he will feel no pain in it (develop analgesia). Phrases such as "numb and senseless" may be used here. At "ten" the hypnotist may pinch the designated hand and ask the subject if he feels it, at the same time watching the subject's face for signs of the flinch which usually accompanies a painful stimulation. If it appears that the hand is analgesic, the subject's other hand may be pinched, by way of contrast, to show how painful a pinch can be. If any of the suggested phenomena appear, they may be removed by some such device as stating that they will disappear when the letters of the alphabet up to "g" have been said slowly.

If the subject has responded to the previous suggestions satisfactorily, the hypnotist may give further suggestions of sleep and drowsiness, perhaps informing the subject that he will hear all that is said and that he can reply to questions, without awakening. Then the hypnotist may attempt to produce hallucinations in the subject, usually visual or auditory, though any modality may be included. He will suggest, for instance, that at a given signal the subject will hear a band playing a favorite tune, or a voice calling to him. Or he may suggest that the subject will see, as if in a dream, a common object, or an animal, or a person whom he knows. He may even suggest that the subject will open his eyes, *without awakening,* and that when his eyes are open, he will see what is suggested to him. Then the hypnotist may direct the subject to close his eyes and relax, or he may continue with other directions, such as to believe that he is a street-cleaner, and ask him to carry out the activities appropriate to his occupation.

At some time, the hypnotist will direct the subject to awaken at a prearranged signal, such as saying the letters up to "g." Before doing this, he may say that the subject will not remember some (or perhaps all) of the events which took place during hypnosis. Perhaps he will state that the subject will carry out a certain action at a designated time after awakening, such as blowing his nose two minutes from the time he opens his eyes, without realizing why he does so. If the subject is unable to remember the specified events after he is dehypnotized, this is taken as evidence of amnesia. If he carries out the designated act, the phenomenon of post-hypnotic suggestion has occurred. If the amnesia is present, or if the post-hypnotic suggestion is carried out, it is imperative that the subject be rehypnotized and reminded of all that has happened, including the instructions regarding the carrying out of suggestions post-hypnotically. This second hypnosis usually takes place rapidly and is often accomplished merely by directing the subject to close his eyes and go to sleep. Most hypnoses proceed more slowly than the foregoing account would seem to indicate; it is often necessary to continue the procedure for short sessions each day over a period of several days in order to accomplish any of the results described above. Many subjects show little response to the efforts of the hypnotist; individual differences are great, as will be shown in a succeeding section.

Because the subject may develop hallucinations and delusions about what took place during the hypnotic procedure, in accordance with his wishes, many hypnotists require that a third person be present as observer. The presence of the latter may allay such fears and doubts as the subject may have, and thus facilitate hypnosis. W. R. Wells (1941 and earlier) has recommended that a subject who has been deeply hypnotized should be instructed under hypnosis that thereafter he cannot be hypnotized by *anyone* unless he has voluntarily signed a statement that he is willing to be a subject for hypnosis. This is intended to protect subjects, who, because of their training, might otherwise be more readily hypnotized by others. The present writer has always exercised this precaution and feels that it is desirable to do so.

Many writers have described the ways in which they induce hypnosis. Among the better of these descriptions are those of Rosenow (1928), Hollander (1928), Bernheim (1900), Hull (1933), and Winn (1939). A detailed description of the techniques for therapeutic purposes is given by Schilder and Kauders (1927). Bramwell (1921) has summarized the methods of some of the earlier investigators and therapists, as well as describing his own techniques.

The Criteria of Hypnosis

The foregoing account includes the principal symptoms of hypnosis. These are: contractures, paralyses, anesthesia (loss of sensation), analgesia (loss of pain sensitivity), hallucinations, delusions (false judgments as indicated by false beliefs), amnesia,[3] and post-hypnotic sug-

---

[3] W. R. Wells (1940) has reported a carefully planned and executed experiment in which three subjects maintained amnesias for a series of nonsense syllables for one year, only to remember the series at the appointed hour, according to a suggestion given a year previously.

gestion.[4] If all of them appear, we say that the subject is deeply hypnotized. If some of them appear and others do not, we give a relative rating to the depth of hypnosis. Some hypnotists would insist on further symptoms than these and the skeptic unfamiliar with hypnotism might readily point out that all of these phenomena might be simulated or "faked" by the subject. The experienced hypnotist, however, is not easily fooled by simulation, though in order to judge the genuineness of these symptoms, he may have to rely on further evidence which he has learned to observe in the course of his experience. He recognizes a relaxation of facial musculature, a lack of humor and of the recognition of incongruity, a lack of initiative, during hypnosis, which could hardly be simulated. The amazement of the subject, either during or after the hypnosis, at what has happened, affords a further means of judging the genuineness of the phenomena. Another objection which may be raised against using the phenomena we have listed as criteria of hypnosis is that some of them may be produced without any suggestion of sleep, and that therefore they are not necessarily symptoms of hypnosis. In fact, Bernheim (1900) and W. R. Wells (1924) demonstrated that all of the phenomena which are listed here as symptoms of hypnosis could be produced without any suggestions of sleep or drowsiness. It should be noted, however, that Wells does not use this demonstration as a basis for denying that these are criteria of hypnosis. Rather, he suggests that the term "waking hypnosis," in spite of its being an etymological paradox, should be applied to the state in which such phenomena occur in the absence of suggestions of sleep or drowsiness.

Individual Differences in Hypnotizability

No precise data are available on the proportion of the general population which is hypnotizable. Practically every hypnotist of wide experience has reported failure to hypnotize some subjects, though usually the term "failure" is avoided; it is stated, instead, that the persons who were not hypnotized were not "good" subjects for hypnosis. In theory, every person can be hypnotized to some extent, but in practice some persons do not respond to hypnotic techniques. Bramwell has devoted a chapter of his book (1921) to a summary of reports from some twenty hypnotists of attempts to hypnotize more than 30,000 persons. The percentages of persons reported as being "susceptible" to hypnosis ranges from 78 to 97. Obviously, the depth of hypnosis must have varied greatly in the subjects reported as "susceptible." Since probably no two of the hypnotists used the same criteria for judging the depth of hypnosis in their subjects, the figures which Bramwell gives for the relative depths of hypnosis reported by various authorities mean little. The percentages for *somnambulism,* the deepest stage of hypnosis, vary from 55 to 7, the former representing children from seven to fourteen years of age, and the latter, persons from 56 to 63 years old. In general, among young

---

[4] Erickson (1941) has described post-hypnotic suggestion in detail.

adults, from 10% to 20% of the subjects were reported as having gone into the somnambulistic state. No marked sex or national differences are reported. It must be remembered that the majority of the subjects covered by these reports were patients who had gone to physicians for treatment, many of them expecting to be hypnotized. The reports generally exclude feebleminded and psychotic persons, who are notoriously difficult to hypnotize. Schilder (1927, 1929) has reported, however, that he has been able to hypnotize schizophrenic patients.

In recent years there have been a number of attempts to standardize scales by which the depth of hypnosis can be designated with fair precision. However, these have not been applied to anything like the number of subjects reported by the older investigators, and most of the recent subjects have been college students. Such scales are described by White (1930), Davis and Husband (1931), Barry, Mackinnon, and Murray (1931), and Friedlander and Sarbin (1938). Numerous "tests of suggestibility" by which it is assumed that "hypnotizability" can be predicted have been devised over a period of years. Among these are those of Estabrooks (1929), Aveling and Hargreaves (1921), and Hull (1933). In the latter, the subject stands erect, blindfolded, and suggestions are given him that he will begin to fall forward. The score is in terms of the amount of postural sway exhibited in response to the suggestions. In an unpublished study by Jenness and J. F. W. McClure, the amount of postural sway was found to be positively correlated with ratings of the vividness of visual and auditory imagery by the subjects. It was anticipated that postural sway would be positively correlated with ratings of vividness of kinesthetic imagery, but actually this correlation was insignificant. The writer knows of no attempt to study the relationship between vividness of imagery and hypnotizability, but it seems a likely hypothesis that persons whose imagery is generally vivid would be more readily hypnotizable than those whose imagery is poor.

Hypnotizability in Relation to Personality Traits.—Attempts to understand individual differences in hypnotizability by correlating the latter with measures of personality traits usually have been unsuccessful or have led to conflicting conclusions. It has often been assumed, for instance, that extraverts generally make "good" hypnotic subjects. It happens that M. M. White (1930) reported a positive correlation of + .70 between hypnotizability and scores on the Neymann-Kohlstedt test of introversion-extraversion, but other experimenters (e.g., Barry, Mackinnon, and Murray, 1931), using the same test, found no significant correlation. Hull (1933), and Friedlander and Sarbin (1938) discuss several studies of hypnotizability in relation to personality traits. The failure to establish the dependence of hypnotizability upon certain personality traits is understandable on the grounds that the scales for rating hypnotizability have not been well standardized and that in many instances, "tests" (really inventories) which purport to measure the same personality traits do not correlate highly with each other. Furthermore, when we realize that each subject has his own unique traits and his own characteristic interrelationship of common traits, and that he is entering into a social relationship with a hypnotist whose personality is also unique, it seems hardly reasonable to expect that individual differences in hypnotizability could be demonstrated to vary concomitantly with individual differences in any one common personality trait. Occasionally a report of a hypnotic experiment or therapeutic procedure describes the personality of the subjects in some detail, but seldom is there any mention of the personality of the hypnotist. Once in a while the reader may draw his own inferences about the hypnotist's personality from his publications, but generally speaking, scientific writing is not an ideal medium for the expression of one's personality. The result is that little is known about the personality of the hypnotist, unless the reader is so fortunate as to be personally acquainted with him. R. W. White (1941a) has suggested that if one wishes to know something about the relation between personality and hypnotizability, it would be well to observe subjects with an eye to (1) their *aptitude* for being hypnotized, and (2) their *motivation*. In order to arrive at an evaluation of the latter in Murray's (1938) terms, as White does, one must consider the *press* (the environmental situation considered from the point of view of what it can do *to* the subject or *for* the subject), and the *needs* of the subject. White reports a positive correlation of $+.43$ between hypnotizability and the need for deference in his subjects, as based on the composite ratings of experts who had extraordinary opportunities to observe the subjects, and a negative correlation of the same magnitude between hypnotizability and the need for dominance. White agrees with the Freudians that not only manifest needs must be considered, but also latent ones, which are more difficult to recognize and evaluate. But he adds, "If motivation is not all on the surface, neither is it all underground, and the student of hypnosis can do no better than keep a watchful lookout at both levels" (1941a, p. 157).

The History of Hypnotism

The history of hypnotism is largely the record of attempts by medical men and other practitioners to cure various disorders by suggestion and to induce anesthesia for surgical purposes. Accounts of the early hypnotists and their work are given by Binet and Féré (1890), Björnström (1889), Brown (1934), Moll (1909), Bernheim (1900), Bramwell (1921), Boring (1931), Hull (1933), Janet (1925), and many others. Of these, the works of Bramwell, Boring, Hull, and Janet are of probably the greatest value to present-day psychologists. Interest in hypnotism for therapeutic purposes was great during the last 60 years of the nineteenth century and many books on the subject appeared during that time. Journals such as *Revue de l'Hypnotisme,* published from 1886 to 1909, and *Zeitschrift für Hypnotismus,* published from 1892 to 1902, carried hundreds of scientific articles on the subject. *The Zoist,* published from 1843 to 1856 and edited by John Elliotson (the first English physician to use the stethoscope), was devoted largely to articles on hypnotism, though at that time the subject was called Mesmerism. Max Dessoir's bibliography (1888) and the supplement (1890) together contained 1182 titles by 774 authors on what was then considered to be modern hypnotism.

It is impossible to give here more than the briefest summary of the findings and claims of the early hypnotists. Suffice it to say that remarkable claims, substantiated in many instances by reputable physicians of the times, were put forth for hypnosis. In general, these may be grouped under four headings:

1. ANESTHESIA FOR SURGICAL AND OBSTETRICAL PURPOSES.—Esdaile was reported to have performed more than three hundred major operations and "many thousand minor ones" painlessly in India (Esdaile, 1852; Bramwell, 1921). Bramwell induced hypnotic anesthesia for numerous surgical and dental operations; he reports cases from many physicians in which hypnotic anesthesia was used for surgical and obstetrical purposes. During the middle of the nineteenth century in England, it was not uncommon to find the words "painlessly during mesmeric trance" at the end of a birth announcement in a newspaper. With the development of ether and other general and local anesthetics, the use of hypnotic anesthesia declined rapidly, ostensibly because hypnosis was not successful with everyone, and the anesthetics were. Today the employment of hypnosis for anesthetic purposes is regarded as a novelty, though occasional reports, such as those of Wells (1941, pp. 86–87) on the extraction of a wisdom tooth under hypnotic anesthesia, appear today.

2. TREATMENT AND CURE OF DISEASE AND ORGANIC DISORDERS.—The ancient Egyptians, Medes, Persians, Greeks, Romans, and Asiatic Indians are all reported to have been familiar with the hypnotic state and may be presumed to have employed it for therapeutic purposes (Dorcus and Shaffer, 1939, p. 208). From medieval ages, through the time of Greatrakes, who stroked diseases out of his patients' bodies through the extremities (Stubbs, 1666), and of Mesmer (1781), to the present, come reports of hypnotic cures of all sorts of ailment. Even the lists of cures reported in more recent books are too varied to summarize here. Bramwell (1921), Brooks (1922), Bernheim (1900), Forel (1907), and others have reported many of them. Baudouin wrote: "Without any other treatment than autosuggestion, you can cure pimples, warts, varicose ulcers, eczema" (1920, p. 187).

3. FUNCTIONAL AND PERSONALITY DISORDERS.—Many of the earlier writers make no distinction between functional and organic disorders. In all probability, many of the early "cures" were of functional disorders. Claims for the therapeutic value of hypnosis in treating functional disorders still appear. Brown (1934), Hollander (1928), Quack-

enbos (1908), Schilder and Kauders (1927), Winn (1939), Wingfield (1920), and Yellowlees (1923) are among the more modern writers who report success in the treatment of functional disorders of many types. The usual criticism against hypnotic therapy, as voiced by Ferenczi (1926) and many others, is that it merely suppresses the symptoms of the disorder, rather than curing it.

4. SPECIAL PHENOMENA OF HYPNOSIS.—In addition to anesthesia, analgesia, contractures, and paralyses of voluntary muscles, amnesia, hallucinations, and post-hypnotic suggestion, which have previously been mentioned as symptoms of hypnosis in its various stages, the early hypnotists reported other phenomena the occurrence of which is not now so widely accepted. There were many reports of improvement in sensory and perceptual capacities, such as increased visual acuity (Bramwell, 1921; Moll, 1909; Bernheim, 1900), increases in the visual field and color sensitivity (Bernheim, 1900), increased auditory acuity (Bramwell, 1921), olfactory hyperesthesia (Braid, 1899), improved discrimination in lifting small weights (Bramwell, 1921), and lowering of the two-point limen on the skin (Bramwell, 1921; Moll, 1909). Hollander (1928) insists that in all modalities the senses are accentuated. Wingfield (1920), Heidenhain (1906), and others have maintained that, on the contrary, sensory limens are raised under hypnosis, i.e., acuity is decreased. Increases in voluntary muscular performance beyond normal capacity have been widely reported. Typical of these are the statements of Rieger (1884), Moll (1909), and McDougall (1926) that a hypnotized person can hold his arm out at a right angle to his body much longer than he could in the normal state. Further evidence of phenomenal strength and endurance in muscular performances was claimed by Hadfield (1924) and Nicholson (1920). Numerous changes in visceral activity and other physiological phenomena have been noted from time to time. These have been summarized in varying degrees of completeness by Bramwell (1921), Dorcus and Shaffer (1939), Jenness and Wible (1937), Hull (1933), and in the reviews of Young (1926, 1931, 1941).

Claims that hypnotized persons often possessed remarkable telepathic and clairvoyant ability were sometimes made (see Esdaile, 1852). Hypermnesia (increased memory) was frequently reported and amnesias for early and unpleasant events were said to have been removed by suggestion under hypnosis (Bernheim, 1900; Bramwell, 1921; McDougall, 1926; Wingfield, 1920; and others). The estimation of time was reported to be more accurate under hypnosis than in the normal waking state (Bramwell, 1921).

Modern Hypnotism

With the perfection of modern anesthetics for surgical purposes and with the development of modern psychiatry and psychoanalysis, interest in hypnotism decreased, though it was kept alive by a few physicians, academic psychologists, and performers who traveled about giving demonstrations. During the first quarter of the twentieth century, a few competent psychologists subjected some of the classical hypotheses regarding hypnosis to experimental investigation, as contrasted with clinical procedure, and made use of hypnosis as a tool for research in psychology. About the end of this period, new impetus for research in hypnotism was provided by Hull, who had reviewed the literature of hypnotism and had decided that the conclusions of many of the investigators of hypnosis were subject to serious criticism, so far as their logic and experimental procedures were concerned. Rather than try to investigate the whole of hypnotism himself, he published a list of hypotheses regarding suggestion and hypnosis from which he deduced special cases, the experimental investigation of which might be presumed to provide criteria for judging the validity of the hypotheses (Hull, 1929, 1930, 1931). Thus he invited all who were interested to share in the scientific investigation of suggestion and hypnosis. Due in part to the interest arising from these articles, Hull was able to publish in 1933 his *Hypnosis and Suggestibility,* a book on these topics based on well-planned and carefully controlled experimental investigation. Hull directed or himself participated in many of the experiments, though in some instances he merely reported the independent work of previous investigators, such as Young (1925, 1926, 1927).

An adequate summary of Hull's book is impossible within the limits of this chapter, and it should be familiar to all who investigate hypnotic phenomena or who wish to know and evaluate the results of research in that field. Many of the important researches of recent times are not described here, because a description of them is readily available in Hull's book. Among these are: Williams's (1930b, 1932) studies of postural sway as a measure of suggestibility; the experiments of Huse (1930), and Mitchell (1932) on the recovery of faint memories; the studies of the duration of post-hypnotic suggestion by Kellogg (1929), Patten (1930), and Strickler (1929); Messerschmidt's (1928) attack on the dissociation hypothesis; Bass's (1931) discovery that the patellar reflex is greatly diminished in sleep, but not in hypnosis; Scott's (1930) demonstration that finger withdrawal, with shock as the stimulus, could be conditioned more readily during hypnosis than in the normal state; Williams's (1929, 1930a) studies of muscular fatigue and catalepsy under hypnosis; Stalnaker and Richardson's (1930) observations of time estimation under hypnosis; the researches of Caster and Baker (1932), Hull and Huse (1930), Jenness (1933), Hull, Patten, and Switzer (1933), Krueger (1931), and Williams (1930b) on comparative suggestibility in the normal and hypnotic states. In general, Hull concludes that the difference between the hypnotic state and the normal state is a quantitative, rather than a qualitative one. Nothing can be accomplished by the use of hypnosis which cannot be accomplished without it, he says, but hypnosis facilitates many phenomena. "The only thing which seems to characterize hypnosis as such and which gives any justification for the practice of calling it a 'state' is its generalized hypersuggestibility" (Hull, 1933, p. 391).

While Hull's work has generally been accepted with high regard, it has been criticized by Wells (1941) on the ground that it "is to a large extent a record of experiments by . . . inexperienced operators, who failed to get maximum results from lack of skill in the hypnotic technique and from lack of opportunity to select a few of the best subjects from large numbers by means of hypnotizing groups wholesale." This criticism might well be applied to the work of many modern investigators. Few, if any, persons living today have had the extensive experience in hypnotizing that some of the earlier practitioners had. Bernheim, for instance, worked with more than 10,000 patients and reported that he hypnotized 85% of them (Bramwell, 1921). It is probable that several other early physicians had as extensive experience as Bernheim. Most of the modern researchers have hypnotized so few subjects, by comparison with most of the early investigators, that one may wonder whether they understand hypnotism as well as did their predecessors who worked with many types of person. The subjects in many recent experiments have been limited to college students. In favor of the modern investigators, it can be said that they have at their disposal better techniques for planning and carrying out experiments and that their research can be checked more easily by others.

Recent Experimental Investigations of Hypnotic Phenomena

In order to enable the reader to evaluate properly the results of recent experimental work in hypnotism, it would be necessary to state the hypotheses held by the investigators, to describe in detail the experimental procedure, and to present the data from the experiments. This is impossible in a work of this kind, but it seems desirable to mention some of the recent reports of investigations of hypnotic phenomena, by way of illustration. The reader who wishes to have a better basis for evaluating the results of the experiments must go to the original sources, unless the particular experiment has been presented by Hull (1933).

Hypnotic Anesthesia.—Sears (1932), in an experiment discussed by Hull (1933), demonstrated that various of the ordinary reactions to painful stimulation were greatly reduced when hypnotic anesthesia was suggested. The reduction was greatest in responses which may be called voluntary or partially voluntary, such as the verbal report, facial flinch, and respiration; it was less marked in the case of measures of non-voluntary response, such as records of pulse and galvanic skin reaction. Control experiments seemed to indicate that the reductions in these reactions were far greater than the subjects could produce voluntarily when they were not hypnotized.

It is well known that hypnotic anesthesias are like functional anesthesias generally, in that they conform to popular conceptions of functional units, rather than to the anatomical distribution of sensory nerves.

Pattie (1937) has reported that hypnotic suggestion that one hand is anesthetic will bring about consistent results only when the subject's hand is in such a position that he would ordinarily know which hand was being stimulated. In Pattie's experiment, the hands of the subject were placed in the position which usually produces the "Japanese illusion" in which the subject incorrectly localizes tactual stimuli, i.e., he reports that a finger of the left hand has been stimulated, whereas actually the stimulus has been applied to a finger of the right hand. Under hypnosis Pattie suggested to five subjects that the right hand and arm would be anesthetic, and had them place their hands in the usual position for the "Japanese illusion." Under these circumstances, the subjects frequently reported when the right hand was stimulated and failed to report when the left hand was stimulated; they made the same errors which normal subjects made under the conditions of the "Japanese illusion." Pattie (1935) has also reported that uniocular blindness as a result of suggestion at first appeared to be genuine blindness, but that careful tests with filters tricked the subjects into reporting things which could be seen only with the "blind" eye. Pattie, after questioning the subjects under hypnosis, concludes that the subjects must have been undergoing severe conflict between the tendency to believe that the eye was blind and the tendency to malinger, knowing that the eye was normal.

Negative After-Images from Visual Hallucinations.—One test of the validity of visual hallucinations has been reported by Erickson and Erickson (1938). Four hypnotized subjects who were shown to be naïve with regard to the principles of negative after-images reported, after a carefully planned series of suggestions, that they saw colors on various sheets of white paper. Whenever a subject reported that he saw the suggested color, he was directed to look at a sheet of white paper and asked what color he saw there. Invariably the subject reported an after-image (after-sensation), the hue of which was complementary to that of the hallucinated color. The experiment failed with a fifth subject who did not hallucinate any color. The conclusions of the Ericksons have been criticized by Hibler (1940), who attempted to test their hypothesis by means of a slightly different technique. Hibler states that his subjects did report after-images, but the hues of the reported after-images were always in accordance with the beliefs of the subject regarding the principles of negative after-images. One subject who believed that after-images were of the same hue as the inducing color, consistently reported the same hue, rather than the complementary hue. Hibler concluded that "hypnotic hallucinations are probably verbal in nature rather than sensory or a function of the central nervous system." E. M. Erickson (1941) seems to have demonstrated, however, that Hibler did not take precautions sufficient either to insure deep hypnosis or to induce hallucinations properly, so that Hibler's experiment was not essentially a repetition of the Erickson and Erickson experiment.

Auditory Anesthesia.—Erickson had previously reported that he had produced auditory anesthesia which was "not distinguishable from neurological deafness by any of the ordinarily competent tests employed" in a number of subjects in response to suggestion under hypnosis (1938a, p. 149). Later (1938b), using two of the subjects from the previous experiment, he conditioned the withdrawal of the hand from an electric shock to the sound of a buzzer. When the conditioned response to the buzzer had become very stable, he suggested that the subjects were deaf; then the withdrawal of the hand ceased, only to reappear when it was suggested that hearing was restored. Lundholm (1928) had previously reported that he had not been able to condition subjects to a click when post-hypnotic auditory anesthesia had been suggested to them. Lundholm attributed this to an attitude or tendency to behave as if there were no click, rather than to a genuine deafness.

Hypermnesia.—Great increases in ability to remember past events, in response to suggestion that the subject will be able to remember well, have been reported in the past. Many of these reports are open to criticism, but two recent experiments seem to have yielded satisfactory evidence of hypnotic hypermnesia. Stalnaker and Riddle (1932) found that their twelve subjects were able to recall verses and prose passages which they had learned a year previously, much better under hypnosis than in the normal state. Their subjects showed a marked tendency to reconstruct or fabricate details which they were unable to recall accurately, a fact which points to the necessity for caution in judging the accuracy of recall under hypnosis. More recently, White, Fox and Harris (1940) have demonstrated that under certain circumstances, recall may be better under hypnosis than in the normal state. If we may accept these results as evidence of hypermnesia, the latter may perhaps be explained on the basis of the limitation of attention and the control of symbolic activity mentioned by Leuba (1941) as possibly responsible for the rapid conditioning in his experiments, which will be discussed later in this chapter.

Is Hypnosis Sleep?

Most hypnotists have used suggestions of sleep and drowsiness to induce hypnosis; because of the fact that the resulting lethargic state resembles sleep, there has been a tendency to assume that hypnosis is identical with sleep. Liébault was an early believer in this doctrine. (See Bramwell, 1921; Hull, 1933.) Forel (1907), Pavlov (1923), and Schilder and Kauders (1927) have argued for the identity of sleep and hypnosis. Binet and Féré (1890) stated that at times hypnosis did not differ from normal sleep. Bernheim (1900) held that hypnotic sleep differed in no way from natural sleep. In opposition, Braid (1899), Moll (1909), Bramwell (1921), Hollander (1928), Hull (1933), and many others have insisted that hypnosis, even in the most lethargic state, is not the same as ordinary sleep. It should be evident to any one who has watched a hypnotized person carry out complicated instructions, read books, and perform difficult mental feats, with the eyes open and otherwise thoroughly active, that the subject is not asleep. The only question which remains is whether the "suggested sleep" of hypnosis, as Bernheim put it, is identical with natural sleep. Walden (1900) considered this to be a physiological problem and he attacked it by taking plethysmographic records of the circulation of hypnotized subjects. He reported a lowering of heart rate during hypnosis, and also a decrease in respiratory rate, comparable to those in normal sleep. However, the "hypnosis" in Walden's experiments lasted for more than four hours without the subjects being disturbed, so that it is probable that much of it was natural sleep.

During the 40 years since Walden's study, many conflicting conclusions based on physiological studies of sleep and hypnosis have been published (see Jenness and Wible, 1937, and Young, 1941). Differences in physiological phenomena during hypnosis may be due, of course, to the various ways in which hypnosis is induced. At present the consensus, except for the Russian and German reflexologists (Young, 1941, p. 94), seems to be that the physiological phenomena of hypnotic sleep resemble those of the waking state, rather than those of sleep. Bass's (1931) finding that the patellar reflex in hypnosis is similar to that in the waking state, but is greatly decreased during sleep, has already been mentioned. Jenness and Wible (1937; Wible and Jenness, 1936) found that electrocardiograms and respiratory records taken during sleeping hypnosis resembled those of the waking state, rather than those of sleep. Their subjects were deeply hypnotized and satisfied all of the criteria for hypnosis mentioned previously. Nygard (1939) studied the cerebral circulation during waking and sleeping in four men and one woman who had recovered from accidents which necessitated removal of portions of their skulls. In two of the subjects, "profound somnambulistic hypnotic trances" were induced. He reports that the characteristics of cerebral circulation prevailing during hypnosis resembled those of the waking state, rather than those of sleep. Loomis, Harvey, and Hobart (1936) describe an experiment on one subject in which the electroencephalograms taken during hypnosis were characteristic of those for the normal waking state, rather than of those for sleep.

The Use of Hypnosis as a Technique of Investigation and Demonstration

Studies of Personality and Unconscious Phenomena.—Hypnosis has long been used as a means of investigating behavior. Many theories of mental activity, particularly the dynamic ones, have grown out of observations of hypnotized persons. Freud's psychoanalytic theory and practice had its beginning in hypnotism. Prince (1929a, 1929b) based his theory of personality and the unconscious largely on observations which he made on subjects whom he hypnotized. Goddard (1927) and

Franz (1933) have reported cases in which the alternations of multiple personality were controlled by the use of hypnosis. Prince's work, in particular, was so extensive that it cannot be recounted here and the reader is referred to his classics on the subject.

Demonstrations of the "Psychopathology of Everyday Life."— Students of abnormal psychology find a particular interest in hypnosis, partly because hypnotic phenomena are themselves abnormal, and partly because hypnosis affords the means of controlling behavior so as to permit further investigation into the nature of behavior itself. Amnesia and hallucinations have been demonstrated to countless generations of students in classes in abnormal psychology who would otherwise have had little or no opportunity to observe these phenomena under controlled conditions. The nature of rationalization has probably been better understood by students after they have observed the efforts of subjects to "explain" actions which were carried out post-hypnotically, especially when the subjects are selected from their own classes. Erickson (1939b) has described a series of demonstrations of "the psychopathology of everyday life" in which attitudes were inculcated during hypnosis so that conflicts, both overt and covert, were bound to result in the post-hypnotic period in which there was amnesia for the events of the hypnotic state.

In one instance the subject was told that upon awakening he would see one of the men present obviously looking for a cigarette, and that he would proffer his own package of cigarettes which the man would absent-mindedly forget to return, but that he would be too courteous to ask for the return of the package, much as he desired it. The subject carried out the instructions post-hypnotically and then engaged in a long conversation in which the words "smoking" and "Camel" occurred frequently, though ostensibly without direct reference to the return of his cigarettes. Interesting *lapsus linguae* occurred several times. The subject was told during hypnosis, for instance, that when he awakened he would be greatly bored by a discussion of an abstruse subject, but that he would try to appear to be interested in what the speaker was saying. After awakening, the subject listened to the discussion for some time, professing great interest, but looking about the room for some distraction. Noticing an open door, he arose and shut it. When asked what he had done, he replied, "Why, I just shut the bore." Upon being informed of what he had said, he was much embarrassed and apologized profusely. Other incidents in the series are equally interesting and informative.

Hypnotic Techniques for Controlling Variables in Psychological Experiments.—Hypnosis has frequently been used as a technique for controlling variables in psychological experiments. In a study of reaction times in response to verbal stimuli during elated and depressed moods, as compared with "normal" reaction time, Fisher and Marrow (1934) used hypnosis to induce the "moods." In general, the subjects were much slower in responding to the stimulus words when they were "depressed" than they were when "elated." Klein (1930) and Welch

(1936) have used hypnosis to induce dreams for experimental purposes. Klein demonstrated that during hypnotic "sleep," dreams would result from external stimuli, without direct suggestion from the hypnotist as to what the dream would be. Stroking the hand with absorbent cotton gave rise to a dream that a cow was licking the subject's hand; allowing the subject to smell asafetida produced a dream of a dead horse. Welch told his subjects what they would dream about and then studied the temporal and spatial aspects of the dreams produced. Whether the "dreams" produced in these experiments were comparable to those of natural sleep is of course open to question, but they afforded the two psychologists concerned an opportunity to refine their hypotheses about dreams in much the same way as psychologists often refine their hypotheses about human behavior by experimenting on rats.

Some of the older writers held that in hypnosis the field of conscious- ness was retracted, so that one central idea could operate, unopposed by conflicting ideas. Leuba (1941) has pointed out, in somewhat differ- ent language, that hypnosis may be employed in conditioning experi- ments to limit the subject's attention and thus eliminate the effects of extraneous stimuli, as well as to control *variables within the subject's own behavior,* such as response to "symbols and possibly other self- initiated stimuli." He disagrees with the widely accepted belief that the most fundamental characteristic of hypnosis is suggestibility (see Hull, 1933). The most fundamental characteristic of hypnosis, he says, is "the limitation of the spontaneous mental life of the subject and the consequent limitation of attention to the stimuli provided by the experi- menter. . . . suggestibility flows from this limitation as a secondary phenomenon" (1941, pp. 271–272). Although it is usually difficult to develop conditioned responses in human adults in the laboratory, Leuba (1940, 1941) has reported a series of experiments in which the sensory responses of subjects were quickly conditioned to various common stimuli, sometimes in only one presentation of the paired stimuli. For example, under hypnosis a subject was asked to sniff at an open bottle of creosote, while a laboratory "cricket" was snapped six or seven times. After the subject was dehypnotized, with amnesia for the hypnotic period, the cricket was snapped and the subject mentioned creosote, inquiring for the source of the odor. Leuba suggests that much ordinary imagery may be interpreted as "conditioned sensation," occurring under circumstances similar to those in which conditioned responses generally appear. Scott's (1930) finding that conditioning of finger withdrawal to the sound of a buzzer (with electric shock as the adequate stimulus), took place more rapidly during hypnosis than in the normal state, is consistent with Leuba's report.

Hypnotic Induction of Conflicts and Complexes.—In view of the current interest in experimentally induced "neurotic" behavior, it is not surprising to find that hypnosis has been employed as a tool for research in this field. Luria (1932), in some of his investigations of affective behavior, employed hypnosis to "insert affective complexes and psychological trauma into the psyche" of his subjects. Luria's apparatus (1932, pp. 24–26) consists essentially of tambours and signal magnets arranged to record synchronously (1) movements of the subject's fingers, (2) instant of verbal stimulation by experimenter, (3) instant of vocal response by the subject. The subject is seated as comfortably as possible in a chair, with the third and fourth fingers of his right hand held lightly in one metal capsule and those of his left hand in another. He is instructed to respond as quickly as possible to the stimulus word given by the experimenter with the first word that occurs to him, and to press downward with the fingers of his right hand at the instant he responds vocally. If the subject makes abortive movements with his right hand before he says a word, this is taken as evidence of a tentative verbal response which was inhibited in favor of the word spoken later. The records for both right and left hands are carefully scrutinized for evidences of movements which are assumed to be the correlates of "concealed and unexpressed speech symbols" and of "affective reactions." This gives a more complete record of the subject's behavior than can be got by the various adaptations of Jung's "free association" technique in which only overt verbal responses and reaction-times are recorded.

One example of Luria's experiments will illustrate their general nature.

A woman medical student was hypnotized and informed vividly and in detail that she had agreed to perform an illegal abortion. The subject was then awakened with amnesia for the hypnotic state. Thus Luria produced what seemed to be a serious conflict in the subject, the cause of which was unknown to her in the post-hypnotic period. In this latter condition, she was presented with a list of words, some of which referred directly to the event suggested under hypnosis. The same words had been given her before she was first hypnotized, and were again presented to her after she had later been rehypnotized and the suggestion about the abortion countermanded. In the latter two instances, she showed no marked affective responses. During the second presentation, shortly after she had been awakened from the hypnosis during which the "complex" was suggested, her responses, particularly to the significant words, were retarded and variable, accompanied in many cases by the conspicuous motor disturbances usually found in affective behavior.

Luria states that experiments such as these enabled him to understand much better the behavior of unconfessed criminals and hysterics whom he had studied by means of his technique.

Huston, Shakow, and Erickson (1934) have reported success in some attempts to induce "complexes" hypnotically, and failure in others. In one instance, a hypnotized subject was persuaded that he had accidentally burned a hole in a girl's dress with his cigarette. The next day he seemed quite upset, complained of a headache and gave up smoking. He was extremely hostile and resentful toward the hypnotist; the latter had considerable difficulty in getting him to consent to be a subject for hypnosis again so that the amnesia for the earlier hypnosis could be removed and he could be given an understanding of how the "complex" had developed. Huston, Shakow, and Erickson stipulate that experiments of this kind are successful only when the subject exhibits amnesia for the period when the "complex" was induced. While they succeeded in getting subjects to believe that they had committed unfortunate acts in the past, they were unsuccessful in getting subjects to accept "complexes" concerning acts to be performed in the future. Yet Erickson, in a previously mentioned experiment (1939b), was able to get a subject to express "unconscious resentment" post-hypnotically against a designated person, at the same time showing "overcompensatory courtesy" to that person.

Hypnosis an Additional Variable in the Experiment.—While there is no doubt that hypnosis provides a means of demonstrating experimentally many normal and abnormal mechanisms of behavior and that hypnosis may be utilized conveniently as a technique for controlling many variables in psychological experiments, it must nevertheless be remembered that the use of hypnosis introduces a new variable, virtually an unknown one, viz., hypnosis itself. The question of whether the "complexes" or the "limitation of the spontaneous mental life of the subject and the consequent limitation of attention to the stimuli provided by the experimenter" are genuine, is not so important as is the question of whether the results of the experiment may not be partly, if not wholly, dependent upon the nature of hypnosis itself. Generally speaking, an experimenter does not deliberately insert an unknown variable into an experiment and then proceed to overlook this variable in accounting for the results of the experiment. While objections may be raised against designating hypnosis as an "unknown" variable, yet it seems to the writer that the nature of hypnosis is still so much of a mystery that skepticism ought to be maintained concerning it as a "control" in psychological experiments. Such skepticism need not *prevent* research in hypnotism, or even the use of hypnosis as a tool in other research; on the contrary, it should facilitate investigation of the fundamental nature of hypnosis itself.

The Subject's Control of His Own Behavior During Hypnosis

Can a person be hypnotized against his will? This is a question which is frequently asked by laymen, and one which is difficult to answer satisfactorily. Much of the difficulty is verbal and arises from the absence of a definition of "will" which is mutually satisfactory to laymen and psychologists. It seems to be generally agreed that if a person refuses to carry out the preliminary instructions of the hypnotist, especially if he walks away and refuses to cooperate, he will not be hypnotized. A possible exception to this statement may be found in cases in which hypnotic drugs have been used to render the subject more suggestible (Moll, 1909; Hull, 1933). If the subject is willing to assume a comfortable position and to carry out the hypnotist's instructions regarding clasping the hands, closing the eyes and similar activities, one may assume that the subject is willing to be hypnotized, even though he may honestly try to resist later commands from the hypnotist. Under circumstances of this kind, there is no test of whether the subject can be hypnotized against his will, because the subject already has shown his willingness to be hypnotized.

In a few instances, persons have been hypnotized without knowing what was taking place, or at least in the absence of a statement on the part of the hypnotist that the person was to be hypnotized. Erickson and Kubie (1941) have reported that an employee of a mental hospital was hypnotized for therapeutic purposes, without her knowing it, while she was under the impression that she was merely observing the hypnotizing of a patient whom she had accompanied to the doctor's office. There is every evidence in the report to indicate that the patient would have refused to allow herself to be hypnotized, had she been asked for her consent.

The problem of whether a deeply hypnotized subject can resist carrying out a simple command of the hypnotist has been subjected to experiment by several investigators. P. C. Young (1927) asked each of several subjects to choose, before he was hypnotized, one of ten of the common phenomena of hypnosis, the appearance of which he would try to prevent when he was later directed to exhibit it under hypnosis. Among these phenomena were: inability to open the eyes, visual hallucinations, inability to walk, analgesia, and post-hypnotic amnesia. Young reported that when the subjects determined in advance of hypnosis that they would not carry out a certain command under hypnosis, they were successful in preventing the appearance of the phenomenon they had chosen. Thus he questioned the "helplessness" of the subjects described by some of the earlier investigators.

W. R. Wells (1940a) has insisted that if a subject does not carry out the instructions of the hypnotist, i.e., if he succeeds in resisting the command of the hypnotist, that is in itself evidence that the subject is not deeply hypnotized (somnambulistic). Wells repeated Young's experiments with what seem to be unimportant variations and reported that in fifteen of his sixteen subjects there was complete inability to resist the command of the hypnotist, regardless of whether the subject had anticipated that he would be able to resist. In many instances, Wells was himself unable to detect which phenomenon the subject had chosen not to exhibit, so completely was the command carried out.

One of the subjects, still unconvinced, demanded a further test. To satisfy him, Wells determined upon a drastic experiment, warning the subject that the consequences might be harmful to him. Wells hypnotized the subject and turned him over to a graduate student who was learning the technique of hypnotizing. The subject was directed to clasp his hands tightly and told that he would be unable to open them until the command to do so was given. A lighted cigarette was placed between the subject's hands so that it would burn him unless he unclasped them. Twice the subject was able to pull his hands apart as the cigarette burned close to them; the third time the subject did not unclasp his hands, though he screamed and the odor of burning flesh was noticeable. As soon as the subject pleaded to have his hands released, the hypnotist suggested that he would be able to open them and he promptly did so. So far as anyone could discover, there were no undesirable consequences of this experiment beyond burns which took several days to heal, and a "deflated ego" on the part of the subject.

"Dangers" in the Use of Hypnosis

Traditional Approach.—Will suggestions given under hypnosis cause persons to harm themselves or others? This is another of the persistent problems of hypnotism which is frequently raised by laymen and others who have misgivings about hypnosis. Many of the earlier investigators attempted to solve it by suggesting to their subjects that they commit fictitious crimes or immoral acts. Although the several investigators placed various interpretations upon the resulting phenomena, they usually arrived at the generalization that persons would not carry out under hypnosis any act which violated their moral principles. Bramwell (1921), after surveying a number of reports of such experiments, concluded that under hypnosis the moral standard of the subject was raised, i.e., that the person was more scrupulous when hypnotized than he would otherwise be. Janet (1925) cited a famous experiment at the Salpêtriere which illustrates the point at issue. At a public demonstration, a hypnotized woman was ordered to stab persons with a paper sword, shoot them with a pistol having blank cartridges, and poison them with fake poison. The subject carried out these suggestions with great vehemence, but later, after the main experiment was over, "had a violent fit of hysterics" and awoke, rather than accept the suggestion that she undress and take a bath under the delusion that she was alone in the hall. From this it was concluded that there is a distinct difference between engaging in fictitious crimes or immoral acts and carrying out *real* acts which are contrary to the principles of the subject.

Bramwell consulted many of the medical hypnotists of his time in an effort to discover whether any harm had ever been done their patients by the use of hypnosis. He reported that Forel, Liébeault, Wetterstrand, van Eeden, de Jong, Moll, and the others consulted "had never seen a single instance in which mental or physical harm had been caused by hypnotism" (1921, pp. 428–429). Including Bramwell's own cases, the observations cover more than 50,000 patients who had been hypnotized by physicians.

Several of the earlier writers on hypnotism do maintain, however, that persons may be induced to commit real crimes under hypnosis or as a result of post-hypnotic suggestion. Björnström (1889) reports an instance in which a person was persuaded under hypnosis to steal a bracelet and then to accuse another person of having committed the theft. Binet

and Féré (1890) insist that subjects may commit crimes post-hypnotically. Forel (1907) was convinced that a "good somnambulist" might
commit serious crimes during hypnosis in response to suggestion, and
that he might not know anything about it later. Hollander (1928), who
has made extensive claims for hypnosis as a therapeutic agent, is convinced that persons may be used for ulterior purposes and greatly
harmed by unscrupulous hypnotists. He says, "I cannot understand
authorities on hypnotism declaring, on the one hand, what a wonderful
power hypnotism is, and on the other hand that hypnotic subjects can
protect themselves against deception by a mountebank or a rogue"
(p. 170).

Schilder, while maintaining "that there is not a single well accredited
case of a real crime having been performed by a hypnotized person on
the command of the hypnotist and against the will of the hypnotized person" (Schilder and Kauders, 1927, p. 51), nevertheless admits that "the
man or woman hypnotized may be more readily induced to perform sexual acts than other 'crimes'" (p. 54). He hastens to add, however, that
this is likely to be the case only when the situation under which hypnosis
takes place is one which might signify "an outright consent or even
challenge to the sexual act—as, let us say, in lay hypnoses performed
without witnesses . . ." (p. 54). In accordance with his theory of
rapport, Schilder holds that there are sexual tendencies inherent in the
hypnotic situation, on the part of both subject and hypnotist, and that for
this reason, a third person should be present during the hypnosis. Bramwell (1921) investigated what seemed to be a well-authenticated report
of the seduction under hypnosis of eleven patients by a Swiss physician,
only to discover that, while there was no denying the seductions, the
physician in question had never hypnotized anyone.

**Difficulties Arising from Popular Misunderstanding of Hypno-
tism.**—Rumors concerning mischief done to hypnotized persons are the
bane of hypnotists. Because of the beliefs which many persons hold,
hypnosis is likely to be blamed for all sorts of harm, regardless of whether
the person concerned has been hypnotized. Those who are familiar with
the psychology of rumor will at once recognize that hypnosis is a topic
which lends itself to rumor and which is likely to be associated with
other topics which have considerable rumor value. For this reason, researchers and others who employ hypnosis must be on guard constantly
lest their efforts be misinterpreted. When prudence and caution are un-
availing, it is sometimes necessary to take drastic steps to quiet such
rumors.

In one instance a professor of psychology, a competent researcher in
hypnotism and abnormal psychology, was plagued by reports that he had
hypnotized a young woman student who shortly thereafter left the university suffering from a "nervous breakdown," and that her physician had
told her parents that her condition was the result of hypnosis. There was

no basis in fact for the rumor, which was easily traced to a woman colleague. In a friendly conference, the latter admitted that the source of her information was unreliable, and agreed to do what she could to correct the matter. The rumor persisted, however, and the psychologist felt that it was necessary to stop it, if he was to continue his work unmolested. He solved the problem by placing $100 on the desk of his classroom, explaining that he did not blame anyone for spreading the story, as it had all the elements necessary for a good rumor. Then he offered $50 of the sum to anyone who could prove that anyone had ever been harmed by hypnosis when the hypnotist was a member of the American Medical Association or of the American Psychological Association. No one made any effort to collect any of the money; the counter-propaganda was effective and the rumor died.

Recent Investigations of the Extent to Which Subjects Will Carry Out Harmful Suggestions.—

ROWLAND'S EXPERIMENT WITH A RATTLESNAKE AND ACID.—The old question of how far a subject will go in harming himself or others under hypnosis, or as a result of suggestions given under hypnosis, has been raised recently by a number of investigators, principally Rowland (1939), Erickson (1939a), and Wells (1941). Rowland constructed a large box with a curved plate glass front so arranged that it reflected no glare and was invisible to several persons who were asked to reach into the box and get a hammer for the experimenter. Wire netting was placed outside the glass, so that the box resembled a cage. A lively rattlesnake was placed in the box. Two hypnotized subjects were instructed to approach the box, reach through an opening in the wire, and pick up the "piece of coiled rubber rope" in the box. One of the subjects saw the snake and "awoke" without touching it, but the other subject reached in, was surprised at finding the glass, and began to explore the surface in an attempt to find an opening. Two other hypnotized subjects, having been appraised of the rattlesnake, nevertheless made serious attempts to pick it up when requested to do so. By way of control, 42 nonhypnotized persons were asked to pick up the snake. Forty-one of them were badly frightened and refused to do so. The other subject boldly reached in and struck the glass. When asked why she did so, she said that of course it was an artificial snake. She was also frightened when she learned that the snake was real. Later Rowland removed the screen and sat behind the glass so that he could be plainly seen reading a book. In two instances a colleague, after demonstrating the effect of strong sulphuric acid on a strip of zinc and emphasizing that it would scar the skin and put out the eyes, directed a hypnotized subject to throw a glass of the acid into Rowland's face. Both of the subjects complied with the request, though one seemed at first reluctant to do so. Unless some defect is demonstrated in these techniques, the possibility remains that persons might harm themselves or others as a result of direct suggestion under hypnosis.

ERICKSON'S INVESTIGATION OF THE POSSIBLE ANTISOCIAL USES OF HYPNOSIS.—Erickson (1939a) reports a series of 35 experiments, involving more than 50 subjects, in which attempts were made to have the subjects carry out "antisocial" acts, either during hypnosis or post-hypnotically. The suggestions included lying, stealing, slapping faces, disclosing confidential information, reading other people's mail, exhibiting the contents of purses, and similar acts which could be carried out without great danger. In no instance was the suggestion carried out as given, though in some instances abortive attempts were made which did not accomplish the stipulations of the experimenter. One subject who had been carefully trained to pick pockets as a means of developing "finger-dexterity," was finally persuaded to pick his roommate's pocket, but he did it so crudely and roughly that it could not help but be noticed. Another subject, who frequently picked the pockets of his friends and distributed what he had taken to the pockets of others, as a practical joke, could not be persuaded to pick pockets when hypnotized, though he expressed eagerness to demonstrate his ability to do so, if only he would be awakened from the hypnosis.

Hence, the conclusion warranted by these experimental findings is that hypnosis cannot be misused to induce hypnotized persons to commit actual wrongful acts either against themselves or others, and that the only serious risk encountered in such attempts is incurred by the hypnotists in the form of condemnation, rejection and exposure. (1939a, p. 414)

WELLS' EXPERIMENT ON THE HYPNOTIC PRODUCTION OF CRIME.— W. R. Wells (1941) has reported that he succeeded in getting a man who had a good reputation for honesty to steal a dollar post-hypnotically and to spend it, with every evidence that the subject remembered neither the instruction regarding stealing, nor the act of stealing. Witnesses who had seen the subject remove the dollar bill from Wells' coat made accusations against the subject, but it was only when he was again hypnotized that he remembered what took place. He even denied having been hypnotized, maintaining that he was not a good subject for hypnosis. He did not offer to return the money until later, though he might have returned it at the time of the subsequent hypnosis if he had had the necessary amount with him. Wells also reports three instances in which a woman graduate student under his direction was able to accomplish much the same thing with three undergraduate women, although it later turned out that, in the case of one of the girls, "stealing was most definitely *not* contrary to the normal character of the subject" (Brenman, 1942). Wells has criticized other hypnotists on the ground that their failure to get subjects to commit crimes in response to hypnotic instructions is due to faulty techniques and lack of ability to practice well the art of hypnosis. "The fact is," says Wells, "failures are only failures; and numerous failures do not invalidate one single success when the latter comes" (1941, p. 88). The question remains, however, as to how serious a "crime" Wells' subject committed and how much against his moral scruples it was. Personally, the writer, who has the utmost confidence in Professor Wells and the highest respect for his integrity, would not be greatly averse to taking a dollar from him at his direction, nor even to spending the dollar as part of a psychological experiment. It should be added that, despite the success of his demonstration, Wells does not feel that hypnosis is likely to be used for criminal purposes, because the opportunities for criminals to learn to use hypnosis *effectively* are extremely limited.

Caution Regarding the Indiscriminate Use of Hypnosis.—Although decisive evidence of *actual* harm resulting from the use of hypnosis is lacking, the possibility still remains that grave mischief *might* result from the use of hypnosis. The reports of success in the experimental production of neurotic behavior under hypnosis lead one to believe that considerable harm might be done to a subject by an ignorant or unscrupulous hypnotist. The widely accepted belief that an amateur hypnotist might put a person to sleep and then be unable to awaken him is groundless, but there are other reasons why only properly trained persons should ever hypnotize. The principal of these reasons is that attitudes may be set up under hypnosis that might harm the person concerned. A simple example will illustrate this. An itinerant hypnotist suggested to a volunteer subject that thereafter he would have a violent distaste for butter and that he would not remember upon awakening that the suggestion had been given him. The next day the subject was violently nauseated when he ate butter. His friends explained the source of his distaste, but his failure to remember receiving the suggestion added to his anxiety. Fortunately, this case came to the attention of a competent psychologist before any permanent harm in the way of a neurotic disorder resulted, but it was clear that worse developments might have ensued, had not the case been handled as it was.

It must be remembered, of course, that suggestions given during hypnosis are not the only means of influencing the attitudes of persons. Day in and day out, many of our actions influence the attitudes of others, whether we intend so or not. A chance remark of a physician may frighten a patient; a criticism of a child by a teacher may lead to a dislike of mathematics or of a foreign language; slight misunderstandings have been known to alienate friends. Certainly the number of instances in which undesirable attitudes have resulted from the use of hypnosis is infinitesimal as compared with the number of instances in which unfortunate attitudes have been developed by other means. Nevertheless, the fact remains that attitudes are readily inculcated or modified under hypnosis. The responsibility for the development of attitudes under hypnosis should not be undertaken lightly. The very possibility that harm *might* result from hypnosis should act as a deterrent against indiscriminate hypnotizing.

Hypnotic Therapy

While this is not the place for consideration of the value of hypnotic therapy, positive or negative, it seems desirable to mention a few of the uses to which hypnosis has recently been put for therapeutic purposes (see Chapter 34 by Appel). Erickson and Kubie (1941) have reported a case in which hypnotic investigation and therapy seem to have been used successfully in the treatment of a case of hysterical depression.

The patient was a capable young woman who was employed in a mental hospital. The depression was precipitated by a proposal of marriage. Several psychiatrists had given a diagnosis of the depressive phase of manic-depressive psychosis. Psychoanalysis was attempted, but was unsuccessful. For various reasons, Erickson decided to attempt to hypnotize the patient without her knowledge, while she was ostensibly chaperoning another patient who was supposed to be receiving hypnotic therapy. The attempt was successful and the patient was gradually directed under hypnosis to regress to a vaguely defined period of her life between the ages of ten and thirteen. She recounted serious misconceptions of sex which were given her at that time by her mother, who had died when the patient was thirteen. During a series of interviews in the hypnotic and waking states, the childhood misunderstandings were corrected and the inhibitions and repressions were removed by means of a technique which seemed to allow the patient to withhold anything she did not wish to mention, but which actually aided her in organizing her ideas before presenting them to the therapist. Even though many aspects of the case were unexplored, the patient developed a satisfactory insight into the situation and made an excellent recovery. Shortly afterward she married the man whose proposal had precipitated the depression. Two years later she was reported to be enjoying a happy life with her husband and infant daughter.

This paper by Erickson and Kubie illustrates the use of hypnoanalysis, i.e., analysis by the patient and the physician of the history and factors of importance in the case. Hypnoanalysis is sometimes used as a short substitute for psychoanalysis, but unless it is supplemented by reports in the waking state, it is likely to be inadequate for that purpose. Hypnoanalysis has been reported to be satisfactory only in so far as it enables the patient to develop insight into his problems and to develop attitudes which enable him actively to attack the solution of his problems. An objection to the employment of hypnoanalysis is that the patient may hallucinate and develop delusions so readily under hypnosis, in response to the unintentional suggestions of the hypnotist, that it is difficult to distinguish fact from fiction in the patient's report of events.

In view of the fact that conditioning is readily accomplished during hypnosis, it might seem that hypnosis would afford an easy means of extinguishing unfortunate conditioned responses and building up desirable conditioned responses. The writer is familiar with a number of instances in which just such a procedure seems to have been successful. The danger incident to this use of hypnosis is that it may provide what seems to be an easy technique for removing the superficial symptoms of what actually may be fundamental personality disorders. There is the added danger that the hypnotist may be tempted to suggest away the patient's symptoms, thus making the patient dependent on the hypnotist, instead of developing the patient's ability to solve his own problems independently.

The Nature of Hypnosis

Earlier Theories.—From the time of Mesmer, when hypnotic phenomena were supposed to result from a kind of magnetic force, to the present, innumerable theories have arisen as to the fundamental nature of hypnosis. We can readily understand how, when the concept of animal magnetism became out of date, hypnosis was thought to be a mysterious influence of one mind over another. With the development of the concept of the reflex, it was perhaps inevitable that hypnosis should be regarded as induced automatism and attributed to the machinery of the reflex, rather than to higher levels of mental activity. Braid (1899) thought of hypnosis as a nervous sleep, distinguished from real sleep, and to be explained on the basis of phrenology. Esdaile (1852) attempted to explain hypnosis in terms of clairvoyance. Heidenhain (1906) invoked the concept of ideo-motor action; he held that the automatic nature of hypnotic phenomena was due to the fact that prolonged stimulation of the sensory nerves "inhibited the activity of the ganglion cells of the cerebral cortex" (p. 46). Hull's (1933) theory is a more sophisticated version of ideo-motor action, without the neurological aspects.

Charcot asserted that hypnosis was an artificially induced neurosis which could be produced only in hysterical persons (Bramwell, 1921). Winn (1939) is the modern representative of Charcot's theory; he admits that hypnosis is not hysteria, but he holds that the similarity between the two is so great that the bodily mechanism responsible for both of them must be the same. He explains hypnosis on the basis of an unorthodox theory of the function of the autonomic nervous system. Many other neurological theories have been offered (Moll, 1909), but they are all open to serious criticism. Bramwell (1921) gives a rather detailed summary of theories of hypnotism, concluding that much is to be said for the interpretation that hypnosis involves the arousal of a secondary (subliminal) consciousness. He does object, on physiological grounds, to the assumption that more than one personality may exist in the same human being. Hollander (1928) appeals to the concept of the subconscious mind, and points out that it is a peculiarity of the subconscious mind that it is highly amenable to suggestion.

Psychoanalytic Theories Regarding Hypnosis.—It was perhaps also inevitable that psychoanalysts should interpret hypnosis as a relationship of unconscious love (sexual attraction) between hypnotist and subject (Jones, 1910; MacCurdy, 1924). Schilder has stated the thesis as follows:

As a matter of fact, hypnosis and suggestibility have an erotic root. If one hypnotizes women, the hypnotizer often has occasion to observe, just before the hypnotic sleep and just after the awakening, the glance of surrender which is characteristic of sexual excitement. A trembling corresponding to the trembling under erotic excitement is not infrequent. The hysteriform rigidities at the beginning of a hypnosis frequently show a very distinct relation with the motions of coitus. (Schilder and Kauders, 1927, p. 34)

The writer has never observed these phenomena in hypnotized subjects, but perhaps his failure to do so may be attributed to the fact that he has not been analyzed. While there is no denying that there may always be an erotic element in human relations, heterosexual or homosexual, it is also possible that this erotic element is merely incidental, rather than fundamental, to hypnosis. Freud himself is less literal in his interpretation of hypnotic rapport:

From being in love to hypnosis is evidently only a short step. . . . It is only that everything is even clearer and more intense in hypnosis, so that it would be more to the point to explain being in love by means of hypnosis than the other way round. The hypnotist is the sole object, and no attention is paid to any but him. . . . *The complete absence of tendencies which are uninhibited in their sexual aims* contributes further towards the extreme purity of the phenomena. The hypnotic relation is the devotion of some one in love to an unlimited degree *but with sexual satisfaction excluded*; whereas in the case of being in love this kind of satisfaction is only temporarily kept back, and remains in the background as a possible aim at some later time. (1922, pp. 77–78; italics not in original)

Another psychoanalytic concept, regression, is frequently invoked as an explanation of hypnosis. Schilder (1927) is one writer who states that hypnosis involves regression. This regression, according to Schilder, does not include the whole personality; part of the personality retains normal relations with the outside world. Ferenczi (1926) describes two types of regression in what he refers to as "father hypnosis" and "mother hypnosis." Recent attempts to verify this hypothesis of hypnotic regression have not met with success (Young, 1941), but the regression hypothesis is one which is difficult to subject to experimental investigation.

Hypnosis Considered as Goal—Directed Behavior.—The most encouraging attempt to deal with the theory of hypnosis which has come to the writer's attention in recent years is that of R. W. White (1941b). Although White refers to his contribution as "a preface to the theory of hypnotism," he has built the foundation for a theoretical structure which is consistent with the architecture of modern psychological theory. A theory of hypnosis, says White, is called upon to explain the following facts:

1. Hypnotized subjects frequently transcend their voluntary capacity, as in the case of insensitivity to pain and certain muscular phenomena.
2. Activities which could be performed voluntarily are carried out during hypnosis in a manner quite different and distinct from the way they are performed in the ordinary waking state. The hypnotized subject "seems literal and humorless, he shows no surprise and makes no apology for bizarre behavior, he appears entirely un-self-conscious, and very often he acts abstracted, inattentive, almost as if he were insulated against his surroundings" (1941b, p. 481).
3. The procedure by which the phenomena of hypnosis are produced does not seem adequate to bring them about.

White points out that the development of a theory of hypnosis which will be acceptable to modern psychologists has been hindered by the tendency of those who are interested in hypnotism to cling to the concepts of behavior which were generally accepted in the days when the older hypnotists were carrying on their extensive investigations in the field. Two of these concepts were those of automatism and dissociation. The concept of automatism was useful enough, perhaps, when there were supposed to be two distinct levels of human behavior: those of (1) reflex activity and (2) intelligent behavior or "purposive volitional striving." Since hypnotic behavior did not seem clearly to be "volitional," and sometimes appeared to take place against the subject's "will," it seemed obvious that it must be some kind of automatism. The concept of dissociation was applied to hypnosis in the days when amnesia and hysteria generally were interpreted as evidence of cleavage between certain organized experiences and functions and the remainder of the mind or personality.

Although these concepts may have been sufficient to provide satisfactory working hypotheses in their day, they have long since been supplanted in most branches of psychology by more modern concepts. In the field of hypnotism, however, the newer concepts of human behavior are seldom encountered. White suggests that the contemporary concept of behavior as "goal-directed striving" is one which will lead to a more acceptable theory of hypnosis.

> As a first step it is proposed that hypnotic behavior be regarded as a meaningful, goal-directed striving, its most general goal being to behave like a hypnotized person as this is continuously defined by the operator and as this is understood by the subject. (1941b, p. 503)

Regardless of which system of terminology is employed, it is obvious that an adequate theory of hypnosis will have to take into account what the subject is trying to do. That the hypnotized subject is trying to behave as he understands a hypnotized person should under the circumstances, is a reasonable assumption. Rosenow (1928), Lundholm (1928), Pattie (1937, 1941), Dorcus (1937), and perhaps others previous to White, have suggested this in recent years. In many instances, the subject has fairly definite ideas regarding the way in which a hypnotized subject should behave. Dorcus, Brintnall, and Case (1941) found that more than half of 669 students whom they questioned at the University of California at Los Angeles had read something about hypnosis and nearly three-fourths of them admitted having discussed hypnosis with others. Since college students have been the subjects in most of the recent experimental investigations of hypnosis, it is safe to conclude that many of the subjects were not literally "naïve," so far as their knowledge of hypnotism was concerned. Even if the subject knows nothing of hypnosis, the hypnotist defines the situation so that the subject has some idea as to how a hypnotized person should act. If the subject behaves as a hypnotized person should, as he understands it and as the hypnotist defines the situation, then he is hypnotized. In order to achieve his goal of behaving like a hypnotized person, he may have to transcend his normal sensory or motor capacity; he may have to become insensitive to stimuli which ordinarily give rise to pain, or he may have to forget what he would ordinarily remember. He may have to undergo experiences which he would not ordinarily undergo, and he may have to accept beliefs which he would not ordinarily accept. He may have to keep his hands clasped at the same time that he is trying to pull them apart. If he fails to achieve the goal of behaving like a hypnotized person, then he is not hypnotized, and he may be dismissed as a poor subject.

The "helplessness" of the hypnotized subject to resist the command of the hypnotist, which Wells (1940a) considers to be an essential feature of deep hypnosis, is not so difficult to understand when one takes into account that the subject is striving to carry out two mutually incompatible actions. Wells makes it a practice to have his subjects write out and sign the statement, "I am willing to be hypnotized today by Professor Wells," before beginning to hypnotize them (1941, p. 71). While many hypnotists do not require such a statement, the willingness to be hypnotized, and often the intention of the subject to act like a hypnotized person, is usually implied before the induction of hypnosis begins. It is reasonable to assume that Wells' subjects in the experiments on the ability to resist his suggestions (1940a) and on the hypnotic production of "crime" (1941), were striving to accomplish two incompatible goals: (1) to act like hypnotized persons, which meant carrying out his commands, (2) to maintain their personal integrities. Serious striving to accomplish two such incompatible goals might well be expected to result in helplessness. In the case of the subject who allowed his hands to be burned, rather than unclasp them (see page 484), the man collapsed and seemed to lose confidence in his ability to manage his affairs for the moment.

White suggests that the "altered state of the person" in hypnosis may be understood when one realizes that the subject is usually required to go through a procedure such as "anyone might use to permit drowsiness and sleep to overtake him in their own natural way" (1941b, p. 499). The conditions are usually such that the subject sees little or nothing; kinesthesis is much reduced, and audition is controlled largely by the voice of the hypnotist. The task of the hypnotist is to bring the subject to a light stage of drowsiness and then to prevent him from becoming more sleepy, and at the same time "to keep regnant the wish to behave like a hypnotized person" in the subject.

> . . . the peculiarities of hypnotic behavior . . . the involuntary feeling, the literal humorless manner, the un-self-consciousness, inattentiveness, and poor subsequent memory, can all be plausibly related to the changes which take place in drowsiness. When a person is drowsy, his images and experiences tend to become more vivid, more concrete, and more absolute. Abstract processes and complex frames of reference seem to be highly vulnerable to fatigue. The operator avails himself of this vulnerability, reduces as far as possible the perceptual supports which might serve to sustain a wider frame of reference, bids the subject relax his mind as well as his body, and thus encourages drowsiness to take a small toll from the higher integrative processes. (1941b, p. 501)

White has pointed out elsewhere (1937a, 1937b, 1941a) that the principal factors which contribute to hypnotizability are (1) the subject's aptitude for hypnosis and (2) his motivation.[5] Except for the psychoanalysts, most students of hypnotism have neglected to provide a place for the subject's motives in their theories about hypnosis. If a competent psychologist were to try to predict the academic success of a college freshman, undoubtedly he would consider carefully the student's aptitudes, his skills, and his motivation, in relation to the incentives to which the student would be exposed during the college years. In predicting the hypnotizability of a subject, the psychologist should do no less; any theory of hypnosis must take into account the factors on which predictions of hypnotizability are based. Among the aptitudes necessary for hypnosis, we should perhaps include (1) a certain minimum of intelligence, (2) the ability to relax properly, (3) sufficient sensory acuity to carry on ordinary conversation. Probably the subject's imagery and his verbal control over the rest of his action are important. So far no one has ascertained the degree of the various aptitudes necessary for the several stages of hypnosis, nor have the aptitudes themselves been accurately identified. Skill in being hypnotized is developed by practice, and it is conceivable that skills previously developed in other situations may be utilized in being a "good" hypnotic subject.

---

[5] The tendency to use hypnosis as a technique for investigating the phenomena of personality and then to explain hypnosis itself by resort to a theory of personality derived in part from observations made by the use of hypnotic technique, is not new at the Harvard Psychological Clinic. Morton Prince exhibited that tendency many years ago (Prince, 1929a). However, the theory of personality which White employs is one which is more consistent with the theories of behavior accepted by psychologists in other fields, than is the theory developed by Prince.

In discussing motivation in hypnosis, White (1941a) has listed a number of the common needs which are often found in the "good" hypnotic subject. White realizes, of course, that it is futile to try to present a statement regarding needs which would fit all cases, as hypnosis involves a relationship between at least two persons, the subject and the hypnotist, and each such relationship is unique. The needs of a given person might be such that one hypnotist might be successful with him, while another hypnotist would fail entirely.

Some Aspects of Suggestion Related to the Theory of Hypnosis.
—In view of the widely accepted assumption that hypnosis is a state of exaggerated suggestibility, it seems obvious that an adequate theory of hypnosis would require and be dependent upon an equally adequate theory of suggestion. The limitations of this chapter preclude a thorough discussion of suggestion, but one approach to the concept of suggestion seems so pertinent that it must be mentioned here.

The term *suggestion* is usually applied to a situation in which one person controls the behavior of another person by means of verbal cues. Guthrie has stated the matter succinctly:

> Suggestibility is the result of learning a language. When we acquire any language, such acquisition lies in associating the sounds of the language with action. The use of suggestion is merely the use of these acquired cues in the direction and control of the behavior of our neighbors. There is no essential difference between causing a man to perform some act by suggestion and causing him to perform that act by request. It is evident that the basis of social cooperation lies in the attachment of action systems to language. Through this attachment it becomes possible to adjust our behavior to the behavior of other persons.
>
> By far the most interesting use of words in the control of action is in the control of one's own action, in other words, self-control. We recognize that an act is our own when it is thus directed. The sneeze is not our own act, but an "outside" interruption in our action because it is not controlled by verbal cues. We cannot say to ourselves "no" and inhibit the sneeze. (1938, pp. 174–175).

To state the matter in another way: In the past, the subject has been drowsy when the word "drowsy" has been spoken, and the state of drowsiness has thereby become conditioned to the word "drowsy." The word "drowsy" repeated later under the proper circumstances tends to elicit drowsiness. It is necessary to emphasize the phrase *under the proper circumstances* here. When the hypnotist uses the word "drowsy," he is in an alert and active state and the sound of the word does not necessarily (though it *may*) make *him* feel drowsy; the subject, however, is relaxed and in the position in which drowsiness usually occurs. The conditioned response of drowsiness (association between sound and action) is therefore more readily elicited in the subject than in the hypnotist. Step by step, the hypnotist uses words to build up attitudes in the subject which make him more and more amenable to the other words which are associated with the behavior which constitutes the phenomena of hypnosis. Thus the hypnotist aids the subject in achieving the goal of behaving like a hypnotized person, a goal which can be understood only when the subject's needs are taken into consideration. It seems to the writer that it is not mere coincidence that one of the most effective methods of discovering what a person's needs are, is to try to hypnotize him.

While we agree with Guthrie that there is no *essential* difference between "causing a man to perform some act by suggestion and causing him to perform that act by request," further consideration of that difference is necessary if we are to understand the nature of suggestion in hypnosis. Here it is necessary to distinguish between *direct* and *indirect* suggestion. In the case of indirect suggestion, the person who uses the verbal cues to get action does so by employing words which detract attention from the action which he wishes to take place, or if the action is mentioned, it is done in a way which will not lead to self-control, as Guthrie has used the latter term. The use of words by the person concerned, to control his own action, might negate the action desired by the suggester. This indirect approach is the one to which the term "suggestion" usually has been applied. Psychologists distinguish a further type, direct suggestion, in which the person who uses the verbal cues to control the behavior of another person does so by using the cues which are directly related to the action desired and, if necessary, using them so strongly that they are sufficient to overcome the use of verbal cues by the other person to control his own behavior. It frequently happens that the person who is amenable to indirect suggestion is not amenable to direct suggestion, and *vice versa*. As a rule, persons who respond well to direct suggestion are likely to be good hypnotic subjects, and it follows logically that direct suggestion is the most effective kind to use in hypnotizing.

W. R. Wells (1931) has argued that when the term "suggestion" has been used in connection with hypnotism, it has often been used in the sense of "indirection," and that the evasiveness and even lies used by some operators arouse such ill-will and resentment on the part of subjects that really deep hypnosis does not result. He prefers to avoid the term "suggestion" and to refer to his use of verbal cues to control the behavior of the subject as "hypnotic technique" (1941). Where Hull (1933) and others use the term "waking suggestion," Wells (1931) would employ the term "waking hypnosis." Wells bespeaks truthfulness and directness on the part of the hypnotist, not only on ethical grounds, but also on the ground that these are necessary to a successful hypnotic technique.

Regardless of the distinction between direct and indirect suggestion, or of that between suggestion and hypnotic technique, the hypnotist does, nevertheless, obtain his results by the use of words which are associated with actions and which therefore elicit these actions on the part of the subject. Hypnotizing is the art of employing words and other appropriate actions in such a manner as to elicit the responses on the part of the subject, which, taken collectively, amount to the definition of hypnosis given at the beginning of this chapter.

Conclusion

As this chapter is little more than an outline of hypnotism, it seems unnecessary to present a further summary. Suffice it to say that hypnotic phenomena must be reckoned with in any broad theory of personality or behavior disorders and that any satisfactory theory of hypnosis must be based on sound theories of personality and behavior. It is perhaps unnecessary to add that hypnotism remains an "intriguing" subject.

BIBLIOGRAPHY

This is not a complete bibliography of hypnotism. More complete bibliographies are those of Dessoir (1888, 1890), Baldwin (1905, vol. 3), Bramwell (1921), and Young (1926, 1931, 1941). Among the most informative general works on hypnotism are Bramwell (1921), Bernheim (1900), Forel (1907), Hull (1933), Moll (1909), Schilder & Kauders (1927), Wingfield (1920). See also Ch. 7 in Dorcus and Shaffer (1939). Works in languages other than English have not been cited if an English translation is available.

AVELING, F., & HARGREAVES, H. L. 1921. Suggestibility with and without prestige in children. *Brit. J. Psychol., 12,* 52–75.
BALDWIN, J. M. 1901–1905. Dictionary of philosophy and psychology. Vols. 1, 3. New York: Macmillan.
BARRY, H., JR., MACKINNON, D. W., & MURRAY, H. A., JR. 1931. Studies in personality: A. Hypnotizability as a personality trait and its typological relations. *Hum. Biol., 3,* 1–36.
BASS, M. J. 1931. Differentiation of the hypnotic trance from normal sleep. *J. exp. Psychol., 14,* 382–399.
BAUDOUIN, C. 1920. Suggestion and autosuggestion. (Trans. by Eden & Cedar Paul). London: Allen & Unwin.
BERNHEIM, H. 1900. Suggestive therapeutics: a treatise on the nature and uses of hypnotism. (Trans. by C. A. Herter.) New York: Putnam's.
BINET, A., & FÉRÉ, C. 1890. Animal magnetism. New York: Appleton-Century.
BJÖRNSTRÖM, F. 1889. Hypnotism: its history and present development. (Trans. by Baron Nils Posse.) New York: Humboldt.
BORING, E. G. 1931. A history of experimental psychology. New York: Appleton-Century. Ch. 7.
BRAID, J. 1899. Neurypnology: (Braid on hypnotism) (Ed. by A. E. Waite.) London: George Ridway.
BRAMWELL, J. M. 1921. Hypnotism: its history, theory and practice. (3rd ed.) London: Rider.
BRENMAN, M. 1942. Experiments in the hypnotic production of anti-social and self-injurious behavior. *Psychiatry, 5,* 49–61.
BROOKS, C. H. 1922. The practice of autosuggestion by the method of Emile Coué. New York: Dodd, Mead.
BROWN, W. 1934. Psychology and psychotherapy. (3rd ed.) Baltimore: Wm. Wood.
CASTER, J. E., & BAKER, C. S., JR. 1932. Comparative suggestibility in the trance and waking states—a further study. *J. gen. Psychol., 7,* 287–301.
DAVIS, L. W., & HUSBAND, R. W. 1931. A study of hypnotic susceptibility in relation to personality traits. *J. abnorm. soc. Psychol., 26,* 175–182.

DESSOIR, M. 1888. Bibliographie des modernen Hypnotismus. Berlin: C. Dunker.
—— 1890. Erster Nachtrag zur Bibliographie des modernen Hypnotismus. Berlin: C. Dunker.
DORCUS, R. M. 1937. Modification by suggestion of some vestibular and visual responses. *Amer. J. Psychol., 49,* 82–87.
DORCUS, R. M., BRINTNALL, A. K., & CASE, H. W. 1941. Control experiments and their relation to theories of hypnotism. *J. gen. Psychol., 24,* 217–221.
DORCUS, R. M., & SHAFFER, G. W. 1939. Textbook of abnormal psychology. (2nd ed.) Baltimore: Williams & Wilkins. Ch. 7.
ERICKSON, E. M. 1941. Critical comments on Hibler's presentation of his work on negative after-images of hypnotically induced hallucinated colors. *J. exp. Psychol., 29,* 164–170.
ERICKSON, M. H. 1938a. A study of clinical and experimental findings on hypnotic deafness: I. Clinical experimentation and findings. *J. gen. Psychol., 19,* 127–150.
—— 1938b. A study of clinical and experimental findings on hypnotic deafness: II. Experimental findings with a conditioned response technique. *J. gen. Psychol., 19,* 151–167.
—— 1939a. An experimental investigation of the possible anti-social use of hypnosis. *Psychiatry, 2,* 391–414.
—— 1939b. Experimental demonstrations of the psychopathology of everyday life. *Psychoanal. Quart., 8,* 338–353.
—— 1939c. The induction of color blindness by a technique of hypnotic suggestion. *J. gen. Psychol., 20,* 61–89.
ERICKSON, M. H., & ERICKSON, E. M. 1938. The hypnotic induction of hallucinatory color vision followed by pseudo negative after-images. *J. exp. Psychol., 22,* 581–588.
—— 1941. Concerning the nature and character of post-hypnotic behavior. *J. gen. Psychol., 24,* 95–133.
ERICKSON, M. H., & KUBIE, L. S. 1941. The successful treatment of a case of acute hysterical depression by a return under hypnosis to a critical phase of childhood. *Psychoanal. Quart., 10,* 583–609.
ESDAILE, J. 1852. Natural and mesmeric clairvoyance. London: Hippolyte Bailliere.
ESTABROOKS, G. H. 1929. Experimental studies in suggestion. *J. genet. Psychol., 36,* 120–139.
—— 1930a. A standardized hypnotic technique dictated to a victrola record. *Amer. J. Psychol., 42,* 115–116.
—— 1930b. The psycho-galvanic reflex in hypnosis. *J. gen. Psychol., 3,* 150–157.
FERENCZI, S. 1926. Further contributions to the theory and technique of psychoanalysis. (Compiled by J. Rickman, trans. by J. I. Suttie.) London: Hogarth.
FISHER, V. E., & MARROW, A. J. 1934. Experimental study of moods. *Character & Pers., 2,* 201–208.
FOREL, A. 1907. Hypnotism: or suggestion and psycho-therapy. (Trans. by H. W. Armit.) New York: Rebman.
FRANZ, S. I. 1933. Persons one and three. New York: McGraw-Hill.
FREUD, S. 1922. Group psychology and the analysis of the ego. (Trans. by J. Strachey.) London: Hogarth.
FRIEDLANDER, J. W., & SARBIN, T. R. 1938. The depth of hypnosis. *J. abnorm. soc. Psychol., 33,* 453–475.
GODDARD, H. H. 1927. Two souls in one body? New York: Dodd, Mead.
GUTHRIE, E. R. 1938. The psychology of human conflict. New York: Harper.
HADFIELD, J. A. 1924. The psychology of power. New York: Macmillan.
HEIDENHAIN, R. 1906. Hypnotism or animal magnetism. (Trans. by L. C. Wooldridge.) London: K. Paul, French, Trübner.
HIBLER, F. W. 1940. An experimental investigation of negative after-images of hallucinated colors in hypnosis. *J. exp. Psychol., 27,* 45–57.
HOLLANDER, B. 1928. Methods and uses of hypnosis and self-hypnosis. London: Allen & Unwin.
HULL, C. L. 1929. Quantitative methods of investigating waking suggestion. *J. abnorm. soc. Psychol., 24,* 153–169.
—— 1930. Quantitative methods of investigating hypnotic suggestion. Part I. *J. abnorm. soc. Psychol., 25,* 200–223.

HULL, C. L.   Quantitative methods of investigating hypnotic suggestion.   Part II. *J. abnorm. soc. Psychol.*, 25, 390–417.

—— 1933. Hypnosis and suggestibility. New York: Appleton-Century.

HULL, C. L., & HUSE, B. 1930. Comparative suggestibility in the trance and waking states. *Amer. J. Psychol.*, 42, 279–286.

HULL, C. L., PATTEN, E. F., & SWITZER, S. A. 1933. Does positive response to direct suggestion as such evoke a generalized hypersuggestibility? *J. gen. Psychol.*, 8, 52–64.

HUSE, B. 1930. Does the hypnotic trance favor the recall of faint memories? *J. exp. Psychol.*, 13, 519–529.

HUSTON, P. E., SHAKOW, D., & ERICKSON, M. H. 1934. A study of hypnotically induced complexes by means of the Luria technique. *J. gen. Psychol.*, 11, 65–97.

JANET, P. 1925. Psychological healing. New York: Macmillan.

JENNESS, A. 1933. Facilitation of response to suggestion by response to previous suggestion of a different type. *J. exp. Psychol.*, 16, 55–82.

JENNESS, A., & WIBLE, C. L. 1937. Respiration and heart action in sleep and hypnosis. *J. gen. Psychol.*, 16, 197–222.

JONES, E. 1910. The action of suggestion in psychotherapy. *J. abnorm. Psychol.*, 5, 217–254.

KELLOGG, E. R. 1929. Duration of the effects of post-hypnotic suggestion. *J. exp. Psychol.*, 12, 502–514.

KLEIN, D. B. 1930. The experimental production of dreams during hypnosis. *Univ. Texas Bull.*, No. 3009, 1–71.

KREUGER, R. G. 1931. The influence of repetition and disuse upon rate of hypnotization. *J. exp. Psychol.*, 14, 260–269.

LEUBA, C. 1940. Images as conditioned sensations. *J. exp. Psychol.*, 26, 345–351.

—— 1941. The use of hypnosis for controlling variables in psychological experiments. *J. abnorm. soc. Psychol.*, 36, 271–274.

LOOMIS, A. L., HARVEY, E. N., & HOBART, G. 1936. Brain potentials during hypnosis. *Science*, 83, 239–241.

LUNDHOLM, H. 1928. An experimental study of functional anesthesias as induced by suggestion in hypnosis. *J. abnorm. soc. Psychol.*, 23, 338–355.

LURIA, A. R. 1932. The nature of human conflicts. New York: Liveright.

MACCURDY, J. T. 1924. Problems in dynamic psychology. New York: Macmillan.

MCDOUGALL, W. 1926. Outline of abnormal psychology. New York: Scribner's.

MESMER, F. A. 1781. Précis historique des faits relatifs au magnétisme-animal jusques en avril 1781. London.

MESSERSCHMIDT, R. 1928. A quantitative investigation of the alleged independent operation of conscious and subconscious processes. *J. abnorm. soc. Psychol.*, 22 325–340.

MITCHELL, M. B. 1932. Retroactive inhibition and hypnosis. *J. gen. Psychol.*, 7, 343–359.

MOLL, A. 1909. Hypnotism. (Trans. by A. F. Hopkirk.) London: Walter Scott Publ.

MURRAY, H. A., JR. 1938. Explorations in personality. New York: Oxford University Press.

NICHOLSON, N. C. 1920. Notes on muscular work during hypnosis. *Johns Hopk. Hosp. Bull.*, 31, 89–91.

NYGARD, J. W. 1939. Cerebral circulation prevailing during sleep and hypnosis. *J. exp. Psychol.*, 24, 1–20.

PATTEN, E. F. 1930. The duration of post-hypnotic suggestion. *J. abnorm. soc. Psychol.*, 25, 319–334.

PATTIE, F. A., JR. 1935. A report of attempts to produce uniocular blindness by hypnotic suggestion. *Brit. J. med. Psychol.*, 15, 230–241.

—— 1937. The genuineness of hypnotically produced anesthesia of the skin. *Amer. J. Psychol.*, 49, 435–443.

—— 1941. The production of blisters by hypnotic suggestion: a review. *J. abnorm. soc. Psychol.*, 36, 62–72.

PAVLOV, I. P. 1923. The identity of inhibition with sleep and hypnosis. *Sci. Mon., N. Y.*, 17, 603–608.

PRINCE, M. 1929a. Clinical and experimental studies in personality. Cambridge: Sci-Art.

—— 1929b. The unconscious. (2nd ed.) New York: Macmillan.

QUACKENBOS, J. D. 1908. Hypnotic therapeutics in theory and practice. New York: Harper.

REIGER, C. 1884. Der Hypnotismus. Jena: G. Fischer.

ROSENOW, C. 1928. Meaningful behavior in hypnosis. *Amer. J. Psychol.*, 10, 205–235.

ROWLAND, L. W. 1939. Will hypnotized persons try to harm themselves or others? *J. abnorm. soc. Psychol.*, 34, 114–117.

SCHILDER, P. 1929. Über das Hypnose-Erlebnis der Schizophrene. *Z. ges. Neurol. Psychiat.*, 120, 700–707.

SCHILDER, P., & KAUDERS, O. 1927. Hypnosis. (Trans. by S. Rothenberg.) New York: Nervous & Mental Disease Publ.

SCOTT, H. D. 1930. Hypnosis and the conditioned reflex. *J. gen. Psychol.*, 4, 113–130.

SEARS, R. R. 1932. An experimental study of hypnotic anesthesia. *J. exp. Psychol.*, 15, 1–22.

STALNAKER, J. M., & RICHARDSON, M. W. 1930. Time estimation in the hypnotic trance. *J. gen. Psychol.*, 4, 362–366.

STALNAKER, J. M., & RIDDLE, E. E. 1932. The effect of hypnosis on long-delayed recall. *J. gen. Psychol.*, 6, 429–440.

STRICKLER, C. B. 1929. A quantitative study of post-hypnotic amnesia. *J. abnorm. soc. Psychol.*, 24, 108–119.

STUBBS (STUBBE), H. 1666. The miraculous conformist. Oxford: R. Davis.

WALDEN, E. C. 1900. A plethysmographic study of the vascular conditions during hypnotic sleep. *Amer. J. Physiol.*, 4, 124–161.

WARREN, H. C. (Ed.) 1934. Dictionary of psychology. Boston: Houghton Mifflin.

WELCH, L. 1936. The space and time of induced hypnotic dreams. *J. Psychol.*, 1, 171–178.

WELLS, W. R. 1924. Experiments in waking hypnosis for instructional purposes. *J. abnorm. Psychol.*, 18, 389–404.

—— 1931. Hypnotizability versus suggestibility. *J. abnorm. soc. Psychol.*, 25, 436–449.

—— 1940a. Ability to resist artificially induced dissociation. *J. abnorm. soc. Psychol.*, 35, 261–272.

—— 1940b. The extent and duration of post-hypnotic amnesia. *J. Psychol.*, 9, 137–151.

—— 1941. Experiments in the hypnotic production of crime. *J. Psychol.*, 11, 63–102.

WHITE, M. M. 1930. The physical and mental traits of individuals susceptible to hypnosis. *J. abnorm. soc. Psychol.*, 25, 293–298.

WHITE, R. W. 1937a. Prediction of hypnotic susceptibility from a knowledge of subject's attitudes. *J. Psychol.*, 3, 265–277.

—— 1937b. Two types of hypnotic trance and their personality correlates. *J. Psychol.*, 3, 279–289.

—— 1941a. An analysis of motivation in hypnosis. *J. gen. Psychol.*, 24, 145–162.

—— 1941b. A preface to the theory of hypnotism. *J. abnorm. soc. Psychol.*, 36, 477–505.

WHITE, R. W., FOX, G. F., & HARRIS, W. W. 1940. Hypnotic hypermnesia for recently learned material. *J. abnorm. soc. Psychol.*, 35, 88–103.

WIBLE, C. L., & JENNESS, A. 1936. Electrocardiograms during sleep and hypnosis. *J. Psychol.*, 1, 235–245.

WILLIAMS, G. W. 1929. The effect of hypnosis on muscular fatigue. *J. abnorm. soc. Psychol.*, 24, 318–329.

—— 1930a. A comparative study of voluntary and hypnotic catalepsy. *Amer. J. Psychol.*, 42, 83–95.

—— 1930b. Suggestibility in the normal and hypnotic states. *Arch. Psychol.*, N. Y., 19, No. 122.

—— 1932. A study of the responses of three psychotic groups to a test of suggestibility. *J. gen. Psychol.*, 7, 302–309.

WINGFIELD, H. E. 1920. An introduction to the study of hypnotism. (2nd ed.) London: Bailliere, Tindall & Cox.

WINN, R. B. 1939. Scientific hypnotism. Boston: Christopher.

YELLOWLEES, H. 1923. A manual of psychotherapy. London: A. & C. Black.

YOUNG, P. C. 1925. An experimental study of mental and physical functions in the normal and hypnotic states. *Amer. J. Psychol.*, *36*, 214–232.

—— 1926a. An experimental study of mental and physical functions in the normal and hypnotic states: additional results. *Amer. J. Psychol.*, *37*, 345–356.

—— 1926b. Hypnotism. *Psychol. Bull.*, *23*, 504–523.

—— 1927. Is rapport an essential characteristic of hypnosis? *J. abnorm. soc. Psychol.*, *22*, 130–139.

—— 1931. A general review of the literature on hypnotism and suggestion. *Psychol. Bull.*, *28*, 367–391.

—— 1940. Hypnotic regression—fact or artifact? *J. abnorm. soc. Psychol.*, *35*, 273–278.

—— 1941. Experimental hypnotism: a review. *Psychol. Bull.*, *38*, 92–104.

PART IV

DETERMINANTS OF PERSONALITY—
BIOLOGICAL AND ORGANIC

Chapter 16

HEREDITY

By L. S. Penrose, M.D.

The genetical aspect of personality is a neglected field of study, though it is one which has great potentialities. The reasons for this backwardness appear to be twofold: first, personality and its attributes are somewhat intangible phenomena and are not easily subjected to rigid types of analysis necessary in dealing with genetical material. Heredity can best be studied when characters are easily distinguishable qualitatively or can be expressed on a graded quantitative scale. The personality itself is a complex attribute determined by the relationships which subsist between more elementary individual characteristics. The behavior of the bricks out of which the personality is built may be susceptible to genetical analysis much more easily than the quality determined by the relationships between them. Unfortunately, students of personality have often been unaware of many possible uses of genetic methods in this field of psychology. Acknowledged authorities, like Allport (1937), make practically no reference to this aspect. The term "genetic psychology," favored by certain schools, is somewhat confusing because, although it includes the study of the development of individual characters, it is not primarily concerned with genetics and pays little heed to the exact way these characters are determined by heredity. Before describing the work which has already been done and future possibilities, therefore, a brief survey of the relevant history of human genetics and a description of some of its most relevant methods will be given. Some specific traits out of which the personality is built have been studied intensively from the hereditary point of view: these are dealt with in the next section. Lastly, work on the genetics of general aspects of personality will be discussed.

Historical Note.—The understanding of the genetics of human personality traits naturally has had to follow the lines of genetical discovery in other fields. Indeed, to a very large extent, human genetics has been found to follow the same general rules that have been discovered in animal and plant genetics. This is probably still true in the field of personality (Jennings, 1930). The scientific study of heredity can be said to have begun when it was realized that it was not the similarities, but the differences, between related individuals which could be most fruitfully analyzed. In consequence, perhaps, of the preoccupation of medical writers with extreme variations, rather than variations within the normal range, the first discoveries in human genetics were made by observing familial concentrations of differences sufficiently marked to be classified as abnormal. Probably the first genetical unit character in man to be clearly recognized was the partly psychological trait, color blindness (Huddart, 1777). Though most early work revolved around physical diseases, such as haemophilia and Huntington's chorea (Lyon, 1863), the psychological side was not altogether neglected. Darwin (1872), for example, noted that the tendency to blush might be a familial characteristic; and Sedgwick (1863) mentions a number of instances of mental peculiarities which could be interpreted as hereditary, for example aversion to specific odors and tastes, as well as tendencies to certain types of temperament. It was not until 1900, according to Gates (1929), when Mendel's work, which had been first published in 1865 on the inheritance of discrete characters, was rediscovered, that the genetic analysis of differences in human beings was undertaken with marked success. Galton (1897), it is true, had already proposed methods for dealing with graded characters, though the formulae he used were not correct, because he assumed that in inheritance the characters of the parents blended. He also collected data about the familial concentration of traits associated with superior intellectual endowment. Like many much more recent studies, his results could not go further than to suggest that certain traits which contributed to social success had genetic foundations. There was no prospect of finding out just how these traits were transmitted.

The beginning of the application of Mendelism to man, carried out by such pioneers as Bateson (1909) and Garrod (1902), at first concerned chiefly physical deviations from normality. Goddard (1914), however, attempted the same type of analysis with feeblemindedness. The contemporary efforts of Pearson (1902) to apply Mendelism to graded characters, physical and mental, evoked much initial criticism from biologists. Since that time, however, it has been accepted, first, that a great many kinds of mental differences between individuals cannot be expressed simply, in terms of the presence or absence of a given character, and ought to be treated quantitatively, and, secondly, that quantitative characters can be satisfactorily analyzed by methods which presuppose the accuracy of the Mendelian laws. The validity of quantitative genetical analysis of graded traits has been upheld by Fisher (1918). Appreciation of the effects of random mating in large populations enabled the results of quantitative genetics to be intelligently interpreted.

Not all transmission in man is Mendelian but, from the point of view of psychological research, other rare possibilities need not be initially considered. Early writers paid much attention to prenatal influences. Sedgwick reported that a lady while in a state of pregnancy was frightened by a ferret and that the child when born (and the sibs which followed it also) had eyes precisely like that animal. Some diseases, like smallpox, can be transmitted from mother to foetus and can affect personality but the effect is not genetical. Moreover, injury to the germ plasm (blastophthoria) by external agencies, poisons such as alcohol or diseases such as syphilis, is not generally believed to be an important factor in individual development, though formerly many types of mental abnormalities (Myerson, 1925) and physical defects (Stockard, 1931) were attributed to this mechanism.

Investigations on the relation between body build and character do not appear as yet to have provided any information about the genetics of personality traits. This may be due to the fact that workers in this anthropometrical field have not usually collected data suitable for the analysis of differences between related individuals. The aims of genetical investigations, in respect of mental and physical traits, are to predict as precisely as possible the traits which will be present in a given person, or a given group of people, when the status of certain of their relatives, with respect to these traits, is known. For this purpose data must be collected which give the measurements of characters in sets of relatives.

Methodology

Inferences from Animal Experiments.—Although many important findings in the genetics of lower animals have been successfully applied to man, little information about the origins of human temperament has been derived in this way. Human personalities are so much more complex than those of even the higher mammals that generalizations from observations on animal behavior applied to human behavior are likely to be fallacious. The direct experimental approach, however, has greater feasibility with the lower mammals than with human beings. It is well known that domestic animals can be selectively bred for specific temperaments or for intelligence, just as they can be bred for color or physique. Excellent examples of artificial selection of desired mental traits are to be found among dogs and horses. Success in the career of sheep dog, watch dog, or lap dog depends as much upon hereditary mental constitution as upon physique or upon environment. In the laboratory, Tryon (1934) demonstrated that rats could be selectively bred for the ability to traverse mazes efficiently. He thus proved that this form of intelligence in rats has a genetic background. In experiments like this, on measurable graded characters in animals, it is usually possible to control environmental conditions sufficiently for the relative contributions of heredity and other variables to be estimated. The statistical method known as analysis of variance can be used to evaluate the relative importance of genetic variations and such environmental influences as diet, temperature, size of litter, and so forth within the experimental universe.

Recently much attention has been focused upon the apparently abnormal behavior of certain strains of rats (Maier, 1939). In response to continuous auditory stimuli, rats and mice can be excited to the point where convulsions ensue. The excitability varies in different strains. Some workers (Humphrey and Marcuse, 1939) have seen resemblances between induced peculiarities of this and other kinds in rats to human mental disorders. Few attempts, however, have been made to assess the importance of genetic components in the susceptibility of animals to these abnormal reactions. The reactions of different strains of rats to situations calculated to induce fear have been studied by Parker (1939) who concluded that about half of the variation from one animal to another in respect of susceptibility to fear was of genetic origin.

Specific pathological behavior in animals is sometimes inherited in a precise manner, as in the case of the waltzing tendency in mice, which was shown by Gates (1927) to be due to a chromosome deletion. Many specific defects, whose genetics are known, undoubtedly exert an influence on the mouse, rat, or dog personality, as the case may be. The main value of knowledge about the genetics of blindness, deafness, and so on in animals to the investigation of the genetics of human personality is to fortify confidence in the search for a genetical background for psychological traits in man.

Methods of Investigating Hereditary Factors in Man.—

PEDIGREES.—A variety of different methods are available for studying the genetic behavior of human attributes. The first is direct observation of families. Formerly, it was considered necessary to investigate large numbers of relatives in any study, but it has been shown by modern workers that this is not always so. Certainly it is advantageous, when information is exact, to make observations on as many members of each family as possible, but it is quite possible to obtain useful information when only one pair of individuals from each family are investigated (Cotterman, 1941). Errors are minimized by confining the study to those members of the family who can be accurately observed. Two types of pairs which are particularly valuable for investigation are brother-sister (sib) pairs, and parent-child pairs. In many special kinds of studies, brothers and sisters are even more useful than parents and children.

The mode of inheritance of characters, which segregate clearly, can be fairly easily detected by the observation of a relatively few families. For example, a dominant character is commonly detected by its almost invariable presence in one parent of the propositus, that is to say, in one parent of the person who possesses the character and comes first under observation. In the case of recessive conditions, the likelihood of a parent's being affected with the same conditions is small and, in rare diseases, inherited recessively, parents are almost always found to be normal. A rare recessive condition, however, is suspected when it is found that usualy more than one sib is affected and that parents are consanguineous in an unduly high proportion of cases. The importance of blood relationship of parents in the genetics of rare recessive traits, first pointed out by Garrod, has been fully investigated by numerous workers since (Lenz, 1919; Bell, 1940). The application of these results to mental traits, as opposed to physical peculiarities, has not yet been undertaken though parental consanguinity increases the variation among sibs in graded traits. For full discussion on other modes of inheritance—sex-linked, partially sex-linked, and numerous theoretical possibilities—technical works on human genetics should be consulted (Roberts, 1940). In view of the indistinct nature of much of the subject matter of personality studies, it is likely that the simplest genetic hypotheses would be, on the whole, most serviceable. Difficulty arises from the lack of sharp segregation in most components of personality and the resulting uselessness of the search for Mendelian ratios in this field.

CORRELATION TECHNIQUE.—For dealing with characters which do not segregate clearly, methods of genetical investigation have been successfully developed, which do not presuppose knowledge of the exact mode of inheritance. All of these methods are ultimately based upon the measurement of variance or covariance of characters within a related group of people. Foremost among such methods is the technique of correlating likenesses in relatives. Pairs of brothers and sisters, of parents and children, or even of more distantly related people, are classified according to their measurements on a given trait and the intra-class product moment correlation coefficient (Fisher, 1934) is calculated. With sib pairs, for example, the mean square difference,

$$\frac{\Sigma(D_g)^2}{N}$$

between the measurements of a trait, g, in N pairs is ascertained (not the mean difference, which is sometimes favored). Briefly, the correlation coefficient, r, is obtained from the formula,

$$r = 1 - \frac{\Sigma(D_g)^2}{2N\sigma^2}$$

where σ is the standard deviation of the trait in question, calculated from the whole set of measurements. Pearson (1902) showed that a correlation of $+\frac{1}{2}$ is to be expected for relatives of the degree of brother-sister or parent-child, when multiple hereditary factors are the sole causes of variation. That is to say, in consequence of the fact that a child receives one-half of its genes from a specified parent, whose measurement on a multifactorial trait deviates a certain amount from the normal, that child's measurement is likely to deviate one-half as much from the normal in the same direction as does the parent's. The expected size of the correlation coefficient varies according to the degree of closeness of relationship in the pair studied. For grandparent-grandchild, uncle-niece and half-sib pairs the expected value is $\frac{1}{4}$; for first cousins, it is $\frac{1}{8}$. The value also varies with the type of inheritance. For example, dominance and recessivity in the factors concerned diminish the size of the coefficient. Sex-linkage increases the value for some types of pairs and diminishes it for others (Hogben, 1932): the father-daughter, mother-son and sister-sister coefficients are raised and the father-son and brother-sister coefficients lowered.

The correlation technique, by itself, is no more perfect an instrument than any other form of family study. The similarity of environment within the family may cause correlations to be spuriously high for traits influenced to a marked degree by environment. The advantage of correlation technique over pedigree work is solely that it enables the genetics of graded characters to be analyzed simply. Moreover, the theory, on which the correlation method is based to some extent, implies a random assortment of marriages in the general population with respect to the trait studied and the supposition of random mating is by no means always correct. In respect of numerous character traits, as well as physical peculiarities, there is a significant tendency for like to mate with like. For example, people of tall stature are prone to marry one another, and short people to marry short people, more often than would be expected from a knowledge of the frequencies of these types. Pearson noted significant tendencies of this kind in mental traits. The correlation between husband and wife for truthfulness was $+.22$; for temper, $+.18$; for sympathetic temperament, $+.15$; and for neglect of duty $+.20$. Selective mating is even more marked in relation to intelligence, both at high and at low levels (Sheldon and Ziegler, 1938). One effect of such assortative mating is to raise the expected values of the correlation coefficients in sib pairs. If r is the interparental correlation with respect to a given trait, the expected sib-sib correlation is altered from the value of $\frac{1}{2}$ to

$$\frac{1+r}{2+r}.$$

TWINS.—Especially interesting, but not always conclusive, are studies made on twins. The methods of analysis here need careful scrutiny before inferences are drawn because the environments of monovular twins, even of those reared apart for long periods, are likely to be more similar than environments of ordinary sibs. Galton first proposed the experiment of comparing twins derived from one egg (monovular) with fraternal twins (binovular) in order to study the comparative effects of environment and heredity. A great deal of work has been expended on the problem of differentiating these two types of twins and it is now possible to classify them with a high degree of accuracy (Newman, 1940), if sufficient trouble is taken. Fraternal twins, however, give scarcely any more information about genetics of a given trait than do pairs of sibs born of different pregnancies. Nor can it be assumed, because both of the twins have the same peculiarity, that this is proof of its hereditary origin. Conversely, though most differences between identical twins are environmental in origin, some can be genetically determined (Dahlberg, 1926). The crude method of measuring the degree of concordance or discordance between sets of twins is, for these reasons, unreliable. It also fails to take into account the frequency of the trait in the general population. Care is needed, also, when the correlation technique is applied to twin groups. Strictly speaking, the correlation for fraternal twins with respect to a trait due to heredity should be ½ and that for monovular twins should be unity. In practice, the coefficients are not usually found to approach expected values very closely, and some authorities interpret discrepancies between observed and expected value in terms of degrees of effect of heredity and environment.

LINKAGE.—One of the most intricate branches of genetical study is the search for a gene linkage. Up to the present time little material has been available for human studies on chromosome topography. The difficulties, in the past, have been partly due to the confusion of gene linkage with physiological association or racial grouping of traits. In gene linkage, the phase of repulsion of the two characters will occur as often as the phase of coupling and the characters will appear uncorrelated in the general population. In order to establish linkage, pairs of sibs must be investigated and it is not sufficient to collect data from one person in each family, as is often done in anthropometric studies. If characters segregate clearly, the linkage value can be calculated by methods developed by Bernstein or by Fisher (1935). Most traits connected with personality, however, are not suitable for this type of analysis. Some temperaments might, however, give rise to interesting results if they were treated by methods available for the study of linkage in graded characters (Penrose, 1938; Cotterman, 1942). To test for linkage between two (uncorrelated) traits, g and h, which are both measured in N pairs of sibs, the function ϕ is calculated from the respective differences, D_g and D_h, in the two measurements for each pair, where

$$\phi = \frac{N \cdot \Sigma[(D_g)^2 \cdot (D_h)^2]}{\Sigma(D_g)^2 \cdot \Sigma(D_h)^2} - 1.$$

In the absence of linkage, this function has the value zero, for perfect linkage its value is ½. Large quantities of data are needed in order to obtain significant results. The fact that the earliest study to be made with the object of detecting genetic linkage of personality with physical qualities (Burks and Tolman, 1932) gave negative results, should not deter future workers from treating fresh data with newer methods.

Inheritance of Specific Traits Which Can Contribute Significantly to the Personality

Normal Traits.—

INTELLIGENCE.—The more specifically an ability is defined, the more easily will its mode of inheritance be investigated. Among normal components of the personality, it is natural first to consider intelligence, though, according to Spearman, this is a "general" character. From the point of view of the total personality, it is a specific component. The mode of inheritance of intelligence has been studied by a variety of methods, among which the correlation technique has played an important part. The earliest investigations of Galton and Pearson used qualitative ratings but, since that time, the advent of intelligence tests has made quantification of this character possible and numerous studies have been made on sibs, twin pairs, and relatives of other degrees. Usually, the object of these investigations is to compare the effects of heredity and environment.

The degree of intellectual resemblance of sibs in random samples has frequently been shown by correlation to be of the order of magnitude of ½ (Fisher, 1918), though some results give a lower value approximating to ⅓ (Herrmann and Hogben, 1933). A recent investigation by Roberts (1939) had the advantage that the material was drawn from a random population sample. The sib-sib correlation coefficient for 650 pairs was +.534. If allowance is made for the probable effects of assortative mating, this result suggests that intelligence is a graded character largely determined by multiple hereditary factors, many of which exert their effects additively. This conclusion applies specifically to the normal intelligence range and not to the group of cases who come under institutional supervision for mental defect.

These conclusions are supported, in the main, by studies on twins. Early workers, Thorndike (1905) and Lauterbach (1925), did not segregate distinctly the monovular type; they showed that intelligence resemblance of like-sexed twins was closer than that of unlike-sexed twins. More recent studies have differentiated the monovular group and the correlations for groups of "identical pairs" usually range from +.80 to +.90. The fact that these correlations do not reach unity may be taken to indicate that a significant component of the likeness between sibs (tested in the same way) can be attributed to nongenetic influences. That prenatal environmental influences can have a marked effect is shown in a study by Hobbs (1941) on monovular twins; in one pair there was a difference of nearly 50 points in the Binet I.Q.

Another way of estimating the importance of heredity in intellectual stature is to compare parents and children. Here, the factor of age difference makes measurement difficult. In general, it can be shown that resemblance of parent and child is close enough to be in harmony with the hypothesis of multifactorial inheritance. Much work on this topic is contained in the "Twenty-Seventh Year Book" (1928) which emphasizes, on the whole, the importance of environmental factors in the development of intellectual capacity. Lawrence (1931), however, showed that the intelligence of illegitimate children was significantly associated with the mental grade of the father as judged by his social status. In the study by Burks (1928) on adopted children, which emphasized the importance of environment, a method was used, which may prove eventually superior to the study of twins, for the purpose of estimating the relative effects of nature and nurture. The differences in environment between adopted and unadopted sibs are likely to be greater than those between identical twins reared apart and the number of cases available for study should be much greater. On the other hand, some of the conclusions reached by studies on adopted children are liable to error on account of selective factors which come into play in the choice of children for adoption.

SPECIAL SKILLS.—The details of technical skills which contribute to a person's ability, but which are not highly correlated with general intelligence, may provide very valuable information for the study of personality. Specific skills, like mechanical aptitude, are comparatively easy to measure. Thus, they become suitable material for the investigation of the mode of inheritance. Unfortunately, much less work has been done on these lines than on the more general and less easily definable traits, such as intelligence. Verbal ability has a great number of degrees, but it is the imperfections of this character which are usually given most attention. One of the most easily measured specific skills is musical ability although there are obviously a large number of factors which enter into this faculty; for example, appreciation of rhythm, aesthetic sense, perception of pitch and manual dexterity, all may vary independently of one another. When discussing the inheritance of musical ability, some writers assume that there is a special trait, which can be measured by such tests as Seashore's. While it is well known that there are strong familial likenesses in respect of musical ability, e.g., the families of Mozart and Bach, very little exact genetical work has been done on this subject. In order to approach the problem more closely, it would be necessary to take groups of sibs at random and record their test results on a number of relevant tasks. It is a mistake from the scientific point of view to pick out just those families in which musical ability is notably high and only to examine them. Relatives are liable to be overlooked if their abilities are not spectacular and special interest also could be derived from investigation of the apparently nonmusical members of so-called musical families.

It is a matter of common knowledge that abilities associated with physical traits, such as skills in special branches of sports or in acrobatics, may show marked familial concentration. As with other abilities, this concentration is partly attributable to environmental likeness within the family. Again, genetical work on these lines is scanty and, until more exact studies are made of families, especially of sibs, in the general population, the mode of inheritance of these specific skills is not likely to be ascertained. Proficiencies in academic subjects, such as mathematics, are culturally significant traits which are known to be partly hereditary and a precise understanding of their modes of inheritance would be valuable.

Among the simpler personal qualities which show large variations in normal people, one of the most easily measured is speed of reaction

(Whipple, 1925). This appears to vary over a considerable range independently of such factors as intelligence and physique. The distribution of tapping speeds probably has a tendency to bimodality and, to geneticists, this would suggest that there may be one main pair of factors which determine speed of reaction in this test. It is surprising that genetical studies do not appear to have been made on this significant and easily measurable trait.

HANDEDNESS.—The inheritance of right- and left-handedness, or, more generally, of degree of dominance of one side of the body over the other, is a field suitable for genetical investigation. The tendency of left-handedness to run in families is a matter of common knowledge. One of the difficulties here is to decide upon the best criterion for measuring handedness. It seems probable that the distribution of degrees of handedness is continuous and that there is a larger number of people intermediately between right- and left-handed than strongly left-handed. Possibly the distribution is a fairly normal one, with its medium point on the side of right-handedness, which stretches from extreme right-handedness to a moderate degree of left-handedness in a graded series. The inheritance of this trait would, therefore, appear to be of a complex type. Writers on twins have called attention to the tendency for reversal of handedness in like-sexed pairs, together with reversal of some physical features. Sometimes careful genetical investigation of handedness leads to surprising results. For instance, it had been claimed that both the mode of clasping hands and the mode of folding arms were inherited peculiarities. By use of correlation technique, Wiener (1932) was able to disprove this assumption and he could attribute the familial differences found in these traits to nothing other than pure chance.

Abnormal Traits.—

INHERITED CONGENITAL APHASIA.—Much attention has been paid to a condition often termed "congenital word blindness" in which there is apparently an inborn aphasia. It is unlikely that this condition represents one single abnormality in all the cases described. Sometimes, it is associated with stammering and sometimes with lack of right- or left-sided dominance. At present, no conclusions can be definitely laid down about the mode of inheritance of abnormalities of this group, though families have been recorded in which the condition appears dominant, and others where it appears to behave as a recessive trait (Brain, 1933).

AUDITORY DEPRIVATION.—Congenital aphasia need not be sufficiently severe to be regarded as abnormal, but there are other ways in which speech may be interfered with and which are definitely abnormal, many of them due to auditory deprivation. For example, deaf mutism cannot but fail to have a marked effect on the personalities of people in whom it occurs. The deprivation is sometimes due to infectious disease of the middle ear in very early life. It is also known as a recessive condition, sometimes associated with blindness (retinitis pigmentosa) and sometimes with dysthyroidism. Deaf mutism was one of the earliest heritable diseases to be studied (Boudin, 1862) and the recessive nature of the condition is clearly shown by the fact that first cousin parents are more frequently found for cases of this kind than for children in the general population.

VISUAL DEPRIVATION.—Sense deprivation, due to eye diseases, has a profound influence on personality and a large proportion of instances of blindness with onset in early life are of hereditary origin.

Among the more important common visual disabilities which affect the capacity and the character of the individual are color blindness and night blindness. The inheritance of color blindness is undoubtedly dependent on a gene or group of allemorphic genes situated on the sex chromosomes. There are various degrees of color blindness, and in severe types, there may be retinal changes. Hysterical color blindness is an entirely different phenomenon, whose mode of inheritance would be much more difficult to study. From the point of view of linkage, the gene for color blindness is of special interest, because of its location on the sex chromosomes. If any other trait, inherited in a like manner, is studied simultaneously in a group of individuals, it is possible to estimate the degree of linkage between the two conditions. So far, this method has only been applied to color blindness and haemophilia, by Bell and Haldane (1937). The search for linkage of characters known to be due to genes located on the sex chromosomes is naturally a much more promising study than the search for linkage of characters due to genes located on one of the 23 pairs of autosomes. Color blindness is sometimes found to be associated with tone deafness, but this is not necessarily to be interpreted as evidence of linkage: there may be some physiological association between these two characters.

Night blindness, though it has been shown to be affected by the amount of vitamin A in the diet and also by psychological factors, seems definitely to be an inherited character in some instances. Nettleship put on record a pedigree in which the records included ten generations of affected persons and stretched back in time to the year 1637. During the present war, this disability has become very significant and its study has been greatly advanced from the physiological point of view. It is undoubtedly a common character, in its milder forms, and possibly has a graded distribution. Its significance as a contributory element in the personality has lately been stressed and further work on the genetic background by study of sibs should prove profitable.

The personality may be affected to a marked degree by the presence of visual refracture errors. The part played by heredity in the genesis of the commoner defects, such as myopia, is not yet clearly defined. There are, however, many types of blindness (i.e., congenital cataract, microphthalmia, retinitis pigmentosa) whose modes of inheritance have been demonstrated in pedigree studies. Albinism, which is due to a single recessive gene, is said to be associated with a timid and somewhat insipid personality, which parallels the physical state and is perhaps engendered by the painful effects of bright light upon eyes which lack normal defensive pigment in the iris.

Inheritance of General Aspects of Personality

Normal Personality.—

RATINGS OF PERSONALITY.—The exact study of the general types of personality from the point of view of heredity is not easy. It is perhaps reasonable to expect to be able to say whether or not two people have the same temperament. It is not possible to say exactly to what degree two people differ, if judgment is made without recourse to measurement. Averages of ratings, however, have been successfully used. For example, with sib pairs, Pearson (1904) found that the average correlation coefficient for a set of traits such as vivacity, temper, and so on, was of the magnitude of $+.52$. By contrast, Newman (1933) assessed, without measurement, the degrees of similarity or difference between the temperaments of pairs of monovular twins reared apart. In the cases of three of these pairs, the temperaments were said to be very similar; for three pairs, there was a moderate difference, and for the other pairs, marked differences. It can be inferred from these results, that, although the general temperaments of sibs tend to be similar to one another, a good deal of the likeness may depend upon environmental similarities. More definite measurements for the assessment of degrees of temperamental differences are required if conclusive results are to be obtained.

BEHAVIOR PATTERNS AND PROFILES.—One of the ways in which the contribution of several different factors to the personality, as a whole, can be easily understood is by references to the concept of profile— sometimes dignified by the term "psychogram" (Hollingworth, 1922). Here, the same group of traits is measured in a number of different persons, but instead of analyzing the participant traits, the different types of profile are classified. The profile is really a quantitative relation between the magnitudes of all the traits concerned and, as a complex quality, the profile has closer kinship with the whole personality than have any of the separate factors. Formerly, it was considered sufficient by most workers in this field to estimate similarity and difference of profile by inspection. It is, however, quite possible to obtain measurements of profile by constructing functions (with weighted scores on the separate contributory tests) which discriminate between profiles. Discriminant scoring functions have been successfully used to detect personal differences with inventory tests. Methods of measuring profiles of subjects who have lost abilities through age or mental infirmity have also been devised. An implication of the measurement of profile is that two profiles may be similar, yet situated at different levels of performance. An intelligent person, for example, with musical talent, might show a marked profile in a group of tests, some of which measured musical ability. A similar profile might describe an imbecile who had much less musical ability than the average person, but whose other abilities were even lower. The study of the inheritance of profile types has received little attention, though it is implied in certain studies on racial differences, for a racial group is usually assumed to be a population of distantly related cousins.

RACIAL DIFFERENCES.—It is generally assumed, if people who belong to one nationality are found to perform in the same way on a test or set of tests and in a different way from other people selected in a corresponding manner, that this is due to genetic determination of the differences in question. Davenport and Steggerda (1929) showed that there were marked differences in profile between white and colored children in Jamaica, for instance. Woodworth (1910) showed racial temperamental differences by means of special tests. There are also relative differences in ability between white and Asiatic, or between American white and American Indian children, especially with linguistic and non-linguistic tests. The differences have been shown to be partly due to nurture. Uniformity in mental traits, moreover, among groups who have similar linguistic, economic or even geographical environments, does not imply underlying genetic similarity. If a genetic analysis by correlation study were applied uncritically to such a thing as language, it is obvious that we should be able to show that native language was apparently a hereditary characteristic. From the physical aspect we find that differences between racial groups are resolved into questions of gene frequency. The blood group B, for example, is more frequent in samples of people of Asiatic origin than in samples of Western European origin, but the difference between the two populations is one of gene frequency—not an absolute distinction. The same type of picture is found when the frequencies of hereditary physical diseases are studied. The infantile form of amaurotic idiocy is a recessive disease almost confined to Jewish populations, as also is pentosuria. Phenylketonuria, on the other hand, seems to be most prevalent among people of Northern European origin; again, as Komai has pointed out, there are some hereditary diseases which are more frequent in Japan than elsewhere, such as hereditary optic atrophy and Oguchi's disease of the retina. We cannot say, at present, how many genes are responsible for differences in skin color, but the difference between a white man and a Negro might not be determined by much more than a dozen genes. Similarly, though there are probably genes, which underlie certain temperaments, more frequent in one racial group than another, the distinction between the personalities of one racial group and another is not absolute but is likely to be, from a genetic point of view, a question of relative frequency. In so far as many mental traits, however, are affected by environment to a greater degree than are physical traits, we may expect to find a strong tendency towards uniformity in personality among groups whose geographical and cultural unity is superimposed upon a fairly homogeneous genetical background.

TYPES OF TEMPERAMENT.—Some investigations on temperament have emphasized especially the expression of personality in one or other variable modes of behavior. For instance, handwriting has a relation to certain qualitative emotional traits and shows interesting similarities in twins. An attempt to measure social competence has been made by Doll (1937), who holds that pedigree studies indicate this aspect of the personality to be inherited. For the most part, however, investigators have not gone far in the examination of the genetics of normal traits of personality. On the other hand, Terman and Miles (1936) have made a great advance in the direction of the study of personality by classifying people's reactions, in respect to certain situations, as expressions of masculine or feminine preferences. A very extensive battery of choice-reaction tests was used. Here, in effect, a single profile was measured; deviations in the direction of the profile indicate the masculine type of reaction, and deviations in the opposite direction, i.e., towards the reverse profile, the feminine type of reaction. This process of measurement is possible on the assumption that the masculinity and femininity are, in fact, positive and negative aspects of the same quality. It is claimed that the results of this test show a definitely bimodal distribution in the general population. Results of this kind should give valuable information about the inheritance of the mental reactions associated with sex in man and indeed information about the inheritance of sex itself. Terman's results from family studies are meagre and difficult to interpret, but on the whole tend to show that there are likenesses with respect to test scores, which pervade the whole family group.

Abnormal Personality.—

SOCIAL ABERRATION.—Among the more important differences in personality are those which influence unfavorably the subject's attitude towards the society in which he lives. Sometimes the degree of social problem presented is most marked in the economic sphere. The tendency for low economic status to affect numerous members of the same family group has been remarked by many observers. In some instances, as in the study of Lidbetter (1933), low economic status was the main object of inquiry, and it is possible to demonstrate from such pedigrees as he collected the apparently genetic origin of pauperism, indigency and so forth. In the work of others, the inferior personal characteristics of the individuals who form these family groups has been emphasized, as with the data compiled on the Jukes (Dugdale, 1877; Estabrook, 1915) the Kallikaks (Goddard, 1913), and the Hill Folk (Danielson and Davenport, 1921). Some of the earliest studies on the inheritance of antisocial tendencies (which involved the subjects in conflict with the law) were undertaken by Goring (1925), who correlated criminal traits in close relatives. The work of Rosanoff (1941) on twins, at least one of whom in each instance had been convicted of a criminal offense, also showed a familial tendency to crime. Much work has been done in Germany on similar problems and investigation of the whole family was usually attempted (Ernst, 1938). The results of all these investigations tend to demonstrate the existence of a fairly marked familial association for all types of antisocial trends. They must be treated with reserve: first, because the criteria of social fitness vary in every environment, and secondly, because environment itself is a very strong factor in molding the personality with respect to antisocial propensities. Analysis of groups of people living in very poor economic circumstances often reveal a high incidence of crime, but area studies made in Chicago recently showed that, when social problem communities were removed to more prosperous surroundings, the antisocial tendencies tended to disappear.

PSYCHONEUROSIS.—The underlying genetical causes of such conditions as hysteria, obsessional and neurasthenic reactions are very difficult to study. Partly, this is due to the elusive nature of the material. It is difficult to know for certain when such symptoms are absent. Nearly every individual has some neurotic symptoms and to examine members of families from the point of view of presence or absence of neurotic constitution is not a very scientific undertaking. Analysis of measurements made on the basis of personality inventories might perhaps eventually give more definite results than can be obtained from clinical surveys. The problem merges into the more specific discussion of the mode of inheritance of psychotic types and is probably best dealt with from that point of view, especially as many families in which psychosis occurs contain members who suffer from psychoneurosis.

SEX PERVERSION.—Some types of sex perversion are so well marked as to provide quite good material for genetical study. Krafft-Ebing (1902) referred to many instances where a subject with sexual perversion had relatives who were either similarly affected or showed other signs of mental instability. Recent work by Lang (1940) on the genetics of homosexuality suggests that this aberration may have a biological basis because affected persons tend towards being intersexes. This phenomenon of intersexes is well-known in animal genetics but has received little serious consideration from workers in the human field. The subject is of great interest in psychiatry and Bosselman and Skorodin (1940) have shown that there is a tendency towards reversal of sex preference in psychotic patients. A genetic hypothesis, which explains the tendency for like-sexed members of the same family to have similar symptoms of mental abnormality in terms of the effects of autosomal sex-determining factors, has recently been advanced (Penrose, 1942). In consequence of the likelihood of discovering endocrine disturbance in cases of sex perversion, the genetics of characters associated with differential activity of the ductless glands is relevant to this study. Most of such work has been devoted to consideration of abnormalities of the thyroid and pituitary glands. The inheritance of cretinism has been studied especially in Switzerland where goitre is common. Thyroid diseases have been found especially prevalent in inbred communities and this fact suggests a recessive determination for some of the characteristics associated with thyroid disturbance. Pituitary activity is a significant factor in sexual development and any abnormality of this gland is likely to affect personality. In the families studied by the Moscow Biological Institute, it was found that pituitary dystrophy behaved as an irregular dominant predisposition.

SCHIZOPHRENIA.—It has been considered since the time of Kraepelin that schizophrenia (formerly known as dementia praecox) is a condition which arises on a constitutional basis. The earliest studies to ascertain its mode of inheritance were carried out by members of the Munich School (Rüdin, 1916). More recently, a much more detailed analysis on the same lines has been undertaken by Kallmann (1938). Schizophrenia is a disease which, for the most part, develops in late adolescence and it diminishes the subject's potential fertility. The average number of children born in families where a parent is schizophrenic is not more than half the normal number. This means that parents are not very often fully affected and the type of inheritance appears to have the general pattern of a recessive condition. Since the disease is so common, marked excess of parental consanguinity is not to be expected. Difficulties arise in deciding whether or not a given member of the family should be called schizophrenic or normal. This difficulty is sometimes resolved by specifying an intermediate class of people who are called "schizophrenic psychopaths." When this description is added to the vocabulary, the condition of schizophrenia is seen to be of a much more graded nature than first appeared probable. It is possible that the predisposition to the disease is recessively inherited but it is just as likely to be the result of many factors. Environmental influences also play a significant part in causing the mental breakdown of a predisposed subject.

MANIC-DEPRESSIVE INSANITY.—The first detailed work to be published on the genetics of manic-depressive disease came from the Munich School. It was held that the condition was probably mainly due to a Mendelian dominant factor. Since then, Rosanoff (1938) and others have suggested that more than one factor is involved. Considerable variations are observed in the severity of the condition in different members of the same family and not infrequently a generation is skipped. The disease has its onset much later in life than schizophrenia and fertility is little diminished by its presence. The hypothesis that a single dominant gene is responsible for all cases seems improbable. A fairly simple hypothesis to cover the facts would be that there are a number of different types of manic-depressive disposition, that most of them are inherited as dominants, but that both environment and further genetic factors influence the development of the disease. On the other hand the tendency of the condition to be graded in members of the same family and the occurrence of minor states of mania and depression even in normal people suggests that it might be wisest to presume that the mode of inheritance is multifactorial.

EPILEPSY.—The type of personality peculiar to the epileptic has been emphasized by many writers on psychiatry and it has been urged by some that the epileptic character is more worthy of study than the seizures, for these are only symptomatic. Direct genetical investigation of the epileptic character never seems to have been undertaken but the discovery of electro-encephalography has made possible the more accurate diagnosis of epilepsy and its subclinical variants. It is stated by Lennox (1941) that potential epileptics may be detected by the presence of abnormal electrical discharges. Lennox has suggested, moreover, that the similarity of wave pattern in members of the same family, where at least one member is epileptic, indicate that the underlying condition is strongly heritable: he found the familial incidence of the disposition very high. The medical significance of this observation, however, is made doubtful by the knowledge that a large percentage of people in the general population are liable to show similar peculiarities. It seems possible that, as with many other traits, the common idiopathic epilepsy is a graded character and that its mode of inheritance may, like other determiners of personality, be multifactorial. There are, however, special types of epilepsy, associated with diseases whose heredity can be described more precisely. Lundborg (1903), for example, showed that myoclonus epilepsy usually behaved as a recessive character. Epilepsy due to tuberose sclerosis is determined by a single dominant gene; it sometimes appears sporadically in an otherwise healthy family on account of fresh mutation.

HUNTINGTON'S CHOREA.—This disease occupies a special position in the genetics of insanity because it is definitely known to be due to a degenerative process in the brain and is inherited as a Mendelian dominant character. The condition gives rise to involuntary jerky or squirming movements and a psychosis develops in the majority of cases. The average age of onset is 35 years, but this shows much variation even among affected members of the same family. A significant amount of the variation in age of onset and in degree of severity from one case to another can be attributed to genetic modification (Haldane, 1941).

SPECIAL TYPES OF MENTAL DEFECT.—Some special types of mental deficiency are closely associated with fairly specific temperaments. For example, mongolism, originally described by Langdon-Down (1866), goes with a fairly definite pattern of personality in the majority of cases. The affected subject is usually of a friendly, sociable and cheerful, though timid, disposition and he enjoys music. This condition is associated with an IQ below 50 and has a genetic background, which is not at present fully understood. Recessive determination seems unlikely and some chromosomal anomaly seems a more probable explanation because the familial incidence is extremely low. The incidence is closely associated with maternal age and about one half the cases are born to mothers over 38 years. Paternal age and number of previous pregnancies do not seem to be significant determinants.

There are many other types of severe mental defect which can be connected with special personalities. Phenylketonurics, whose disability is due to a recessive gene, are usually cooperative and friendly. Unless the mental grade is too low, their temperaments are liable to be stolid but they may show a tendency to hyperactivity. Cerebral diplegia, either associated with athetosis or without this, often carries with it a temperament of a particular kind; such subjects are almost invariably more intelligent than they superficially appear to be, are optimistic in outlook and not unduly weighed down by their disabilities. Especially when athetosis is present, there is a tendency to emotional lability with the emphasis on the side of cheerfulness. Formerly, many of these conditions were attributed to birth injury but this view has been strongly disputed by competent neurologists. Some recent writers, who have carefully studied the personalities of these cases (Doll, Phelps, and Melcher, 1932) have reverted to the previous view that birth injury is the main cause. However, since then, evidence has accumulated which indicates that familial incidence is not uncommon in cases where both sides of the body are affected and that recessive heredity accounts for many of these cases. Haldane (1941) analyzed the genetic material and offered the hypothesis that recessive genes responsible for cerebral diplegia are located on the non-sex-determining part of the sex chromosomes.

Idiots and imbeciles are, on the whole, genetically distinct from the subjects whose mental disability is much less severe—morons, simpletons, and borderline cases. The distinction is mainly due to the impossibility for most idiots to have children of their own. The predominant type of inheritance is recessive and different recessive genes cause different types. It is noteworthy how many of the cases which suffer from hereditary defects have temperaments of a cooperative kind and are amenable to elementary training. Defects caused by secondary disease or injury to the brain often produce cases whose characters are less well integrated and who are more difficult to handle. Noteworthy examples are cases of mental disability due to encephalitis, where character changes in an antisocial direction form part of the symptomatology. The milder types of defect come within range of the normal distribution of intelligence. All types of character are found among these subjects and the genetics of intelligence are multifactorial here, as they are in the normal population.

Conclusion

Personality is a complex attribute of man, not easily reducible to a form suitable for genetical investigation. Animal genetics deals primarily with definite qualitative and quantitative differences between members of the same species. Since human genetics is analogous to animal genetics, it is most efficiently advanced by the study of well-defined characters. Moreover, special methods are available for analyzing quantitative human characters where the influence of heredity is suspected to he important. Many of the elements out of which personality is built are suitable for genetic analysis, especially those which are associated with rare physical defects. As the concept of total personality is approached, exact measurement or precise description becomes difficult. When sound genetical methods are used, however, there is no reason why the contribution of heredity to the elusive phenomenon of personality should not be estimated. The value of attempts of this kind depends very largely upon the accuracy with which various types of personality can be distinguished from one another in the first instance.

BIBLIOGRAPHY

ALLPORT, G. W. 1937. Personality, a psychological interpretation. New York: Holt.
BATESON, W. 1909. Mendel's principles of heredity. Cambridge: Cambridge Univ. Press.
BELL, J. 1940. A determination of the consanguinity rate in the general hospital population of England and Wales. *Ann. Eugen., Camb., 10,* 370.
BELL, J., & HALDANE, J. B. S. 1937. The linkage between the genes for colour blindness and haemophilia in man. *Proc. roy. Soc. Lond.,* B123, 119–150.
BOSSELMAN, B., & SKORODIN, B. 1940. Masculinity and femininity in psychotic patients. *Amer. J. Psychiat., 97,* 699–702.
BOUDIN, M. 1862. Du danger des unions consanguines. *Rec. Mem. Med. Chir. Milit.*
BRAIN, R. 1933. Diseases of the nervous system. New York: Oxford University Press.
BURKS, B. S. 1928. The relative influence of nature and nurture upon mental development. *27th Yearb. nat. Soc. Stud. Educ.,* Part 1, 219–316.
BURKS, B. S., & TOLMAN, R. S. 1932. Is the mental resemblance related to physical resemblance in sibling pairs. *J. genet. Psychol., 40,* 3–5.
COTTERMAN, C. W. 1941. Relatives and human genetic analysis. *Sci. Mon., N. Y., 53,* 227–234.
—— 1942. The biometric approach in human genetics. *Amer. Nat., 76,* 144–155.
DAHLBERG, G. 1926. Twin births and twins from a hereditary point of view. Stockholm: Tidens Tryckeri.
DANIELSON, F. H., & DAVENPORT, C. B. 1921. The hill folk. Report on a rural community of hereditary defectives. *Eugen. Rec. Off. Mem.,* No. 1, p. 56.
DAVENPORT, C. B., & STEGGERDA, M. 1929. Race crossing in Jamaica. Washington: Carnegie Instn.
DARWIN, C. 1872. The expression of the emotions. New York: Appleton.
DOLL, E. A. 1937. The inheritance of social competence. *J. Hered., 28,* 5.
DOLL, E. A., PHELPS, W. M., & MELCHER, R. T. 1932. Mental deficiency due to birth injuries. New York: Macmillan.
DUGDALE, R. L. 1877. The Jukes. (3rd ed.) New York: Putnam.
ERNST, K. 1938. Über Gewalttätigkeits-verbrecher und ihre Nachkommen. Berlin: J. Springer.
ESTABROOK, A. H. 1916. The Jukes in 1915. Washington: Carnegie Institn.
FISHER, R. A. 1918. The correlation between relatives on the supposition of Mendelian inheritance. *Trans. roy. Soc. Edinb., 52,* 399.
—— 1934. Statistical methods for research workers. (5th ed.) Edinburgh: Oliver & Boyd.
—— 1935. The detection of linkage with recessive abnormalities. *Ann. Eugen., Camb., 6,* 339.
GALTON, F. 1897. The average contribution of each several ancestor to the total heritage of the offspring. *Proc. roy. Soc. Lond., 61,* 401–413.

GARROD, A. E. 1902. Incidence of alkaptonuria. *Lancet,* Part 2, 1616.
GATES, R. R. 1929. Heredity in man. New York: Macmillan.
GODDARD, H. H. 1913. The Kallikak family. New York: Macmillan.
—— 1914. Feeble-mindedness: its causes and consequences. New York: Macmillan.
GORING, C. 1925. On the inheritance of the diathesis of phthisis and insanity. A statistical study based upon the family history of 1500 criminals. Cambridge: Cambridge University Press.
HALDANE, J. B. S. 1941. The partial sex-linkage of recessive spastic paraplegia. *J. Genet., 41,* 141–148.
HERRMAN, L., & HOGBEN, L. H. 1933. Intellectual resemblance of twins. *Proc. roy. Soc. Edinb., 53,* 105–139.
HOBBS, G. E. 1941. Mental disorder in one of a pair of identical twins. *Amer. J. Psychiat., 98,* 447–450.
HOGBEN, L. 1932. Correlation of relatives on a supposition of sex-linked inheritance. *J. Genet., 26.*
HOLLINGWORTH, H. L. 1922. Judging human character. New York: Appleton-Century.
HUDDART, J. 1777. An account of persons who could not distinguish colors. *Philos. Trans., 67,* 260–265.
HUMPHREY, G., & MARCUSE, F. 1939. New methods of obtaining neurotic behavior in rats. *Amer. J. Psychol., 52,* 616–619.
JENNINGS, H. F. 1930. The biological basis of human nature. New York: Norton.
KALLMANN, F. J. 1938. The genetics of schizophrenia. New York: J. J. Augustin.
KRAFFT-EBING, R. VON. 1902. Psychopathia sexualis. (12th ed.) (Trans. by F. J. Rebman) New York: Physicians & Surgeons Book Co., 1932.
LANG, T. 1940. Studies on the genetic determination of homosexuality. *J. nerv. ment. Dis., 92,* 55–64.
LANGDON-DOWN, J. 1866. Ethnic classification of idiots. *Clin. Lect. Rep., Lond. Hosp., 3,* 259.
LAUTERBACH, C. 1925. Studies in twin resemblance. *Genetics, 10,* 525–566.
LAWRENCE, E. M. 1931. An investigation into the relation between intelligence and inheritance. *Brit. J. Psychol. Monogr. Suppl., 16,* 1–80.
LENNOX, W. G. 1941. Science and seizures; new light on epilepsy and migraine. New York: Harper.
LENZ, F. 1919. In *Münch. med. Wschr.,* 1930, Vol. 66.
LIDBETTER, E. J. 1933. Heredity and the social problem group. London: Edward Arnold.
LUNDBORG, H. B. 1903. Die progressive Myoklonus-Epilepsie. Upsala: Almquist & Wiksells Buchdruckerei.
LYON, I. W. 1863. Chronic hereditary chorea. *Amer. med. Times, 7,* 289–290.
MAIER, N. R. F. 1939. Studies of abnormal behavior in the rat. New York: Harper.
MYERSON, A. 1925. The inheritance of mental diseases. Baltimore: Williams & Wilkins.
NEWMAN, H. H. 1933. Effects of hereditary and environmental differences upon human personality as revealed by studies of twins. *Amer. Nat., 67,* 193–205.
—— 1940. Multiple human births. New York: Doubleday-Doran.
PARKER, M. M. 1939. Experimental studies in the psychobiology of temperament in the adult albino rat. *Abstr. doct. Diss., Ohio St. Univ.,* No. 30.
PEARSON, K. 1902. The law of ancestral heredity. *Biometrika, 2,* 211–228.
—— 1904. On the inheritance of mental and moral characters in man. *Biometrika, 3,* 131.
PENROSE, L. S. 1938. Genetic linkage in graded human characters. *Ann. Eugen., Camb., 8,* 233–237.
—— 1942. Auxiliary genes for determining sex as contributory causes of mental illness. *J. ment. Sci., 88,* 308–316.
ROBERTS, J. A. F. 1939. Resemblances in intelligence between sibs selected from a complete sample of urban population. *Proc. int. genet. Congr.* Cambridge: Cambridge University Press.
—— 1940. An introduction to medical genetics. New York: Oxford University Press.

ROSANOFF, A. J. 1938. Manual of psychiatry and mental hygiene. New York: Wiley.

ROSANOFF, A. J., HANDY, L. M., & PLESSET, I. R. 1941. The etiology of child behavior. *Psychiat. Monogr.*, No. 1.

RÜDIN, E. 1916. Zur Vererbung und Neuentstehung der Dementia Praecox. Berlin: J. Springer.

SEDGWICK, W. 1863. On the influence of sex in hereditary disease. *Brit. med.-chir. Rev.*, Vol. 21.

SHELDON, C. P., & ZIEGLER, L. H. 1938. Marriage among mental defectives. *J. Amer. med. Assn., 3,* 1982.

STOCKARD, C. R. 1931. The physical basis of personality. London: Allen & Unwin.

TERMAN, L. M., & MILES, C. C. 1936. Sex and personality. New York: Mc-Graw-Hill.

THORNDIKE, E. L. 1905. Measurement of twins. *Arch. Phil. Psychol. sci. Meth., 1,* 64.

TRYON, R. C. 1934. In Moss, F. A., *Comparative psychology.* New York: Macmillan. Ch. 13.

WHIPPLE, G. M. 1925. Manual of mental and physical tests. (3rd ed.) Baltimore: Warwick & York.

WIENER, A. S. 1932. The manner of clasping the hands and folding the arms. *Eugen. News, 17,* 121–122.

WOODWORTH, R. S. 1910. Race differences in mental traits. *Science* (n. s.), *31,* 171–186.

SUPPLEMENTARY GENERAL REFERENCES

ANASTASI, A. 1937. Differential psychology. New York: Macmillan.

BURLINGAME, L. L. 1940. Heredity and social problems. New York: McGraw-Hill.

HALDANE, J. B. S. 1938. Heredity and politics. London: Allen & Unwin.

HOGBEN, L. 1931. Genetic principles in medicine and social science. London: Williams & Norgate.

MYERSON, A., AYER, J. B., PUTNAM, T. J., KEELER, C. E., ALEXANDER, L. 1936. Eugenical sterilization: a reorientation of the problem. New York: Macmillan.

NEWMAN, H. H., FREEMAN, F. N., & HOLZINGER, K. J. 1937. Twins: a study of heredity and environment. Chicago: University Chicago Press.

POLLOCK, H. M., MALZBERG, B., & FULLER, R. G. 1939. Hereditary and environmental factors in the causation of manic-depressive psychoses and dementia praecox. Utica, N. Y.: State Hospitals Press.

Chapter 17

CONSTITUTIONAL FACTORS IN PERSONALITY

By WILLIAM H. SHELDON, Ph.D.

IN MEDICINE IT IS COMMON to hear an experienced clinician make such an observation as this: The patient *looks like* one of those who are susceptible to cancer, or to ulcer, or to infantile paralysis. But when pressed for a detailed explanation the cautious clinician generally declines to specify the signs which led him to his intuition.

Through the ages there have always been a few—physicians as well as others—who are less cautious in the rationalization of their subjective impressions of people, and these less cautious ones have from time to time devised "systems" of various sorts for diagnosing and judging men. Such systems have for the most part been scientifically sterile, for they have rarely been associated with any experimental or validating program. Yet in many of them some truth or usefulness must have resided, if viability is at all a criterion of either.

One of the most conspicuous threads in the intellectual history of the past 2500 years is the persistent recurrence of certain fundamentally similar assumptions concerning the relationship between physical and mental characteristics. Since the time of Hippocrates and probably long before him, systems for the analysis of personality and character have risen, flourished for a time, and disappeared. Usually the enthusiasm of one generation has withered under the scrutiny of the next, but the underlying idea of a systematic connection between physique, temperament, and immunity or susceptibility to various (constitutional) diseases has persisted.

In this chapter we shall first review our heritage of constitutional thought, and then examine briefly a modern attempt to reduce the problem of constitution to workable dimensions.

A General Historical Orientation

Hippocrates, about 425 B.C., described two antithetical physical types, which he called the *habitus apoplecticus* (thick, strong, muscular) and the *habitus phthisicus* (delicate, linear, weak). The former he found particularly suspectible to apoplexy and the latter, especially susceptible to tuberculosis (*phthisis*). He describes the two "types" as different both temperamentally and physically. Throughout the succeeding centuries various more or less similar typologies have flourished, some of them, like that of Hippocrates, resting on a simple dichotomy of polar variants, and some depending on a trichotomy instead of a dichotomy.

During the nineteenth century in particular, several reincarnations of the early typologies were brought forth. Most of these were variations of the more modern French threefold typology which describes a *digestive, muscular,* and *respiratory-cerebral* type (Rostan, 1828). Of the present-day examples of this family of typologies the best known is that of the German psychiatrist Kretschmer.

Between the time of Hippocrates and the late eighteenth century there are, so far as we know, no attacks on the problem of constitutional description which can be said to contribute materially to the modern effort in that direction. There are discursive references to types, but no consistent efforts even to establish typologies. The nineteenth and early twentieth centuries, however, are the golden age of typologies, and a short review of the principal constitutional literature of this period is first in order. We shall do well at least to glance at the French, Italian, German, American-British, and psychoanalytic developments, although in the space available we can, of course, do full justice to none of these.

The French Typologies.—During the early nineteenth century the French literary and scientific influence was already waning rapidly but several French writers of this period contributed to the development of a three-fold typology which is now most closely associated with the names of Rostan (1828) and the German, Kretschmer, who revived it nearly 100 years later. The approach (of the entire French group) is literary and anecdotally observational rather than systematically scientific. There is rich, shrewd insight, based both on clinical and general observation, but there is no attempt to cross the difficult barrier which intervenes between an intelligently generalized insight and the objective structuralization of a taxonomy.

To the French probably belongs most of the credit for the formulation of the three-fold typology which we now associate more with German than with French names. Rostan's descriptions of the *digestive* type (which Kretschmer has called pyknic), of the *muscular* type (athletic) and of the two subtypes which Rostan called *respiratory* and *cerebral* (asthenic or athletic-asthenic to Kretschmer) are classic. Yet Rostan made little "scientific" contribution, in the sense in which we use that term. He elaborated and in a literary sense sharpened certain rather universal concepts which had been taken for granted both by himself and by a long line of predecessors. Neither Rostan nor any other of the French group made what could be called a serious attempt to translate the ancient intuitions into the quantitative language of modern science.

In the midnineteenth century, and even as late as the present day, many schools of phrenology, physiognomy, and character reading have flourished. Nearly all of these trace their genealogy back to the French influence. Many of them are attributed to Gall and Spurzheim, two French anatomists who were contemporary with Rostan. Both of these men made notable contributions in the field of brain anatomy, but Spurzheim in particular became interested during his later years in the problem of brain localization, and in the question of general human typologies. He developed a system of personality analysis based in part on skull configuration.

History has shown that such ideas are dangerous when put prematurely before a public, without norms, controls, and quantitative procedures. Many later opportunists have made stock of the speculations of Gall and Spurzheim, in some cases distorting their ideas to provide a rationalization for "systems" of phrenology which approach the miraculous.

The Italian Contribution.—Next to the French, a group of Italian anthropologists and clinicians of the late nineteenth and early twentieth centuries have pioneered most actively in the constitutional field. It was this group who first seemed to feel the impact of the new scientific spirit as applied to the constitutional sphere of interest. Darwin, Huxley, Spencer, and their followers in and out of England had prepared the ground, and the idea of applying measuremental, statistical methods to problems of human life was growing in men's minds. To the Italians belongs the credit of the first vigorous attempt to make use of anthropometry in defining constitutional differences. At Padua, about 1885, di Giovanni founded a school of clinical anthropology. He standardized many of the now common anthropometric techniques—methods of measuring precisely various parts of the body.

Viola, a pupil of di Giovanni, developed what he called the morphological index. This is really an index measuring the linearity (as compared with the mass) of a human body. It is derived by adding the length of an arm to the length of a leg, and dividing the resulting sum by a number arrived at by multiplying together eight trunk measurements (one of them used twice). Thus a person with a high morphological index is *microsplanchnic* (small-bodied) while the *megalosplanchnic* (large-bodied) individual has a low morphological index. The microsplanchnics are people with small trunks and relatively long limbs. The megalosplanchnics (or macrosplanchnics) have large, heavy bodies and relatively short limbs. The former represent the old *phthisic habitus* of Hippocrates, the latter the *habitus apoplecticus*. It is the ancient dichotomy in new (this time anthropometric) clothing.

Viola thus brought quantification into one aspect of the constitutional problem. He was able to measure one variable which seemed to him important and meaningful. He believed that the microsplanchnic is a *hyperevolute* and relatively intelligent type of human being, in contrast with the *hypoevolute* characteristics and relatively low intelligence which he associated with macrosplanchny. In several studies carried on by followers of Viola, low positive correlations were found between microsplanchny and intelligence test scores. Naccarati (1921) reported a correlation of $+.36$ between these two variables for a group of 75 Columbia University students. But this finding was exceptional. Several other investigators failed to find such a relationship. In one study of 450 University of Chicago students (Sheldon, 1927), the correlation between microsplanchny and intelligence test scores was $+.14$.

No discussion of the constitutional problem can fairly omit mention of Lombroso, who worked and wrote during the closing decades of the nineteenth century and into the twentieth century. He stands as a man of great genius, possibly of the greatest genius, in the constitutional field. Although he never developed a system of physical or mental classification, and never laid any particular claim to scientific objectivity in his methods, the scope and penetration of his insights were gigantic. From youth he trained himself to watch and to study man, and as he put it, "to observe relationships." Also he was a prodigious reader. He held the chair of Legal Medicine at the University of Turin.

Lombroso is remembered principally for his theory of atavistic retrogression, which offers one explanation for the phenomena of criminality and degeneracy. In criminals he observed signs of "throwback" to remote ancestors. His extensive writings constitute reading which is both entertaining and instructive, but since he made no pretense of establishing a system of scientific objectivity his work has been an easy target for representatives of what might be called the school of impatient criticism.

Probably the present consensus of opinion would be that di Giovanni, Viola, and later Pende (1928) have made a contribution of lasting importance in their procedures of anthropometric quantification. Also they may fairly be said to have been the first to demonstrate a statistically supported relationship between a general morphological variable and a psychological variable. Their work has constituted a stimulus to much of the American research in the field.

The German Contribution.—Beneke (1878), a German pathologist, deserves a share of the credit for whatever may have been accomplished by modern constitutional studies. He recorded precise measurements upon the internal organs of persons who had succumbed to various maladies, and kept systematic records of his work. In his theoretical conception he followed in substance the French three-fold classification of types (Rostan), although he changed the terminology. At first he used the terminology of another German (Carus, 1852) calling the first type (French *digestive*) the *phlegmatic* type; the second (French *muscular*) the *athletic* type; and the third group of subtypes (French subtypes *respiratory* and *cerebral*) the *asthenic* and *cerebral* types respectively.

In 1878 Beneke published a monograph on pathological anomalies associated with constitutional variation and suggested for the three constitutional types the following names: *Rachitic, Carcinomatous,* and *Scrofulous-phthisical.* As the names imply, Beneke associated rickets with the first type, cancer with the second, and tuberculosis and scrofula with the third.

Here then was one of the first documented modern contributions to constitutional medicine. Unfortunately Beneke, like the Italians, made no attempt to establish norms for physical variation *at large,* or to develop a basic taxonomy aimed at isolating and describing *components* of physique. He merely collected isolated anthropometric measurements and reported them as such, or rather as averages, and then added the verbal typology as something of an afterthought.

Beneke's third (*scrofulous-phthisical*) type is once more the old *phthisic habitus* of Hippocrates, but his other two "types" present somewhat newer concepts. The idea of a cancer type (carcinomatous) appears here for the first time, so far as the writer is aware. Beneke found that the majority of people dying from cancer were of heavy, muscular make-up, corresponding to the old muscular type of the French, or to the athletic type of Carus. This is a lead which may yet be of value in constitutional medicine, and it may be added that our own preliminary studies have tended to confirm it. That is to say, the component which we now call *mesomorphy* (see page 540) appears to be one factor showing a positive relationship with cancer. The "rachitic type" seems to be more vague, and is probably a mixture of the old French digestive and cerebral types, or of what we now call *endomorphy* and *ectomorphy.*

In the work of the German psychiatrist Kretschmer we find a revival of the French typology just about as Rostan defined it, except that Kretschmer has substituted one more new term (*pyknic* instead of *digestive*) for the first type, and he has taken over the older terms *athletic* and *asthenic* for the other two general types (later he substituted the term *leptosomic* for *asthenic*). Also he has added the idea of dysplastic or incompatible mixtures of types, so that he really has four designative groups, pyknics, athletics, asthenics, and dysplastics.

Kretschmer has made at least four contributions to the constitutional field, exclusive of the work of some hundreds of his followers and associates. First he has revived the typology concept in what had previously been its most highly developed form. He redefined and sharpened it and for the first time made it widely and popularly available, thus stimulating a vast amount of work in the field. Moreover, he has kept this work alive during a period when the tide of academic attitude and fashion has seemed to run strongly against him.

Second, he added for the first time the idea of dysplasia, or mixture of types. This represents a long stride in constitutional research, for it leads quite naturally to another step—the idea of continuous distributions and measurable elemental components *instead of* types. This last step, however, Kretschmer never has taken. He is still engaged in a Laocoön-like struggle with his types, and consequently has never found a dimensional frame of reference in which to establish norms for an attack on *general* problems.

Third, he demonstrated a statistical relationship between physical constitution and two psychiatric entities. This work has been repeated in many clinics, and the majority of the reports confirm (at least in a measure) Kretschmer's findings that the asthenic physique predisposes toward schizoid psychopathology while the massive (pyknic) physique predisposes toward the more vigorously expressive (manic-depressive or circular) forms of psychopathology.

Fourth, Kretschmer has extended the type concept beyond morphology to include temperament. Working from the point of view of a psychiatrist, and therefore dealing mainly with psychopathology, he has described with what even his severest critics call penetrative insight, a dichotomy of temperamental types which he associates respectively with schizoid and circular characteristics manifest in everyday behavior.

His *Physique and Character,* translated into English in 1925, presents all four of these basic ideas. The work has been harshly criticized, but in some quarters it has been warmly defended. The least that can be said for Kretschmer is that he has given impetus to constitutional research. The worst that his critics have said of him is that his generalizations are not supported by a sufficiently rigorous method.

Kretschmer has not quite escaped from the "type approach." His conception of polar types implies a kind of multimodal distribution of both physical and temperamental patterns which is not true to life. There are not three kinds of physique, or of temperament. There is unquestionably a continuous (although multidimensional) distribution of both. Failure to grasp the idea of varying *components* (instead of types), and the consequent effort to describe the variations of human morphology without the aid of a device for scaling structural variables, have left Kretschmer's work singularly open to attack.

Several other typologies which are more strictly psychological, rather than constitutional, have originated among the modern German-speaking group. The typologies of Jung, Freud, the Jaensch brothers, and Spranger will doubtless be encountered in another section of this book.

The American and British Developments.—On both sides of the Atlantic, the contributions of the English-speaking people to the constitutional field have been rather isolated and eclectic. There has been but little suggestion of a focus or "school" of constitutional research either in England or America. Numerous individuals here and there have attacked the problem, however. These investigators have for the most part contented themselves with attempting to correlate anthropometric measurements or indices with isolated fragments of conscious behavior (psychological test scores, attitudes, and the like). Such studies have failed to penetrate to the heart of the problem. The assumption seems too often to have been implicit that a direct correlation should be found between segmental fragments of the physical or constitutional pattern and isolated behavioral fragments like specific motor skills, general information, verbal attitudes, and so on.

Significant correlations between such remote variables are not to be found, however, and should never have been expected. To seek them is to ignore the obvious complexity of human personality, and the multiplication of futile studies of this nature has tended not only to discourage research in an already difficult field, but also to discount in some quarters the good sense of psychologists. We have gradually learned that in order to reach the heart of the constitutional problem, it is necessary (1) to deal with integrated personality patterns rather than with isolated segments of structure and behavior, and (2) to contrive to measure elemental components ("first-order" components, see page 543) at those levels of personality at which we choose to work. When the physical and mental expressions of personality are viewed as expressions of primary, first-order components, significant enough relationships are found to emerge (see page 544).

In England, Havelock Ellis was fond of calling himself, facetiously, a "criminal anthropologist." In *The Criminal* (1890) he summarized and pointed the then already controversial doctrine that a close relationship existed between criminality and constitutional (or more accurately, degenerative and atavistic) factors. His point of view and methods of supporting it are very similar to those of Lombroso. Ellis added no original researches, except of an anecdotal and literary nature. He wrote at a time when the tide of reaction against generalization drawn from anecdotal material was rising. He was swept away by this tide, so far as his anthropology is concerned, although he later applied the same methods to the study of sexuality with greater resultant acclaim.

Goring's *The English Convict* (1913) is the best known British contribution to the constitutional field. Goring took precise anthropometric measurements on a large sampling of English convicts, and demonstrated convincingly the statistical untenability of Lombroso's more or less unguarded assumptions concerning relationships between specific bodily (especially head and facial) measurements and specific criminal tendencies. Goring wrote as the timely champion of hard-headed skepticism, and his carefully elaborated study dealt a lethal blow to that kind of (anecdotal) science of which Lombroso and Ellis were probably terminal representatives.

By many modern students of the biological and psychological sciences, Goring's work has been taken as a conclusive discrediting of the entire constitutional approach. Yet Goring did not deal with any systematized description of constitutional patterning, but only with isolated anthropometric measurements and indices which were handled as if they were discrete entities. To try to relate such data to the complex psychological and sociological behavior of an individual is much like asking a dismembered finger to point, or a dismembered brain to think.

Constitutional research in America has consisted chiefly of isolated reports pursuing correlations between anthropometric and psychological "fragments" of personality. During the nineteen twenties in particular, a host of such studies were reported, nearly all of them yielding either very low correlations, or none at all, between mental and physical measurements. Paterson in *Physique and Intellect* (1930) presented an exhaustive, pessimistic summary of these studies and sounded what was accepted as a death knell to the whole question, so far as academic psychology was concerned. However, the Kretschmerian influence was just then beginning to be felt in this country, and a good deal of support for Kretschmer's findings was being brought forward in other countries, particularly by Krasusky (1927), Ssucharewa (1928), Willemse (1932), Enke (1933), and Stevenson (1939).

There have been a number of American reports on the correlation between Kretschmer's types and psychiatric or psychological data, and the majority of these have tended to confirm his general thesis, at least in part. Among the better known of the more or less confirmatory Kretschmerian studies are those of Wertheimer and Hesketh (1926), Shaw (1925), Burchard (1936), Campbell (1932), and Garvey (1933). These workers found correlations of some degree between the Kretschmer types and psychotic classifications. On the other hand, Klineberg, Asch, and Block (1934) attempted to correlate Kretschmerian ratings of type with various mental tests and similar psychological data, and found only extremely low correlation. Similarly, Cabot (1938) made a careful analysis of the relation of school teachers' ratings on bodily build to various psychological and temperamental traits in a group of school children. He, too, reported virtually negative results. Mohr and Gundlach (1927) had reported nearly the same finding for a group of Illinois convicts, although they found a few significantly positive correlations between physical type and tests of temperament. For an excellent further summary of the specific researches on this question, see Cabot's monograph (1938, pp. 10–22).

The American experiments with Kretschmer's typology might be summarized about as follows: (1) The descriptions of the physical types and the criteria for their recognition were found to be confusing and unsatisfactory. In fact, it was soon made evident that types as such do not exist. (2) Yet in a number of instances where investigators sidestepped this stumbling block, accepting what may possibly be called *the spirit rather than the letter* of Kretschmer's claims, and proceeding to grade physiques according to their manifest general tendencies—in a considerable number of such instances significant positive correlations were found between physical tendency and psychotic tendency. (3) However, no American students, using Kretschmer's technique as he presented it, have been able to demonstrate significant relationships between physical type and temperamental or normal psychological characteristics.

Another, perhaps stronger impetus to constitutional thinking in this country has come from the practice of medicine. During the past two decades there has been an increasingly articulate emphasis in the medical schools upon the point of view that the physiological organism must be considered as an integrated unit which reacts as a whole, not in parts. This emphasis has been especially noticeable in the teaching of psychiatry, and in endocrinology. The words "constitution" and "constitutional factors" are now heard frequently in the clinics, although they are ordinarily used without more specific meaning than a vague designative reference to the *general fact* that hereditary, innate, or very deepseated and relatively permanent individual differences must exist. However, the prevalent use of the term constitution in medicine seems to indicate at least that the need for a method of constitutional analysis is being strongly felt.

Tucker and Lessa (1940) have published a good summary of the rather bewildering mass of medical and anthropological literature which bears in one way or another on the problem of relating constitutional factors to clinical symptoms and procedures. Their paper includes a comprehensive bibliography and brings into relief the long groping of clinicians for a meaningful taxonomy of elemental constitutional factors.

From the physical anthropologists themselves has come little to help the psychologist and the clinician in their efforts to deal with constitution. The complaint is usually made that the anthropologist measures for the sake of measuring. Even when the measurements are applied to the classification of "races," the psychologist protests that with "race" he is left with a psychologically meaningless variable. But not all anthropological studies are devoid of constitutional interest.

The anthropologist Hooton (*Crime and the Man,* 1939) carried out a variant of the unaided anthropometric attack. In a survey of criminal and noncriminal population, he found certain statistically tenable anthropometric differences which appear to establish a degree of association between bodily build and type of crime. Since his criteria of bodily build depend almost entirely on stature and weight, and since we know that people of the same height and weight actually vary greatly in bodily build or somatotype (see page 539), Hooton's findings may be of greater importance than appears on the surface. If with such a tool alone he found a valid positive relationship, a more discriminative classification of physical constitution might, as Hooton indicates, open the way to a still more important contribution in the field of criminology.

The Constitutional Implications of the Psychoanalytic Movement.—Psychoanalysis, if literally interpreted, is a rather ambitious undertaking. The psychoanalysts attempt to penetrate deeply into the motivating mechanisms lying behind consciousness. One of their most insistent claims has been that of the discovery of a close relationship between physical and mental processes. They speak sometimes of "psychogenic factors affecting the organism" and sometimes of "somatogenic factors affecting the mind." In either case a step is taken toward recognition of the inevitability of substituting the conception of a continuum for the rudimentary dichotomy of mind and body.

Among the psychoanalysts, Franz Alexander of Chicago (1935) has taken the lead in emphasizing the proposition that any system of analysis aimed at comprehension of *a fragment* of personality (such as the conscious processes, for example) must in the end deal with *the total personality,* inclusive of both mental and physical processes, if it is not to fail in its purpose. Traditionally, psychoanalysis attempts to reach an understanding of the whole individual through a deep penetration "from the top," that is to say, through something suggesting a small incision made in consciousness itself. By free association, dream analysis and the like, the analysts have found that it is possible to penetrate to remarkably obscure, deep-lying characteristics of the individual.

Alexander and some others have felt that when once a systematic description of physical and physiological variation becomes available, couched in terms of concepts which have common roots (common components, possibly) with a similarly systematic description of psychological variables, the way will be open to a more effective attack on the general problem of analysis. Analysis might then become, not merely *psycho*analysis, but general, *constitutional* analysis, or total analysis. The descriptive adjective is unimportant, so long as it refers to a process by which the analyst directs his attack upon more than one level of description. By approaching the individual through both a physical and a psychological attack, the analyst can effect a kind of "pincers movement," and the efficiency of the analytic attack should be enhanced.

In line with this conception Draper (1924) has for the past quarter century taught a point of view in his Constitution Clinic at the New York Presbyterian Hospital which advocates, ideally at least, a four-fold simultaneous attack on the problem of constitutional analysis. He postulates four "panels" of personality, a morphological, physiological, immunological, and a psychological panel. This is a most useful general conception, and one which has exerted a good influence on a generation of medical students. By way of implementation Draper uses the Freudian psychoanalytic approach to the psychological panel, and has access to the usual clinical approaches to physiology and immunology. On the morphological side he has unfortunately relied heavily upon anthropometric measurements used alone, without a constitutional frame of reference, or without reference to the *general* component factors in morphological differentiation. So used, measurements tend merely to cancel one another out, and only low correlations are found.

The general movement toward integrating psychological and somatic studies has been spreading among the younger generation of psychoanalysts and kindred scientists. In 1939 the new *Journal of Psychosomatic Medicine* was founded. Dunbar (1935), in her *Emotions and Bodily Changes,* wrote a general review aimed at integration of psychoanalytic concepts with recent developments in physiology, endocrinology, metabolism, homeostasis, and in the study of "functional" illness. This book provides a good modern orientation, on the clinical side, for the student of constitutional analysis (see also Chapters 8, 17, 18, and 19).

In summary, for the step of progression from the ancient dichotomy of Hippocrates to the trichotomy with which we are more lately familiar, we are indebted most immediately to a group of French anatomists. Italian anthropologists have played a principal role in the development of anthropometric technique and in a vigorous although rather fruitless attempt to apply it to the problem of constitutional differentiation. Lombroso stands as the classic, probably tragic, example of what happens when a brilliant, active mind tackles the constitutional problem without benefit of a scientifically acceptable basic taxonomy.

In Germany, Beneke made the first real beginning toward constitutional medicine with his systematic, comparative studies of autopsy material, while Kretschmer, with making at least four definable contributions, has become probably the most articulate figure in the modern constitutional approach. He has added a certain scientific respectability to the French typology; he has introduced the idea of dysplasia and thereby opened the way to a conception of scalable components; he has shown a statistically sound relationship between morphological and psychiatric variables; and he has extended his typological approach into the field of temperamental analysis. In referring thus to Kretschmer we also include the scores of his collaborators, followers, and friendly critics who have attempted to validate and carry on his work.

England has made but little contribution to this field. Havelock Ellis is closely comparable to Lombroso, and Goring's ponderous labor on criminal anthropology has, in the present writer's opinion, probably achieved more actual harm than good. For by attacking a good problem with inadequate tools, thereby arriving at negative results, he has, in a sense, vaccinated a generation of anthropologists against one of the fields for which anthropology exists. An accusation of sterility can be directed against the work of the physical anthropologists between the time of Goring and Hooton's recent revitalizing of this field. They appear to have incubated all their eggs in the basket of random anthropometry. Eggs so treated do not hatch. Anthropometric measurements, *used merely as such,* will no more tell the story of a physique than would some of the words of a narrative, rearranged at random, tell its story.

In America, psychological, anthropological, and clinical students alike have for more than a generation relied mainly upon unaided anthropometry. This has been relatively a sterile period, but the psychoanalytic and Kretschmerian influences appear to have touched off a revival of interest in a more vital approach. A group of psychoanalytically inclined investigators, led particularly by Alexander, have lately been developing a point of view which postulates the total organism as the primary focus of study. This point of view seems already to have found a warm welcome in some of the clinical centers, although the problem of its adequate implementation still confronts us.

Statement of the Present-Day Problem

The history of the constitutional approach makes it plain that we are still confronted with the existence of a general problem having to do with the definition of the *most basic nature* of individual differences, or with the definition and measurement of *first-order* constitutional differences among people. It is an ancient problem, and many efforts have been made to direct a fruitful attack upon it. Some of these attacks have succeeded in part, but the formulation of a comprehensive constitutional psychology remains a goal of first importance.

Schemes for the classification of morphology, physiology, temperament, and of consciousness itself have not been wanting. The question is, have any of these systems resulted in the definition and measurement of variables which can be regarded as *basic components* common to the various levels of the expression of personality? Have we yet been able to carry out a crucial test of the relationships between structure and function, or between different levels of personality? Most of the published research on the correlation between physical and mental characteristics has rested on a relatively casual choice of variables. Under such circumstances it is easy to understand why correlations are low or absent. For if measurable relationships between constitutional variables are to be discovered, these variables need to be chosen against some criterion of basic relevance.

Therefore a first step in an investigation which would measure and correlate constitutional factors must be that of isolating and defining first-order variables at different levels of personality. Further, since psychological reactions are processes in which the living individual plays a part as an integrated unit, our efforts to study the relationship between psychological reactions and constitutional factors must not only find a way of analyzing both into their most basic recognizable components, but must then also contrive to work with the *patterning* of these basic components, not merely with the isolated components themselves.

In short, to achieve a constitutional psychology, it is necessary to make peace not only with the need for a factorial analysis, but with a concomitant need for a meaningful synthesis. The two needs are obviously not incompatible. They are complementary, supporting one another like the two slopes of a roof.

An Approach to the Problem—A Summary

Of the many contemporary efforts to systematize a constitutional approach to personality we shall now examine the one with which the author is naturally most familiar. Beginning with a doctoral thesis in 1924 a constitutional research project has been in progress through more than a decade. Its object has been to lay a skeletal foundation for a constitutional psychology—a psychology of basic individual differences—first by devising a technique for describing human morphology in terms of continuous variables, and second by defining and measuring analogous first-order variables of temperament.

Indispensable collaboration has come from many workers. Dr. S. S. Stevens of Harvard has played a particularly indispensable part in systematizing and ordering the philosophical assumptions and mathematical principles underlying the central idea of component analysis.

The Basic Components of Morphology.—The procedures employed in the morphological analyses of human beings have already been described (*The Varieties of Human Physique,* 1940). Having failed to arrive at useful results with anthropometric techniques alone, we came to the conclusion that in order to set up the framework of a morphological taxonomy *ab initio*, it would first be necessary to *scrutinize* a large collection of physiques, and if possible to see them all at one time. Photography not only would make this possible, but also would permit us to see each physique from as many directions at once as we might desire. Accordingly, a procedure was adopted in which the individual is photographed in a standardized posture from the frontal, lateral, and dorsal positions on a single film.

Four thousand college students were photographed in this manner, and later many more who were not college students. When the four thousand cases were assembled so that they could be studied in one place, and could be arranged experimentally in series, it was found that a certain orderliness of nature could be made out by the unaided eye. Certainly there were no "types," but only dimensions of variation.

The first problem was to determine how many dimensions or components of structural variation could be recognized by inspectional examination. The criteria we employed in seeking to discover "primary structural components" were two: (1) Could the entire collection of photographs be arranged in an ascending (or descending) progression of strength of the characteristic under consideration, with agreement between experimenters working independently? (2) In the case of a suspected new component of structural variation, is it, upon examination of the photographs, found to be impossible to define this apparently new component in terms of mixtures, regular or dysplastic, of the other already accepted components?

Application of these two criteria revealed the presence of three primary components of structural variation, and although a set of photographs was virtually worn out by experimental sortings and rearrangements, we were unable to find a fourth structural variant which was not obviously the result of a mixture of these three.

To arrange the entire series of four thousand along each of the three accepted axes of variation was relatively easy, not only for the body as a whole, but also for different regions of the body separately (thus providing a method for the ultimate measurement of dysplasia). The distributions for the body as a whole were then scaled tentatively by the method of equal-appearing intervals, and we had at hand a rough approximation to the general patterning of a continuous tridimensional distribution. This was not yet an objectively defined distribution, but the first step toward meaningful objectification had been taken. We now had a fairly good idea of what it was that needed to be measured, and were ready to make use of anthropometry.

The second problem was to find such anthropometric measurements as would, (1) most reliably reflect those obvious differences in physique that our anthroposcopic inspection had already shown to be present, and (2) refine and objectify these differences so that precise allocations of physiques on the tridimensional distribution could be made. Such measurements were selected by trial and error. We found by experiment that the measurements most valuable for the purpose were certain diameters expressed as ratios to stature, and that most of these diameters could be taken with needle point dividers from the film more accurately (more reliably) than from the living subjects, provided the photographs were perfectly posed.

The question of how many such diameters to use is simply the question of how precisely accurate an allocation is desired. In dealing with groups statistically, we scale the strength of each of the primary components on a 7-point scale. For this purpose a minimum of seventeen diameter measurements is adequate for determining what is called the somatotype. In the detailed analysis of an individual, more precise differentiation may be made by using a greater number of measurements.

In order more readily to determine the somatotype from a series of seventeen measurements, a machine has been constructed into which the measurements may be entered. The manipulation of switches then discloses the correct somatotype. This machine, as at present constructed, may be used for the somatotyping of any male individual in the age range of 16 to 21.

The somatotype is a series of three numerals, each expressing the approximate strength of one of the primary components in a physique. The first numeral always refers to *endomorphy* (see below), the second to *mesomorphy,* and the third to *ectomorphy.* Thus when a 7-point scale is used, a 7-1-1 is the most extreme endomorph, a 1-7-1 is the most extreme mesomorph, and a 1-1-7 the most extreme ectomorph. The 4-4-4 falls at the mid-point (of the scale, not the frequency distribution) with respect to all three components. Seventy-six different somatotypes have been described, and photographic illustrations of most of them are presented in *The Varieties of Human Physique* (Sheldon, Stevens, and Tucker, 1940).

As these components occur in nature they are complex, continuous variables. The somatotype is an oversimplification which merely serves the purpose of bracketing a physique within certain defined boundaries. When the somatotype is determined, analysis of the physique is of course only begun, but the somatotype provides the basis for a morphological taxonomy which is both comprehensive and statistically manipulable. The bugaboo of types thus disappears in a continuous distribution in which every physique has a place, and the establishment of norms becomes a routine.

When *endomorphy* predominates, the digestive viscera are massive and highly developed, while the somatic structures are relatively weak and undeveloped. Endomorphs are of low specific gravity. They float high in the water. Nutrition may of course vary to some degree independently of the primary components. Endomorphs are usually fat but they are sometimes seen emaciated. In the latter event they do not change into mesomorphs or ectomorphs any more than a starved spaniel will change into a mastiff or a collie. They become simply emaciated endomorphs.

When *mesomorphy* predominates, the somatic structures (bone, muscle, and connective tissue) are in the ascendancy. The mesomorphic physique is high in specific gravity and is hard, firm, upright, and relatively strong and tough. Blood vessels are large, especially the arteries. The skin is relatively thick with large pores, and it is heavily reinforced with underlying connective tissue. The hallmark of mesomorphy is uprightness and sturdiness of structure, as the hallmark of endomorphy is softness and sphericity.

Ectomorphy means fragility, linearity, flatness of the chest, and delicacy throughout the body. There is relatively slight development of both the visceral and somatic structures. The ectomorph has long, slender, poorly muscled extremities with delicate, pipestem bones, and he has, relative to his mass, the greatest surface area and hence the greatest sensory exposure to the outside world. He is thus in one sense overly exposed and naked to his world. His nervous system and sensory tissue have relatively poor protection. It might be said that the ectomorph is biologically "extraverted," as the endomorph is biologically "introverted." Psychologically, as we shall see later, these characteristics are usually reversed—the ectomorph is the introvert, the endomorph is *one type* of extravert. The hallmark of ectomorphy is the stooped posture and hesitant restraint of movement.

The digestive viscera (dominant in endomorphy) are derived principally from the endodermal embryonic layer. The somatic tissues (dominant in mesomorphy) are derived from the mesodermal layer, while the skin and nervous system, which are relatively predominant in ectomorphy, come from the ectodermal embryonic layer.

The anthropometric measurements are standardized for normal or average nutrition, within a particular age range. Therefore those measurements which change with nutritional changes readily detect the under- or overnourished individual. But apparently no nutritional change can cause the measurements of a person of one somatotype to stimulate those of another somatotype. Nutritional changes are recognized as such by the somatotyping process. When an individual's measurements are posted in the somatotyping machine, the machine indicates where the somatotype lies. If a severe nutritional disturbance is present, the machine does not indicate a false somatotype, but indicates only an unusual aberration from the normal pattern. We have as yet seen no case in which metabolic or nutritional changes led us to the assignment of two different somatotypes for the same individual, although we have somatotyped people from photographs taken at different periods in their (adult) lives when a weight change of as much as 100 pounds had taken place.

When the relative strength of the three primary components of morphology has been determined, the physical analysis may be said to be anchored. But identification of the somatotype is only a beginning. So many secondary variables still remain to be described that the horizon of individuality seems only to broaden and to recede to greater distance as the techniques of physical description mature to usefulness.

Some of the important secondary variables are dysplasia, gynandromorphy (bisexuality), texture (fineness or coarseness of tissue), aesthetic harmony of structure, secondary local dysplasias or hereditary local patternings of the primary components (often called racial characteristics), pigmentation, distribution of secondary sexual characteristics (gynandromorphic dysplasias and characteristic patterns), hair and hair distribution, and so on. We have tried to standardize the scaling of most of these characteristics just mentioned, but many other important physical variables lie on beyond these. Furthermore the work on secondary factors is for the most part new and incomplete, since none of this work could be done in a meaningful frame of reference until the somatotyping techniques and the norms for the primary components were well established.

The Basic Components of Temperament.—As in the studies of physique, the first problem at this more complex level of personality was to discover and define criteria for a useful basic taxonomy. It was necessary at the beginning to determine what first-order components are present in temperament. The method which has finally yielded fruitful results is a variation on the technique of factor analysis applied to quantitative ratings on a group of traits.

The literature on temperament and especially on the measurement of extraversion and introversion, contains many hundreds of references to alleged traits of temperamental differentiation. This literature was first combed for differentiative behavioral traits. The trait definitions were then modified and rewritten until they appeared to embrace or to imply all of the specific characteristics mentioned in the literature. A number of trait definitions were added which were drawn from our own clinical and general observation of people, and finally the list was boiled down to exactly 50 traits.

A group of 33 young men, mostly graduate students and instructors, were then studied by the writer through the course of a series of weekly analytic interviews extending through a period of one year. These men were finally rated on each of the 50 experimental traits, a 7-point scale being used. The intercorrelations for the 50 traits were then run, and were posted on a correlation chart (See App. 4, Sheldon and Stevens, 1942). That is to say, the basic procedure of what is now called factor analysis was carried out. The purpose was to discover whether or not there were any "nuclear clusters" of traits showing positive correlation among themselves and also negative correlation with other nuclear clusters which might be present.

The result was clear-cut. Clusters of the sort just indicated were present, and clearly defined. After some statistical experimenting had been done, two criteria were adopted for qualification of a trait within a nuclear cluster. (1) The trait must show a positive correlation of at least $+.60$ with each of the other traits already accepted in the cluster, and (2) it must show a negative correlation of at least $-.30$ with every trait found in any of the other clusters. When the criteria of positive intracorrelation and negative intercorrelation were applied, it was found that three clusters of traits were present in the material. Six traits then defined what was designated as group 1, seven defined group 2, and nine defined group 3. Twenty-two of the original 50 traits had qualified. These 22 appear in Table I.

TABLE I

TWENTY-TWO TRAITS ORIGINALLY DEFINING THE THREE PRIMARY TEMPERAMENTAL COMPONENTS

Group 1		Group 2		Group 3	
V- 1[1]	Relaxation	S- 1	Assertive Posture	C- 1	Restraint in Posture
V- 2	Love of Comfort	S- 3	Energetic Characteristic	C- 3	Overly Fast Reaction
V- 6	Pleasure in Digestion	S- 4	Need of Exercise	C- 8	Sociophobia
V-10	Dependence on Social Approval	S- 7	Directness of Manner	C- 9	Inhibited Social Address
V-15	Deep Sleep	S-13	Unrestrained Voice	C-10	Resistance to Habit
V-19	Need of People when Troubled	S-16	Quality of Seeming Older	C-13	Vocal Restraint
		S-19	Need of Action when Troubled	C-15	Poor Sleep Habits
				C-16	Youthful Intentness
				C-19	Need of Solitude when Troubled

[1] The number before each trait refers to its position in Table II.

This was the beginning of what is called the Scale for Temperament. It now consists of 60 traits, 20 in each group. The additional 38 items were added as rapidly as traits meeting the criteria could be discovered and tested—a tedious process, since each individual used as a subject was analyzed through a period of at least one year. The scale in its present form is shown in Table II.

Names have been given to the three correlated groups of traits. *Viscerotonia,* the first component, in its extreme manifestation is character-

TABLE II

The Scale for Temperament

| Name | | Date | | Photo No. | | Scored by | |

I VISCEROTONIA....	II SOMATOTONIA...	III CEREBROTONIA ...
( ) 1 Relaxation in Posture and Movement	( ) 1. Assertiveness of Posture and Movement	( ) 1. Restraint in Posture and Movement, Tightness
( ) 2. Love of Physical Comfort	( ) 2. Love of Physical Adventure	— 2. Physiological Over-response
( ) 3 Slow Reaction	( ) 3 The Energetic Characteristic	( ) 3. Overly Fast Reactions
— 4 Love of Eating	( ) 4 Need and Enjoyment of Exercise	( ) 4. Love of Privacy
— 5 Socialization of Eating	— 5. Love of Dominating, Lust for Power	( ) 5. Mental Overintensity, Hyperattentionality, Apprehensiveness
— 6. Pleasure in Digestion	( ) 6 Love of Risk and Chance	( ) 6 Secretiveness of Feeling, Emotional Restraint
( ) 7 Love of Polite Ceremony	( ) 7 Bold Directness of Manner	( ) 7. Self-conscious Motility of the Eyes and Face
( ) 8. Sociophilia	( ) 8 Physical Courage for Combat	( ) 8. Sociophobia
— 9 Indiscriminate Amiability	( ) 9. Competitive Aggressiveness	( ) 9. Inhibited Social Address
— 10 Greed for Affection and Approval	— 10 Psychological Callousness	— 10. Resistance to Habit, and Poor Routinizing
— 11. Orientation to People	— 11. Claustrophobia	— 11. Agoraphobia
( ) 12. Evenness of Emotional Flow	— 12. Ruthlessness, Freedom from Squeamishness	— 12. Unpredictability of Attitude
( ) 13. Tolerance	( ) 13. The Unrestrained Voice	( ) 13. Vocal Restraint, and General Restraint of Noise
( ) 14. Complacency	— 14. Spartan Indifference to Pain	— 14. Hypersensitivity to Pain
— 15. Deep Sleep	— 15. General Noisiness	— 15. Poor Sleep Habits, Chronic Fatigue
( ) 16. The Untempered Characteristic Easy	( ) 16. Overmaturity of Appearance	( ) 16. Youthful Intentness of Manner and Appearance
( ) 17. Smooth,/Communication of Feeling, Extraversion of Viscerotonia	— 17. Horizontal Mental Cleavage, Extraversion of Somatotonia	— 17. Vertical Mental Cleavage, Introversion
— 18. Relaxation and Sociophilia under Alcohol	— 18. Assertiveness and Aggression under Alcohol	— 18. Resistance to Alcohol, and to other Depressant Drugs
— 19. Need of People when Troubled	— 19. Need of Action when Troubled	— 19. Need of Solitude when Troubled
— 20. Orientation toward Childhood and Family Relationships	— 20. Orientation toward Goals and Activities of Youth	— 20. Orientation toward the Later Periods of Life

NOTE: The thirty traits with brackets constitute collectively the short form of the scale.

ized by general relaxation, love of comfort, sociability, conviviality, gluttony for food, for people, and for affection. The viscerotonic extremes are people who "suck hard at the breast of mother earth" and love physical proximity with others. The motivational organization is dominated by the gut and by the function of anabolism. The personality seems to center around the viscera. The digestive tract is king, and its welfare appears to define the primary purpose of life.

Somatotonia, the second component, is roughly a predominance of muscular activity and of vigorous bodily assertiveness. The motivational organization seems dominated by the soma. These people have vigor and push. The executive department of their internal economy is strongly vested in their somatic muscular systems. Action and power define life's primary purpose.

Cerebrotonia, the third component, is roughly a predominance of the element of restraint, inhibition, and of the desire for concealment. These people shrink away from sociality as from too strong a light. They "repress" somatic and visceral expression, are hyperattentional, and sedulously avoid attracting attention to themselves. Their behavior seems dominated by the inhibitory and attentional functions of the cerebrum, and their motivational hierarchy appears to define an antithesis to both of the other extremes.

Concerning the Relationship Between Physique and Temperament.—We have been less interested in the statistical relationship between physique and temperament than in the problem of standardizing a procedure for the general (physical and temperamental) analysis of the individual. The project may be regarded as in one sense an effort to make a contribution to the theory and technique of psychoanalysis. Constitutional psychology and Freudian analysis are, as we see it, something like upward and downward extensions, respectively, of a continuum. The Freudians start with consciousness and go as far (down) as they can. We start with the solid bone and flesh of the individual and go as far (up) as we can. The two procedures need to be carried on conjointly, and indeed in certain cases where the two analyses have been so conducted, excellent results have obtained.

The correlation between physique and temperament is, however, an interesting byproduct of constitutional analysis. In a study extending over a period of five years we have been able to analyze 200 cases, both morphologically and temperamentally. The intracorrelations among the three primary components at each level, and the intercorrelations between the two levels are shown in Table III.

The correlations between the same components at the two levels, morphological and temperamental, are seen to be of the order of +.81

TABLE III

INTRACORRELATIONS AND INTERCORRELATIONS AMONG THE PRIMARY COMPONENTS

	Viscero-tonia	Meso-morphy	Somato-tonia	Ecto-morphy	Cerebro-tonia
Endomorphy	+.79	−.29	−.29	−.41	−.32
Viscerotonia		−.23	−.34	−.41	−.37
Mesomorphy			+.82	−.63	−.58
Somatotonia				−.53	−.62
Ectomorphy					+.83

(endomorphy-viscerotonia, +.79; mesomorphy-somatotonia, +.82; and ectomorphy-cerebrotonia, +.83). These correlations are higher than we had previously expected, and they contradict the current academic supposition that physical constitution plays only a small part in motivation and temperament. However, this common supposition can hardly be regarded as founded upon any convincing evidence, since there have been no previous studies which attempted to break down both physical and temperamental factors into comparable component elements.

In any event the correlation between the two levels is by no means perfect, and we have found that from the point of view of individual analysis, it is the disagreements or inconsistencies between the physical and temperamental patterns that are most valuable in throwing light on motivation.

Roughly, we find at least four general factors at work in the development of a personality: (1) The amount of the endowment; (2) the quality of the endowment; (3) the mixture of the components, or their order of predominance; and (4) the dyscrasias or incompatibilities between morphology and manifest temperament. Of the latter, there are several subvarieties, the most important being those cases in which the temperamental manifestation reverses a relationship of dominance between two of the morphological components. Beyond these general factors there are many secondary variables which can be measured with a greater or less degree of reliability, once the analysis of the primary components is made secure. Such factors as peripheral and central concentration of strength, endowment of sexuality, and gynandrophrenia (mental bisexuality) appear to play an important part, and these factors are closely related to the primary morphological components.

Conclusion

Comparable primary components of morphology and of manifest temperament can be identified and can be quantitatively measured. The relationship between these two levels of personality appears to be a closer one than has generally been supposed. Description of people in terms of the primary components, and in terms of other secondary components which are more or less related to them, offers the framework for a basic taxonomy of individual differences, and provides an orientation upon which constitutional analysis or psychoanalysis can be conducted. With further standardization, the methods of constitutional analysis appear also to offer promise of usefulness in attacking the problems of practical human genetics, and those of isolating and controlling the so-called constitutional diseases, such as cancer, ulcer, epilepsy, tuberculosis, and hereditary mental afflictions. In the field of constitutional medicine the frustrating obstacle has been lack of a taxonomy of individual differences adequate for comparative classifications of patients. In the component approach may lie the basis upon which such a taxonomy can be standardized.

BIBLIOGRAPHY

ALEXANDER, F. 1935. The psychoanalysis of the total personality. (Trans. by B. Glueck & B. D. Lewin.) New York: Nervous & Mental Diseases Publ.
—— 1936. The medical value of psychoanalysis. New York: Norton.
BAKWIN, H., & BAKWIN, R. M. 1929. Types of body build in infants. *Amer. J. Dis. Child., 37*, 461–472.
BARDEEN, C. R. 1920. The height, weight index of build in relation to linear and volumetric proportion, etc. *Contr. Embryol., Carneg. Instn., 46*, 483–552.
BAUER, J. 1924. Die konstitutionelle Disposition zu inneren Krankheiten. Berlin: Springer.
BEAN, R. B. 1912. Morbidity and morphology. *Johns Hopk. Hosp. Bull., 23*, 363.
—— 1923. The two European types. *Amer. J. Anat., 31*, 359.
BENEDETTI, P. 1931. Das Problem der Disposition zur Krebskrankheit. *Z. menschl. Vererb.-u. KonstLehre, 16*, 261–291.
BENEKE, F. W. 1878. Die anatomischen Grundlagen der Konstitutionsanomalien des Menschen. Marburg.
BLEULER, E. 1921. Körperliche wud geistige Konstitutionen. *Naturwissenschaften, 9*, 753.
BRANDT, W. 1936. Die biologischen Unterschiede des Pyknikers und des Leptosomen. *Dtsch. med. Wschr., 62*, 501–502.
BRYANT, J. 1914. The carnivorous and herbivorous types of man. *Boston med. surg. J., 170*, 795; *172*, 321; *173*, 384.
BURCHARD, E. M. L. 1936. Physique and psychosis—an analysis of the postulated relationship between bodily constitution and mental disease syndrome. *Comp. Psychol. Monogr., 13*, No. 61.
CABOT, P. S. DEQ. 1938. The relationship between characteristics of personality and physique in adolescents. *Genet. Psychol. Monogr., 20*, No. 1.
CAMPBELL, J. K. 1932. The relation of the types of physique to the types of mental diseases. *J. abnorm. soc. Psychol., 27*, 147–151.
CIOCCO, A. 1936a. Studies on constitution: III. Somatological differences associated with diseases of the heart in white females. *Hum. Biol., 8*, 38–91.
—— 1936b. The historical background of the modern study of constitution. *Bull. Inst. Hist. Med., 4*, 23–38.
CONNOLLY, C. J. 1939. Physique in relation to psychosis. *Stud. Psychol. Psychiat., Catholic Univ. Amer., 4*, No. 5.
DAVENPORT, C. B. 1923. Body build, its development and inheritance. *Publ. Carnegie Instn.*, No. 329.
DI GIOVANNI, A. 1909. Clinical commentaries deduced from the morphology of the human body. (Trans. by J. J. Eyre.) London and New York: Rebman.
DRAPER, G. 1924. Human constitution: a consideration of its relationship to disease. Philadelphia and London: Saunders.
DUNBAR, H. F. 1935. Emotions and bodily changes. New York: Columbia University Press.
ELLIS, H. 1890. The criminal. London: Walter Scott; New York: Scribner's.
ENKE, W. 1933. The affectivity of Kretschmer's constitutional types as revealed in psycho-galvanic experiments. *Character & Pers., 3*, 225–233.
FEIGENBAUM, J., & HOWAT, D. 1934. The relation between physical constitution and the incidence of disease: the disease groups include peptic ulcer, cholecystitis and diabetes mellitus. *J. clin. Invest., 13*, 121–138.
FREEMAN, W. 1934. Human constitution: a study of the correlations between physical aspects of the body and susceptibility to certain diseases. *Ann. intern. Med., 7*, 805–811.
GARRETT, H. E., & KELLOGG, W. N. 1928. The relation of physical constitution to general intelligence, social intelligence and emotional stability. *J. exp. Psychol., 11*, 113–129.
GARVEY, C. R. 1933. Comparative body build of manic-depressives and schizophrenic patients. *Psychol. Bull., 30*, 567–568.
GILDEA, E. F., KAHN, E., & MAN, E. B. 1936. The relationship between body build and serum lipoids and a discussion of these qualities as pyknophilic and leptophilic factors in the structure of the personality. *Amer. J. Psychiat., 92*, 1247–1260.

GOLDTHWAIT, J. E. 1915. An anatomic and mechanistic conception of disease. *Boston med. surg. J., 172,* 881.

GORING, C. 1913. The English convict. London: H. M. Stationery Office.

GRAVES, W. W. 1924. The relations of scapular types to problems of human heredity, longevity, morbidity and adaptability in general. *Arch. intern. Med., 34,* 1 26.

GREULICH, W. W., & THOMS, H. 1939. Pelvic type and its relationship to body build in white women. *J. Amer. med. Assn., 112,* 485–493.

HACKEL, W. 1932. Pathologisch-anatomische und anthropometrische Studien über Konstitution. *Z. menschl. Vererb.-u. f. KonstLehre, 16,* 63–80.

HARRIS, J. A. 1930. The measurement of man in the mass. In Harris, Jackson, Paterson & Scammon, *The measurement of man.* Minneapolis: University Minnesota Press.

HENCKEL, K. O. 1925. Konstitutionstypen und europäische Rassen. *Klin. Wschr., 4,* 2145.

HESS, A. F., & BLACKBERG, S. N. 1932. Constitutional factors in the etiology of rickets. *Amer. J. Physiol., 102,* 8.

HIPPOCRATES. On ancient medicine: The genuine works of Hippocrates. (Trans. by F. Adams.) New York: Wood.

HNAT, F. 1933. The importance of the study of human constitution in the practice of medicine. *J. med. Soc., N. J., 30,* 557–559.

HOOTON, E. A. 1939. Crime and the man. Cambridge: Harvard University Press.

JAENSCH, E. 1930. Eidetic imagery and typological methods of investigation. (Trans. by Oeser.) New York: Harcourt, Brace.

KLINEBERG, O., ASCH, S. E., & BLOCK, H. 1934. An experimental study of constitutional types. *Genet. Psychol. Monogr., 16,* 145–221.

KRASUSKY, W. S. 1927. Kretschmers konstitutionele Typen unter den Kindern im Schulalter. *Arch. Kinderheilk., 82–83,* 22–32.

KRETSCHMER, E. 1921. Körperbau und Charakter. Berlin: Springer. (Trans. from the second German edition as *Physique and Character,* by W. J. H. Sprott.) London: Kegan Paul, Trench, Trubner, 1925.

KROGMAN, W. M. 1941. Bibliography of human morphology. 1914–1939. Chicago: University Chicago Press.

KUGELMAN, I. N. 1935. Growing superior children. New York: Appleton-Century.

LAVATER, J. C. 1804. Essays on physiognomy: for the promotion of the knowledge and the love of mankind. (2nd ed., 4 vols.) (Trans. by Thomas Holcroft.) London: C. Whittingham.

LAYCOCK, T. 1862. Physiognomical diagnosis. *Med. Times, Lond.,* Part 1, 1.

LEDERER, R. Konstitutionspathologie in den medizinischen Specialwissenschaften. Vol. 1. Berlin: Springer.

LOMBROSO, C. 1889. L'uomo deliquente. (4th ed.) Torino: Flli. Bocca.

—— 1911. Crime, its causes and remedies. (Trans. by Horton.) Boston: Little, Brown.

LUCAS, W. P., & PRYOR, H. B. 1933. The body build factor in the basal metabolism of children. *Amer. J. Dis. Child.,* Part 1, *46,* 941–948.

MANOUVRIER, L. 1902. Étude sur les rapports anthropométriques en général et sur les principales proportions du corps. *Mém. Soc. Anthrop. Paris,* Ser. 3, T. 2.

McCLOY, C. H. 1936. Appraising physical status and the selection of measurements. *Univ. Ia Stud. Child Welf., 12,* No. 2.

MILLER, E. 1927. Types of mind and body. New York: Norton.

MILLS, R. W. 1917. The relation of body habitus to visceral form, position, tonus and motility. *Amer. J. Roentgenol., 4,* 155.

MOHR, G. J., & GUNDLACH, R. H. 1927. The relation between physique and performance. *J. exp. Psychol., 10,* 117–157.

NACCARATI, S. 1921. The morphologic aspect of intelligence. *Arch. Psychol., N. Y.,* No. 45.

PATERSON, D. G. 1930. Physique and intellect. New York: Appleton-Century.

PEARL, R. 1933. Constitution and health. London: Kegan Paul, Trench, Trubner.

PEARL, R., & PEARL, R. D. 1934. Studies on human longevity: VI. *Hum. Biol., 6,* 98–222.

PEARL, R., SUTTON, A. C., HOWARD, W. T., JR., & RIOCH, M. 1929. Studies on constitution: I. *Hum. Biol., 1,* 10–56.

PEARSON, K. 1906. Relationship of intelligence to size and shape of the head and other mental and physical characters. *Biometrika, 5,* 105–146.

PENDE, N. 1928. Constitutional inadequacies. (Trans. by S. Naccarati.) Philadelphia: Lea & Febiger.

PETERSON, W. F. 1932. Constitution and disease. *Physiol. Rev., 12,* 283–308.

PIGNET. 1901. Du coefficient de robusticité. *Bull. méd., Paris, 15,* 373–376.

PLATTNER, W. 1934. Metrische Körperbaudiagnostik. *Z. ges. Neurol. Psychiat., 151,* 374–404.

RIPPY, E. L. 1936. Physical types and their relation to disease. *Dallas med. J., 22,* 112–115.

RITALA, A. M. 1935. Inheritance of constitution of the parents by the new-born child as demonstrated by body measurements. *Acta Soc. Med. 'Duodecim.'* (Ser. B, parts 1–3, no. 20), *23,* 1–56.

ROSTAN, L. 1828. Cours élémentaire d'hygiène. (2nd ed., 2 vols.) Paris.

SHAW, F. C. 1924–1925. A morphologic study of the functional psychoses. *St. Hosp. Quart., N. Y., 10,* 413–421.

SHELDON, W. H. 1927a. Morphological types and mental ability. *J. person. Res., 5,* 447–451.

—— 1927b. Social traits and morphological types. *Person. J., 6,* No. 1.

—— 1927c. Ability and facial measurements. *Person. J., 6,* No. 2.

SHELDON, W. H., & STEVENS, S. S. 1942. The varieties of temperament. New York: Harper.

SHELDON, W. H., STEVENS, S. S., & TUCKER, W. B. 1940. The varieties of human physique. New York: Harper.

SIGAUD, C. 1914. La forme humaine. Paris: A. Maloine.

SLYE, M. 1927. Cancer and heredity. *Ann. intern. Med., 1,* 951.

SNYDER, L. H. 1926. Human blood groups: their inheritance and racial significance. *Amer. J. phys. Anthrop., 9,* 233–263.

SOMMERVILLE, R. C. 1924. Physical, motor and sensory traits. *Arch. Psychol., N. Y., 12,* 1–108.

SPRANGER, E. 1928. Types of men. (Trans. by Pigors.) Halle: Niemeyer.

SPURZHEIM, J. G. 1833. Phrenology in connexion with the study of physiognomy. Boston: Marsh, Capen & Lyon.

SSUCHAREWA, G. E. 1928. Körperbau, Motorik und Charakter der Oligophrenen. II. *Z. ges. Neurol. Psychiat., 114,* 22–37.

STERN-PIPER, L. 1923. Kretschmers psycho-physische Typen und die Rassenformen in Deutschland. *Arch. Psychiat. Nervenkr., 67,* 569.

STEVENSON, P. H., SUNG, S. M., PAI, T., & LYMAN, R. S. 1937. Chinese constitutional differentiation and Kretschmerian typology. *Hum. Biol., 9,* 451–481.

STILLER, B. 1907. Die asthenische Konstitutionskrankheit. Stuttgart: F. Enke.

STOCKARD, C. R. 1923. Human types and growth relations. *Amer. J. Anat., 31,* 261.

—— 1931. The physical basis of personality. New York: Norton.

TODD, T. W. 1930. Behavior patterns of the alimentary tract. Beaumont Foundation Lectures, Series No. 9. Baltimore: Williams & Wilkins.

TREADGOLD, H. A. 1934. Functional efficiency and body-build in the young male adult. *Lancet,* Part 1, 1377–1382.

TSCHERNING, R. 1923. Über die somatische und psychische Konstitution bei Ulcus ventriculi. *Arch. VerdauKr., 31,* 351–360.

TSCHERNORUTZKY, M. W. 1931. Wechselbeziehungen zwischen Funktionseigenschaften und Konstitutionstypus. *Z. menschl. Vererb.-u. KonstLehre, 15,* 134.

TUCKER, W. B., & LESSA, W. A. 1940. Man: a constitutional investigation. *Quart. Rev. Biol., 15,* 265–289; 411–455.

VAN DER HORST. 1924. Experimentell-psychologische Untersuchungen zu Kretschmers "Körperbau und Charakter." *Z. ges. Neurol. Psychiat., 93,* 341–380.

VIOLA, G. 1933. La costituzione individuale. Bologna: L. Cappeli.

VOLLMER, H. 1937. The shape of the ear in relation to body constitution. *Arch. Pediat., 54,* 574–590.

VON ROHDEN, F. 1925. Über Beziehungen zwischen Konstitution und Rasse. *Z. ges. Neurol. Psychiat., 98,* 255.

WARSTADT, A., & COLLIER, W. A. 1935. Über den angeblichen Zusammenhang von Schizophrenie und Tuberkulose. *Allg. Z. Psychiat., 103,* 355–365.

WEIDENREICH, F. 1926. Rasse und Körperbau. Berlin: Springer.

WEISMAN, S. A. 1938. Your chest should be flat. (Foreword by R. E. Scammon.) Philadelphia: Lippincott.

WERTHAM, F. 1930. Progress in psychiatry: IV. Experimental type psychology. *Arch. Neurol. Psychiat., Chicago, 21,* 605 611.

WERTHEIMER, F. I., & HESKETH, F. E. 1926. The significance of the physical constitution in mental disease. Medical Monographs. Vol. 10. Baltimore: Williams & Wilkins.

WESTPHAL, K. 1931. The use of indices as an auxiliary method in the establishment of physical types. *Hum. Biol., 3,* 420–428.

WHEELER, W. M. 1927. Physiognomy of insects. *Quart. Rev. Biol., 2,* 1.

WILLEMSE, W. 1932. Constitution-types in delinquency. New York: Harcourt, Brace.

YOUNG, M. 1933. A study of rheumatic fever and asthmatic children with special reference to physical type. *J. Hyg., Camb., 33,* 435.

ZWEIG, H. 1919. Habitus und Lebensalter. *Z. angew. Anat., 4,* 255.

Chapter 18

PERSONALITY AS AFFECTED BY LESIONS OF THE BRAIN

By STANLEY COBB, M.D.

Historical

THE CONCEPT THAT THE BRAIN is the organ of mind and that injury to that organ causes mental symptoms goes back to the dawn of medicine. To trace it through the centuries would be the work of a careful historian; I can only touch on some of the recent leaders. During the nineteenth century speculation in medicine gave way to a search for evidence and some great names in Neurology stand as milestones in the development of the present body of knowledge concerning the effect of lesions of the brain upon personality. Meynert (1833–1892), a great anatomist and student of the structure of the brain, gave some thought as early as 1865 to the relation of the cerebral cortex to the life of reason and in 1884 wrote a book on psychiatry. His neurologizing of psychiatry gave it a certain respectability which it then lacked. During these same years Hughlings Jackson (1835–1911) in England was using his great clinical and analytical gifts in studying the levels of neurological integration and their relation to consciousness, speech and many mental symptoms (Jackson, 1931; Levin, 1933, 1936). His brilliant insight into the mechanism of the brain gave many of the hypotheses that were later proved to be correct by the careful work of Sherrington (1906, 1933) and other physiologists. Wernicke (1848–1905) went further and considered mental disease as due to abnormality of the organ of association (the cerebrum) and described three types of consciousness: allopsychic (the consciousness of the outer world), somatopsychic (the consciousness of the soma) and autopsychic (the consciousness of the ego). This last he considered particularly related to personality (1900).

Von Monakow (1853–1930) in his great book *Gehirnpathologie* (1897) gave an important place to psychological symptoms, for the first time authoritatively accepting them on an equal footing with neurological disorders. Pavlov (1849–1936) throughout this epoch was trying to explain all mental functions as physiological reflexes. He made a great contribution to psychology by his experiments on dogs (1927), never realizing that his antagonism to psychology was merely a play on words —he worked in the field most of his life but called it by another name!

The next epoch was that of the World War, where experiments on the human were performed by the thousand. Much use of all this misery was made to advance neurology and psychology by such investigators as Goldstein (1927), Reichmann (1920), Kleist (1934), and Head (1912). Many other neurologists and neurosurgeons contributed to the great store of knowledge gained from this clinical material. Almost every part of the brain was injured in a focal way; the subjects were healthy young men and the physicians were keen observers both in the military hospitals and in the years of follow-up in veterans' homes after the war. Another source of neuropsychiatric advance was the epidemic of encephalitis. This disease, well described by Economo (1919, 1931), had such varied motor symptoms that it helped greatly to elucidate the physiology of the brain stem and basal ganglia. Patients with the disease gave evidence of great importance as to the relation of motor function to the more highly integrated psychological functions (Jelliffe, 1930).

In America, Adolf Meyer's (Muncie, 1939) synthesizing philosophy of psychobiology has done much to bring together physiology, neurology, psychology, and sociology. His battle for unity, the concept of a patient as "he" or "she" in a complex setting, has been won so thoroughly that most well-trained physicians now think in terms of personality. From the physiological side, working with comparative anatomy and embryology, two thoughtful neurologists have done much to coordinate anatomy and psychology. Herrick (1924, 1926) has helped an army of students with his clear expositions of what the brain does. Coghill (1929) has shown that integration is not the simple addition of reflex plus reflex; it is a complex hereditary and embryological organization of neural mechanisms with clear biological meanings, that functions immediately and is only broken down into simple reflexes by disease or experiment.

Since 1920, except for the continued observation of the wounded men, there has been little advance in the understanding of the higher neurological integrations of man. The present war will doubtless make its contributions. Important knowledge has been gained through the experimental operations on the brains of higher monkeys and apes in Fulton's (1938) laboratory at Yale, and the closely following "lobotomies" of the neurosurgeons (Freeman and Watts, 1939, 1941, 1942).

Definitions

There has been much loose thinking and confused writing upon the subject of whether certain phenomena are "mental or physical," "psychic or somatic," "functional or organic." The current medical vernacular that divides all diseases into either "organic" or "functional" is convenient, but entirely indefensible on either scientific or philosophical grounds. It must be perfectly clear to any physician who will stop to think about it, that all disease is *both* organic and functional because without functional disturbance there can be no symptoms, and without organic involvement there can be no disturbance of function. The latter statement is obviously true because function is not an abstraction; it is the result of some organ in action; function cannot exist without an organ which is functioning. No physiologist would doubt these statements and it would not be worth while writing these paragraphs were it not true that many clinicians thoughtlessly use the dichotomy "organic or functional," thus beclouding their own thinking and confusing their students who have just come from physiology and are amazed at the jargon of their teachers in the different branches of clinical medicine. To a physiologist, for example, an exaggerated knee jerk following cord lesion is accepted, as a matter of course, as a functional disturbance. Definitions, however, must be made before exposition and discussion can be undertaken. I want to emphasize the importance of physiological thinking and the stultifying effect of clinical slang, such as "functional heart disease" and "functional psychosis." The following terms are submitted, and will be used in this chapter:

The main clinical syndromes known to psychiatrists can be roughly grouped according to etiology under four main headings: hereditary, neuropathological, chemical, and psychopathological. More dynamically one could speak of these as genogenic, histogenic, chemogenic, and psychogenic disorders (Cobb, 1941). Of course there are no "pure" cases of any one etiology and most cases probably have elements of all four, nevertheless the concept is useful if the terms are clearly defined. From a broad point of view all behavior is dependent upon histogenic function; inherited disturbances arise from disorders of the gonadal tissues; interpersonal relations are dependent upon physical stimuli (sound, light, smell, touch, heat, etc.) acting upon body cells that have been conditioned in various ways. For classification, however, one must use narrower meanings:

Genogenic disorders of personality are those that are known to have their source largely in heredity. The abnormal genes may or may not cause recognizable lesions or malformations of the nervous system. For example, manic-depressive psychosis is strongly inherited, but no lesion is known. Hereditary chorea, on the other hand, has well-recognized lesions.

Histogenic disorders of the personality are those that are largely due to non-hereditary lesions of the nervous system, i.e., to inflammation, degeneration, asphyxia, toxin, trauma, or tumor. A lesion is defined as an abnormality of tissue either microscopically or grossly visible.

Chemogenic disorders of personality come from the effects of chemical agents. The normal chemical balance of a tissue may be upset by either too much or too little of a substance. This group is, however, defined arbitrarily to omit cases where chemical substances lead to visible lesions on the one hand, and cases where emotional stress is obviously the immediate cause of chemical change in the body, on the other hand.

Psychogenic disorders of personality are those that seem to arise largely because of disturbed interpersonal relations, social maladjustments, and the like.

If one uses these terms and definitions the problem at hand resolves itself into *a discussion of histogenic symptoms in man in so far as they are psychological in their phenomenology.* "Psychological" is here taken to mean symptoms pertaining to disorders of the more highly integrated neural processes (Pavlov, 1927), so only lesions of the brain will be discussed although it is obvious that personality is affected by any and every lesion of the body. These effects are secondary, however, and belong to another chapter in psychology. For example, pneumonia may cause confusion and delirious symptoms through a sustained hypoxemia in the brain; a withered arm from obstetrical injury, like that of Kaiser Wilhelm II, may cause an inferiority complex with dire and far-reaching results (Ludwig, 1926).

Lesions of the brain may affect personality in a direct and primary way, or secondarily by complex psychological reactions such as fear and discouragement. A person may have a hemianopsia from a lesion of the occipital areas and never notice the visual defect. After a neurological examination has brought this blind area to his attention, he may become preoccupied with his defect and become anxious, afraid to cross the street and restricted in social relations. In this case the lesion itself did not cause a psychological effect, because it was a lesion of the lowest cortical level of integration. *Fear,* aroused by discovering the trouble, did cause psychological reactions of the highest levels. A more obvious example is the varied responses of old people to hemiplegic "strokes" from thrombotic lesions of the motor cortex. This common neurological disorder is borne by some with courage and equanimity. Others are thrown into a deep depression. The variability of reaction is rarely a question of the type or location of the lesion, but an expression of the whole life experience of the *person who gets the stroke.*

The lesions directly effecting the more highly integrated levels of the brain (which are the subject of this chapter) cause even more varied effects.[1] In understanding such clinical phenomena one must start with the fact that no two human brains are alike. Lesions destroying exactly the same areas in two different brains would not cause exactly similar symptoms. This is because the life experience of each person has conditioned and changed the brain so that it is unique. Take, for example, the effect upon two Swiss brothers of cerebral softenings in the left parieto-temporal regions. One brother lived on the farm in his native valley and carried on with a vocabulary of 2500 words or so. The other became a waiter in hotels, learned five languages, and ended up in a large metropolis. Semantic aphasia in the first would be an inconvenience soon overcome. In the waiter such an aphasia would be an economic catastrophe; he might easily get back enough native German to run a farm, but never could he regain his five learned languages.

This hypothetical example is taken at the language level because it is

---

[1] See also experimental and test studies of deficit in Chapter 32 by Hunt and Cofer. (Editor)

simpler; lesions affecting the higher associative levels can be even more varied in their effects from person to person. The brain is the organ of mind and the psychological reactions to injury must necessarily depend upon what was in the brain when it was injured. Essentially this means memories (engrams, conditioned reflexes, associations). How these are stored is not known, but that they *are* stored and form a principal basis of personality is proven.

Having mentioned these preliminary propositions one can take up more specific aspects of the psychological study of cerebral lesions. Three main factors are involved: the *type* of pathological process, the *timing* of this process, that is to say, its mode of onset and course, and lastly, the *topography* of the lesion or its location within the brain. These will be taken up as separate topics.

Types of Pathological Process

The types of pathological process that may cause changes in personality can be quickly enumerated as tumor, trauma, inflammation, metabolic disorder. Etiologically these may be due to genogenic, chemogenic, histogenic, and psychogenic causes. To discuss each one separately with all its varied effects would be to write a textbook of several volumes on cerebral neurology. For the purposes of this chapter some examples and contrasts must suffice.

Cerebral Tumors.—Tumors of the brain have given the clinician a great deal of data concerning cerebral function. The slow clinical course, the operative technique itself, and the post-operative recovery phase have all contributed important data, most of which have to do with localization. Some more general facts, however, appear from a study of this extensive literature. It is seen that slowly expanding lesions can distort the brain to a great degree and cause much destruction with little or no functional change, i.e., with no overt symptoms. A similar amount of distortion produced by a suddenly expanding lesion such as a hemorrhage would cause profound symptoms and perhaps death.

A few neurologists working in surgical clinics have made careful studies of the psychological effects of tumors of the brain. Benda (1934) surveyed a series of 200 cases, paying especial attention to the development of the symptoms, a genetic as opposed to a symptomatic approach. He states:

> After discussing anatomical localization and localization of function, a third aspect of localization ought to be considered which may be called the psychological one. This approach has met with some suspicion from the standpoint of exact neurology, and yet if one studies the history of neurology, one might easily recognize that the psychological aspect of neurology is a legitimate offspring of its classic development, and is likely to yield important results if one avoids unfounded psychologism.
>
> Studies in the behavior patterns of men and animals have brought

forth evidence that sensory and motor activity are not independent entities which could be studied separately. The development of sensory functions is dependent upon the motor pattern. Sensory function represents a regulation of motor activity and vice versa, increased sensory regulation is the fundament of improved motor specialization. From animal observations and pathological conditions of men, it seems safe to conclude that the center of motor activity is placed in the axis of the central nervous system. Motor activity seems to originate from the lower centers and if we accept this view, the development of the brain pallium represents an inhibition and deviation of primary impulses. The pallium splits the primitive action into several phases and produces a retardation of the response through lengthening of the way between perception and reaction.[2] The pallium is a projection-field which is inserted into the course of central action in order to differentiate and specialize the response. In this way, normal brain function represents a complex integration while under pathological conditions some links in the chain may be missing. Focal pathology, therefore, does not reveal the center of a function but does reveal the loss of an interpolation. If in a picture, parts of the painting are destroyed, the meaning may be beyond recognition, and yet it is obvious that the significance of the painting and its material representation are not identical.

It may appear as if the psychological aspect of neurology is merely of theoretical value, and yet a more careful analysis of the situation shows that a recognition of the situation is of an extreme practical value. If the observation of a patient is centered on a study of his pathological behavior and the examination includes testing of reflexes and ocular function as well as memory, perception and understanding, it is obvious that any partition of functions into organic and psychological becomes meaningless. The main subject of the study of a patient is his response to various test situations, and every method which yields more information is welcome but none is of exclusive value because we realize that any method reveals only limited aspects of a complex function which represents a highly integrated entity. (Trans. from Benda, 1934)

In his analysis he brings out the point that tumors of the upper frontal areas and frontal poles cause slowing of speech and thought, protracted reactions, cloudiness, and difficulty in grasping problems. In contrast to these can be shown cases where the tumor is basal, either growing from the dura or from the suprasella region. The symptoms in this group may be quite different, some patients having quick responses of a jocose, even hypomanic nature (*Witzelsucht*) with euphoric mood. Changes in "consciousness" from this hyperactivity to drowsiness, somnolence, and coma are conspicuous features. The frequently associated vegetative symptoms make it seem probable that the physiological mechanisms involved are those related to the nuclei in the walls of the third ventricle and the hypothalamus. Under this localization they will be further discussed.

---

[2] See "long-circuiting" as used by Fulton (1938) and Cobb (1941).

Several cases of bilateral removal of the cerebral frontal areas for tumor have been carefully studied by competent psychologists, but these are special cases and will be discussed under localization. Rylander (1939) in Stockholm has recently reported 30 cases of frontal tumor in which psychological tests were carried out before and after operation. Since the symptoms seem to be due to the surgical lobectomy rather than the tumor, the results are discussed under localization below.

Harrower-Erickson (1940) in Penfield's clinic at the Montreal Neurological Institute has used the Rorschach technique on a series of 25 patients with cerebral tumors. The results of the tests have been presented in a simplified, diagrammatic way and it is clearly demonstrated that the patient 'with a cerebral tumor responds to the Rorschach test quite differently from the normal. They show an extraordinarily uniform restriction of response, both in total number of responses and in special categories, indicating greatly "constricted personality." Thus the old clinical "hunch" of the experienced neurologist that his patient suffered from a brain tumor because he had "that peculiar blank look" yet showed no obvious intellectual defect, is beginning to be analyzed and explained in scientific terms.

After operative removal of the tumors the test score improved somewhat. The striking fact was that the location of the lesion was not important: 26 of the 28 records differed so greatly from the normal records that the smaller differences between records of patients with lesions in various locations became relatively insignificant.

In differential diagnosis the Rorschach method thus becomes useful in distinguishing between personality changes due to cerebral lesion and such conditions as manic-depressive psychosis, schizophrenia, and neurosis. The attempt to differentiate more exactly, within the large group of patients suffering from cerebral lesions of all sorts, can be aided by isolating this comparatively uniform group of patients with cerebral tumors. Then further careful work with the Rorschach and other psychological tests may show the diagnostician further refinements. At present the work is in its infancy as is shown by authors who are naïve enough to talk of "the organic personality" (Piotrowski, 1937a), meaning the type of personality found in patients suffering from cerebral lesions. It would be difficult to find a noun and an adjective less compatible when exact meanings are considered. To such depths does medical slang descend!

Trauma.—Injury to the brain affects many aspects of the personality. In the first place a blow on the head may instantly change the state of consciousness [3] from one of acute awareness to complete oblivion. This may be due to a simple *concussion* of the brain; consciousness may return in a few seconds and no ill effects need follow. The mechanism of this remarkable phenomenon is entirely unknown; many theories have

---

[3] "Consciousness" is here taken as meaning *awareness of the environment*.

been promulgated but none is satisfactory. If the blow is more severe a *contusion* of the brain results. The period of unconsciousness is longer and after effects are usually severe. The swelling of the brain causes increased intracranial pressure with concomitant headache, focal symptoms in accordance with the location of the lesion, and perhaps long-continued dazed states or coma.

Laceration (Munro, 1938) of the brain results from the most severe types of injury to the head, usually with fracture or penetration of the skull. Consciousness is impaired or lost, often for a period of days. Symptoms vary with the location of the injury. On returning to an awareness of his surroundings the patient may be dazed, dull, and slow in his reactions for weeks (Goldstein, 1927). This is seen commonly in bullet or shrapnel wounds of the brain. Complete recovery may follow, or the cerebral injury may lead to atrophy and scar formation within the brain, causing mental deterioration with or without epilepsy. Goldstein and Reichmann (1920) had a great experience with such cases between 1916 and 1920. They state that gunshot injuries of the brain may cause subjective symptoms resembling psychoneurotic disorders. Objectively one observes loss of bodily and spiritual efficiency and a change in the whole personality ("hirntraumatische Leistungsschwäche"). In early cases the apathetic symptom complex was commonly seen consisting of difficulty of intellectual grasp, loss of interest, slowing of all motor reactions and psychological processes. The amnesic phenomena which are often seen following concussion were rare in late cases but Forster and Gagel (1933) reported Korsakow's syndrome as common in fresh cases. "Traumatic dementia" in the sense of a general impairment of the highest intellectual process has also been described by other German authors.

Persons who have had several concussions or contusions of the brain often develop a clinical picture that is quite characteristic: after each injury, but usually more conspicuously after the third or fourth, the patient has persistent headache, increased by using the eyes or exposure to the sun; transient diplopia is common. He avoids lifting or leaning over because of increased headache and dizzy feelings. After a few months this state becomes one of general invalidism with many aches, easy fatigability, lack of initiative, and varying degrees of apathy. Close psychiatric supervision may keep him socially acceptable, but he usually drifts off, becomes a "rolling stone" and "irresponsible." Alcohol affects him strongly and may precipitate epileptic attacks of various kinds. Psychological examination shows little intellectual deficit in such fields as memory, retention, and alertness, but as the process goes on, such symptoms of deterioration may appear. During the first year of his disorder the patient seems to be simply unreliable; later he becomes incorrigible, a pathological liar, always taking the easy way out and avoiding sustained effort. Some of these patients are difficult to distinguish from the "ne'er do well" and chronic delinquent diagnosed "psychopathic personality" and "moral imbecile." The best positive evidence is gained from encephalography and from a careful history which brings out the repeated traumas. The pneumoencephalogram will often reveal somewhat enlarged cerebral ventricles and slight frontal atrophy. The electroencephalogram may show abnormal, slow waves. The pathological process is not thoroughly understood, but is supposed to be the result of scattered petechial extravasation of blood in the brain substance. The hemorrhages are absorbed and heal, forming multiple small scars which cause contraction and atrophy of the brain by slow gliosis. When the injury is largely basal, as from pugilistic blows on the jaw, the functional effects may be largely in the motor sphere and the tremulous, staggering "punch drunk" results. In the cases under discussion the injury is more in the cerebral cortex and white matter. If epilepsy comes on, as it often does after months or years, the symptoms and course are those of traumatic epilepsy (see Chapter 31 by Lennox).

Remarkable improvement both in the fits and in the mental status may follow clean, operative removal of injured frontal lobes. Hebb and Penfield (1940) have made the most recent and one of the best case reports of a bilateral frontal lobectomy on a young man injured at the age of 16, epileptic for ten years, and operated upon at age 27. The studies are thorough from the points of view of psychology and anatomy. Their emphasis, however, is upon the significance of the great postoperative improvement following the removal of abnormal frontal poles and the great diminution of abnormal electrical activity. The areas mutilated by the trauma were approximately 8, 9, 10, and 11, while the surgical procedure removed in addition normal parts of 6, 8, 25, 32, 33, 46, and 47 (see Figures 1, 2, and 3, below). The patient changed from being an irresponsible, stubborn, restless, and forgetful epileptic, to a "pleasant personality, considerate of other patients," with only two seizures in 15 months. The case demonstrated the detrimental effect of the presence of pathological tissue in the brain. Moreover, it has been shown by Stein, Marshall, and Nims (1941) that injury to the cerebral cortex in one focal area can result in marked chemical changes in adjacent or remote areas. These changes affect the phosphorylating glycolytic cycle along with the acid-base equilibrium and the lactic acid content; they can be partly explained by changes in blood flow, but the exact mechanism is still unknown.

Another extraordinary personality change occurs in certain cases of cerebral hemorrhage when the blood spreads into the arachnoid space or ventricles. At first there is extreme, sudden headache; coma and death may follow, but those cases that keep or regain consciousness may become wildly active, thrashing about in a confused way, screaming, and striking themselves or others. Such disturbed states go on for hours and are only terminated by proper sedation and lumbar puncture or by exhaustion and death.

Inflammation.—When the author of a nineteenth century novel had ensnarled himself hopelessly in a plot that could not fit the characters, he gave the worst offender an attack of "brain fever," had him emerge a different man, and ended his book happily. What this disease might be no medical man seems to know, but it seems to be generally accepted that inflammation of the brain may explain a change in personality. On what basis this common belief stands is the subject of this section.

The term "encephalitis" is usually used to denote inflammatory reaction within the brain due to invasion by micro-organisms. But any infection of the blood, skull, or meninges may spread to the brain. If it is severe enough to cause necrosis of tissue an abscess forms, so all types of meningo-encephalitis, focal encephalitis, and abscess are possible. Since the symptoms depend on the location of the lesion, focal encephalitic lesions will be discussed under localization.

A severe meningitis usually causes acute and marked personality change. The patient becomes confused, restless, and sometimes loses all control, screaming and fighting, probably because of the intense headache. The lesions in the brain even in these severe cases of meningitis may be negligible and the delirium and behavior is best explained as a delirious reaction to toxin and pain—a chemogenic syndrome.

There are two types of encephalitis, however, that have fairly definite clinical pictures and pathological findings. These are the inflammations of the brain caused by syphilis (Jacob, 1930) and by viruses (Hendrick, 1928; Fothergill, 1939). A syphilitic infection of the meninges is possible within weeks or a few months of the primary infection, but the symptomatology is largely neurological, and psychological phenomena are secondary or resemble those of any acute meningitis. It is the late (tertiary) lesions of the brain that cause the syndrome of *dementia paralytica* (general paresis, G. P., general paralysis of the insane, G. P. I., or paresis). The lesions are largely cortical, causing a subacute or chronic atrophy of the gray matter, especially the association and motor areas. The patient may come first to the physician complaining of fatigue and nervousness. Unless the reflexes, pupils, and spinal fluid are examined he may be sent away with a diagnosis of neurosis and some psychotherapeutic advice, only to return a year later, when it is too late to cure the disease, with more overt mental symptoms. The neurological symptoms at this time will be more conspicuous, a slurring speech is probably beginning to show. The family will complain that the patient is becoming coarse and ill-mannered, irritable and forgetful. The jovial megalomania so often described may be present, but it is not the rule; a mood of depression is not uncommon instead of the textbook euphoria. But when the elated, expansive mood is present, it is a most remarkable phenomenon: one sees a man in the prime of life, who has previously been modest and reliable, rather suddenly break forth with ideas of omnipotence and actions dishonest and spectacular. The usual picture, however, is less striking, with emphasis on the gradual loss of culture and memory.

I remember well, when acting as clinical clerk at Queen Square for Kinnier Wilson, I saw him present a new case to a group of students in the out-patient clinic. I was seated at the table taking notes, Wilson was standing, having just dismissed a patient, and there was an empty chair beside my table. Wilson rang for the next patient, the door opened and a man entered, followed by his wife. He walked across the fifteen feet of classroom, smiled at the students and at me, and sat down. Wilson turned to me instantly and said, "Write down G. P. I. as the diagnosis." Probably my jaw dropped, for he went on, "Well, Cobb, what else could it be? Here is a middle-aged man coming to a nerve clinic. He enters the room smiling, pushes ahead of his wife, does not take off his hat, takes the only chair without asking and likes an audience!" Subsequent neurological and serological studies proved the correctness of the diagnosis.

It is almost impossible to correlate the type and distribution of the cerebral lesions with the mental picture. Perhaps the memory defect can be related to the predilection of the atrophy for the associative areas (areas 9, 10, 11, see Figure 1 below). The speech defect and later motor paresis are probably caused by atrophy of areas 4, 6, 44, and 45. Beyond this little can be stated except that no two cases are alike. Perhaps this is the crux of the situation. No two adult brains are alike. The life history of each person is somehow written into his cortex, so similar lesions cause dissimilar results. But the whole problem cannot be dismissed as simply as that; certain other clinical observations have to be explained. For example, senile dementia has lesions of an atrophic nature largely in the frontal areas. One would expect mental symptoms similar to G. P. There is a marked memory defect in both disorders, but even this is usually clinically distinguishable because of the excellent memory for remote events often retained by the senile patient. The striking difference is that most patients with senile psychoses retain their veneer of good manners and culture almost to the end, while the G. P. is likely to lose his at the onset of the disease. Systematized paranoid delusions are common in the senile and rare in the G. P. True, the lesions are not exactly alike, but to my mind the autopsy findings alone will never explain the differences in the clinical pictures. The senile atrophy is more widespread, more complete and slower in development than the paretic atrophy, which is more superficial and affects blood vessels and meninges to a greater extent.

The *timing* of the process is not sufficiently considered by most neuropathologists. Wertham (1934) has written a good discussion of the subject; he believes that the factor of time is of great importance and that the genetic development of lesions is insufficiently known.

In the case of the G. P. as contrasted with the senile atrophy I would suggest that important considerations are: (1) the time of life at which the symptoms began; (2) the rapidity of the progress of the disease process. The first is important from the endocrine and metabolic standpoints. A man in his forties has energy, sex drive, and ambition. A loss of his highest levels of integration will affect him very differently at that age than at seventy. He would then have much less energy and his outlook might well be so narrowed that a querulous suspiciousness would develop out of memory loss. One does not want to speculate too much, but it seems true that similar processes attacking persons at different times of life have quite different psychological effects.

An even more marked example of this is seen in inflammation of the brain due to the virus of epidemic encephalitis (lethargic encephalitis, the "sleeping sickness" of temperate climates). The lesions are found widely scattered throughout the nervous system, from peripheral nerve to cerebral cortex, but the greatest concentration of lesions is in the brain stem, with cortex often affected. Adults suffering from this infection usually have a mild, acute illness with fever, headache, diplopia, and interferences with sleep rhythm. They may entirely recover, or if unlucky, they go on to have chronic encephalitis (often incorrectly called "*post*-encephalitic syndrome"). In this they have a variety of motor and oculomotor symptoms, of which Parkinson's syndrome is the commonest. In spite of severe and disabling motor symptoms, however, they rarely show much emotional disorder or intellectual deficit. The disease slowly reduces their motor initiative and speed until they become almost like slow-moving, wooden puppets, but retaining to the end alert and normal minds.

Quite different is the picture in children under the age of twelve. The virus strikes its quota of victims in this age group, but in my experience none of them develop Parkinson's syndrome; most of them have severe and lasting disorders of behavior (Jasper, *et al.*, 1938). They become restless and cannot concentrate long enough to attend classes; they are impulsive, moody, stubborn, and combative. These symptoms often have remissions and exacerbations, the latter being so explosive at times as to resemble epileptic seizures. In fact, the electroencephalograms in most of these children show abnormal slow waves. Some of them go on to motor fits that bring them into the classification of epilepsy. Some gradually deteriorate and by the age of sixteen or eighteen are less of a behavior problem and merely need institutional protection. Others continue to be most difficult social problems and are loose in the community labeled "ne'er do wells," "psychopaths" and "delinquents." The milder cases may resemble the post-traumatic patients described above.

The number of brains studied at autopsy from this group is not large, but there is no evidence that the lesions differ much in their form or distribution from those found in adults. Once more the difference in symptomatic result from similar lesions must be explained on the basis of the seed and the soil. The virus (seed) is the same in both cases, but in the child it lands on younger soil, where cerebrum is less developed and growth processes in the rest of the body are active. In the adult the nervous system is more static and the endocrine balance different. Many other differences might be mentioned. These are suggested as important. It would seem as if the explanation would never be obtained from the autopsy material available. Many more autopsies are needed. Experimental methods are necessary to watch the timing and development of the disease process. But behavior in animals is not to be compared with human behavior, so a research project to elucidate the problem is difficult.

Degeneration.—Under this heading are grouped a large number of diseases of the brain. Some, like *cerebral arteriosclerosis,* have a known basis; others, like *senile dementia,* are probably due to nutritional deficiency related to circulation of blood, but not due to arteriosclerosis. The causes of other degenerations of the brain are largely unknown (congenital diplegia, Alzheimer's disease, tuberous sclerosis, the diffuse sclerosis of Schilder, and multiple sclerosis). Many are hereditary—for example, the familial ataxias and Huntington's chorea. The psychological pictures associated with the cerebral and bulbar degenerations are varied and numerous. Good descriptions of the disorders are found in Nielsen's (1941) *Textbook of Clinical Neurology,* Chapter 19. Wertham has attempted the difficult task of correlating lesions with psychopathological phenomena. He says:

> The present possibilities of making direct correlations between histopathological findings in the central nervous system and psychopathological phenomena are infinitely fewer than neurohistologists have generally supposed. . . .
>
> In considering the possibility of correlations, it must be pointed out that in proportion to the extraordinary complexity and differentiation of the finer functions mediated by the central nervous system, histological lesions are very gross. However we may conceive of the functional processes going on in the central nervous system,—physiological, physicochemical, metabolic, electrical, etc.,—it should be obvious that only the grossest miscarriages and defects would become morphologically visible. Structural lesions are the effect of functional reactions that are not histologically demonstrable. Physicochemical changes, metabolic processes, functional changes of blood vessels, and similar biological phenomena that cannot be microhistologically demonstrated, *precede* the anatomically visible lesions, which occur only where the processes have attained a certain intensity. Many histopathological findings, such as the proliferation of fibrous glia (sclerosis), may be thought of as the reaction to the whole changed nutritional situation in the tissue and its altered consistency in pathological processes. (1934, pp. 358–359)

When the degenerations are focal in distribution as in Pick's disease with its circumscribed areas of cortical atrophy, the symptoms follow fairly well the description of reactions given under "Localization" (see page 565). Arteriosclerotic softenings are notably of this sort. There is usually in addition a general loss of what Goldstein (1927) calls *Grundfunktion,* a diffuse deterioration difficult to recognize by clinical tests and in the case of aphasic disturbances, exemplified by Head's "semantic aphasia." In other words, more of the brain is affected than one can see by microscopical technique.

One group of degenerative disorders has recently come into prominence because of the rapid advance of our knowledge of nutrition. I refer to the vitamin deficiencies. Those affecting the brain are known to be mainly in the "B complex" (thiamin, riboflavin, nicotinic acid, etc.), but the exact fractions of vitamin B responsible for the different symptoms are not as yet known (see also Chapter 19 by Shock). The data even now are extensive and it is probable that some of the disorders listed above as of unknown cause and some of the others now considered circulatory or inherited, will be found to have a factor of vitamin deficiency. Table I gives an idea of the neuropsychiatric disorders related to vitamin B and the general distribution of the lesions:

TABLE I

NEUROPSYCHIATRIC DISORDERS RELATED TO DEFICIENCIES OF VITAMIN B

	Distribution of Lesion				
	Cerebral	Spinal	Peri. nerve	Skin	Mucosa
Pellagra	++	+	+	++	++
Korsakow's psychosis...	+++	+	++	+	+
Subacute degeneration of the cord	+	++	+		+
Alcoholic neuritis			++	+	+
Beri-beri			++	++	+

A glance at this diagram suggests that the clinical syndromes are not clearly separated from one another and that the causative deficiencies are overlapping. Pellagra is the most diffuse, and the mental symptoms may be slight or marked; when the psychosis is the conspicuous part of the picture the name is changed to "Korsakow." The processes are the same and alcohol is a common, though not necessary, precipitating cause. In pernicious anemia (and allied disorders) there is marked subacute degeneration of the spinal cord causing spastic and ataxic paraplegia; cerebral lesions are also found, often expressed as a mild paranoid reaction with confusion at night. Alcoholic neuritis may be a part of Korsakow's syndrome, but when found alone is nothing but "white man's beri-beri." In these last two conditions there are no mental symptoms other than those concerned with the social implications of alcoholism and famine.

Thus one sees that certain degenerative lesions of the brain have certain psychological pictures associated with them. They are not clear-cut, but often give syndromes that lead to correct clinical diagnosis. It must be remembered, however, that the degenerative process is at work on the brain of an individual man or woman. As Meyer would put it, upon a "him" or a "her." The past history of the individual is of importance in determining in what way and to what extent psychological symptoms will appear. Rothschild and Sharp bring this out well in a recent paper on senile psychosis. They report several cases:

. . . to illustrate the discrepancies that may occur between anatomic changes and mental phenomena in the field of senile conditions.

The discrepancies are explained on the basis of differences in the capacity of different individuals to resist or compensate for cerebral damage. In certain cases, defects of personality are associated with such a high vulnerability that unusually slight changes lead to an outspoken psychosis. It is believed that mental stress may lower the compensatory capacity and thereby upset an equilibrium which had hitherto been well maintained. Other persons remain normal mentally in spite of severe senile involvement of the brain. These observations suggest that the qualities of the living person rather than the neuropathologic alterations determine whether or not a psychosis will occur in some cases. The role of the structural disturbances probably varies from one extreme, at which they wholly account for the psychosis, to the other at which they are only a minor factor. A picture of the true situation is revealed, not by isolated consideration of any single feature, but by a scrutiny which seeks to determine the relative importance of anatomic factors and factors of a more personal nature in each case. (1941, p. 50)

Aplasia

Lack of normal development accounts for many mental abnormalities from the total amentia of anencephalic monsters to the various degrees of personality defect caused by congenital endocrine disorders. The endocrine disorders are discussed in Chapter 19 by Shock, so only a brief account will be given here of congenital and hereditary cerebral defects, although it is obvious that the endocrine development of the embryo runs parallel to the development of the nervous system, and disease, dysfunction, or retardation of one probably affects the other.

Great numbers of patients with poorly developed brains inhabit our institutions for the feebleminded and epileptic. Some of the lesions are due to trauma, infection, and tumor; many are congenital or hereditary. Infants born with truly rudimentary brains are classed as "monsters" and do not live long enough to become a public charge. Those with less marked defects show variations in size of the brain, from the microcephalic idiots to the hydrocephalics with enormous heads and thinned out cortices that appear to function remarkably well. The gyri may be malformed in many idiots and imbeciles (macrogyria and microgyria). These patients are of low mental grade and their psychological reactions are so defective that they can hardly be said to have a personality. They are neurological curiosities and live vegetative lives, kept alive by careful hospitalization. At best they go through monotonous routines with a dull appreciation of the world about them. The lesions causing these defects are usually sporadic congenital affairs, caused by some embryological fault, and are not hereditary as the defect does not often run through a family tree. Many of them have convulsions and other sorts of fits, so are classed as "epileptic," but the more logical viewpoint is to consider the brain defect as primary and the fit as one of many symptoms thereof.

Mental deficiency of the higher grades (less severe, with IQ 50 to

80) is both genogenic and histogenic; at present the best guess is that the proportion is about 50:50 (Hopwood, *et al.*, 1941). Many cases are certainly due to cerebral trauma and infections in infancy and childhood. Most people who have looked into the subject, however, agree that mental defect of this grade runs strongly in families and that the brains of these familial cases show no lesions and rare developmental anomalies. Since the disorder is genogenic it must rely on abnormal structure, but that abnormality has not been found in the brain and may be outside it. With improved techniques one hopes some day to solve these riddles of mental defect, dullness and, on the other hand, brightness and genius. At present about all that is known is that genealogical data prove that some infants are born "with brains" and others with "less brains." Whether or not they make the most of their allotment is a question of environment. Even special gifts are inheritable, such as music, mathematics, and drawing. What the basis of such inheritance may be is for future research to tell. At present I take my stand with Forel and Vogt (1919) that careful anatomical studies of the brain with new methods will surely increase our knowledge of psychiatry and psychology.

Localization

A number of disease processes have been discussed in relation to their effect on personality. Some of these show a slight, and others show an important relationship, but in the majority of cases it is not *what* the disease is, but *where* the disease is in the brain, that is important to the student of personality. In other words, a knowledge of cerebral functional localization is essential to the understanding of psychology. There need be no argument as to the facts; they are accepted now by all informed neuropsychiatrists and psychologists. Thorndike (1941) puts it: "Localization of abilities in centers has been discarded a generation ago, and replaced by localization in groups of conductors and synapses . . . the localization within the cerebrum is far more complex and indeterminate than had been supposed." Twenty years ago a wave of anti-localizationalism disturbed the small pond wherein worked the specialists in cerebral function. The brain was said to be "equipotential" and clinical localization was belittled. The experimentalists, however, have enlarged their sphere, used more highly developed mammals (Fulton, 1938; Klüver and Bucy, 1939), and shown that the quite definite areas of functional localization in the cerebral cortex of man are phylogenetically predicted by less and less definite, but still recognizable, areas, all the way down the mammalian ladder. In short, rats show less specific localization and more equipotentiality, while man shows the opposite (Lashley, 1929). "Centers" are still under suspicion, but "areas" are quite proper.

Thus previous stimulation of a spot in the motor area of a monkey may cause "reversal" of function, flexion changes to extension. Again, a motor point may be stimulated repeatedly, causing a certain muscular movement; immediately after this, stimulation of an appropriate point in the sensory area will cause the same movement, although previous stimulation of this point in the sensory area would have had no motor effect. Similar sorts of variability and facilitation have been found in the human cortex by Penfield and Erickson (1941). Thus the evidence shows that although the cerebral cortex has a great deal of functional localization, there is also much potential variability of function even in man.

The historical and bibliographical aspects of the study of localization are excellently given in von Monakow's book in 1914 and Goldstein's monograph in 1927. At present the best way of showing the data is by illustrations (see Figures 1, 2, and 3) modified from Brodmann (1925) and using his numbered designations for the various histologically

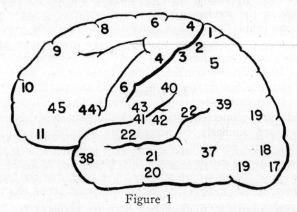

Figure 1

Lateral aspect of the left cerebral hemisphere, showing general localization of the principal cortical areas, after Brodmann.

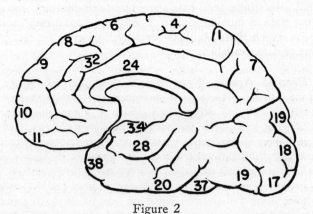

Figure 2

Mesial aspect of the right cerebral hemisphere, showing some of the main cortical areas, after Brodmann.

recognizable fields. These designations are now being more and more widely used and have a great advantage over description in terms of gyri or lobes, because the latter are variable surface landmarks, variously defined by different authors.

Looking at Figs. 1 and 2 one can quickly grasp the lay of the land by locating the four main receiving stations for stimuli: area 17 (vision), area 41 (hearing), areas 1, 2, 3, and 5 (somatic sensory, e.g., touch and pressure from skin and deep end organs) and the olfactory bulb and olfactory areas that show only on the mesial surface of the brain (areas 28 and 34). Around each of these receiving stations is said to be a more complex area related to sensory perception and its elaboration. For example, area 18, surrounding "visual-sensory" area 17, is said to be "visuo-psychic." The evidence for this subdivision is not entirely conclusive, but clinical facts suggest its correctness. Areas 4 and 6 are the motor areas (4 "pyramidal" and 6 "extrapyramidal"). These are the outflow side of the mechanistically conceived sensori-motor projection system of the brain, "projection" simply signifying that the area, be it sensory or motor, is connected with lower centers by long fibre tracts. Having designated the more simple and phylogenetically older areas (Kappers, 1920), there remain to be explained two main groups of cortical areas, the frontal (areas 9, 10, 11, 45, and 32 on the mesial aspect) and the parieto-temporal (areas. 39, 40, 41, 42, 43, and 44). These areas are connected intimately with each other by associative fibres, they are similarly connected with the projection areas and their longest fibres probably go as far as the thalamus. In short, they are association areas, and as such are of especial interest to the student of personality. The frontal group appears to be related to the highest emotional and social integrations, the parieto-temporal group has to do with language, learned skills, and meanings of acts and symbols. Neither can alone be said to be the "seat of the intellect"—if either had to be chosen

I think I would call the functions associated with language the more intellectual. But these are broad generalizations that are speculative at the present state of our knowledge. I will therefore present some of the evidence on which these opinions are based, to give the reader an idea of the sort of data available.

The Frontal Areas.—Experimental work on laboratory animals clearly forecast the present opinions concerning the functions of the frontal areas of the cerebral cortex in man. For example, Bianchi (see trans., 1922), in 1893, after frontal ablations on monkeys, said that the animals no longer showed any restraint or resourcefulness in small difficulties and that "utilization of past experience was absolutely wanting." Franz in 1907 found that cats and monkeys lost recent memory, i.e., their training in opening a food box. Recently Fulton (1938) and his colleagues have done remarkable work on functional localization in the brains of the higher apes, work which apparently led directly to the present operation of "lobotomy."

Clinical observations, however, must be the foundation because no mammal except man possesses much personality. The study of certain cases where operations for tumor caused bilateral damage to the frontal areas of the cerebrum give important data. Unfortunately no perfectly satisfactory scientific evidence is available because no case is known where a normal man has been examined and then deprived of his frontal areas and reexamined. Hebb and Penfield (1940) say that it may be that no clinical study will be adequate to reveal the defects that follow frontal injury because of the difficulty of obtaining a good premorbid rating of ability. One must rely on observations concerning, first, brains already deformed and partially destroyed by tumors and, second, patients with epilepsy or mental symptoms who undergo cerebral operation for the relief of their symptoms. Obviously in neither case can satisfactory examinations be made before operation, so no scientific controls exist. The best one can do is to examine the cases and amass such data as are available.[4] Harlow's case of the "crow-bar skull" is of more historical than neurological interest, because the exact injury to the brain is not known, it had to be reconstructed from the skull. The same can be said of a great deal of literature on the effects of frontal injuries in the last war. The data are interesting, but not convincing.

There is an extensive literature on unilateral lesions of the frontal areas. The more careful observers have been able to detect slight changes in personality, loss of initiative, a loss of the power of abstraction, and incapacity to resolve situations. Some authors such as Grünthal (1930) even believe that they can localize symptoms; for example, "emotional" disturbances are likely to result from lesions of the orbital surface of the frontal lobe (area 11) whereas "intellectual" deterioration results from injury to the lateral convex surface (area 10). Benda (1934) confirms and perhaps partly explains these observations by finding that tumors at the base of the frontal lobe are similar in symptomatology to tumors of the suprasellar region, both show the silly, slightly manic reaction known as *Witzelsucht,* rare in cases with tumor of the more frontal convexity of the lobe, where the principal symptoms are slowing of speech and thought, difficulty in grasping situations, cloudiness, and protracted reactions.

In a monograph on *Personality Changes After Operations on the Frontal Lobes,* Rylander (1939) of Stockholm has given a careful report of 32 cases of unilateral excision of the frontal areas. The patients were examined psychologically and there was a careful follow-up. The weakness of the evidence is due to the fact that no exact delineation of the lesions was possible by autopsy methods. Most of the patients are still alive, and although he believes the lesions he removed to have been unilateral, it is possible, even probable in some cases, that damage had been

---

[4] For a more extended discussion of this subject with full bibliography, see Cobb, S., 1940, *Arch. int. Med., 66,* 1431 ff, and also summary of studies in Chapter 32.

done to the other frontal areas by pressure. In 32 cases of these frontal excisions he lists the mental changes as follows:

"Intellectual changes" in 21 cases, itemized as:

Memory loss in 21	Euphoria in 20 cases
Weakened association in 20	Restlessness in 14
Slower thinking, "can't keep up" in 14	Loss of initiative in 12
Loss of attention in 10	Depression in 8

He sums up by saying that the loss of the frontal areas disables the patient "not to such a degree as to destroy his ability to lead a normal social existence" but to a degree that "can be fatal to persons doing qualified intellectual work."

These findings of Rylander's are not corroborated by other surgeons. Most reports of unilateral removal of the frontal areas are remarkable for their lack of psychological results. My own conclusion is that careful psychological examinations before and after operation and a follow-up a year later, would usually show slight psychological defects in most unilateral cases (for example, see the Rorschach tests of Harrower-Erickson discussed under "tumors" above). In other words, the lack of symptoms may be because of insufficient search for them. But on the whole I believe a man can lose one frontal pole with insignificant disability.

When both frontal areas are injured or removed the case is much more plain. Psychological changes are quite conspicuous and are the rule. Four cases have been reported in which *both* frontal areas were excised in order to remove a large tumor. The first and most carefully reported is Dandy's case; he operated on this man in 1930, and after prolonged and careful study, Brickner published the psychological observations in 1936. A reconstruction of the specimen removed from the left hemisphere indicates that it probably contained most of area 8, and the whole of 9, 10, 11, 45, 46, 47, and 32; the excision on the right was slightly larger including probably a little more of area 8 and area 44. The results on the patient's mentality can be summarized as follows: (1) a limitation of the capacity to associate and synthesize, e.g., the patient showed distractability with impairment of selection, retention and learning; (2) impairment of restraint of emotion with boasting, anger and hostility; (3) additional symptoms such as impairment of abstraction, judgment, initiative, with euphoria and increased slowness, stereotypy, and compulsiveness.

Ackerly (1935) reported a similar case operated upon in 1933 by Spurling. The left frontal area, however, though greatly compressed, was not actually removed. The symptoms were more like those reported by Rylander than those reported by Brickner, but all have points of similarity. Euphoria was marked and the patient said of the surgeon: "He cut out my worry!" The case reported by Karnosh in 1935 showed emotional instability and distractability. David and Askanasy's (1939) patient is interesting because she remarked after recovery, "I understand things better now, but they don't stir me up."

The most convincing data, however, came from the surgeons who perform "lobectomies" and "lobotomies" on psychotic patients for the relief of mental symptoms. As emphasized above, one must admit that

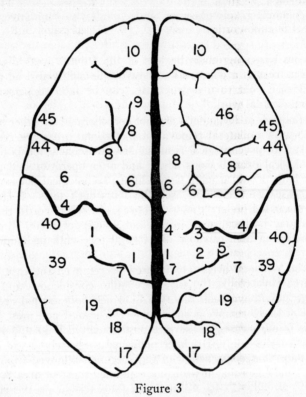

Figure 3

Vertical aspect of the brain, showing general arrangement of the principal cortical areas, after Brodmann. They are not all indicated and some are only indicated on one side but this is to avoid crowding. All areas are somewhat symmetrical, right and left.

the evidence as to the normal function of the frontal areas is not conclusive, because all the patients were psychotic before operation and there could be no normal controls. Moreover as Hebb and Penfield (1940) point out, disconnected and perhaps asphxiated tissue is left in the brain after lobotomy, and this pathological tissue may cause symptoms. Nevertheless, the mass of data accumulating is impressive and points in the direction already indicated by the tumor cases cited above. Moniz (see Freeman and Watts, 1942) started this form of treatment in Portugal; he believes that the best results are with patients suffering from agitated depression. Out of the 20 cases he cured 7, ameliorated 7. and had no effect upon 6. Only one case of the 20, however, is given in enough detail to allow the reader to judge for himself as to diagnosis and result.

In this country Freeman and Watts (see 1942), and Lyerly have taken up the work, and a few such operations have been done by other surgeons. Altogether well over 100 lobotomies and lobectomies have been performed. In these operations the frontal areas are either removed through bilateral craniotomy, or more commonly, the connections between the frontal cortical areas (9, 10, 11, 47, and 45?), and the lower centers are severed by cutting the white matter in the center of the frontal lobes just anterior to the tips of the anterior horns of the ventricles. The results of the work are best summarized by Freeman and Watts (1942). The main symptoms relieved by the operation have been depression (80% of 49 instances), agitation (70% of 51), compulsion (70% of 27), suspiciousness (55% of 17), and irritability (33% of 14). Symptoms produced have been inertia ("emotional flattening" or laziness) in most cases, hypomania (euphoria, playfulness, and poor judgment) in about half the cases, and in 40% a marked gain in weight. Freeman and Watts (1939) divide their results into two classes: the primary results consist of inertia, lack of ambition, reduction in consecutive thinking, loss of "self-consciousness," indifference to opinion of others, satisfaction with results of inferior quality. The secondary results are euphoria, evasion, bluffing, talkativeness, aggressiveness, teasing, indecency in speech and act, inattention, and poor judgment.

In other words, when accident, disease, or a surgeon destroys the frontal areas bilaterally, the subject usually becomes a little stupid, a little silly, lazy, and fat. If the operation saves the patient from death or incurabe psychosis, it is obviously worth while. If the disease is curable by other means or liable to remission, and if the patient is young, the operation seems to me unjustifiable.

After analyzing such case histories, it still remains difficult to describe "typical frontal lobe symptoms." Probably one is on safest ground at present if one holds that the loss of the frontal areas causes no specific qualitative defect; rather the defect is quantitative and related to loss of association fibres. That the most important association fibres are those that go from the frontal areas to the thalamus and other diencephalic nuclei, is suggested by the observations of Grünthal (1930) and Benda (1934, mentioned above) and by Bostroem (1936) in his chapter on "General and Psychic Symptoms in Diseases of the Cerebrum." Bostroem believes that understanding and mental grasp may be effected (a) by lack of interest, the patient has lost initiative and does not attend to the stimuli presented by the environment; or (b) the brain is incapable of analyzing the stimuli. These take place in basal or frontal lesions. Evidence from tumors and stimulation of the walls of the third ventricle at operation on man (Foerster and Gagel, 1933), suggests that maniacal reactions are related to a diencephalic center, not frontal. This agrees with the experiments on animals by Ranson (1939), who postulates a "wakefulness" center in this region which stimulates the cortex perhaps by way of the thalamo-cortical circuits described by Campion and Smith (1934) and considered so important for "consciousness." Degrees of consciousness (defined as "awareness of environment") are surely affected by lesions in many parts of the brain, and, if consciousness is to be considered a faculty, it is probably best not to try to localize it narrowly, but to realize that any interference with the neuron connections from hypothalamus to thalamus and thence to cortex and back, may cause changes in the degree of consciousness.

The Parieto-temporal Areas.—Perhaps even more complex in their psychological functions and certainly more intricate in their localization, are the association areas that lie in the parieto-occipital region between the stations for somatic-sensory, visual and auditory perception. In Fig. 1 these are numbered, 39, 40, 41, 42, 43, and 44. They are unique in that they are only well developed in the leading hemisphere (the left in right-handed persons). Man alone has this specialization of a leading hemisphere in respect to handedness and language.

In a chapter on personality as affected by lesions of the brain one cannot review and discuss the great subject of language, eugnosia, and eupraxia from Broca to Nielsen (see history in Head, 1926), but it is important to emphasize that just as much, if not more, "intellectual" function is centered in these areas as in the frontal areas.

The senses most important to language are vision and hearing. The two main senses each have three levels of integration (Nielsen, 1941). Visual *perception* is localized in area 17 (Figure 1), visual *recognition* in area 18, and *revisualization* in parts of area 19. A lesion at the first level causes blindness; at the second, loss of recognition (the patient does not know what the perceived object means, hence visual agnosia). Lesions in parts of area 19 cause a loss of power to revisualize scenes or persons. This faculty has to do with remembering sequences. The patient cannot remember the plan of a house. On the street he is lost and cannot get home even though he may recognize the street or house he is seeing at the moment. Recognition of learned symbols for words seen is the third level and is in the angular gyrus, area 39. Lesions here cause visual verbal agnosia or "word blindness."

The auditory sense has three levels, but they are not so clearly defined. The first level is not in the cortex; primary auditory perception is in the mesial geniculate bodies of the thalami. Each cochlea sends fibres to both geniculates. Thence fibres go to the temporal lobes, where cortical areas 41 and 42 make the center for auditory recognition (level 2). Since the innervation is bilateral a single cerebral lesion cannot cause complete agnosia and never can cause deafness. Acoustic agnosia (for sounds) and acoustic verbal agnosia result from lesions in these areas but they are less unilateral than the visual areas, so a bilateral lesion in 41 is usually needed for complete word deafness.

The motor side of language is equally complex and depends on an understanding of the fact that no learned motor skill can be practiced without an *ideational plan;* the normal individual knows how to do a thing quickly and almost automatically when requested. A defect of such performance in response to command is apraxia. It is a symptom of injury to the sensori-motor elaboration areas of the cortex. In relation to most performances eupraxia is bilateral, the acts of one hand, for example, being planned in the opposite precentral (area 6) and supramarginal gyri (area 40). Apraxia of the organs of speech (tongue, lips, larynx) causes "motor aphasia"; the patient loses the memory of how to make the movements to articulate words, he may know just what he wants to say but he cannot get the plan of the word into his mind. Lesions of Broca's area, 44, cause this symptom.

Area 39 has the functions of symbolic visual recognition (Nielsen, 1941), i.e., understanding letters and words by sight. Because words were first learned by hearing, however, area 39 cannot function if cut off from 41 and 42. During the process of learning to read, words were sounded out or spoken, so the portion of the temporal lobe lying between 39 and 42 is of great importance (the posterior part of area 22 and the upper part of 37). A lesion here may cause in some persons as much loss of reading (alexia) as a lesion directly in 39. Moreover, because language is learned by associating vision and hearing with objects and symbols, this area is particularly important in relation to nouns. That this is true is shown by temporal lobectomies where this language formation area of the leading hemisphere was removed. The result was "amnesic aphasia" or "anomia." When the patient is shown a pen he uses circumlocution and may express "It's to write with" but cannot say "pen."

If one takes these main symptoms, agnosia, motor aphasia, and anomia, as examples and considers the many possible variables, it is seen that various special sorts of aphasia are possible. For example, music has meaning, though not with the exactness of words, therefore "amusia" is found. One can learn several languages and have marked aphasia in one but little in another. Symbols used for mathematics are different from letters, so one may have agnosia for figures. In fact, loss of the ability to calculate is found after lesions in various areas. One could go on with special cases and the results of focal lesions; suffice it to say that there is a great mass of well-studied data available for the student who wishes to go into the subject.

A new and important attack on these problems has been made possible by the work of factor analysts (see Thurstone, 1938). Their analysis of mental abilities by batteries of performance tests, mathematically analyzed, is bringing to light functional variables of a new type which cannot be expressed in the classical terms of psychology. According to Lashley (1941), this method

> distinguishes between the ability to think in terms of the spatial relations of objects and to comprehend nonspatial relations. It distinguishes facility in manipulating separate symbols, as in recognition of words in jumbled letters, from facility with combinations of

symbols as in grammatical speech. It is difficult to describe these variables except in terms of the tests from which they are derived, for they do not correspond to any familiar classification of functions. They do seem, however, to correspond to functions which may be independently lost as a result of localized brain injury. Certain types of apraxia are marked by difficulty in dealing with spatial relations; the function represented by manipulation of isolated symbols resembles the ability which suffers in verbal aphasia as defined by Henry Head [see, 1926], and there are other less clear correspondences.

The Neurological Approach to Mental Disorder

Since writing the main part of this chapter, I received from Charles P. Symonds a reprint of his address to the Royal Society of Medicine as President of the Section of Psychiatry. This paper has the title that appears in the heading above and so closely agrees with my point of view on most important issues that I quote freely. It is certainly important to see how trends of thought are turning, and it is interesting to note that a neurologist, trained in the English school of Jackson, Sherrington, Head, Wilson, and Holmes, with a couple of years in America 20 years ago, comes independently to much the same point of view as mine. This is not only interesting to me but comforting, for in being critical of what one considers prevalent misapprehensions one often feels lonely!

Symonds says in his introductory paragraphs:

Sherrington and his followers have succeeded in building knowledge of function level by level, on Jacksonian principles, from the lowest towards the highest, reaching up towards those at which functional activity is, more or less, associated with consciousness. Sherrington has summarized in his Rede lecture the extent of physiological achievement and outlined the gap between physiology and psychology. That gap is still so wide that it is beyond imagination to pass it. Yet physiological experiment has confirmed Jackson's view that the nervous system from first to last is a sensorimotor arrangement, in which, at higher levels, there is re-representation in ever-increasing complexity of all parts and functions already represented.

The variability of function at forebrain level is indeed bewildering. Even in the excitable motor cortex, where functional pattern is relatively stable, it is evident that response depends upon recent individual experience. Stimulation of a point may determine now flexion, now extension, of the same digit. Which will happen depends upon what has just happened, not only at this point, but in the sensory cortex behind it.

The neurologist conceives the nervous system, even at forebrain level of complexity, governed by the same principles as obtain at spinal segmental level. There the rule is afferent impulse and response by excitation or inhibition, but even at the spinal level subliminal excitation and inhibition, unseen but legitimately inferred, determine complex variety of response. Long circuiting at the higher levels allows more and more opportunity for delayed reaction, and so for the interplay of impulses seemingly remote in space and time. With such evidence before him the neurologist approaches the study of mental disorder prepared for what indeed he finds, no fixed clinical syndromes, but types of reaction roughly and arbitrarily defined, with, in the individual patient, inexplicable vagaries of response. (1941, pp. 289–290)

I applaud Symonds' emphasis of Jackson's principles (see Jackson's *Selected Writings,* 1931). Only by accepting psychology as a part of physiology can one make any sense out of it. The gap between physiology and certain aspects of psychology is certainly wide, but I do not believe it is too wide for "imagination" to cross. In fact, it is just such constructive thinking as that of Jackson and Sherrington that gives us a bridge. The idea of "long circuiting" gives one plan for the bridge; conditioned reflex phenomena give another (see Chapter 12 by Liddell) and "psychosomatic" investigations a third (see Chapter 8 by Saul). For example, studies of the learning process by the methods of experimental neurology (Klüver and Bucy, 1939; Lashley, 1929) and observations on agnosia, aphasia, and amnesia in relation to human cerebral lesions (Hebb and Penfield, 1940; Nielsen, 1936) are spanning this gap from below while careful studies of personality, of the physiology of emotional reactions, Pavlovian technique applied to man (Finesinger and Finesinger, 1937), and experimental neurosis in laboratory animals (Liddell and Bayne, 1927), are bridging it from above (Cobb, 1941). In fact, the job of each student of cerebral function is to bring his stone to this bridge. To use another metaphor, we all are working at the great mosaic; a great many important stones (valid observations) have been put together, both in the area of psychology and in the areas of physiology, pathology, and other fundamental sciences. Each of the areas is developing into a meaningful picture, but the connecting zones are blank or scarcely filled. When each of us has added one or more stones, I strongly believe that the relation between physiology and psychology will be seen to be merely that of more simple to more complex. Qualitatively they are the same. In degree of complexity they differ widely and physiology has so far only attempted to solve the simpler problems. To say that these psychological problems never can be solved scientifically is to prophesy pusillanimously. To say that psychology is something apart, that must be studied by nonscientific methods and by "psychologically minded" people is surrendering to metaphysics and the supernatural. These especially gifted people certainly exist and make a great contribution to psychology by their flair for understanding interpersonal relations. As long as they stick to their field, they do much good. When they try to dichotomize, dividing the world into "mental or physical," and when they ignore the importance of neurology, they create a harmful schism in neuropsychiatry.

On this subject Symonds (1941) says:

> The psychologist may ask at this stage whether the neurologist from his study of micturition has anything of practical value to offer to the investigation and treatment of disordered function. He will probably admit contribution if the disorder be "organic" but may deny it if "functional." Here we are faced with a division which for medicine has become a source of much error and confusion. It is in part due to double usage of the terms. "Functional" for some means disorder of a kind which has never been proved due to demonstrable lesion. For others it means mentally as opposed to physically caused. Neither distinction is wholly valid. Disordered function not yet traced to demonstrable lesion may be so traced tomorrow. We have no right to speak of mental *or* physical causes. We can at most say that certain causes operate at levels of neural integration usually attended by consciousness, others not.
>
> There is another meaning sometimes given to these terms functional and organic which has more validity—disorder of the former type is reversible, of the latter not. But it would be better to say so, implying in each instance physical change. Physiogenic and psychogenic are terms which have better value as indicating factors in *causation* to be described respectively in terms of physiology and psychology, but it should be understood that the distinction is made for convenience in description only, and that all cerebral activity whether conscious or unconscious must have its physical basis.

I would give the term "functional" even shorter shrift and say categorically that it is modern medical slang and harmful to clear thinking. Symonds' words "physiogenic and psychogenic" are better, but "physiogenic" is too vague and does not stick to the etiological significance that such terms should have. Physiology, to my mind, is the study of normal function, so pathological states should not be generated by physiological processes. I submit that chemogenic, histogenic, and genogenic disorders as defined cover the field of "physiogenic" etiology more satisfactorily. No classification will be correct until etiology is thoroughly understood.

Symonds takes for the elaboration of his arguments a discussion of the "affective" psychoses and neuroses. He states that affective disorder is not a disorder of mood alone, but also of somatic and visceral sensation which add important elements to the picture. He regards the affective disorders as a central disturbance of feeling, a disorder of the central nervous system at a hypothetical level, at which there is representation of "feeling tone, and together with this, direction of the vegetative functions." If he means by this level the diencephalon, especially the thalamic and hypothalamic regions, I agree. The experimental and clinical observations indicate to me that too much function is often relegated to the hypothalamus. Masserman (1941) puts the thing well, saying that it is not a center of emotional life, but a center where afferent impulses are integrated for the expression of the emotions. The feeling aspect of the phenomena are probably taken care of by the thalamus and thalamo-cortical connections (Papez, *et al.*, 1940).

Speaking of the etiology of manic-depressive psychosis, Symonds (1941) says:

> Apart from heredity there is little known of cause. What is important, perhaps, is that precipitating cause when definite may be so various—emotional disturbance, infective or toxic illness, fatigue, or head injury. This to the neurologist is not surprising, for he is accustomed to different causes operating at the same level producing the same symptoms. What is indeed remarkable is the absence of apparent cause in so many cases. . . . Causeless onset in a disorder of this kind is at the same time a reminder of our ignorance of cerebral function, and of the almost infinite variety of combinations made possible by the cerebral nerve net. . . . What perhaps is even more noteworthy is that the affective disorder can persist so long and yet be so completely reversible. There can, therefore, be no structural alteration of a kind we should call lesion, and it is possible, if not probable, that there is a cause outside the brain itself—physical or chemical.

A more important clinical problem could hardly have been chosen. The sorrows caused by manic-depressive psychosis are common and great. Mild depressions cause much unhappiness and inefficiency, while mild manic states disrupt social relationships to an extraordinary degree. I agree with Symonds entirely, but would like to underline, for emphasis, the words *"of a kind we should call a lesion."* I *do* believe that there is "structural alteration" in every case of manic-depressive psychosis. I have not discussed it above, in the main body of the chapter, because the structural alteration may not be in the brain. Nevertheless, the disease is strongly inherited, and to carry this taint the gene must have structural abnormality; function is action and cannot be inherited. The defect in the gene has not as yet been microscopically detected, but it must be there. No abnormality of any organ is regularly discovered in the bodies of persons suffering from this psychosis. Perhaps the lesion escapes notice because it consists of the imbalance of two or more organs, no one of which shows enough abnormality to be recognized by our present methods. Such a deviation from the normal would coincide with Symonds' conception. Another possibility is that a lesion (defined as visible structural change) will be found in the diencephalon when methods are improved. In that case manic-depressive symptoms will form a large chapter in the discussion of lesions that affect the personality. One thing is certain, and that is that the term "functional" cannot reasonably be applied to this disease. Etiologically speaking, manic-depressive psychosis is strongly genogenic, a large chemogenic factor is probable and psychogenic precipitants are known to occur in some cases.

In upholding the importance of the neurological approach to mental disorder, Symonds (1941) discusses the position of what in England is called "Medical Psychology," i.e., the practice of psychotherapy by persons not trained in neuropsychiatry. He says:

The medical psychologist also asserts that for his purpose training in neurology is unnecessary. He may be prepared to admit that all mental activity has its physical basis, and that brain is the organ of mind, but these propositions are, for him, of theoretical value only. They have no real bearing upon the practical diagnosis and treatment of the neuroses. An approach to these problems in terms of neurophysiology and neuropathology may be an interesting intellectual exercise, but has no practical significance. I have already attempted to indicate the fallacies in such argument, with especial reference to the affective disorders. I would take as another example the diagnosis and treatment of neurosis following head injury. Here we have a patient whose adjustments to inner need and external stimulus are faulty. How far is this due to inherited disposition, training, experience, present needs and difficulties; how far to the nature and situation of cerebral damage? Is the cerebral injury of reversible or irreversible character? If there is headache, how much is due to meningeal adhesion, alterations in the cerebrospinal fluid pressure or circulation, or disordered cortical rhythm? How much to fear, depression, or defeatism arising from difficulty in coping with the situation as a whole? If there is insomnia, how much is due to anxiety, how much to hypothalamic damage? I submit that the answers to some of these questions are impossible without neurological training, and that unless they are all answered diagnosis and treatment must be at fault. I do not think this is an unfair example. There are many other instances in which knowledge of cerebral function in health and disease, in relation to nutrition—including vitamin supply, effect of drugs, endocrine disorders, or oxygen need—is essential to the proper understanding and treatment of neurosis.

This brings us back to the central problem: What effect may cerebral injury have upon personality? Moreover it points out that personality certainly has an effect upon what will happen after cerebral injury. Trauma is the easiest example to think about, and has been discussed somewhat at length, but to envisage the problem correctly one must admit its complexity and consider that changes in the brain are of paramount importance to all psychiatric disorders, from the miscalled "functional" neuroses and psychoses to those with known and visible lesions. To my mind it is only a matter of time, work, and improved technique; structure and function will be shown to be the same thing. Already physics and chemistry are practically unified.

BIBLIOGRAPHY

ACKERLY, S. 1935. Instinctive, emotional and mental changes following prefrontal lobe extirpation. *Amer. J. Psychiat., 92,* 717–729.
BENDA, C. E. 1934. Die topische Diagnostik der Hirntumoren. *Mschr. Psychiat. Neurol., 89,* 53–80.
—— 1934. Die topische Diagnostik der Hirntumoren. *Mschr. Psychiat. Neurol., 89,* 105 ff.
BIANCHI, L. 1922. The mechanism of the brain and the function of the frontal lobes. (Trans. by J. H. MacDonald.) Edinburgh: E. & S. Livingstone.
BOSTROEM, A. 1936. Allgemeine und psychische Symptome bei Erkrankungen

des Grosshirns. In Bumke, O., & Foerster, O., *Handbuch der Neurologie, Bd. 6.* Berlin: Springer. Pp. 961–1021.

BRICKNER, R. M. 1936. The intellectual functions of the frontal lobes. New York: Macmillan.

BRODMANN, K. 1925. Vergleichende Lokalisationslehre der Grosshirnrinde. Leipzig: Barth.

CAMPION, G. S., & SMITH, G. E. 1934. The neural basis of thought. New York: Harcourt, Brace.

COBB, S. 1941. Foundations of neuropsychiatry. Baltimore: Williams & Wilkins.

COGHILL, G. E. 1929. Anatomy and the problem of behavior. New York: Macmillan.

DAVID, M., & ASKANASY, H. 1939. Tumeur sous-frontale bilatérale à symptomatologie affective; étude psychologique après ablation de la tumeur et des deux pôles frontaux. *Encéphale, 1,* 34–41.

ECONOMO, C. VON. 1919. Chronic lethargic encephalitis. *Münch. med. Wschr.,* 1933.

—— 1931. Encephalitis lethargica. (Trans. by K. O. Newman.) London: Oxford University Press.

FINESINGER, J. E., & FINESINGER, G. L. 1937. Modification of the Krasnogorski method for stimulating and measuring the secretion from the parotid glands in human beings. *J. Lab. clin. Med., 23,* 267 ff.

FOERSTER, O., & GAGEL, O. 1933. Ein Fall von Ependymcyste des III Ventrikels. *Z. ges. Neurol. Psychiat., 149,* 312–344.

FOTHERGILL, L. D. 1939. Tentative classification of virus diseases in the central nervous system with the consideration of certain epidemic types of encephalitis. In *Virus and ricketsial diseases; a symposium.* Cambridge: Harvard University Press, 1940. Pp. 617–641.

FRANZ, S. I. 1907. On the functions of the cerebrum; the frontal lobes. *Arch. Psychol., N. Y.,* No. 2.

FREEMAN, W. 1939. Intellectual and emotional changes following prefrontal lobotomy. *Trans. 3rd int. neurol. Congr.* Copenhagen: Munksgaard, 1940. Pp. 773–782.

FREEMAN, W., & WATTS, J. W. 1939. Interpretation of functions of frontal lobe based upon observations in 48 cases of prefrontal lobotomy. *Yale J. Biol. Med., 11,* 527–539.

—— 1941. Frontal lobes and consciousness of self. *Psychosom. Med., 3,* 111–120.

—— 1942. Psychosurgery. Springfield, Ill.: Thomas.

FULTON, J. F. 1938. Physiology of the nervous system. London: Oxford University Press.

GOLDSTEIN, K. 1927. Die Lokalisation in der Grosshirnrinde. In *Handbuch der normalen und pathologischen Physiologie.* Bd. 10. Berlin: Springer. Pp. 600–842.

GOLDSTEIN, K., & REICHMANN, F. 1920. Über praktische und theoretische Ergebnisse aus den Erfahrungen an Hirnschussverletzten. *Ergebn. inn. Med. Kinderheilk., 18,* 406–530.

GRÜNTHAL, E. 1930. Über ein Brüderpaar mit Pickscher Krankheit. *Z. ges. Neurol. Psychiat., 129,* 350–375.

HARROWER-ERICKSON, M. 1940. Personality changes accompanying cerebral lesions; Rorschach studies of patients with cerebral tumors. *Arch. Neurol. Psychiat., Chicago, 43,* 859–890.

HEAD, H. 1926. Aphasia and kindred disorders of speech. (2 Vols.) New York: Macmillan.

HEAD, H., & HOLMES, G. 1912. Sensory disturbances from cerebral lesions. London: John Bale.

HEBB, D. O., & PENFIELD, W. 1940. Human behavior after extensive bilateral removal from the frontal lobes. *Arch. Neurol. Psychiat., Chicago, 44,* 421–438.

HENDRICK, I. 1928. Encephalitis lethargica and the interpretation of mental diseases. *Amer. J. Psychiat., 7,* 989–1015.

HERRICK, C. J. 1926. Brains of rats and men. Chicago: University Chicago Press.

—— 1924. An introduction to neurology. Philadelphia: Saunders.

HOPWOOD, A. T., KIRK, C. C., & KEISER, F. L. 1941. The hereditary factor in mental deficiency. *Amer. J. Psychiat., 98,* 22–28.

JACKSON, J. H. 1931. Selected writings. (Ed. by James Taylor.) London: Hodder and Stoughton.

JACOB, A. 1930. Die Syphilis des Gehirns und seiner Häute. In Bumke, O., *Handbuch der Geisteskrankheiten*. Bd. 11. Berlin: Springer. Pp. 349–417.

JASPER, H. H., SOLOMON, P., & BRADLEY, C. 1938. Electroencephalographic analyses of behavior problem children. *Amer. J. Psychiat., 95,* 641–659.

JELLIFFE, S. E. 1930. Oculogyric crises; psychopathologic considerations of affective states. *Arch. Neurol. Psychiat., Chicago, 23,* 1227–1247.

KAPPERS, C. U. A. 1920. Die vergleichende Anatomie des Nervensystems der Wirbeltiere und des Menschen. Haarlem: Bohn.

KARNOSH, L. J. 1935. Clinical aspects of frontal lobe disease. *J. Indiana med. Assn., 28,* 568–572.

KLEIST, K. 1934. Gehirn-pathologie vornehmlich auf Grund der Kriegserfahrungen. In *Handbuch der ärztlichen Erfahrungen im Weltkriege*. Bd. 4. Leipzig: Barth. Pp. 343–1408.

KLÜVER, H., & BUCY, P. C. 1939. Preliminary analysis of the functions of the temporal lobes in monkeys. *Trans. Amer. neurol. Assn., 65,* 170.

LASHLEY, K. S. 1929. Brain mechanisms and intelligence: a quantitative study of injuries to the brain. Chicago: University Chicago Press.

—— 1941. Coalescence of neurology and psychology. *Proc. Amer. phil. Soc., 84,* 461–470.

LEVIN, M. 1933. Hughlings Jackson's views on mentation. *Arch. Neurol. Psychiat., Chicago, 30,* 848–874.

—— 1936. On the causation of mental symptoms. *J. ment. Sci., 82,* 1–27.

LIDDELL, H. S., & BAYNE, T. L. 1927. Development of experimental neurasthenia in the sheep during the formation of difficult conditioned reflexes. *Amer. J. Physiol., 81,* 494.

LUDWIG, E. 1926. Wilhelm der Zweite. Berlin: E. Rowohet.

MASSERMAN, J. 1941. Is the hypothalamus a center of emotion? *Psychosom. Med., 3,* 3–25.

MEYNERT, T. 1884. Psychiatrie. Wien. W. Braumüller.

—— 1890. Klinische Vorlesungen über Psychiatrie. Wien. W. Braumüller.

MUNCIE, W. 1939. Psychobiology and psychiatry. St. Louis: Mosby.

MUNRO, D. 1938. Cranio-cerebral injuries. London: Oxford Univ. Press.

NIELSEN, J. M. 1936. Agnosia, apraxia, aphasia. *Bull. Los Angeles neurol. Soc., 1,* 11–14.

—— 1941. A textbook of clinical neurology. New York: Hoeber.

PAPEZ, J., BULL, H. B., & STOTLER, W. A. 1940. Cortical softening with atrophy of internal capsule and dorsal thalamus. *Arch. Neurol. Psychiat., Chicago, 44,* 977–990.

PAVLOV, I. P. 1927. Conditioned reflexes, an investigation of the physiological activity of the cerebral cortex. (Trans. and ed. by G. V. Anrep.) London: Oxford Univ. Press.

PENFIELD, W., & ERICKSON, T. C. 1941. Epilepsy and cerebral localization. Springfield, Ill.: Thomas.

PIOTROWSKI, Z. 1937a. Rorschach inkblot method in organic disturbance of the central nervous system. *J. nerv. ment. Dis., 86,* 525–537.

—— 1937b. Rorschach studies of cases with lesions of frontal lobes. *Brit. J. med. Psychol., 17,* 105–118.

RANSON, S. W. 1939. Regulation of body temperature. *Res. Publ. Assn. Res. nerv. ment. Dis., 20,* 342–400.

ROTHSCHILD, D., & SHARP, M. L. 1941. The origin of senile psychoses: neuropathologic factors and factors of a more personal nature. *Dis. nerv. Syst., 2,* 49–54.

RYLANDER, G. 1939. Personality changes after operation on the frontal lobes London: Oxford Univ. Press. Also: *Acta psychiat., Kbh.,* 1939, Suppl. 20.

SHERRINGTON, C. S. 1906. Integrative action of the nervous system. New York: Scribner's.

—— 1933. The brain and its mechanism. London: Oxford Univ. Press.

STEIN, W. E., MARSHALL, C., & NIMS, L. F. 1941. Chemical changes in the brain produced by injury and anoxia. *Amer. J. Psychiat., 132,* 770–775.

SYMONDS, C. P. 1941. The neurological approach to mental disorder. *Proc. R. Soc. Med., 34,* 289–302.

THORNDIKE, E. L. 1941. Mental abilities. *Proc. Amer. phil. Soc., 84,* 503–513.

THURSTONE, L. L. 1938. Primary mental abilities. *Psychomet. Monogr.*, No. 1. Chicago.

VOGT, C., & VOGT, O. 1919. Allgemeinere ergebnisse unserer Hirnforschung. *J. Psychol. Neurol., Lpz., 25, 277.*

VON MONAKOW, C. 1897. Gehirnpathologie. In Nothnagel, II., *Spezielle Pathologie und Therapie,* Bd. 9. Part I. Vienna: Alfred Hölder.

WERNICKE, C. 1900. Grundriss der Psychiatrie. Leipzig: Barth.

―― 1900. Über Hallucinationen, Ratlosigkeit, und Desorientierung in ihren wechselseitigen Beziehungen. *Neurol. Zbl.,* P. 1131 ff.

WERTHAM, F., & WERTHAM, F. 1934. The brain as an organ. New York: Macmillan.

WORCHEL, P., & LYERLY, J. G. 1941. Effects of prefrontol lobotomy on depressed patients. *J. Neurophysiol., 4, 62–67.*

Chapter 19

PHYSIOLOGICAL FACTORS IN BEHAVIOR

By Nathan W. Shock, Ph.D.

We may assume at the outset that alterations in the physiological state of an animal will be followed by changes in its behavior. This is one of the major tenets of physiological psychology, and it is well established. Much experimental work has been directed toward specifying the amount and character of physiological alterations which will be followed by measurable changes in behavior. Interesting and useful results have been obtained in this field, ranging from the effects of reduction in oxygen content of the inspired air on relatively simple perceptual processes to the effect of drug preparations on such complex functions as learning ability. A brief survey of the ambitions, difficulties and results in this area of research will be made in the following sections.

The guiding hope of many investigators has been to demonstrate not only the immediate behavior effects of acute alterations in physiological states but also, more ambitiously, to determine the constant effects of slight, chronic deviations in physiological processes on behavioral characteristics—commonly regarded as personality.

However, there are two stumbling blocks to successful research in this field. The first one is on the psychological side: the more complex a given form of behavior, the harder it is to find adequate measuring devices. For instance, it is much easier to demonstrate the effect of oxygen deprivation in reducing the visual field than it is to demonstrate its effect on reducing the adequacy of judgment. Until more adequate psychological tests of complex mental functions and capacities become available, much of the precision of physiological measurements is wasted. When we consider nonintellectual functions the available measuring devices are even less reliable. Nevertheless, in recent years, new types of measuring techniques have been developed which may prove of great value for the future. Some of these tests have been worked out in connection with studies on the effect of head injuries on mental capacities (Conkey, 1938; Rylander, 1939; Benton and Howell, 1941). Another promising type of test of intellectual capacity in adults has been developed by Wechsler (1941). A third possible measuring technique is the factor analysis approach of Thurstone (1935) and others. Such methods have already been applied to certain aspects of complex social behavior (Horst, 1941) and may prove useful for other aspects of behavior.

The second stumbling block in the way of the worker in this field is the complexity of the interrelationships involved. All too often attempts are made to show that one single physiological factor is responsible for a whole complex behavior pattern. The fallacy of such an approach has been demonstrated by Beach (1937, 1938, 1940) in his studies of maternal and copulatory behavior in the rat. In these studies the interrelationship between endocrine changes in the animal, changes in environmental temperature and, finally, the integrative action of subcortical neural areas in contributing to the complex activity of nest building and maternal behavior is beautifully illustrated. It is this complexity which makes evaluation of many isolated experiments, particularly those designed to demonstrate the relation of endocrines to behavior, especially difficult. To this we shall return in a later section.

In discussing physiological factors in behavior, the implicit assumption is usually made that the kind of behavior observed is somehow the direct result of the physiological state. This general concept dominates, for example, the study of the effects of oxygen deprivation or drugs on behavior. It is assumed, and not without some justification, that the behavior so characteristic of the inebriate is directly related to the amount of alcohol circulating in his blood, or present in his tissues. Similarly, the impairment in handwriting and in such functions as judgment which accompanies exposure to lowered oxygen content of the air is regarded as the result of the depletion of available oxygen in the cells of the nervous system. While the assumption of such direct relations may be most satisfying to investigators trained in physiology and medicine, other more indirect modes of affecting more complex behavior must be considered. For example, social factors only incidentally associated with physiological processes may have far-reaching effects on behavior. The production and excretion of caprylic acid through the sweat glands of the skin is a physiological process which in itself may have little influence on behavior (Eller, 1941). However, accumulation of such substances on the skin, with the resultant odor may have extensive reverberations in the social behavior of the negligent, the horrors of which have been extensively described in, and increased by, modern advertising. This and other examples, such as obesity, or the skin rashes so prevalent at puberty, show that any physiological deviation which sets an individual off as different from his fellows is, potentially, a social determinant of behavior, depending on the way in which other members of the social group react toward the physical or physiological deviation.

To add to our confusion, it has recently been recognized that not only is it possible for physiological changes to alter behavior, but also for psychological events to have physiological reverberations which are both definite and, in turn, exasperating (Kerr, Dalton, and Gliebe, 1937; for a survey of these "psychosomatic" effects, see Chapter 8 by Saul). Anxiety, especially, may set in motion a whole train of physiological processes. This fact was illustrated by the so-called "soldier's heart" of the First World War. In many soldiers who complained of shortness of breath, heart palpitation, precordial pain, tremor, and dizziness—in fact, of most of the classical symptoms of heart disease—no medical examiner could find objective evidence of organic heart damage; hence the concept and diagnosis of "soldier's heart" or "effort syndrome." Similar symptoms also occur in large numbers of civilians, particularly women. Subsequent research showed that anxiety in many persons is a stimulus to excessive breathing. Such persons breathe faster or deeper than normal—beyond their own requirements for carbon dioxide elimination or oxygen absorption. Far from benefiting by this increased respiration, the extra loss of carbon dioxide results in many uncomfortable symptoms —which by the unfortunate victim are often attributed to the heart. Both "anxieties" then, the one precipitating the physiological symptoms and the one caused by their worrisome interpretation, may join in the production of symptoms of cardiac disease (Soley and Shock, 1938).

Another aspect of this concept of anxiety has been shown by Liddell (1938), Anderson and Parmenter (1941), and Maier (1939) in their experiments with animals. A "neurosis" can be induced in sheep, pigs or goats simply by requiring the animals to make sensory discriminations that become more and more difficult—to a point beyond their capacities. Such animals show respiratory and cardiovascular changes that are quite marked in such situations (Anderson and Parmenter, 1941). In human beings, of course, the possibilities for such psychological events to produce physiological changes are even greater, especially where rapid cultural and mechanical development tax adaptability. One of the most important unsolved questions in this field is what determines the organ system in which the physiological symptoms occur. As has been well established, anxiety may precipitate a train of physiological events in one person which will result in cardiovascular symptoms as outlined in the preceding paragraph, while in another person anxiety will result in the symptoms of peptic ulcer (Kerr, Dalton, and Gliebe, 1937). In still others the symptoms may be chiefly respiratory (Sutherland, Wolf, and Kennedy, 1938; Finesinger and Mazik, 1940; Alexander and Saul, 1940). In so far as we assume that the determining factors are physiological in character, this represents a most important area for research.[1]

Physiology of the Central Nervous System

Comparative physiology offers a valid basis for the assumption that the central nervous system of humans has important functions in coordinating and mediating complex types of behavior. Experimental

---

[1] Shock and Erickson (1943) found that in normal adolescents it is not enough to look for the physiological expression of psychological disturbances as caused by specific verbal stimuli in any single system. Whether or not a disturbance has taken place can be ascertained only by the simultaneous use of a battery of physiological tests. Shifts in organ systems in which displacements occur may appear in the same individual during the course of development.

studies of behavior in animals and man have shown that alterations in the physiological state of the nervous system may have widespread effects on behavior. In this section we shall first examine, briefly, experimental studies which have demonstrated the immediate effect of physiological changes in the nervous system on behavior. Secondly, we shall seek information on the long-term effects.

Effects of Anoxia on Behavior.—

IMMEDIATE EFFECTS OF ANOXIA[2]—When the amount of oxygen in the inspired air is reduced, a more or less regular progression of psychological events occurs, the first of which is the loss of critical ability, including the capacity for self-criticism (McFarland, 1937, 1939, 1941). Examples of this may be found in many laboratory experiments. For instance, in an experiment in which Haldane subjected himself to low oxygen concentrations in a chamber, he was sufficiently himself to wish to investigate the color of his lips in the glass, but insufficiently himself to be aware of the fact that he was looking into the back and not the front of the mirror (Barcroft, 1920). Other examples of mental confusion, emotional outbursts and changes in personality have been reported (Barcroft, 1925; Haldane, 1922). In aviation this lack of critical ability due to slight oxygen lack is so well recognized that pilots flying at high altitudes are required to turn on their extra oxygen supply from pressure tanks at a specified altitude—whether they think they need it or not. Leedham (1938) describes an interesting reaction to oxygen want in an airplane pilot. Each day, before daylight, the pilot made a routine flight to an altitude of 12,000 feet for weather observations. On the particular flight described, the altimeter was in error, so that the actual altitude attained was 22,500 feet when the altimeter read only 12,500 feet. The pilot reported weakness, dizziness, and slight confusion. The altitude record showed repeated tail-spins, followed by repeated climbs over a period of three hours, even after the emergency gasoline supply had to be turned on. Although the pilot reported emotional upset and frustration at being unable, as he thought, to attain an altitude of over 12,500 feet, at no time did he attribute his symptoms of dizziness, vocal incoordination, and constriction of visual field, to oxygen lack. Such clinical reports of lack of judgment under lowered oxygen intake more strikingly demonstrate the actual impairment than do objective tests in controlled laboratory situations, for which adequate tests of judgment have yet to be derived (Goldie, 1941).

With this loss in judgment and incapacity for self-criticism during anoxia, feelings of exhilaration and of well-being, strikingly similar to the early stages of alcoholic intoxication, are frequently reported (McFarland, 1939). As anoxia progresses, impairment is frequently reported in many other intellectual processes such as in the speed and accuracy

---

[2] For a recent review of the physiological effects of anoxia, see Van Liere (1942).

in computation (Barach, McFarland, and Seitz, 1937) and in the powers of attention and concentration (McFarland, 1939). Mental test scores also decline (Kranes, 1937). However, it is only with rather severe degrees of anoxia that defects in motor performance of habitual tasks or in sensory processes appear. Handwriting is one of the first neuromuscular functions affected; tremor, ataxia, changes in size of letters, omissions, and repetitious perseveration are reported (McFarland, 1939; Goldie, 1941). In reading, the eyes fixate longer and more frequently as the oxygen intake is diminished (McFarland, Evans, and Halperin, 1941). Similarly, in tests such as color naming, there is an increase in the length and frequency of mental blocks such as occur in mental fatigue (Bills, 1937). As the severity of anoxia further increases, perception is impaired: first vision, then hearing (McFarland, 1939). Ultimately, when the blood leaving the brain is less than 24% saturated with oxygen, consciousness is lost (Lennox, Gibbs, and Gibbs, 1935). Beyond this point there occurs a loss of motor control that causes clonic and tonic contractions.

Some differences of opinion exist as to the ultimate effect of repeated exposures to anoxia. J. B. S. Haldane (1922) originally contended that "anoxemia not only stops the machine, but wrecks the machinery." Barcroft (1920) believes, however, that "no degree of anoxia which produces a less effect than that of complete unconsciousness leaves anything more than the most transient effects; if the anoxia be pushed to the point at which the subject is within a measurable distance of death the results may take days or weeks to get over." Recent studies, however, all emphasize the fact that permanent damage by anoxia to nervous tissue is possible (Van Liere, 1942). Armstrong (1939) has described a group of symptoms consisting of gastric disturbances, nervous irritability, mental fatigue, insomnia, and increased motor activity which develop in airplane pilots. This condition of "aeroneurosis" has been attributed to the cumulative effect of repeated exposure to the lowered oxygen tensions encountered in flight, but its exact etiology is unknown. Armstrong and Heim (1938) have shown that in rabbits, daily exposure to oxygen tensions low enough to produce coma reduced their capacity to withstand low oxygen and finally resulted in death. When Shock and Scow (1942) subjected rats repeatedly to reduced oxygen tensions, the rats' abilities to discriminate between upright and inverted triangles diminished.

Repeated exposures to anoxia are potentially hazardous, and further work is necessary to determine the degree of anoxia which may be experienced repeatedly without danger of permanent damage to the nervous system.

SOME PERMANENT EFFECTS OF ANOXIA.—Thorner and Lewy (1940) have reported structural changes in the brain involving actual destruction of nerve cells in animals repeatedly subjected to only mild anoxia. The permanent and devastating effects of severe anoxia on the central nervous system are illustrated by clinical reports of victims of carbon monoxide poisoning. Carbon monoxide exerts its toxic effects in the organism by interfering with the normal transport of oxygen to the tissues (Yant, *et al.,* 1934). When carbon monoxide is present in the air breathed, it combines with the hemoglobin of the blood and forms a stable compound which prevents the combination of hemoglobin with oxygen. Thus extreme and persisting degrees of anoxia may be produced in the tissues. Since the body is unable to store oxygen, and since the central nervous system, of all tissues, is most susceptible to oxygen lack, unconsciousness quickly ensues. Thus the physiological effects of carbon monoxide poisoning are those of anoxia. In many case studies in which persons have been rendered unconscious by carbon monoxide, but have subsequently been revived, varying degrees of mental impairment are reported (Beck, 1937; Nichols and Keller, 1937; Last and Meyer, 1932; Cohen, 1936; Raskin and Mullaney, 1940). It is significant to note that often the victim will appear normal after resuscitation, but loss of memory, increased irritability, and even severe motor paralyses may develop after several days or weeks (Raskin and Mullaney, 1940). In a few cases followed to autopsy, actual destruction of brain tissue has been established. The extent of personality change is no doubt related to the particular brain areas involved and to the relative amount of tissue destroyed.

In recent years unfortunate accidents have occasionally occurred in the use of nitrous oxide as an anaesthetic (Lowenberg and Zbinden, 1938; O'Brien and Steegmann, 1938). Loss of memory, and even motor involvement have followed such slight operations as removal of birthmarks, cysts, or tonsils. Courville (1936) attributes these accidents to the anoxia which may easily occur where deep anaesthesia is attempted, since it may be necessary for the patient to breathe 90% nitrous oxide, thus reducing the oxygen content of the inspired gas mixture to 10%. Examination of numerous clinical reports, however, leads to the suspicion that individuals who show mental impairment after nitrous oxide anaesthesia are those who have been subjected to anoxia on several occasions, and in whom the anoxia may have been particularly severe (Soley and Jump, 1939).

Severe anoxia at birth may result in brain damage with attendant motor disturbances which often persist throughout life and markedly alter personal characteristics. The relation between head injury during birth and subsequent mental development has received a great deal of discussion, which has generated more heat than light. Birth injuries may be an important factor in the production of many motor disturbances. Where frank head injury has occurred from instrumental deliveries, the etiology is clear. Eastman (1936b), for instance, has collected statistics showing that a large proportion of deaths within the first month after birth can be traced to head injuries of varying degree Birth, however, may also subject the infant to severe anoxia (Eastman, 1936a), and Schriber (1938, 1939) has offered striking evidence of the relation between anoxia at birth and subsequent mental retardation. When he examined the birth records of 252 mentally defective children for whom there was no history of inherited defect, infection, or trauma unassociated with birth, he found that 76% of these cases had a history of asphyxia at birth. Experiments with guinea pigs have shown that neonatal asphyxia may induce irreparable destruction of regions of the brain, and in such animals behavioral changes and impaired ability to learn simple mazes were observed (Windle and Becker, 1942). Since many of the drugs and anaesthetic agents used to reduce the mother's pain at birth depress respiration in the fetus and thereby increase the degree of anoxia, controlled studies of the effects of birth anoxia on subsequent behavioral development should have great practical significance.[3]

The use of such heroic measures as insulin or metrazol convulsions in the treatment of the psychoses (for their description, see Chapter 35 by Appel) has focused attention on the role of cerebral anoxia in these procedures (Gellhorn, 1938). The original assumption that metrazol produced its effects because of anoxia of the brain alone has not been confirmed in recent work (Libet, Fazekas, and Himwich, 1940), but there is evidence that destruction of the brain tissue ensues. The use of low oxygen concentrations has also been tried in the treatment of schizophrenics, but the results have not been promising (Fraser and Reitmann, 1939). At any rate psychiatrists seem justified in being sceptical of therapeutic devices which are known to produce physiological damage of brain tissues (Gildea and Cobb, 1930).

LONG-CONTINUED ANOXIA.—A low-grade tissue anoxia may persist over a period of years in persons suffering from anemia. Mental changes such as apathy, indolence, decreased capacity for work, melancholia, or even dementia have been observed in cases with this disease, but a causal relation with anoxia is far from established (Hunt, 1934; Schou, 1933). Clinical cases have also been reported in which a cure of anemia was followed by disappearance of the psychosis (Handelsman, 1933).

In people living at high altitudes for long periods of time, physiological adjustments take place which tend to raise the oxygen concentration in their tissues. These compensatory factors are not equally effective in all individuals. As a result, many individuals living at high altitude develop the symptoms which are attributed to chronic anoxia. Some of these individuals become irritable and are unable to get along with their fellows (McFarland, 1937). They may show a mild mental depression and often lack the ability to concentrate. They feel that mental tasks become more difficult, and their errors become more frequent (Barcroft, 1925).

Many of the psychological characteristics of senescence, such as loss of memory, irritability, etc., are similar to the effects of low oxygen in younger individuals. This similarity may be based on the universal his-

---

[3] In this connection, see also Ribble's discussion of the importance of anoxia at birth and in early development (Chapter 20).

tological finding of increased fibrin and collagen in the tissues of aged animals. With this increase of inert substance within the cells, the density of the medium through which oxygen must diffuse to reach the functional protoplasm is greatly increased. Thus, cells in the aged are actually farther removed from their sources of oxygen than are cells in young animals. The hypothesis that mental deteriorioration in the aged is partly a result of persistent anoxia of cells of the central nervous system thus is an attractive one which should be experimentally tested.

Effect of Blood Sugar Levels on Behavior.—

IMMEDIATE EFFECTS OF CHANGES IN BLOOD SUGAR.—As is the case in anoxia, when the sugar content of the blood drops below a critical level, loss of consciousness occurs. The explanation is that nervous tissue is unable to maintain its normal metabolism in the absence of adequate carbohydrates (glucose) and is thus particularly sensitive to decreased glucose concentrations. Here, too, experimental studies have shown that more complex mental functions, such as association and memory, suffer first (see review by Shock, 1939). The time required for the performance of simple mental tests, such as mental calculations, increases as does the number of errors. Unfortunately, precise estimates of the blood sugar levels at which impairment of mental function begins have not been made.

In rats, a slight reduction in the blood sugar level produced by insulin injections reduces the time required to establish a conditioned response (Heron and Skinner, 1937; Wentink, 1938). This increase in the rate of learning may be the effect of increasing the hunger drive of the animal rather than the effect of altering the amount of glucose available to its nervous system. When the blood sugar level was raised in animals by the injection of epinephrine, rats, previously trained to press a lever to obtain food, showed a 25% to 30% decrement in the rate of response (Heron and Skinner, 1937; Wentink, 1938). These results are in accord with the inhibition of gastric motility produced by epinephrine, which may thus reduce the hunger stimuli in the experimental animals. In human subjects intramuscular injections of epinephrine have been followed by decreased performance in substitution tests, free association, mental calculations and color naming tests, but speed of tapping and muscle strength were improved (Jersild and Thomas, 1931). Akimov (1936), on the other hand, has reported an acceleration in maze learning in rats following the injection of small doses of epinephrine.

Clinically most outstanding are the alterations in mood, increased irritability, and vague feelings of apprehension which are reported in many subjects when the blood sugar level is diminished (Graham and Womack, 1933). All these observed changes, in both general behavior and specific mental performance, may be reversed by raising the blood sugar level.

When extremely low blood sugar levels are repeatedly induced with convulsions, as is the case in insulin shock therapy for schizophrenia, permanent damage may result to cells in the central nervous system (Baker, 1939). Gellhorn (1941, 1943) has shown in animals that hypoglycemia has more severe effects on the cerebral cortex than on the hypothalamus or the medulla, and that the effects of hypoglycemia and anoxia are additive. Both conditions lead to a general decrease in cortical activity.

The development of the electroencephalogram as an index of cortical activity has produced additional evidence of the depressing effect of low blood sugar levels on the central nervous system. Both in the case of low oxygen and of blood glucose levels below 50 mg. per cent, the alpha waves become less frequent and slower waves with larger potentials (delta waves) appear (Lennox, Gibbs and Gibbs, 1938). In contrast to this, a moderate and temporary increase in blood sugar does not seem to influence cerebral function as measured by the electroencephalogram (see Chapter 34 by Lindsley).

EFFECT OF CONTINUED HYPO- OR HYPERGLYCEMIA.—Our chief sources of information about the possible effects of persistent low blood sugar levels are clinical reports of such changes in behavior as disturbances of speech, loss of memory, listlessness, and emotional instability in patients suffering from tumors of the islet of Langerhans (Tedstrom, 1934). Since these symptoms disappear in cases whose tumors are surgically removed, which removal restores blood sugar to normal levels, there is no evidence of permanent damage to the nervous system. Powell (1936) has reported a case of low blood sugar level whose unsatisfactory school performance was improved by increasing the carbohydrate intake.

Studies of the behavior of diabetic patients provide some information concerning the effects of prolonged blood sugar levels above normal. Boudreau (1937) has reported cases in which mental confusion was apparently associated with diabetic hyperglycemia. Joslin's (1937) original clinical observation that diabetic children exhibit superior intelligence has not been confirmed by later studies in which socio-economic factors have been more adequately controlled. Brown (1938) compared the mental test scores of 60 diabetic children with those of 28 of their normal siblings and found no differences. The social and emotional adjustments of diabetic children, however, are often inadequate. Mc-Gaven, et al. (1940) found that 32 of the 49 diabetic children they carefully interviewed and tested in their clinic were "maladjusted," but the diabetes itself was not the only factor. Physical and intellectual defects and social problems all contributed to their maladjustment. Children who developed diabetes at an early age accepted the handicap as a part of growing up with less emotional upset than did children who developed the disease after the age of seven or eight years.

From studies of the curves of blood sugar tolerance in many psychotic patients, it has been found that depressive mental states are generally associated with the sort of curve found in diabetics, which represents an inability of the body to absorb administered glucose from the blood stream quickly. In a most illuminating experiment on a patient who passed through several cycles of depression (Raphael, Ferguson, and Searle, 1928), a diabetic type of curve was found in periods of depression, while the utilization of carbohydrates approached normal when the mental state improved. From this and similar studies, it appears that depressed function of the vegetative processes involved in carbohydrate metabolism is associated with mental depressions, but no experiments have been made that enable one to differentiate cause and effect in this association.

As was the case for anoxia, the immediate effects of extremely low blood sugar levels on behavior have been experimentally demonstrated, but the effects of slight and persistent reduction of blood sugar can only be inferred from clinical reports. This also represents a fertile field for future investigation. The so-called "four o'clock" slump in work output and the reports of anxiety, apprehension, and irritability in patients with lowered blood sugar require careful quantitative investigation before useful conclusions can be drawn.

Acid-base Balance of the Blood.—The belief that changes in the acid-base equilibrium of the blood may have a bearing on behavior originates from the clinical observation of two behavioral extremes: first, tetany as observed under conditions of increased alkalinity, where the nervous system responds indiscriminately with maximum motor response to almost any internal or external stimulus; and secondly, coma as observed in the extremely acid conditions of diabetes and nephritis, where the nervous system does not respond to any stimuli.

Effect of Increased Alkalinity of the Blood.—Physiological studies on animals show that under conditions of increased alkalinity, muscles and nerves are more readily excited than when subjected to acid environments. Studies on human beings have not offered clear cut results on the relation between acid base balance and complex behavior (see review by Shock, 1941), although preliminary results of several authors tend toward the assumption that "emotionally unstable" or "excitable" individuals tend to secrete an alkaline saliva and urine. The widely quoted results of Ludlum (1918), Starr (1922), and Rich (1928) have led to the additional assumption that the alkalinity in excitable persons is a metabolic characteristic of the individual which in part determines his excitability. However, from the data obtained in these studies (pH determinations on saliva; titratable acidity in the urine) it is impossible to be certain that the alkalinity is associated with true individual metabolic differences. Hamilton and Shock (1936) correlated hydrogen ion content (acidity) and the bicarbonate content of the blood with a number of personality measures in 112 male college freshmen. The correlations found led to the conclusion that persons who were "unadjusted," "excitable," "nervous," or "introverted," rendered their blood more alkaline by changes in respiration when they were confronted with such new situations as being measured in the nude or having blood samples withdrawn. In other words, the physiological displacement toward the alkaline side found in excitable individuals was a part of the general picture of increased excitability rather than its cause.

Slight displacements of the acid-base equilibrium toward the alkaline side are associated with self reports of well-being (Shock, 1930), while feelings of emotional depression are reported after slight displacements toward the acid side (Hoff, 1935; Haldane, et al., 1928). Some evidence has been presented for increased mental performance, particularly in children, following the ingestion of small doses of disodium hydrogen phosphate, which may have a slight alkalinizing effect (see review by Shock, 1941)

Alkalinity of the blood may also be markedly increased by the loss of carbon dioxide brought about by increased respiration (Shock and Hastings, 1935). The increase in neuromuscular excitability found under such circumstances may easily be experienced by the reader if he will exhale forcibly about 30 times a minute for one or two minutes. The dizziness, the feeling of muscular tenseness about the mouth, and the contracture of the fingers are all physiological results of the increased alkalinity which has been produced by excessive loss of carbon dioxide through the lungs. Experimental studies show as the results of hyperventilation: diminished sensory acuity (Gellhorn and Spiesman, 1935a, 1935b), increased sensory latent periods, decreased sensitivity to pain, decreased speed in mental calculations, idiosyncrasy of responses to association words (Gellhorn and Kraines, 1937) and even amnesia. Since loss of CO_2 produces vaso-constriction of the blood vessels of the brain (Cobb and Fremont-Smith, 1931); Wolff and Lennox, 1930), it is believed that many of these mental effects of carbon dioxide loss should be attributed to cerebral anoxia (Gellhorn, 1936). This hypothesis is supported by the increased mental performance possible under low oxygen tension when small amounts of carbon dioxide (5%) are added to the inspired air. The added carbon dioxide produces a vaso-dilatation in the brain with increased blood flow and greater delivery of oxygen.

Patients suffering from anxiety and such physical symptoms as cardiac palpitation, nausea, sense of suffocation and gastric pain, which can be attributed to the periodic hyperventilation frequently associated with anxiety, show certain psychological characteristics. If psychotherapy can determine the source of anxiety and resolve it, hyperventilation and the associated physiological symptoms disappear. Spontaneous alleviation of anxiety or the removal of its source also results in a cure of the physiological symptoms mentioned (Kerr, Gliebe, Soley, and Shock, 1939).

EFFECT OF INCREASED BLOOD ACIDITY.—That an increased amount of carbon dioxide has a narcotic effect on nerve and muscle has long been known. The increase of the carbon dioxide concentration in inspired air to 20–30% will produce anaesthesia. Loevenhart, Lorenz and Waters (1929) were able to produce intervals of mental lucidity in resistive, mute, catatonic, schizophrenic patients fifteen to twenty minutes after the administration for three to five minutes of 20–40% carbon dioxide. Because of the rapidity with which the blood returns to normal acid-base balance after carbon dioxide has been administered (Shock and Hastings, 1935), it is doubtful that the cerebral stimulation observed can be attributed to alterations in the acid-base balance. Later experiments by d'Elseaux and Solomon (1933) lend support to the hypothesis that the heightened carbon dioxide concentration itself is not the effective stimulus, for any intense stimulus which the patient regarded as a threat to his life caused the same effect. For instance, the above authors found similar cerebral stimulation in catatonics when low oxygen concentrations, large doses of sodium bicarbonate, or metrazol were administered.

Extensive displacement of the acid-base equilibrium in either direction from the norm will result in impaired mental function and in loss of consciousness. However, slight increases in alkalinity tend to increase motor reactivity to stimuli, particularly at the reflex level, but to decrease functions involving higher levels of the central nervous system. A slight decrease in alkalinity, or increase in carbonic acid, of the blood may facilitate higher mental processes.

Effects of Disease Processes on Behavior.—Disease processes may affect behavior not only directly by virtue of physiological processes within the body, as occurs in encephalitis, but also by causing the development of attitudes and habits of dependency and lack of self-sufficiency which may become established during the course of almost any protracted or debilitant illness. The psychological effects of severe illness, particularly in growing children, deserve careful attention as an aid in understanding adult behavior. Too few studies of this aspect of illness have been made (for a few, see Chapter 21 by Murphy).

Diseases of the Nervous System.[4]—Of the diseases known to produce alterations in behavior, encephalitis has received the most attention from psychiatrists and psychologists because of the perplexing anti- or asocial behavior which frequently appears in children suffering its ravages. The changes in conduct characterized by exaggeration of instinctive, affectionate, or aggressive expressions, overactivity, and inability to inhibit impulsive actions, persist long after the infectious process has disappeared (Bender, 1940). This behavior may be associated with some degree of mental deterioration and retardation in development, particularly in younger children, but the intellectual capacity is

---

[4] In connection with the effects of cerebral lesions on personal behavior, see especially Chapter 18 by S. Cobb, and for their effects on various kinds of test performance, see also Chapter 32 by Hunt and Cofer.

usually not greatly affected (Brown, Jenkins, and Cisler, 1938). Prognosis in such cases is poor, even when special schooling and training are provided. Bond and Smith (1935) report good results in only 20 out of 76 post-encephalitics receiving special schooling. Thirty-three of the 76 cases appeared in State Hospitals within a ten-year period. The persistence of abnormal behavior in such cases has led to the assumption that irreversible organic changes in the brain have been produced by the infection, but macroscopic and microscopic studies of the brain have failed to demonstrate the site or nature of such lesions.

Poliomyelitis (or infantile paralysis) is a disease which specifically attacks the cells of the anterior horn of the spinal cord, thus producing the well-known loss of motor function. No evidence has been found for impairment of higher intellectual functions in such patients (Gordon, Roberts, and Griffiths, 1939). The degree of neural involvement will obviously determine changes in motor behavior of such patients. Studies of such patients indicate that the attitude of parents and associates toward the disability produced by the disease has an important influence on the subsequent personality characteristics of the patient. Thus, again, the importance of the reaction of others in the social environment to a physiological (or anatomical) deviation is found to be of extreme importance for behavior.

INFECTIOUS DISEASES WITHOUT DIRECT EFFECTS ON THE NERVOUS SYSTEM.—The effect of other infectious diseases on mental development and behavior are difficult to evaluate because of possible uncontrolled selective factors. Even though a positive relationship may be demonstrated between incidence of syphilis and mental defect we cannot be sure to what extent this is due to the tendency for duller individuals to expose themselves to infection and to neglect adequate prophylactic measures, rather than to the deleterious effect of the disease on mental development (Shock and Jones, 1942). By comparing Binet IQ of syphilitic children with their nonsyphilitic sibs, Jenkins, Brown, and Cisler (1940) have minimized this selective error. Their results led to the conclusion that syphilis in childhood has a retarding influence on mental development. In such congenital syphilitic children the retardation is minimized with early and intensive treatment of the disease (Kiss and Rajka, 1934).

Moorman (1940) has assembled a great deal of semi-scientific and popular opinions in support of his thesis that the tuberculosis bacillus produces a substance which excites the central nervous system and produces symptoms of genius. This hypothesis is less attractive than "the simpler assumption that greater mental output in tuberculous patients (if it exists) is a result of heightened motivation in the face of physical handicaps and enforced physical inactivity" (Shock and Jones, 1942).

NON-INFECTIOUS DISEASES.—The clinical impression that allergic children are more intelligent than normal has not received confirmation in quantitative studies (Piness, Miller, and Sullivan, 1937). Riess and de Cillis (1940) reported greater "ascendance" among 139 allergic children than among 117 normal children to whom personality questionnaires were administered. They also reported small statistically insignificant increases in extraversion and in emotional instability for the allergic group. These results were not confirmed by Chobat, *et al.* (1939) who studied a group of 20 girls and 45 boys and concluded that "allergic children show all degrees of ascendancy and submission, extraversion and introversion, the tendency being slightly toward submission and introversion for the group as a whole." It is thus doubtful whether any real differences in intellectual or personality traits exist between allergic and nonallergic children.

Although diseases with their site of focus within the nervous system often result in alteration of behavior and mental capacities, present information is still inadequate to predict the direction or degree of their effect on behavior. Once established, abnormal behavior is extremely difficult to eradicate. While hereditary syphilis may interfere with mental development in young children if left untreated, there is no good evidence that diabetes, tuberculosis, heart disease, or allergy causes significant alterations in behavior because of their physiological effects. On the other hand, any disease process may have profound effects on behavior by influencing the social environment of the patient. One might say that it is more the effect of the child's allergy on the parent than the physiological effect of the allergy on himself that influences his personal development.

Nutritional Factors in Behavior

The young science of nutrition has brought to light the importance of adequate diet for normal growth and development. Although a certain minimum food intake is required for adequate growth and development, qualitative deficiencies in diet may be even more potent in retarding development. The importance of adequate vitamin intake for the growing animal cannot be minimized. Only recently has the importance of nutrition in maintaining adequate physiological and psychological functions in the adult been recognized (Sebrell, 1940). Future research will indicate the importance of adequate nutrition in maintaining normal functional capacities in the total population.

Special Diets.—We may dismiss as unworthy of serious comment the claims of diet faddists for the effects of certain foods on human temperament. An example of such uncontrolled fantasy is the claim (Braune, 1935) that people who follow a meatless diet are more peaceable, less irritable, and have greater self-control than those who consume meat. No experimental or clinical evidence of correlation between behavior and the consumption (or exclusion) of any specific food has yet been demonstrated.

Restriction of Food Intake.—Hunger, as a motivating stimulus for behavior, has received extensive treatment in the psychological literature. The theory has grown up around animal experimentation, and, when transferred to human behavior, the generalizations are often far-fetched at best, even for newborn infants. The changes in behavior and in mental performance with starvation are slight in human beings subjected to standardized tests (Glaze, 1928). In fact, some enthusiasts have concluded that mental efficiency is improved during short periods of total fasting and recovery (Hoelzel, 1938). While it is probable that the diet consumed by the average American adult contains a greater caloric value than is necessary or even desirable, the quantitative measurements of increased mental efficiency after fasting have not been made on a large enough sample to permit valid generalizations. Starvation in young animals produces retardation of the rate of development as measured by time of eruption of teeth, bone ossification, and rate of elimination of errors in a water T-maze (Biel, 1939). No evidence of permanent damage was found, since, at maturity, the learning capacity of the starved animals was equal to, if not slightly superior to that of normal animals.

In children low positive correlations between nutritional state and intelligence test scores have been reported (see review by Shock, 1939). These results cannot be interpreted, however, for they usually refer to children from marginal economic groups where poor genetic stock as well as gross inadequacies of both quality and quantity of diet complicate the picture.

Some of the difficulties in studies of the effect of diet on human behavior are illustrated in the study by Seymour and Whitaker (1938). Fifty underprivileged children six and one-half years of age were divided into two groups with the same average intelligence. The experimental group was provided at school with breakfast of fruit juice, porridge made with bread, butter, and cocoa made with milk. The control group had their usual inadequate breakfast of bread and tea at home. The two groups were taught in the same class throughout the experimental period of eight weeks. During this time arithmetic and English grades showed 7–10% more gain in the experimental than in the control group. The output of the experimental group on standard tests showed more improvement than did that of the controls. Differences in output did not become apparent until the tenth day of the experiment, and they diminished again within one week after the breakfasts were discontinued. Although one is tempted to conclude that the improvement in mental performance was due specifically to the improvement in nutrition, it is difficult to know to what extent the experimental group may have been responding with better rapport and with stronger positive motivation to the special attention received.

Excessive Food Intake.—The results of overeating may range from a "pleasing plumpness" to revolting fatness. Although much has been written about the endocrine basis of obesity, the stark physiological fact remains that the accumulation of fat can take place only when the caloric intake is in excess of the energy used. Changes in appetite, changes in rate of utilization of the food ingested, or changes in activity may have their ultimate basis in endocrine dysfunction. For instance, the frequent increase in weight of women following castration is partly due to the reduction in metabolism and physical activity due to removal of the sex glands coupled with the same diet as was consumed before operation. This combination of circumstances appears normally at the menopause in women, when obesity is also frequent. In obese children, Bruch (1940, 1941a, 1941b) has found that the excessive eating may be the child's overcompensation for unconscious parental rejection or for feelings of insecurity. In such patients endocrine therapy failed to correct the obesity.

Effects of Vitamins on Behavior.—The effect of vitamin deficiencies on behavior is one of the most promising fields of research. At present great hiatuses exist between the results of rigorously controlled experiments on animals and the clinical reports of the effects of vitamin administrations in human beings. Because of the known physiological effects of vitamins of the B group on the nervous system, and their importance in maintaining normal cellular oxidation (Peters, 1936; Wortis, 1941), it is reasonable to suppose that their lack might hinder proper functioning of the brain by interfering with the utilization of dextrose, its essential food stuff. In an attempt to test such a hypothesis O'Shea and Elsom (1942) maintained four women, aged 43 to 65 years, on a low vitamin B intake for from 62 to 98 days. No diminution in general intelligence scores, reasoning ability, or speed of hand-eye coordination was observed, but scores on the Porteus maze test decreased and later improved after vitamin B_1 (thiamine or yeast) therapy. On the basis of these results these investigators concluded that foresight and judgment are impaired by vitamin B deficiency. These experiments should be repeated with a larger number of younger subjects and with other psychological tests.

Physical fitness and speed of recovery after physical exertion diminished within a week in thirteen young men kept on a diet deficient in vitamin B while doing manual labor (Johnson, et al., 1942). These symptoms do not appear so quickly in sedentary workers (Egaña, et al., 1942). Most of the subjects in these studies complained of being fatigued easily, of loss of ambition, and of inefficiency in their daily work. A similar reduction in the capacity for work with generalized weakness was found in four women maintained on a low intake of vitamin B_1 for from ten to fourteen weeks (Williams, et al., 1940).

In human beings, dietary deficiency in vitamin A produces an inability for rapid visual adaptation to faint illumination called "night blindness." This visual defect is associated with failure to resynthesize the visual purple of the retina. After 35 days of vitamin A deprivation, the minimum human threshold for the cones may be increased by three-fold and that of the rods by nine-fold. Some investigators have reported the restoration of normal thresholds of sensitivity in less than one hour after the administration of B carotene, the precursor of vitamin A (Hecht and Mandelbaum, 1940). Such striking results have not been confirmed by others (Olmsted, 1941). Retinal sensitivity appears to increase somewhat when large amounts of B-carotene are administered or when raw carrots are added to the diet. These findings have important practical applications in night flying (Armstrong, 1939). Extreme deficiencies of vitamin A may also produce lesions of the cochlea which reduce auditory sensitivity in puppies (Melanby, 1938) but not in rabbits (Lawrence, 1941).

In human beings it is dangerous to induce extreme degrees of vitamin deficiency, and, in addition, the control of other factors is extremely difficult. Hence, our most illuminating experiments on the effects of vitamins on behavior have been made on animals. Some impairment of learning ability with low vitamin B intake has been found (see reviews by Shock, 1939, and by Shock and Jones, 1942). Many of the early experiments in this field, however, suffered from the criticism that the vitamin deficient animals suffered from poor coordination due to poor physical condition and from poor appetite so that hunger was not an effective motivation in the learning experiments. Wickens and Biel (1940) avoided most of this difficulty by using the eyelid response to a puff of air as their criterion of learning ability. Vitamin B deficient animals were significantly slower in acquiring this conditioned response than were animals on normal diet. Furthermore, both vitamin B_1 deficiency and inanition have been found to be important contributing factors to increased susceptibility of rats to convulsive seizures induced by high pitched sounds (Patton, 1941; Patton and Karn, 1941; Patton, Karn, and King, 1941). Diets low in magnesium have also been shown to sensitize rats to this "audiogenic seizure" (Kleiber, et al., 1941; for a description of this epileptoid-like seizure and of the factors related to its incidence, see Chapter 13 by Finger).

Other important implications for the effects of diet on behavior are found in clinical observations. One of the symptoms of even slight vitamin B deficiency in human subjects is their increased irritability, moodiness, lack of cooperation and "meanness" (Williams, et al., 1941 and 1942; Egaña, et al., 1942; Johnson, et al., 1942). With more severe B-vitamin deficiency such mental states as apathy, depression, and emotional instability have often been observed. A most striking study is that of Williams, et al. (1942) who restricted the B-vitamin (thiamin) intake of eleven women to .45 mg. daily, which is an amount little, if any, below that obtained in many American diets. Within six or eight weeks the subjects began to show such symptoms of emotional instability as irritability, moodiness, quarrelsomeness, lack of cooperation, and vague fears progressing to agitation and mental depression. When thiamin was restored to their diets, or even when riboflavin was reduced in the presence of adequate thiamin, no such symptoms were observed. This experiment was made on the inmates of an institution for mental patients who had manifested no physical or emotional abnormalities for from eight to twelve weeks. It is to be hoped that a similar study will be made on a noninstitutional population so as to allay any suspicion that the results were due to the selection of subjects prone to such behavior.

Since the effects of vitamin deficiencies on behavior have been demonstrated both experimentally and clinically, the question of whether beneficial effects on either performance or development can be produced by the administration of amounts of vitamins grossly in excess of the known physiological needs arises. Colby, et al. (1937), reported an acceleration in the development of such behavioral landmarks as visual pursuit, sustained visual fixation, eye-hand coordination and manual prehension in 25 infants artificially fed supplementary vitamin B. The superiority of the experimental group had disappeared, however, by the time the children were one year old. Fatigue of the central nervous system, as measured by the frequency at which the perceived flicker of a regularly intermittent light disappears, is reduced by the administration of extra vitamin B, i.e., fusion occurs at a higher rate of intermittent stimulation (Simonson, et al., 1942). Although Droese (1941) reported an increase in maximal work output from the addition of vitamin B_1 to an already adequate diet, other investigators have failed to find such effects on the recovery from voluntary muscular fatigue (Foltz, Ivy, and Baborka, 1942). Neither vitamin B nor C, when increased in the diet, improved the muscular endurance, resistance to fatigue, or recovery from exertion in healthy young adults (Keys and Henschel, 1942; Simonson, et al., 1942).

In psychotics the administration of vitamin concentrates has resulted in improved appetite and physical condition and frequently in an improvement in the mental condition itself (Cleckley, Sydenstricker, and Gieslin, 1939; Lewald and Alexander, 1939; Jolliffe, 1939, 1941, 1942; Sydenstricker and Cleckley, 1941; Aring, 1943). Sydenstricker and Cleckley (1941) administered nicotinic acid to 38 patients who were in stuporous states or in active psychoses but who lacked the usual clinical signs of pellagra. All showed prompt and very impressive improvement, often within 24 hours. Although the brains of pellagrins have shown a lowered utilization of oxygen (Himwich, Spies, Fazekas, and Nesin, 1940), the beneficial effects of nicotinic acid may be due to the dilation of cerebral arterioles (Aring, et al., 1941) rather than to a correction of an actual state of deficiency. Since the amide of nicotinic acid is equally effective in correcting vitamin deficiency, but has no vasodilator effect (Aring, et al., 1941), the amide should be administered to psychotics in order to distinguish between the metabolic and the circulatory effects of nicotinic acid. The studies in which vitamin administrations have appeared effective in improving the mental status of psychotic patients have been reviewed by Jolliffe (1941), by Morbury (1940), and by Aring (1943).

At the present time no evidence available indicates a causal relationship between any specific vitamin and specific mental symptoms. For instance, numerous workers (Spies, *et al.,* 1940; Jolliffe, 1941; Sebrell and Butler, 1939) who have treated pellagrins with nicotinic acid have observed improvement in the alimentary symptoms and in the skin lesions, without improvement in: the pain of the calves, the numbness of the extremities, the weakness, the difficulty of walking, the dizziness, the lassitude, the fatigue, the increased irritability to light and noise, the loss of memory, the sleeplessness, and the general irritability. Administrations of thiamin were followed by relief from many of these neuropathic signs. Nevertheless, many patients who improved following treatment with nicotinic acid and thiamin, developed lesions characteristic of riboflavin deficiency, and these lesions disappeared following administrations of adequate amounts of riboflavin (Sebrell and Butler, 1939). In still other patients these symptoms of extreme nervousness, insomnia, and irritability were not relieved until vitamin B_6 (pyridoxin) was administered (Spies and Ashe, 1939).

Although the recent advances in our knowledge of the chemical nature and the biological importance of vitamins have been rapid and startling, exaggerated claims have too frequently appeared in print, and under the names of responsible investigators who should know better. Statements that vitamin feeding can overcome feeblemindness are wishful, for there is room for considerable doubt that vitamin administrations can compensate for a niggardly heredity. So also are statements that vitamin feeding is potentially capable of fostering intelligence or morality (R. J. Williams, 1942). Such statements simply supply the wherewithal for unscrupulous advertising.

In the words of Professor A. J. Carlson:

> When we have vitamins that prevent dishonesty and injustice, the millennium will have come. But as I read and listen to the modern propaganda for vitamin pills, I am led to suspect that at least some vitamin vendors do not take their own medicine. They just sell it. (1942)

Endocrine Factors in Behavior

Because they are physiologically so potent, the endocrine secretions have often been regarded as equally potent determinants of behavior in human beings. Many of the most appealing of these claims have not been confirmed by critical experiments. Since the literature on this topic is so voluminous, no attempt will be made to review it exhaustively. In the following section, we aim instead to present a theory concerning how endocrine secretions may regulate behavior with illustrative examples from the literature. It is the hazard of such a subjective technique of exposition in a field with so many contradictory experimental results that almost any selection of fantastic claims could be provided with some evidence. The only protection from this hazard is the maintenance

TOTAL ORGANISM RESPONSES IN MAINTENANCE OF HOMEOSTASIS.— Such regulatory processes might be regarded as purely physiological with little or no importance for more complex forms of human behavior, were it not for the fact that when a breakdown of these adjustments occurs, the resulting displacement may produce marked alterations in behavior. Numerous examples in which the total behavior of the organism may become directed toward maintaining a constant internal environment have recently appeared (Richter, 1941a). For example, animals in which the normal regulation of water excretion was upset by removal of the posterior lobes of the pituitary drank very large amounts of water and thus maintained themselves in good health indefinitely. Richter and his coworkers have shown experimentally that the total overt behavior of an animal may be directed toward the maintenance of homeostasis when the normal process is interfered with. Rats threatened with a seriously lowered body temperature following removal of the pituitary or thyroid glands built large nests and thereby conserved their body heat. Those in which the internal salt balance was disturbed by removal of the adrenal glands drank large amounts of salt solution and thereby kept themselves alive and free from symptoms of salt deficiency. When the parathyroid glands were removed they selected solutions containing calcium to maintain normal calcium balance. Rats rendered diabetic by the surgical removal of the pancreas avoided sugar, which they could not utilize in the absence of their pancreas, and in its stead they ate large amounts of fat, thus freeing themselves of diabetic symptoms.

Examples where the total organism responses were directed toward the maintenance of homeostasis may also be found in human beings. Wilkins and Richter (1940) have described the case of a 3½-year-old boy brought to the hospital because of precocious sex development who died unexpectedly in seven days. At autopsy destruction of the adrenal cortex was found, indicating a marked upset in regulation of the stores of salt in the body. Inquiry into this boy's history disclosed that since the age of one year he had shown a marked craving for salt. He ate salt as most other children eat candy. At the age of 3½ years, when he was brought to the hospital and placed on an ordinary diet without access to extra salt, he quickly developed symptoms of insufficiency of the adrenal cortex and died. He had kept himself alive previously by increasing his salt intake.

It is interesting to note that babies, given free access to a variety of natural foods, will make selections which result in normal growth and development (Davis, 1928). Thus it is possible that many dietary cravings which seem peculiar are but attempts of the total organism to compensate for failure of some regulatory mechanism within the body. Pursuing this concept further, one is led to wonder how much other behavior commonly regarded as abnormal may in reality be an attempt of the organism to maintain homeostasis of its internal environment in the face of some nonapparent physiological breakdown or need.

Endocrine Factors Determining Complex Periodic Behavior.— The importance of endocrine secretions in regulating and controlling certain complex behavior patterns of a transient or periodic nature has been demonstrated in animal experiments on sex and maternal behavior. Early observations led to the emphasis on hormones as the sole determiners of these types of behavior. Recent experiments, however, have tended to show that other factors such as neural and environmental ones play a part in determining mating and maternal acts in animals (Stone, 1939; Bard, 1939, 1940).

Prolactin, a hormone secreted by the anterior lobe of the pituitary gland, has been shown to increase greatly the strength of the maternal urge in rats. Riddle (1935) has shown that normal young female rats ignore newborn animals placed in their cages. If such animals, previously sensitized with estrin, are given adequate doses of prolactin, not only are their mammary glands stimulated to secrete milk, but they will eagerly adopt as many young as are offered to them, build elaborate nests, and mother them. Beach (1937, 1938) has found that although such maternal behavior may be induced by administering hormones, an intact nervous system is required for its mediation and organization. With the ablation of increasing amounts of the cerebral cortex in rats, the mothers become clumsy and inept in their activities with the result that many of the offspring die.

Richter and his coworkers (1941a) have found that any rat, male or female, will resort to nest building whenever the body temperature falls below a certain critical level. The same activity may be induced in males by removing the pituitary gland and decreasing environmental temperature, the result of which is a drop in body temperature.

The importance of the nervous system for normal copulatory behavior has been conclusively demonstrated (Bard, 1939, 1940; Stone, 1939). A more extensive review of the literature only serves to strengthen the conception illustrated above, viz., complex behavior patterns, which may normally be induced by endocrine changes, are also found to be subject to other forms of stimuli and may be dependent on many interrelationships for their normal progression.

Endocrine Factors Involved in Persisting Behavior Patterns.—

INTELLECTUAL BEHAVIOR.—The dependence of intellectual development on normal secretion of the thyroid gland has been firmly established by both clinical and experimental studies. Inadequacy of thyroid secretion in the young results in a stunting of physical and mental development known as *cretinism*. Some improvement follows thyroid therapy in most cretins. The degree of improvement is greater where treatment is begun early and continued vigorously (Gesell, Amatruda, and Culotta, 1936). Even though complete mental normality cannot be restored to all cretins (Brown, Bronstein, and Kraines, 1939), it seems that the social adjustments of such children are improved by glandular therapy. McDonald, Brown, and Bronstein (1940) found that cretins aged from six

to seven and from seventeen to twenty-one years made the best social
and family adjustment after therapy. This is perhaps because the
younger cretins are still considered babies by parents, while the older
ones are accepted because they are able to take care of themselves and
cause little trouble. Cretins between the ages of seven and twelve years
are reported to have the greatest difficulty in adjusting to other children.
The effectiveness of thyroid therapy in the field of social adjustments is
probably based on the fact that with even slight physical improvement
the children experience an improvement in their acceptance by other
children and especially by their parents.

Thyroid administration has also resulted in the development of language facility in certain cretins during the short span of six weeks
(Schreiber, Bronstein, and Brown, 1940). Reports of permanent intellectual improvement in cretin children receiving transplants of the
thyroid gland from other persons have appeared (Le Fort, 1937; Voronoff, 1937), but the chances of a successful glandular graft are few.

Lesser degrees of hypothyroidism may be present in persons suffering
from endemic goiter. Kimball and Marinus (1930) surveyed the children in special classes of the Detroit schools and found 8% suffering
from endemic goiter. No studies using standard test procedures for intelligence have been successful in demonstrating a significant correlation
between the size of the thyroid gland and intelligence (Olesen and
Fernald, 1926; Stocks, Stocks, and Karn, 1927). These negative results
are not very illuminating, however, because they assume that the size
of the gland is an index of its functional activity. Numerous physiological studies have shown that this assumption is fallacious; a large thyroid
gland may be producing less thyroxin than a small one.

Since the level of activity of the thyroid gland is best indicated by the
basal rate of oxygen consumption (or the BMR), a number of studies
have attempted to relate intellectual performance and the basal metabolic rate. Hinton (1939) has reported correlations of the order of 0.80
between Binet IQ scores and the BMR in six-, seven-, eight-, and nine-
year-old children. In ten- to eleven-year-olds the correlations drop to .70
and in twelve- to fifteen-year-olds to .50. These correlations are in striking contrast to the low or zero correlations reported in adolescents
(Shock and Jones, 1940; Rothbart, 1935; Molitch and Eccles, 1934) or
college students (Patrick and Rowles, 1933; Steinberg, 1934). The
weight of available evidence favors the conclusion that slight variations
in the functional activity of the thyroid gland are not reflected in changes
in mental capacity.

Crile (1941) has recently expanded his general thesis that "variation
in the size of the brain, the heart, the thyroid gland and the adrenal-
sympathetic system is the sole cause of the variation in the intelligence,
power, and personality of wild and domestic animals." Crile argues that
the relatively large brain of man requires a larger thyroid gland for the
maintenance of constant oxidations but enables him to get along with
smaller adrenal glands required for the emergency release of energy. In

the increasing incidence of thyroid, heart and vascular disorders, he sees
evidence that evolution cannot continue further in the direction of a
larger thinking brain and a larger thyroid gland. Even if we pass by the
fallacy of regarding the size of a gland as an index of its function, little
support for this theory exists in experimental studies.

In animal studies concerning the effect of thyroid substance on mental
performance, the results have been inconclusive. Increased sensitivity to
stimuli, shown in the respiratory response to CO_2 or anoxia (Landolt,
1936; Sos, 1939) and by reductions in the thresholds for light and for
sound (Asher, 1937), has been reported following the administration of
small doses of thyroxin to animals. Brody (1941) found no significant
change in the reaction time of adult rats which were fed thyroid hormone, even though the BMR was increased by as much as 50% in individual animals. Partial thyroidectomy with slight diminution (5% to
26%) in the BMR caused a slight, statistically insignificant, decrease in
reaction time. Burnham and Leonard (1941) found that thyroid removal had no effect on learning, or on either the retention or the reversal
of a discrimination habit by a small group of rats. Morrison and Cunningham (1941) reported that in cretinous rats the establishment of conditioned responses was impaired; this was remedied by the administration of thyroid substance. Some investigators have accorded to other
endocrine secretions, as well, an influence on intellectual performance, but
the evidence is often meager and inadequate. Blatz and Heron (1924)
reported that rats fed dried anterior pituitary gland learned mazes more
quickly than did animals receiving the usual diet. Later feeding experiments in animals have failed to confirm these results; in fact, they have
led most physiologists to believe that the hormones present in the pituitary gland are destroyed by the secretions of the gastrointestinal tract,
and that in order to have any physiological effects, the pituitary extracts
must be administered by injections into the skin or muscle. Nevertheless,
clinical reports continue to appear in which dried pituitary gland administered by mouth is thought to have physiological effects (Lurie, 1938).
For instance Mateer (1935) is convinced that the administration of
pituitary gland by mouth is effective treatment for the reading difficulties
of retarded children. The evidence for this belief is clinical and contains
many uncontrolled variables (see review by Shock, 1938).

Studies on animals in which the pituitary gland has been removed
have not demonstrated any impairment of learning ability where other
factors of motivation have been adequately controlled (Burnham and
Leonard, 1941). Kriaschew (1939) reported that removal of the pituitary gland actually increased the speed with which a conditioned reflex
was established in dogs, but extinction also occurred more rapidly.

Human beings suffering from such skeletal defects as dwarfism
(Foster, Brown, and Bronstein, 1939), gargoylism, and acromegaly, or
from retarded sexual development, all symptoms based on pituitary
pathology, have not shown any measurable psychological impairment
(Schott, 1938). Although no impairment of intellectual function has

been found, individuals suffering from pituitary disorders often manifest many undesirable personal characteristics. Experimental removal of the pituitary gland in puppies not only produced retardation in growth and development, but Dandy and Reichert (1938) found their hypophysectomized puppy fatigued easily, never played, and was always snappy and cranky.

In summary, we may say that extreme underactivity of the thyroid gland has been shown to result in retardation of both physical and mental development. Within the range of normal variation no relation between thyroid function and intellectual capacity has been clearly demonstrated. No adequate evidence indicates that secretions of the pituitary gland have any influence on intellectual functions, but they may affect social behavior. Claims for an effect of other glands on intellectual performance are without proof.

EMOTIONAL BEHAVIOR AND TEMPERAMENT.—The part that endocrine secretions play in emotional and other emergency reactions is well known from the work of Cannon (1929) and others (see Bard, 1933). In these reactions, the secretion of the adrenal medulla, adrenalin or epinephrine, has received the greatest emphasis. However, the injection of epinephrine in amounts sufficient to produce the same physiological effects, such as increased blood pressure, pulse rate, blood sugar, etc., does not produce "emotion" in the human. To experience "emotion" there must be something more than the physiological upheaval in which the adrenal glands participate (Carr, 1925). A discussion of the "something more" is beyond the scope of the present chapter, or of the capabilities of the writer.

Evidence for an association between endocrine function and behavior in human beings has been obtained chiefly from studies on persons who show marked deviations either in endocrine function or in behavior. It is from such studies that relationships in normal persons have been inferred.

A connection between glandular dysfunction and mental disturbance is clearer in the case of the thyroid than in that of any other gland. The basal metabolic rate of schizophrenics is slightly below normal (Hoskins and Jellinek, 1934), indicating a hypofunction of the thyroid gland, which extensive and thorough studies have demonstrated to be part of a total picture of physiological depression. Varying degrees of hypothyroidism (myxodema) cause irascibility, depression, melancholia, suspiciousness, and delusions, and make such patients difficult. Since they frequently have a long life, patients with hypothyroidism wreck many a home. Stoll (1932) has reported a series of such cases in which thyroid therapy removed the behavior symptoms.

The increased function of the thyroid gland in cases of mania (Cahane and Cahane, 1938) is more difficult to demonstrate quantitatively because of the technical difficulties involved in measuring the basal metabolic rate in excited patients. Hyperactivity of the thyroid gland, as present in Graves' disease, is often associated with hyperirritability, hyperactivity, distractibility, hyperemotivity, and wide swings in mood. Numerous instances of improvement of such behavior following removal of the overactive thyroid gland have been cited in clinical reports. Again the difficulties of living with such individuals are well characterized by Crile who has said, "Pity the man who marries a hyperthyroid—for his nights will be filled with anguish and his days with remorse." Thus extreme thyroid deviations in either direction are associated with undesirable behavior. On the other hand, an attractive, though unconfirmed, hypothesis is that slight hyperactivity of the thyroid gland may provide the internal stimulus to the greater energy and drive that sets an individual off as one kind of leader in his community or profession.

The first experiments on the relation between sex glands and behavior were performed unwittingly by stock men who have long made a practice of castrating domestic animals (see Hoskins, 1941). The difference between the fiery aggressive stallion and his placid brother, the work horse, has long been known. The pugnacious bull and the gentle ox owe their differences to the removal of the sex glands. All degrees of masculine or feminine behavior have been experimentally induced in animals by castration, gland grafting, or sex hormone injections (Allen, 1939). However, in human beings the effects of castration on behavior are not as striking as in animals. If the operation is performed before puberty, genital libido fails to develop; on the other hand libido does not always disappear when an adult is castrated. Castration in human beings, with loss of sexual potency, is apt to have secondary psychological implications which are more powerful than the primary effects of the removal of the sex hormone itself (Codet, 1937). Thus Ley (1938) believes that the dangers of castration when *asked for* or *freely consented to* by the subject are extremely small. Reports of decreased energy and drive, and of increased lassitude and depression following castration have not been confirmed experimentally in human beings. Steinach (1936) believed that increased tonicity of muscles and feelings of wellbeing with return of libido could be induced in aged males by an increased resorption of male hormone. He thought he could produce increased hormone resorption by ligating the spermatic ducts. These results were not confirmed by other investigators, however, and Steinach's operation has fallen into disrepute. With the isolation and commercial preparation of crystalline male hormone, reports of its good effects on energy and libido in males have appeared (Davidoff and Goodstone, 1942; Simonson, *et al.*, 1941). These reports actually concern the feelings of the patients treated, for controlled measurements of these increases of energy and libido have not been made.

Administration of sex hormone in young boys suffering from retarded sexual development has increased genital growth, libido, and aggressive behavior (Miller, Hubert, and Hamilton, 1938). Again the social effects of the treatment have not been adequately separated from the physiological effects. Experimental studies on animals have demonstrated a relation between male sex hormone and aggressiveness. Allee, *et al.*

(1939) have found that the social organization in flocks of hens may be altered by the administration of male sex hormone. Submissive animals treated with the male hormone became the most aggressive and domineering members of the flock, while dominant animals treated with female sex hormone became submissive (Allee and Collias, 1940).

In women, the ovaries sometimes are able to produce their hormones only in deficient amounts, and persistence of such imbalance may give rise to the hypogonadal temperament defined by Rowe and Lawrence (1929) as follows: "An insistently expressed egoism is the keynote of the hypogonad character. Coupled with, and dependent upon this is an active resentment toward a world that is but inadequately mindful of the patient's many excellences. Hyperemotionalism and self-pity are united with an attitude of acid criticism of environmental conditions that are always unsatisfactory." Thus Rowe and Lawrence believe that ovarian deficiency renders difficult the maintenance of the graciousness and charm which are considered a characteristic of the feminine personality.

In women many of the physiological effects usually associated with castration occur at the menopause. Nervousness, excitability, disturbed sleep with headaches, dyspnea, tachycardia, hot flushes with cold hands and feet are symptoms disturbing enough; but the worst of all is the depression that often makes the victim yearn for death. Werner and his associates (1934, 1936) have reported success in alleviating these psychological symptoms by the administration of female sex hormone. His belief that the sex hormone has a *direct* influence on these psychological symptoms, however, is not shared by other investigators (Ripley, Shorr, and Papanicolaou, 1940, see also Chapter 34 by Appel), but the reduction in the physiological symptoms following sex hormone therapy, and thus a secondary influence on experience and behavior, is not disputed (Burlingame and Patterson, 1941).

The cyclic changes in the activity of the sex glands in normal women after puberty have often been considered the cause of accompanying changes in behavior. No changes in the capacity for mental or physical work have been established (Seward, 1934). However, many subjects report changes in mood, fatigue, ability, irritability, and libido with the sex cycle (Brush, 1938; McCance, *et al.* 1937). Altman, *et al.* (1941) report the presence of elation associated with ovulation, while the premenstrual phase is characterized by feelings of depression coupled with a critical feeling toward others. Benedik and Rubenstein (1939) have shown an interesting relation between activity of the sex glands in women, as indicated by vaginal smears, and the psychological content of dream reports obtained in a psychoanalytic interview. Patients under psychoanalytic treatment for various neurotic disturbances were used as subjects. During the time when ovarian follicles were maturing and when the amount of estrone (female sex hormone) in the body was increasing, the psychological material was dominated by heterosexual interest. In neurotic persons this increasing estrone production seemed to activate the psychological conflict and thus intensify the neurotic symptoms. With ovulation, the psychic tension was suddenly relieved. With the increased production of progesterone after ovulation, the psychological material showed the tendency of the subject to be passive and receptive. Thus, more and more evidence is accumulating to indicate a relation between psychodynamic processes and the cyclic activity of the sex glands.

SOCIAL BEHAVIOR.—Certain physical deviations produced by glandular dysfunction are associated with significant alterations in personality. However, because of the secondary effects of the mental attitude subsequently adopted by the patient toward the physical abnormality, the endocrine disturbance itself can only be regarded as an indirect cause of the behavioral deviation (Lurie, 1938). It is not difficult, for instance, to understand why the adolescent boy, who is suffering from eunuchoidism as a result of gonadal insufficiency, should develop a marked feeling of inferiority which in turn leads him to shun his companions, to become morose, and gradually to withdraw from the world of reality to live in a world of fantasy. In a similar way obesity may have far-reaching effects on the adolescent girl, and these effects will depend on the way her associates react to her size. Moreover, the presence of facial hair because of adrenal cortex involvement in girls may arouse feelings of self-pity leading to withdrawal and ultimate neurotic manifestations.

Studies of delinquent children have given support to the belief that in certain instances the asocial behavior may be an overcompensation for a physical or physiological inadequacy. A high incidence of hypogonadism is reported among certain groups of delinquents (Molitch, 1937).

In other instances the delinquent behavior may be more directly associated with an endocrine disturbance. For instance, Lurie (1938) reports the case of a boy who suffered from dystrophia-adoposo-genitalis and stole. After oral administration of extract of whole pituitary gland, he stopped stealing. Lurie believes that the stealing served the simple purpose of obtaining additional sweets to satisfy a craving for food caused by the pituitary dysfunction.

Summary.—The endocrine glands have many important regulatory functions in maintaining the constancy of the internal environment, so essential to normal function in human beings. With the breakdown of physiological functions involved in the maintenance of homeostasis, responses of the total organism will be directed toward this end. Such behavior may appear "abnormal." Although normal mental development requires the presence of adequate secretion of the thyroid gland, slight variations in functional activity of the thyroid gland are not reflected in changes in mental capacity of mature persons. Energy output and "drive," as well as certain temperamental differences, may be influenced by thyroid activity, but quantitative proof is still lacking. The influence of sex hormones in conditioning sexual and maternal behavior is only part of the total physiological mechanism involved. In women, fluctuations in mood and psychodynamic processes are associated with the endocrine secretions dominating the two chief phases of the menstrual cycle. There is no quantitative evidence for attendant changes in physical or mental capacities. Evidence for a direct influence on behavior from other endocrine secretions is not impressive, although any dysfunction which results in obvious physical or physiological deviations may influence behavior by way of the social or cultural environment.

Conclusion

In conclusion, the necessity for an interchange and coordination of clinical and experimental techniques in the study of physiological factors in behavior must be emphasized if progress is to be made. Investigators will need to consider carefully the strengths and limitations of clinical and experimental methods. The essence of the experimental technique is the abstraction of specific variables for quantitative measurement with the elimination or neutralization of the simultaneous effects of all other variables. Unfortunately, complex human behavior cannot be adequately evaluated outside of its social setting. The clinician sees the behavior of his patient within the total social and cultural pattern, and the importance of his observations must not be underestimated by ardent experimentalists. It is equally true that care and caution must be exercised in drawing sweeping conclusions from clinical material alone. As we stated previously, the clinical observations and hunches of today should provide the basis for the experiments of tomorrow.

BIBLIOGRAPHY

AKIMOV, N. E.   1936.   The effect of adrenalin on maze learning in white rats. *Refleksi, Instinkti, Naviki, 2,* 111–138.

ALEXANDER, F., & SAUL, L. J.   1940.   Respiration and personality—a preliminary report: I.   Description of the curves.   *Psychosom. Med., 2,* 110–118.

ALLEE, W. C., & COLLIAS, N.   1940.   The influence of estradiol on the social organization of flocks of hens.   *Endocrinology, 27,* 87–94.

ALLEE, W. C., COLLIAS, N. E., & LUTHERMAN, C. Z.   1939.   Modification of the social order in flocks of hens by the injection of testosterone propionate. *Physiol. Zool., 12,* 412–440.

ALLEN, E., DANFORTH, C. H., & DOISY, E. A.   1939.   Sex and internal secretions. (2nd ed.)   Baltimore: Williams & Wilkins.

ALTMANN, M., KNOWLES, E., & BULL, H. D.   1941.   A psychosomatic study of the sex cycle in women.   *Psychosom. Med., 3,* 199–225.

ANDERSON, O. D., & PARMENTER, R.   1941.   A long term study of the experimental neurosis in the sheep and dog, with nine case histories.   *Psychosom. Med. Monogr., 2,* 1–150.

ARING, C. D.   1943.   The use of vitamins in clinical neurology.   *Bull. N. Y. Acad. Med., 19,* 17–33.

ARING, C. D., RYDER, H. W., ROSEMAN, E., ROSENBAUM, M., & FERRIS, E. B., JR. 1941.   Effect of nicotinic acid and related substances on intracranial blood flow in man.   *Arch. Neurol. Psychiat., Chicago, 46,* 649–653.

ARMSTRONG, H. G.   1939.   Aviation medicine.   Baltimore: Williams & Wilkins.

ARMSTRONG, H. G., & HEIM, J. W.   1938.   The effect of repeated daily exposures to anoxemia.   *J. Aviat. Med., 9,* 92–96.

ASHER, L.   1937.   Nervous system and internal secretion.   *Ohio J. Sci., 37,* 349–354.

BAKER, A. B.   1939.   Cerebral damage in hypoglycemia; a review.   *Amer. J. Psychiat., 96,* 109–127.

BARACH, A. L., McFARLAND, R. A., & SEITZ, C. P. 1937. The effects of oxygen deprivation on complex mental functions. *J. Aviat. Med., 8*, 197–207.

BARCROFT, J. 1920. Anoxaemia. *Lancet, 199*, 485–489.

—— 1925. The respiratory function of the blood: Part I. Lessons from high altitudes. Cambridge: Cambridge University Press.

BARD, P. 1933. The neuro-humoral basis of emotional reactions. In Murchison, C., *Handbook of general experimental psychology*. Worcester, Mass.: Clark University Press.

—— 1939. Central nervous mechanisms for emotional behavior patterns in animals. *Res. Publ. Assn. Res. nerv. ment. Dis., 19*, 190–218.

—— 1940. The hypothalamus and sexual behavior. *Res. Publ. Assn. Res. nerv. ment. Dis., 20*, 551–579.

BEACH, F. A., JR. 1937. The neural basis of innate behavior: I. Effects of cortical lesions upon the maternal behavior pattern in the rat. *J. comp. Psychol., 24*, 393–436.

—— 1938. The neural basis of innate behavior: II. Relative effects of partial decortication in adulthood and infancy upon the maternal behavior of the primiparous rat. *J. genet. Psychol., 53*, 109–148.

—— 1940. Effects of cortical lesions upon the copulatory behavior of male rats. *J. comp. Psychol., 29*, 193–245.

BECK, H. G. 1937. Chronic carbon monoxide anoxemia: clinical syndrome. *Sth. med. J., 30*, 824–829.

BENDER, L. 1940. The Goodenough test (drawing a man) in chronic encephalitis in children. *J. nerv. ment. Dis., 91*, 277–286.

BENEDEK, T., & RUBENSTEIN, B. B. 1939. The correlation between ovarian activity and psychodynamic processes: I. The ovulative phase. *Psychosom. Med., 1*, 245–270.

BENTON, A. L., & HOWELL, I. L. 1941. The use of psychological tests in the evaluation of intellectual function following head injury: report of a case of post-traumatic personality disorder. *Psychosom. Med., 3*, 138–151.

BERNARD, C. 1859. Leçons sur les propriétés physiologiques et les alterations pathologiques des liquides de l'organisme. Paris: Bailliere.

BIEL, W. C. 1939. The effects of early inanition on a developmental schedule in the albino rat. *J. comp. Psychol., 28*, 1–15.

BIEL, W. C., & WICKENS, D. D. 1941. Effect of vitamin B_1 deficiency on conditioning eyelid responses in the rat. *J. comp. Psychol., 32*, 329–340.

BILLS, A. G. 1937. Blocking in mental fatigue and anoxemia compared. *J. exp. Psychol., 20*, 437–452.

BLATZ, W. E., & HERON, W. T. 1924. The effect of endocrine feeding upon the learning performance of white rats. *J. exp. Psychol., 7*, 291–311.

BOND, E. D., & SMITH, L. H. 1935. Postencephalitic behavior disorders: ten year review of Franklin School. *Amer. J. Psychiat., 92*, 17–33.

BOUDREAU, E. N. 1937. Psychic states associated with hyperglycemia. *N. Y. St. J. Med., 37*, 1627–1634.

BRAUNE. 1935. Über den Einfluss fleischloser Kost auf die Geistestätigkeit des Menschen. *Veröff. Medverw., 44*, 586–606.

BRODY, E. B. 1941. The influence of age, hypophysectomy, thyroidectomy, and thyroxin injection on simple reaction time in the rat. *J. gen. Physiol., 24*, 433–436.

BROWN, A. W., BRONSTEIN, I. P., & KRAINES, R. 1939. Hypothyroidism and cretinism in childhood: VI. Influence of thyroid therapy on mental growth. *Amer. J. Dis. Child., 57*, 517–523.

BROWN, A. W., JENKINS, R. L., & CISLER, L. E. 1938. Influence of lethargic encephalitis on intelligence of children. *Amer. J. Dis. Child., 55*, 304–321.

BROWN, G. D. 1938. The development of diabetic children, with special reference to mental and personality comparisons. *Child Develpm., 9*, 175–184.

BRUCH, H. 1940. Obesity in childhood: III. Physiologic and psychologic aspects of the food intake of obese children. *Amer. J. Dis. Child., 59*, 739–781.

—— 1941a. Obesity in childhood and endocrine treatment. *J. Pediat., 18*, 36–56.

—— 1941b. Obesity in childhood and personality development. *Amer. J. Orthopsychiat., 11*, 467–474.

BRUSH, A. L. 1938. Attitudes, emotions and physical symptoms commonly associated with menstruation in 100 women. *Amer. J. Orthopsychiat., 8*, 286–301.

BURLINGAME, C. C., & PATTERSON, M. B. 1941. Estrogen therapy in the psychoses. *J. nerv. ment. Dis., 94,* 265–276.

BURNHAM, R. W., & LEONARD, S. T. 1941. Hypophysectomy and thyroidectomy as related to learning in the rat: I. Preliminary investigation. *J. comp. Psychol., 31,* 233–242.

CAHANE, M., & CAHANE, T. 1938. Recherches sur les hormones hypophysaires dans certains psychoses. *Ann. Méd. phys., 15,* 311–320.

CANNON, W. B. 1929. Bodily changes in pain, hunger, fear, and rage. (2nd. ed.) New York: Appleton-Century.

—— 1939. The wisdom of the body. (2nd ed.) New York: Norton.

CARLSON, A. J. 1942. How bad is the American diet? *West. J. Surg. Obstet. Gynec., 50,* 483–497.

CARR, H. A. 1925. Psychology: a study of mental activity. New York: Longmans, Green.

CHOBOT, R., SPADAVECCHIA, R., & DE SANCTIS, R. M. 1939. Intelligence rating and emotional pattern of allergic children. *Amer. J. Dis. Child., 57,* 831–837.

CLECKLEY, H. M., SYDENSTRICKER, V. P., & GEESLIN, L. E. 1939. Nicotinic acid in the treatment of atypical psychotic states associated with malnutrition. *J. Amer. med. Assn., 112,* 2107–2110.

COBB, S., & FREMONT-SMITH, F. 1931. The cerebral circulation: XVI. Changes in the human retinal circulation and in the pressure of the cerebrospinal fluid during inhalation of a mixture of carbon dioxide and oxygen. *Arch. Neurol. Psychiat., Chicago, 26,* 731–736.

CODET, H. 1937. Troubles psychopathiques de la castration feminine. *Ann. méd.-chir., 2,* 86–90.

COHEN, L. 1936. Speech perseveration and astasia-abasia following carbon monoxide intoxication. *J. Neurol. Psychopath., 17,* 41–47.

COLBY, M. B., MACY, I. G., POOLE, M. W., HAMIL, B. M., & COOLEY, T. B. 1937. Relation of increased vitamin B (B_1) intake to mental and physical growth of infants. Preliminary report. *Amer. J. Dis. Child., 54,* 750–756.

COURVILLE, C. B. 1936. Asphyxia as a consequence of nitrous oxide anesthesia. *Medicine, Baltimore, 15,* 129–245.

CRILE, G. 1941. A neuro-endocrine formula for civilized man. *Educ. Rec., 22,* Suppl. 14, 57–76.

DANDY, W. E., & REICHERT, F. L. 1938. Studies on experimental hypophysectomy in dogs: III. Somatic, mental and glandular effects. *Johns Hopk. Hosp. Bull., 62,* 122–155.

DAVIDOFF, E., & GOODSTONE, G. L. 1942. Use of testosterone propionate in treatment of involutional psychosis in the male. *Arch. Neurol. Psychiat., Chicago, 48,* 811–817.

DAVIS, C. M. 1928. Self selection of diets by newly weaned infants. *Amer. J. Dis. Child., 36,* 651.

D'ELSEAUX, F. C., & SOLOMON, H. C. 1933. Use of carbon dioxide mixtures in stupors occurring in psychoses. *Arch. Neurol. Psychiat., Chicago, 29,* 213–230.

DROESE, W. 1941. Ueber den Einfluss von B_1 Traubenzucker-kombinationen auf der körperlichen Leistungsfähigkeit und einen funktionellen Nachweiss von B_1 Hypovitaminosen. *Münch. med. Wschr., 88,* 909–910.

EASTMAN, N. J. 1936a. Fetal blood studies. The role of anesthesia in the production of asphyxia neonatorum. *Amer. J. Obstet. & Gynaec., 31,* 563–572.

—— 1936b. Asphyxia neonatorum. *Int. Clin., 2,* 274–300.

EGAÑA, E., JOHNSON, R. E., BLOOMFIELD, R., BROUHA, L., MEIKELJOHN, A. P., WHITTENBERGER, J., DARLING, R. C., HEATH, C., GRAYBIEL, A., & CONSOLAZIO, F. 1942. The effects of a diet deficient in the vitamin B complex on sedentary men. *Amer. J. Physiol., 137,* 731–741.

ELLER, J. J. 1941. Body odor. *Med. Rec., N. Y., 154,* 167–171.

FINESINGER, J. E., & MAZICK, S. G. 1940. The respiratory response of psychoneurotic patients to ideational and to sensory stimuli. Respiratory response in psychoneuroses. *Amer. J. Psychiat., 97,* 27–46.

FOLTZ, E. E., IVY, A. C., & BABORKA, C. J. 1942. Influence of components of the vitamin B complex on recovery from fatigue. *J. Lab. clin. Med., 27,* 1396–1399.

FOSTER, R., BROWN, A. W., & BRONSTEIN, I. P. 1939. The mental development of a group of dwarfish children. *Proc. Amer. Assn. ment. Def., 63,* 143–153.

FRASER, R., & REITMANN, F. 1939. A clinical study of the effects of short periods of severe anoxia with special reference to the mechanism of action of cardiazol "shock." *J. Neurol. Psychiat., 2,* 125–136.

GELLHORN, E. 1936. Value of carbon dioxide in counteracting oxygen lack. *Nature, London, 137,* 700–701.

—— 1938. Effects of hypoglycemia and anoxia on the central nervous system. A basis for the rational therapy of schizophrenia. *Arch. Neurol. Psychiat., Chicago, 40,* 125–146.

—— 1941. The internal environment and behavior: II. The influence of variations in blood sugar on the functions of the brain. *Amer. J. Psychiat., 97,* 1204–1218.

—— 1943. Autonomic regulations. New York: Interscience Publishers.

GELLHORN, E., & KRAINES, S. H. 1937. Word associations as affected by deficient oxygen, excess of carbon dioxide and hyperpnea. *Arch. Neurol. Psychiat., Chicago, 38,* 491–504.

GELLHORN, E., & SPIESMAN, I. G. 1935a. The influence of hyperpnea and of variations of the oxygen and carbon dioxide tension in the inspired air upon after-images. *Amer. J. Physiol., 112,* 620–625.

—— 1935b. The influence of hyperpnea and of variations of oxygen and carbon dioxide tension in the inspired air upon hearing. *Amer. J. Physiol., 112,* 519–528.

GESELL, A., AMATRUDA, C. S., & CULOTTA, C. S. 1936. Effect of thyroid therapy on mental and physical growth of cretinous infants. *Amer. J. Dis. Child., 52,* 1117–1292.

GILDEA, E. F., & COBB, S. 1930. The effects of anemia on the cerebral cortex of the cat. *Arch. Neurol. Psychiat., Chicago, 23,* 876–903.

GLAZE, J. A. 1928. Psychological effects of fasting: the effects of prolonged fasting. *Amer. J. Psychol., 40,* 236–253.

GOLDIE, E. A. G. 1941. The clinical manifestations of oxygen lack. *Proc. R. Soc. Med., 34,* 631–632.

GORDON, R. G., ROBERTS, J. A. F., & GRIFFITHS, R. 1939. Does poliomyelitis affect intellectual capacity? *Brit. med. J., 2,* 803–805.

GRAHAM, E. A., & WOMACK, N. A. 1933. Application of surgery to hypoclycemic state due to tumors of the pancreas and to other conditions. *Surg., Gynec., Obstet., 56,* 728–742.

HALDANE, J. B. S. 1922. Respiration. New Haven: Yale University Press.

HALDANE, J. B. S., LINDER, G. C., HILTON, R., & FRASER, F. R. 1928. Arterial blood in ammonium chloride acidosis. *J. Physiol., 65,* 412.

HALDANE, J. S., & PRIESTLY, J. G. 1935. Respiration. Oxford: Clarendon Press.

HAMILTON, J. A., & SHOCK, N. W. 1936. An experimental study of personality, physique and the acid-base equilibrium of the blood. *Amer. J. Psychol., 48,* 467–473.

HANDELSMAN, J. 1933. Contribution à la pathogénie des troubles psychiques organiques. Troubles psychiques au cours de l'anémie pernicieuse. *Roczn. Psychjat., 21,* 440–441.

HECHT, S., & MANDELBAUM, J. 1940. Dark adaptation and experimental human vitamin A deficiency. *Amer. J. Physiol., 130,* 651–654.

HERON, W. T., & SKINNER, B. F. 1937. The effects of certain drugs and hormones on conditioning and extinction. *Psychol. Bull., 34,* 741–742.

HIMWICH, H. E., SPIES, T. D., FAZEKAS, J. F., & NESIN, S. 1940. Cerebral carbohydrate metabolism deficiencies during deficiency of various members of the vitamin B complex. *Amer. J. med. Sci., 199,* 849–853.

HINTON, R. T., JR. 1939. A further study on the role of the basal metabolic rate in the intelligence of children. *J. educ. Psychol., 30,* 309–314.

HOELZEL, F. 1938. Mental efficiency, carbohydrate metabolism and nutritional hydration. *Science, 87,* 218.

HOFF, F. 1935. Über Änderungen der seelischen Stimmungslage bei Verschiebungen des Säurebasengleichgewichts. *Münch. med. Wschr., 82,* 1478–1479.

HORST, P. 1941. The prediction of personal adjustment. *Soc. Sci. Res. Coun. Bull., No. 48.*

HOSKINS, R. G. 1941. Endocrinology. The glands and their function. New York: Norton.

HOSKINS, R. G., & JELLINEK, E. M. 1934. The schizophrenic personality with special regard to psychologic and organic concomitants. *Res. Publ. Assn. Res. nerv. ment. Dis., 14,* 211–233.

HUNT, E. L. 1934. Neurological and mental symptoms of pernicious anemia. *N. Y. St. J. Med., 34,* 99–100.

JENKINS, R. L., BROWN, A. W., & CISLER, L. E. 1940. Influence of syphilis on intelligence of children. *Amer. J. Dis. Child., 60,* 341–351.

JERSILD, A. T., & THOMAS, W. S. 1931. The influence of adrenal extract on behavior and mental efficiency. *Amer. J. Psychol., 43,* 447–456.

JOHNSON, R. E., DARLING, R. C., FORBES, W. H., BROUHA, L., EGAÑA, E., & GRAYBIEL, A. 1942. The effects of a diet deficient in part of the vitamin B complex upon men doing manual labor. *J. Nutrit., 24,* 585–596.

JOLLIFFE, N. 1939. Effects of vitamin deficiency on mental and emotional processes. *Res. Publ. Assn. Res. nerv. ment. Dis., 19,* 144–153.

—— 1941. Treatment of neuro-psychiatric disorders with vitamins. *J. Amer. med. Assn., 117,* 1496–1502.

—— 1942. The neuropsychiatric manifestations of vitamin deficiencies. *J. Mt Sinai Hosp., N. Y., 8,* 658.

JOSLIN, E. P. 1937. The treatment of diabetes mellitus. Philadelphia: Lea & Febiger.

KERR, W. J., DALTON, J. W., & GLIEBE, P. A. 1937. Some physical phenomena associated with the anxiety states and their relation to hyperventilation. *Ann. intern. Med., 2,* 961–992.

KERR, W. J., GLIEBE, P. A., SOLEY, M. H., & SHOCK, N. W. 1939. Treatment of the anxiety states: with special attention to certain physiologic manifestations. *J. Amer. med. Assn., 113,* 637–640.

KEYS, A., & HENSCHEL, A. F. 1942. Vitamin supplementation of U. S. Army rations in relation to fatigue and the ability to do muscular work. *J. Nutrit., 23,* 259–269.

KIMBALL, O. P., & MARINUS, J. C. 1930. The relation of endemic goiter to mental deficiency. *Ann. intern. Med., 4,* 569–577.

KISS, P. v., & RAJKA, T. 1934. Intelligenzprüfungen an Kindern mit angeborener Syphilis. *Arch. Kinderheilk., 102,* 25–36.

KLEIBER, M., BOELTER, M. D., & GREENBERG, D. M. 1941. Fasting catabolism and food utilization of magnesium deficient rats. *J. Nutrit., 21,* 363–372.

KRAINES, S. H. 1937. The correlation of oxygen deprivation with intelligence, constitution and blood pressure. *Amer. J. Psychiat., 93,* No. 2, 1435–1446.

KRIASCHEW, W. J. 1933. Der Charakter der bedingten Reflexe von hypophysektomierten Hunden. *Pflüg. Arch. ges. Physiol., 232,* 389–401.

LANDOLT, H. 1936. Die Einwirkung von Thyroxin auf das Zentralnervensystem bzw. Atemzentrum beim Kaninchen. *Z. Biol., 90,* 327–333.

LAST, S. L., & MEYER, A. 1932. Zur Frage pseudodemenz-ähnlicher psychischer Störungen nach CO-Vergiftung und anderen Hirnschädigungen. *Arch. Psychiat. Nervenkr., 96,* 73–83.

LAWRENCE, M. 1941. Vitamin A deficiency and its relation to hearing. *J. exp. Psychol., 29,* 37–48.

LEEDHAM, C. L. 1938. An interesting reaction to oxygen want. *J. Aviat. Med., 9,* 150–154.

LE FORT, R. 1937. Greffe de thyroid humaine dans un cas de myxoidime infantile: Résultats suivis pendant 12 ans. *Pr. méd., 45,* 1171–1173.

LENNOX, W. G., GIBBS, F. A., & GIBBS, E. L. 1935. Relationship of unconsciousness to cerebral blood flow and to anoxemia. *Arch. Neurol. Psychiat., Chicago, 34,* 1001–1013.

—— 1938. The relationship in man of cerebral activity to blood flow and to blood constituents. *Res. Publ. Assn. Res. nerv. ment. Dis., 19,* 277–297. Also: *J. Neurol. Psychiat.,* 1938, *1,* 211–225.

LEWALD, J., & ALEXANDER, E. J. 1939. A report on thiamine chloride (Vitamin B₁) in mental deficiency. *Proc. Amer. Assn. ment. Def., 44,* 34–39.

LIBET, B., FAZEKAS, J. F., & HIMWICH, H. E. 1940. A study of the central action of metrazol. *Amer. J. Psychiat., 97,* 366–371.

LIDDELL, H. S. 1938. The experimental neurosis and the problem of mental disorder. *Amer. J. Psychiat., 94,* 1035–1041.

LOEVENHART, A. S., LORENZ, W. F., & WATERS, R. M. 1929. Cerebral stimulation. *J. Amer. med. Assn., 92,* 880–883.

LOWENBERG, K., & ZBINDEN, T. 1938. Destruction of the cerebral cortex following nitrous oxide-oxygen anesthesia. *Curr. Res. Anaesth., 17,* 101–108.

LUDLUM, S. D. W. 1918. Physiologic psychiatry. *Med. Clin. N. Amer., 2,* No. 1, p. 895.

LURIE, L. A. 1935. Endocrinology and behavior disorders of children. A study of the possible causal relationships between endocrinopathic states and behavior disorders of children. *Amer. J. Orthopsychiat., 5,* 141–153.

—— 1938. Pituitary disturbances in relation to personality. *Res. Publ. Assn. Res. nerv. ment. Dis., 17,* 547–560.

MAIER, N. R. F. 1939. Studies of abnormal behavior in the rat: I. The neurotic pattern and an analysis of the situation which produces it. New York: Harper.

MARAÑON, G. 1924. Contribution à l'étude de l'action émotive de l'adrénaline. *Rev. franc. Endocrinol., 2,* 301–325.

MATEER, F. 1935. Glands and efficient behavior. New York: Appleton-Century.

McCANCE, R. A., LUFF, M. C., & WIDDOWSON, E. E. 1937. Physical and emotional periodicity in women. *J. Hyg., Camb., 37,* 571–611.

McDONALD, J. W., BROWN, A. W., & BRONSTEIN, I. P. 1940. VIII. Background and social adjustment of thyroid-deficient children receiving glandular therapy. *Amer. J. Dis. Child., 59,* 1227–1244.

McFARLAND, R. A. 1937. Psychophysiological studies at high altitudes in the Andes. *J. comp. Psychol., 23,* 191–258; *ibid., 24,* 147–220.

—— 1939. The psycho-physiological effects of reduced oxygen pressure. *Res. Publ. Assn. Res. nerv. ment. Dis., 19,* 112–143.

—— 1941. The internal environment and behavior: I. Introduction and the role of oxygen. *Amer. J. Psychiat., 97,* 858–877.

McFARLAND, R. A., EVANS, J. N., & HALPERIN, M. H. 1941. Ophthalmic aspects of acute oxygen deficiency. *Arch. Ophthal., Chicago, 26,* 886–913.

McGAVEN, A. P., SCHULTZ, E., PEDEN, G. W., & BOWEN, B. D. 1940. The physical growth, the degree of intelligence and the personality adjustment of a group of diabetic children. *New Engl. J. Med., 223,* 119–127.

MELLANBY, E. 1938. The experimental production of deafness in young animals by diet. *J. Physiol., 94,* 380–398.

MILLER, N. E., HUBERT, G., & HAMILTON, J. B. 1938. Mental and behavioral changes following male hormone treatment of adult castration, hypogonadism, and psychic impotence. *Proc. Soc. exp. Biol., N. Y., 38,* 538–540.

MOLITCH, M. 1937. Endocrine disturbances in behavior problems. *Amer. J. Psychiat., 93,* 1175–1180.

MOLITCH, M., & ECCLES, A. K. 1934. The relation between mental level and basal metabolism in juvenile delinquents. *J. juven. Res., 18,* 135–139.

MOLITCH, M., & POLIAKOFF, S. 1936. Pituitary disturbances in behavior problems. *Amer. J. Orthopsychiat., 6,* 125–133.

MOORMAN, L. J. 1940. Tuberculosis and genius. Chicago: University Chicago Press.

MORRISON, G. W., & CUNNINGHAM, B. 1941. Characteristics of the conditioned response in cretinous rats. *J. comp. Psychol., 31,* 413–426.

NICHOLS, I. C., & KELLER, M. 1937. Apraxias and other neurological sequelae of carbon monoxide asphyxia. *Amer. J. Psychiat., 93,* 1063–1071.

NORBURY, F. G. 1940. Applications of vitamin B_1 to neuropsychiatry. *Illinois med. J., 78,* 228–232.

O'BRIEN, J. D., & STEEGMANN, A. T. 1938. Severe degeneration of the brain following nitrous oxide-oxygen anesthesia. *Ann. Surg., 107,* 486–491.

OLESEN, R., & FERNALD, M. R. 1926. Endemic goiter and intelligence. *Publ. Hlth Rep., Wash., 41,* 971–986.

OLMSTED, J. M. D. 1941. The special senses. In Bard, P., *MacLeod's physiology in modern medicine.* St. Louis: Mosby. Pp. 247–290.

O'SHEA, H. E., & ELSOM, K. O. 1942. Studies of the B vitamins in the human subject: IV. Mental changes in experimental deficiency. *Amer. J. med. Sci., 203,* 388–397.

PATRICK, J. R., & ROWLES, E. 1933. Intercorrelations between metabolic rate, vital capacity, blood pressure, intelligence, scholarship, personality and other measures on university women. *J. appl. Psychol., 17,* 507–521.

PATTON, R. A. 1941. The effect of vitamins on convulsive seizures in rats subjected to auditory stimulation. *J. comp. Psychol., 31,* 215–221.

PATTON, R. A., & KARN, H. W. 1941. Abnormal behavior in rats subjected to repeated auditory stimulation. *J. comp. Psychol., 31,* 43–46.

PATTON, R. A., KARN, H. W., & KING, C. G. 1941. Studies on nutritional basis of abnormal behavior in albino rats. Effect of vitamin B_1 and vitamin B complex deficiency on convulsive seizures. *J. comp. Psychol., 32,* 543–550.

PETERS, R. A. 1936. The biochemical lesion in vitamin B_1 deficiency. Application of modern biochemical analysis in its diagnosis. *Lancet,* Part 1, 1161–1164.

PINESS, G., MILLER, H., & SULLIVAN, E. B. 1936. The intelligence rating of the allergic child. *J. Allergy, 8,* 168–174.

POWELL, E. 1936. Cerebral malnutrition and mental malfunction. *Med. Rec., N. Y., 144,* 318–322.

RAPHAEL, T., FERGUSON, W. G., & SEARLE, O. M. 1928. Long section blood sugar tolerance study in a case of depression. *Arch. Neurol. Psychiat., Chicago, 19,* 120–124.

RASKIN, N., & MULLANEY, O. C. 1940. The mental and neurological sequelae of carbon monoxide asphyxia in a case observed for fifteen years. *J. nerv. ment. Dis., 92,* 640–659.

RICH, G. I. 1928. A biochemical approach to the study of personality. *J. abnorm. soc. Psychol., 23,* 158.

RICHTER, C. P. 1941a. The internal environment and behavior: V. Internal secretions. *Amer. J. Psychiat., 97,* 878–893.

—— 1941b. Biology of drives. *Psychosom. Med., 3,* 105–110.

RICHTER, D. 1940. The action of adrenaline in anxiety. *Proc. R. Soc. Med., 33,* 615–618.

RIDDLE, O. 1935. Aspects and implications of the hormonal control of the maternal instinct. *Proc. Amer. phil. Soc., 75,* 521.

RIESS, B. F., & DE CILLIS, O. E. 1940. Personality differences in allergic and non-allergic children. *J. abnorm. soc. Psychol., 35,* 104–113.

RIPLEY, H. S., SHORR, E., & PAPANICOLAOU, G. N. 1940. The effect of treatment of depression in the menopause with estrogenic hormone. *Amer. J. Psychiat., 96,* 905–911.

ROTHBART, H. B. 1935. Basal metabolism in children of normal and sub-normal intelligence: with blood cholesterol and creatinine values. *Amer. J. Dis. Child., 40,* 672–688.

ROWE, A. W., & LAWRENCE, C. H. 1929. Studies of the endocrine glands: IV. Male and female gonads. In *Publications from the Robert Dawson Evans Memorial for clinical research and preventive medicine.* No. 1. Endocrine studies. Boston.

RYLANDER, G. 1939. Personality changes after operations on the frontal lobes. London: Oxford Univ. Press. Also: *Acta psychiat. Kbh.,* Suppl. 20, 1–337.

SCHOTT, E. L. 1938. Superior intelligence in patients with Fröhlich's syndrome. *J. appl. Psychol., 22,* 395–399.

SCHOU, H. I. 1933. Anemia psychoses and anemia neuroses. *Acta psychiat., Kbh., 8,* 483–506.

SCHREIBER, F. 1938. Apnea of the newborn and associated cerebral injury. A clinical and statistical study. *J. Amer. med. Assn., 111,* 1263–1269.

—— 1939. Mental deficiency from paranatal asphyxia. *Proc. Amer. Assn. ment. Def., 63,* 95–106.

SCHREIBER, S. L., BRONSTEIN, I. P., & BROWN, A. W. 1940. VII. Speech studies in cretins: speech sounds. *J. nerv. ment. Dis., 92,* 169–192.

SEBRELL, W. H. 1940. Nutritional diseases in the United States. *J. Amer. med. Assn., 115,* 851–854.

SEBRELL, W. H., & BUTLER, B. E. 1939. Riboflavin deficiency in man (ariboflavinosis). *Publ. Hlth Rep., Wash., 54,* 2121–2131.

SEWARD, G. H. 1934. The female sex rhythm. *Psychol. Bull., 31,* 153–193.

SEYMOUR, A. H., & WHITAKER, J. E. F. 1938. An experiment on nutrition. *Occup. Psychol., Lond., 12,* 215–223.

SHOCK, N. W. 1930. Mental performance and the acid base balance of the blood in normal individuals. *Proc. Indiana Acad. Sci., 40,* 193–202.

—— 1939a. Physiological factors in mental development. *Rev. educ. Res., 9,* 103–110.

—— 1939b. Some psychophysiological relations. *Psychol. Bull., 36,* 447–476.

—— 1941. The internal environment and behavior: IV. Carbon dioxide and acid-base balance. *Amer. J. Psychiat., 97,* 1374–1396.

SHOCK, N. W., & ERIKSON, E. H. 1944. Physiological responses of adolescents to work stimuli selected for the individual on the basis of his life history. (Unpublished)

SHOCK, N. W., & HASTINGS, A. B.   1935.   Studies of the acid-base balance of the blood: IV.   Characterization and interpretation of displacement of the acid-base balance.   *J. biol. Chem., 112,* 239–262.

SHOCK, N. W., & JONES, H. E.   1940.   The relationship between basal physiological functions and intelligence in adolescents.   *J. educ. Psychol., 31,* 369–375.

—— 1941.   Mental development and performance as related to physical and physiological factors.   *Rev. educ. Res., 11,* 351–352.

SHOCK, N. W., & SCOW, R. O.   1942.   The effect on learning of repeated exposures to lowered oxygen tension of the inspired air.   *J. comp. Psychol., 34,* 55–63.

SIMONSON, E., ENZER, N., BAER, A., & BRAUN, R.   1942.   The influence of vitamin B (complex) surplus on the capacity for muscular and mental work.   *J. industr. Hyg., 24,* 83–90.

SIMONSON, E., KEARNS, W. M., & ENZER, N.   1941.   Effect of oral administration of methyltestosterone on fatigue in eunuchoids and castrates.   *Endocrinology, 28,* 506–512.

SOLEY, M. H., & JUMP, K. B.   1939.   Cerebral anoxemia and its sequelae.   *Calif. West. Med., 51,* 1–3.

SOLEY, M. H., & SHOCK, N. W.   1938.   The etiology of effort syndrome.   *Amer. J. med. Sci., 196,* 840–851.

SÓS, J.   1939.   Trennung der zentralnervösen und der peripheren Thyroxinwirkungen.   *Arch. exp. Path. Pharmak., 192,* 78–84.

SPIES, T. D., & ASHE, W. F.   1939.   A note on the use of vitamin B₆ in human nutrition.   *J. Amer. med. Assn., 112,* 2414.

STARR, H. E.   1922.   The (H) concentration of the mixed saliva considered as an index of fatigue and of emotional excitation, and applied to a study of the metabolic etiology of stammering.   *Amer. J. Psychol., 33,* 394–418.

STEINACH, E.   1936.   Zur Geschichte des männlichen Sexualhormons und seiner Wirkungen am Saugetier und beim Menschen.   *Wien. klin. Wschr., 49,* No. 1, 161–172, 196–205.

STEINBERG, J.   1934.   The relation between basal metabolism and mental speed.   *Arch. Psychol., N. Y., 26,* No. 172, 5–39.

STOCKS, P., STOCKS, A. V., & KARN, M. N.   1927.   Goiter in adolescence; anthropometric study of relation between size of thyroid gland and physical and mental development.   *Biometrika, 19,* 292–353.

STOLL, H. F.   1932.   Chronic invalidism with marked personality changes due to myxedema.   *Ann. intern. Med., 6,* 806–814.

STONE, C. P.   1939.   Sex Drive.   In Allen, E., Danforth, C. H., & Doisy, E. A., *Sex and internal secretions.*   (2nd ed.)   Baltimore: Williams & Wilkins.   Pp. 1213–1262.

SUTHERLAND, G. F., WOLF, A., & KENNEDY, F.   1938.   The respiratory "fingerprint" of nervous states.   *Med. Rec., N. Y., 148,* 101–103.

SYDENSTRICKER, V. P., & CLECKLEY, H. M.   1941.   The effect of nicotinic acid in stupor, lethargy and various other psychiatric disorders.   *Amer. J. Psychiat., 98,* 83–92.

TEDSTROM, M. K.   1934.   Hypoglycemia and hyperinsulinism.   *Ann. intern. Med., 7,* 1013–1025.

THORLEY, A. S.   1942.   The action of adrenalin in neurotics.   *J. Neurol. Psychiat., 5,* 14–21.

THORNER, M. W., & LEWY, F. H.   1940.   The effects of repeated anoxia on the brain.   A histopathologic study.   *J. Amer. med. Assn., 115,* 1595–1600.

THURSTONE, L. L.   1935.   The vectors of mind.   Chicago: Univ. Chicago Press.

VAN LIERE, E. J.   1942.   Anoxia; its effect on the body.   Chicago: University Chicago Press.

VORONOFF, S.   1937.   Résultats après vingt ans de la greffe de la glande thyroide aux enfants cretins myxoedemateaux.   *Rev. path. comp. 37,* 1133–1169.

WECHSLER, D.   1941.   The measurement of adult intelligence.   (2nd ed.)   Baltimore: Williams & Wilkins.

WECHSLER, I. S.   1936.   The complications and sequellae of head injuries.   *Bull. Menninger Clin., 1,* 9–18.

WENTINK, E. A.   1938.   The effects of certain drugs and hormones upon conditioning.   *J. exp. Psychol., 22,* 150–163.

WERNER, A. A., JOHNS, G. A., HOCTOR, E. F., AULT, C. C., KOHLER, L. H., & WEIS, M. W.   1934.   Involutional melancholia.   Probable etiology and treatment.   *J. Amer. med. Assn., 103,* 13–16.

WERNER, A. A., KOHLER, L. H., AULT, C. C., & HOCTOR, E. F. 1936. Involutional melancholia. Probable etiology and treatment. *Arch. Neurol. Psychiat., Chicago, 35,* 1076–1080.

WICKENS, D. D., & BIEL, W. C. 1940. The effects of vitamin B₁ deficiency on the conditioning of eyelid responses in the rat. *Psychol. Bull., 37,* 478. (Abst.)

WILKINS, L., & RICHTER, C. P. 1940. A great craving for salt by a child with cortico-adrenal insufficiency. *J. Amer. med. Assn., 114,* 866–868.

WILLIAMS, R. D., MASON, H. L., WILDER, R. M., & SMITH, B. F. 1940. Observations on induced thiamine (vitamin B₁) deficiency in man. *Arch. intern. Med., 66,* 785–799.

—— 1942. Induced thiamine (B₁) deficiency and the thiamine requirement of man. Further observations. *Arch. intern. Med., 69,* 721.

WILLIAMS, R. J. 1942. Vitamins and the future. *Science, 95,* 340.

WINDLE, W. F., & BECKER, R. F. 1942. Brain damage and impairment of mental processes by asphyxia neonatorium. Experiments in the guinea pig. *Trans. Amer. neurol. Assn., 68,* 170–171.

WOLFF, H. G., & LENNOX, W. G. 1930. Cerebral circulation: XII. The effect on pial vessels of variations in the oxygen and carbon dioxide content of the blood. *Arch. Neurol. Psychiat., Chicago, 23,* 1097–1120.

WORCHEL, P., & LYERLY, J. G. 1941. Effects of prefrontal lobotomy on depressed patients. *J. Neurophysiol., 4,* 62–67.

WORTIS, H. 1941. Some nutritional aspects of brain metabolism. *Psychiat. Quart., 15,* 693–714.

YANT, W. P., CHORNYAK, J., SCHRENK, H. H., PATTY, F. A., & SAYERS, R. R. 1934. Studies in asphyxia. *Publ. Hlth Bull., Wash.,* No. 221, 1–61.